D1786447

977.6 155175
Nei

    Neill.
    The history of Minnesota.

MID-AMERICAN
★ FRONTIER ★

This is a volume in the Arno Press collection

MID-AMERICAN ★ FRONTIER ★

Advisory Editor
Jerome O. Steffen

Editorial Board
Richard S. Brownlee
William W. Savage, Jr.

*See last pages of this volume
for a complete list of titles*

THE

HISTORY OF MINNESOTA

EDWARD DUFFIELD NEILL

ARNO PRESS
A New York Times Company
New York – 1975

Editorial Supervision: ANDREA HICKS

Reprint Edition 1975 by Arno Press Inc.

Reprinted from a copy in
The Newark Public Library

THE MID-AMERICAN FRONTIER
ISBN for complete set: 0-405-06845-X
See last pages of this volume for titles.

Manufactured in the United States of America

Library of Congress Cataloging in Publication Data

Neill, Edward Duffield, 1823-1893.
   The history of Minnesota.

   (The Mid-American frontier)
   Reprint of the 1858 ed. published by Lippincott, Philadelphia.
   1. Minnesota--History--To 1858. I. Title. II. Series.
F606.N42 1975   977.6   72-112
ISBN 0-405-06879-4

THE
HISTORY OF MINNESOTA:

FROM THE

EARLIEST FRENCH EXPLORATIONS

TO THE

PRESENT TIME.

BY

EDWARD DUFFIELD NEILL,

SECRETARY OF THE MINNESOTA HISTORICAL SOCIETY.

"NEC FALSA DICERE, NEC VERA RETICERE."

PHILADELPHIA:
J. B. LIPPINCOTT & CO.
1858.

Entered, according to Act of Congress, in the year 1858, by
EDWARD DUFFIELD NEILL,
in the Clerk's Office of the District Court of the Eastern District of Pennsylvania.

MEARS & DUSENBERY, STEREOTYPERS.

TO

ANNA EARL RAMSEY,

MY WIFE'S FRIEND,

THE NAME OF WHOSE HUSBAND,

AS THE

First Governor,

MUST ALWAYS BE IDENTIFIED

WITH THE

HISTORY OF MINNESOTA,

This Work

IS INSCRIBED.

PREFACE.

NINE years ago, the writer wished to obtain some information in relation to Minnesota, but could find no reliable history. Even the devout astronomer and geologist, Nicollet, was misled by the fable of Baron La Hontan, more wonderful than any Munchausen story, and inclined to the belief that the Long river, on which that writer said he travelled in a canoe in winter, was really a stream of Minnesota.

The most costly Atlas ever published in America, which adorns libraries and is a work of reference used by our public men, in the description of this portion of the Union, is full of errors. As the historian of a government exploring expedition, informed the world, that "with the most active vigilance, it was impossible to subsist upon the grain" raised in the vicinity of Chicago, so the editor of the geographical descriptions accompanying the work to which we have alluded, with the same incorrectness, states that the summers of Minnesota are too brief for agricultural success.

The design of this History, is first, to show where Minnesota is, its characteristics and adaptations for a dense and robust population, and then consider the past and present dwellers on the soil.

In addition to the knowledge obtained from a residence of many years, during the hours not occupied by professional duties, the works of Charlevoix, La Harpe, Hennepin, the Jesuit Relations, French Official Documents, and the atlases of De l'Isle, Robert, Buache, Vaugondy, Moll, and others, besides separate charts, have been examined. The result is presented in the following pages.

Much assistance has been derived from the Documents pertaining to the Colonial History of New York, the Documentary History of Wisconsin, and kindred works.

For information concerning the aborigines of Minnesota, I am indebted to frequent conversations with the Reverend Messrs. POND, RIGGS, and WILLIAMSON, whose years of toil for the welfare of the Dahkotah Nation, need no comment.

It has been necessary in many places to sift the statements of mere tourists and letter-writers, but the endeavour has been always to bear in mind the essential of the historian, neither to state false things nor suppress the truth; "Nec falsa dicere, nec vera reticere."

CONTENTS.

INTRODUCTORY.

Physical characteristics, Page xxvii	Minnesota well watered, . xxxv
Boundaries of the state, . xxvii	Cascades of Pigeon river, . xxxvi
Climate of Minnesota, . xxviii	Falls of Kettle river, . . xxxvi
Eulogy on climate by Maury, xxviii	Vermillion Falls, . . xxxvi
Report of Minnesota and Pacific Railroad, . . xxix	Minne-ha-ha, . . . xxxvii
	Falls of St. Anthony, . xxxviii
Temperature of Minnesota, xxix	Early French maps, . . xli
Table illustrative of temperature, ... xxx	De l'Isle's maps, . . xlii
	Jeffery's map, 1762, . . xliii
Annual temperature equal to Central New York, . xxxi	Pronunciation of certain Indian names, . . xliv
Table showing mean fall o rain and melted snow at various places, . . xxxii	Census of Minnesota, 1857, xlv
	Rev. Albert Barnes' description of Minnesota scenery, ... xlvi
Less snow than on the Atlantic border, . . xxxiii	Meaning of the word Minnesota, ... xlvii
Table showing mean force of wind in winter for several years, . . . xxxiv	Dahkotah used in place of Sioux, ... xlvii

CHAPTER I.

Dahkotahs, a distinct group, . 49	Yanktons, ... 52
Language difficult, . . . 49	Teetwawns, ... 52
Mille Lac region, . . . 50	Assineboines, . . . 52
Dahkotah, its signification, . 50	Revolt of the Assineboines, . 53
Origin of term Sioux, . . 51	Religious characteristics, . 54
Divisions of the Dahkotahs, . 51	No idea of a Supreme Being, . 54
M'dewakantonwans, . . 52	Oanktayhee, ... 55

(7)

viii CONTENTS.

Hayokah,	. . .	56
Takushkankan,	. . .	57
Wahkeenyan,	. . .	58
Thunder Nest,	. . .	58

Poem on Thunder Bird,	. .	59
Sun worship,	. . . .	60
Offerings to stones,	. .	60

CHAPTER II.

Dahkotahs priestridden, .	.	61
Sacred men, ...		61
Sacred or medicine dance,	.	62
Initiation as a sacred man,	.	62
Ceremonies, ...		63
Sacred song, ...		64
Medicine sack, . . .		64
Dahkotah doctors, . . .		65
Vapour bath, ...		65
Hennepin steamed, . .		65
Medicine man, signification,	.	66
Cause of disease, . . .		66
Manner of calling a doctor,	.	67
Mode of medical practice,	.	67
Fondness for war, . . .		68
Vows of a young warrior,	.	68
The return of a war party,	.	69
Scalp, its preparation, .	.	69
Scalp dance, ...		69
Feathers, signs of prowess,	.	69

Maternal affection, . . .		70
Lament over an infant, .	.	71
Mode of obtaining wives,	.	72
Custom of son-in-law, .	.	72
Penalty for adultery, .	.	73
The woodpecker charm, .	.	73
Love of dress, . . .		73
Games, plum stones, .	.	74
Ball play, ...		74
Ball play at Oak Grove,	.	75
Dog dance, ...		76
Fish dance, ...		76
Cormorant dance, . . .		77
Secret clubs, ...		77
Crow Feather in Cap Club,	.	78
Strong Heart Club, .	.	78
Uncleanness, ...		79
Dog meat, a delicacy, .	.	80
Irregular mode of life, .	.	81

CHAPTER III.

Dahkotah women, . . .		82
Hardships of women, .	.	82
Husbands cruel, . . .		83
Disposition to be suicides,	.	84
Disguised girl, . . .		84
Chiefs, no authority, .	.	85
Absence of law, . . .		85
Names of months, . . .		86
Moon eaten by mice, .	.	87
Looking-glass, . . .		87
Peculiar views, . . .		87
Belief in relation to future,	.	87
Burial ceremonies, . . .		88
Death song, ...		89

Schiller's poem, . . .		89
Translations of Bulwer and Herschell, ...		89
Legends, ...		90
Eagle-Eye and Scarlet Dove, .	.	90
Anpetusapa, ...		91
Weenonah, ...		93
Hogan-wanke-kin, St. Croix River, ...		94
Language of Dahkotahs,	.	95
Hennepin collecting a vocabulary, ...		95
Riggs's Lexicon, . . .		96
Dahkotah Alphabet, . .		97

CHAPTER IV.

Source of St. Lawrence in Minnesota,	99
Cartier discovers the mouth,	99
Champlain in Huron country,	99
Nicolet, in Wisconsin,	100
Le Jeune's mention of Dahkotahs,	101
Jogues and Raymbault at Sault St. Marie,	101
Traders west of Lake Superior,	102
Garreau and Dreuilletes,	102
Puritan Eliot,	102
Two traders visit Dahkotahs,	103
Their description,	103
Grosellier,	103
Murder of Garreau,	104
René Menard,	104
His farewell letter,	104
Arrival in Lake Superior,	105
Hurons at La Pointe,	106
Guerin, Menard's companion,	106
Menard lost,	107
Allouez succeeds Menard,	107
Arrives at La Pointe,	108
Grand Council,	108
Allouez meets Dahkotahs,	109
First mention of the "Messipi,"	110
Description of Dahkotahs,	110
Marquette succeeds Allouez,	111
His opinion of the Dahkotahs,	111
Number of Dahkotah villages,	112
La Pointe Mission abandoned,	113
Dahkotahs killed at Sault St. Marie,	113
Ojibways intermarry with Dahkotahs,	113

CHAPTER V.

Fur trade,	115
Fascination of the business	115
Licenses granted to old officers,	115
Clerks,	115
Voyageurs,	116
Careless and hardy class,	116
Fondness for the frontier,	117
Complaints against coureurs des bois,	117
Meaning of the expression,	117
Number of annual licenses,	118
Profits of the trade,	119
Nicholas Perrot,	119
Perrot a Canadian,	119
Visits tribes of Lake Michigan,	120
Council at Sault St. Marie,	120
French take possession of North-west,	121
Trading post at head of Lake Superior,	121
Du Luth visits Minnesota,	122
Intendant of Canada displeased,	122
Mille Lac called Lake Buade,	122
Perrot's account attracts La Salle,	123

CHAPTER VI.

La Salle at Kingston,	124
Louis Hennepin,	124
His early life,	124
Not a Jesuit,	125
Embarks for Canada,	125
At the Falls of Niagara,	126
Visits Albany,	126
La Salle launches the Griffin,	127
He builds Fort Crevecœur,	127
Sends Hennepin to Upper Mississippi,	127
Hennepin seized by the Dahkotahs,	128
Indians astonished at prayer-book,	129
First mention of a Dahkotah word,	129
Hennepin at Lake Pepin,	130
Old mode of kindling fire,	130
Indians land near St. Paul,	131
Journey to Mille Lac,	131
Hennepin's robe,	131
Sweating cabin,	132
Astonishment at mariner's compass,	132
The mystery of an iron pot,	132
Amazement at writing,	133
Ridicule of the Indians,	133
First infant baptism in Minnesota,	134
Arrival of distant Indians,	134
Hope of a Northern Pacific route,	135
Hennepin's falsehoods,	135
List of editions of his travels,	136
Calliere's opinion of Hennepin,	137
Louis XIV. orders his arrest,	137
Hennepin in Italy,	137
Du Luth, discoverer of Mille Lac,	138
Du Luth in France,	138
Du Luth at Mackinaw,	138
Perrot near the mouth of Wisconsin,	138
Droll strategy of Dahkotahs,	139
Miamies bring lead,	139
Du Luth and Perrot obtain allies for Iroquois war,	139
Louis XIV. censures Du Luth	140
Du Luth at a post above Detroit,	140
Du Luth and Tonty at Detroit,	141
Du Luth captures Englishmen,	141
Du Luth in New York,	141
Afflicted with gout,	142
Notice of his death,	142

CHAPTER VII.

Formal occupation of Minnesota,	143
First official document,	143
Boisguillot at the Wisconsin,	144
Mantantons,	144
First French post in Minnesota,	145
Frontenac's opposition to Jesuits,	145
Perrot visits Montreal,	146
Grand feast of Frontenac,	146
Frontenac sings the war song,	147
Long-expected furs,	147
Le Sueur at La Pointe,	148
Second post in Minnesota,	148
First Dahkotah in Montreal,	148
Ojibway chief from La Pointe,	148
His speech,	149
Dahkotah's speech,	149
Dahkotah woman in Montreal,	150
Dahkotah chief dies,	151

CONTENTS.

Le Sueur goes to France, . 151
Perrot about to be burned, . 151
Le Sueur's mining project, . . 152
Louis XIV. revokes his license, 153
Le Sueur's second visit to France, ... 153

CHAPTER VIII.

D'Iberville Governor of Louisiana, ... 154
Relative of Le Sueur, . . 154
Le Sueur arrives with miners, 154
Ascends the Mississippi, . 154
Marest's letter to Le Sueur, . 154
Le Sueur meets Dahkotah warriors, ... 155
At the mines near Galena, . 155
Canadians attacked by Wisconsin Indians, . . . 156
Le Sueur at mouth of Wisconsin, ... 156
War party returning from Minnesota, ... 157
Le Sueur at Chippeway river, 158
Lake Pepin, ... 159
Cannon river, . . . 159
La Place, a deserter, killed by Dahkotahs, . . . 160
Denis, Canadian voyageur, . 160
St. Croix river named after a Frenchman, . . . 161
River St. Pierre entered, . 161
Blue Earth river, . . . 162
Post established, . . . 162
Dahkotahs desire a post near Mendota, ... 162
Dahkotahs described, . . 163
Fort L'Huillier finished, . 164
Dahkotahs sue for favour, . 164
Canoes filled with blue earth, 165
Mantantons visit the post, . 165
M'dewakantons at Mille Lac, 165
Assineboines, . . . 166
Ioways and Ottoes moving west, ... 166
Dahkotahs mourn the death of Tioscaté, ... 167
Le Sueur makes presents, . 168
Cultivation of the earth proposed, ... 168
Mantantons give a feast, . 168
M'dewakantons at the post, . 169
Catalogue of Dahkotah villages, ... 170
Le Sueur returns to Gulf of Mexico, ... 171
Acccompanies D'Iberville to France, ... 171
D'Iberville's manuscript, . 171
State of the tribes, . . 172
Census of Indians, Mississippi valley, . . . 173
Frenchmen should not follow Indians, ... 173
Canada and Louisiana governments, ... 174
Workmen leave Mahkahto, . 175
Le Sueur's death, . . . 175

CHAPTER IX.

Westward tendency of Dahkotahs, ... 176
Sauk and Fox hostility to French, ... 176
Sauks and Foxes defeated by Dahkotahs and Ioways, . 176
Language of the Foxes, not Algonquin, . . . 176

xii   CONTENTS.

Foxes attack Detroit,	. .	177
Their repulse,	. . .	177
Defeat near Lake St. Clair,	.	178
Louvigny invades the Fox country,	. . . .	178
Foxes break their treaty,	.	179
Licenses to traders renewed,	.	179
Prediction of English mastery,		179
Captain St. Pierre sent to La Pointe,	. . . .	180
De Lignery concludes peace with Foxes,	. . .	180
Peace between Ojibways and Dahkotahs,	. . . .	181
La Pointe Ojibways at Montreal,	. . . . .	181
Foxes again faithless,	. .	182
Lake Pepin re-occupied by French,	. . . .	183
Importance of the post urged,		184
De Lignery's expedition against Foxes,	. . . .	185
Foxes leave their country,	.	186
Father Guignas captured,	.	186
Returns to Lake Pepin,	. .	186
Establishment at Lake Ouinipigon,	. . . .	186
Veranderie discovers Lake Winnipeg,	. . . .	187
Alleged pillars of stone,	.	187
Aiton's letter on stone heaps,		187
Stone heaps near Red Wing,	.	188
Dahkotahs attack Veranderie,		189
Extermination of Foxes determined,	. . . .	189
Moran, captain of the expedition,	. . . . .	189
Moran's strategy,	. . .	190
Final defeat of the Foxes,	.	190
De Lusignan visits Dahkotahs,		191
Coureurs des bois refuse to return,	. . . . .	191
Trading-post burned,	. .	191
St. Pierre at Mackinaw,	.	191
His character,	. . .	191
Escape of Indian prisoners,	.	192

CHAPTER X.

Canada and English colonies at war,	. . . .	193
French enlist savages,	. .	193
Le Duc robbed at Lake Superior,	. . . . .	194
La Ronde, officer at La Pointe,		194
Veranderie at Fond du Lac,	.	194
Marin at Green Bay,	. .	194
List of Upper Indian allies,	.	194
St. Pierre in the state of Pennsylvania,	. . . .	195
Beaujeu and De Lignery at Fort Duquesne,	. . .	195
Beaujeu killed while attacking Braddock,	. . .	195
St. Pierre killed at Lake Champlain,	. . . . .	195
Langlade of Wisconsin, at Ticonderoga,	. . . .	196
Ioways and Ojibways at Ticonderoga,	. . . .	197
List of Upper Indians,	. .	197
Rogers and Jonathan Carver at Fort George,	. . .	198
Rogers's amusing note,	. .	198
Ojibways returning, die of small-pox,	. . . .	199
French deliver up their posts,		199
English troops at Green Bay,	.	199
Dahkotahs visit, and make peace,	. . . . .	199
Penneshaw a French trader,	.	199
His influence with Dahkotahs,		200
Friendly to the English,	.	200

CHAPTER XI.

Indians partial to French traders,	201
Jonathan Carver's early life,	202
At Fort William Henry,	202
Visits Mackinaw,	202
Arrives at Green Bay,	202
Carver's description of Prairie du Chien,	203
Artificial earth works,	203
Lake Pepin,	206
Nehogatawonahs, Mawtawbauntowahs, Shashweentowahs,	206
Carver's Cave in suburb of St. Paul,	207
Indian burial place,	207
Minnesota river,	208
Falls of St. Anthony in 1766,	208
Mound near St. Paul opened,	208
Exploration of Carver's Cave,	208
Dahkotahs at Carver's Cave,	210
Speech over dead chief,	211
Versification, by Schiller,	212
Sir Wm. Johnson in relation to Ojibways,	212
Rogers makes a treaty with Dahkotahs and Ojibways,	213
Prediction of speedy route to New York,	213
Carver's Pacific route,	214
Supposed origin of Dahkotahs,	214
Analogies of language,	215
Carver's death,	215
Claim of his heirs,	215
Marriage of Carver's daughter,	216
Alleged deed given at Cave near St. Paul,	216
Agent of Carver's heirs murdered,	216
Rev. Samuel Peters purchases Carver claim,	217
Testimony before Senate committee,	217
General Leavenworth's letter,	218
Indians do not recognise the grant,	218
Frenchmen cut timber on Chippeway,	219
Report of Senate committee in 1823,	219
British government prohibited grants,	220
Lord Palmerston finds no papers about the grant,	221

CHAPTER XII.

Dahkotahs formerly at Leech Lake,	222
Driven from Sandy Lake,	222
Fight at mouth of Crow Wing,	222
Pillagers, origin of name,	223
Battle of Falls of St. Croix,	223
Foxes and Dahkotahs defeated,	224
English trader killed by Dahkotahs,	225
Murder near Mendota,	225
British withdraw their trade,	226
Wapashaw,	226
Determines to visit Quebec,	227
Delivers himself,	227
Winters in Canada,	227
Wapashaw dies an exile,	228
Depeyster commands Mackinaw,	228
Wapashaw visits him,	228
Song for Wapashaw,	228
Troop leaves Mackinaw,	229
Langlade at Prairie du Chien,	229

xiv CONTENTS.

Wapashaw at Prairie du Chien, 1780,	230
Speech to the Foxes,	230
Peltries taken by British to Mackinaw,	230
M'dewakantonwans in one band,	231
Penneshaw's village,	231
History of North-west Company,	231
Clerks,	232
Pork Eaters,	232
Winterers,	232
Kay in Minnesota,	233
Kay intoxicated,	233
Winters at Pine river,	234
Kay stabbed by an Indian,	235
Perrault and Harris at Leech Lake,	236
Dubuque at Prairie du Chien,	236
The lead mines of Dubuque,	236
Renville, Grignon, and Dickson,	236
Perlier falls in love on the St. Croix,	237
North-west Company build at Sandy Lake,	238
British do not surrender posts,	238
Jay's treaty,	239

CHAPTER XIII.

Indiana organized,	240
Louisiana transferred,	240
Territory of Upper Louisiana,	241
Territory of Michigan,	241
First United States officer in Minnesota,	241
Pike's expedition,	241
Pike at Kaposia,	242
J. B. Faribault, sketch of	242
Sketch of Fisher, the trader,	242
Pike's council on island,	243
Articles of treaty,	243
Pike's speech to Dahkotahs,	244
Flag lost,	248
Portage at Falls of St. Anthony,	248
Sergeant breaks a blood-vessel,	249
Pike's block house,	249
Complaints against Dickson,	250
Dickson visits Pike,	251
Ascent of the Mississippi,	252
Sled falls into the river,	253
Baggage wet,	253
Ignorance and inattention of voyageurs,	254
Ojibway encampment	254
Pike's indignation at British flag,	255
Tent on fire,	256
Sandy Lake,	256
North-west Company's post at Sandy Lake described,	257
Arrival from Fond du Lac,	258
Leech Lake,	259
North-west Company's post,	259
American flag hoisted,	259
English flag lowered,	260
Council with Ojibways,	260
Pike at Red Cedar Lake,	261
Shabby actions of Pike's sergeant,	262
Peculiar hospitality,	265
Arrival at mouth of Minnesota,	266
Carver's Cave not found,	267
Conference with Little Crow,	268
Pike at Red Wing,	269
The murderer, Roman Nose,	270
Pike ascends the Barn bluff,	271
Pike visits Wapashaw,	272
Pike at Prairie du Chien,	273
Ball play,	274
Red Thunder, Yankton chief,	275

CONTENTS. xv

CHAPTER XIV.

Traders disregards Pike's instructions,	276
Cameron, principal trader,	276
His grave,	276
Milor, old voyageur,	276
His perilous journey,	277
Indians combine against United States,	278
Nicholas Jarrot,	278
Messengers from Tecumseh,	279
Dickson, his character and influence,	279
Dickson a British partisan,	280
Mackinaw surprised,	280
Rolette and Langlade present,	280
Kaposia and Wapashaw bands at Fort Meigs,	281
Refuse to eat an American,	282
Americans fortify Prairie du Chien,	283
Site of Fort Shelby,	283
British attack the fort,	284
Joseph Rolette, British guide,	284
Americans capitulate,	285
Americans attacked near Rock Island,	285
Fort Shelby called McKay,	285
Zachary Taylor retreats from Rock Island,	286
Daring of Paul Harpole,	286
One-eyed Sioux,	286
Dickson imprisons him,	287
British evacuate Prairie du Chien,	287
Sketch of one-eyed Sioux,	288
Dickson at Lake Traverse,	287
Prejudice against Selkirk,	290
O'Fallon's letter,	290
Dickson's character misrepresented,	291
Ramsay Crooks on Dickson,	291
Wapashaw and Little Crow visit British,	292
Treaty of Portage des Sioux,	293
Astor organizes a fur company,	293
History of Astor's company,	293
Lockwood trader in Minnesota,	294
Indian trade in 1816,	294
First grist-mill above Prairie du Chien,	298
Saw-mill on Black river,	298
Spartan conflict of Ojibways,	298

CHAPTER XV.

Red River difficulties,	300
Early posts on the northern border,	300
Formation of North-west Company,	301
Earl of Selkirk's project,	301
Selkirk's grant described,	302
Pioneers of Selkirk colony,	303
Winter at Pembina,	303
Colony augmented,	304
The North-west Company oppose,	305
Duncan Cameron,	305
Selkirk storehouse broken open,	306
First Selkirk emigrants Presbyterians,	306
Colonists driven away,	307
Return to Red river,	308
Earl of Selkirk comes to America,	308
Messenger to Red river robbed,	309
Governor Semple attacked,	310
Massacre of his party,	311

CONTENTS.

Selkirk settlers again exiled,	.	312
Owen Keveny seized,	.	312
His murder, ...		313
His trunks opened and papers read, ...		313
Earl of Selkirk seizes Fort William, ...		314
John Tanner discovered,	.	314
Sketch of Tanner, . .	.	314
Selkirk's interest in Tanner,	.	315
Sufferings at Pembina, 1817, 1818, ...		315
Grasshopper invasion, .	.	316
Complete devastation, .	.	316
Mackinaw boats from Prairie du Chien to Pembina,	.	317
Selkirk's agent visits Switzerland, ...		318
Compromise of Hudson Bay and North-west Company,	.	318

CHAPTER XVI.

United States fortify the Northwest, ...		319
Orders to proceed to Mendota,		319
Crawford county, Wisconsin, organized, ...		320
Colonel Leavenworth ascends Mississippi, . . .		320
Primitive mode of living,	.	320
Troops move to Camp Coldwater, ...		321
Lumber cut on Rum river,	.	322
Cass expedition, . . .	.	322
Negro and Indian offspring,	.	322
Arrival of Cass at Sandy Lake,		323
At Upper Red Cedar Lake,	.	323
This lake the supposed source of Mississippi, . . .		323
Emaciated and suffering voyageur, ...		324
Buffalo hunt above Elk river,		324
Cass at Fort Snelling, .	.	325
Description of Little Crow,	.	326
Red Wing and Wapashaw in 1820, ...		327
Colonel Snelling met by Cass,		327
First infant of European parents, ...		327
Wanata hostile, . . .		328
Chief offers himself as a substitute for son, . . .		328
Solemnity of surrender,	.	329
Saw-mill in Chippeway valley,		330
Columbia Fur Company formed, ...		330
Names of partners, .	.	330
Mill at Minneapolis, .	.	331
J. R. Brown visits Minne Tonka, ...		331
Family of Hess murdered,	.	332
Rescue of a daughter, .	.	332
Swiss come to United States, from Red river, . .	.	333
First steamboat above Rock Island, ...		334
Passengers on board, .	.	334
Grand illumination, .	.	335
Arrival of steamboat at Mendota, ...		336
Astonishment of natives,	.	336
Reminiscences of Taliaferro,	.	337
Origin of name Lake Calhoun and Harriet, . .		338
Flat Mouth at Fort Snelling,	.	339
Penneshaw's mother kills Ojibway girl, . . .	.	340

CHAPTER XVII.

Major Long's expedition to Red river,	341
Arrival at Fort Snelling,	341
Renville, interpreter,	342
J. Snelling, assistant,	342
Beltrami, Italian refugee,	342
Arrival at Big Stone Lake,	342
Wanata's appearance and character,	343
Wanata's vow to the Sun,	344
Cuttings of the flesh,	344
Wanata feasts Long and party,	346
Dog meat presented,	347
Origin of word Pembina,	348
Boundary line at that point fixed,	348
Tanner wounded by an Indian,	349
Beltrami separates from Major Long,	349
Returns by way of Red Lake,	350
Beltrami's characteristics,	350
Beltrami deserted by his guides,	353
Awkward attempt at paddling,	354
The difficulties of travel,	355
Indians' astonishment at umbrella,	357
Ludicrous appearance of Beltrami,	357
Fear of the Dahkotahs,	358
Beltrami at Red Lake,	359
Dogs tear his clothing,	360
Ojibways mourn the loss of a brave,	361
Half-breed hut described,	362
Notice of Red river,	363
Topography of Red Lake,	364
Theory of old geographers in relation to what constitutes the sources of a stream,	366
Beltrami leaves Red Lake,	367
Table land of North America,	368
Beltrami discoverer of northern source of Mississippi,	369
Beautiful description,	370
Indian stories unreliable,	371
Beltrami suggests western source of Mississippi,	371
Leech Lake described,	372
Interview of the Italian with Pillagers,	373
Pike makes Leech Lake source of Mississippi,	374
Beltrami's tribute to Pike,	375
William Morrison's letter,	375
Morrison at Leech Lake, 1802,	375
Morrison at Lake Itasca, 1804,	376
Wintered there in 1811–12,	376
Beltrami at Sandy Lake,	377
Government mill,	378
Beltrami returns to Fort Snelling,	379
Cordial reception,	380
Accuracy of Beltrami's map,	380
Underrated by Long and Keating,	380
Findlay and party killed at Lake Pepin,	381
Degraded state of traders and Indians,	382
Traders among Dahkotahs, 1825–26,	382

CHAPTER XVIII.

Prairie du Chien treaty of 1825,	383
Boundary fixed between Dahkotahs and Ojibways,	383

2

CONTENTS.

Fond du Lac treaty, 1826, . 384	Dahkotah coward, . . . 393
Commissioners Cass and McKenney, ... 384	Troops removed from Prairie du Chien, ... 394
Aged woman scalped when a girl, ... 385	Methode and family killed, . 394
	Red Bird at Prairie du Chien, 395
Woman in council, . . 385	Attempts to kill Mrs. Lockwood, ... 395
Agreement to deliver up murderers, ... 386	Murders the Gagnier family, . 395
Cass orders a canoe, . . 386	Dahkotahs unruly, . . 396
Building of birch bark canoe, 387	Winnebagoes attack keel-boats, 396
Murderers surrender themselves, ... 387	The father's wail, . . . 397
	Fort Crawford put in a state of defence, ... 397
Severe snow storm, 1825, . 388	
Famine, ... 388	Cass at Buttes des Morts, . 397
Freshet in Red River valley, . 389	Soldiers march from Green Bay, ... 398
Swiss emigrants home-sick, . 389	
Swiss move to vicinity of St. Paul, ... 390	General Atkinson starts for the scene, ... 398
Swiss, the first farmers in Minnesota, ... 390	Red Bird described, . . 398
	His dress, ... 399
Ojibways at Fort Snelling, 1826, 391	The surrender, . . . 399
Slaughtered by the Dahkotahs, 391	Death in prison, . . . 399
Ojibway revenge, . . . 392	

CHAPTER XIX.

Prairie du Chien treaty, 1830, 400	Grand scalp dance, . . 406
Half-breed tract of Lake Pepin, ... 400	Indian burial place, . . 406
	Elk or Itasca Lake, . . 407
Attempt to erect a mill, . . 400	Lieut. Allen surveys and makes a map, ... 407
Holmes builds a mill on Chippewa river, . . 401	
	Allen's canoe upsets, . . 408
Schoolcraft visits Ojibways in 1831, ... 401	Flat Mouth's lodge at Leech Lake, ... 408
Snake river chief, . . . 402	Vaccination of Indians, . 409
Schoolcraft's expedition of 1832, ... 403	Beautiful country, . . . 409
	Good soil, ... 410
Associates of Schoolcraft, . 403	Falls of St. Anthony, . . 410
Child of Rev. S. Hall, first child of pure European stock on Lake Superior, . . 404	Schoolcraft talks with Dahkotahs, ... 411
	Haste of Schoolcraft, . . 411
Portage of St. Louis river, . 404	Hostile intentions of Black Hawk, ... 412
Strength of Indian women, . 404	
Dahkotah scalp at Cass Lake, ... 405	Dahkotahs, allies of United States, . . . 412

CONTENTS.

Black Hawk routed by Dodge,	412	Nicollet's early life,	417
Battle of Bad Axe,	413	Arrival in Minnesota,	417
General Z. Taylor present,	413	Pillagers molest Nicollet,	418
Preservation of Indian babe,	414	Rev. Mr. Boutwell assists him,	418
Black Hawk surrenders,	414	Nicollet visits Itasca Lake,	418
Alleged speech of that chief,	414	Surveys the sources of Itasca,	418
First land mail to Fort Snelling,	415	Explorations beyond Schoolcraft,	419
Traders in Minnesota, 1833–34,	415	Devotion to science,	419
Missouri Territory attached to Michigan,	416	Nicollet's second tour,	419
		J. C. Fremont, his assistant,	419
Wisconsin Territory organized,	416	Valuable map,	420
Iowa organized,	416	Leech Lake Ojibways kill a trader,	421
George Catlin, the artist,	416		
Featherstonhaugh, geologist,	416	Sibley's tribute to Nicollet,	421
Nicollet, the astronomer,	417		

CHAPTER XX.

History of missions,	422	Mode of carrying goods at a portage,	429
Frontispiece of La Hontan's travels,	422	Mr. Ayer arrives at Yellow Lake,	431
Savages no regard for law,	422		
Youth trained to war,	423	Rev. W. T. Boutwell at Leech Lake,	432
Error in the teachings of Marquette,	423	First mission in Minnesota west of Mississippi,	432
Rev. Dr. Morse visits Mackinaw,	424	E. F. Ely, teacher at Sandy Lake,	432
Rev. Mr. Ferry opens mission school,	424	Indian children in missionary's lap,	433
On manual labour principle,	424		
Warren trader at La Pointe,	425	Indians laugh at missionary,	434
Introduction of missionaries by him,	425	Number and locality of Leech Lake Indians,	435
Rev. Sherman Hall,	425	Fish of the Lake,	436
Mr. Frederic Ayer,	425	Wild rice,	436
Mode of travel through Lake Superior,	426	Soil around the lake,	436
		Danger of gifts to the Indians,	437
Rev. S. Hall's arrival at La Pointe,	427	Polygamy common,	438
		Mr. Boutwell married,	439
Aitkin requests a school at Sandy Lake,	428	Primitive mode of life,	440
Hall's tour to Oakes' trading post,	428	Jesuits did not stay with Dahkotahs,	441
		S. W. Pond,	441

CONTENTS.

G. H. Pond, ...	441
First to labour for the welfare of Dahkotahs, . . .	441
Rev. T. S. Williamson, M. D.,	442
Arrives at Fort Snelling, May, 1835, ...	442
First church and communion in Minnesota, . . .	443
Indian mode of gathering corn,	443
Fondness of Dahkotahs for meat, ...	444
Rev. J. D. Stevens preaches at Fort Snelling, . . .	445
Indian mourning at Lake Harriet, ...	445
Mourners cut their flesh, .	446
Church at Fort Snelling, .	446
Indian school at Lake Harriet,	447
Presbyterian church, Lac qui Parle, ...	447
Rev. S. R. Riggs joins the mission, ...	447

CHAPTER XXI.

Buffaloes unknown in Lower Canada, ...	448
Rumour in relation to lions' skins, ...	448
Marquette's description of the buffalo, ...	448
First engraving of the buffalo,	449
Hudson Bay Co. buffalo hunters,	449
Carts of the half-breeds, .	449
Hunters' camp described, .	450
Rules of the camp, . .	450
Great buffalo hunt in Minnesota, ...	450
Last buffalo east of Mississippi,	451
Pemmican, ...	451
Dickson's proposed invasion, .	452
McLeod and Bottineau's perilous journey, . . .	452
Swiss missionaries at Red Wing, ...	452
Methodist mission at Kaposia,	452
Treaty of 1837 with Ojibways,	453
Dahkotah treaty of 1837, .	453
Faribault's claim to Pike Island, ...	453
Baker, Taylor, and Steele at Falls of St. Croix, . .	453
Visit of Captain Maryatt, .	453
Small-pox among Dahkotahs,	454
G. H. Pond buries slaughtered Dahkotahs, . . .	455
Ojibways chase lumbermen, .	456
First steamboat in the St. Croix, ...	456
Ratification of treaty of 1837,	456
Marine mills, . . .	456
Dahkotah killed at Lake Harriet, ...	457
Battles of Rum river and Stillwater, ...	457
Settlers on Fort Snelling reserve, ...	458
Forcible ejection, . . .	459
Death of Arctic explorer in Minnesota, . . .	460
Supposed insanity, . .	461
J. R. Brown makes a claim near Stillwater, . . .	462
St. Croix county, . . .	463
Lake Pokeguma, . . .	463
Mission at Pokeguma, . .	464
Pleasing prospect, . . .	464
Little Crow's son killed at Falls of St. Croix, . .	465
Battle of Lake Pokeguma, .	466
Daring feat, ...	467
Scene after the fight, . .	468
Christian burial, . . .	468

CONTENTS.

Ojibway attack below St. Paul,	469
Mr. Ayer visits Red Lake,	470
Governor Doty makes treaties with Dahkotahs,	470
Stillwater commenced,	471
Captain Allen's tour to Big Sioux,	472
Mill at Little Canada,	472
Drovers lose their way,	472
Captain Sumner and dragoons visit Red River,	472
Murderer of one of the drovers arrested,	473
Death of Joseph Renville,	474
Sketch of Renville,	474
One-eyed whiskey-seller,	475
Residence at St. Paul,	476
His shanty called Pig's Eye,	478
Henry Jackson settles at St. Paul,	479
Roberts and J. W. Simpson,	480
Little Crow requests a missionary,	480
Dr. Williamson comes to Kaposia,	480
Procures a teacher for St. Paul,	481
Miss H. E. Bishop,	482
First school-room in St. Paul,	482
First court in St. Croix county, Wisconsin,	483
Rev. Mr. Boutwell moves near Stillwater,	483
H. M. Rice selects a new home, for Winnebagoes,	483
Winnebago removal,	484
Halt at Wapashaw,	484
Excitement,	485
Battle array,	486
Winnebagoes arrive at Watab,	487

CHAPTER XXII.

Act for Wisconsin to form a constitution,	488
Bill for organization of Minnesota, 1846,	488
Sioux and Red River of North, proposed boundary,	488
Wisconsin desires to extend to Rum river,	488
Remonstrance of citizens of St. Croix,	489
Wisconsin admitted into the Union,	490
Debate on the name of Minnesota Territory,	490
Discussion on territorial organization,	490
First meeting in St. Paul,	490
Public meeting at Stillwater,	490
Catlin's letter to Holcombe,	491
Catlin resides at Stillwater,	492
The delegate from Wisconsin resigns,	492
H. H. Sibley elected successor,	492
Minnesota Territory created, March 3, 1849,	492
Boundaries of territory,	492
Sparse settlements,	493
St. Paul in 1849,	494
Steamer brings news of the existence of Minnesota Territory,	494
Joyful demonstrations,	494
Goodhue arrives with press,	494
Governor Ramsey and family arrive,	495
List of early citizens at the capital,	495
First newspaper,	495
Sketch of Governor Ramsey,	496
Anna Earl Ramsey,	497

CONTENTS.

Sketch of Governor Sibley,	497
Notice of Mrs. Sibley,	498
Sketch of H. M. Rice, U. S. Senator,	498
Notice of Mrs. Rice,	500
Franklin Steele,	500
Notice of Mrs. Steele,	501
Fish dance at Kaposia,	501
Proclamation of Governor Ramsey, organizing the territory,	502
C. K. Smith,	502
A. Goodrich,	502
D. Cooper,	502
B. B. Meeker,	502
J. L. Taylor,	502
H. L. Moss,	502
Temporary judicial districts,	503
Major Wood's expedition to Pembina,	503
Governor Ramsey commences housekeeping at St. Paul,	504
H. M. Rice and family remove to St. Paul,	504
Fourth of July at St. Paul,	504
First census,	504
Recognition and death of a young chief,	505
Indian fight in Cheyenne valley,	506
Tipsinna or Dahkotah turnip,	506
H. M. Rice transports goods by horse-boats,	507
First election,	507
A. M. Mitchell, U. S. Marshal,	507
Vote at first election,	507
Newspapers, when established,	508
Old printing press,	508
Court at Stillwater,	509
Court at Minneapolis,	509
Court at Mendota,	509
Temperance reform among Dahkotahs,	510
Session of first legislature,	511
Names, age, and nativity of members,	511
Officers of first legislature,	511
Governor Ramsey's message,	512
Funeral of child of a member of legislature,	512
Counties formed,	513
Resolution in relation to pipe stone slab,	513
Sibley's letter on red pipe stone,	514
History of Pipe Stone Quarry,	514
Nicollet's description of red pipe stone,	515
Allusions to pipe stone in Hiawatha,	515
Territorial seal described,	516
Captain and Mrs. Eastman,	516
Poem by Mrs. Eastman,	517
Ramsey and Chambers, commissioners to treat with Indians,	518
The project unsuccessful,	518
Organization of Democratic party,	518
Death of David Lambert,	519
Notice of D. Lambert,	519
Meeting in behalf of public schools,	520
Names of first school teachers,	520
County elections,	520
St. Anthony Library Association,	521

CHAPTER XXIII.

Historical Society,	522
First public meeting of Historical Society,	522
Carrier Boys' Address, Jan. 1, 1850,	523
Marriage at Fort Snelling,	523

CONTENTS.

Road by land to Prairie du Chien opened, . . . 524
First trial for murder, . . 525
Apple river battle, . . 526
Scalp dance in Stillwater, . 526
Captive boy sent back by Gov. Ramsey, ... 526
High water in 1850, . . 527
"Hole-in-the-Day" scalps near St. Paul, . . . 527
First Presbyterian church burned, ... 528
Indian council at Fort Snelling, 528
Description of council ground, 529
Speech of Governor Ramsey, . 530
Dahkotah rudeness, . . 533
Ojibway gallantry, . . . 533
Ojibways visit St. Paul, . . 534
Navigation on Minnesota begun, ... 534
Trip of the Yankee, . . 534
Steamer at Traverse des Sioux, 535
Passengers on steamer, . . 536
Steamer at Blue Earth, . . 537
Supposed buffaloes, . . 537
Mosquitoes, ... 537
Ice fails on board the boat, . 538
Uncomfortable night, . . 538
Return of steamer, . . . 538
Traverse des Sioux in 1850, . 539
Shokpay's village, . . . 540
The ministry needed for the West, ... 541
Election in September, . . 542
Sibley and Mitchell candidates, 543
Sibley elected delegate to Congress, ... 543
Official vote, ... 543
Miss Bremer visits St. Paul, . 543
Fredrika Bremer's sketch of the capital, . . . 543
The Dahkotah Friend published, ... 544
D. A. Robertson, . . . 544
Minnesota Democrat commenced, ... 544
C. J. Henniss, editor, . . 545
First Thanksgiving Day, . 545

CHAPTER XXIV.

Legislature of 1851, . . 546
Age and birth-place of members of the legislature, . 546
Editor stabbed, . . . 547
Bitter party feeling, . . 547
University of Minnesota, . 547
Apportionment bill, . . 548
Members resign their seats, . 548
Sufferings of Ojibways, . . 549
Mortality at Sandy Lake, . 550
Hole-in-the-Day addresses legislature, ... 551
Alleged cannibalism, . . 552
Debate on school lands at Washington, . . . 553
Remarks of Stevens, of Pennsylvania, ... 554
Sibley's reply, . . . 555
Chronicle and Register suspended, ... 555
Murder of Andrew Swartz, . 555
Remarkable escape of murderers, ... 556
First newspaper beyond the capital, ... 556
Treaties of 1851, . . . 556
Lea and Ramsey, commissioners, ... 556
Rev. Mr. Hopkins drowned, . 557
Thunder Bird dance, . . 558
Treaty at Traverse des Sioux concluded, ... 559
Provisions of the treaty, . 559
Treaty at Mendota concluded, 560

xxiv   CONTENTS.

Provisions of the treaty,	560	J. P. Owens, editor of Minnesotian,	562
Indians as horse purchasers,	561	October election,	563
Shokpay as it was in 1851,	562	Second Thanksgiving Day,	563
New paper started at St. Paul,	562	Governor's Proclamation,	563

CHAPTER XXV.

Legislature of 1852,	564	Birch Bark Fort,	571
Names of members,	564	Lake Neill,	572
Occupation of members,	564	Special election on liquor law,	572
Liquor law enacted,	565	Vote on liquor law,	572
Memorial to discontinue "St. Peter's" as a name of Minnesota river,	565	Claims before ratification of treaties,	573
Superintendent of Public Instruction report,	565	Death of James M. Goodhue,	574
		Sketch of pioneer editor,	574
Number of school-houses in Minnesota,	569	Editorial hoax,	576
		Trial of Yuhazee for murder,	577
Rae, Arctic explorer, in St. Paul,	570	Escort of dragoons,	578
Exploration between Watab and Long Prairie,	570	Judge Hayner's decision against liquor law,	579

CHAPTER XXVI.

Legislature of 1853,	580	J. T. Rosser, Secretary,	589
Officers chosen,	580	W. H. Welch, Chief Justice,	589
Governor Ramsey's last message,	581	Moses Sherburne, Associate,	589
		A. G. Chatfield, Associate,	589
Rapid growth of Minnesota,	581	Indian villages below St. Paul, 1853,	589
Advantages of Minnesota,	582		
Hopeful future,	583	Villages near Fort Snelling,	590
Prospective railways,	584	Alleged fraud of Ramsey and Sibley,	590
Roman Catholic petitions,	585		
Proposed school law,	586	Presbyterian missionaries among Dahkotahs,	590
Counties west of Mississippi,	587		
Baldwin School,	587	Honourable exculpation of Ramsey by United States Senate,	591
College of St. Paul,	587		
Ojibway and Dahkotah skirmish at the capital,	587		
		Robertson retires from editorial duties,	591
Burial scaffold at Kaposia,	588	David Olmsted,	591
Appointments by President Pierce,	588	October election for delegate,	591
Governor W. A. Gorman,	589	Official vote,	591

CHAPTER XXVII.

New political coalitions,	592
Legislature of 1854,	592
Governor Gorman's message,	593
Members of legislature, age and birth-place,	593
Mission-house at Lac qui Parle burned,	594
Minnesota and North-western Railroad incorporated,	594
E. S. Goodrich becomes editor of Pioneer,	594
Great railroad excursion,	595
Names of distinguished visiters,	595
Pursuit of pleasure under difficulties,	596
Guests at Fort Snelling,	597
Speeches of Fillmore and Bancroft,	597
Railroad sermon,	597
Railways in a religious view,	599
Antidotes to bigotry,	601
Savers of time,	603
Extend Christianity,	605
Land grant of Congress,	606
Repeal of land grant,	607
Debate on the repeal,	607
Rice's letter about the repeal,	610
Minnesota and North-western Railroad suit,	610
Appeal to United States Supreme Court,	611
Case dismissed,	611
Execution of Yuhazee,	611
Governor's letter to ladies declining to pardon Yuhazee,	612

CHAPTER XXVIII.

Legislature of 1855,	613
First bridge over the Mississippi,	613
Wire bridge,	613
Governor's message,	613
Governor opposes Minnesota and North-western Railroad Company,	613
United States Senate refuse to annul charter of Minnesota and North-western Railroad,	613
General illumination,	613
Governor Gorman vetoes an act amending charter of Minnesota and North-western Railroad Company,	614
Act passed by a two-thirds vote,	614
Formation of Republican party,	614
W. R. Marshall nominated delegate to Congress,	614
David Olmsted candidate for Congress,	614
H. M. Rice elected delegate,	614
Votes for delegate enumerated,	614
Express arrives at St. Paul with relics of Sir John Franklin,	615
Legislature of 1856,	615
Railroad discussion,	615
Governor Gorman signs a bill giving extension of time to Minnesota and North-western Railway Company,	615
His message on the subject,	615
List of members of Council of 1856,	617

CONTENTS

Members of House of Representatives, 1856,	617
State organization agitated by J. E. Warren,	618
Ojibways scalp Dahkotah child at a farm-house,	618
Legislature of 1857,	618
Presiding officers of legislature,	618
Bill removing capital to St. Peter passes the House,	618
Council resolutions of Mr. Balcombe,	619
Rolette, Chairman of Committee of Enrolled Bills, absent,	619
Call of the Council,	619
Sergeant-at-arms ordered to report absent member in his seat,	619
Council remains in session under the call for several days,	619
Last night of session proceedings under the call dispensed with,	620
Committee on Enrolled Bills report,	620
Report,	620
Call of the Council again moved,	621
Under the call the session expired,	621
Council adjourned,	621
Massacre at Spirit Lake and Springfield,	621
Inkpadootah,	621
Indians fire house of settlers,	622
The inmates killed,	622
Murder of the Gardners,	622
White women captives,	623
United States troops and volunteers bury the dead,	623
Captive women maltreated,	623
Mrs. Thatcher shot,	624
Two Indian youths rescue Mrs. Marble,	624
Paul and party rescue Miss Gardner,	625
Killing of Mrs. Noble,	625
Inkpadootah's son shot,	626
Outlaws' retreat beyond the Missouri,	626
Enabling act passed by Congress,	626
Special session of legislature,	626
Election for delegates to form constitution,	636
Meeting of constitutional convention,	627
Division into two bodies,	627
Compromise,	627
Constitution adopted by the people,	628
Meeting of first state legislature,	628
Election of United States Senators,	628
Admission of Minnesota into the Union,	628

INTRODUCTORY.

THE physical characteristics of a land should be known, to correctly understand the history of its people. In an important sense, when the skies do change, men also change. Grand scenery, leaping waters, and a bracing atmosphere, produce men of different cast from those who dwell where the land is on a dead level, and where the streams are all sluggards. We associate heroes like Tell and Bruce with the mountains of Switzerland and the Highlands of Scotland, and not with regions of country where the outline is unbroken, and the horizon appears as a continuation of the earth.

Minnesota occupies the elevated plateau of North America; and from its gently sloping plains descend the rivulets that feed the mighty Mississippi, that flows into the Gulf of Mexico; the noble St. Lawrence, emptying its volume into the Atlantic; and the winding Red River of the North, flowing into Hudson's Bay. It extends from 43° 30′ to 49° north latitude, and its boundaries are: on the north, the British Possessions;

on the south, the state of Iowa; on the east, Lake Superior and the state of Wisconsin; and on the west Red river, Sioux Wood river, Lake Traverse, and Big Stone Lake, and from the latter a due south line to the northern boundary of Iowa.

The climate of Minnesota has elicited an eulogy from every observing traveller, and yet erroneous impressions prevail in the public mind. During the summer, the temperature corresponds with that of Philadelphia; and while the thermometer has a high range during the day, the evenings are generally cool and refreshing. Nights, so frequent on the Atlantic border, when the body welters in perspiration, and the individual arises exhausted rather than refreshed by sleep, are unknown. Nor is the winter any more trying to the constitution than the summer. The air is dry and bracing, and the skies are by day generally cloudless, and at night are studded with stars. Maury, the author of the Physical Geography of the Sea, and Superintendent of the National Observatory at Washington, has remarked:—

"At the small hours of the night, at dewy eve and early morn, I have looked out with wonder, love, and admiration upon the steel-blue sky of Minnesota, set with diamonds, and sparkling with brilliants of purest ray. The stillness of your small hours is sublime. I feel constrained, as I gaze and admire, to hold my breath, lest the eloquent silence of the night should be broken by the reverberations of the sound, from the seemingly solid but airy vault above.

"Herschell has said, that in Europe, the astronomer might consider himself highly favoured, if by patiently watching the skies for one year, he shall, during that period find, all told, one hundred hours suitable for satisfactory observations. A telescope mounted here, in this atmosphere, under the skies of Minnesota, would have its powers increased many times over what they would be under canopies of a heaven less brilliant and lovely."

Corroborative of these statements are tables which appear in the report of the Minnesota and Pacific Railroad Company.

No region which at present engages the public mind, as a field for settlement, has been so grossly misrepresented, in regard to peculiarities of climate, as Minnesota. Fabulous accounts of its arctic temperature, piercing winds, and accompanying snows of enormous depth, embellish the columns of the Eastern press. An examination of this subject, and especially in relation to the snows and winds of winter, as opposed to the operation of lines of railroad, seems necessary to correct existing prejudices; and fortunately the means are at hand for conducting this examination with an exactness nearly reaching mathematical precision. The data employed are compiled from the "Army Meteorological Register," and "Blodgett's Climatology of the United States," both standard authorities, based upon the system of meteorological observations which have been conducted by the surgeons of the United States army, and other scientific gentlemen, through a series of upwards of thirty years.

In the following table, illustrative of the temperature of Minnesota, St. Paul is inserted in the place of Fort Snelling (six miles distant), where the observations were made:—

SPRING. MEAN TEMPERATURE, 45° 36'.	No. of Years.[1]	SUMMER. MEAN TEMPERATURE, 70° 36'.	No. of Years.
St. Paul,	35½	St. Paul,	35½
Boston, Massachusetts,	20	Lowell, Massachusetts,	7
Springfield, Massachusetts,	2	Trenton, New Jersey,	5
Worcester, Massachusetts,	7	Middletown, New Jersey,	3
Kinderhook, New York,	17	Flatbush, Long Island, New York,	24
Utica, New York,	9	Newburg, New York,	18
Cooperstown, New York,	16	Philadelphia, Pennsylvania,	10
Onondaga, New York,	16	Mifflintown, Pennsylvania,	3
Lewiston, New York,	18	Warren, Pennsylvania,	1½
Detroit, Michigan,	13	Hudson, Ohio,	7
Ann Arbor, Michigan,	3	Oberlin, Ohio,	5
Battle Creek, Michigan,	5½	Chicago, Illinois,	5
Chicago, Illinois,	5	Beloit, Wisconsin,	6
Beloit, Wisconsin,	6	Portage City, Wisconsin,	16
Portage City, Wisconsin,	16	Pembina, M. T. lat. 49°	7–12th

AUTUMN. MEAN TEMPERATURE, 45° 54'.	No. of Years.	WINTER. MEAN TEMPERATURE, 16° 6'.	No. of Years.
St. Paul,	35½	St. Paul,	35½
Portland, Maine,	31	Houlton, Maine,	17
Burlington, Vermont,	6	Hanover, New Hampshire,	3
Montreal, Canada,	15	Williamstown, Massachusetts,	13
Lake Simcoe, Canada West,	1	Montreal, Canada,	15
Lowville, Lewis County, New York,	19	Sault St. Marie,	31
Plattsburg, New York,	11		
Fairfield Academy, New York,	19		
Mexico, Oswego County, New York,	11		
Cherry Valley, New York,	15		
Ebensburg, Pennsylvania,	2¼		
Smethport, Pennsylvania,	3		
Green Bay, Wisconsin,	21		
Manitowoc, Wisconsin,	21		
Baraboo, Wisconsin,	1		

Taking a map of the United States, and applying to it lines of mean temperature for the seasons and year, passing through the places indicated in the foregoing table, we find that while the winter temperature of St.

[1] The column headed "No. of years" gives the duration of the observations at each station.

Paul does not fall below the average of places on its parallel of latitude, its spring temperature coincides with that of Central Wisconsin, Northern Illinois, Southern Michigan, Central New York, and Massachusetts; its summer with that of Central Wisconsin, Northern Illinois, Northern Ohio, Central and Southern Pennsylvania, and New Jersey; its autumn with that of Central Wisconsin, Northern New York, a small part of Northern Pennsylvania, Northern Vermont, and Southern Maine; and its entire year with that of Central Wisconsin, Central New York, Southern New Hampshire, and Southern Maine.

Viewing this subject with reference to the extremes of latitude touched by these isothermal lines, we discover that St. Paul has a temperature in spring equal to Chicago, which is two and a half degrees of latitude south; in autumn, equal to Northern New York, one and a half degrees south; and during the whole year, equal to Central New York, two degrees south.

These statements do not admit of the slightest doubt or question, no matter how widely they may differ from preconceived opinions, for they are founded on facts of experience which have occupied an entire generation in their development.

This condition of temperature not only obtains in Minnesota, but it is a well established fact, that there extends hundreds of miles to the north-west of her an immense area of fertile and arable soil, possessed of a climate hardly inferior in warmth to her own. The closing chapter of Blodgett's Climatology is an admirable treatise on the climate and resources of this vast region.

The obstruction opposed by snows to the rapid and

regular passage of trains, is among the chief difficulties of winter operation, and in order to submit in the plainest and most concise manner possible the magnitude of this obstacle, as found here in comparison with other districts, a table of mean results, compiled from the same sources with the preceding table, is here introduced.

The results given in the table are all reduced to water, but in order to convert them into equivalents of snow, we have only to consider the figures in the columns as representing feet and decimals of a foot. The rule adopted in the "Register," gives ten inches of snow as equivalent to one inch of water, but the proportion of twelve to one is believed to be more correct, particularly as regards snows of our latitude.

Mean Fall of Rain and Melted Snow at various places for the different seasons and the entire year. Also, the Maximum and Minimum Fall during the winter months.

DEPTH IN INCHES AND DECIMALS OF AN INCH.

PLACES.	SPRING. Mean.	SUMMER. Mean.	AUTUMN. Mean.	WINTER. Minim.	WINTER. Mean.	WINTER. Maxim.	YEAR. Mean.	No. of Years.
St. Paul, M. T.	6.61	10.92	5.98	0.35	1.92	3.56[1]	25.43	19
Montreal, Canada	11.54	11.18	16.60		7.26		47.28	2
Houlton, Me.	7.62	11.92	9.95	4.02	7.48	10.00	36.97	9¼
Eastport, Me.	8.88	10.05	9.85	8.91	10.61	11.95	39.39	8¼
Portsmouth, N. H.	9.03	9.21	8.95	4.44	8.38	11.08	35.57	13
Hanover, N. H.	9.90	11.40	10.50		9.10		41.00	18
Burlington, Vt.	7.41	10.83	9.82		6.02		34.11	20
Cambridge, Mass.	10.85	11.17	12.57		9.89		44.48	12
Worcester, Mass.	10.89	10.71	13.51		11.85		46.96	13
New York City	11.69	11.64	9.93	4.99	10.39	19.27	43.65	14
Plattsburg, N. Y.	8.36	10.03	10.05	2.90	4.95	9.33	33.39	10
Potsdam, N. Y.	6.20	10.15	8.38		3.90		28.63	20
Utica, N. Y.	9.26	12.83	9.76		8.72		40.57	19
Rochester, N. Y.	6.82	8.86	9.38		5.38		30.44	19
Fort Niagara, N. Y.	6.87	9.81	8.68	3.23	6.41	9.24	31.77	5½
Pittsburgh, Pa.	9.38	9.87	8.23	4.39	7.48	11.97	34.96	18
Hudson, O.	9.76	8.87	6.16		8.00		32.79	7
Cincinnati, O.	12.14	13.70	9.90		11.15		46.89	20
Detroit, Mich.	8.51	9.29	7.41	2.84	4.86	6.01	30.07	12½
Sault St. Marie, Mich.	5.44	9.97	10.76	2.85	5.18	11.57	31.35	16¾
Athens, Ill.	12.20	13.30	9.20		7.10		41.80	10
Muscatine, Iowa	11.19	15.08	10.34		6.72		44.33	10
Milwaukee, Wis.	6.60	9.70	6.80		4.20		27.20	7
Green Bay, Wis.	9.00	14.45	7.84	2.90	3.36	4.80	34.65	7¼
Portage City, Wis.	5.58	11.46	7.63	1.92	2.82	3.84	27.49	9
Beloit, Wis.	13.16	18.12	10.44		6.43		48.15	4

[1] In the winter of 1849. The next less fall was in the winter of 1837—2.96 inches.

Without going into a detailed review of the contents of the foregoing table, which presents the facts in a light that argument cannot strengthen, it may be well to inquire what proportion of the winter precipitation is in the form of snow, and in the absence of positive knowledge we may arrive at general conclusions by other means.

Since Houlton, Hanover, Plattsburg, Montreal, and Sault St. Marie, coincide in mean winter temperature with St. Paul, we must infer that the precipitation at those places assumes the form of snow in the same proportion as here. Admitting this, and supposing the *entire* winter precipitation to be a successive accumulation of snows, the resulting depths would be as follows, viz., Average annual depth at St. Paul, 3 feet; Houlton, 7½ feet; Hanover, 9 feet; Plattsburg, 5 feet; Montreal, 7 feet; Sault St. Marie, 11½ feet. Maximum depth, at St. Paul, 3½ feet; Houlton, 10 feet; Plattsburg, 9⅔ feet; and Sault St. Marie, 11½ feet. It is hardly necessary to add that such immense depths of snow are never known, and it must follow that a great part of the fall at all these localities is dissipated during the higher fluctuations of temperature. This is confirmed by Mr. Blodgett, who estimates the average depth of snow constantly occupying the ground in winter among the *elevated and northern* districts of New England at two feet, and the experience of the present winter, 1857–8, at St. Paul, is, that, out of a total fall of upwards of twenty inches of snow, the depth on the ground has at no time exceeded six inches.

Although no reliable evidence can be adduced upon this point, it seems entirely safe to assume that the average of *extreme* depths of snow in Minnesota, during the nineteen years through which the observations extend, does not exceed ten inches, and it is certain that the average here falls quite below that in Wisconsin, Illinois, Michigan, or New York, and very far below that in the Eastern States.

Table showing the Mean Force of the Wind at Various Places during the Months of January, February, March, and December, in each Year for a Series of Years.[1]

PLACES.	1845 Mean Force.	1846 Mean Force.	1847 Mean Force.	1848 Mean Force.	1849 Mean Force.	1850 Mean Force.	1851 Mean Force.	1852 Mean Force.	1853 Mean Force.	1854 Mean Force.	Whole No. of Years.	Mean Force Whole Term.
Fort Snelling, M. T., near St. Paul,	1.59	1.72	1.63	1.74	1.55	2.05	2.18	2.00	1.80	2.41	10	1.87
Fort Trumbull, New London, Conn.,	2.53	2.85	....	....	3.41	2.98	2.31	2.45	2.16	....	7	2.67
Fort Hamilton, New York City,	3.28	3.43	3.18	3.08	3.40	3.14	3.40	3.14	1.90	1.66	10	2.96
Fort Niagara, New York,	3.33	3.28	....	....	3.30	3.24	2.59	3.54	2.20	2.57	8	3.01
Plattsburg Barracks, Plattsburg, N. Y.	2.58	1.69	....	....	....	1.48	1.54	2.19	....	....	5	1.90
Fort Sullivan, Eastport, Maine,	3.29	....	....	....	....	....	2.31	2.37	2.55	2.63	5	2.63
Fort Constitution, Portsmouth, N. H.	2.44	....	....	....	....	....	2.18	2.53	2.70	2.65	5	2.50
Alleghany Arsenal, Pittsburgh, Pa.	2.13	1.85	2.08	1.86	2.08	2.29	2.15	2.74	2.31	2.55	10	2.20
Detroit Barracks, Detroit, Mich.	2.52	2.46	....	....	1.72	2.11	2.32	....	....	....	5	2.26
Fort Atkinson, Winneshiek County, Iowa,	2.88	2.07	....	....	....	....	....	....	....	....	2	2.48
Fort Leavenworth, Kansas,	2.30	2.19	1.70	1.99	2.55	1.45	1.61	2.03	2.07	2.30	10	2.09
Average force at all places,	2.63	2.40	2.15	2.17	2.57	2.32	2.30	2.59	2.22	2.30	....	2.42

[1] In this classification 0 signifies a calm, 1 a barely perceptible breeze, 2 a gentle breeze, 3 a moderate breeze, 4 a brisk breeze, and so on to 10, which represents a violent hurricane.

"It appears that the mean force of the wind at Fort Snelling for the whole term is less than at any other station, and twenty-five per cent. less than the average of all stations for the whole term, and that the mean force in any year is below the average at all stations for the year, except in 1854, when it slightly exceeds the average."

Like the Garden of Eden, the state is encircled by rivers and lakes. There is "water, water everywhere;" and in view of this characteristic, Nicollet called the country Undine. To naiads and all water spirits it would be a perfect paradise. The surface of the country is dotted with lakes, and in some regions it is impossible to travel five miles without meeting a beautiful expanse of water. Many of these lakes are linked together by small and clear rivulets, while others are isolated. Their configuration is varied and picturesque; some are large, with precipitous shores, and contain wooded islands, others are approached by gentle grassy slopes. Their bottoms are paved with agates, carnelians, and other beautiful quartz pebbles. Owens, in his Geological Report, says: "Their beds are generally pebbly, or covered with small boulders, which peep out along the shore, and frequently show a rocky line around the entire circumference. Very few of them have mud bottoms. The water is generally sweet and clear, and north of the water-shed is as cool and refreshing during the heats of summer as the water of springs or wells. All the lakes abound with various species of fish, of a quality and flavour greatly superior to those of the streams of the Middle or Western States.

The country also contains a number of ha-ha, as the Dahkotahs call all waterfalls. As the state of New

York shares with Great Britain the sublimest cataract, so Minnesota has a joint ownership in a picturesque fall. It is about a mile and a half above the mouth of Pigeon river. The perpendicular descent is sixty feet, after which the river chafes its way for many yards. About one mile below the west end of Grand Portage, the old depôt of the North-west Company, are the great cascades of Pigeon river. "The scenery at the cascades presents the singular combination of wild grandeur and picturesque beauty, with an aspect the most dreary and desolate imaginable. In the distance of four hundred yards, the river falls one hundred and forty-four feet. The fall is in a series of cascades through a narrow gorge, with perpendicular walls, varying from forty to one hundred and twenty feet, on both sides of the river."[1] The streams in the north-east county of Minnesota nearly all come into Lake Superior with a leap. Half a mile from the lake, the Kawimbash hurries through perpendicular walls of stone, seventy-five feet in height, and at last pitches down a height of eighteen or twenty feet.

On Kettle river, a tributary of the St. Croix, there are also interesting rapids and falls. The Falls of St. Croix, thirty miles above Stillwater, elicit the admiration of the traveller. Between lofty walls of trap rock, the river rushes, "at first with great velocity, forming a succession of whirlpools, until it makes a sudden bend, then glides along placidly, reflecting in its deep waters the dark image of the columnar masses, as they rise towering above each other to the height of a hundred to a hundred and seventy feet." On the Vermillion

---

[1] Owens' Report, p. 409, 4to.

river, which is a western tributary of the Mississippi, opposite the St. Croix, there are picturesque falls, about a mile from Hastings.

A drive of less than fifteen minutes from Fort Snelling, in the direction of St. Anthony, brings the tourist to a waterfall that makes a lifetime impression.

> "Stars in the silent night
> Might be enchained,
> Birds in their passing flight
> Be long detained,
> And by this scene entrancing,
> Angels might roam,
> Or make their home,
> Hearing, in waters dancing,
> 'Mid spray and foam,
> Minnehaha!"

These, within a brief period, have obtained a world-wide reputation, from the fact that "a certain one of our own poets" has given the name of Minne-ha-ha to the wife of Hiawatha. Longfellow, in his vocabulary, says: "Minne-ha-ha—Laughing-water; a waterfall or a stream running into the Mississippi, between Fort Snelling and the Falls of St. Anthony." All waterfalls, in the Dahkotah tongue, are called Ha-ha, *never Minne-ha-ha*. The "h" has a strong guttural sound, and the word is applied because of the *curling* or laughing of the waters. The verb *I-ha-ha* primarily means, *to curl;* secondarily *to laugh*, because of the curling motion of the mouth in laughter. The noise of Ha-ha is called by the Dahkotahs I-ha-ha, because of its resemblance to laughter.

A small rivulet, the outlet of Lake Harriet and Calhoun, gently gliding over the bluff into an amphitheatre, forms this graceful waterfall. It has but little of "the cataract's thunder." Niagara symbolizes the sublime; St. Anthony the picturesque; Ha-ha the beautiful. The fall is about sixty feet, presenting a parabolic curve, which drops, without the least deviation, until it has reached its lower level, when the stream goes on its way rejoicing, curling along in laughing, childish glee at the graceful feat it has performed in bounding over the precipice.

Five miles above this embodiment of beauty, are the more pretentious Falls of St. Anthony. This fall was not named by a Jesuit, as Willard says, in her History of the United States, but by Hennepin, a Franciscan of the Recollect Order. He saw it while returning from Mille Lac, in the month of July, 1680, and named it after his patron Saint, Anthony of Padua.

In the last edition of his travels, the adventurous father says, "the navigation is interrupted by a fall, which I called St. Anthony of Padua's, in gratitude for the favours done me by the Almighty through the intercession of that great saint, whom we had chosen patron and protector of all our enterprises. This fall is forty or fifty feet high, divided in the middle by a rocky island of pyramidal form." As Hennepin was passing the falls, in company with a party of buffalo hunters, he perceived a Dahkotah up in an oak opposite the great fall weeping bitterly, with a well dressed beaver robe, whitened inside, and trimmed with porcupine quills, which he was offering as a sacrifice to the falls, which is in itself admirable and frightful. I heard him while shedding copious tears say, as he spoke to the great cataract: "Thou who art a spirit, grant that our nation may pass here quietly without accident, may kill buffalo in abundance, conquer our enemies, and bring in slaves, some of whom we will put to death before thee; the Messenecqz [to this day the Dahkotahs call the Fox Indians by this name] have killed our kindred, grant that we may avenge them."

The only other European, during the time of the French dominion, whose account of the falls is preserved, is Charleville. He told Du Pratz, the author of a history of Louisiana, that, with two Canadians and two Indians, in a birch canoe laden with goods, he proceeded as far as the Falls of St. Anthony. This cataract he describes as caused by a flat rock, which forms the bed of the river, and causing a fall of eight or ten feet. It was not far from a century after Hennepin saw the "curling waters," that it was gazed upon by a British subject. Jonathan Carver, a native of Connecticut, and captain of a Provincial troop, was the Yankee who first looked on this valuable water-power, and began to make calculations for further settlement. His sketch of the falls in 1766 was the first ever taken, and was well engraved in London.

Carver, like Hennepin, speaks of a rocky island dividing the falls, and estimates its width about forty feet, and its length not much more, "and about half way between this island and the eastern shore, is a rock, lying at the very edge of the fall, that appeared to be about five or six feet broad, and thirty or forty long."

During the two generations that have elapsed, since this description was penned, some changes have taken place in the appearance of the falls. The small island about forty feet broad, which is now some distance in front of the falls, was probably once in its midst. The geological character of the bed of the river is such, that an undermining process is constantly at work. The upper stratum is limestone, with many large crevices, and about fifteen feet in thickness. Beneath is the saccharoid sandstone, which is so soft, that it cannot resist the wearing of the rapid waters. It is more than probable that in an age long passed, the falls were once in the vicinity of Fort Snelling. In the course of two years they have receded many feet. The numbers of pine logs that pitch over the falls, have increased the recession. As the logs float down they are driven into the fissures, and serve as levers, other logs and the water communicating the power, to wrench the limestone slabs from their localities. In time the falls will recede until they become nothing more than rapids.

The fall of water on the west side of the dividing island, is several rods above that on the east side, and the difference is occasioned by the greater volume of water on the former side, causing a more rapid recedence.

There are two islands of great beauty in the rapids above the falls. The first juts some feet beyond the falls, and contains about fifteen acres. It is now generally known as Hennepin Island, not, as some blunderer says in Harper's Magazine for July, 1853, because the *Jesuit father was placed there by the Indians,* but in accordance with the following suggestion, in an address before the Historical Society of Minnesota, on January first, 1850:—

" As a town in the state of Illinois has already taken

the name of Hennepin, which would have been so appropriate for the beautiful village of St. Anthony, we take leave of the discoverer of those picturesque falls, which will always render that town equally attractive to the eye of the poet and capitalist, by suggesting that the island which divides the laughing waters, be called Hennepin."

When Du Luth left Minnesota, in 1680, one of the Dahkotah chiefs drew on birch bark a map of the Mississippi, and it was agreed that the French should bring goods to the Mississippi, and that the Dahkotahs would come down and traffic with them. Perrot, in carrying into effect this arrangement, appears to have erected the trading establishment, called Fort St. Nicholas, in the vicinity of Prairie du Chien.

When forts are spoken of in connection with the French explorations of the North-west, the reader must divest himself of the idea of massive walls of masonry, and turrets and buttresses, and angles with ordnance protruding their muzzles;—and picture before him a log cabin, surrounded by a few pickets.

The early French maps on America, are both curious and instructive. Without their aid it is impossible to trace with certainty the progress of discovery in Minnesota, and the whole North-west.

The earliest chart representing Minnesota that has been examined is that of Coronellis, corrected by Tillemon, published at Paris, 1688.

Mille Lac is called Lac Buade, and the map states that it was named by Du Luth.

The St. Croix river appears as Magdeline, and Snake river is marked Prophet.

The second map that attempts a representation of

the region now known as Minnesota, is attached to the Utrecht edition of Hennepin's Travels, published in 1698. Lake Pepin is on this marked Lac des Pleurs, and the St. Croix as Riviere du Tombeau, and Mille Lac is the Lake of the Issati. North-east of this lake are placed the Ouadebaton band of Dahkotahs; and near by the Chongas-kabions, and Songasquitons.

A member of the Franciscan priesthood, Hennepin, was very jealous of the influence of the Jesuits, yet he is frequently by loose writers called a Jesuit. To convey the impression that his order were the pioneers in the evangelization of the North-west, he has marked beyond Sauk Rapids, in a region where a white man's footsteps were not seen for years subsequent, a house which is called Mission of the Recollects.

The maps on the North-west that were the basis of the French and English charts, for half a century, were prepared by William de l'Isle, a member of the Royal Academy of Sciences at Paris. In his preparation of the chart of Louisiana, he was assisted by the observations of the early explorer of Minnesota, Le Sueur. The map was issued about the year 1700, and as the section of it accompanying another chapter of this work shows,[1] attempted to designate the villages of the Sioux of the East and Sioux of the West. It places a coal mine on the Minnesota river, in the neighbourhood of the present town of Carver, and calls Lake St. Croix, Lake Pepin. The fort built by Le Sueur on the island below Hastings, and by Perrot at an earlier period, opposite the Chippeway river, and Fort Huillier on the small tributary of the Mahkahto, are clearly designated.

[1] See page 164.

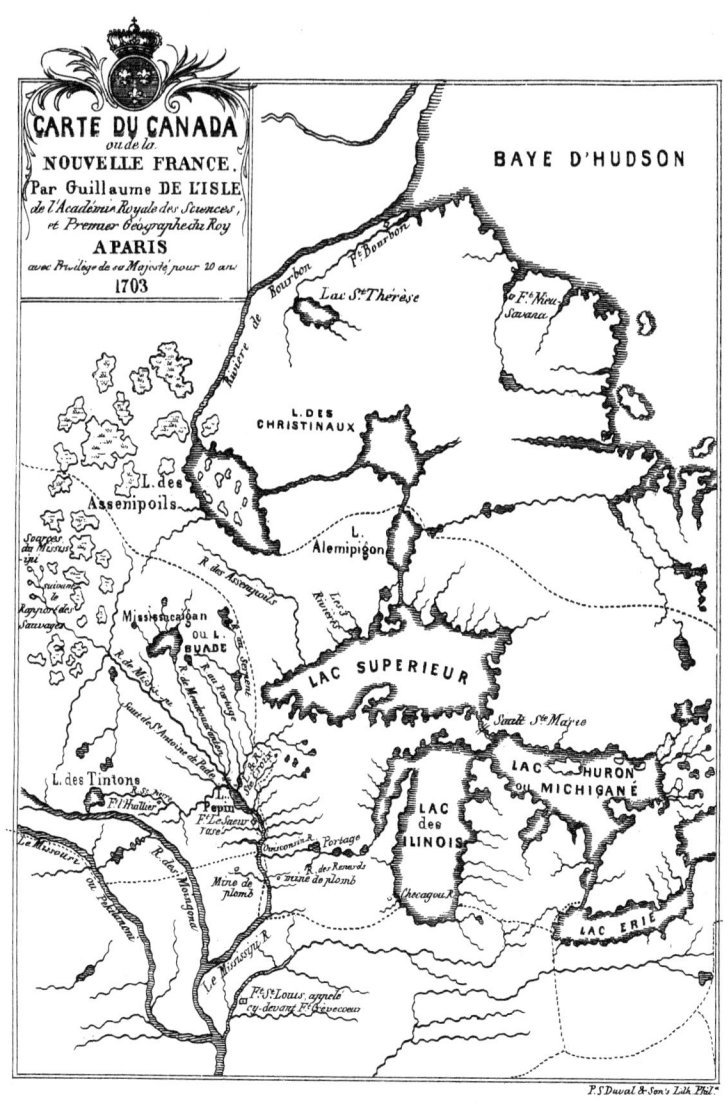

Section of a Map of Canada.

In the map of Canada, by the same author, Minnesota is more fully delineated. Pepin is attached to the lake which now bears the name. Mille Lac is called Buade, after the family name of Frontenac, and also by an Ojibway word Missisacaigan, conveying the idea expressed by the French term Mille Lacs.

Rum river is called the Mendeouacanton, after the division of Dahkotahs that dwelt in the valley. Snake river bears its present name, and the mines of lead near Galena and Dubuque are noted. In the year 1750, after Veranderie's tour by the chain of lakes that form the northern boundary of Minnesota, Philip Buache[1] revised and improved the maps of De l'Isle. The fort at the mouth of Pigeon river, built by Du Luth, appears, and this locality was afterwards occupied by Fort Charlotte, and was the great depôt of the North-west Company. The post on Rainy Lake, and Lake Winnipeg and Lake of the Woods, are also presented for the first time. Previous to the treaty of peace at Paris, in 1763, Thomas Jefferys, Geographer to the King of England, prepared a map which embodied all of the latest corrections, and exhibits the sites of all the French establishments in Minnesota.[2]

So recent has been the removal of the Dahkotahs, there is danger, in reading the history of Minnesota, of supposing that the emigrant will be exposed to the scalping knife of the savage. It is true that there was a massacre by some outlaws on the extreme southwestern frontier, not long since; but this barbarity was condemned by the Indian bands, as much as by American citizens. Although the war-whoop has scarcely

---

[1] See page 188.   [2] See page 300.

ceased to resound through the vales, and over the prairies, yet, since 1853, the Indian population has receded westward one hundred and fifty miles, and an Indian, when he appears on the site of what was only yesterday his village, is gazed at with curiosity.

At Weenonah,[1] so lately the residence of Wapashaw,[2] there is already an embryo city with three thousand inhabitants, and two newspapers; at Raymneecha, the recent village of the Red Wing band, at the head of Lake Pepin, there is a busy town, the seat of a Methodist University, with comfortable church edifices of brick, and an industrious population. At Shokpay,[3] which was one of the largest Dahkotah[4] villages, is a thriving county seat, with a population that is rapidly increasing. Near the old mission-house of Traverse des Sioux, is springing up St. Peter, a town of ardent aspirations, which may be the future capital of the state.

Notwithstanding the erroneous impressions that have prevailed, that Minnesota was too far north for agricultural success, and the emigration to Kansas, Nebraska, and California, its growth has been surprising. In 1849, the population was less than five thousand, including all of the soldiers of the forts; in 1857, a census that was not fully completed, presented the following figures:—

---

[1] In several places we write Winona as it is pronounced, because some are beginning to talk of the town of *Wyenonay*, a barbarism that would shock a Dahkotah.

[2] Wapashaw is used for Wabasha, because more correct and euphonious —See *Dahkotah Lexicon*, vol. iv. Smithsonian Publications.

[3] Shokpay or Shakpay, is now written Shakopee, but we prefer the old method.

[4] Dahkotah is also spelled Dakota, Dacota, Dahcotah, and Dakotah. The accent is emphatic, and on the penult.

DESCRIPTION OF FALLS OF ST. ANTHONY, 1848. xlv

Houston,	5,264	Benton,	688	
Winona,	8,163	Stearns,	2,840	
Fillmore,[1]	6,595	Meeker,	1,014	
Olmsted,	8,458	Morrison,	751	
Dodge,	3,680	Manomin,[2]	——	
Mower,[2]	——	Washington,	6,182	
Freeborn,	2,485	Chisago,	1,763	
Faribault,	689	Pine,	102	
Waseca,	2,595	St. Louis,	1,559	
Steele,	2,598	Isanti,	184	
Blue Earth,	3,628	Pierce,[2]	——	
Wabashaw,	5,115	Cass,	196	
Goodhue,	6,951	Pembina,	——	
Rice,	6,440	Crow Wing,	176	
Le Sueur,	3,610	Mille Lac,[2]	——	
Nicollet,	5,437	Todd,	81	
Brown,	1,689	Buchanan,	120	
Sibley,[2]	——	Carlton,	239	
Scott,	5,302	Lake,	1,212	
Carver,	3,117	Itasca,[2]	——	
Renville,	245	Cotton Wood,	173	
McLeod,	822	Murray,	81	
Dahkotah,	8,158	Nobles,	16	
Hennepin,	13,064	Rock,	52	
Ramsey,	12,748	Jackson,	50	
Anoka,	2,559	Martin,	55	
Wright,	2,233	Pipe Stone,	24	
Sherburne,	507			
Total,				136,464

In 1848, Minnesota seemed a wilderness to a divine, the Rev. Albert Barnes, of Philadelphia, who visited the country on a tour of pleasure; and he thus presents his views of a locality, which is now spanned by two bridges, the seat of the State University, and of two towns, the abode of five thousand active inhabitants :—

"I visited the Falls of St. Anthony. I know not how other men feel when standing there, nor how men will feel a century hence, when standing there—then,

[1] Partial return. [2] No returns.

not in the *West*, but almost in the centre of our great nation. But when I stood there and reflected on the distance between that and the place of my birth and my home; on the prairies over which I had passed; and the stream—the 'Father of Rivers'—up which I had sailed some five hundred miles, into a new and unsettled land—where the children of the forest still live and roam—I had views of the greatness of my country, such as I have never had in the crowded capitals and the smiling villages of the East. Far in the distance did they then seem to be; and there came over the soul the idea of greatness, and vastness, which no figures, no description, had ever conveyed to my mind. To an inexperienced traveller, too, how strange is the appearance of all that land! * * * * You ascend the Mississippi amidst scenery unsurpassed in beauty probably in the world. You see the waters making their way along an interval of from two to four miles in width—between bluffs of from one hundred to five hundred feet in height. Now the river makes its way along the eastern range of bluffs, and now the western, and now in the centre, and now it divides itself into numerous channels, forming thousands of beautiful islands, covered with long grass, ready for the scythe of the mower. Those bluffs, rounded with taste and skill, such as could be imitated by no art of man, and set out with trees here and there, gracefully arranged like orchards, seem to have been sown with grain to the summit, and are clothed with beautiful green. You look out instinctively for the house and barn; for flocks and herds; for men, and women, and children; but they are not there. A race that is gone seems to have cultivated those fields, and then to have silently disappeared—leaving them for the first man that should come from the older parts of our own country, or from foreign lands, to take possession of them. It is only by a process of reflection that you are convinced that it is not so."

The state of Minnesota derives its name from the principal tributary of the Mississippi within its boundaries. The name is a compound Dahkotah word. This nation call the Missouri, Minneshoshay, muddy water, and this stream Minnesota. The precise signification of Sota is difficult to express. Featherstonhaugh says it means clear, Schoolcraft bluish green, others turbid. Nicollet remarks:—

"The adjective Sotah is of difficult translation. The Canadians translated it by a pretty equivalent word brouillé, perhaps more properly rendered into English by blear, as for instance Minisotah, blear water. I have entered upon this explanation because the word sotah really means neither clear nor turbid, as some authors have asserted, its true meaning being readily found, in the Sioux expression Ishta-sotah, blear eyed."

From the fact that the word signifies neither white nor blue, but the peculiar appearance of the sky on certain days, the Historical Society publications, define Minnesota to mean the *sky-tinted water*, which is certainly poetic, and according to Gideon H. Pond, one of the best Dahkotah scholars, correct.

Throughout the work, we have called the tribe who were the aborigines of Minnesota, Dahkotahs, a name by which they recognise themselves. The term Sioux is a mere nickname given for convenience by the early voyageurs.

Minnesota, as a state, ought to have the highest aspirations. The birthplace of many rivers, flowing north, south, east, and west; with varied scenery, the prairie, the forest, the lofty bluff, the placid lake, and the laughing waterfall; the summit of the central valley of North America; with an atmosphere peculiarly dry and bracing, it must ever be attractive to emigrants from all regions of the world. If the aims of her citizens only correspond with the elevated natural position and advantages, the cattle upon a thousand hills will soon occupy the old pasture-grounds of the elk and bison, and school-houses will crown the eminences but lately adorned with burial scaffolds; and the State will become the birth-place of not only majestic rivers, but great men.

If the perusal of the following pages shall tend to foster a proper State pride, and interest the generation now springing up in the history of their country, the chief end of the work will have been attained.

HISTORY OF MINNESOTA.

CHAPTER I.

MINNESOTA is the "land of the Dahkotahs." Long before their existence was known to civilized men, they wandered through the forests, between Lake Superior and the Mississippi, in quest of the bounding deer, and over the prairies beyond in search of the ponderous buffalo.

They are an entirely different group from the Algonquin and Iroquois, who were found by the early settlers of the Atlantic States, on the banks of the Connecticut, Mohawk, and Susquehanna rivers. Their language is much more difficult to comprehend; and, while they have many customs in common with the tribes who once dwelt in New England, New York, Pennsylvania, and Illinois, they have peculiarities which mark them as belonging to a distinct family of the aborigines of America.

Winona, Wapashaw, Mendota, Anoka, Kasota, Mahkahto, and other names designating the towns, hamlets, and streams of Minnesota, are words derived from the Dahkotah vocabulary.

Between the head of Lake Superior and the Mississippi river, above the Falls of Saint Anthony, is a country of many lakes. So numerous are they, and interlaced by clear and sparkling brooks, to an aeronaut they would appear like a necklace of diamonds, on silver filaments, gracefully thrown upon the bosom of Earth.

Surrounded by forests of the sugar maple—the neighbouring marshes fertile in the growth of wild rice—the waters abounding in fish—the shores once alive with the beaver, the otter, the bear, and the fox—they were sites just adapted for the residence of an Indian population.

When the Dahkotahs were first noticed by the European adventurer, large numbers were occupying this region of country, and appropriately called by the voyageur, " People of the Lakes."[1] And tradition, asserts that here, was the ancient centre of this tribe. Though we have traces of their warring and hunting on the shores of Lake Superior, there is no satisfactory evidence of their residence, east of the Mille Lac region.[2]

The word Dahkotah, by which they love to be designated, signifies allied or joined together in friendly compact, and is equivalent to " E pluribus unum," the motto on the seal of the United States.

In the history of the mission at La Pointe, Wisconsin, published nearly two centuries ago, a writer, referring to the Dahkotahs, remarks:—

" For sixty leagues from the extremity of the Upper Lake, toward sunset; and, as it were in the centre of the western nations, they have all *united their force by a general league.*"

---

[1] Gens du Lac.

[2] They have no name for Lake Superior.—G. H. Pond, in "*Dahkotah Tawaxitku Kin.*"

THE NAMES SIOUX, AND DAHKOTAH.

The Dahkotahs in the earliest documents, and even until the present day, are called Sioux, Scioux, or Soos. The name originated with the early "voyageurs." For centuries the Ojibways of Lake Superior waged war against the Dahkotahs; and, whenever they spoke of them, called them Nadowaysioux, which signifies enemies.

The French traders, to avoid exciting the attention of Indians, while conversing in their presence, were accustomed to designate them by names, which would not be recognised.

The Dahkotahs were nicknamed Sioux, a word composed, of the two last syllables, of the Ojibway word, for foes.

Charlevoix, who visited Wisconsin in 1721, in his history of New France says: "The name of Sioux, that we give to these Indians, is entirely of our own making, or rather it is the last two syllables of the name of Nadouessioux, as many nations call them."

From an early period, there have been three great divisions of this people, which have been subdivided into smaller bands. The first are called the Isanyati, the Issati of Hennepin, after one of the many lakes at the head waters of the river, marked on modern maps, by the unpoetic name of Rum. It is asserted by Dahkotah missionaries now living, that this name was given to the lake because the stone from which they manufactured the knife (isan) was here obtained. The principal band of the Isanti was the M'dewakantonwan.[1] In the journal of Le Sueur, they are spoken of as residing on a lake east of the Mississippi. Tra-

[1] Pronounced as if written Medday-wawkawn-twawn.

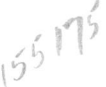

dition says that it was a day's walk from Isantamde or Knife Lake.

On a map prepared in Paris in 1703, Rum River is called the river of the M'dewakantonwans, and the Spirit Lake on which they dwelt, was, without doubt, Mille Lac of modern charts.

The second great division is the IHANKTONWAN, commonly called YANKTON. They appear to have occupied the region west of the M'dewakantonwan, and north of the Minnesota river. The geographer De Lisle places their early residence in the vicinity of Traverse des Sioux, extending northward.

The last division, the TITONWAN, hunted west of the Ihanktons, and all the early maps mark their villages at Lac-qui-parle and Big Stone Lake.

Hennepin, in August, 1679, in the vicinity of the Falls of Niagara, met the Senecas returning from war with the Dahkotahs, and with them some captive Tintonwans (Teetwawns).

This division is now the most numerous, and comprises about one-half of the whole nation. They have wandered to the plains beyond the Missouri, and are the plundering Arabs of America. Whenever they appear in sight of the emigrant train, journeying to the Pacific coast, the hearts of the company are filled with painful apprehensions.

North of the Dahkotahs, on Lake of the Woods and the watercourses connecting it with Lake Superior, were the Assiniboine. These were once a portion of the nation. Before the other divisions of the Dahkotahs had traded with the French, they had borne their peltries to the English post, Fort Nelson, on Hudson's Bay, and had received in return British manufactures. By association with the English, they learned to look upon the French with distrust, and in time to be hostile towards those who had formed alliances with the French.

Le Sueur writes, in relation to their separation from the rest of the nation, in these words:—

"The Assinipoils speak Scioux, and are certainly of that nation. It is *only a few years* since they became enemies. It thus originated: The Christianaux having the use of arms before the Scioux, through the English at Hudson's Bay, they constantly warred upon the Asssinipoils, who were their nearest neighbours. The latter being weak sued for peace, and, to render it more lasting, married the Christianaux women. The other Scioux, who had not made the compact, continued to war, and seeing some Christianaux with the Assinipoils, broke their heads." After this there was alienation. A letter, however, written at Fort Bourbon, on Hudson's Bay, about 1695, remarks: "It is said that the Assiniboins are a nation of the Sioux, which separated from them *a long time ago.*"

The Dahkotahs call these alienated tribes Hohays, and make woman the cause of the separation. They are said to have belonged to the Ihanktonwan (Yankton) division of the nation. A quarrel, tradition asserts, occurred between two families hunting at the time in the vicinity of Lake Traverse. A young man seduced the wife of one of the warriors. The injured husband, in attempting to rescue his wife, was killed in the tent of the seducer. His father and some relatives wanted to secure the corpse. On the road, they were met, by some of the friends of the guilty youth, and three of their number were killed. The father then turned back and raised a party of sixty warriors, who waged war against the seducer and his friends, which continued until the whole band were involved, and ended in a revolt upon the part of the aggressor and his friends, who in time became a separate people.

In the valleys of the Blue Earth, the Des Moines, and the eastern tributaries of the Missouri, within the limits of the territory of Minnesota, there also dwelt in ancient days bands of the Ioways, Ottoes, Cheyennes, Aricarees, and Omahaws, who sought other hunting-grounds as the Dahkotahs advanced westward.

The Dahkotahs, like all ignorant and barbarous people, have but little reflection beyond that necessary to gratify the pleasure of revenge and of the appetite.

It would be strange to find heroes among skulking savages, or maidens like "Minnehaha" of the poet, among those whose virtue can be easily purchased. While there are exceptions, the general characteristics of the Dahkotahs, and all Indians, are indolence, impurity, and indifference to the future.

The religion of this people is exceedingly indistinct, and with reluctance do they converse on the subject. That a nation so low in the scale of humanity should have preserved the idea of one great spirit, the father of all spirits, the supreme and most perfect of beings, is not to be supposed. To attribute to them more elevated conceptions than those of the cultivated Athenians, is perfect absurdity. The Dahkotahs, in their religious belief, are polytheists. The hunter, as he passes over the plains, finds a granite boulder: he stops and prays to it, for it is "*Wawkawn*"—mysterious or supernatural. At another time, he will pray to his dog; and at another time, to the sun, moon, or stars.

In every leaf, in every stone, in every shrub, there is a spirit. It may be said of them, as Cotton Mather said of the Massachusetts Indians, in his Life of Eliot: "All the religion they have amounts to thus much: they believe that there are many gods, who made and own the several nations of the world. They believe that every remarkable creature has a peculiar god within or about it; there is with them a sun god or a moon god and the like; and they cannot conceive but that the fire must be a kind of god, inasmuch as a spark of it will soon produce very strange effects. They believe that when any good or ill happens to them, there is the favour or anger of a god expressed in it."

The Dahkotahs have greater and minor deities, and they are supposed to multiply as men and animals, and the superior to have power to exterminate the inferior.

The Jupiter Maximus of the Dahkotahs is styled Oanktayhee. As the ancient Hebrews avoided speaking the name of Jehovah, so they dislike to speak the name of this deity, but call him "Taku-wakan," or "That which is supernatural." This mighty god manifests himself as a large ox. His eyes are as large as the moon. He can haul in his horns and tail, or he can lengthen them, as he pleases. From him proceed invisible influences. In his extremities reside mighty powers.

He is said to have created the earth. Assembling in grand conclave all of the aquatic tribes, he ordered them to bring up dirt from beneath the water, and proclaimed death to the disobedient. The beaver and others forfeited their lives. At last the muskrat went beneath the waters, and, after a long time, appeared at the surface nearly exhausted, with some dirt. From this,

Oanktayhee fashioned the earth into a large circular plain.

The earth being finished, he took a deity, one of his own offspring, and grinding him to powder, sprinkled it upon the earth, and this produced many worms. The worms were then collected and scattered again. They matured into infants; and these were then collected and scattered and became full-grown Dahkotahs.

The bones of the mastodon, the Dahkotahs think, are those of Oanktayhee, and they preserve them with the greatest care in the medicine bag. It is the belief of the Dahkotahs that the Rev. R. Hopkins, who was drowned at Traverse des Sioux, on July 4th, 1851, was killed by Oanktayhee, who dwells in the waters, because he had preached against him.

This deity is supposed to have a dwelling-place beneath the Falls of Saint Anthony. A few years ago, by the sudden breaking up of a gorge of ice, a cabin near Fort Snelling, containing a soldier, was swept off by the flood. The Dahkotahs supposed that this great god was descending the river at the time, and, being hungry, devoured the man.

HAY-O-KAH (*the anti-natural god*).—There are four persons in this godhead. The *first* appears like a tall and slender man with two faces, like the Janus of ancient mythology. Apollo-like, he holds a bow in his hand streaked with red lightning, also a rattle of deer claws. The *second* is a little old man with a cocked hat and enormous ears, holding a yellow bow. The *third*, a man with a flute suspended from his neck. The *fourth* is invisible and mysterious, and is the gentle zephyr which bends the grass and causes the ripple of the water.

Hayokah is a perfect paradox. He calls bitter sweet,

and sweet bitter; he groans when he is full of joy; he laughs when he is in distress; he calls black, white, and white, black; when he wishes to tell the truth he speaks a lie, and when he desires to lie, he speaks the truth; in winter he goes naked, and in summer he wraps up in buffalo robes. The little hills on the prairies are called Hay-o-kah-tee, or the house of Hay-o-kah. Those whom he inspires, can make the winds blow and the rain fall, the grass to grow and wither.

There is said to exist a clan who especially adore this deity, and at times dance in his honour. At dawn of day they assemble within a tēēpēē, in the centre of which is a fire, over which are suspended kettles. With cone-shaped hats and ear-rings, both made of bark, and loins girded with the same material, they look like incarnate demons. On their hats are zigzag streaks of paint— representations of lightning.

The company remain seated and smoking around the fire, until the water in the kettle begins to boil, which is a signal for the commencement of the dance. The excitement now becomes intense. They jump, shout, and sing around the fire, and at last plunge their hands into the cauldron, seize and eat the boiled meat. Then they throw the scalding water, on each others backs, the sufferers never wincing, but insisting that it is cold.

TAKU-SHKAN-SHKAN.—This deity is supposed to be invisible, yet everywhere present. He is full of revenge, exceedingly wrathful, very deceitful, and a searcher of hearts. His favourite haunts are the four winds, and the granite boulders strewn on the plains of Minnesota. He is never so happy as when he beholds scalps, warm and reeking with blood.

The object of that strange ceremony of the Dahkotahs, in which the performer being bound hand and foot with the greatest care, is suddenly unbound by an invisible agent, is to obtain an interview with Taku-shkan-shkan.

The name of another one of the superior divinities is Wahkeenyan. His tēēpēē is supposed to be on a mound on the top of a high mountain, in the far West. The tēēpēē or tent has four openings, with sentinels clothed in red down. A butterfly is stationed at the east, a bear at the west, a fawn at the south, and a reindeer at the north entrance. He is supposed to be a gigantic bird, the flapping of whose wings makes thunder. He has a bitter enmity against Oanktayhee, and attempts to kill his offspring. The high water a few years ago was supposed to be caused by his shooting through the earth, and allowing the water to flow out. When the lightning strikes their tēēpēēs or the ground, they think that Oanktayhee was near the surface of the earth, and that Wahkeenyan, in great rage, fired a hot thunderbolt at him.

By him wild rice, is said to have been created, also the spear, and tomahawk.

A bird of thunder was once killed, the Indians assert, near Kaposia. Its face resembled the human countenance. Its nose was hooked like the bill of an eagle. Its wings had four joints, and zigzag like the lightning.

About thirty miles from Big Stone Lake, near the head waters of the Minnesota, there are several small lakes bordered with oak-trees. This is the supposed birth-place of the Thunder Bird, and is called the Nest of Thunder. The first step the spirit ever took in this world was equal to that of the hero, in the child's story, who wore seven-league boots, being twenty-five miles in length. A rock is pointed out which has a foot-like impression, which they say is his track; and the hill is called Thunder Tracks.

A son of Colonel Snelling, the first commander of the fort of that name, in a poem, which is published in Griswold's collection of American poetry, alludes to the foregoing incidents:—

"The moon that night withheld her light.
By fits, instead, a lurid glare
Illumed the skies; while mortal eyes
Were closed, and voices rose in prayer
While the revolving sun
Three times his course might run,
The dreadful darkness lasted;
And all that time the red man's eye
A sleeping spirit might espy,
Upon a tree-top cradled high,
Whose trunk his breath had blasted.
So long he slept, he grew so fast,
Beneath his weight the gnarlèd oak
Snapped, as the tempest snaps the mast:
It fell, and Thunder woke!
The world to its foundation shook,
The grizzly bear his prey forsook,
The scowling heaven an aspect bore
That man had never seen before;
The wolf in terror fled away,
And shone at last the light of day.

"'Twas here he stood; these lakes attest
Where first WAW-KEE-AN's footsteps press'd.
About his burning brow a cloud,
Black as the raven's wing, he wore;
Thick tempests wrapt him like a shroud,
Red lightnings in his hand he bore;
Like two bright suns his eyeballs shone,
His voice was like the cannon's tone;
And, where he breathed, the land became,
Prairie and wood, one sheet of flame.

"Not long upon this mountain height
The first and worst of storms abode,

> For, moving in his fearful might,
>   Abroad the God-begotten strode.
> Afar, on yonder faint blue mound,
> In the horizon's utmost bound,
> At the first stride his foot he set;
>   The jarring world confessed the shock.
> Stranger! the track of Thunder yet
>   Remains upon the living rock.
>
> "The second step, he gained the sand
> On far Superior's storm-beat strand:
> Then with his shout the concave rung,
> As up to heaven the giant sprung
>   On high, beside his sire to dwell;
> But still, of all the spots on earth,
> He loves the woods that gave him birth.—
>   Such is the tale our fathers tell."

After an individual has dreamed in relation to the sun, there are sacred ceremonies. Two persons are the participants, who assume a peculiar attitude. Almost naked, holding a small whistle in their mouths, they look towards the sun, and dance with a strange and awkward step. One of their interpreters remarks, "The nearest and best comparison I can make of them when worshipping, is a frog held up by the middle with its legs half drawn up."

During the continuance of the ceremony, which may last two or three days, the parties fast.

When a Dahkotah is troubled in spirit, and desires to be delivered from real or imaginary danger, he will select a stone that is round and portable, and, placing it in a spot free from grass and underbrush, he will streak it with red paint, and, offering to it some feathers, he will pray to it for help. The stone, after the ceremony is over, does not appear to be regarded with veneration. If visitors request them, they can be obtained.

CHAPTER II.

In all nations where the masses are unenlightened, their spiritual nature is uncultivated, and they believe whatever a class of men pretending to have authority from the spirit world, may impose upon them. All ignorant communities are superstitious and easily priest-ridden. The early Britons looked upon the Druids, as a supernatural, and wonder-working class, and they fed, and feared them. The Wawkawn, or medicine men, hold the same relation to the Dahkotahs as the Druids to the ancient Britons. They are the most powerful and influential of the tribe. They are looked upon as a species of demi-gods. They assert their origin to be miraculous. At first they are spiritual existences, encased in a seed of some description of a winged nature, like the thistle. Wafted by the breeze to the dwelling-place of the gods, they are received to intimate communion. After being instructed in relation to the mysteries of the spirit world, they go forth to study the character of all tribes. After deciding upon a residence, they enter the body of some one about to become a mother, and are ushered by her into the world. A great majority of the M'dewakantonwans are medicine men.

When an individual desires to belong to this priesthood, he is initiated by what is termed a "medicine dance." This dance is said to have been instituted by Oanktayhee, the patron of medicine men. The editor of the "Dahkotah Friend," in a description of this dance, remarks:—

"When a member is to be received into this society, it is his duty, to take the hot bath, four days in succession. In the mean time, some of the *elders* of the society instruct him in the mysteries of the medicine, and Wahmnoo-*h*ah—shell in the throat. He is also provided with a dish (wojute) and spoon. On the side of the dish is sometimes carved the head of some voracious animal, in which resides the spirit of Eeyah (glutton god). This dish is always carried by its owner to the medicine feast, and it is his duty, ordinarily, to eat all which is served up in it. Gray Iron has a dish which was given him at the time of his initiation, on the bottom of which is carved, a bear complete. The candidate is also instructed with what paints, and in what manner, he shall paint himself, which must always be the same, when he appears in the dance. There is supernatural virtue in this paint, and the manner in which it is applied; and those who have not been furnished with a better, by the regular war prophets, wear it into battle, as a life-preserver. The bag contains besides, the claws of animals, with the toanwan of which they can, it is believed, inflict painful diseases and death on whomsoever, and whenever, they desire.

"The candidate being thus duly prepared for initiation, and having made the necessary offerings for the benefit of the institution, on the evening of the day previous to the dance a lodge is prepared, and from ten to twenty of the more substantial members pass the night in singing, dancing, and feasting. In the morning, the tent is opened for the dance. After a few appropriate ceremonies preliminary to the grand operation, the candidate takes his place on a pile of blankets which he has contributed for the occasion, naked, except the breech-cloth and moccasins, duly painted and prepared for the mysterious operation. An elder having been stationed in the rear of the novice, the master of the ceremonies, with his knee and hip joints bent to an angle of about forty-five degrees, advances, with an unsteady, unnatural step, with his bag in his *hand,* uttering, "*Heen, heen, heen,*" with great energy, and raising the bag near a painted spot on the breast of the candidate, gives the discharge, the person stationed in the rear gives him a push forward at the same instant, and as he falls headlong throws the blankets over him. Then, while the dancers gather around him and chant, the master throws off the covering, and, chewing a piece of the bone of the Oanktay*h*ee, spirts it over him, and he revives, and resumes a sitting posture. All then return to their seats except the master; he approaches, and, making indescribable noises, pats upon the breast of the novice, till the latter, in agonizing throes, heaves up the Wahmnoo-*h*ah or shell, which falls from his mouth upon the bag which had been previously spread before him for that purpose. Life being now completely restored, and with the mysterious shell in his open hand, the new-made member passes around and exhibits it to all the members and to the wondering bystanders, and the ceremonies of initiation are closed. The dance continues, interspersed with shooting each other, rests, smoking, and taking refreshments, till they have jumped to the music of four sets of singers. Besides vocal music, they make use of the drum and the gourd-shell rattle. The following chants, which are used in the dance, will best exhibit the character of this mysterious institution of the Oanktayhee :—

"Waduta ohna micage.
Waduta ohna micage.
Miniyata ite wakan de maqu,
Tunkanixdan.

"He created it for me enclosed in red down.
He created it for me enclosed in red down.
He in the water with a mysterious visage gave me this,
My grandfather.

"Tunkanixdan pejihuta wakan micage,
He wicake.
Miniyata oicage wakan kin maqu ye,
Tunkanixdan ite kin yuwinta wo.
Wahutopa yuha ite yuwinto wo.

"My grandfather created for me mysterious medicine,
That is true.
The mysterious being in the water gave it to me.
Stretch out your hand before the face of my grandfather,
Having a quadruped, stretch out your hand before him."

The medicine pouch is the skin of an otter, fox, or similar animal, containing certain articles which are held sacred.

A warrior leaving his village to hunt, gave his pouch to a friend of the writer, who had dwelt as a missionary among the Dahkotahs for a score of years. The owner having died, he retained it, and, being at his house one day, it was, at my request, opened. The contents were some dried mud, a dead beetle, a few roots, and a scrap of an old letter, which had probably been picked up about the walls of Fort Snelling.

Where the science of medicine is not understood, the

inhabitants are very superstitious concerning the sick. Those who are prominent in their devotion to the sacred rites of a heathen tribe, generally act as physicians. The Druids of the early Britons performed the duties of doctors, and the conjurers, or medicine men, as they are generally termed, are called to attend the sick Dahkotahs. This tribe of Indians are well acquainted with the bones of the body; but no Dr. Hunter has yet risen among them to explain the circulation of the blood, and therefore they have but a single word for nerves, arteries, and veins. When a young man is sick, he is generally well watched; but old persons, and those that have some deformity, are often neglected. To effect a cure, they often practise what is called steaming. They erect a small tent covered with thick buffalo robes, in which they place some hot stones. Stripping the sick person of his blanket, they place him in the tent. Water is then thrown upon the hot stones, which creates considerable vapour. After the patient has been confined in this close tent for some time, and has perspired profusely, they occasionally take him out and plunge him into the waters of an adjacent river or lake.

This custom is very ancient. One of the first white men who appear to have resided amongst them, was a Franciscan priest, named Hennepin. He was made their prisoner in the year 1680, while travelling on the Mississippi, above the Wisconsin river. The Dahkotahs took him to their villages on the shores of Rum river, at Mille Lac, where he was quartered in a chief's lodge, whose name was Aquipaguetin. The chief observing that Hennepin was much fatigued, ordered an oven to be made, which, to use the words of the Franciscan, "he ordered me to enter, stark naked, with four savages. The oven was covered with buffalo hides, and in it they placed red-hot flint and other stones. They ordered me to hold my breath as long as I could. As soon as the savages that were with me let go their breath, which they did with a great force, Aquipaguetin began to sing. The others seconded him; and laying their hands on my body began to rub, and at the same time cry bitterly. I was near fainting, and forced to leave the oven. At my coming out, I could scarcely take up my cloak. However, they continued to make me sweat thrice a week, which at last restored me to my former vigour."

When a Dahkotah is very sick, the friends call in a conjurer or medicine man. Before we proceed, it is proper to explain the meaning of the term "medicine man." Anything that is mysterious or wonderful, the Dahkotahs call "Wawkawn." The early explorers and traders in Minnesota were French, and they always call a doctor "medecin." As the Indian doctors are all dealers in mysteries, the word "medicine" has at last obtained a local signification, meaning anything that is mysterious or unaccountable. A "medicine man" means, then, a doctor who calls to his aid charms and incantations. The medicine men are divided into war prophets, and conjurers or doctors.

A Dahkotah, when he is sick, believes that he is possessed by the spirit of some animal, or insect, or enemy. The medicine men, are supposed to have great power of suction in their jaws, by which they can draw out the spirit that afflicts the patient, and thus restore him to health. They are much feared by all the tribe. The doctor is called to see a sick person by sending some one with a present of a horse or blankets, or something as valuable. The messenger sometimes carries a bell, and rings around the lodge until the conjurer makes his appearance; at other times he bears to the doctor's lodge a lighted pipe, and presenting it to him, places his hands on his head and moans.

"The person sent to call on the doctor, strips himself for running, retaining only his breech cloth, and carrying a bell. He enters the lodge, and without further ceremony, strikes the doctor with his foot, jingles his bell, and suddenly issuing from the lodge, runs with all his might for the sick man's lodge, with the doctor at his heels. If the latter overtakes and kicks him before he reaches the lodge, he does not proceed any further, but returns home. Another person is then despatched, and it is not until one is sent who is too swift for him, that the doctor's services can be secured."

The doctor having entered the tent, without touching the patient, begins to strip himself, leaving nothing upon his body but the breech cloth, and moccasins. Having obtained a sacred rattle, which is nothing more than a dried gourd, filled with a few kernels of corn, or beads, he begins to shake and sing in unearthly monotones. He now gets upon his knees, and, to use a vulgarism, "crawls on all fours," up to his patient. After a few moments we see him rise again retching violently, and picking up a bowl of water thrusts his face therein, and begins to make a gurgling noise. Into this bowl he professes to expectorate the spirit which has incited the disease. The doctor having decided what animal has possessed his patient, he has an image of the animal made out of bark, and placed outside near the tent door in a vessel of water. Mr. Prescott, United States Interpreter of the Dahkotahs, in a communication upon this subject says: "The animal made of bark is to be shot. Two or three Indians are in waiting, standing near the bowl, with loaded guns, ready to shoot when the conjurer gives the signal. To be sure that the conjuring shall have the desired effect, a woman must stand astride the bowl, when the men fire into it, with her dress raised as high as the knees. The men are instructed how to act by the conjurer; and as soon as he makes his appearance out of doors, they all fire into the bowl, and blow the little bark animal to pieces. The woman steps aside, and the juggler makes a jump at the bowl on his hands and knees, and commences blubbering in the water. While this is going on, the woman has to jump on the juggler's back, and stand there a moment; then she gets off, and as soon as he has finished his incantations, the woman takes him by the hair of his head, and pulls him back into the lodge. If there are any fragments found of the animal that has been shot, they are buried. If this does not cure, a similar ceremony is performed, but some other kind of animal is shaped out."

Among the earliest songs, to which a Dahkotah child listens, are those of war. As soon as he begins to totter about, he carries as a plaything, a miniature bow, and arrow. The first thing he is taught, as great and truly noble, is taking a scalp, and he pants to perform an act, which is so manly. At the age of sixteen, he is often on the war path. When a boy is of the proper age to go to war, he is presented with weapons, or he makes a war club. He then consecrates certain parts of animals, which he vows, not to eat. After he has killed an enemy, he is at liberty, to eat of any one of those portions of an animal, from which he agreed to abstain. If he kills another person, the prohibition is taken off from another part, until finally he has emancipated himself from his oath, by his bravery. Before young men go out on a war party, they endeavour to propitiate the patron deity by a feast. During the hours of night, they celebrate the " armour feast," which is distinguished by drumming, singing, and agonizing shrieks.

The war prophets or priests, by the narrating of pretended dreams, or by inspiring oratory, incite the tribe against an enemy. If a party are successful in securing scalps, they paint themselves black, and return home in mad triumph. As they approach their village, those who are there run forth to greet them, and strip them of their clothes, and supply them with others. The scalp is very carefully prepared for exhibition, being painted red, and stretched upon a hoop, which is fastened to a pole. If the scalp is from a man, it is decked with an eagle's feather, if from a woman, with a comb. At a scalp dance, which we once attended at Kaposia, the braves stood on one side of the circle, drumming and rattling, and shouting a monotonous song, reminding one of a song of chimney sweeps of a city. The women, standing opposite to the men, advanced and retreated from the men, squeaking in an unearthly manner, a sort of chorus. This is the chief dance, in which the women, engage. If a scalp is taken in summer, they dance until the falling of the leaves; if in winter, until the leaves begin to appear. When the scalp is freshly painted, as it is four times, it is a great occasion. After their mad orgies, have ceased, they burn or bury it. An eagle's feather, with a red spot, in the head of some of those Indians walking through our settlements, is a badge that the possessor has killed a foe. If the feather is notched and bordered with red, or clipped and topped with red, it signifies that a throat has been cut. The red hand on a blanket, shows that the man has been wounded by an enemy; but the black hand, that he has killed his enemy. The Dahkotahs, like other savages in war, show no sympathy for sex, infancy, or old age. At Pokeguma, the Kaposia band scalped two little girls that attended the mission school; buried a tomahawk in their brains; severed the hands from the bodies; and then set them up in the sand. Mr. Riggs narrates an incident of some of the upper bands of Dahkotahs, pursuing a weak Ojibway mother. To save her life she swam a stream. Half naked she reached the opposite bank, and dropped down, too much exhausted to attempt to proceed. With the delight of demons just let loose from hell, her pursuers came over, stabbed and scalped her. Prematurely, ushering her unborn babe into existence, they dashed its brains out, upon the ground. Returning with a poor, sick mother's scalp, they came home as " conquering heroes come," and were received with pride and honour. Such is savage warfare, and the savage idea of what constitutes true glory. But, notwithstanding their horrid mode of warfare, they are not destitute of affection for their own offspring or friends.

The Dahkotahs assert that a mother is with her absent children whenever they think of her, and that she feels a pain in her breast (or heart) whenever anything of moment happens to them. When a child dies, like Rachel, they refuse to be comforted. The following paraphrase of the lament of a bereaved Indian mother, prepared for the " Dakota Friend," is full of poetry : " *Me choonkshee! Me choonkshee!* (my daughter, my daughter,) alas! alas! My hope, my comfort has departed, my heart is very sad. My joy is turned into sorrow, and my song into wailing. Shall I never behold thy sunny smile? Shall I never more hear the music of thy voice? The Great Spirit has entered my lodge in anger, and taken thee from me, my first born and only child. I am comfortless and must wail out my grief. The pale faces repress their sorrow, but we children of nature must give vent to ours or die. Me choonkshee! me choonkshee!

"The light of my eyes is extinguished; all, all is dark. I have cast from me all comfortable clothing, and robed myself in comfortless skins, for no clothing, no fire, can warm thee, my daughter. Unwashed and uncombed, I will mourn for thee, whose long locks I can never more braid; and whose cheeks I can never again tinge with vermillion. I will cut off my dishevelled hair, for my grief is great, me choonkshee! me choonkshee! How can I survive thee? How can I be happy, and you a homeless wanderer to the spirit land? How can I eat if you are hungry? I will go to the grave with food for your spirit. Your bowl and spoon are placed in your coffin for use on the journey. The feast for your playmates has been made at the place of interment. Knowest thou of their presence? Me choonkshee! me choonkshee!

"When spring returns, the choicest of ducks shall be your portion. Sugar and berries also shall be placed near your grave. Neither grass nor flowers shall be allowed to grow thereon. Affection for thee will keep the little mound desolate, like the heart from which thou art torn. My daughter, I come, I come. I bring you parched corn. Oh, how long will you sleep? The wintry winds wail your requiem. The cold earth is your bed, and the colder snow thy covering. I would that they were mine. I will lie down by thy side. I will sleep once more with you. If no one discovers me, I shall soon be as cold as thou art, and together we will sleep that long, long sleep from which I cannot wake thee, Me choonkshee! me choonkshee!"

A Dahkotah obtains his wives (for they are polygamists) not by courtship, but by a practice as old as the book of Genesis, that of purchase. A young man, when he wants a wife, announces the fact, and begs his friends to give him an outfit. He then proceeds to the parents and makes a purchase. The ancestors of some of the first families of Virginia, purchased their wives from the London company, for one hundred and twenty or fifty pounds of tobacco, at three shillings a pound, but a Dahkotah pays a higher price for the article, and takes more. Usually they pay a horse, or four or five guns, or six or eight blankets, a value equal to thirty or forty dollars.

The chief of the Kaposia band has three wives, who are sisters. His second wife he purchased of her father while he was drunk, and she but ten years of age. It is said that a friend throws a blanket over the bride and bears her to the lodge of the purchaser. Though a son-in-law lives near the parents of his wife, he never names or talks to them, and never looks his wife's mother in the face. He thinks it is respectful to act in this manner. He occupies a large lodge, while his wife's parents frequently live in a small one, in the rear, whom he supplies with game until he has a family of his own. Should the parents accidentally meet him, they hide their faces. If the mother starts for the daughter's lodge and perceives her husband inside, she does not enter.

If a woman proves faithless to her husband, she is frequently shot or has her nose cut off. This latter practice was noticed by Le Sueur, in 1700. There is much system in relation to the place in which each should sit in a Dahkotah lodge. The wife always occupies a place next to the entrance on the right. The seat of honour, to which a white man is generally pointed, is directly opposite to the door of the lodge.

Like the rest of mankind, they are by no means insensible to flattery. When one thinks that he cannot obtain a horse, or some other article that he wishes, by a simple request, he will take a number of woodpeckers' heads, and sing over them in the presence of the individual he hopes to influence, recounting the honourable deeds of the man to whom he gives the birds' heads. This process acts like a charm, and is often successful.

A Parisian dandy is known the world over, but he is not to be compared with a Dahkotah fop. An Indian young man passes hours in attiring himself. That green streak of paint upon the cheek; those yellow circles around the eyes, and those spots upon the forehead, have cost him much trouble and frequent gazings into his mirror, which he always keeps with him. That head-dress, which appears to hang so carelessly, is all designed. None knows better than he how to attitudinize and play the stoic or majestic. No moustachioed clerk, with curling locks, and kid gloves, and cambric handkerchief, and patent-leather boots, and glossy hat, is half so conscious as he who struts past us with his streaming blanket and ornamented and uncovered head, holding a pipe or a gun in the place of a cane, and wearing moccasins in the place of boots. The rain upon his nicely decorated head and face, causes as much of a flutter as it does when it falls upon the hat of the nice young man who smokes his cigar and promenades in Broadway.

When the Dahkotahs are not busy with war, or the chase, or the feasts and dances of their religion, time hangs heavily, and they either sleep or resort to some game to keep up an excitement. One of their games is like " Hunt the Slipper;" a bullet or plum-stone is placed by one party in one of four moccasins or mittens, and sought for by the opposite. There is also the play of "plum-stones." At this game much is often lost and won. Eight plum-stones are marked with certain devices. This game is played by young men and females. If, after shaking in a bowl, stones bearing certain devices turn up, the game is won.

The favourite and most exciting game of the Dahkotahs is ball playing. It appears to be nothing more than a game which was often played by the writer in schoolboy days, and which was called "*shinny.*" A smooth place is chosen on the prairie or frozen river or lake. Each player has a stick three or four feet long and crooked at the lower end, with deer strings tied across forming a sort of a pocket. The ball is made of a rounded knot of wood, or clay covered with hide, and is supposed to possess supernatural qualities. Stakes are set at a distance of a quarter or half mile, as bounds. Two parties are then formed, and the ball being thrown up in the centre, the contest is for one party to carry the ball from the other beyond one of the bounds. Two or three hundred men are sometimes engaged at once. On a summer's day, to see them rushing to and fro, painted in divers colors, with no article of apparel, with feathers in their heads, bells around their wrists, and fox and wolf tails dangling behind, is a wild and noisy spectacle. The eye-witnesses among the Indians become more interested in the success of one or the other of the parties than any crowd at a horse race, and frequently stake their last piece of property on the issue of the game.

On the 13th of July, 1852, the last great ball-play in the vicinity of Saint Paul took place. The ground selected was Oak Grove, in Hennepin county, and the parties were, Shokpay's band, against the Good Road, Sky Man, and Gray Iron bands. The game lasted several days; about two hundred and fifty were participants, encompassed by a cloud of witnesses. About two thousand dollars' worth of property was won by Shokpay's band the first day. The second day they were the losers. On the third day Shokpay lost the first game, and the stake was renewed. Shokpay lost again; but while a new stake was being made up, a dispute arose between the parties concerning some of the property which had been won from Shokpay's band, but which they kept back. They broke up in a row, as they usually do. Gray Iron's band leaving the ground first, ostensibly for the reason above named, but *really* because Shokpay's band had just been reinforced by the arrival of a company from Little Crow's band. During the play four or five thousand dollars' worth of goods changed hands.

Like the ancient Greeks, they also practise foot racing. Before proceeding to other topics, it is well to give a brief account of the dog dance and the fish dance. The first is seldom performed, and is said to be peculiar to this nation. A dog being thrown into the midst of the crowd of dancers, is speedily "tomahawked" by one of the sacred men. The liver is then extracted and cut into slices, after which it is hung upon a pole. Now the dancers hop around, their mouths apparently watering with the desire for a bite. After a time some one dances up to the pole and takes a mouthful of the raw liver. He is then succeeded by others, until the whole is devoured. If another dog is thrown into the circle, the same process is repeated.

"Not long since a Dahkotah chief was sick, and the gods signified to him that if he would make a *raw fish feast*, he would live till young cranes' wings are grown. So he must make the feast or die. Fifteen or twenty others, who, like himself, were inspired by the cormorant, joined with him in the ceremonies of the feast, of which the chief was master.

"After one or two days spent in 'vapour baths' and 'armour feasts,' a tent is prepared, opening towards the east. The railing extending from the tent is composed of bushes. Within the enclosure each of those who are to participate in the feast has a bush set, in which is his nest. Early in the morning, on the day of the feast, the master informs two others where the fish are to be taken, and sends them forth to spear and bring them in, designating the kind and number to be taken. On this occasion two pike, each about one foot in length, were taken, and after having been painted with vermillion and ornamented with red down about the mouth and along the back, were laid on some branches in the enclosure, entire, as they were taken from the water. Near the fish were placed birch-bark dishes filled with sweetened water. Their implements of war were solemnly exhibited in the tent, and the dancers, who were naked, except the belt, breech-cloth, and moccasins, and fantastically painted and adorned with down, red and white, being in readiness, the singers, of whom there are four ranks, commenced to sing, each rank in its turn. The singing was accompanied with the drum and rattle.

" The cormorant dancers danced to the music, having a little season of rest as each rank of singers ended their chant, until the fourth rank struck the drum and made the welkin ring with their wild notes; then, like starving beasts, they tore off pieces of the fish, scales, bones, entrails, and all, with their teeth, and swallowed it, at the same time drinking their sweetened water, till both the pike were consumed, except the heads and fins and large bones, the latter of which were deposited in the nests. Thus the feast ended, and the chief will of course live till the young cranes can fly. At the close of the ceremony, whatever of clothing is worn on the occasion is offered in sacrifice to the gods."

Sufficient has been said to show that the Dahkotahs are *Odd Fellows;* but not the half has been told. Among the Ojibways there are totems, or family symbols, of the name of some ancestor, which is honoured as much as the coat of arms among the nobility of Europe. If a man dies, his totem is marked upon his grave post with as much formality as the heraldic design of an English nobleman. It was this custom among the Algonquin Indians, that led the unscrupulous La Hontan to publish engravings of the fabulous coats of arms of the various savage nations of the northwest. That of the " Outchipoues" (Ojibways) is an eagle perched upon a rock, devouring the brain of an owl. That of the Sioux, or Dahkotahs, is a squirrel perched upon a citron or pumpkin, and gnawing its rind. While the Dahkotahs do not appear to have totems or family designs, like the Ojibways, yet, from time immemorial, secret clans, with secret signs, have existed among them. It is impossible to force any member of these clans to divulge any of their proceedings. Culbertson, who visited the Dahkotahs of the Missouri, at the request of the Smithsonian Institution, was struck with this peculiarity. His remarks, for the entire accuracy of which we do not vouch, are as follows:—

"The Sioux nation has no general council, but each tribe and band determines its own affairs. These bands have some ties of interest analogous to the ties of our secret societies. The 'Crow-Feather-in-Cap' band are pledged to protect each others' wives, and to refrain from violating them. If the wife of one of their number is stolen by another of their number, she is returned, the band either paying the thief for returning the stolen property, or forcing him to do it, whether he will or not. * * * * * The 'Strong-Heart' band is pledged to protect each other in their horses. Should a 'Strong-Heart' from a distance steal some horses, and they be claimed by a brother 'Strong-Heart,' his fellows would tell him that he must give them up, or they would give the robbed man some of their own horses, regarding it as the greatest disgrace to themselves to allow him to go away on foot. And thus I suppose that all these bands have some common object that unites them together, and here we have the origin of this system of banding. In the absence of law, it takes the place of our system of justice."

The heathen, in their manner of life, are essentially the same all over the world. They are all given up to uncleanness. As you walk through a small village, in a Christian land, you notice many appearances of thrift and neatness. The day-labourer has his lot fenced, and his rude cabin white-washed. The widow, dependent upon her own exertions, and alone in the world, finds pleasure in training the honeysuckle or the morning-glory to peep in at her windows. The poor seamstress, though obliged to lodge in some upper room, has a few flower-pots upon her window-sill, and perhaps a canary bird hung in a cage outside. But in an Indian village all is filth and litter. There are no fences around their bark huts. White-washing is a lost art if it was ever known. Worn-out moccasins, tattered blankets, old breech-cloths, and pieces of leggins are strewn in confusion all over the ground. Water, except in very warm weather, seldom touches their bodies, and the pores of their skins become filled with grease and the paint with which they daub themselves. Neither Monday, or any other day, is known as washing-day. Their cooking utensils are incrusted with dirt, and used for a variety of purposes. A few years ago, a band of Indians, with their dogs, ponies, women, and children, came on board of a steamboat on the Upper Mississippi, on which the writer was travelling. Their evening meal, consisting of beans and wild meat, was prepared on the lower deck, beneath the windows of the ladies' cabin. After they had used their fingers in the place of forks, and consumed the food which they had cooked in a dirty iron pan, one of the mothers, removing the blanket from one of her children, stood it up in the same pan, and then, dipping some water out of the river, began to wash it from head to foot. The rest of the band looked on with Indian composure, and seemed to think that an iron stew-pan was just as good for washing babes as for cooking beans. Where there is so much dirt, of course vermin must abound. They are not much distressed by the presence of those insects which are so nauseating to the civilized man. Being without shame, a common sight, of a summer's eve, is a woman or child with her head in another's lap, who is kindly killing the fleas and other vermin that are burrowing in the long, matted, and uncombed hair.

The Dahkotahs have no regular time for eating. Dependent, as they are, upon hunting and fishing for subsistence, they vacillate from the proximity of starvation to gluttony. It is considered uncourteous to refuse an invitation to a feast, and a single man will sometimes attend six or seven in a day, and eat intemperately. Before they came in contact with the whites, they subsisted upon venison, buffalo, and dog meat. The latter animal has always been considered a delicacy by these epicures. In illustration of these remarks, I transcribe an extract from a journal of a missionary, who visited Lake Traverse in April, 1839:—

"Last evening, at dark, our Indians chiefly returned, having eaten to the full of buffalo and dog meat. I asked one how many times they were feasted. He said, 'Six, and if it had not become dark so soon, we should have been called three or four times more.' * * * This morning, 'Burning-Earth' (chief of the Sissetonwan Dahkotahs), came again to our encampment, and removing we accompanied him to his village at the southwestern end of the lake. * * * In the afternoon, I visited the chief; found him just about to leave for a dog feast to which he had been called. When he had received some papers of medicine I had for him, he left, saying, 'The Sioux love dog meat as well as white people do pork.'"

In this connection, it should be stated that the Dahkotahs have no regular hours of retiring. Enter a New England village after nine o'clock, and all is still. Walk through Philadelphia after the State House clock has struck eleven, and everybody and thing, hacks, hackmen, and those on foot, appear to be hastening to rest; the lamp in the store, the entry and parlour, is extinguished, and lights begin to flicker in the chambers and in the garrets, and soon all are quiet, except rogues and disorderly persons, and those who watch; and you can hear the clock tick in the entry, and the watchman's slow step as he walks up and down the street. But there is nothing like this in an Indian village. They sleep whenever inclination prompts; some by day and some by night.

If you were to enter a Dahkotah village, at midnight, you might, perhaps, see some few huddled round the fire of a teepee, listening to the tale of an old warrior, who has often engaged in bloody conflict with their ancient and present enemies, the Ojibways; or you might hear the unearthly chanting of some medicine man, endeavouring to exorcise some spirit from a sick man; or see some lounging about, whiffing out of their sacred red stone pipes, the smoke of kinnikinnick, a species of willow bark; or some of the young men sneaking around a lodge, and waiting for the lodge-fire to cease to flicker before they perpetrate some deed of sin; or you might hear a low, wild drumming, and then a group of men, all naked, with the exception of a girdle round the loins, daubed with vermillion and other paints, all excited, and engaged in some of their grotesque dances; or a portion may be firing their guns into the air, being alarmed by some imaginary evil, and supposing that an enemy is lurking around.

CHAPTER III.

DAHKOTAH females deserve the sympathy of every tender heart. From early childhood they lead " worse than a dog's life." Like the Gibeonites of old, they are the hewers of wood, and the drawers of water for the camp. On a winter's day, a Dahkotah mother is often obliged to travel five or eight or ten miles with the lodge, camp-kettle, axe, child, and small dogs upon her back. Arriving late in the afternoon at the appointed camping-ground, she clears off the snow from the spot upon which she is to erect the tēēpēē. She then, from the nearest marsh or grove, cuts down some poles about ten feet in length. With these she forms a frame work for the tent. Unstrapping her pack, she unfolds the tent-cover, which is seven or eight buffalo skins stitched together, and brings the bottom part to the base of the frame. She now obtains a long pole, and fastening it to the skin covering, she raises it. The ends are drawn around the frame until they meet, and the edges of the covering are secured by wooden skewers or tent pins. The poles are then spread out on the ground, so as to make as large a circle inside as she desires. Then she, or her children, proceed to draw the skins down so as to make them fit tightly. An opening is left where the poles meet at the top, to allow the smoke to escape. The fire is built upon the ground in the centre of the lodge. Buffalo skins are placed around, and from seven to fifteen lodge there through a winter's night, with far more comfort than a child of luxury upon a bed of down. Water is to be drawn and wood cut for the night. The camp-kettle is suspended, and preparations made for the evening meal. If her lord and master has not by this time arrived from the day's hunt, she is busied in mending up moccasins. Such is a scene which has been enacted by hundreds of females this very winter in Minnesota. How few of the gentle sex properly appreciate the everlasting obligations they are under to the Son of Mary, after the flesh, who was the first that taught the true sphere and the true mission of woman!

The Dahkotah wife is subject to all of the whims of her husband, and woe unto her when he is in bad humour! As a consequence, the females of this nation are not possessed of very happy faces, and frequently resort to suicide to put an end to earthly troubles. Uncultivated, and made to do the labour of beasts, when they are desperate, they act more like infuriated brutes than creatures of reason. Some years ago a lodge was pitched at the mouth of the St. Croix. The wife, fearing her husband would demand the whiskey keg, when he came from hunting, hid it. Upon his return, she refused to tell him where it was, and he flogged her. In her rage, she went off and hung herself. At Oak Grove, a little girl, the pet of her grandmother, was whipped by her father. The old woman, sympathizing with the child, flew into a passion and went off. At last, the screaming of the grandchild was heard, for she had discovered her " grandma' " hanging by a portage collar from a burial scaffold. An assistant female teacher in the mission school, being attracted by the noise, went and cut the " old granny" down before life had fled. On another occasion, at the same place, a son-in-law refused to give his mother some whiskey, and in a rage she went on to the burial scaffold, tied the portage strap around her neck, and was about to jump off, when Mr. Pond came up to her and cut the strap. Still she did not relinquish her intention of suicide. At last, he climbed on to the scaffold and told her he would stay there as long as she. Other females from the village then came out, and succeeded in persuading her to live a little while longer. In this connexion, an incident may be told, which, for romantic interest, cannot be surpassed. The girl, since the occurrence, which we substantially narrate as we find it in the " Pioneer," without being responsible for every particular, became a pupil in the Rev. Mr. Hancock's mission school at Remnica or Red Wing Village.

In the spring of 1850, a young girl, fourteen years of age, shot another girl with whom she was quarrelling. The deceased was a daughter of a sullen man by the name of Black Whistle. The affrighted girl, after she fired the gun, fled to the trader's house, and was by him aided to make her escape down to Wapashaw's village. While stopping at Red Wing's village, some hundred miles from the place where the deed was committed, the incensed father overtook her. His first plan was to carry her home and sacrifice her at his daughter's burial scaffold; but, through the influence of some of the whites, he changed his plan, and resolved to make her his slave or his wife. For some time she endured what to her was a living death, but on one night she suddenly disappeared. Not many days after, there appeared at Good Road's village, a young Indian boy, stating that he was a Sisseton, and had just arrived from the plains. He was well received, no one dreaming that he was the Indian maid. While in this disguise, she went out one day to spear fish, when her husband and enemy, the revengeful father of the girl she had shot, met her, and inquired for her, and avowed his intention to kill her. She very coolly assented to the justice of what he said, and left. At last, her real sex being suspected, she came down to Little Crow or Kaposia village. Here she passed herself off as a Winnebago orphan, which disguise succeeded for a time. But soon she was suspected, and was again obliged to seek safety in flight, and at last took up her residence at Red Wing's village, though for a long time no one knew what had become of her.

It is an erroneous idea that chiefs have any authority. Popularity is the source of power, and they resort to measures which vie with those of the modern demagogue, to gain the ear of the people. They never express an opinion on any important point, until they have canvassed the band over which they preside, and their opinions are always those of the majority.

The Dahkotahs suffer much for want of law. The individual who desires to improve his condition is not only laughed at, but maltreated. Moreover, if he acquires any property, there is no law which secures it to him, and it is liable to be taken away at any time by any ill-disposed person. Until this state of things is altered by the interposition of the United States government, or tl interposition of Providence in some unforeseen way, there is little hope of elevating this tribe. Their missionary will be forced to look upon this degradation, and say, in view thereof, "My whole head is sick, my whole heart faint."

T' e superstitions and peculiarities of the Dahkotahs are so various that we can but barely glance at them. They count years by winters, and compute distances by the number of nights passed upon a journey; their months are computed by moons, and are as follows:—

1. WI-TERI, *January;* the hard moon.
2. WICATA-WI, *February;* the raccoon moon.
3. ISTAWICAYAZAN-WI, *March;* the sore-eye moon.
4. MAGAOKADI-WI, *April;* the moon in which the geese lay eggs: also called Wokada-wi; and, sometimes, Watopapi-wi, the moon when the streams are again navigable.
5. WOJUPI-WI, *May;* the planting moon.
6. WAJUSTECASA-WI, *June;* the moon when the strawberries are red.
7. CANPASAPA-WI, and WASUNPA-WI, *July;* the moon when the choke-cherries are ripe, and when the geese shed their feathers.
8. WASUTON-WI, *August;* the harvest moon.
9. PSINHNAKETU-WI, *September;* the moon when rice is laid up to dry.
10. WI-WAJUPI, *October;* the drying rice moon; sometimes written Wazupi-wi.
11. TAKIYURA-WI, *November;* the deer-rutting moon.
12. TAHECAPSUN-WI, *December;* the moon when the deer shed their horns.

They believe that the moon is made of something as good as green-cheese. The popular notion is that when the moon is full, a great number of very small mice commence nibbling until they have eaten it up. A new moon then begins to grow until it is full, then it is devoured.

Though almost every Dahkotah young man has his pocket mirror, a maid does not look at a looking-glass, for it is "wakan" or sacred. Almost everything that the man owns is wakan or sacred, but nothing that the woman possesses is so esteemed. If one has a toothache, it is supposed to be caused by a woodpecker concealed within, or the gnawing of a worm. Coughs are occasioned by the sacred men operating through the medium of the down of the goose, or the hair of the buffalo. It is considered a sin to cut a stick that has once been placed on the fire, or to prick a piece of meat with an awl or needle. It is wrong for a woman to smoke through a black pipe-stem, and for a man to wear a woman's moccasins. It is also sinful to throw gunpowder on the fire.

This tribe of Indians believe that an individual has several souls. Le Sueur said that they thought that they had three souls, but the sacred men say that a Dahkotah has four souls. At death one of these remains with or near the body; one in a bundle containing some of the clothes and hair of the deceased, which the relatives preserve until they have an opportunity to throw them into the enemy's country; one goes into the spirit land; and one passes into the body of a child or some animal.

They have a fear of the future, but no fixed belief in relation to the nature of future punishment. They are generally taciturn on such topics. The more simple-minded believe that a happy land exists across a lake of boiling water, and that an old woman sits on the shore holding a long narrow pole, that stretches across the water to the earth. Warriors who can show marks of wounds on their flesh, can walk the pole with security; also infants, whose blue veins are a passport as good as war marks. Others slip into the boiling water.

Their theology makes no difference between the condition of the thief and liar and the correct and good man. Those who commit suicide are thought to be unhappy. They believe that a woman who commits suicide will have to drag through another world that from which she hung herself in this, and that she will often break down the corn in another land by the pole or tree which dangles at her feet, and for this will be severely beaten by the inhabitants of the spirit land.

When any one dies, the nearest friend is very anxious to go and kill an enemy. A father lost a child while the treaty of 1851 was pending at Mendota, and he longed to go and kill an Ojibway. As soon as an individual dies, the corpse is wrapped in its best clothes. Some one acquainted with the deceased then harangues the spirit on the virtues of the departed; and the friends sit around with their faces smeared with a black pigment, the signs of mourning. Their lamentations are very loud, and they cut their thighs and legs with their finger nails or pieces of stone, to give free vent, as it would appear, to their grief. The corpse is not buried, but placed in a box upon a scaffold some eight or ten feet from the ground. Hung around the scaffold are such things as would please the spirit if it was still in the flesh—such as the scalp of an enemy or pots of food. After the corpse has been exposed for some months, and the bones only remain, they are buried in a heap, and protected from the wolves by stakes.

On the bluff, above the dilapidated cave which forms the eastern limit of Saint Paul, there is an ancient burial place. Here the Dahkotahs formerly brought their dead, and performed solemn services.

Carver, in his Travels, publishes the alleged speech over the remains of a Dahkotah brave—the reading of which so attracted the attention of the great German poet, Schiller, that he composed a poem called the "Song of a Nadowessee Chief." Goethe considered it one of his best, "and wished he had made a dozen such."

Sir John Herschell and Sir E. L. Bulwer have each attempted a translation, both of which seem to convey the spirit of the original.

SIR E. L. BULWER'S.	SIR JOHN HERSCHELL'S.

See on his mat—as if of yore,
  All life-like sits he here!
With that same aspect which he wore
  When light to him was dear.
	See, where upon the mat, he sits
	  Erect, before his door,
	With just the same majestic air
	  That once in life he wore.

But where the right hand's strength? and where
  The breath that loved to breathe,
To the Great Spirit aloft in air,
  The peace-pipe's lusty wreath?
	But where is fled his strength of limb,
	  The whirlwind of his breath,
	To the Great Spirit, when he sent
	  The peace-pipe's mounting wreath?

And where the hawk-like eye, alas!
  That wont the deer pursue,
Along the waves of rippling grass,
  Or fields that shone with dew?
	Where are those falcon eyes, which late
	  Along the plain could trace,
	Along the grass's dewy wave,
	  The reindeer's printed pace?

Are these the limber, bounding feet
  That swept the winter's snows?
What stateliest stag so fast and fleet?
  Their speed outstripped the roe's!
	Those legs, which once, with matchless speed,
	  Flew through the drifted snow,
	Surpassed the stag's unwearied course,
	  Outran the mountain roe?

These arms, that then the steady bow
  Could supple from its pride,
How stark and helpless hang they now
  Adown the stiffened side!
	Those arms, once used with might and main,
	  The stubborn bow to twang?
	See, see, their nerves are slack at last,
	  All motionless they hang.

SIR E. L. BULWER'S.	SIR JOHN HERSCHELL'S.

Yet weal to him—at peace he stays
  Where never fall the snows;
Where o'er the meadows springs the maize
  That mortal never sows.
	'Tis well with him, for he is gone
	  Where snow no more is found,
	Where the gay thorn's perpetual bloom
	  Decks all the field around;

Where birds are blithe on every brake—
  Where forests teem with deer—
Where glide the fish through every lake—
  One chase from year to year!
	Where wild birds sing from every spray,
	  Where deer come sweeping by,
	Where fish from every lake, afford
	  A plentiful supply.

With spirits now he feasts above;
  All left us—to revere
The deeds we honour with our love,
  The dust we bury here.
	With spirits now he feasts above,
	  And leaves us here alone,
	To celebrate his valiant deeds,
	  And round his grave to moan.

Here bring the last gift! loud and shrill
  Wail, death dirge for the brave!
What pleased him most in life may still
  Give pleasure in the grave.
	Sound the death-song, bring forth the gifts,
	  The last gifts of the dead,—
	Let all which yet may yield him joy
	  Within his grave be laid.

We lay the axe beneath his head
  He swung when strength was strong—
The bear on which his banquets fed—
  The way from earth is long!
	The hatchet place beneath his head,
	  Still red with hostile blood;
	And add, because the way is long,
	  The bear's fat limbs for food.

And here, new sharped, place the knife
  That severed from the clay,
From which the axe had spoiled the life,
  The conquered scalp away!
	The scalping-knife beside him lay,
	  With paints of gorgeous dye,
	That in the land of souls his form
	  May shine triumphantly.

The paints that deck the dead bestow—
  Yes, place them in his hand—
That red the kingly shade may glow
  Amid the spirit-land.	

The legends of the Dahkotahs are numerous, and while many are puerile, a few are beautiful.

EAGLE-EYE, the son of a great war prophet, who lived more than one hundred years ago, was distinguished for bravery. Fleet, athletic, symmetrical, a bitter foe and warm friend, he was a model Dahkotah. In the ardour of his youth, his affections were given to one who was also attractive, named Scarlet Dove.

A few moons after she had become an inmate of his lodge, they descended the Mississippi, with a hunting party, and proceeded east of Lake Pepin.

One day, while Eagle-Eye was hid behind some bushes, watching for deer, the arrow of a comrade found its way through the covert, into his heart. With only time to lisp the name Scarlet Dove, he expired.

For a few days the widow mourned and cut her flesh, and then, with the silence of woe, wrapping her beloved in skins, she placed him on a temporary burial scaffold, and sat beneath.

When the hunting party moved, she carried on her own back the dead body of Eagle-Eye. At every encampment she laid the body up in the manner already mentioned, and sat down to watch it and mourn.

When she had reached the Minnesota river, a distance of more than a hundred miles, Scarlet Dove brought forks and poles from the woods, and erected a permanent scaffold on that beautiful hill opposite the site of Fort Snelling, in the rear of the little town of Mendota, which is known by the name of Pilot Knob. Having adjusted the remains of the unfortunate object of her love upon this elevation, with the strap by which she had carried her precious burden, Scarlet Dove hung herself to the scaffold and died. Her highest hope was to meet the beloved spirit of her Eagle-Eye, in the world of spirits.[1]

Many years before the eye of the white man gazed on the beautiful landscape around the Falls of Saint Anthony, a scene was enacted there of which this is the melancholy story:—

Anpetusapa was the first love of a Dahkotah hunter. For a period they dwelt in happiness, and she proved herself a true wife.

---

[1] For this legend we are indebted to Rev. G. H. Pond.

> "With knife of bone she carved her food,
>   Fuel, with axe of stone procured—
>   Could fire extract, from flint or wood;
>   To rudest savage life inured.
>
> "In kettle frail of birchen bark,
>   She boiled her food with heated stones;
>   The slippery fish from coverts dark
>   She drew with hooked bones."

But her heart was at length clouded. The husband, in accordance with the custom of his nation, introduced a second wife within the tēēpēē, and the first wife's eyes began to grow sad, and her form from day to day drooped. Her chief joy was to clasp the little boy, who was the embodiment of hopes and happiness fled for ever. Faithful and unmurmuring, she followed her husband on his hunts. One day the band encamped on the picturesque shores near the Falls of Saint Anthony. With tearless eye, and nerved by despair, the first wife, with her little son, walked to the rapid waters. Entering a canoe, she pushed into the swift current, and the chanting of her death dirge arrested the attention of her husband and the camp in time to see the canoe on the bank, and plunge into the dashing waves. The Dahkotahs say, that in the mist of the morning, the spirit of an Indian wife, with a child clinging around her neck, is seen darting in a canoe through the spray, and that the sound of her death-song is heard moaning in the winds, and in the roar of the waters.

On the eastern shore of Lake Pepin, about twelve miles from its mouth, there stands a bluff which attracts attention by its boldness. It is about four hundred and fifty feet in height, the last hundred of which is a bald, precipitous crag. It is seen at a distance of miles; and as the steamer approaches, the emergence of passengers to the upper deck, and the pointing of the finger of the captain, or some one familiar with the country, evinces that it is an interesting locality—it is the Maiden's Rock of the Dahkotahs.

The first version of the story, in connection with this bluff, differs from those more modern, but is preferable.

In the days of the great chief Wapashaw, there lived at the village of Keoxa, which stood on the site of the town which now bears her name, a maiden with a loving soul. She was the first-born daughter, and, as is always the case in a Dahkotah family, she bore the name of Weenōnah. A young hunter of the same band, was never happier than when he played the flute in her hearing. Having thus signified his affection, it was with the whole heart reciprocated. The youth begged from his friends all that he could, and went to her parents, as is the custom, to purchase her for his wife, but his proposals were rejected.

A warrior, who had often been on the war path, whose head-dress plainly told the number of scalps he had wrenched from Ojibway heads, had also been to the parents, and they thought that she would be more honoured as an inmate of his teepee.

Weenōnah, however, could not forget her first love; and, though he had been forced away, his absence strengthened her affections. Neither the attentions of the warrior, nor the threats of parents, nor the persuasions of friends, could make her consent to marry simply for position.

One day the band came to Lake Pepin to fish or hunt. The dark green foliage, the velvet sward, the beautiful expanse of water, the shady nooks, made it a place to utter the breathings of love. The warrior sought her once more, and begged her to accede to her parents' wish, and become his wife, but she refused with decision.

While the party were feasting, Weenōnah clambered to the lofty bluff, and then told to those who were below, how crushed she had been by the absence of the young hunter, and the cruelty of her friends. Then chanting a wild death-song, before the fleetest runner could reach the height, she dashed herself down, and that form of beauty was in a moment a mass of broken limbs and bruised flesh.

The Dahkotah, as he passes the rock, feels that the spot is Wawkawn.

The Dahkotahs call the St. Croix river, Hogan-wanke-kin. The legend is that in the distant past, two Dahkotah warriors were travelling on the shores of Lake St. Croix, one of whom was under a vow to one of his gods not to eat any flesh which had touched water. Gnawed by hunger, the two perceived, as they supposed, a raccoon, and pursued it to a hollow tree. On looking in, the one who could not eat flesh that had touched water, saw that the animal was a fish and not a quadruped. Turning to his companion, he agreed to throw it to the ground if he was not urged to eat. Hunger, however, was imperious, and forced him to break his vow and partake of the broiled fish.

After the meal, thirst usurped the place of hunger. He called for water to cool his parched tongue, until the strength of his companion failed, and he was then told to lie down by the lake and drink till his thirst was quenched. Complying with the advice, he drank and drank, till at last he cried to his friend, "come and look at me." The sight caused the knees of his comrade to smite together with fear, for he was fast turning to a fish. At length, he stretched himself across the Lake, and formed what is called Pike Bar. This, tradition says, is the origin of the sand-bar in the Lake, which is so conspicuous at low stage of water.

Having full faith in the legend, to this day they call the river, which is part of the boundary between Wisconsin and Minnesota, "THE PLACE WHERE THE FISH LIES." (Hogan-wanke-kin.)

The Dahkotahs, from the Minnesota to the plains beyond the Missouri, speak essentially the same language. Though difficult to acquire, it is allied to that of the Ottoes, Winnebagoes, Ioways, and Omahaws.[1]

After ten years' close study by an observing missionary, he was obliged to confess that he had not mastered it, which admission forms quite a contrast to the vaunting statement of Jonathan Carver, who wintered in Minnesota in 1767. He remarks: "To render my stay as comfortable as possible, I first endeavoured to learn their language. This I soon did, to make myself perfectly intelligible."

Hennepin made the first effort to collect a vocabulary of the language, while he was a captive on Rum river, or Mille Lacs. His description of the attempt is very quaint: "Hunger pressed me to commence the formation of a vocabulary of their language, learned from

---

[1] The ancient Arkansas seem to have belonged to the Dahkotah family. A letter published in Kip's Jesuit Mission, written by a missionary at the mouth of the Arkansas, in October, 1727, speaks of "a river which the Indians call Ni ska (Minne ska) or White Water." Again: "They place the hand upon the mouth, which is a sign of admiration among them." Ouakan tague they cry out, "it is the Great Spirit." They said probably, Wakan de, This is wonderful.

the prattle of their children. When once I had learned the word Taketchiabein, which means 'How call you this?' I began to be soon able to talk of such things as are most familiar. For want of an interpreter this difficulty was hard to surmount at first. For example, if I had a desire to know what *to run* was in their tongue, I was forced to increase my speed, and actually run from one end of the lodge to the other, until they understood what I meant and had told me the word, which I presently set down in my Dictionary."

The first printed vocabulary is that appended to Carver's Travels, which is exceedingly incorrect, though it contains many Dahkotah words. The Smithsonian Institution have published, under the patronage of the Historical Society of Minnesota, a quarto Grammar and Dictionary of this language, which will be gazed upon with interest by the "wise men of the East" long after the Dahkotah dialect has ceased to be spoken. This work is the fruit of eighteen years of anxious toil among this people, and is the combined work of the members of the Dahkotah Presbytery, edited by the Rev. S. R. Riggs, of Lac qui Parle; and should be preserved in the library of every professional man and lover of letters in Minnesota.

The vocabulary is, of course, meagre, compared with that of the civilized European; for living, as they have until of late, far away from any but those of like habits and modes of thought, they are defective in many words which have their place in the dictionary of a Christian people. Accustomed to cut poles from a forest and spread buffalo skins thereon, under which they pass the night, and then decamp early the next day in quest of game or the scalp of an enemy, they have no word which expresses the comfortable idea of our noble Saxon word "home." Still, in the language of a missionary, "it is in some of its aspects to be regarded as a noble language, fully adequate to all the felt wants of a nation, and capable of being enlarged, cultivated, and enriched, by the introduction of foreign stores of thought. Nothing can be found anywhere more full and flexible than the Dahkotah verb. The affixes, and reduplications, and pronouns, and prepositions, all come in to make it of such a stately pile of thought as is to my knowledge found nowhere else. A single paradigm presents more than a thousand variations."

THE DAHKOTAH ALPHABET.

NAME				NAME.			
A	ah,	sounds as *a*	in far.	O	o,	sounds as *o*	in go.
B	be,	"	*b* in but.	P	pe,	"	*p* in pea.
C	che,	"	*ch* in cheat.	Q	qe, indescribable.		
D	de,	"	*d* in deed.	R	re, high guttural.		
E	a,	"	*a* in say.	S	se,	sounds as *s*	in sea.
G	ge, low guttural.			T	te,	"	*t* in tea.
H	he,	sounds as *h*	in he.	U	oo,	"	*oo* in noon.
I	e,	"	*e* in see.	W	we,	"	*w* in we.
J	je,	"	*si* in hosier.	X	she,	"	*sh* in sheet.
K	ke,	"	*k* in key.	Y	ye,	"	*y* in yeast.
M	me,	"	*m* in me.	Z	ze,	"	*z* in zeta.
N	ne,	"	*n* in neat.				

The vowels represent each but one sound. *G* represents a low guttural or gurgling sound. *R* represents a rough hawking sound, higher than that of *g*. Besides their simple sounds, *c*, *k*, *p*, *s*, *t*, and *x*, have each a close compound sound, which cannot be learned except from a living teacher. They are printed in italics when they represent these sounds, except *k*, which is never italicised for this purpose; but *q* is used instead of it. The last-named letter might as well, perhaps, be expunged from the Dahkotah alphabet, and *k* held responsible for the performance of this service. When *n* follows a vowel at the end of a syllable, except in contracted words, with very few exceptions, it is not full, but sounds like *n* in *tinkle, ankle*.

It was intended that the Dahkotah orthography should be strictly phonetic, and it fails but little of being so. To learn the names of the letters is to learn to read it, and no English scholar need spend more than a few hours, or even a few moments, in learning to read the Dahkotah language.[1]

[1] G. H. Pond, in "*Tawaxitku Kin.*"

CHAPTER IV.

MORE than three centuries ago, an enterprising naval officer, Jacques Cartier, discovered the mouth of the great river of North America, that empties into the Atlantic, and whose extreme head waters are in the interior of Minnesota, within an hour's walk of a tributary of the Mississippi.

Having erected, in the vicinity of Quebec, a rude fort, in 1541, more than a half century before the settlement of Jamestown, in Virginia, from that time the river Saint Lawrence became known to the bold mariners of France, and there was an increasing desire to explore its sources.

In the year 1608, Champlain selected the site in the vicinity of Cartier's post as the future capital of New France. Burning to plant a colony in the New World, he, with great assiduity, explored the country. In 1609 he ascended a tributary of the Saint Lawrence, till he came to the beautiful lake in New York, which, to this day, bears his name.

After several visits to France, in 1615 he is found, with unabated zeal, accompanying a band of savages to their distant hunting-grounds, and discovering the waters of Lake Huron.

Before the emigrants of the "May Flower" trod on New England soil, and while Massachusetts was an unknown country to the geographers of Europe, he had gained an inkling of the Mediterranean of America, Lake Superior. In a map accompanying the journal of his discoveries, this lake appears as "Grand Lac," and a great river is marked flowing from the lake toward the south, intended to represent the Mississippi, as described by the Indians, who, from the earliest period, had been accustomed, by slight portages, to pass from the waters of Lake Superior into those of the "grand" river which flows into the Gulf of Mexico.

About the time that Champlain returned from his expedition to the Huron country, there arrived in Canada a youth from France of more than ordinary promise, who, by his aptness in the acquisition of the Indian dialects, became interpreter and commissary of the colony.

Determined to press beyond others, he, in 1639, arrived at the lake of the Winnebagoes, in the present state of Wisconsin, which had been described by Champlain, though erroneously located on the map accompanying his narrative.

While in this region he concluded a friendly alliance with the Indians in the valley of the Fox river.

Paul le Jeune, in a letter to his superior, Vimont, written in the month of September, 1640, alludes to Nicolet, and is also the first writer who makes distinct mention of the Dahkotahs. Speaking of the tribes on Lake Michigan, the father remarks:—

"Still further on, dwell the Ouinipegou (Winnebago), a sedentary people and very numerous. Some Frenchmen call them the 'Nation of Stinkers,' because the

Algonquin word Ouinipeg signifies stinking water. They thus designate the water of the sea, and these people call themselves Ouinipegou, because they come from the shores of a sea, of which we have no knowledge, and therefore we must not call them the nation of 'Stinkers,' but the nation of the sea.

"In the neighbourhood of this nation are the Nadouessi (Dahkotahs), and the Assinipouars (Assiniboines). * * * * * I will say, by the way, that the Sieur Nicolet, interpreter of the Algonquin and Huron languages for 'Messieurs de la Nouvelle France,' has given me the names of these nations, whom he has visited, for the most part, in their own countries."

Two years elapse, and, in 1641, Jogues and Raymbault, of the "Society of Jesus," after a journey of seventeen days, in frail barks, over tempestuous waters, arrive at the barrier of rocks at the entrance of Lake Superior; and then, at Sault St. Marie, met the Pottowattomies flying from the Dahkotahs, and were told that the latter lived to the west of the Falls, about eighteen days' journey, the first nine across the lake, the other up a river which leads inland, referring, probably, to the stream which interlocks with the head waters of the river Saint Croix.

We would not detract from the zeal of the man of God, but it is a fact that those in the service of mammon have ever outrun those in the service of Christ. The "insacra fames auri," the unholy thirst for gold, has always made the trader the pioneer of the missionary in savage lands.

In a communication made as early as 1654, it was stated that it was only nine days' journey from the Lake of the Winnebago (Green Bay) to the sea that separates America from China; and, that, if a person could be found who would send thirty Frenchmen into that country, they would obtain the finest peltries and amass wealth.

This year two adventurous Frenchmen went to seek their fortunes in the region west of Lake Michigan; and, in August, 1656, with a flotilla of canoes, laden with treasures, and two hundred and fifty Ojibways, they arrived at Quebec, and interested "voyageurs" with a recital of their hair-breadth escapes—merchants with their packs of valuable furs, and ecclesiastics with narrations of the miserable condition of immortal souls, and of the numerous villages of the "Nadouesiouack" (Dahkotahs) and other tribes.

Thirty young Frenchmen, excited by the reports, equipped themselves to trade with the lodges in the distant wilderness; and, two Fathers, Leonard Garreau and Gabriel Dreuilletes, were summoned by their Superior to return with the brigade, and were rejoiced to find themselves chosen to be the first to carry the name of Jesus Christ into a country alike replete with tribulation, darkness, and death.

The latter missionary had been a visiter to the house of the Puritan minister, Eliot, in the vicinity of Boston, and they had frequently taken sweet counsel together in relation to the amelioration of the condition of the aborigines.

This expedition failed to reach its destination, owing to a murderous attack of the Iroquois, in which Garreau was killed, and the Ojibways so alarmed that they refused to receive the surviving "black robe."

In the year 1659 two traders travelled extensively among the distant tribes. Six days' journey south-west of La Pointe, now Bayfield, Wisconsin, they found villages of Hurons, who, retreating across rocky ridges, over deep streams, wide lakes, and dense thickets, had reached the shores of the Mississippi, and found a shelter among the Dahkotahs from the fierce onslaught of the Iroquois. In the vicinity of the Hurons they saw Dahkotah settlements, "in five of which were counted all of five thousand men." They noticed women with the tips of their noses cut off, and heads partly scalped, and were informed that this was the penalty inflicted upon adulteresses.

They also heard of " another warlike nation who, with their bows and arrows, have rendered themselves as formidable to the upper Algonquins as the Iroquois have to the lower. They bear the name of Poualak (Assineboine), that is to say, the warriors." Continues the relation:—" As wood is scarce and very small with them, nature has taught them to burn stones in place of it, and to cover their wigwams with skins. Some of the most industrious among them have built mud cabins nearly in the same manner that swallows build their nests; nor would they sleep less sweetly beneath these skins, or under this clay, than the great ones of earth beneath their golden canopies, was it not for the fear of the Iroquois, who come here in search of them from a distance of five or six hundred leagues."

On the early French maps of Lake Superior, a tributary from Minnesota is called the River Grosellier.[1] It

---

[1] Grosellier was a native of Touraine, and married Helen, daughter of Abraham Martin, King's Pilot, who has left his name to the celebrated plains of Abraham, near Quebec. Returning by Lake Superior, he offered to carry French ships to Hudson's Bay. Rejected by the court, he crossed over to England, where his offers were accepted. With

appears to have been named after a French pilot who, about this time, roamed into the Assiniboine country, in the region of Lake Winnepeg, and was conducted by them to the shores of Hudson's Bay.

During the summer of 1660 the traders of the far West returned to Quebec with sixty canoes, manned by Algonquins, and laden with fox, beaver, and buffalo skins. The narrative of these men increased the existing enthusiasm of the Jesuits, and the Superior at Quebec had a zeal which "caused him to wish that he might be an angel of glad tidings to the far nations; and, at the expense of a thousand lives, to go and search in the depths of the forest the lost sheep for whose welfare he had crossed the sea."

The murder of Garreau, four years before, did not intimidate, but his blood increased the courage of the church, and René Menard was the one selected to be the cross-bearer to the barbarians in the regions round about Lake Superior.

His hair whitened by age, his mind ripened by long experience, and acquainted with the peculiarities of Indian character, he seemed the man for the mission.

The night before he started, the eyes of the venerable priest were not closed. He thought much of his friends, and, knowing that he was about to go into a land of barbarians, two hours after midnight he penned a letter,

---

Raddisson, another Frenchmen, he piloted an English vessel, commanded by Captain Gillam, a Yankee, to the River Nemiscau, on the east side of James Bay, where Fort Rupert was built. See O'Callaghan's note, vol. ix. p. 797, Paris Doc.: Col. History of New York.

[1] MY REVEREND FATHER—THE PEACE OF CHRIST BE WITH YOU:

I write to you probably the last word, which I hope will be the seal of our friendship until eternity. Love whom the Lord Jesus did not disdain to love, though the greatest of sinners, for he loves whom he

touching in its simplicity, and which will be embalmed in the literature of the future dwellers on the shores of Lake Superior.

Early on the morning of the 28th of August, 1660, he, in company with eight Frenchmen, departed with the Ottawa convoy from "Three Rivers." After much ridicule from the wild companions of his voyage, he arrived at a bay on Lake Superior, on the 15th of October, St. Theresa's day, on which account he so designated the sheet of water.

During the following winter they remained at this point. Their supply of provisions being exhausted, they nearly starved. "At times they scraped up a mess of the 'tripe de roche,' which slightly thickened their water, foaming upon it a kind of foam or slime, similar to that of snails, and which served rather to nourish their imagination than their bodies:" at other times they

loads with his cross. Let your friendship, my good father, be useful to me by the desirable fruits of your daily sacrifice. In three or four months, you may remember me at the memento for the dead, on account of my old age, my weak constitution, and the hardships I lay under amongst these tribes. Nevertheless, I am in peace, for I have not been led to this mission by any temporal motive, but I think it was by the voice of God. I was afraid, by not coming here, to resist the grace of God. Eternal remorse would have tormented me, had I not come when I had the opportunity. We have been a little surprised, not being able to provide ourselves with vestments and other things; but he who feeds the little birds and clothes the lilies of the fields, will take care of his servants; and though it should happen we should die with want, we would esteem ourselves happy. I am loaded with affairs. What I can do is to recommend our journey to your daily sacrifices, and to embrace you with the same sentiments of heart, as I hope to do in eternity.

My reverend father, your most humble and affectionate servant in Jesus Christ,

R. MENARD.

From the Three Rivers, this 27th August, 2 o'clock after midnight, 1660.

subsisted on pounded fish-bones and acorns. When the vernal breezes began to blow, ducks, geese, and wild pigeons made their appearance, and their bodies strengthened.

The refugee Hurons, at La Pointe, hearing that a "black gown" was on the shores of the lake, invited him to visit them.

Menard appointed three young Frenchmen to act as pioneers, and reconnoitre the country and make presents. On their journey their canoe was stolen, and after many difficulties they returned. Their report was discouraging, but did not deter the aged enthusiast. His last written sentences, penned in July, 1661, are:—

"I hear every day four populous nations spoken of, that are distant from here about two or three hundred leagues. I expect to die on my way to them; but as I am so far advanced, and in health, I shall do all that is possible to reach them. The route, most of the way, lies across swamps, through which it is necessary to feel your way in passing, and to be in danger every moment of sinking too deep to extricate yourself; provisions which can only be obtained by carrying them with you, and the mosquitoes, whose numbers are frightful, are the three great obstacles which render it difficult for me to obtain a companion."

Some Hurons having come to treat with the Ojibways, agreed to act as guides. Selecting John Guerin, a faithful man, as his companion, he started, with some dried fish and smoked meat for provisions. The Indians, full of caprice, soon moved off, and left the priest and his friend in an unknown country. Bruised in limb, and faint in body, on the 10th of August, Menard, while following his companion, lost himself by mistaking the trail.

The agony of Guerin is great when he looks behind and beholds not the aged traveller. He calls at the top of his voice, but he only hears the echo. He fires his gun repeatedly, to lead him to the right path; at last he wanders to a Huron village, and, by gestures and tears, and the promise of reward, induced a youth to go in search. He soon returned, weary; and from that day there have been no traces of his body.

A century ago, the report was current in Canada, that, some years after his disappearance, his robe and prayer book were found in a Dahkotah lodge, and were looked upon as " wawkawn" or supernatural.

In the summer of 1663 the mournful intelligence of the loss of Menard reached Quebec, and one was soon found to be his successor—Father Claude Allouëz, who anxiously awaited the means of conveyance to his scene of labour. In the year 1665 a hundred canoes, laden with Indians and peltries, arrived at Montreal from Lake Superior. A Frenchman, who accompanied them, reported that the Outaouaks (Ojibways) were attacked on one side by the Iroquois, and on the other by the Nadouessioux (Dahkotahs), a warlike people, who carry on cruel wars with nations still more distant. Allouëz rejoiced at the sight of the frail barks, and greeted the besmeared savages as if they were visitants from a better land. In a letter written at the time, his full heart thus speaks: " At last it has pleased God to send us the *angels* of the Upper Algonquins to conduct us to their country."

On the 8th of August, 1665, with six Frenchmen

and four hundred savages, returning from their trading expedition, he embarked.

Having made a portage at Sault St. Marie, on the 2d of September their birch canoes glided on the waters of Lake Superior. On the 1st of October they arrived at the Chegoimegon, a beautiful bay (Bayfield, Wisconsin), where were two large villages, one of which was occupied by the Hurons, who had been driven from the Dahkotah country under the following circumstances:—

Having claimed superiority, on account of the possession of fire-arms, they taunted the Dahkotahs, who had received them when they were outcasts and flying from the Iroquois, on account of their simplicity. At last, provoked beyond endurance, they decoyed a number of Hurons into a wild rice marsh, and killed many with their primitive, but not to be despised, stone-tipped arrows, and drove the remnant to Chegoimegon.

The second village was composed of several bands of Ojibways, whose ancestors had, a long time before, lived east of Lake Michigan, but had been driven westward by the Iroquois.

This point was a centre of trade for many nations. Even the Illinois came here to fish and exchange commodities.

Allouëz, when he landed at La Pointe, as the French named the place, in consequence of a tongue-like projection of land, found a scene of great confusion. In the language of Bancroft, " It was at a moment when the young warriors were bent on a strife with the warlike Sioux. A grand council of ten or twelve neighbouring nations was held to wrest the hatchet from the hands of the rash braves, and Allouëz was admitted to an audience before the vast assembly. In the name of

Louis XIV. and his viceroy, he commanded peace, and offered commerce and alliance against the Iroquois— the soldiers of France would smooth the path between the Chippewas and Quebec—would brush the pirate canoes from the rivers—would leave to the Five Nations no choice, but between tranquillity and destruction. On the shore of the bay to which the abundant fisheries attracted crowds, a chapel soon rose, and the mission of the Holy Spirit was founded. There admiring throngs, who had never seen an European, came to gaze on the white man, and on the pictures which he displayed of the realms of hell, and of the last judgment. There a choir of Chippewas were taught to chant the pater and the ave. * * * * The Sacs and Foxes travelled on foot from their country, which abounded in deer, beaver, and buffalo. The Illinois also, a hospitable race, unaccustomed to canoes, having no weapon but the bow and arrow, came to rehearse their sorrows. * * * * * * * Curiosity was roused by their tale of the noble river on which they dwelt, and which flowed toward the south. Then, too, at the very extremity of the lake, the missionary met the wild and impassioned Sioux, who dwelt to the west of Lake Superior, in a land of prairies, with wild rice for food, and skins of beasts instead of bark for roofs to their cabins, on the bank of the great river, of which Allouëz reported the name to be Messipi."

While on an excursion to Lake Alempigon (Saint Anne), he met, at Fond du Lac, in Minnesota, some Dahkotah warriors; and, in describing them, he is the first to give the name of the great river of which the Indians had told so many wonderful stories.

In the relations of the mission of the Holy Spirit, the following remarks are made of the Dahkotahs:—

"This is a tribe that dwells to the west of this (Fond du Lac), toward the great river called MESSIPI. They are forty or fifty leagues from here, in a country of prairies, abounding in all kinds of game. They have fields in which they do not sow Indian corn, but only tobacco. Providence has provided them with a species of marsh rice, which, toward the end of summer, they go to collect in certain small lakes that are covered with it. They know how to prepare it so well that it is quite agreeable to the taste and nutritive. They presented me with some when I was at the extremity of Lake Tracy (Superior), where I saw them. They do not use the gun, but only the bow and arrow, which they use with great dexterity. Their cabins are not covered with bark, but with deerskins well dried, and stitched together so well that the cold does not enter. These people are, above all other, savage and warlike. In our presence they seemed abashed, and were motionless as statues. They speak a language entirely unknown to us, and the savages about here do not understand them."

After two years passed among the Algonquins at La Pointe and vicinity, Allouëz was convinced that his mission would not prosper, unless he had some assistance. He determined to go in person to Quebec, and implore labourers for the field. Arriving there on the 3d day of August, 1667, he worked night and day; and, after two days, the bow of his canoe was again turned towards the far West. His party consisted at first of Father Louis Nicholas, and another Jesuit, with four labourers; but, when they came to the canoes, the whimsical savages only allowed Allouëz, Nicholas, and one of their men, to enter. But, notwithstanding the help obtained, the savage hearts could not be subdued; and, " weary of their obstinate unbelief," he resolved to leave La Pointe. On the 13th of September, 1669, the renowned Marquette took his place; and, writing to his Superior, describes the Dahkotahs in these words:—

" The Nadouessi are the Iroquois of this country, beyond La Pointe, but less faithless, and never attack till attacked.

" They lie south-west of the mission of the Holy Spirit, and we have not yet visited them, having confined ourselves to the conversion of the Ottawas.

" Their language is entirely different from the Huron and Algonquin; they have many villages, but are widely scattered; they have very extraordinary customs; they principally use the calumet; they do not speak at great feasts, and when a stranger arrives give him to eat of a wooden fork, as we would a child.

" All the lake tribes make war on them, but with small success. They have false oats (wild rice), use little canoes, and keep their word strictly. I sent them a present by an interpreter, to tell them to recognise the Frenchman everywhere, and not to kill him or the Indians in his company; that the black gown wishes to pass to the country of the Assinipouars (Assineboines), and to that of the Kilistinaux (Cnistineaux); that he was already with the Outagamis (Foxes), and that I was going this fall to the Illinois, to whom they should leave a free passage.

" They agreed; but as for my present waited till all came from the chase, promising to come to La Pointe in the fall, to hold a council with the Illinois and speak with me. Would that all these nations loved God as they feared the French."

The relations of the Jesuits for 1670–71, allude to the Dahkotahs, and their attack on the Hurons and Ojibways of La Pointe:—

" There are certain people, called Nadouessi, dreaded by their neighbours, and although they only use the bow and arrow, they use it with so much skill and so much dexterity that, in a moment, they fill the air. In the Parthian mode, they turn their heads in flight, and discharge their arrows so rapidly, that they are no less to be feared in their retreat than in their attack.

" They dwell on the shores of, and around the great river, Messipi, of which we shall speak. They number no less than fifteen populous towns, and yet they know not how to cultivate the earth by seeding it, contenting themselves with a species of marsh rye, which we call wild oats.

" For sixty leagues, from the extremity of the upper lakes towards sunset, and, as it were, in the centre of the western nations, *they have all united their force*, by a general league, which has been made against them, as against a common enemy.

" They speak a peculiar language, entirely distinct from that of the Algonquins and Hurons, whom they generally surpass in generosity, since they often content themselves with the glory of having obtained the victory, and freely release the prisoners they have taken in battle.

" Our Outaouacs and Hurons, of the Point of the Holy Ghost, had, to the present time, kept up a kind

LA POINTE MISSION ABANDONED.—OJIBWAYS DIVIDED. 113

of peace with them, but affairs having become embroiled during last winter, and some murders having been committed on both sides, our savages had reason to apprehend that the storm would soon burst upon them, and judged that it was safer for them to leave the place, which in fact they did in the spring."

La Pointe being abandoned, the nearest French settlement is Sault St. Marie, at the foot of the lake. In the year 1674 a party of Dahkotahs arrived there to make an alliance with the French, having been defeated in recent engagements with their foes. They visited the mission-house of Father Dreuilletes, where some of their nation were under religious instruction; and a council of the neighbouring tribes was called to deliberate on the proposed peace. A Cree Indian insulted a Dahkotah chief by brandishing his knife in his face. Fired at the indignity, he drew his own stone knife from his belt, and shouted the war cry. A fierce conflict now took place, in which the ten Dahkotah envoys were scalped and the mission-house burned.

The Saulteurs[1] or Ojibways divided into two bands, not far from this period. One remained at the Falls of Saint Mary, and subsisted on the delicious white fish, the other retired towards the extremity of Lake Superior, and settled at two places, making an alliance with the Dahkotahs, who were anxious for French goods, which they strengthened by intermarriages. The Dahkotahs, who had their villages near the Mississippi,

---

[1] Name applied because they lived at Sault St. Marie. The Dahkotahs call them Ha-ha-twawns, Dweller at the Falls. The Algonquin tribes called them Pauotig-oueieuhak, Inhabitants of the Falls, or Pahouitingdachirini, Men of the Shallow Cataract.

8

about the forty-sixth degree of latitude, shared their country with their new allies. During the winter, the Ojibways hunted, and in the spring they returned to the shores of Lake Superior. While in the land of the Dahkotahs, they took care not to assist them in their wars, lest they should be embroiled with surrounding nations.[1]

[1] Perrot in La Potherie.

CHAPTER V.

THE trade in furs has produced a class of men of marked peculiarities. Under the French dominion, military officers, and the descendants of a decayed nobility, were licensed, by authority, to trade in a particular district. These men were well educated, polished in their manners, and fond of control. Living in a savage land, surrounded by a few dependents, they acted as monarchs of all they surveyed. The freedom from the restraints of civilized life, and the adulation received from the barbarians, who are so easily impressed by tinsel and glare, had a wonderful fascination, so that a "lodge in some vast wilderness" became preferable to the drawing-rooms of ancient France, and the gay assemblies of Quebec.

These licensed officers did not harass themselves with the minutiæ of the Indian trade. In their employ were a few clerks, chiefly natives of Canada, who had received the rudiments of an education. Upon these devolved the task of conducting European articles of merchandise, to the tribes on the various watercourses that radiated from the centre of trade, with whom they wintered, and then returned in the spring or summer with the peltries that had been obtained in exchange for powder, lead, rum, and tobacco.

Under each clerk were a few men of no cultivation, the children of poverty or shame, who from their earliest youth had led a roving life, and who acted as canoe men, hewers of wood, and drawers of water.

Mercurial in temperament, and with no sense of responsibility, they were a "jolly set" of fellows, in their habits approximating to the savage, rather than the European.

The labours of the day finished, they danced around the camp-fire to the sound of the viol, or they purchased the virtue of some Indian maiden, and engaged in debauch as disgusting as that of sailors sojourning in the isles of the South Sea, or

> "Worn with the long day's march, and the chase
> Of the deer, and the bison,
> Stretched themselves on the ground and slept
> Where the quivering fire-light
> Flashed on their swarthy cheeks, and their
> Forms wrapped up in their blankets."[1]

Inured to toil, they arose in the morning "when it was yet dark," and pushing the prow of their light canoes into the water, swiftly they glided away "like the shade of a cloud on the prairie," and did not break fast until the sun had been above the horizon for several hours.

Halting for a short period they partook of their coarse fare, and sang their rude songs; then re-embarking, they pursued their course to the land of the beaver and the buffalo, until the " shades of night began to fall."

From early youth accustomed to descend rapids, and ascend lofty bluffs with heavy burdens, they guided

---

[1] Evangeline.

their canoes, and carried their packs through places that would have been impassable to any but the "coureurs des bois."[1] When old age relaxed their sinewy joints, they returned to Mackinaw, or some other entrepôt, and with an Indian woman obtained, after the manner of the country, to mend their moccasins and hoe their gardens, passed the remainder of life in whiffing the pipe and recounting hair-breadth escapes.

The "bois brulé"[2] offspring naturally became enamoured with the rover's life, a retrospect of which infused fire into the dim eyes of the old man, and as soon as employment could be obtained they left the homestead to follow in the footsteps of their ancestors.

The voyageur seldom remains in a settled country. As civilization advances he feels cramped and uncomfortable, and follows the Indian in his retreat. On the confines of Minnesota are many of this class, whose fathers, a generation ago, dwelt at La Pointe, Green Bay, or Prairie du Chien. Before France had taken formal possession of the region of the Lakes, hundreds of "coureurs des bois" had ventured into the distant North-West. The absence of so many from regular pursuits, was supposed to be disastrous to the interests of the colony, and measures were taken by the French government to compel them to return, which resulted in only partial success.

Du Chesneau, Intendant of Canada, was worried by the lawlessness of the rovers, and writes to the Minister of Marine[3] and Colonies of France:—

---

[1] So called because they wandered through the woods, to obtain peltries from the savages.

[2] This term, meaning "burnt wood," applied to half-breeds because of their dark complexions.

[3] Nov. 10, 1679, Paris Documents, Col. Hist. N. Y. vol. ix. p. 133.

"Be pleased to bear in mind, my lord, that there was a general complaint, the year previous to my arrival in this country, that the great quantity of people who went to trade for peltries to the Indian country, ruined the colony, because those who alone could improve it, being young and strong for work, abandoned their wives and children, the cultivation of lands, and rearing of cattle; that they became dissipated; that their absence gave rise to licentiousness among their wives, as has often been the case, and is still of daily occurrence; that they accustomed themselves to a loafing and vagabond life, which it was beyond their power to quit; that they derived little benefit from their labours, because they were induced to waste in drunkenness and fine clothes the little they earned, which was very trifling, those who gave them licenses having the larger part, besides the price of the goods, which they sold them very dear, and that the Indians would no longer bring them peltries in such abundance to sell to the honest people, if so great a number of young men went in search of them to those very barbarians, who despised us on account of the great cupidity we manifested."

At one period, three-fourths of the revenue of Canada was derived from the fur trade.

Only twenty-five licenses were granted each year; and when a "poor gentleman" or "old officer" did not wish to go West, he disposed of his permit, which was valued at six hundred crowns, to the merchants of Quebec or Montreal. Each license allowed the possessor to send two canoes into the Indian country. Six "voyageurs" were employed for the canoes, and were furnished with goods valued at one thousand crowns, with an addition of fifteen per cent. The losses and risk were great, but when a venture was successful the profits were enormous.

The two canoes sometimes brought to Montreal beautiful furs valued at eight thousand crowns. The merchants received from the "coureurs des bois" six hundred crowns for the license, one thousand for the goods, and forty per cent. on the balance of sales; the residue was divided among the "coureurs," giving to each five or six hundred crowns, which was disposed of as quickly, and much in the same way, as mariners discharged from a ship of war spend their wages.

During the latter part of the seventeenth century, the name of Nicholas Perrot was familiar, not only to the men of business, and officers of government at Montreal and Quebec, but around the council fires of the Hurons, Ottawas, Otchagras, Ojibways, Pottawotamies, Miamies, and Dahkotahs. A native of Canada, accustomed from childhood to the excitement and incidents of border life, he was to a certain extent prepared for the wild scenes witnessed in after days.

If the name of Joliet is worthy of preservation, the citizens of the North-West ought not to be willing to let the name of that man die, who was the first of whom we have any account that erected a trading post on the upper Mississippi.

Perrot was a man of good family, and in his youth applied himself to study, and, being for a time in the service of the Jesuits, became familiar with the customs and languages of most of the tribes upon the borders of our lakes.

Some years before La Salle had launched the "Griffin" on Lake Erie, and commenced his career of discovery, Perrot, at the request of the authorities in Canada, who looked upon him as a man of great tact, visited the various nations of the North-West, and invited them to a grand council at Sault St. Marie, for the purpose of making a treaty with France. Of mercurial temperament, he performed the journey with great speed, going as far south as Chicago, the site of the present city.

On the 3d of September, 1670, Talon, the Intendant of Canada, ordered Sieur de St. Lusson to proceed to the "countries of the Outaouais, Nez Percés, Illinois, and other nations discovered" near Lake Superior or the Fresh Sea, and search for mines, particularly copper. He was also delegated to take possession of all the countries through which he passed, planting the cross and the arms of France.

In May, 1671, there was seen at the Falls of St. Mary, what has been of late, a frequent occurrence. Here was the first convocation of civilized men, with the aborigines of the North-West, for the formation of a compact, for the purposes of trade and mutual assistance.[1]

It was not only the custom but policy of the court of France to make a great display upon such an occasion. It is not to be wondered at, therefore, that we should see the ecclesiastic and military officers, surrounded "with all of the pomp and circumstance" peculiar to their profession in that age of extravagance in externals.

Allouëz, the first ecclesiastic who saw the Dahkotahs

---

[1] The Europeans present, besides De Lusson and Perrot, were the Jesuits, André, Dreuilletes, Allouëz, and Dablon; also Joliet, the explorer of the Mississippi; Mogras, of Three Rivers, Canada; Touppine, a soldier of the castle of Quebec; Dennis Masse; Chavigny; Chevriottiere; Lagillier; Mayseré; Dupuis; Bidaud Joniel; Portcet; Du Prat; Vital Oriol; Guillaume.

face to face, and the founder of the mission among the Ojibways at La Pointe, opened council by detailing to the painted, grotesque assemblage, enveloped in the robes of the beaver and buffalo, the great power of his monarch who lived beyond the seas.

Two holes were then dug, in one of which was planted a cedar column, and in the other a cross of the same material. After this the European portion of the assemblage chanted the hymn which was so often heard in the olden time from Lake Superior to Lake Pontchartrain :—

> "Vexilla regis prodeunt
> Fulget crucis mysterium,
> Qua vita mortem pertulit,
> Et morte, vitam pertulit."

The arms of France, probably engraved on leaden plates, were then attached to both column and cross, and again the whole company sang together the " Exaudiat," of the Roman Catholic service, the same as the 20th Psalm, of the King James' version of the Bible. The delegates from the different tribes having signified their approval of what Perrot had interpreted of the speech of the French Envoy, St. Lusson, there was a grand discharge of musketry, and the chanting of the noble " Te Deum Laudamus."

After this alliance was concluded, Perrot, in a spirit of enterprise, opened the trade with some of the more remote tribes.

The first trading posts on Lake Superior, beyond Sault St. Marie, were built of pine logs, by Daniel Greysolon du Luth, a native of Lyons, at Kamanistigoya, the entrance of Pigeon river, Minnesota. On the

1st of September, 1678, he left Quebec, to explore the country of the Dahkotahs and Assineboines.

The next year, on the 2d of July, he caused the king's arms to be planted "in the great village of the Nadouessioux (Dahkotahs), called Kathio, where no Frenchman had ever been, also at Songaskicons, and Houetbatons,[1] one hundred and twenty leagues distant from the former."

On the 15th of September, he met the Assineboines and other nations, at the head of Lake Superior, for the purpose of settling their difficulties with the Dahkotahs, and was successful.

On this tour he visited Mille Lac, which he called Lake Buade, the family name of Frontenac, governor of Canada.[2]

Du Chesneau, the intendant of Canada, appears to have been hostile to Du Luth, and wrote to Seignelay, Minister of the Colonies, that he and Governor Frontenac were in correspondence, and enriching themselves by the fur trade. He also intimated that the governor clandestinely encouraged Du Luth to sell his peltries to the English. From the tone of the correspondence, Du Chesneau was excitable and prejudiced.[3]

---

[1] The Chongasketons and Ouadebatons of the early French maps. The former were the same as the Sissetoans.

[2] Coronellis' map, corrected by Tillemon, published at Paris, 1688.

[3] "The man named La Taupine, a famous 'coureur de bois,' who set out in the month of September of last year, 1678, to go to the Outawacs, with goods, and who has always been interested with the governor, having returned this year, and I being advised that he had traded in two days, one hundred and fifty beaver robes in a single village of this tribe, amounting in all to nearly nine hundred beavers, which is a matter of public notoriety, and that he left with Du Luth, two men, whom he had with him, considered myself bound to have him arrested and to question him, but having presented a license from the governor

He attempted to imprison several of Du Luth's friends, among others his uncle, named Patron, who was a merchant, and his agent for the sale of furs.

The account that Perrot gave of his explorations beyond Lake Michigan, attracted the attention of La Salle, and induced him to project those enterprises which have given distinction to his name.

permitting him and his comrades, Lamonde, and Dupuy, to repair to the Outawac nation to execute his secret orders, I had him set at liberty. Immediately on his going out, Sieur Prevost, Town-Mayor of Quebec, came at the head of some soldiers, to force the prison, with written orders in these terms from the governor:—

"'Count de Frontenac, Councillor of the King in his Council, Governor and Lieutenant-General of His Majesty in New France:

"Sieur Prevost, Mayor of Quebec, is ordered, in case the Intendant arrest Pierre Moreau, alias La Taupine, whom WE have sent to Quebec, as bearer of despatches, upon pretext of his having been in the bush, to set him forthwith at liberty, and employ every means for this purpose at his peril. Done at Montreal, 5th September, 1679.

FRONTENAC.'"

CHAPTER VI.

THE same autumn that Du Luth left Montreal for the region west of Lake Superior, La Salle was at Fort Frontenac, the modern Kingston, busily engaged in maturing his plans for an occupation of the Mississippi valley. During the winter and the following spring his employees were occupied in building a vessel to navigate the lakes. Among those who were to accompany him on the voyage was Louis Hennepin, a Franciscan priest, of the Recollect order.

The first European to explore the Mississippi above the mouth of the Wisconsin; the first to name and describe the Falls of Saint Anthony; the first to present an engraving of the Falls of Niagara to the literary world; the Minnesotian will desire to know something of the antecedents and subsequent life of this individual.

The account of Hennepin's early life is chiefly obtained from the introduction to the Amsterdam edition of his book of travels. He was born in Ath, an inland town of the Netherlands. From boyhood he longed to visit foreign countries, and it is not to be wondered at that he assumed the priestly office, for next to the army, it was the road, in that age, to distinction. For several years he led quite a wandering life. A member of the Recollect branch of the Franciscans, at one time he is on a begging expedition to some of the towns on the sea coast. In a few months he occupies the post of chaplain at an hospital, where he shrives the dying and administers extreme unction. From the quiet of the hospital he proceeds to the camp, and is present at the battle of Seneffe, which occurred in the year 1674.

His whole mind, from the time that he became a priest, appears to have been on "things seen and temporal," rather than on those that are "unseen and eternal." While on duty at some of the ports on the Straits of Dover, he exhibited the characteristic of an ancient Athenian more than that of a professed successor of the Apostles. He sought out the society of strangers "who spent their time in nothing else but either to tell or to hear some new thing." With perfect nonchalance he confesses that notwithstanding the nauseating fumes of tobacco, he used to slip behind the doors of sailors' taverns, and spend days, without regard to the loss of his meals, listening to the adventures and hair-breadth escapes of the mariners in lands beyond the sea.

In the year 1676 he received a welcome order from his Superior, requiring him to embark for Canada. Unaccustomed to the world, and arbitrary in his disposition, he rendered the cabin of the ship in which he sailed anything but heavenly. As in modern days, the passengers in a vessel to the new world were composed of heterogeneous materials. There were young women going out in search for brothers or husbands, ecclesiastics, and those engaged in the then new, but profitable, commerce in furs. One of his fellow passengers was the talented and enterprising, though unfortunate, La Salle, with whom he afterwards associated. If he is to be credited, his intercourse with La Salle was not very pleasant on ship-board. The young women, tired of being cooped up in the narrow accommodations of the ship, when the evening was fair sought the deck, and engaged in the rude dances of the French peasantry of that age. Hennepin, feeling that it was improper, began to assume the air of the priest, and forbade the sport. La Salle, feeling that his interference was uncalled for, called him a pedant, and took the side of the girls, and during the voyage there were stormy discussions.

Good humour appears to have been restored when they left the ship, for Hennepin would otherwise have not been the companion of La Salle in his great Western journey.

Sojourning for a short period at Quebec, the adventure-loving Franciscan is permitted to go to a mission station on or near the site of the present town of Kingston, Canada West.

Here there was much to gratify his love of novelty, and he passed considerable time in rambling among the Iroquois of New York, even penetrating as far eastward as the Dutch Fort Orange, now the city of Albany.

In 1678 he returned to Quebec, and was ordered to join the expedition of Robert La Salle.

On the 6th of December Father Hennepin and a portion of the exploring party had entered the Niagara river. In the vicinity of the Falls, the winter was passed, and while the artisans were preparing a ship above the Falls, to navigate the great lakes, the Recollect wiled away the hours in studying the manners and customs of the Seneca Indians, and in admiring the sublimest handiwork of God on the globe.

On the 7th of August, 1679, the ship being completely rigged, unfurled its sails to the breezes of Lake Erie. The vessel was named the "Griffin," in honour of the arms of Frontenac, Governor of Canada, the first ship of European construction that had ever ploughed the waters of the great inland seas of North America.

After encountering a violent and dangerous storm on one of the lakes, during which they had given up all hopes of escaping shipwreck, on the 27th of the month, they were safely moored in the harbour of "Missilimackinack." From thence the party proceeded to Green Bay, where they left the ship, procured canoes, and continued along the coast of Lake Michigan. By the middle of January, 1680, La Salle had conducted his expedition to the Illinois river, and on an eminence near Lake Peoria, he commenced, with much heaviness of heart, the erection of a fort, which he called Crevecœur, on account of the many disappointments he had experienced.

La Salle, in the month of February, selected Hennepin and two traders for the arduous and dangerous undertaking of exploring the unknown regions of the upper Mississippi.

Daring and ambitious of distinction as a discoverer, he was not averse to such a commission, though perhaps he may have shrunk from the undertaking at so inclement a season as the last of February is, in this portion of North America.

On the 29th of February, 1680, with two voyageurs, named Picard du Gay and Michael Ako, Hennepin embarked in a canoe on the voyage of discovery.

The venerable Ribourde, a member of a Burgundian family of high rank, and a fellow Franciscan, came down to the river bank to see him off, and, in bidding him farewell, told him to acquit himself like a man, and be of good courage. His words were, "Viriliter age et confortetur cor tuum."

The canoe was loaded with about one hundred and fifty dollars' worth of merchandise for the purpose of trade with the Indians, and in addition La Salle presented to Hennepin ten knives, twelve awls or bodkins, a parcel of tobacco, a package of needles, and a pound or two of white or black beads.

The movements of Hennepin, during the month of March, are not very clearly related. He appears to have been detained at the junction of the Illinois with the Mississippi by the floating ice, until near the middle of that month. He then commenced the ascent of the river for the first time by civilized man, though Marquette had, seven years before, descended from the Wisconsin.

Surrounded by hostile and unknown natives, they cautiously proceeded. On the 11th of April, 1680, thirty-three bark canoes, containing a Dahkotah war party against the Illinois and Miami nations, hove in sight, and commenced discharging their arrows at the canoe of the Frenchmen. Perceiving the calumet of peace, they ceased their hostile demonstrations and approached. The first night that Hennepin and his companions passed with the Dahkotah party was one of anxiety. The next morning, a chief named Narrhetoba asked for the peace calumet, filled it with willow bark, and all smoked. It was then signified that the white men were to return with them to their villages.

In his narrative the Franciscan remarks :—" I found it difficult to say my office before these Indians. Many seeing me move my lips, said in a fierce tone, 'Ouakanche.' Michael, all out of countenance, told me, that if I continued to say my breviary, we should all three be killed, and the Picard begged me at least to pray apart, so as not to provoke them. I followed the latter's advice, but the more I concealed myself, the more I had the Indians at my heels, for when I entered the wood, they thought I was going to hide some goods under ground, so that I knew not on what side to turn to pray, for they never let me out of sight. This obliged me to beg pardon of my canoe-men, assuring them I could not dispense with saying my office. By the word 'Ouakanche,' the Indians meant that the book I was reading was a spirit, but by their gesture they nevertheless showed a kind of aversion, so that to accustom them to it, I chanted the Litany of the Blessed Virgin in the canoe, with my book opened. They thought that the breviary was a spirit which taught me to sing for their diversion, for these people are naturally fond of singing."

This is the first mention of a Dahkotah word in a European book. The savages were annoyed rather than enraged, at seeing the white man reading a book, and exclaimed " Wakan-de !" this is wonderful or supernatural. The war party was composed of several bands of the M'dewakantonwan Dahkotahs, and there was a diversity of opinion in relation to the disposition that should be made of the white men. The relatives of those who had been killed by the Miamis, were in favour of taking their scalps, but others were anxious to retain the favour of the French, and open a trading intercourse.

Perceiving one of the canoe-men shoot a wild turkey, they called the gun Manza Ouackange—iron that has understanding; more correctly, Maza Wakande, this is the supernatural metal.

Aquipaguatin, one of the head men, resorted to the following device to obtain merchandise. Says the Father, "this wily savage had the bones of some distinguished relative, which he preserved with great care in some skins dressed and adorned with several rows of black and red porcupine quills. From time to time he assembled his men to give it a smoke, and made us come several days to cover the bones with goods, and by a present wipe away the tears he had shed for him, and for his own son killed by the Miamis. To appease this captious man, we threw on the bones several fathoms of tobacco, axes, knives, beads, and some black and white wampum bracelets. * * * * * * * We slept at the point of the Lake of Tears,[1] which we so called from the tears which this chief shed all night long, or by one of his sons whom he caused to weep when he grew tired."

The next day, after four or five leagues' sail, a chief came, and telling them to leave their canoes, he pulled up three piles of grass for seats. Then taking a piece of cedar, full of little holes, he placed a stick into one, which he revolved between the palms of his hands, until he kindled a fire, and informed the Frenchmen that they would be at Mille Lac in six days. On the nineteenth day after their captivity, they arrived in the

[1] Lake Pepin.

vicinity of Saint Paul, not far, it is probable, from the marshy ground on which the Kaposia band once lived, and now called "Pig's Eye."

The journal remarks, "Having arrived, on the nineteenth day of our navigation, five leagues below St. Anthony's Falls, these Indians landed us in a bay, broke our canoe to pieces, and secreted their own in the reeds."

They then followed the trail to Mille Lac, sixty leagues distant. As they approached their villages, the various bands began to show their spoils. The tobacco was highly prized, and led to some contention. The chalice of the Father, which glistened in the sun, they were afraid to touch, supposing it was "wakan."[1] After five days' walk they reached the Issati (Dahkotah) settlements in the valley of the Rum river. The different bands each conducted a Frenchman to their village, the chief Aquipaguetin taking charge of Hennepin. After marching through the marshes towards the sources of Rum river, five wives of the chief, in three bark canoes, met them and took them a short league to an island where their cabins were.

An aged Indian kindly rubbed down the way-worn Franciscan—placing him on a bear-skin near the fire, he anointed his legs and the soles of his feet with wild-cat oil.

The son of the chief took great pleasure in carrying upon his bare back the priest's robe with dead men's bones enveloped. It was called Père Louis Chinnien— in the Dahkotah language Shinna or Shinnan signifies

---

[1] The word for supernatural, in the Dahkotah Lexicon, is thus spelled, but pronounced "wakon," or "wawkawn."

a buffalo robe. Hennepin's description of his life on the island is in these words :—

"The day after our arrival, Aquipaguetin, who was the head of a large family, covered me with a robe made of ten large dressed beaver skins, trimmed with porcupine quills. This Indian showed me five or six of his wives, telling them, as I afterwards learned, that they should in future regard me as one of their children.

"He set before me a bark dish full of fish, and, seeing that I could not rise from the ground, he had a small sweating-cabin made, in which he made me enter naked with four Indians. This cabin he covered with buffalo skins, and inside he put stones red-hot. He made me a sign to do as the others before beginning to sweat, but I merely concealed my nakedness with a handkerchief. As soon as these Indians had several times breathed out quite violently, he began to sing vociferously, the others putting their hands on me and rubbing me while they wept bitterly. I began to faint, but I came out and could scarcely take my habit to put on. When he made me sweat thus three times a week, I felt as strong as ever."

The mariner's compass was a constant source of wonder and amazement. Aquipaguetin having assembled the braves, would ask Hennepin to show his compass. Perceiving that the needle turned, the chief harangued his men, and told them that the Europeans were spirits, capable of doing anything.

In the Franciscan's possession was an iron pot with lion paw feet, which the Indians would not touch unless their hands were wrapped in buffalo skins.

The women looked upon it as "wakan," and would not enter the cabin where it was.

"The chiefs of these savages, seeing that I was desirous to learn, frequently made me write, naming all the parts of the human body; and as I would not put on paper certain indelicate words, at which they do not blush, they were heartily amused."

They often asked the Franciscan questions, to answer which it was necessary to refer to his lexicon. This appeared very strange, and, as they had no word for paper, they said, "That white thing must be a spirit which tells Père Louis all we say."

Hennepin remarks: "These Indians often asked me how many wives and children I had, and how old I was, that is, how many winters; for so these natives always count. Never illumined by the light of faith, they were surprised at my answer. Pointing to our two Frenchmen, whom I was then visiting, at a point three leagues from our village, I told them that a man among us could only have one wife; that, as for me, I had promised the Master of life to live as they saw me, and to come and live with them to teach them to be like the French.

"But that gross people, till then lawless and faithless, turned all I said into ridicule. 'How,' said they, 'would you have these two men with thee have wives? Ours would not live with them, for they have hair all over their face, and we have none there or elsewhere.' In fact they were never better pleased with me than when I was shaved, and from a complaisance, certainly not criminal, I shaved every week.

"As I often went to visit the cabins, I found a sick child, whose father's name was Mamenisi. Michael Ako would not accompany me; the Picard du Gay alone followed me to act as sponsor, or rather to witness the baptism.

"I christened the child Antoinette, in honour of St. Anthony of Padua, as well as for the Picard's name, which was Anthony Auguelle. He was a native of Amiens, and nephew of the Procurator-General of the Premonstratensians both now at Paris. Having poured natural water on the head and uttered these words:— 'Creature of God, I baptize thee in the name of the Father, and of the Son, and of the Holy Ghost,' I took half an altar cloth which I had wrested from the hands of an Indian who had stolen it from me, and put it on the body of the baptized child; for as I could not say mass for want of wine and vestments, this piece of linen could not be put to better use, than to enshroud the first Christian child among these tribes. I do not know whether the softness of the linen had refreshed her, but she was the next day smiling in her mother's arms, who believed that I had cured the child—but she died soon after, to my great consolation.

"During my stay among them, there arrived four savages, who said they were come alone five hundred leagues from the west, and had been four months upon the way. They assured us there was no such place as the Straits of Anian, and that they had travelled without resting, except to sleep, and had not seen or passed over any great lake, by which phrase they always mean the sea.

"They further informed us that the nation of the Assenipoulacs (Assiniboines) who lie north-east of Issati, was not above six or seven days' journey; that none of the nations, within their knowledge, who lie to the east or north-west, had any great lake about their countries, which were very large, but only rivers which came from the north. They further assured us that there were very few forests in the countries through which they passed, insomuch that now and then they were forced to make fires of buffaloes' dung to boil their food. All these circumstances make it appear that there is no such place as the Straits of Anian, as we usually see them set down on the maps. And whatever efforts have been made for many years past by the English and Dutch, to find out a passage to the Frozen Sea, they have not yet been able to effect it. But by the help of my discovery, and the assistance of God, I doubt not but a passage may still be found, and that an easy one too.

"For example, we may be transported into the Pacific Sea, by rivers which are large and capable of carrying great vessels, *and from thence it is very easy to go to China and Japan, without crossing the equinoctial line, and, in all probability, Japan is on the same continent as America.*"

It is painful to witness a member of the sacred profession so mendacious as Hennepin. After publishing a tolerably correct account of his adventures in Minnesota, in 1683, at Paris, fifteen years after he issued another edition greatly enlarged, in which he claims to have descended the Mississippi towards the Gulf of Mexico, as well as discovered the Falls of St. Anthony. As the reader notes his glaring contradictions in this last work, he is surprised that the author should have been bold enough to contend, that the statements were reliable. Though a large portion was plagiarized from the accounts of other travellers, it had a rapid sale, and was translated into several languages.[1]

[1] The following will give some idea of the popularity of Hennepin's narrative. It was prepared by Dr. O'Callaghan, for the Historical Magazine, Jan. 1858, and is believed to be nearly a complete list of the several editions of Hennepin's books:

No. 1. Description de la Louisiane. 12mo. Paris, 1683. Meusel. Ternaux, No. 985.

2. The same. 12mo. Paris, 1684. Rich., in No. 403 of 1683.

3. Descrizione della Luisiana. 12mo. Bologna, 1686. Rib. Belg. Meusel Ternaux, No. 1012. Translated by Casimir Frescot.

4. Description de la Louisiane. 12mo. Paris, 1688. Richarderie Faribault.

5. Beschryving van Louisiana. 4to. Amsterdam, 1688. Harv. Cat.

6. Beschreibung, &c. 12mo. Nurnberg, 1689. Meusal. Ternaux, No. 1041.

7. Nouvelle Decouverte. 12mo. Utrecht, 1697. Ternaux, 1095. "Nouvelle Description," Meusel. Faribault.

8. The same. 12mo. Amsterdam, 1698. Ternaux, No. 1110.

9. New Discovery. London, 1698. Ternaux, No. 1119, who calls it a 4to.; all the other catalogues an 8vo. J. R. B. says 2v.; but see Rich.

10. Another, same title. 8vo. London, 1698. J. R. B.

11. Nouveau Voyage. 12mo. Utrecht, 1698. Ternaux, No. 1111. 2v. Bib. Belg. Hennepin calls this his third vol.; No. 1 sup., being his first, and No. 7 sup. his second. Rich.

12. An edition in Dutch. 4to. Utrecht, 1698. J. R. B.

13. Nouveau Voyage. Amsterdam, 1698. Faribault.

14. A New Discovery of a Vast Country, &c. 8vo. London, Bonwick, 1699. t. f. Ded. 4ff. Pref. 2ff. Cont. 3ff. Text, pp. 240 and 216, with tit., pref. and cont. to part II.; two maps, six plates. [Not in any catalogue.]

15. Relaçion, de un Pays, &c. 12mo. Brusselas, 1699. Ternaux, 1126. A translation into Spanish by Seb. Fern. de Medrano.

16. Neue Entdekungen vieler grossen Landschaften in Amerika. 12mo. Bremen, 1699. Ternaux, 1049, who gives the date incorrectly, 1690. Translated by Langen. Meusel, No. 6 of J. R. B., and an edition in German of No. 7. *Supra*.

17. Voyage ou Nouvelle Decouverte. 8vo. Amsterdam, 1704. Meusel, Rich., No. 8.

18. The same. 8vo. Amsterdam, 1711. Meusel. Faribault says "Nouvelle Description."

19. The same. 12mo. Amsterdam, 1712. J. R. B.

20. A Discovery of a large, rich, &c. 8vo. London, 1720. Rich., No. 12.

21. Nouvelle Description. Amsterdam, 1720. Faribault.

22. Nouvelle Decouverte. 4to. Amsterdam, 1737. Richarderie. In

No doubt much of the information which the author obtained in relation to Minnesota, was obtained from Du Luth, whom he met in the Dahkotah country, and with whom he descended the Mississippi on his return to Canada.

Having made a favourable acquaintance with English gentlemen, he dedicated the edition of his work, published at Utrecht, in 1698, to King William, and the contents induced the British to send vessels to enter the Mississippi river. Callieres, Governor of Canada, writing to Pontchartrain,[1] the Minister, says, "I have learned that they are preparing vessels in England and Holland to take possession of Louisiana, upon the relation of Père Louis Hennepin, a Recollect who has made a book and dedicated it to King William."

After he had earned a reputation, not to be coveted, he desired to return to America, and Louis XIV., in a despatch to Callieres, writes, "His majesty has been informed that Father Hennepin, a Dutch Franciscan, who has formerly been in Canada, is desirous of returning thither. As his majesty is not satisfied with the conduct of the friar, it is his pleasure, if he return thither, that they arrest and send him to the Intendant of Rochefort."

In the year 1701 he was still in Europe, attached to a Convent in Italy.[2] He appears to have died in obscurity, unwept and unhonoured.

Histoire des Incas. A translation of Garcilasso de la Vega by Rousseler.

23. Neue Entdekungen, &c. Bremen, 1742. The same as No. 15, with a new title page.

[1] May 12, 1699. See Smith's Hist. Wisconsin, vol. i., p. 318.

[2] Historical Magazine, Boston, p. 316, vol. i.

Du Luth and not Hennepin was considered the real discoverer of Minnesota. Le Clercq remarks, that "in the last year of M. de Frontenac's first administration, Sieur du Luth, a man of talent and experience, opened a way to the missionaries and the gospel in many different nations, turning toward the north of that lake (Superior), where he even built a fort. He advanced as far as the Lake of the Issati (Mille Lac), called Lake Buade, from the family name of M. de Frontenac."

In the month of June, 1680, he left his post on Lake Superior, and with two canoes, an Indian, and four Frenchmen, entered a river, eight leagues below, ascending to the sources of which, he made a portage to a lake, which is the head of a river that entered into the Mississippi. Proceeding toward the Dahkotah villages he met Hennepin, with a party of Indians.

Returning to Quebec, Du Luth visited France, and conferred with the Minister of the Colonies, but in 1683, he was at Mackinaw fortifying the post against a threatened attack by the savages, and sending expresses to the Indians north and west of Lake Superior, who traded at Hudson's Bay with the English, to come and traffic with the French.

In the spring of 1683, Governor De La Barre sent twenty men, under the command of Nicholas Perrot, to establish frendly alliances with the Ioways and Dahkotahs. Proceeding to the Mississippi, he established a post below the mouth of the "Ouiskonche"[1] (Wisconsin), which was known as Fort St. Nicholas.[2]

He found the Miamies, Foxes, and Maskoutens, at war

---

[1] La Potherie. [2] Bellin.

with the Dahkotahs, who were at that time in alliance with their old foes, the Ojibways.

Frenchmen visited the Dahkotahs during the winter; and, at the opening of navigation, a deputation of them came down to the post, and carried Perrot with great parade, on a robe of beavers, to the lodge of their chief, chanting songs, and weeping over his head according to custom.

He learned from the Dahkotahs a droll adventure. The Hurons, who had fled to them for refuge, at length excited them to war. The Hurons secreted themselves in marshes, keeping their heads only out of water. The Dahkotahs, knowing that they would travel in the night, devised an ingenious stratagem. Cutting up beaver-skins into cords, they stretched them around the marshes, and suspended bells on them which they had obtained from the French. When night came the Hurons marched, and, stumbling over the unseen cords, they rung the bells, which was a signal for the attack of the Dahkotahs, who killed the whole party with one exception.

While they were in the neighbourhood, they pillaged the goods of some Frenchmen; but, under the threats of Perrot, they were brought back.

The Miamies brought to the post lumps of lead, which they said were found between the rocks, on the banks of a small stream which flowed into the Mississippi, about two days' journey below that point. These were probably the mines of Galena, which are marked on De l'Isle's maps of the Mississippi.

In the month of March, 1684, notwithstanding all the attempts of the French to keep the peace, a band of Seneca and Cayuga warriors, having met seven canoes manned by fourteen Frenchmen, with fifteen or sixteen thousand pounds of merchandise, who were going to trade with the "Scioux," pillaged and made them prisoners; and, after detaining them nine days, sent them away without arms, food, or canoes. This attack caused much alarm in Canada; and Du Luth, who appeared to have been in command at Green Bay, was ordered by the Governor of Canada to come and state the number of allies he could bring.

Perrot, who happened to be engaged in trade among the Outagamis (Foxes), not very far distant from the bay, rendered him great assistance in collecting allies.

With great expedition he came to Niagara, the place of rendezvous, with a band of Indians, and would alone have attacked the Senecas, had it not been for an express order from De La Barre, the governor, to desist.

When Louis XIV. heard of this outbreak of the Iroquois, he felt, to use his words, "that it was a grave misfortune for the colony of New France," and then, in his letter to the governor, he adds: "It appears to me that one of the principal causes of the war arises from one Du Luth having caused two Iroquois to be killed who had assassinated two Frenchmen in Lake Superior, and you sufficiently see how much this man's voyage, which cannot produce any advantage to the colony, and which was permitted only in the interest of some private persons, has contributed to distract the repose of the colony."

The English of New York, knowing the hostility of the Iroquois to the French, used the opportunity to trade with the distant Indians. In 1685, one Roseboom, with some young men, had traded with the Ottawas in Michigan.

In the year 1686, an old Frenchman, who had lived among the Dutch and English in New York, came to Montreal, to visit a child at the Jesuit boarding-school; and he stated that a Major McGregory, of Albany, was contemplating an expedition to Mackinac.

Denonville having declared war in 1687, most of the French left the region of the Mississippi. Perrot and Boisguillot, at the time trading near the Wisconsin, leaving a few "coureurs des bois" to protect their goods from the Dahkotahs, joined Du Luth, who was in command at Green Bay.

The Governor of Canada ordered Du Luth to proceed to the present Detroit river, and watch whether the English passed into Lake St. Clair. In accordance with the order, he left Green Bay. Being provided with fifty armed men, he established a post called Fort St. Joseph, some thirty miles above Detroit.

In the year 1687, on the 19th of May, the brave and distinguished Tonty, who was a cousin of Du Luth, arrived at Detroit, from his fort on the Illinois. Durantaye and Du Luth, knowing that he had arrived, came down from Fort St. Joseph with thirty captive English. Here Tonty and Du Luth joined forces and proceeded toward the Iroquois country. As they were coasting Lake Erie, they met and captured Major McGregory, of Albany, then on his way with thirty Englishmen, to trade with the Indians at Mackinac.

Du Luth having reached Lake Ontario, we find him engaged in that conflict with the Senecas of the Genesee valley, when Father Angleran, the superintendent of the Mackinac mission, was severely but not mortally wounded. After this battle, he returned, in company with Tonty, to his post on the Detroit river.[1]

[1] Baron La Hontan speaks of Grisolon de la Tourette being at Niagara in August, 1687, and calls him a brother of Du Luth.

In 1689, immediately previous to the burning of Schenectady, we find him fighting the Iroquois in the neighbourhood, and there is reason to suppose that he was engaged in the midnight sack of that town. As late as the year 1696, he is on duty at Fort Frontenac; but after the peace of Ryswick, which occasioned a suspension of hostilities, we hear but little more of this man, who was the first of whom we have any account, who came by way of Lake Superior to the upper Mississippi.

The letter of one of the Jesuit fathers, shows that in some things he was as superstitious as the Dahkotahs, with whom he once traded. While in command of Fort Frontenac, in 1696, he gave the following certificate:

"I, the subscriber, certify to all whom it may concern, that having been tormented by the gout for the space of twenty-three years, and with such severe pains that it gave me no rest for the space of three months at a time, I addressed myself to Catherine Tegahkouita, an Iroquois virgin, deceased at the Sault Saint Louis, in the reputation of sanctity, and I promised her to visit her tomb if God should give me health through her intercession. I have been so perfectly cured at the end of one novena which I made in her honour, that after five months I have not perceived the slightest touch of my gout.

"Given at Fort Frontenac, this 18th day of August, 1696.

"J. DE LUTH, Capt. of the Marine Corps, Commander Fort Frontenac."

He died in 1710. The despatch announcing the fact to the Home Government, is expressive in its simplicity: Capt. Du Luth is dead, "he was an honest man." Who would wish more said of him? His name is spelled Du Luth, Du Lut, Dulhut, and De Luth, in the old documents.

CHAPTER VII.

ALTHOUGH Du Luth and Hennepin had visited Minnesota, France laid no formal claim to the country, until the year 1689, when Perrot, accompanied by Le Sueur, Father Marest, and others, planted the cross and affixed the arms of France.

The first official document pertaining to Minnesota is worthy of preservation, and thus reads:—

"Nicholas Perrot, commanding for the King, at the post of the Nadouëssioux, commissioned by the Marquis Denonville, Governor and Lieutenant-Governor of all New France, to manage the interests of commerce among all the Indian tribes, and people of the Bay des Puants,[1] Nadouëssioux,[2] Mascoutins, and other western nations of the Upper Mississippi, and to take possession in the King's name of all the places where he has heretofore been, and whither he will go.

"We, this day, the eighth of May, one thousand six hundred and eighty-nine, do, in the presence of the Reverend Father Marest of the Society of Jesus, missionary among the Nadouëssioux; of Monsieur de Borie-

---

[1] Green Bay, Wisconsin.   [2] Dahkotahs.

guillot,[1] commanding the French in the neighbourhood of the Ouiskonche[2] on the Mississippi; Augustin Legardeur, Esquire, Sieur de Caumont, and of Messieurs Le Sueur, Hebert, Lemire, and Blein:

"Declare to all whom it may concern, that, being come from the Bay des Puants, and to the Lake of the Ouiskonches, and to the river Mississippi, we did transport ourselves to the country of the Nadouëssioux, on the border of the river St. Croix,[3] and at the mouth of the river St. Pierre,[4] on the bank of which were the Mantantans;[5] and, farther up to the interior to the north-east of the Mississippi, as far as the Menchokatonx,[6] with whom dwell the majority of the Songeskitons, and other Nadouëssioux, who are to the northeast of the Mississippi, to take possession for, and in the name of the King, of the countries and rivers inhabited

---

[1] Charlevoix writes Boisguillot.

[2] Wisconsin, (Fort St. Nicholas,) Ouiskonche, Mesconsing, Ouisconsing, Wiskonsan, are some of the former spellings of this word.

[3] This is not ecclesiastical in its associations, but named after Mons. Saint Croix, who was drowned at its mouth.—*La Harpe's Louisiana.*

[4] Nicollet supposes that this river bore the name of Capt. St. Pierre.

[5] The Dahkotahs have a tradition, that a tribe called Onktokadan, who lived on the St. Croix just above the lake, was exterminated by the Foxes.

At an early date the Mde-wa-kanton-wan division of the Dahkotah tribe split into two parties, one of which was denominated Wa-kpa-a-ton-we-dan, and the other Ma-tan-ton-wan. The former name signifies, —Those-who-dwell-on-the-creek, because they had their village on Rice Creek, a stream which empties into the Mississippi seven miles above the Falls of St. Anthony. The signification of the latter name is unknown. It is said that Ta-te-psin, Wa-su-wi-ca-xta-xni, Ta-can-rpi-sa-pa, A-nog-i-na jin, Ru-ya-pa, and Ta-can-ku-wa-xte, whose names signify, respectively, Bounding-Wind, Bad-Hail, Black-Tomahawk, He-stands-both-sides, Eagle-Head, and Good-Road, are descendants of the Wa-kpa-a-ton-we-dan.—Wa-ku-te, Ta-o-ya-te-du-ta, Ma-za-ro-ta, Ma-rpi-ya-ma-za, Ma-rpi-wi-ca-xta, and Xa-kpe-dan, are said to be Ma-tan-ton-wans. The respective signification of their names is as follows: Shooter, His-scarlet-people, Grey-Iron, Iron-Cloud, Sky-Man, and Little-six.

[6] M'daywawkawntwawns.

by the said tribes, and of which they are proprietors. The present act done in our presence, signed with our hand and subscribed."[1]

The first French establishment in Minnesota was on the west shore of Lake Pepin, a short distance above the entrance.[2] On a map of the year 1700, it was called Fort Bon Secours; three years later it was marked Fort Le Sueur, and abandoned;[3] but in a much later map it is correctly called Fort Perrot.[4]

The year that Perrot visited Minnesota, Frontenac, who had been recalled seven years before, was recommissioned as Governor of Canada. He issued orders that the Frenchmen in the upper Mississippi country should return to Mackinaw.

Frontenac was dogmatic and overbearing, though deeply interested in the extension of the power of France. During the first term of office he had opposed the ecclesiastics, who deplored the ill effects of rum and licentious "coureurs des bois" upon the morals of the savages, and desired both excluded from the country. He had no interest in Christianity, and still less confidence in the Jesuits. In a communication to the government he bluntly said, to Colbert the minister, "To speak frankly to you, they think as much about the conversion of beavers as of souls. The majority of their missions are mere mockeries."

Learning that Durantaye, the Commandant at Macki-

---

[1] Then are given the names of those already mentioned. This record was drawn up at Green Bay, Wisconsin.

[2] Bellin's description of Map of North America.

[3] De l'Isle's Maps 1700, and 1703. This last name appears incorrect.

[4] See Jeffery's Map, 1762.

naw, was disposed to be friendly to missionary schemes, he superseded him by the appointment of Louvigny.

Perrot, who was on a visit to Montreal, conducted the new commander to his post, where he found the Ottawas wavering, and about to carry their peltries to the English; but by his uncommon tact he regained their confidence, and a flotilla of one hundred canoes, with furs valued at one hundred thousand crowns, started towards Montreal.

On the eighteenth of August, 1690, the citizens of that city perceived the waters of the Saint Lawrence darkened by descending canoes, and supposing that they were filled by the dreaded Iroquois, alarm-guns were fired to call in the citizens from the country; but this terror was soon turned to joy, by a messenger arriving with the intelligence that it was a party of five hundred Indians, of various tribes near Mackinaw, who had come to the city to exchange their peltries. So large a number from the North-West had not appeared for years; and, on the twenty-fifth, Count Frontenac gave them a grand feast of two oxen, six large dogs, two barrels of wine, and some prunes, with a plentiful supply of tobacco.

The Ottawas in council demanded the meaning of the hatchet Perrot had hung in their cabin.

Frontenac told them that they were aware of the tidings he had received, that a powerful army was coming to ravage his country; that all that was necessary to conclude was the mode of proceeding, whether to go and meet this army, or to wait for it with a firm foot; that he put into their hands the hatchet which had been formerly given them, and had since been kept suspended for them, and he doubted not they would make good use of it.

He then, hatchet in hand, sung the war song, in which the Indians joined.

The increasing Iroquois and English hostility made it a dangerous undertaking to transport in canoes to or from Mackinaw.

Lieutenant D'Argenteuil was despatched by Frontenac in 1692, with eighteen Canadians on increased pay to Mackinaw, with an order to Louvigny, the commander, to send down all the Frenchmen that could be spared from the North-West, and the large amount of peltries that had accumulated at his post.

On the seventeenth of August two hundred canoes filled with Frenchmen and Ottawas arrived from the upper country at Montreal with the long-detained furs.

"The merchant, the farmer, and other individuals who might have some peltries there, were dying of hunger, with property they could not enjoy. Credit was exhausted, and the apprehension universal that the English might seize this last resource of the country while it was on the way. Terms sufficiently strong were not to be found to praise and bless him by whose care so much property had arrived."[1]

The Indians were entertained at the governor's table, and on Sunday, the sixth of September, there was a grand war dance. The next day they received presents, and during the week returned to their own country.

The French soon followed under the direction of Tonty, Commandant of the Illinois. La Motte, Cadillac, and D'Argenteuil shortly after were ordered to Mackinaw, Louvigny being recalled. Perrot was sta-

[1] Paris Doc. vol. ix. N. Y. Col. Hist.

tioned among the Miamis, at a place called "Malamek," in Michigan; and Le Sueur was sent to La Pointe of Lake Superior to maintain the peace that had just been concluded between the Ojibways and Dahkotahs.

The mission of Le Sueur was important. As the Foxes and Mascoutins had become inimical, the northern route to the Dahkotahs was the only one that could be used in transporting goods.

In the year 1695, the second post in Minnesota was built by Le Sueur. Above Lake Pepin, and below the mouth of the St. Croix, there are many islands, and the largest of these was selected as the site.[1] The object of the establishment was to interpose a barrier between the Dahkotahs and Ojibways, and maintain the peaceful relations which had been created. Charlevoix speaks of the island as having a very beautiful prairie, and remarks that "the French of Canada have made it a centre of commerce for the western parts, and many pass the winter here, because it is a good country for hunting."

On the fifteenth of July, Le Sueur arrived at Montreal with a party of Ojibways, and the *first Dahkotah brave* that had ever visited Canada.

The Indians were much impressed with the power of France by the marching of a detachment of seven hundred picked men, under Chevalier Cresafi, who were on their way to La Chine.

On the eighteenth, Frontenac, in the presence of Callieres and other persons of distinction, gave them an audience.

The first speaker was the chief of the Ojibway band at La Pointe, Shingowahbay, who said :—

[1] Bellin in his description of the Chart of North America.

"That he was come to pay his respects to Onontio,[1] in the name of the young warriors of Point Chagouamigon, and to thank him for having given them some Frenchmen to dwell with them; to testify their sorrow for one Jobin, a Frenchman, who was killed at a feast accidentally, and not maliciously. We come to ask a favour of you, which is to let us act. We are allies of the Sciou. Some Outagamies or Mascoutins have been killed. The Sciou came to mourn with us. Let us act, Father; let us take revenge.

"Le Sueur alone, who is acquainted with the language of the one and the other, can serve us. We ask that he return with us."

Another speaker of the Ojibways was Le Brochet.

Tēēoskahtay, the Dahkotah chief, before he spoke, spread out a beaver robe, and laying another with a tobacco pouch and otter skin, began to weep bitterly. After drying his tears he said :—

"All of the nations had a father who afforded them protection; all of them have iron. But he was a bastard in quest of a father; he was come to see him, and begs that he will take pity on him."

He then placed upon the beaver robe twenty-two arrows, at each arrow naming a Dahkotah village that desired Frontenac's protection. Resuming his speech, he remarked :—

"It is not on account of what I bring that I hope he who rules this earth will have pity on me. I learned from the Sauteurs that he wanted nothing; that he was the Master of the Iron; that he had a big heart, into which he could receive all the nations. This has

---

[1] The title the Indians always gave to the Governor.

induced me to abandon my people to come to seek his protection, and to beseech him to receive me among the number of his children. Take courage, Great Captain, and reject me not; despise me not though I appear poor in your eyes. All the nations here present know that I am rich, and the little they offer here is taken from my lands."

Count Frontenac in reply told the chief that he would receive the Dahkotahs as his children, on condition that they would be obedient, and that he would send back Le Sueur with him.

Tēēoskahtay, taking hold of the governor's knees, wept, and said:—" Take pity on us; we are well aware that we are not able to speak, being children; but Le Sueur, who understands our language, and has seen all our villages, will next year inform you what will have been achieved by the Sioux nations, represented by those arrows before you."

Having finished, a Dahkotah woman, the wife of a great chief whom Le Sueur had purchased from captivity at Mackinaw, approached those in authority, and with downcast eyes embraced their knees, weeping and saying:—

"I thank thee, Father; it is by thy means I have been liberated, and am no longer captive."

Then Tēēoskahtay resumed:—

" I speak like a man penetrated with joy. The Great Captain; he who is the Master of the Iron, assures me of his protection, and I promise him that if he condescends to restore my children, now prisoners among the Foxes, Ottawas, and Hurons, I will return hither, and bring with me the twenty-two villages whom he has just restored to life by promising to send them Iron."

On the 14th of August, two weeks after the Ojibway chief left for his home on Lake Superior, Nicholas Perrot arrived with a deputation of Sauks, Foxes, Menomonees, Miamis of Maaramek, and Pottowattamies.

Two days after, they had a council with the governor, who thus spoke to a Fox brave:—

"I see that you are a young man; your nation has quite turned away from my wishes; it has pillaged some of my young men, whom it has treated as slaves. I know that your father, who loved the French, had no hand in the indignity. You only imitate the example of your father, who had sense, when you do not co-operate with those of your tribe who are wishing to go over to my enemies, after they grossly insulted me, and defeated the Sioux, whom I now consider my son. I pity the Sioux; I pity the dead whose loss I deplore. Perrot goes up there, and he will speak to your nation from me, for the release of their prisoners; let them attend to him."

Tēēoskahtay never returned to his native land. While in Montreal he was taken sick, and in thirty-three days he ceased to breathe; and, followed by white men, his body was interred in the white man's grave.

Le Sueur, instead of going back to Minnesota that year, as was expected, went to France, and received a license, in 1697, to open certain mines supposed to exist in Minnesota. The ship in which he was returning, was captured by the English, and he was taken to England. After his release, he went back to France, and, in 1698, obtained a new commission for mining.

While Le Sueur was in Europe, the Dahkotahs waged war against the Foxes and Miamis. In retaliation, the latter raised a war party, and entered the land of the Dahkotahs. Finding their foes intrenched, and assisted by "coureurs des bois," they were indignant; and on their return they had a skirmish with some Frenchmen, who were carrying goods to the Dahkotahs.

Shortly after, they met Perrot, and were about to burn him to death, when prevented by some friendly Foxes. The Miamis, after this, were disposed to be friendly to the Iroquois. In 1696, the year previous, the authorities at Quebec decided that it was expedient to abandon all the posts west of Mackinaw, and withdraw the French from Wisconsin and Minnesota.

The "voyageurs" were not disposed to leave the country, and the governor wrote to Pontchartrain for instructions, in October, 1698. In his despatch he remarks:—

"In this conjuncture, and under all these circumstances, we consider it our duty to postpone, until new instructions from the court, the execution of Sieur Le Sueur's enterprise for the mines, though the promise had already been given him to send two canoes in advance to Missilimackinac, for the purpose of purchasing there some provisions and other necessaries for his voyage, and that he would be permitted to go and join them early in the spring with the rest of his hands. What led us to adopt this resolution has been, that the French who remained to trade off with the Five Nations the remainder of their merchandise, might, on seeing entirely new comers arriving there, consider themselves entitled to dispense with coming down, and perhaps adopt the resolution to settle there; whilst, seeing no arrival there, with permission to do what is forbidden, the reflection they will be able to make during the winter, and the apprehension of being guilty of crime, may oblige them to return in the spring.

"This would be very desirable, in consequence of the great difficulty there will be in constraining them to it, should they be inclined to lift the mask altogether and become buccaneers; or should Sieur Le Sueur, as he easily could do, furnish them with goods for their beaver and smaller peltry, which he might send down by the return of other Frenchmen, whose sole desire is to obey, and who have remained only because of the impossibility of getting their effects down. This would rather induce those who would continue to lead a vagabond life to remain there, as the goods they would obtain from Le Sueur's people would afford them the means of doing so."

In reply to this communication, Louis XIV. answered that—

"His majesty has approved that the late Sieur de Frontenac and De Champigny, suspended the execution of the license granted to the man named Le Sueur to proceed, with fifty men, to explore some mines on the banks of the Mississippi. He has revoked said license, and desires that the said Le Sueur, or any other person, be prevented from leaving the colony on pretence of going in search of mines, without his majesty's express permission."

Le Sueur, undaunted by these drawbacks to the prosecution of a favourite project, again visited France.

CHAPTER VIII.

FORTUNATELY for Le Sueur, D'Iberville, who was a friend, and closely connected by marriage, was appointed governor of the new territory of Louisiana.[1]

In the month of December he arrived from France, with thirty workmen, to proceed to the supposed mines in Minnesota.

On the thirteenth of July, 1700, with a felucca, two canoes, and nineteen men, having ascended the Mississippi, he had reached the mouth of the Missouri, and six leagues above this he passed the Illinois. He there met three Canadians, who came to join him, with a letter from Father Marest, who had once attempted a mission among the Dahkotahs, dated July 13, Mission Immaculate Conception of the Holy Virgin, in Illinois.

"I have the honour to write, in order to inform you that the Saugiestas have been defeated by the Scioux and Ayavois (Iowas). The people have formed an alliance with the Quincapous (Kickapoos), some of the Mecoutins, Renards (Foxes), and Metesigamias, and gone to revenge themselves, not on the Scioux, for they are too much afraid of them, but perhaps on the Ayavois, or very likely upon the Paoutees, or more probably upon

[1] Charlevoix says that he was the father of the governor, perhaps wife's father?

the Osages, for these suspect nothing, and the others are on their guard.

"As you will probably meet these allied nations, you ought to take precaution against their plans, and not allow them to board your vessel, since *they are traitors, and utterly faithless*. I pray God to accompany you in all your designs."

Twenty-two leagues above the Illinois, he passed a small stream which he called the River of Oxen, and nine leagues beyond this he passed a small river on the west side, where he met four Canadians descending the Mississippi, on their way to the Illinois. On the 30th of July, nine leagues above the last-named river, he met seventeen Scioux, in seven canoes, who were going to revenge the death of three Scioux, one of whom had been burned, and the others killed, at Tamarois, a few days before his arrival in that village. As he had promised the chief of the Illinois to appease the Scioux, who should go to war against his nation, he made a present to the chief of the party to engage him to turn back. He told them the King of France did not wish them to make this river more bloody, and that he was sent to tell them that, if they obeyed the king's word, they would receive in future all things necessary for them. The chief answered that he accepted the present, that is to say, that he would do as had been told him.

From the 30th of July to the 25th of August, Le Sueur advanced fifty-three and one-fourth leagues to a small river which he called the River of the Mine.[1] At the mouth it runs from the north, but it turns to the north-east. On the right seven leagues, there is a lead

[1] This is the first mention of the Galena mines.

mine in a prairie, one and a half leagues; the river is only navigable in high water, that is to say, from early spring till the month of June.

From the 25th to the 27th he made ten leagues, passed two small rivers, and made himself acquainted with a mine of lead, from which he took a supply. From the 27th to the 30th he made eleven and a half leagues, and met five Canadians, one of whom had been dangerously wounded in the head. They were naked, and had no ammunition except a miserable gun, with five or six loads of powder and balls. They said they were descending from the Scioux to go to Tamarois; and, when seventy leagues above, they perceived nine canoes in the Mississippi, in which were ninety savages, who robbed and cruelly beat them. This party were going to war against the Scioux, and were composed of four different nations, the Outagamis (Foxes), Saquis (Sauks), Poutouwatamis (Pottowattamies), and Pauns (Winnebagoes), who dwell in a country eighty leagues east of the Mississippi from where Le Sueur then was.

The Canadians determined to follow the detachment, which was composed of twenty-eight men. This day they made seven and a half leagues. On the 1st of September, he passed the Wisconsin river. It runs into the Mississippi from the north-east. It is nearly one and a half miles wide. At about seventy-five leagues up this river, on the right, ascending, there is a portage of more than a league. The half of this portage is shaking ground, and at the end of it is a small river which descends into a bay called Winnebago Bay. It is inhabited by a great number of nations who carry their furs to Canada. Monsieur Le Sueur came by the Wisconsin river to the Mississippi, for the first time, in 1683, on his way to the Scioux country, where he had already passed seven years at different periods. The Mississippi, opposite the mouth of the Wisconsin, is less than a half mile wide. From the 1st of September to the 5th, our voyageur advanced fourteen leagues. He passed the river " Aux Canots," which comes from the north-east, and then the Quincapous, named from a nation which once dwelt upon its banks.

From the 5th to the 9th, he made ten and a half leagues, and passed the Rivers Cachee and Aux Ailes. The same day he perceived canoes, filled with savages, descending the river, and the five Canadians recognised them as the party who had robbed them. They placed sentinels in the wood, for fear of being surprised by land; and, when they had approached within hearing, they cried to them that if they approached farther they would fire. They then drew up by an island, at half the distance of a gun shot. Soon, four of the principal men of the band approached in a canoe, and asked if it was forgotten that they were our brethren, and with what design we had taken arms when we perceived them. Le Sueur replied that he had cause to distrust them, since they had robbed five of his party. Nevertheless, for the surety of his trade, being forced to be at peace with all the tribes, he demanded no redress for the robbery, but added merely that the king, their master and his, wished that his subjects should navigate that river without insult, and that they had better beware how they acted.

The Indian who had spoken was silent, but another said they had been attacked by the Scioux, and that if they did not have pity on them, and give them a little powder, they should not be able to reach their village. The consideration of a missionary, who was to go up among the Scioux, and whom these savages might meet, induced them to give two pounds of powder.

M. Le Sueur made the same day three leagues; passed a stream on the west, and afterwards another river on the east, which is navigable at all times, and which the Indians call Red river.

On the 10th, at daybreak, they heard an elk whistle, on the other side of the river. A Canadian crossed in a small Scioux canoe, which they had found, and shortly returned with the body of the animal, which was very easily killed, "quand il est en rut," that is from the beginning of September until the end of October. The hunters at this time make a whistle of a piece of wood, or reed, and when they hear an elk whistle, they answer it. The animal, believing it to be another elk, approaches, and is killed with ease.

From the 10th to the 14th, M. Le Sueur made seventeen and a half leagues, passing the rivers Raisin and Paquilenettes, (perhaps the Wazi Ozu and Buffalo.) The same day he left, on the east side of the Mississippi, a beautiful and large river, which descends from the very far north, and called Bon Secours (Chippeway), on account of the great quantity of buffalo, elk, bears, and deers, which are found there. Three leagues up this river there is a mine of lead, and seven leagues above, on the same side, they found another long river, in the vicinity of which there is a copper mine, from which he had taken a lump of sixty pounds, in a former voyage. In order to make these mines of any account, peace must be obtained between the Scioux and Outagamis (Foxes), because the latter, who dwell on the east side of the Mississippi, pass this road continually when going to war against the Scioux.

In this region, at one and a half leagues on the north-west side, commenced a lake, which is six leagues long and more than one broad, called Lake Pepin. It is bounded on the west by a chain of mountains; on the east is seen a prairie; and on the north-west of the lake there is another prairie two leagues long and one wide. In the neighbourhood is a chain of mountains quite two hundred feet high, and more than one and a half miles long. In these are found several caves, to which the bears retire in winter. Most of the caverns are more than seventy feet in extent, and three or four feet high. There are several of which the entrance is very narrow, and quite closed up with saltpetre. It would be dangerous to enter them in summer, for they are filled with rattlesnakes, the bite of which is very dangerous. Le Sueur saw some of these snakes which were six feet in length, but generally they are about four feet. They have teeth resembling those of the pike, and their gums are full of small vessels in which their poison is placed. The Scioux say they take it every morning, and cast it away at night. They have at the tail a kind of scale which makes a noise, and this is called the rattle.

Le Sueur made on this day seven and a half leagues, and passed another river called Hiambouxecate Ouataba, or the River of Flat Rock.[1]

On the 15th he crossed a small river, and saw, in the neighbourhood, several canoes filled with Indians, descending the Mississippi. He supposed they were

---

[1] This is evidently the Inyanbosndata, or Cannon river.

Scioux, because he could not distinguish whether their canoes were large or small. The arms were placed in readiness, and soon they heard the cry of the savages, which they are accustomed to raise when they rush upon their enemies. He caused them to be answered in the same manner; and, after having placed all the men behind the trees, he ordered them not to fire until they were commanded. He remained on shore to see what movement the savages would make, and perceiving that they placed two on shore, on the other side, where from an eminence they could ascertain the strength of his forces, he caused the men to pass and repass from the shore to the wood, in order to make them believe that they were numerous. This ruse succeeded, for as soon as the two descended from the eminence, the chief of the party came, bearing the calumet, which is a signal of peace among the Indians.

They said, that never having seen the French navigate the river with boats like the felucca,[1] they had supposed them to be English, and for that reason they had raised the war cry, and arranged themselves on the other side of the Mississippi; but, having recognised their flag, they had come without fear to inform them, that one of their number, who was crazy, had accidentally killed a Frenchman, and that they would go and bring his comrade, who would tell how the mischief had happened.

The Frenchman they brought was Denis, a Canadian, and he reported that his companion was accidentally killed. His name was Laplace, a deserting soldier from Canada, who had taken refuge in this country.

[1] The felucca is a small vessel propelled both by oars and sails, and had never before been seen on the waters of the Upper Mississippi.

Le Sueur replied, that Onontio (the name they give to all the governors of Canada), being their father and his, they ought not to seek justification elsewhere than before him; and he advised them to go and see him as soon as possible, and beg him to wipe off the blood of this Frenchman from their faces.

The party was composed of forty-seven men of different nations, who dwell far to the east, about the forty-fourth degree of latitude. Le Sueur, discovering who the chiefs were, said the king whom they had spoken of in Canada, had sent him to take possession of the north of the river; and that he wished the nations who dwell on it, as well as those under his protection, to live in peace.

He made this day three and three-fourth leagues; and, on the 16th of September, he left a large river on the east side, *named St. Croix, because a Frenchman of that name was shipwrecked at its mouth.* It comes from the north-north-west. Four leagues higher, in going up, is found a small lake, at the mouth of which is a very large mass of copper. It is on the edge of the water, in a small ridge of sandy earth, on the west of this lake.

From the 16th to the 19th, he advanced thirteen and three-fourth leagues. After having made from Tamarois two hundred and nine and a half leagues, he left the navigation of the Mississippi, to enter the river St. Pierre,[1] on the west side. By the 1st of October, he

---

[1] The Saint Pierre, like the Saint Croix, just below it, was evidently named after a Frenchman. Charlevoix speaks of an officer by that name, who was at Mackinaw in 1692, and prominent in the Indian affairs in that age. Carver, in 1776, on the shores of Lake Pepin, discovered the ruins of an extensive trading post, that had been under the control

had made in this river forty-four and one-fourth leagues. After he entered into Blue river, thus named on account of the mines of blue earth found at its mouth, he founded his post, situated in forty-four degrees, thirteen minutes, north latitude. He met at this place nine Scioux,[1] who told him that the river belonged to the Scioux of the West, the Ayavois (Iowas), and Otoctatas (Ottoes), who lived a little farther off; that it was not their custom to hunt on ground belonging to others, unless invited to do so by the owners, and that when they would come to the fort to obtain provisions, they would be in danger of being killed in ascending or descending the rivers, which were narrow, and that if they would show their pity, *he must establish himself on the Mississippi, near the mouth of the St. Pierre,*[2] where the Ayavois, the Otoctatas, and the other Scioux, could go as well as they.

Having finished their speech, they leaned over the head of Le Sueur, according to their custom, crying out, "Ouaechissou ouaepanimanabo," that is to say, "Have pity upon us." Le Sueur had foreseen that the establishment of Blue Earth river, would not please the Scioux of the East, who were, so to speak, *masters of the other Scioux*, and of the nations which will be hereafter mentioned, *because they were the first with whom trade was commenced*, and in consequence of which they had already quite a number of guns.

As he had commenced his operations, not only with a view to the trade of beaver, but also to gain a

of a Captain Saint Pierre, and there is scarcely a doubt that Le Sueur named the Minnesota river in honour of his fellow explorer and trader.

[1] Scioux, is the orthography of Lahontan, Le Sueur, and the Jesuits of that period in their relations, and it has not been altered to Dahkotah in this chapter.

[2] Neighbourhood of Mendota.

knowledge of the mines, which he had previously discovered, he told them he was sorry that he had not known their intentions sooner; and that it was just, since he came expressly for them, that he should establish himself on their land, but that the season was too far advanced for him to return. He then made them a present of powder, balls, and knives, and an armful of tobacco, to entice them to assemble as soon as possible, near the fort which he was about to construct, that when they should be all assembled he might tell them the intention of the king, their and his sovereign.

The Scioux of the West, according to the statement of the Eastern Scioux, have more than a thousand lodges. They do not use canoes, nor cultivate the earth, nor gather wild rice. They remain generally in the prairies, which are between the Upper Mississippi and Missouri rivers, and live entirely by the chase. The Scioux generally say they have three souls, and that after death, that which has done well goes to the warm country, that which has done evil to the cold regions, and the other guards the body. Polygamy is common among them. They are very jealous, and sometimes fight in duel for their wives. They manage the bow admirably, and have been seen several times to kill ducks on the wing. They make their lodges of a number of buffalo skins interlaced and sewed, and carry them wherever they go. They are all great smokers, but their manner of smoking differs from that of other Indians. There are some Scioux who swallow all the smoke of the tobacco, and others who, after having kept it some time in their mouth, cause it to issue from the nose. In each lodge there are usually two or three men with their families.

On the third of October, they received at the fort several Scioux, among whom was Wahkantape, chief of the village. Soon two Canadians arrived who had been hunting, and had been robbed by the Scioux of the East, who had raised their guns against the establishment which M. Le Sueur had made on Blue Earth river.

On the fourteenth the fort was finished and named Fort L'Huillier,[1] and on the twenty-second two Canadians were sent out to invite the Ayavois and Otoctatas to come and establish a village near the fort, because these Indians are industrious and accustomed to cultivate the earth, and they hoped to get provisions from them, and to make them work in the mines.

On the twenty-fourth, six Scioux Oujalespoitons wished to go into the fort, but were told that they did not receive men who had killed Frenchmen. This is the term used when they have insulted them. The next day they came to the lodge of Le Sueur to beg him to have pity on them. They wished, according to custom, to weep over his head and make him a present of packs of beavers, which he refused. He told them he was surprised that people who had robbed should come to him; to which they replied that they had heard it said that two Frenchmen had been robbed, but none from their village had been present at that wicked action.

Le Sueur answered, that he knew it was the Mendeoucantons and not the Oujalespoitons; "but," continued he, "you are Scioux; it is the Scioux who have robbed me, and if I were to follow your manner of

---

[1] The farmer general at Paris who had encouraged Le Sueur in his projects.

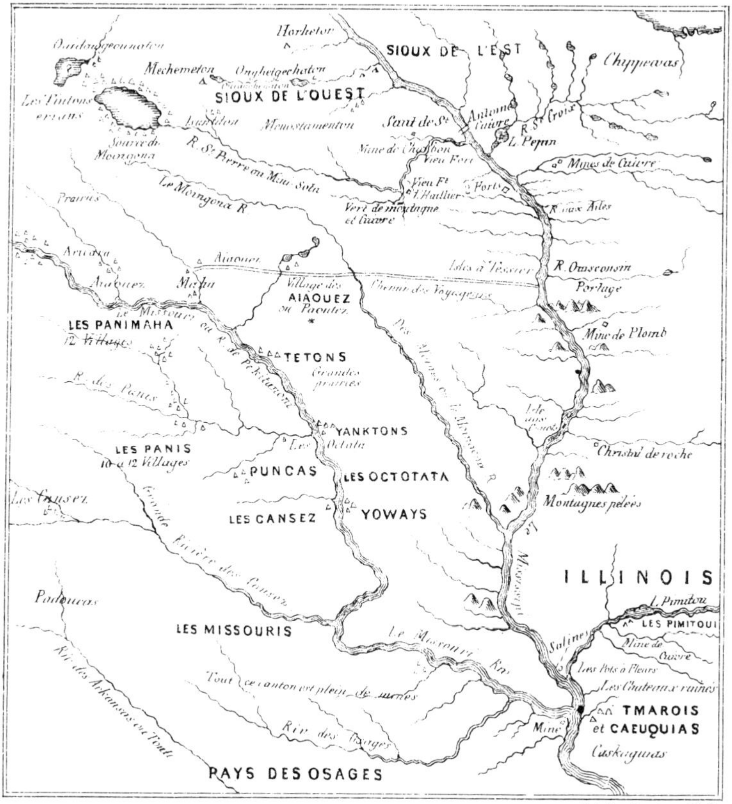

P.S. Duval & Son. Phil.a

SECTION OF A CHART
of
LOUISIANA,
by
WILLIAM DE L'ISLE
of the
Royal Academy of Sciences.

acting, I should break your heads; for is it not true, that when a stranger (it is thus they call the Indians who are not Scioux) has insulted a Scioux, Mendeoucanton, Oujalespoitons, or others—all the villages revenge upon the first one they meet?"

As they had nothing to answer to what he said to them, they wept and repeated, according to custom, "Ouaechissou! ouaepanimanabo!" Le Sueur told them to cease crying, and added, that the French had good hearts, and that they had come into the country to have pity on them. At the same time he made them a present, saying to them, "Carry back your beavers and say to all the Scioux, that they will have from me no more powder or lead, and they will no longer smoke any long pipe until they have made satisfaction for robbing the Frenchman."

The same day the Canadians, who had been sent off on the 22d, arrived without having found the road which led to the Ayavois and Otoctatas. On the 25th Le Sueur went to the river with three canoes, which he filled with green and blue earth.[1] It is taken from the hills near which are very abundant mines of copper, some of which was worked at Paris in 1696 by L'Huillier, one of the chief collectors of the king. Stones were also found there, which would be curious, if worked.

On the 9th of November, eight Mantanton Scioux arrived, who had been sent by their chiefs to say that the *Mendeoucantons were still at their lake on the east of the Mississippi,* and they could not come for a long time; and that, for a single village which had no good sense,

[1] The locality was a branch of the Blue Earth, about a mile above the fort, called by Nicollet Le Sueur river, and on a map published in 1773, the river St. Remi.

the others ought not to bear the punishment; and that they were willing to make reparation if they knew how. Le Sueur replied that he was glad that they had a disposition to do so.

On the 15th the two Mantanton Scioux, who had been sent expressly to say that all of the Scioux of the east, and part of those of the west, were joined together to come to the French, because they had heard that the Christianaux and the Assinipoils were making war on them. These two nations dwell above the fort on the east side, more than eighty leagues on the Upper Mississippi.

The Assinipoils speak Scioux, and are certainly of that nation. It is only a few years since that they became enemies. The enmity thus originated: The Christianaux, having the use of arms before the Scioux, through the English at Hudson's Bay, they constantly warred upon the Assinipoils, who were their nearest neighbours. The latter, being weak, sued for peace, and to render it more lasting, married the Christianaux women. The other Scioux, who had not made the compact, continued the war; and, seeing some Christianaux with the Assinipoils, broke their heads. The Christianaux furnished the Assinipoils with arms and merchandise.

On the 16th the Scioux returned to their village, and it was reported that the Ayavois and Otoctatas were gone to establish themselves towards the Missouri river, near the Maha, who dwell in that region. On the 26th the Mantantons and Oujalespoitons arrived at the fort; and, after they had encamped in the woods, Wahkantape[1] came to beg Le Sueur to go to his lodge. He

[1] Wakandapi or Esteemed Sacred, was the name of one of the head men at Red Wing, in 1850.

there found sixteen men with women and children, with their faces daubed with black. In the middle of the lodge were several buffalo skins, which were sewed for a carpet. After motioning him to sit down, they wept for the fourth of an hour, and the chief gave him some wild rice to eat (as was their custom), putting the first three spoonsful to his mouth. After which, he said all present were relatives of Tioscaté,[1] whom Le Sueur took to Canada in 1695, and who died there in 1696.

At the mention of Tioscaté they began to weep again, and wipe their tears and heads upon the shoulders of Le Sueur. Then Wahkantape again spoke, and said that Tioscaté begged him to forget the insult done to the Frenchmen by the Mendeoucantons, and take pity on his brethren by giving them powder and balls whereby they could defend themselves, and gain a living for their wives and children, who languish in a country, full of game, because they had not the means of killing them. "Look," added the chief, "Behold thy children, thy brethren, and thy sisters; it is to thee to see whether thou wishest them to die. They will live if thou givest them powder and ball; they will die if thou refusest."

Le Sueur granted them their request, but as the Scioux never answer on the spot, especially in matters of importance, and as he had to speak to them about his establishment, he went out of the lodge without saying a word. The chief and all those within followed him as far as the door of the fort; and when he had gone in, they went around it three times, crying with all their strength, "Atheouanan!" that is to say, "Father, have pity on us." (Ate unyanpi, means Our Father.)

[1] Teeoskahtay.

The next day, he assembled in the fort the principal men of both villages; and as it is not possible to subdue the Scioux or to hinder them from going to war, unless it be by inducing them to cultivate the earth, he said to them that if they wished to render themselves worthy of the protection of the king, they must abandon their erring life, and form a village near his dwelling, where they would be shielded from the insults of their enemies; and that they might be happy and not hungry, he would give them all the corn necessary to plant a large piece of ground; that the king, their and his chief, in sending him, had forbidden him to purchase beaver skins, knowing that this kind of hunting separates them and exposes them to their enemies; and that in consequence of this he had come to establish himself on Blue river and vicinity, where they had many times assured him were many kinds of beasts, for the skins of which he would give them all things necessary; that they ought to reflect that they could not do without French goods, and that the only way not to want them was, not to go to war with our allied nations.

As it is customary with the Indians to accompany their word with a present proportioned to the affair treated of, he gave them fifty pounds of powder, as many balls, six guns, ten axes, twelve armsful of tobacco, and a hatchet pipe.

On the first of December, the Mantantons invited Le Sueur to a great feast. Of four of their lodges they had made one, in which were one hundred men seated around, and every one his dish before him. After the meal, Wahkantape, the chief, made them all smoke one after another in the hatchet pipe which had been given them. He then made a present to Le Sueur of a slave and a sack of wild rice, and said to him, showing him his men: "Behold the remains of this great village, which thou hast aforetimes seen so numerous! all the others have been killed in war; and the few men whom thou seest in this lodge, accept the present thou hast made them, and are resolved to obey the great chief of all nations, of whom thou hast spoken to us. Thou oughtest not to regard us as Scioux, but as French, and instead of saying the Scioux are miserable, and have no mind, and are fit for nothing but to rob and steal from the French, thou shalt say my brethren are miserable and have no mind, and we must try to procure some for them. They rob us, but I will take care that they do not lack iron, that is to say, all kinds of goods. If thou dost this, I assure thee that in a little time, the Mantantons will become Frenchmen, and they will have none of those vices with which thou reproachest us."

Having finished his speech, he covered his face with his garment, and the others imitated him. They wept over their companions who had died in war, and chanted an adieu to their country in a tone so gloomy, that one could not keep from partaking of their sorrow.

Wahkantape then made them smoke again, and distributed the presents, and said that he was going to the Mendeoucantons, to inform them of the resolution, and invite them to do the same.

On the twelfth, three Mendeoucanton chiefs and a large number of Indians of the same village, arrived at the fort, and the next day gave satisfaction for robbing the Frenchmen. They brought 400 pounds of beaver skins, and promised that the summer following, after their canoes were built and they had gathered their wild rice, that they would come and establish themselves near the French. The same day they returned to their village east of the Mississippi.

NAMES OF THE BANDS OF SCIOUX OF THE EAST, WITH THEIR SIGNIFICATION.

MANTANTONS—That is to say, Village of the Great Lake which empties into a small one.

MENDEOUCANTONS—Village of Spirit Lake.

QUIOPETONS—Village of the Lake with one River.

PSIOUMANITONS—Village of Wild Rice Gatherers.

OUADEBATONS.—The River Village.

OUATEMANETONS.—Village of the Tribe who dwell on the Point of the Lake.

SONGASQUITONS—The Brave Village.

THE SCIOUX OF THE WEST.

TOUCHOUASINTONS—The Village of the Pole.

PSINCHATONS—Village of the Red Wild Rice.

OUJALESPOITONS—Village divided into many small Bands.

PSINOUTANHHINTONS—The Great Wild Rice Village.

TINTANGAOUGHIATONS—The Grand Lodge Village.

OUAPETONS—Village of the Leaf.

OUGHETGEODATONS—Dung Village.

OUAPETONTETONS—Village of those who Shoot in the Large Pine.

HINHANETONS—Village of the Red Stone Quarry.

The above catalogue of villages concludes the extract that La Harpe has made from Le Sueur's Journal.[1]

---

[1] The "History of Louisiana, by La Harpe," who was a French officer, remained in manuscript more than one hundred years. In 1805, a copy was taken from the original, and deposited among the archives of the American Philosophical Society, from which a few extracts were published by Professor Keating, in his narrative of Major

In the narrative of Major Long's second expedition, there are just the same number of villages of the Gens du Lac or M'dewakantonwan Scioux mentioned, though the names are different. After leaving the Mille Lac region, the divisions evidently were different, and the villages known by new names.

Charlevoix, who visited the valley of the Lower Mississippi in 1722, says that Le Sueur spent a winter in his fort on the banks of the Blue Earth; and that in the following April he went up to the mine about a mile above. In twenty-two days they obtained more than thirty thousand pounds of the substance, four thousand of which were selected and sent to France.

On the tenth of February, 1702, Le Sueur came back to the post on the Gulf of Mexico, and found D'Iberville absent, who, however, arrived on the eighteenth of the next month, with a ship from France, loaded with supplies. After a few weeks, the Governor of Louisiana sailed again for the old country, Le Sueur being a fellow passenger.

On board of the ship, D'Iberville wrote a memorial upon the Mississippi Valley, with suggestions for carrying on commerce therein, which contains many facts furnished by Le Sueur. A copy of the manuscript is in possession of the Historical Society of Minnesota, from which are the following extracts:—

"If the Sioux remain in their own country they are useless to us, being too distant. We could have no commerce with them except that of the beaver. *M.*

Long's expedition. In the year 1831, the original was published at Paris, for the first time, in the French language. The first English translation of that part which pertains to Minnesota, appeared in a St. Paul newspaper in 1850.

Le Sueur, who goes to France to give an account of this country, is the proper person to make these movements. He estimates the Sioux at four thousand families, who could settle upon the Missouri.

"He has spoken to me of another which he calls the Mahas, composed of more than twelve hundred families, the Ayooues (Ioways) and the Octoctatas their neighbours, are about three hundred families. They occupy the lands between the Mississippi and the Missouri, about one hundred leagues from the Illinois. These savages do not know the use of arms, and a descent might be made upon them in a river, which is beyond the Wabash on the west. * * * * * * * * * *

"The Assinibouel, Quenistinos, and people of the North, who are upon the rivers which fall into the Mississippi, and trade at Fort Nelson (Hudson Bay), are about four hundred men. We could prevent them from going there if we wish."

"In four or five years we can establish a commerce with these savages of sixty or eighty thousand buffalo skins; more than one hundred deer skins, which will produce, delivered in France, more than two million four hundred thousand livres yearly. One might obtain for a buffalo skin four or five pounds of wool, which sells for twenty sous, two pound of coarse hair at ten sous.

"Besides, from smaller peltries, two hundred thousand livres can be made yearly."

In the third volume of the "History and Statistics of the Indian Tribes," prepared under the direction of the Commissioner of Indian Affairs, by Mr. Schoolcraft, a manuscript, a copy of which is in possession of General Cass, is referred to as containing the first enumeration of the Indians of the Mississippi Valley. The following was made thirty-four years earlier:—

"The Sioux, . Families,	4,000	Chicachas,	2,000
Mahas,	12,000	Mobiliens and Chohomes, .	350
Octata and Ayoues,	300	Concaques, (Conchas)	2,000
Canses, (Kansas),	1,500	Ouma, (Houmas)	150
Missouri,	1,500	Colapissa,	250
Arkansas, &c.,	200	Bayogoula,	100
Manton, (Mandan)	100	People of the Fork,	200
Panis, (Pawnee)	2,000	Counica, &c., (Tonicas)	300
Illinois, of the great village and Camaroua (Tamaroa)	800	Caensa, (Taensa)	150
Meosigamea, (Metchigamias)	200	Nadeches,	1,500
Kikapous and Mascoutens,	450	Belochy, (Biloxi) Pascoboula.	100
Miamis,	500	Total,	23,850
Chactas,	4,000		

"The savage tribes located in the places I have marked out, make it necessary to establish three posts on the Mississippi. One at the Arkansas, another at the Wabash (Ohio), and the third at the Missouri. At each post it would be proper to have an officer with a detachment of ten soldiers, with a sergeant and corporal. All Frenchmen should be allowed to settle there with their families, and trade with the Indians, and they might establish tanneries for properly dressing the buffalo and deer skins for transportation.

"No Frenchman *shall be allowed to follow the Indians on their hunts, as it tends to keep them hunters*, as is seen in Canada, and when they are in the woods they do not desire to become *tillers of the soil.* * * * *

"I have said nothing in this memoir of which I have not personal knowledge or the most reliable sources. The most of what I propose is founded upon personal reflection, in relation to what might be done for the defence and advancement of the colony. * * * *

* * * It will be absolutely necessary that the king should define the limits of this country, in relation to the government of Canada. It is important that the commandant of the Mississippi should have a report of those who inhabit the rivers that fall into the Mississippi, and principally those of the river Illinois.

"The Canadians intimate to the savages that they ought not to listen to us, but to the governor of Canada, who always speaks to them with large presents; that the governor of the Mississippi is mean, and never sends them anything. This is true, and what I cannot do. It is imprudent to accustom the savages to be spoken to by presents, for, with so many, it would cost the king more than the revenue derived from the trade. When they come to us, it will be necessary to bring them in subjection, make them no presents, and *compel* them to do what we wish, *as if they were Frenchmen.*

"The Spaniards have divided the Indians into parties on this point, and we can do the same. When one nation does wrong, we can cease to trade with them, and threaten to draw down the hostility of other Indians. We rectify the difficulty by having missionaries, who will bring them into obedience *secretly.*

"The Illinois and Mascoutens have detained the French canoes they find upon the Mississippi, saying that the governors of Canada have given them permission. I do not know whether this is so, but, if true, it follows that we have not the liberty to send any one on the Mississippi.

"M. Le Sueur would have been taken if he had not been the strongest. Only one of the canoes he sent to the Sioux was plundered." * * * * * *

On the third of March, 1703, the workmen left at

Mahkahto returned to Mobile, having left Minnesota on account of the hostility of the Indians, and the want of means.

Le Sueur, on his return from France, does not appear to have visited Minnesota. His name appears in the history of Louisiana as a leader of expeditions against the Natchez and other southern tribes. It is said that he died on the road while passing through the colony of Louisiana.[1]

[1] La Harpe.

CHAPTER IX.

At the commencement of the eighteenth century, the Dahkotahs were still dwelling at the Spirit Lake, east of the Mississippi; but influences were beginning to operate, which eventually led to dislodgment from their ancient stronghold.

When the French traders first visited Green Bay, they found the Sauks a fierce and haughty people, wandering about the country between the head waters of the Fox and Chippeway rivers. Below them, and above the Illinois, resided the Fox or Outagami nation,[1] with whom they were closely allied by intermarriage. The French, from the first, seemed to be unsuccessful in obtaining their good-will, the early voyageurs having behaved themselves as bandits rather than civilized men.

In the year 1700 the Sauks and Foxes were defeated in a contest with the Dahkotahs and Ioways; and

---

[1] The Ojibways assert that the Foxes, before their incorporation with the Sauks, spoke a different language, and they called them "O-dug-aum-eeg," or people of the opposite side.

A French memoir on the Indians between Lake Erie and Mississippi, prepared in 1718, confirms this statement. "The Foxes are eighteen leagues from the Sacs, they number five hundred men, abound in women and children, are as industrious as they can be, and have a different language from the Ottawas. An Ottawa interpreter would be of no use with the Foxes." Paris Doc. vii. in N. Y. C. H. vol. ix.

ATTACK OF FOXES ON DETROIT.

shortly after this they began to manifest open hostility against the French. Under the direction of the noted warriors Lamina and Pemoussa, they marched to the post at Detroit, which was the key to the commerce of the upper lakes, with the intention of exterminating the small garrison of thirty men, and delivering the post to the English, who, from the year 1687, had been looking wistfully towards the beautiful peninsula which now comprises the commonwealth of Michigan.

For days they prowled around the rude stockade, watching every opportunity for insult and murder.

To prevent the burning of the post, Du Buisson, the commander, ordered the chapel, storehouse, and other outbuildings to be destroyed.

After a few days De Vincennes and eight Frenchmen arrived, but brought no news that was cheering; and the commander, in his despatch to the governor of Canada, admits his alarm, and writes, " I did not know on what saint to call."

The hour now came for decided action. The gates of the little fort were closed; the garrison divided into four companies; arms and ammunition duly inspected; two swivels, mounted on logs, loaded with slugs; all were waiting, with anxious impatience, for the attack to commence, when the commander, ascending the bastion, descried a friendly force of Osages, Missouris, Illinois, and other allies, issuing from the forest. The gates being thrown open, they were warmly greeted.

A moment's silence, a terrific war-whoop, that made the very earth tremble, and the battle began in earnest; and murderous missiles flew like hail-stones. To protect themselves from the fire of the fort, the Sauks and Foxes dug holes in the ground, but they were soon besieged. After being surrounded for nineteen days, they succeeded in making their escape, on a dark and rainy night, after the attacking party were asleep. The discovery was not made till morning, when they were found at Presque Isle, near Lake St. Clair. The fight was here renewed, and the Foxes were thoroughly defeated, losing about one thousand men, women, and children.[1]

Maddened by their want of success, they came back with the portion of the Sauks who were their allies to their residence in Wisconsin, and revenged themselves by scalping every French trader they could find, and waging war on the Ojibways and other tribes who had aided the French.

Travel to Louisiana by way of the Wisconsin river was entirely cut off; and in 1714 the governor of Canada determined to subdue or exterminate them. A force of eight hundred men marched to their villages, and the Foxes, under the pressure of necessity, formed a friendly alliance with their old foes, the Dahkotahs of Minnesota. The invading army found the foe, to the number of five hundred men and three thousand women, strongly intrenched. De Louvigny, the commander, planted his field pieces and a grenade mortar, and began the attack; but the Foxes soon capitulated, and six hostages were given by them as security for the presence of their deputies at Montreal, to perfect the terms of the treaty. While at Montreal, Pemoussa, the great warrior, and others of the hostages, died of smallpox.

Fearing that this calamity might defeat the arrange-

---

[1] This must be an exaggeration of the French report, from which the facts were obtained.

ments for the final treaty, De Louvigny was sent to Mackinaw with one of the hostages, who had recovered from the small-pox with the loss of one eye. Arriving in May, 1717, he despatched the one-eyed chief with suitable presents to cover the dead. The Fox chiefs promised to comply with the provisions of the original capitulation, and the pock-marked warrior departed for Mackinaw, with the interpreter, but he soon eloped, and in a little while the truce-breaking Foxes were again shedding blood. They not only harassed the French, but leagued with the Chickasaws of the south, as well as the fierce Dahkotahs of the north.

For a number of years the French government had discountenanced traders dwelling with the Indians west of Mackinaw, and the old license system was abolished. But, in 1726, it was observed that the English were obtaining such an influence over the distant nations, that, to counteract it, the licensing of traders to dwell among the upper tribes was renewed.

A despatch on this point, made a prediction, which has been fully verified:—

" From all that precedes, it is more and more obvious, that the English are endeavouring to *interlope* among all the Indian nations, and to attach them to themselves. They entertain constantly the idea of becoming *masters of North America*, persuaded that the European nation which will be possessor of that section, will, in course of time, *be also master of all America*, because it is there alone that *men live in health*, and produce *strong and robust children*."

To thwart them it was proposed to restore the twenty-five licenses for trading, which had been suppressed, by which seventy-five " coureurs des bois" would proceed annually to the upper tribes, and be absent eighteen months; also, to abolish the prohibitory liquor law, which had been enacted through the influence of the missionaries. The argument in favour of this measure was in these words:—

" 'Tis true, that the Indians are crazy when drunk, and when they have once tasted brandy, that they give all they possess to obtain some more, and drink it to excess.

" Missionaries will complain that this permission destroys the Indians and the religion among them. But, apart from the fact that they will always have rum from the English, the question is, whether it be better that the English penetrate into the continent by favour of that rum, which attracts the Indians to them, than to suffer the French to furnish them with liquor in order to preserve these nations, and to prevent them declaring eventually in favour of the English."[1]

In view of the troubles among the tribes of the northwest, in the month of September, 1718, Captain St. Pierre, who had great influence with the Indians of Wisconsin and Minnesota, was sent with Ensign Linctot and some soldiers to re-occupy La Pointe on Lake Superior, now Bayfield, in the north-western point of Wisconsin. The chiefs of the band there and at Keweenaw, had threatened war against the Foxes, who had killed some of their number.

On the seventh of June, 1726, peace was concluded by De Lignery with the Sauks, Foxes, and Winnebagoes, at Green Bay; and, Linctot, who had succeeded Saint Pierre in command at La Pointe, was ordered, by

[1] Written May 7th, 1726.

presents and the promise of a missionary, to endeavour to detach the Dahkotahs from their alliance with the Foxes. At this time Linctot made arrangements for peace between the Ojibways and Dahkotahs, and sent two Frenchmen to dwell in the villages of the latter, with a promise that, if they ceased to fight the Ojibways, they should have regular trade, and a "black robe" reside in their country.

The Ojibways, after the treaty, came down to Montreal, and were thus addressed by Longeuil,[1] the governor:—

"I am rejoiced, my children of the Sauteurs, at the peace which Monsieur De Linctot has procured for you with the Sioux, your neighbours, and also on account of the prisoners you have restored to them. I desire him, in the letter which I now give you, my son Cabina, for him, that he maintain this peace, and support the happy reunion which now appears to exist between the Sioux and you. I hope he will succeed in it, if you are attentive to his words, and if you follow the lights which he will show you.

"My heart is sad on account of the blows which the Foxes of Green Bay have given you, of which you have just spoken, and of which the commandant has written in his letter. It appears to me that Heaven has revenged you for your losses, since it has given you the flesh of a young Fox to eat. You have done well to listen to the words of your commandant to keep quiet, and respect the words of your Father.

"It would not have been good to embroil the whole land in order to revenge a blow struck by people with-

[1] The Baron Longeuil, was Charles Le Moyne, a native of Canada. He died in 1729.

out sense or reason, who have no authority in their own villages.

"I invite you by this tobacco, my children, to remain in tranquillity in your lodges, awaiting the news of what shall be decided in the council at the bay (Green Bay), by the commandant of Mackinaw.

"There is coming from France a new Father, who will not fail to inform you, as soon as he shall be able to take measures and stop the bad affair which the Foxes wish to cause in future.

"And to convince you, my children, of the interest I take in your loss, here are two blankets, two shirts, and two pairs of leggings, to cover the bodies of those of your children who have been killed, and to stop the blood which has been spilled upon your mats. I add to this, four shirts to staunch the wounds of those who have been hurt in this miserable affray, with a package of tobacco to comfort the minds of your young men, and also to cause them to think hereafter of good things, and wholly to forget bad ones.

"This is what I exhort you all, my children, while waiting for news from your new Father, and also to be always attentive to the words of the French commandant, who now smokes his pipe in security among you."

The Foxes again proved faithless, having received belts from the English, and determined to attack the French. The authorities at Quebec now determined to send a regular army into their country. Their preparations were kept secret; for, says Beauharnois, "they already had an assurance of a passage into the country of the Sioux of the Prairies, their allies, in such a manner, that if they had known of our design of making war, it would have been easy to have withdrawn in that direction, before we could block up the way and attack them in their towns."

To hem in the Fox nation as much as possible, Fort Perrot, or a site a few miles above, on the shores of Lake Pepin, was re-occupied.[1] Shortly after the arrival of the French, the Indians moved off, and joined the Dahkotahs of the Plains, in a war with the Omahaws.

The governor of Canada felt that the occupancy of this post was of vital importance. In a despatch to the French government he eloquently urges his views:—

"The interests of religion, of the service, and of the colony are involved in the maintenance of this establishment, which has been the more necessary as there is no doubt but the Foxes, when routed, would have found an asylum among the Scioux, had not the French been settled there, and the docility and submission manifested by the Foxes cannot be attributed to any cause except the attention entertained by the Scioux for the French, and the offers which the former made the latter, of which the Foxes were fully cognisant.

"It is necessary to retain the Scioux in these favourable dispositions, in order to keep the Foxes in check,

[1] "The fort the French built among the Scioux on the border of Lake Pepin, appears to be badly situated on account of the freshets. But the Indians assure that the waters rose higher in 1727 than it ever did before; and this is credible, inasmuch as it did not reach the fort this year. * * * * * As the waters might possibly rise as high as 1727, this fort could be removed four or five arpents from the shore without prejudice to the views entertained in building it on its present site. Paris Doc. N. Y. Col. D. vol. ix., p. 1016. The fort seems to be higher up than Perrot's, and was built by Laperriere. Pike in his journal appears to have this fort in view, when he says: "Just below the (point of sand) Pt. de Sable, the French, under Frontenac, who had driven the Renards from the Wisconsin, and chased them up the Mississippi river, built a stockade on this lake (Pepin), as a barrier against the savages. It became a noted factory for the Sioux."

and counteract the measures they might adopt to gain over the Scioux, who will invariably reject their propositions so long as the French remain in the country, and their trading post shall continue there. But, despite all these advantages and the importance of preserving that establishment, M. de Beauharnois cannot take any steps until he has news of the French who asked his permission this summer to go up there with a canoe load of goods, and until assured that those who wintered there have not dismantled the fort, and that the Scioux continue in the same sentiments. Besides, it does not seem very easy in the present conjuncture, to maintain that post, unless there be a solid peace with the Foxes; on the other hand, the greatest portion of the traders, who applied in 1727 for the establishment of that post, have withdrawn, and will not send thither any more, as the rupture with the Foxes, through whose country it is necessary to pass in order to reach the Scioux in canoe, has led them to abandon the idea. But the one and the other case might be remedied. The Foxes will, in all probability, come or send next year to sue for peace; therefore, if it be granted to them on advantageous conditions, there need be no apprehension when going to the Scioux, and another company could be formed, less numerous than the first, through whom, or some responsible merchants able to afford the outfits, a new treaty could be made whereby these difficulties would be soon obviated. One only trouble remains, and that is, to send a commanding and sub-officer, and some soldiers up there, which are absolutely necessary for the maintenance of good order at that post; the missionaries would not go there without a commandant. This article, which regards the service, and the expense of which must be on his majesty's account, obliges them to apply for orders. They will, as far as lies in their power, induce the traders to meet that expense, which will possibly amount to 1000 livres or 1500 livres a year for the commandant, and in proportion for the officer under him; but, as in the beginning of an establishment the expenses exceed the profits, it is improbable that any company of merchants will assume the outlay, and in this case they demand orders on this point, as well as his majesty's opinion as to the necessity of preserving so useful a post, and a nation which has already afforded proofs of its fidelity and attachment.

"These orders could be sent them by way of Ile Royale, or by the first merchantmen that will sail for Quebec. The time required to receive intelligence of the occurrences in the Scioux country, will admit of their waiting for these orders before doing anything."

On the fifth of June, 1728, an army of four hundred Frenchmen and eight or nine hundred savages, embarked at Montreal, on an expedition to destroy the Fox nation and their allies, the Sauks. De Lignery[1] was the head of the expedition—a man like Braddock at Fort Duquesne, who moved his army with precision and pomp, as if the savages were accustomed to fight in platoons, and observe the laws of war, recognised by all civilized nations.

On the seventeenth of August, in the dead of night, the army arrived at the post at the mouth of Fox river. Before dawn the French crossed over to the Sauk village, but all had escaped with the exception of four. Ascending the stream on the twenty-fourth, they came

[1] Taught by experience, he afterwards became an able officer in the French war.

to a Winnebago village which was also deserted. Passing over the Little Fox Lake, on the twenty-fifth, they entered a small river leading to marshy ground, on the borders of which there was a large Fox village. Here again was another disappointment, for the swift-footed savages had gone many miles on their trail long before the army came in sight.

Orders were then given to advance upon the last stronghold of the enemy, near the portage of the Wisconsin, and on their arrival they found all as still as the desert. On the return of the army from this fruitless expedition, the Indian villages on the line of march were devastated, and the fort at Green Bay abandoned. The Foxes, having abandoned everything, retired to the country of the Ioways and Dahkotahs, and probably at this time they pitched their tents and hunted in the valley of the Sauk river in Minnesota.

During the year of this badly managed expedition, Father Guignas visited the Dahkotahs, and would have remained there if there had not been hostility between the Foxes and French. While travelling to the Illinois country he fell into the hands of the Kickapoos and Mascoutens, allies of the Foxes, in the month of October. He was saved from being burned to death by an aged man adopting him as a son. For five months he was in captivity. In the year 1736, while St. Pierre was the commander at Lake Pepin, Father Guignas was also there, and thought that the Dahkotahs were very friendly.

About the period of the revival of the post on Lake Pepin, an establishment was built on Lake Ouinipigon, west of Lake Superior.

Veranderie, a French officer, was, at this early date, commissioned to open a northern route to the Pacific.

Proceeding westward from the Grand Portage of Lake Superior, he followed the chain of lakes which form the boundary line of Minnesota and British America, to Lake Winnipeg. Ascending the Assiniboine, he struck out on the plains, and for several days journeyed towards the Rocky Mountains. Kalm, the Swedish traveller, who saw him in Canada, says that he found on the prairies of Rupert's Land, pillars of stone.

At one place, nine hundred leagues from Montreal, he discovered a stone with characters inscribed, which the learned at Paris, where it was sent, supposed were Tartarean; but probably it was a pictograph set up by some passing war or hunting party.[1]

---

[1] Stone heaps are seen on the prairies of Minnesota. Having written to a gentleman some years ago, to inquire of the Dahkotahs "what mean ye by these stones?" I received an interesting reply:—

Dear Sir: Your letter of the third instant, relating to the stone heaps near Red Wing, was duly received.

I am happy to comply with your request, hoping that it may lead to an accurate survey of these mounds.

In 1848 I first heard of stone heaps on the hill-tops, back of Red Wing. But business, and the natural suspicion of the Indian, prevented me from exploring. The treaty of Mendota emboldened me to visit the hills, and try to find the stone heaps. Accordingly, late last autumn, I started on foot and alone from Red Wing, following the path marked P. on the map, which I herewith transmit. I left the path after crossing the second stream, and turning to the left, I ascended the first hill that I reached. This is about a mile distant from the path that leads from Fort Snelling to Lake Pepin. Here, on the brow of the hill, which was about two hundred feet high, was a heap of stones. It is about twelve feet in diameter and six in height. The perfect confusion of the stones and yet the entireness of the heap, and the denuded rocks all around, convinced me that the heap had been formed from stones lying around, picked up by the hand of man.

But *why* and *when* it had been done, were questions not so easily decided. For solving these I resolved to seek internal evidence. Prompted by the spirit of a first explorer, I soon ascended the heap; and the coldness of the day, and the

He established some six commercial posts on the line of his route, some of which are in existence to this day, and bear the same names.

His journey was ended by difficulties with the Indians, and he was obliged to return.

The Dahkotahs were suspected of having molested this expedition. The king of France, writing to the

proximity of my gun, tended to suppress my dread of rattlesnakes. The stones were such that I could lift, or roll them, and soon reached a stick about two feet from the top of the heap. After descending about a foot further, I pulled the post out; and about the same place found a shank bone, about five inches long. The post was red cedar half decayed, *i. e.* one side, and rotted to a point in the ground; hence I could not tell whether it grew there or not. The bone is similar to the two which you have. I left it and the post on the heap, hoping that some one better skilled in osteology might visit the heap. The stones of the heap are magnesian limestone, which forms the upper stratum of the hills about Red Wing.

Much pleased, I started over the hill top, and was soon greeted by another silent monument of art. This heap is marked B. on the map. It is similar to the first which is marked A., only it is larger, and was so covered with a vine, that I had no success in opening it. From this point there is a fine view southward. The valleys and hills are delightful. Such hills and vales, such cairns and bushy glens, would, in my father's land, have been the thrones and playgrounds of fairies. But I must stick to facts. I now started eastward to visit a conical appearing hill, distant about a mile and a half. I easily descended the hill, but to cross the plain and ascend another hill, "*hic labor est.*" But I was amply repaid. The hill proved to be a ridge with several stone heaps on the summit. Near one heap there is a beautiful little tree with a top like "Tam O'Shanter's" bonnet. In these heaps I found the bones which I left with you. I discovered each about half-way down the heaps.

I then descended northward about two hundred feet, crossed a valley, passed some earth mounds, and ascended another hill, and there found several more stone heaps similar to the others. In them I found no bones, nor did I see anything else worthy of particular notice at present.

If these facts should, in any measure, help to preserve correct information concerning any part of this new country, I shall be amply rewarded for writing.

Your obedient servant,
J. F. AITON.
Kaposia, Jan. 17, 1852.

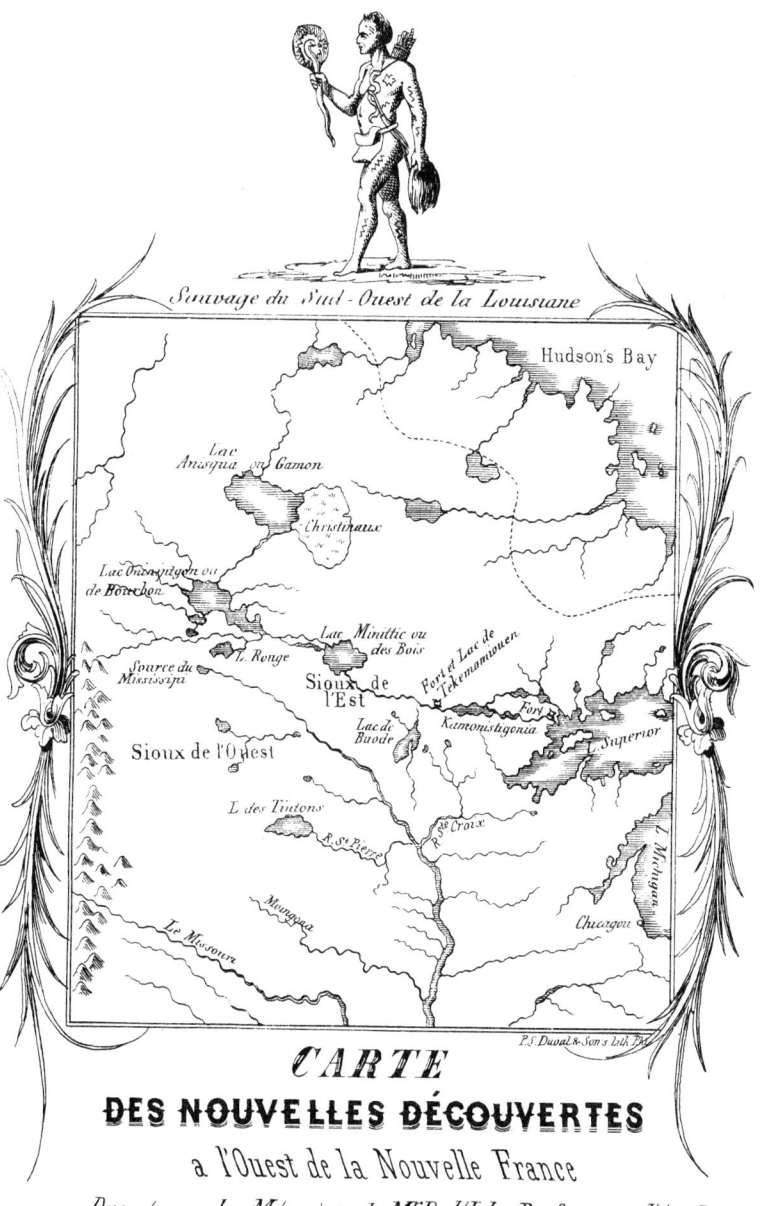

CARTE
DES NOUVELLES DÉCOUVERTES
a l'Ouest de la Nouvelle France

Dressée sur les Mémoires de M.^r De l'Isle, Professeur à l'Académie Royale des Sciences   Par Philippe Buache. —— 1750.

Drawn from the Original by R. Ormsby Sweeny.

governor of Canada, under date of May tenth, 1737, says:—

"As respects the Scioux, according to what the commandant[1] and missionary[2] have written to Sieur de Beauharnois, relative to the disposition of these Indians, nothing appears to be wanting on that point. But their delay in coming down to Montreal since the time they promised to do so, must render their sentiments somewhat suspected, and nothing but facts can determine whether their fidelity can be absolutely relied on. But what must still further increase the uneasiness to be entertained in their regard, is the attack on the convoy of M. de la Veranderie."

The Foxes having killed some Frenchmen in the Illinois country, in 1741, the governor of Canada, Marquis de Beauharnois, assembled at his house, some of the most experienced officers in the Indian service, the Baron de Longeuil, La Corne, De Lignery, and others, and it was unanimously agreed, that the welfare of the French demanded the complete extermination of the Foxes, and that the movements against them should be conducted with the greatest caution.

Louis XV. was glad to hear of the determination of the governor of Canada, but he was afraid that it would not be conducted with sufficient secrecy. He, with great discernment, remarks, "If they foresee their inability to resist, they will have adopted the policy of retreating to the Scioux of the Prairies, from which point they will cause more disorder, in the colony, than if they had been allowed to remain quiet in their village."

The officer in charge of the incursion, was Moran,[3]

---

[1] Saint Pierre.   [2] Guignas.
[3] Probably Sieur Marin, of the French Documents.

who once had charge of the post St. Nicholas near the mouth of the Wisconsin, on the Mississippi. His strategy was not unlike that of the besiegers of ancient Troy. At that time the Fox tribe lived at the Little Butte des Morts, on the Fox river of Wisconsin. Whenever a trader's canoe hove in sight, they lighted a torch upon the bank, which was a signal for Frenchmen to land, and pay for the privilege of using the stream.

Moran having placed his men in canoes, with their guns primed, had each canoe covered with canvas, as if he was bringing into the country an outfit of merchandise, and desired to protect it from storms. When near Little Butte des Morts the party was divided, a portion proceeding by land to the rear of the Fox village, and the remainder moving up the stream.

The oarsmen having paddled the canoes within view of the Foxes, they, according to custom, planted the torch, supposing it was a trader's "brigade."[1]

Curiosity brought men, women, and children to the river's bank, and as they gazed, the canoes were suddenly uncovered, and the discharge of a swivel, and volleys of musketry, were the presents received. Before they could recover from their consternation, they received "a fire in the rear" from the land party, and many were killed. The remnant retreated to the Wisconsin, twenty-one miles from Prairie du Chien, where, the next season Moran and his troops, on snow shoes, surprised them while they were engaged in a game, and slew nearly the whole settlement.[2]

During the winter of 1745-6, De Lusignan visited

---

[1] In the North-West a collection of traders' canoes is called a brigade. Recollections. Vol. iii., Wis. His. Soc. Col.

[2] Snelling's North-West, Grignon's

the Dahkotahs, ordered by government to hunt up the "coureurs des bois," and withdraw them from the country. They started to return with him, but learning that they would be arrested at Mackinaw, for violation of law, they ran away. While at the villages of the Dahkotahs of the lakes and plains, the chiefs brought to this officer nineteen of their young men, bound with cords, who had killed three Frenchmen at the Illinois. While he remained with them they made peace with the Ojibways of La Pointe, with whom they had been at war for some time. On his return, four chiefs accompanied him to Montreal, to solicit pardon for their young braves.

The lessees of the trading post lost many of their peltries that winter, in consequence of a fire.

English influence produced increasing dissatisfaction among the Indians that were beyond Mackinaw. Not only were voyageurs robbed and maltreated at Sault St. Marie, and other points on Lake Superior, but even the commandant at Mackinaw was exposed to insolence, and there was no security anywhere. The Marquis de Beauharnois determined to send St. Pierre to the scene of disorder. In the language of a document of the day, he was "a very good officer, much esteemed among all the nations of those parts—none more loved and feared."

On his arrival, the savages were so cross, that he advised that no Frenchman should come to trade.

By promptness and boldness, he secured the Indians who had murdered some Frenchmen, and obtained the respect of the tribes.

While the three murderers were being conveyed in a canoe down the St. Lawrence to Quebec, in charge of a sergeant and seven soldiers, the savages, with characteristic cunning, though manacled, succeeded in killing or drowning the guard. Cutting their irons with an axe, they sought the woods, and escaped to their own country.

"Thus," writes Galassoniere, in 1748, to Count Maurepas, "was lost in a great measure the fruit of Sieur St. Pierre's good management, and of all the fatigue I endured to get the nations who surrendered these rascals to listen to reason."

CHAPTER X.

CANADA was now fairly involved in the war with New York and the New England colonies. The Home Governments were anxious lookers on, for momentous issues depended upon the failure or success of either party.

The French knew that they must enlist the Upper Indians on their side, or lose Detroit, Mackinaw, and indeed all the keys of the valley of the Mississippi, and the region of the lakes. They, therefore, sent officers with presents to Mackinaw, to induce the tribes of the far West to unite with them in expelling the English.

It was impossible to form regiments of the North American savages, as the French of modern days have done in Algeria, or as the British with the Sepoys.

Indians can never be made to move in platoons. From youth they have marched in single file, and have only answered to the call of their inclinations, and over them their chiefs have not the slightest authority. To their capricious natures enlistment for a fixed time is repugnant. At the same time, under the guidance of colonial officers who humoured them in their whims, they frequently rendered efficient service. They were conversant with the recesses of the forest, and walked through the tangled wilderness with the same ease that the French military officers promenaded the gardens of Paris. They discovered the trail of men with the instinct that their dogs scented the tracks of wild beasts. Adroit in an attack, they would also, amid a shower of musket balls, feel for the scalp of an enemy.

With such allies it is no wonder that New England mothers and delicate maidens turned pale when they heard that the French were coming.[1]

On the twenty-third of August, 1747, Philip Le Duc arrived at Mackinaw from Lake Superior, stating that he had been robbed of his goods at Kamanistigoya,[2] and that the Ojibways of the lake were favourably disposed toward the English. The Dahkotahs were also becoming unruly in the absence of French officers.

In the few weeks after Le Duc's robbery, St. Pierre left Montreal to become commandant at Mackinaw, and Vercheres was appointed for the post at Green Bay.

On the twenty-first of June of the next year, La Ronde started for La Pointe, and La Veranderie for West Sea[3]—Fond du Lac, Minnesota.

For several years there was constant dissatisfaction among the Indians, but under the influence of Sieur Marin, who was in command at Green Bay in 1753, tranquillity was in a measure restored.

---

[1] The following are some of the arrivals in a few weeks at Montreal, in 1746. July 23—31 Ottawas of Detroit.
July 31, 16 Folles Avoines for war.
" " 14 Kiskakons " "
" " 4 Scioux, to ask for a commandant.
Aug. 2, 50 Pottowattamies for war.
" " 15 Puans " "
" " 10 Illinois " "
" 6, 50 Ottawas of Mackinaw.
Aug. 6, 40 Ottawas of the Fork.
" 10, 65 Mississagues.
" " 80 Algonkins and Nepissings.
" " 14 Sauteurs.
" 22, 38 Ottawas of Detroit.
" " 17 Sauteurs
" " 24 Hurons.
" " 14 Poutewatamis.

[2] Pigeon river, part of northern boundary of Minnesota.

[3] Carver's map calls it West Bay.

As the war between England and France, in America became desperate, the officers of the north-western posts were called into action, and stationed nearer the enemy.

Legardeur de St. Pierre, whose name it is thought was formerly attached to the river from which the state of Minnesota derives its name, was in command of a rude post in Erie county, Pennsylvania, in December, 1753, and to him Washington, then just entering upon manhood, bore a letter from Governor Dinwiddie of Virginia.[1]

On the ninth of July, 1755, Beaujeu and De Lignery, who had pursued so unsuccessfully the Foxes, in the valley of the Wisconsin, in 1728, were at Fort Duquesne, and marched out of the fort with soldiers, Canadians, and Indians, to seek an ambush, but about noon, before reaching the desired spot, they met the enemy under Braddock, who discharged a galling fire from their artillery, by which Beaujeu was killed. The sequel, which led to the memorable defeat of Braddock, is familiar to all who have read the life of Washington.

Under Baron Dieskaw, St. Pierre commanded the Indians, in September, 1755, during the campaign on Lake Champlain, where he fell gallantly fighting the English, as did his commander. The Reverend Claude Cocquard, alluding to the French defeat, in a letter to his brother, remarks:—

"We lost, on that occasion, a brave officer, M. de St. Pierre, and had his advice, as well as that of several other Canadian officers been followed, Jonckson[2] was irretrievably destroyed, and we should have been spared the trouble we have had this year."

---

[1] St. Pierre's reply was manly and dignified. See Pennsylvania Colonial Records, v. 715.

[2] Johnson.

Other officers who had been stationed on the borders of Minnesota, also distinguished themselves during the French war. The Marquis Montcalm, in camp at Ticonderoga, on the twenty-seventh of July, 1757, writes to Vaudreuil, Governor of Canada.

"Lieutenant Marin, of the Colonial troops, who has exhibited a rare audacity, did not consider himself bound to halt, although his detachment of about four hundred men was reduced to about two hundred, the balance having been sent back on account of inability to follow. He carried off a patrol of ten men, and swept away an ordinary guard of fifty, like a wafer; went up to the enemy's camp, under Fort Lydius (Edward), where he was exposed to a severe fire, and retreated like a warrior. He was unwilling to amuse himself making prisoners; he brought in only one, and thirty-two scalps, and must have killed many men of the enemy, in the midst of whose ranks it was neither wise nor prudent to go in search of scalps. The Indians generally all behaved well. * * * * * The Outaouais, who arrived with me, and whom I designed to go on a scouting party towards the lake, had conceived a project of administering a corrective to the English barges. * * * * On the day before yesterday, your brother formed a detachment to accompany them. I arrived at his camp on the evening of the same day. Lieutenant de Corbiere, of Colonial troops, was returning in consequence of a misunderstanding, and as I knew the zeal and intelligence of that officer, I made him set out with a new instruction to rejoin Messrs. de Langlade[1] and Hertel de Chantly. They remained in ambush all day

---

[1] This officer has relatives in Wisconsin, and an interesting sketch of his life is in Grignon's Recollections, Wis. Hist. Soc. Collections, vol. iii.

and night yesterday; at break of day the English appeared on Lake St. Sacrament (Champlain), to the number of twenty-two barges, under the command of Sieur Parker. The whoops of our Indians impressed them with such terror that they made but feeble resistance, and only two barges escaped."

After De Corbiere's victory on Lake Champlain, a large French army was collected at Ticonderoga, with which there were many Indians from the tribes of the North-west,[2] and the Ioways appeared for the first time in the east.

It is an interesting fact that the English officers who

[1] INDIANS OF THE UPPER COUNTRY.

		OFFICERS.
Tetes de Boule	3	
Outaouais Kiskakons	94	De Langlade.
" Sinagos	35	Florimont.
" of the Forks	70	Herbin.
" of Mignogan	10	Abbe Matavet.
" of Beaver Island	44	Sulpitian.
" of Detroit	30	
" of Saginau	54	
Sauteurs of Chagoamigon	33	La Plante.
" of Beaver	23	De Lorimer.
" of Coasekimagen	14	Chesne, Interpreter.
" of the Carp	37	
" of Cabibonkè	50	
Poutouatamis of St. Joseph	70	
" of Detroit	18	
Folles Avoines of Orignal	62	
" of the Chat	67	
Miamis	15	
Puans of the Bay	48	De Tailly, Interpreter.
Ayeouais (Ioways)	10	
Foxes	20	Marin, Langus.
Ouillas	10	Reaume, Interpreter.
Sacs	33	
Loups	5	

were in frequent engagements with St. Pierrè, Lusignan, Marin, Langlade, and others, became the pioneers of the British, a few years afterwards, in the occupation of the outposts on the Lakes, and in the exploration of Minnesota.

Rogers, the celebrated captain of rangers, subsequently commander of Mackinaw, and Jonathan Carver, the first British explorer of Minnesota, were both on duty at Lake Champlain—the latter narrowly escaping at the battle of Fort George.

On Christmas eve, 1757, Rogers approached Fort Ticonderoga, to fire the out-houses, but was prevented by discharge of the cannons of the French.

He contented himself with killing fifteen beeves, on the horns of one of which he left a laconic and amusing note, addressed to the commander of the post.[1]

On the thirteenth of March, 1758, Durantaye, formerly at Mackinaw, had a skirmish with Rogers. Both had been trained on the frontier, and they met "as Greek met Greek." The conflict was fierce, and the French victorious. The Indian allies, finding a scalp of a chief underneath an officer's jacket, were furious, and took one hundred and fourteen scalps in return. When the French returned, they supposed that Captain Rogers was among the killed.

At Quebec, when Montcalm and Wolfe fell, there were Ojibways present, assisting the French.

The Indians, returning from the expeditions against

---

[1] "I am obliged to you, Sir, for the repose you have allowed me to take; *I thank you for the fresh meat you have sent me*, I request you to present my compliments to the Marquis du Montcalm. ROGERS, Commandant Independent Companies."

the English were attacked with small-pox, and many died at Mackinaw.

On the eighth of September, 1760, the French delivered up all their posts in Canada. A few days after the capitulation at Montreal, Major Rogers was sent with English troops, to garrison the posts of the distant North-west.

On the eighth of September, 1761, a year after the surrender, Captain Belfour, of the eightieth regiment of the British army, left Detroit, with a detachment, to take possession of the French forts at Mackinaw and Green Bay. Twenty-five soldiers were left at Mackinaw, in command of Lieutenant Leslie, and the rest sailed to Green Bay, where they arrived on the twelfth of October. The fort had been abandoned for several years, and was in a dilapidated condition. In charge of it, there was left a lieutenant, a corporal, and fifteen soldiers. Two English traders arrived at the same time—McKay from Albany, and Goddard from Montreal.

On the first of March, 1763, twelve Dahkotah warriors arrived at the fort, and proffered the friendship of the nation. They told the English officer, with warmth, that if the Ojibways, or other Indians, wished to obstruct the passage of the traders coming up, to send them a belt, and they would come and cut them off, as all Indians were their slaves or dogs. They then produced a letter written by Penneshaw, a French trader, who had been permitted, the year before, to go to their country. On the nineteenth of June, Penneshaw returned from his trading expedition among the Dahkotahs. By his influence the nation was favourably affected toward the English. He brought with him a pipe from them, with a request that traders might be sent to them.[1]

[1] Extracts from the journal of Lt. Gorell, an English officer at Green Bay, Wis. His. Coll. vol. i.

"On March 1, 1763, twelve warriors of the Sous came here. It is certainly the greatest nation of Indians ever yet found. Not above two thousand of them were ever armed with fire-arms, the rest depending entirely on bows and arrows, which they use with more skill than any other Indian nation in America. They can shoot the wildest and largest beasts in the woods at seventy or one hundred yards distant. They are remarkable for their dancing, and the other nations take the fashions from them. * * * * This nation is always at war with the Chippewas, those who destroyed Mishamakinak. They told me with warmth that if ever the Chippewas or any other Indians wished to obstruct the passage of the traders coming up, to send them word, and they would come and cut them off from the face of the earth, as all Indians were their slaves or dogs. I told them I was glad to see them, and hoped to have a lasting peace with them. They then gave me a letter wrote in French, and two belts of wampum from their king, in which he expressed great joy on hearing of there being English at his post. The letter was written by a French trader, whom I had allowed to go among them last fall, with a promise of his behaving well, which he did, better than any Canadian I ever knew. * * * * With regard to traders, I told them I would not allow any to go amongst them, as I then understood they lay out of the government of Canada, but made no doubt they would have traders from the Mississippi in the spring. They went away extremely well pleased. 'June 14th, 1763, the traders came down from the Sack country, and confirmed the news of Landsing and his son being killed by the French. There came with the traders some Puans and four young men, with one chief of the Avoy (Ioway) nation to demand traders.' * * * *

"On the nineteenth, a deputation of Winnebagoes, Sacs, Foxes, and Menominees arrived with a Frenchman named Pennensha. This Pennensha is the same man who wrote the letter the Sous brought with them in French, and at the same time held council with that great nation in favour of the English, by which he much promoted the interest of the latter, as appeared by the behaviour of the Sous. He brought with him a pipe from the Sous, desiring that as the road is now clear, they would by no means allow the Chippewas to obstruct it, or give the English any disturbance, or prevent the traders from coming up to them. If they did so they would send all their warriors and cut them off."

CHAPTER XI.

THOUGH the treaty of 1763, made at Versailles, between France and England, ceded all the territory comprised within the limits of Wisconsin and Minnesota to the latter power, the English did not for a long time obtain a foothold.

The French traders having purchased wives from the Indian tribes, they managed to preserve a feeling of friendship towards their king, long after the trading posts at Green Bay and Sault St. Marie had been discontinued.

The price paid for peltries by those engaged in the fur trade at New Orleans, was also higher than that which the British could afford to give, so that the Indians sought for French goods in exchange for their skins.

Finding it useless to compete with the French of the lower Mississippi, the English government established no posts of trade or defence beyond Mackinaw. The country west of Lake Michigan appears to have been trodden by but few British subjects, previous to him who forms the subject of the present chapter, and whose name has become somewhat famous in consequence of his heirs having laid claim to the site of St. Paul, and many miles adjacent.

Jonathan Carver was a native of Connecticut. It has been asserted that he was a lineal descendant of John Carver, the first governor of Plymouth colony; but the only definite information that the writer can obtain concerning his ancestry is, that his grandfather, William Carver, was a native of Wigan, Lancashire, England, and a captain in King William's army during the campaign in Ireland, and for meritorious services received an appointment as an officer of the colony of Connecticut.

His father was a justice of the peace in the new world, and in 1732, at Stillwater, or Canterbury, Connecticut, the subject of this sketch was born. At the early age of fifteen he was called to mourn the death of his father. He then commenced the study of medicine, but his roving disposition could not bear the confines of a doctor's office, and feeling, perhaps, that his genius would be cramped by pestle and mortar, at the age of eighteen he purchased an ensign's commission in one of the regiments Connecticut raised during the French war. He was of medium stature, and of strong mind and quick perceptions.

In the year 1757, he was present at the massacre of Fort William Henry, and narrowly escaped with his life.

After the peace of 1763, between France and England, was declared, Carver conceived the project of exploring the North-west. Leaving Boston in the month of June, 1766, he arrived at Mackinaw, then the most distant British post, in the month of August. Having obtained a credit on some French and English traders from Major Rogers, the officer in command, he started with them on the third day of September. Pursuing the usual route to Green Bay, they arrived there on the eighteenth.

The French fort at that time was standing, though much decayed. It was, some years previous to his arrival, garrisoned for a short time by an officer and thirty English soldiers, but they having been captured by the Menominees, it was abandoned.

In company with the traders he left Green Bay on the twentieth, and ascending Fox river, arrived on the twenty-fifth at an island at the east end of Lake Winnebago, containing about fifty acres.

Here he found a Winnebago village of fifty houses. He asserts that a woman was in authority. In the month of October the party was at the portage of the Wisconsin, and descending that stream, they arrived, on the ninth, at a town of the Sauks. While here he visited some lead mines about fifteen miles distant. An abundance of lead was also seen in the village, that had been brought from the mines.

On the tenth they arrived at the first village of the "Ottigaumies" (Foxes), and about five miles before the Wisconsin joins the Mississippi, he perceived the remnants of another village, and learned that it had been deserted about thirty years before, and that the inhabitants, soon after their removal, built a town on the Mississippi, near the mouth of the "Ouisconsin," at a place called by the French La Prairie les Chiens, which signified the Dog Plains. It was a large town, and contained about three hundred families. The houses were built after the Indian manner, and pleasantly situated on a dry rich soil.

He saw here many horses of a good size and shape. This town was the great mart where all the adjacent tribes, and where those who inhabit the most remote branches of the Mississippi, annually assemble about the latter end of May, bringing with them their furs to dispose of to the traders. But it is not always that they conclude their sale here. This was determined by a general council of the chiefs, who consulted whether it would be more conducive to their interest to sell their goods at this place, or to carry them on to Louisiana or Mackinaw.

At a small stream called Yellow river, opposite Prairie du Chien, the traders who had thus far accompanied Carver took up their residence for the winter.

From this point he proceeded in a canoe, with a Canadian voyageur and a Mohawk Indian, as companions.

Just before reaching Lake Pepin, while his attendants were one day preparing dinner, he walked out and was struck with the peculiar appearance of the surface of the country, and thought it was the site of some vast artificial earth-work.

It is a fact, worthy of remembrance, that he was the first to call the attention of the civilized world to the existence of ancient monuments in the Mississippi valley. We give his own description :—

" On the first of November I reached Lake Pepin, a few miles below which I landed, and, whilst the servants were preparing my dinner, I ascended the bank to view the country. I had not proceeded far before I came to a fine, level, open plain, on which I perceived, at a little distance, a partial elevation, that had the appearance of entrenchment. On a nearer inspection, I had greater reason to suppose that it had really been intended for this many centuries ago. Notwithstanding it was now covered with grass, I could plainly see that it had once been a breast-work of about four feet in height, extending the best part of a mile, and sufficiently capacious to cover five thousand men. Its form was somewhat circular, and its flanks reached to the river.

"Though much defaced by time, every angle was distinguishable, and appeared as regular and fashioned with as much military skill as if planned by Vauban himself. The ditch was not visible; but I thought, on examining more curiously, that I could perceive there certainly had been one. From its situation, also, I am convinced that it must have been designed for that purpose. It fronted the country, and the rear was covered by the river, nor was there any rising ground for a considerable way that commanded it; a few straggling lakes were alone to be seen near it. In many places small tracks were worn across it by the feet of the elks or deer, and from the depth of the bed of earth, by which it was covered, I was able to draw certain conclusions of its great antiquity. I examined all the angles, and every part with great attention, and have often blamed myself since, for not encamping on the spot, and drawing an exact plan of it. To show that this description is not the offspring of a heated imagination, or the chimerical tale of a mistaken traveller, I find, on inquiry, since my return, that Mons. St Pierre and several traders have, at different times, taken notice of similar appearances, upon which they have formed the same conjectures, but without examining them so minutely as I did. How a work of this kind could exist in a country that has hitherto (according to the generally received opinion) been the seat of war to untutored Indians alone, whose whole stock of military knowledge has only, till within two centuries, amounted to drawing the bow, and whose only breastwork, even at present, is the thicket, I know not. I have given as exact an account as possible of this singular appearance, and leave to future explorers, of those distant regions, to discover whether it is a production of nature or art. Perhaps the hints I have here given, might lead to a more perfect investigation of it, and give us very different ideas of the ancient state of realms, that we at present believe to have been, from the earliest period, only the habitations of savages."

Lake Pepin excited his admiration, as it has that of every traveller since his day, and here he remarks: "I observed the ruins of a French factory, where it is said Captain St. Pierre resided, and carried on a very great trade with the Naudowessies, before the reduction of Canada."

Carver's first acquaintance with the Dahkotahs commenced near the river St. Croix. It would seem that the erection of trading posts on Lake Pepin had enticed them from their old residence on Rum river and Mille Lac.

He says: "Near the river St. Croix, reside bands of the Naudowessie Indians, called the River Bands. This nation is composed at present of eleven bands. They were originally twelve, but the Assinipoils, some years ago, revolting and separating themselves from the others, there remain only at this time eleven. Those I met here are termed the River Bands, because they chiefly dwell near the banks of this river; the other eight are generally distinguished by the title of Naudowessies of the Plains, and inhabit a country more to the westward. The name of the former are Nehogatawonahs, the Mawtawbauntowahs, and Shashweentowahs.

Arriving at what is now a suburb of the capital of Minnesota, he continues, "about thirteen miles below the Falls of St. Anthony, at which I arrived the tenth day after I left Lake Pepin, is a remarkable cave of an amazing depth. The Indians term it Wakon-teebe (Wakan-tipi). The entrance into it is about ten feet wide, the height of it five feet. The arch within is near fifteen feet high, and about thirty feet broad; the bottom consists of fine clear sand. About thirty feet from the entrance, begins a lake, the water of which is transparent, and extends to an unsearchable distance, for the darkness of the cave prevents all attempts to acquire a knowledge of it. I threw a small pebble towards the interior part of it with my utmost strength; I could hear that it fell into the water, and, notwithstanding it was of a small size, it caused an astonishing and terrible noise, that reverberated through all those gloomy regions. I found in this cave many Indian hieroglyphics, which appeared very ancient, for time had nearly covered them with moss, so that it was with difficulty I could trace them. They were cut in a rude manner upon the inside of the wall, which was composed of a stone so extremely soft that it might be easily penetrated with a knife; a stone everywhere to be found near the Mississippi.

"At a little distance from this dreary cavern, is the burying-place of several bands of the Naudowessie Indians. Though these people have no fixed residence, being in tents, and seldom but a few months in one spot, yet they always bring the bones of the dead to this place.[1]

[1] The cave has been materially altered by nearly a century's work of those effective tools, frost, water, and the atmosphere. Years ago the top fell in, but on the side walls, not covered by debris, pictographs gray

"Ten miles below the Falls of St. Anthony, the river St. Pierre, called by the natives Wadapaw Menesotor, falls into the Mississippi from the west. It is not mentioned by Father Hennepin, though a large, fair river. This omission, I consider, must have proceeded from a small island (Faribault's), that is situated exactly in its entrance."

When he reached the Minnesota river, the ice became so troublesome that he left his canoe in the neighbourhood of what is now the ferry, and walked to St. Anthony, in company with a young Winnebago chief, who had never seen the curling waters. The chief, on reaching the eminence some distance below Cheever's, began to invoke his gods, and offer oblations to the spirit in the waters.

"In the middle of the Falls stands a small island, about *forty feet* broad, and somewhat longer, on which grow a few cragged hemlock and spruce trees, and about half way between this island and the eastern shore, is a rock, lying at the very edge of the Falls, in an oblique position, that appeared to be about five or six feet broad, and thirty or forty long. At a little distance below the

with age, are visible. In 1807, the present mouth of the cave was so covered up, that Major Long, to use a vulgarism, was obliged to "creep on all fours" to enter. In 1820, it seems to have been closed, as Schoolcraft describes another cave three miles above, as Carver's. Featherstonhaugh made the same mistake.

In 1837 Nicollet the astronomer and his assistants, worked many hours and entered the little cavity that remained.

It is now walled up and used as a root-house by the owner of the land.

On the bluff above are numerous mounds. Under the supervision of the writer, one eighteen feet high and two hundred and sixty feet in circumference at the base, was opened to the depth of three or four feet. Fragments of skull, which crumbled on exposure, and perfect shells of human teeth, the interior entirely decayed, were found.

Falls, stands a small island of about an acre and a half, on which grow a great number of oak trees."

From this description, it would appear that the little island, now some distance in front of the Falls, was once in the very midst, and shows that a constant recession has been going on, and that in ages long past, they were not far from the Minnesota river. A century hence, if the wearing of the last five years is any criterion, the Falls will be above the town of St. Anthony.

No description is more glowing than Carver's, of the country adjacent:—

"The country around them is extremely beautiful. It is not an uninterrupted plain, where the eye finds no relief, but composed of many gentle ascents, which in the summer are covered with the finest verdure, and interspersed with little groves that give a pleasing variety to the prospect. On the whole, when the Falls are included, which may be seen at the distance of four miles, a more pleasing and picturesque view I believe cannot be found throughout the universe."

He arrived at the Falls on the seventeenth of November, 1766, and appears to have ascended as far as Elk river.

On the twenty-fifth of November, he had returned to the place opposite the Minnesota, where he had left his canoe, and this stream as yet not being obstructed with ice, he commenced its ascent, with the colours of Great Britain flying at the stern of his canoe. There is no doubt that he entered this river, but how far he explored it cannot be ascertained. He speaks of the Rapids near Shokopay, and asserts that he went as far as two hundred miles beyond Mendota. He remarks:—

" On the seventh of December, I arrived at the utmost

extent of my travels towards the West, where I met a large party of the Naudowessie Indians, among whom I resided some months."

After speaking of the upper bands of the Dahkotahs and their allies, he adds that he "left the habitations of the hospitable Indians the latter end of April, 1767, but did not part from them for several days, as I was accompanied on my journey by near three hundred of them to the mouth of the river St. Pierre. At this season these bands annually go to the great cave (Dayton's Bluff), before mentioned."

When he arrived at the great cave, and the Indians had deposited the remains of their deceased friends in the burial-place that stands adjacent to it, they held their great council, to which he was admitted.

When the Naudowessies brought their dead for interment to the great cave (St. Paul), I attempted to get an insight into the remaining burial rites, but whether it was on account of the stench which arose from so many bodies, or whether they chose to keep this part of their custom secret from me, I could not discover. I found, however, that they considered my curiosity as ill-timed, and therefore I withdrew. * * *

One formality among the Naudowessies in mourning for the dead, is very different from any mode I observed in the other nations through which I passed. The men, to show how great their sorrow is, pierce the flesh of their arms above the elbows with arrows, and the women cut and gash their legs with sharp broken flints till the blood flows very plentifully. * * * * * *

After the breath is departed, the body is dressed in the same attire it usually wore, his face is painted, and he is seated in an erect posture on a mat or skin, placed in the middle of the hut, with his weapons by his side. His relatives seated around, each harangues in turn the deceased; and, if he has been a great warrior, recounts his heroic actions nearly to the following purport, which in the Indian language is extremely poetical and pleasing:—

"You still sit among us, brother, your person retains its usual resemblance, and continues similar to ours, without any visible deficiency, except it has lost the power of action! But whither is that breath flown, which a few hours ago sent up smoke to the Great Spirit? Why are those lips silent that lately delivered to us expressions and pleasing language? Why are those feet motionless that a short time ago were fleeter than the deer on yonder mountains? Why useless hang those arms that could climb the tallest tree, or draw the toughest bow? Alas! every part of that frame which we lately beheld with admiration and wonder, is now become as inanimate as it was three hundred years ago! We will not, however, bemoan thee as if thou wast for ever lost to us, or that thy name would be buried in oblivion—thy soul yet lives in the great country of Spirits with those of thy nation that have gone before thee; and, though we are left behind to perpetuate thy fame, we shall one day join thee.

"Actuated by the respect we bore thee whilst living, we now come to tender thee the last act of kindness in our power; that thy body might not lie neglected on the plain and become a prey to the beasts of the field or fowls of the air, we will take care to lay it with those of thy predecessors who have gone before thee; hoping at the same time that thy spirit will feed with their spirits and be ready to receive ours when we shall also arrive at the great country of souls."

For this speech Carver is principally indebted to his imagination, but it is well conceived, and suggested one of Schiller's poems.[1]

It appears from other sources that Carver's visit to the Dahkotahs was of some effect in bringing about friendly intercourse between them and the commander of the English force at Mackinaw.

The earliest mention of the Dahkotahs, in any public British documents that we know of, is in the correspondence between Sir William Johnson, Superintendent of Indian Affairs for the Colony of New York, and General Gage, in command of the forces.

On the eleventh of September, less than six months after Carver's speech at Dayton's Bluff, and the departure of a number of chiefs to the English fort at Mackinaw, Johnson writes to General Gage:—" Though I wrote to you some days ago, yet I would not mind saying something again on the score of the vast expenses incurred, and, as I understand, still incurring at Michilimackinac, chiefly on pretence of making a peace between the Sioux and Chippeweighs, with which I think we have very little to do, in good policy or otherwise."

Sir William Johnson, in a letter to Lord Hillsborough, one of his Majesty's ministers, dated August seventeenth, 1768, again refers to the subject:—

" Much greater part of those who go a trading are men of such circumstances and disposition as to venture their persons everywhere for extravagant gains, yet the

[1] For translations of Schiller, see Chapter III. p. 89.

consequences to the public are not to be slighted, as we may be led into a general quarrel through their means. The Indians in the part adjacent to Michilimackinac have been treated with at a very great expense for some time previous.

"Major Rodgers brings a considerable charge against the former for mediating a peace between some tribes of the Sioux and some of the Chippeweighs, which, had it been attended with success, would only have been interesting to a very few French, and others, that had goods in that part of the Indian country, but the contrary has happened, and they are now more violent, and war against one another."

Though a wilderness of over one thousand miles intervened between the Falls of St. Anthony and the white settlements of the English, he was fully impressed with the idea that the state now organized under the name of Minnesota, on account of its beauty and fertility, would attract settlers.

Speaking of the advantages of the country, he says that the future population will be "able to convey their produce to the seaports with great facility, the current of the river from its source to its entrance into the Gulf of Mexico, being extremely favourable for doing this in small craft. *This might also in time be facilitated by canals or shorter cuts, and a communication opened by water with New York, by way of the Lakes.*"

The subject of this sketch was also confident that a route could be discovered by way of the Minnesota river, which "would open a passage for conveying intelligence to China, and the English settlements in the East Indies."

Carver, having returned to England, interested Whitworth, a member of Parliament, in the Northern route. Had not the American Revolution commenced, they proposed to have built a fort at Lake Pepin, to have proceeded up the Minnesota, until they found, as they supposed they could, a branch of the Missouri, and from thence journeying over the summit of lands, until they came to a river which they called Oregon, they expected to descend to the Pacific.

Carver, in common with other travellers, had his theory in relation to the origin of the Dahkotahs. He supposed that they came from Asia. He remarks, " But this might have been at different times and from various parts—from Tartary, China, Japan, for the inhabitants of these places resemble each other. * * * *

" It is very evident that some of the names and customs of the American Indians resemble those of the Tartars, and I make no doubt but that in some future era, and this not very distant, it will be reduced to certainty that during some of the wars between the Tartars and the Chinese, a part of the inhabitants of the northern provinces were driven from their native country, and took refuge in some of the isles before mentioned, and from thence found their way into America. * * * * *

" Many words are used both by the Chinese and Indians which have a resemblance to each other, not only in their sound but in their signification. The Chinese call a slave Shungo; and the Naudowessie Indians, whose language, from their little intercourse with the Europeans, is least corrupted, term a dog Shungush (Shoankah). The former denominate our species of their tea Shoushong; the latter call their tobacco Shousas-sau (Chanshasha). Many other of the words used by the Indians contain the syllables *che, chaw,* and *chu,* after the dialect of the Chinese." The comparison of languages has become a rich source of historical knowledge, yet very many of the analogies traced are fanciful. The remark of Humboldt in "Cosmos" is worthy of remembrance:—" As the structure of American idioms appears remarkably strange to nations speaking the modern languages of Western Europe, and who readily suffer themselves to be led away by some accidental analogies of sound, theologians have generally believed that they could trace an affinity with the Hebrew, Spanish colonists with the Basque and the English, or French settlers with Gaelic, Erse, or the Bas Breton. I one day met on the coast of Peru, a Spanish naval officer and an English whaling captain, the former of whom declared that he had heard Basque spoken at Tahiti; the other, Gaelic or Erse at the Sandwich Islands.'"

Carver became very poor while in England, and was a clerk in a lottery office. He died in 1780, and left a widow, two sons, and five daughters, in New England, and also a child by another wife that he had married in Great Britain.

After his death a claim was urged for the land upon which the capital of Minnesota now stands, and for many miles adjacent. As there are still many persons who believe that they have some right through certain deeds purporting to be from the heirs of Carver, it is a matter worthy of an investigation.

Carver says nothing in his book of travels in relation to a grant from the Dahkotahs, but after he was buried, it was asserted that there was a deed belonging to him in existence, conveying valuable lands, and that said deed was executed at the cave now in the eastern suburbs of Saint Paul.[1]

The original deed was never exhibited by the assignees of the heirs. By his English wife Carver had one child, a daughter Martha, who was cared for by Sir Richard and Lady Pearson. In time she eloped and married a sailor. A mercantile firm in London, thinking that money could be made, induced the newly married couple, the day after the wedding, to convey the grant to them, with the understanding that they were to have a tenth of the profits.

The merchants despatched an agent by the name of Clarke to go to the Dahkotahs, and obtain a new deed; but on his way he was murdered in the State of New York.

---

[1] DEED PURPORTING TO HAVE BEEN GIVEN AT THE CAVE IN THE BLUFF BELOW ST. PAUL.

"To Jonathan Carver, a Chief under the most mighty and potent George the Third King of the English, and other nations, the fame of whose warriors has reached our ears, and has now been fully told us by our *good brother Jonathan*, aforesaid, whom we rejoice to have come among us, and bring us good news from his country.

"We, Chiefs of the Naudowessies, who have hereunto set our seals, do by these presents, for ourselves and heirs forever, in return for the aid and other good services done by the said Jonathan to ourselves and allies, give, grant, and convey to him, the said Jonathan, and to his heirs and assigns forever, the whole of a certain tract of territory of land, bounded as follows, viz: from the Falls of St. Anthony, running on east bank of the Mississippi, nearly south-east, as far as Lake Pepin, where the Chippewa joins the Mississippi, and from thence eastward, five days travel accounting twenty English miles per day, and from thence again to the Falls of St. Anthony, on a direct straight line. We do for ourselves, heirs, and assigns, forever give unto the said Jonathan, his heirs and assigns, with all the trees, rocks, and rivers therein, reserving the sole liberty of hunting and fishing on land not planted or improved by the said Jonathan, his heirs and assigns, to which we have affixed our respective seals.

"At the Great Cave, May 1st, 1767."

"Signed, HAWNOPAWJATIN.
OTOHTONGOOMLISHEAW.

In the year 1794, the heirs of Carver's American wife, in consideration of fifty thousand pounds sterling, conveyed their interest in the Carver grant to Edward Houghton of Vermont. In the year 1806, Samuel Peters,[1] who had been a tory and an Episcopal minister during the Revolutionary war, alleges, in a petition to Congress, that he had also purchased of the heirs of Carver their rights to the grant.

Before the Senate Committee, the same year, he testified as follows:—

"In the year 1774, I arrived there (London), and met Captain Carver. In 1775, Carver had a hearing before the king, praying his majesty's approval of a deed of land dated May first, 1767, and sold and granted to him by the Naudowissies. The result was his majesty approved of the exertions and bravery of Captain Carver among the Indian nations, near the Falls of St. Anthony, in the Mississippi, gave to said Carver 1373l. 13s. 8d. sterling, and ordered a frigate to be prepared, and a transport ship to carry one hundred and fifty men, under command of Captain Carver, with four others as a committee, to sail next June to New Orleans, and then to ascend the Mississippi to take possession of said territory conveyed to Captain Carver, but the battle of Bunker Hill prevented."[2]

In 1821, General Leavenworth, having made inquiries of the Dahkotahs, in relation to the alleged claim, addressed the following to the commissioner of the land office:—

---

[1] Said to have been the author of a fictitious work called "*Connecticut Blue Laws.*"

[2] Peters also testified that he was the great-grandson of Governor John Carver, the first Chief Magistrate of Plymouth Colony.

"Sir:—Agreeably to your request, I have the honour to inform you what I have understood from the Indians of the Sioux Nation, as well as some facts within my own knowledge, as to what is commonly termed Carver's Grant. The grant purports to be made by the chiefs of the Sioux of the Plains, and one of the chiefs uses the sign of a serpent, and the other a turtle, purporting that their names are derived from those animals.

"The land lies on the east side of the Mississippi. The Indians do not recognise or acknowledge the grant to be valid, and they among others assign the following reasons:—

"1. The Sioux of the Plains never owned a foot of land on the east side of the Mississippi. The Sioux Nation is divided into two grand divisions, viz: The Sioux of the Lake, or perhaps more literally Sioux of the River, and Sioux of the Plain. The former subsists by hunting and fishing, and usually move from place to place by water, in canoes, during the summer season, and travel on the ice in the winter, when not on their hunting excursions. The latter subsist entirely by hunting, and have no canoes, nor do they know but little about the use of them. They reside in the large prairies west of the Mississippi, and follow the buffalo, upon which they entirely subsist; these are called Sioux of the Plain, and never owned land east of the Mississippi.

"2. The Indians say they have no knowledge of any such chiefs, as those who have signed the grant to Carver, either amongst the Sioux of the River, or Sioux of the Plain. They say that if Captain Carver did ever obtain a deed or grant, it was signed by some foolish young men who were not chiefs, and who were not authorized to make a grant. Among the Sioux of the River there are no such names.

"3. They say the Indians never received anything for the land, and they have no intention to part with it, without a consideration. From my knowledge of the Indians, I am induced to think they would not make so considerable a grant, and have it go into full effect, without receiving a substantial consideration.

"4. They have, and ever have had, the possession of the land, and intend to keep it. I know that they are very particular in making every person who wishes to cut timber on that tract, obtain their permission to do so, and to obtain payment for it. In the month of May last, some Frenchmen brought a large raft of red cedar timber out of the Chippewa river, which timber was cut on the tract before mentioned. The Indians at one of the villages on the Mississippi, where the principal chief resided, compelled the Frenchmen to land the raft, and would not permit them to pass until they had received pay for the timber; and the Frenchmen were compelled to leave their raft with the Indians until they went to Prairie du Chien, and obtained the necessary articles, and made the payment required."

On the twenty-third of January, 1823, the Committee of Public Lands made a report on the claim to the Senate, which, to every disinterested person, is entirely satisfactory. After stating the facts of the petition, the report continues:—

"The Rev. Samuel Peters, in his petition, further states that Lefei, the present Emperor of the Sioux and Naudowessies, and Red Wing, a Sachem, the heirs and successors of the two grand chiefs who signed the said deed to Captain Carver, have given satisfactory and positive proof, that they allowed their ancestors' deed to be genuine, good, and valid, and that Captain Carver's heirs and assigns are the owners of said territory, and may occupy it free of all molestation.

"The committee have examined and considered the claims thus exhibited by the petitioners, and remark that the original deed is not produced, nor any competent legal evidence offered, of its execution; nor is there any proof that the persons, whom it is alleged made the deed, were the chiefs of said tribe, nor that (if chiefs) they had authority to grant and give away the land belonging to their tribe. The paper annexed to the petition, as a copy of said deed, has no subscribing witnesses; and it would seem impossible at this remote period, to ascertain the important fact, that the persons who signed the deed comprehended and understood the meaning and effect of their act.

"The want of proof as to these facts, would interpose in the way of the claimants insuperable difficulties. But, in the opinion of the committee, the claim is not such as the United States are under any obligation to allow, even if the deed were proved in legal form.

"The British government, before the time when the alleged deed bears date, had deemed it prudent and necessary, for the preservation of peace with the Indian tribes under their sovereignty, protection, and dominion, to prevent British subjects from purchasing lands from the Indians; and this rule of policy was made known and enforced by the proclamation of the king of Great Britain, of seventh October, 1763, which contains an express prohibition.

"Captain Carver, aware of the law, and knowing that such a contract could not vest the legal title in him, applied to the British government to ratify and confirm the Indian grant, and though it was competent for that government then to confirm the grant, and vest the title of said land in him, yet, from some cause, that government did not think proper to do it.

"The territory has since become the property of the United States, and an Indian grant, not good against the British government, would appear to be not binding upon the United States government.

"What benefit the British government derived from the services of Captain Carver, by his travels and residence among the Indians, that government alone could determine, and alone could judge what remuneration those services deserved.

"One fact appears from the declaration of Mr. Peters, in his statement in writing, among the papers exhibited, namely, that the British government did give Captain Carver the sum of one thousand three hundred and seventy-five pounds six shillings and eight pence sterling.[1] To the United States, however, Captain Carver rendered no services which could be assumed as any equitable ground for the support of the petitioners' claim.

"The committee being of opinion that the United States are not bound, in law or equity, to confirm the said alleged Indian grant, recommend the adoption of the following resolution:—

"'*Resolved*, that the prayer of the petitioners ought not to be granted."'

[1] Lord Palmerston stated in 1839, that no trace could be found in the records of the British office of state papers, showing any ratification of the Carver grant.

CHAPTER XII.

SUSTAINED by French influence and fire-arms, the Ojibways began to advance into the Dahkotah country. Carver found the two nations at war in 1766, and was told that they had been fighting forty years. Pike, when at Leech Lake, in 1806, met an aged Ojibway chief, called "Sweet," who said that the Dahkotahs lived there when he was a young man.

Ojibway tradition says that about one hundred and twenty-five years ago, a large war party was raised to march against a Dahkotah village at Sandy Lake; the leader's name was Biauswah, grandfather of a well known chief of that name at Sandy Lake.

Some years after Sandy Lake had been taken by this chief, sixty Ojibways descended the Mississippi. On their return, at the confluence of the Crow Wing and Mississippi, they saw traces of a large Dahkotah party that had ascended to their village, and probably killed their wives and children. Digging holes in the ground they concealed themselves, and awaited the descent of their enemies. The Dahkotahs soon came floating down, singing songs of triumph and beating the drum, with scalps dangling from poles. The Dahkotahs were five times as many as the Ojibways, but when the latter beheld the reeking scalps of their relatives they were nerved to fight with desperation. The battle soon commenced, and when arms and ammunition failed, they dug holes near to each other and fought with stones. The bravest fought hand to hand with knives and clubs. The conflict lasted three days, till the Dahkotahs at last retreated. The marks of this battle are still thought to be visible.

The band of Ojibways, living at Leech Lake, have long borne the name of "Pillagers," from the fact that, while encamped at a small creek on the Mississippi, ten miles from Crow Wing river, they robbed a trader of his goods.

Very near the period that France ceded Canada to England, the last conflict of the Foxes and Ojibways took place at the Falls of the St. Croix.

The account which the Ojibways give of this battle is, that a famous war chief of Lake Superior, whose name was Waub-o-jeeg, or White Fisher, sent his war club and wampum of war to call the scattered bands of the Ojibway tribes, to collect a war party to march against the Dahkotah villages on the St. Croix and Mississippi. Warriors from St. Marie, Keweenaw, Wisconsin, and Grand Portage joined his party, and with three hundred warriors, Waub-o-jeeg started from La Pointe to march into the enemy's country. He had sent his war club to the village of Sandy Lake, and they had sent tobacco in return, with answer that on a certain day, sixty men from that section of the Ojibway tribe would meet him at the confluence of Snake river with the St. Croix. On reaching this point on the day designated, and the Sandy Lake party not having arrived as agreed upon, Waub-o-jeeg, not confident in the strength of his numbers, continued down the St. Croix. They arrived at the Falls of St. Croix early in the morning, and, while preparing to take their bark canoes over the portage, or carrying place, scouts were sent in advance to reconnoitre. They soon returned with the information that they had discovered a large party of Foxes and Dahkotahs landing at the other end of the portage.

The Ojibways instantly prepared for battle, and the scouts of the enemy having discovered them, the hostile parties met as if by mutual appointment, in the middle of the portage. The Foxes, after seeing the comparatively small number of the Ojibways, and over confident in their own superior numbers and prowess, requested the Dahkotahs not to join in the fight, but to sit by and see how quickly they could rout the Ojibways. This request was granted. The fight between the contending warriors, is said to have been fiercely contested, and embellished with many daring acts of personal valour. About noon the Foxes commenced yielding ground, and at last were forced to flee in confusion. They would probably have been driven into the river and killed to a man, had not their allies the Dahkotahs, who had been quietly smoking their pipes and calmly viewing the fight from a distance, at this juncture, yelled their war whoop, and rushed to the rescue of their discomfited friends.

The Ojibways resisted their new enemies manfully, and it was not until their ammunition had entirely failed that they in turn showed their backs in flight. Few would have returned to their lodges to tell the sad tale of defeat, and death of brave men, had not the party of sixty warriors from Sandy Lake, who were to have joined them at the mouth of Snake river, arrived at this opportune moment, and landed at the head of the portage.

Eager for the fight and fresh on the field, this band withstood the onset of the Dahkotahs and Foxes, till their retreating friends could rally again to the battle. The Dahkotahs and Foxes in turn fled, and it is said that the slaughter in their ranks was great. Many were driven over the rocks into the boiling flood below; and every crevice in the cliffs contained a dead or wounded enemy.

From this time the Foxes retired to the south, and for ever gave up the war with their victorious enemies.

Tradition says that, while the English had possession of what is now Minnesota, and while they occupied a trading post near the confluence of the waters of the Minnesota and Mississippi rivers, the M'de-wa-kan-ton-wan Dahkotahs sent the "bundle of tobacco" to their friends, the Wa-rpe-ton-wan, Si-si-ton-wan, and I-han-kton-wan bands, who joined them in an expedition against the Ojibways of Lake Superior. Notwithstanding the great strength of the party, they found and scalped only a single family of their enemies.

Soon after their return to their own country, a quarrel arose between a M'dewakantonwan named Ixkatape (Toy) and their trader. The Indian name of the trader was Pagonta, Mallard Duck. The result of the quarrel was, that one day as the unsuspecting Englishman sat quietly smoking his Indian pipe in his rude hut near Mendota, he was shot dead.

At this time some of the bands of the Dahkotahs had learned to depend very much upon the trade for the means by which they subsisted themselves. At an earlier period it would have been to them a matter of trifling importance whether a white man wintered with them or not.

In consequence of the murder, the trade was temporarily withdrawn. This was at that time a severe measure, and reduced these bands to sufferings which they could not well endure. They had no ammunition, no traps, no blankets. For the whole long dreary winter, they were the sport of cold and famine. That was one of the severest winters that the M'dewakantonwans ever experienced, and they had not even a pipe of tobacco to smoke over their unprecedented misery. They hardly survived.

On the opening of spring, after much deliberation, it was determined that the brave and head men of the band should take the murderer, and throw themselves at the feet of their English Fathers in Canada. Accordingly, a party of about one hundred of their best men and women left Mendota early in the season, and descended the Mississippi in their canoes to the mouth of the Wisconsin. From thence they paddled up the Wisconsin, and down the Fox river to Green Bay. By this time, however, more than half their number had meanly enough deserted them. While they were encamped at Green Bay, all but six, a part of whom were females, gave up the enterprise, and disgracefully returned, bringing the prisoner with them. The courage, the bone and sinew of the M'dewakantonwan band might have been found in that little remnant of six men and women.

Wapashaw, the grandfather of the present chief who bears that name, was *the* man of that truly heroic little half-dozen. With strong hearts, and proud perseverance, they toiled on till they reached Quebec.

Wapashaw, placing himself at the head of the little deserted band, far from home and friends, assumed the guilt of the cowardly murderer, and nobly gave himself up into the hands of justice for the relief of his suffering people.

After they had given him a few blows with the stem of the pipe through which Pagonta was smoking when he was killed, the English heard Wapashaw with that noble generosity which he merited.

He represented the Dahkotahs as living in seven bands, and received a like number of chiefs' medals; one of which was hung about his own neck, and the remaining six were to be given, one to each of the chief men of the other bands.

It would be highly gratifying to know who were the persons who received those six chiefs' medals; but, although not more than one century, at the longest, has passed, since Wapashaw's visit to Canada, it cannot now be certainly ascertained to which divisions of the Dahkotah tribe they belonged; it seems most probable, however, that the following were the seven divisions to which Wapashaw referred, viz.:—M'de-wa-kan-ton-wan, Wa-rpe-kute, Wa-rpe-ton-wan, Si-si-ton-wan, I-han-kton-wan, I-han-kton-wan-nan, and Ti-ton-wan.

The names of this little band of braves are all lost but that of Wapashaw. They wintered in Canada, and all had the small-pox. By such means Wapashaw reopened the door of trade, and became richly entitled to the appellation of the Benefactor of the Dahkotah tribe. Tradition has preserved the name of no greater nor better man than Wapashaw.

Wapashaw did not, however, end his days in peace. The vile spirit of the fratricidal Cain sprung up among his brothers, and he was driven into exile by their murderous envy. To their everlasting shame be it recorded, that he died far away from the M'dewakantonwan village, on the Hoka river. It is said that the father of Wakute was his physician, who attended on him in his last illness. The Dahkotahs will never forget the name of Wapashaw.[1]

During the war of the Revolution, De Peyster was the British officer in command at Mackinaw. Having made an alliance with Wapashaw, the chief desired that, on his annual visit, he should be received with more distinction than the chiefs of other nations. This respect was to be exhibited by firing the cannon charged with ball, in the place of blank cartridge, on his arrival, so that his young warriors might be accustomed to firearms of large calibre.

On the sixth of July, 1779, a number of Choctaws, Chickasaws, and Ojibways were on a visit to the fort, when Wapashaw appeared; and great was their astonishment when they beheld balls discharged from the cannons of the fort flying over the canoes, and the Dahkotah braves lifting their paddles as if to strike them, and crying out, " Taya ! taya !"

De Peyster, who was fond of rhyming, composed a rude song, suggested by the scene, which is copied as a curiosity :—

> " Hail to the chief! who his buffalo's back straddles,
> When in his own country, far, far, from this fort;
> Whose brave young canoe-men, here hold up their paddles,
> In hopes, that the whizzing balls, may give them sport.

[1] G. H. Pond.

> Hail to great Wapashaw!
> He comes, beat drums, the Scioux chief comes.
>
> "They now strain their nerves till the canoe runs bounding,
>   As swift as the Solen goose skims o'er the wave,
> While on the Lake's border, a guard is surrounding
>   A space, where to land the Scioux so brave.
>   Hail! to great Wapashaw!
>   Soldiers! your triggers draw!
>   Guard! wave the colours, and give him the drum.
>   Choctaw and Chickasaw,
>   Whoop for great Wapashaw;
>   Raise the portcullis, the King's friend is come.[1]

When the news reached Mackinaw that Colonel George R. Clark, in command of Virginia troops, was taking possession of the Wabash and Mississippi settlements, and establishing the jurisdiction of Virginia, the English traders became uneasy lest the Americans should advance to the far North-west. As a precautionary measure they formed themselves into a militia company, of which John McNamara was captain, and a trader by the name of J. Long lieutenant.

In the month of June, 1780, the intelligence was received from the Mississippi that the traders had deposited their furs at the Indian settlement of Prairie du Chien, and had left them in charge of Langlade, the king's interpreter; and also that the Americans were in great force in the Illinois country.

By request of the commanding officer at Mackinaw, Long went to Prairie du Chien, with twenty Canadians,

---

[1] These uncouth lines are from a volume of miscellanies published by De Peyster, at Dumfries, Scotland, in 1812, in the possession of Hon. L. C. Draper, Secretary of the Wisconsin Historical Society. De Peyster's wife accompanied him to Mackinaw, and he seems to have been popular with the traders. When he was ordered to another post, they presented him with a silver punch bowl, gilt inside, holding a gallon and a half, and a silver ladle, as a mark of regard.

and thirty-six Fox and Dahkotah Indians, in nine large birch canoes.

One day, while camping on the Wisconsin river, they discovered a small log hut, in which was a trader, with his arms cut off, lying on his back, who had been murdered by the Indians.

The next day the expedition arrived at the "Forks of the Mississippi," where two hundred Fox Indians, on horseback, armed with spears, bows, and arrows, awaited them. Among the Dahkotah Indians of the party was Wapashaw, by whose order the birch canoes were brought to the shore. Upon landing the Foxes greeted Wapashaw and his party, and invited them to a feast of dog, bear, and beaver meat.

After the feast a council was called, when the chief of the Foxes addressed Wapashaw to this effect:—

"Brothers, we are happy to see you; we have no bad heart against you. Although we are not the same nation by language, our hearts are the same. We are all Indians, and are happy to hear that our Great Father has pity on us, and sends us wherewithal to cover us, and enable us to hunt."

To which Wapashaw replied:—

"It is true, my children, our Great Father, has sent me this way to take the skins and furs that are in the Dog's Field (Prairie du Chien), under Captain Langlade's charge, lest the Great Knives (Americans) should plunder them. I am come with the white men to give you wherewithal to cover you, and ammunition to hunt."

Arriving at Prairie du Chien, the peltries were found in a log-house, guarded by Captain Langlade and some Indians. After resting a short period, the canoes were filled with three hundred packs of the best skins, and the balance burned to keep them from the Americans, who a few days afterwards arrived for the purpose of attacking the post.

At this period the M'dewakantonwan Dahkotahs had retired from the region of Mille Lac, and were residing at Penneshaw's[1] post, on the Minnesota, a few miles above its mouth.

After the disturbance of commerce, incident to the cession of Canada, had ceased, the trade in furs began to revive. In the year 1766, traders left Mackinaw, and proceeded as far as Kamanistigoya, thirty miles east of Grand Portage. Thomas Curry shortly after ventured as far as the valley of the Saskatchewan, and his success in obtaining furs induced a Mr. James Finlay to establish a post in the same valley, as high as the forty-eighth and a half degree of latitude.

The Hudson Bay Company were uneasy at this encroachment of private enterprise upon the territory, and endeavoured to counteract it, though without success.

About the year 1780, two establishments on the Assiniboine river were destroyed by the Indians, and a plot laid to extirpate the traders, but that "noisome pestilence," the small pox, breaking out among the tribes, their attention was diverted.

During the winter of 1783-4, there was a partnership formed by a number of traders, which was called the North-west Company. There were at first but sixteen shares, and the management of the whole was entrusted to the brothers Frobisher and McTavish, at Montreal.

A few that were dissatisfied, formed an opposition

[1] The same individual called Penneshon and Pinchon.

company, one of the members of which was the explorer and author Alexander Mackenzie. After a keen rivalry, this company was merged with the North-west in 1787, and the number of shares was increased to twenty.

From that time the fur trade of the north-west was systematized. The agents at Montreal received the goods from England, and two of them went every year to the Grand Portage of Lake Superior, to receive packs and ship the furs for Europe.

In 1798, the company was re-organized, new partners admitted, and the shares increased to forty-six.

The magnitude of the operations of the company surprise us. At the close of the last century, they employed fifty clerks, seventy-one interpreters, eleven hundred and twenty canoe-men. Five clerks, eighteen guides, and three hundred and fifty canoe-men were employed between the head of Lake Superior and Montreal. The others were in Minnesota, and the country above. The canoe-men were known as " Pork Eaters," or " Goers and Comers," and " Winterers," the latter so called because they entered the interior and passed the winter in traffic with the Indians, received double wages, and were hired from one to three years. The clerks were a kind of apprentices, and received a salary of one hundred pounds, with their board and clothing, with the prospect of being taken into partnership, if they proved good business men. The guides and interpreters were paid in goods.

In July the " Winterers" began to assemble at Grand Portage to settle their accounts and receive new outfits, and at times more than one thousand were congregated. The mode of living at the Portage was truly baronial. The proprietors, clerks, guides, and interpreters all ate in one large hall, at different tables, and, the labours of the day over, the fiddlers were brought in and there was a merry time. The trader in his lonely outpost, considered the reunions at Lake Superior halcyon days, and was buoyed up by anticipating the annual visit.

The love of adventure has often led educated young men "into the woods," as well as "before the mast." Sailor life and Indian trade, unless there is strong religious principle, are apt to render one "earthly, sensual and devilish." There have been scenes enacted in Minnesota which will never be known till the judgment day, for ignorance of which we should be grateful.

The history of one trader at an outpost, is substantially the history of all.

In the year 1784, Alexander Kay visited Montreal to obtain an outfit for the purpose of trading at Fon du Lac, Leech Lake, and vicinity in Minnesota. A young man, educated at the College of Quebec, named Perrault, became his clerk. They arrived at La Pointe on the first of November.

On the little lake at the entrance of the St. Louis river, they found the quarters of Default, a clerk of the North-west Company.

Kay while here was mad, in consequence of intoxication, and with obstinacy pushed up the St. Louis river, with only a bag of flour, a keg of butter, and of sugar, while his party consisted of his squaw mistress, Perrault, and fourteen employees. At the portage of the river he met his partner, Mr. Harris, also without food, except some salt meat.

The men now remonstrated with Kay about proceeding inland, with no provision for the winter; but drawing a pistol, he threatened to shoot those that did not follow.

Taking Mr. Harris, an Indian named Big Marten, and seven men, he pushed on in advance, and the next day sent back word that he had gone on to Pine River,[1] and desiring his clerk to winter at the Savanne portage if possible.

After eleven days' hard toil amid ice and snow, subsisting on the pods of the wild rose, and the sap of trees, Perrault and the men reached the point designated. For a time they lived there on a few roots and fish, but about Christmas, hunger compelled them to seek their employer at Pine River. Weak in body, they passed through Sandy Lake, descended the river, and at last arrived at Kay's post at Pine River. After he was recruited, Perrault was despatched to the Savanne portage, where, with his men, he built a log hut.

Toward the close of February, Brechet, Big Marten, and other Ojibway Indians, brought in meat. Mr. Kay shortly after visited his clerk, and told the troubles he had with the Indians, who exceedingly hated him. In April Kay and Perrault visited Sandy Lake, where Bras Cassé, or Broken Arm, or Bo-koon-ik, was the Ojibway chief. On the second of May, Kay went out to meet his partner Harris coming from Pine River.

During his absence, Katawabada,[2] and Mongozid, and other Indians, came and demanded rum. After much entreaty Perrault gave them a little. Soon Harris, Kay, and Pinot arrived, all intoxicated. The Indians were ripe for mischief. An Indian, named Le Cousin

---

[1] Pine River is a tributary of the Mississippi, about a day's journey in a canoe from Sandy Lake. It is possible to reach Leech Lake by this stream.

[2] Katawabada or Parted Teeth, died at Sandy Lake 1828.

by the French, came to Kay's tent, and asked for rum, Kay told him "No," and pushed him out; the Indian then drew a concealed knife, and stabbed him in the neck. Kay, picking up a carving knife, chased him, but before he could reach his lodge, the passage was blocked up by Indians.

The assailant's mother, approaching Kay, said, "Englishman! do you come to kill me?" and, while imploring for her son, with savage cruelty stabbed him in the side.

Le Petit Mort, a friend of the wounded trader, took up his quarrel, and sallying forth, seized Cul Blanc, an Ojibway, by the scalp lock, and, drawing his head back, he plunged a knife into his breast, exclaiming "Die, thou dog!"

The Indian women, becoming alarmed at this bacchanal, went into the lodges and emptied out all the rum they could find.

On the fifth of May, Kay's wound was better, and sending for Harris and Perrault to come to his tent, he said:—

"Gentlemen, you see my situation; I have determined to leave you at all hazards, to set out for Mackinaw, with seven men, accompanied by the Bras Cassé and wife. Assort the remainder of the goods, ascend to Leech Lake, and wait there for the return of the Pillagers, who are out on the prairies. Complete the inland trade."

Kay, then taking hold of Perrault's hand, Harris having retired, said:—

"My dear friend! you understand the language of the Ojibways. Mr. Harris would go out with me, but he must accompany you. He is a good trader, but he has, like myself and others, a strong passion for drinking, which takes away his judgment."

In the afternoon Kay left, in a litter, for Mackinaw. Perrault and Harris proceeded to Leech Lake, where they had a successful trade with the Pillagers.

Returning to the Savannah river, they found J. Reaume there, and a Mr. Piquet. The former had wintered at the fort of Red Lake, at its entrance into Red River.

They all proceeded by way of the Fond du Lac to Mackinaw, where they arrived on the twenty-fourth of May, and found Kay in much pain. The latter soon after this started for Montreal, but his wound suppurated on the journey, and he died at the Lake of the Two Mountains, August twenty-eighth, 1785.[1]

About the period of this occurrence, Prairie du Chien made its transition, from a temporary encampment of Indians and their traders, to a hamlet. Among the first settlers were Giard, Antaya, and Dubuque.

In the year 1780, the wife of Peosta, a Fox warrior, discovered a large vein of lead, in Iowa, on the west bank of the Mississippi.

At a council held at Prairie du Chien, in 1788, Julien Dubuque obtained permission to work the lead mines, on and near the site of the city that bears his name, and the bluff, on which is the little stone house that covers his remains.

Towards the close of the last century we find Dickson, Renville, Grignon, and others, trading with the Ojibways and Dahkotahs of Minnesota. In the employ-

---

[1] "History, condition, and prospects of the Indian Tribes of the United States," vol. iii.   Mr. Schoolcraft says that Harris was a native of Albany, and was alive in 1830.

ment of the latter, at his trading-house on the river St. Croix, was James Perlier, a youth, who in the next century became one of the most useful citizens of Green Bay, Wisconsin. He was a native of Montreal, and arrived at Green Bay in 1791. Two years after he was employed by an old trader, Pierre Grignon, to act as clerk, at his trading post on the St. Croix. While there he found, with a band of Menomonees, an interesting girl, the daughter of a woman that had been abandoned by a French trader, with whom he fell in love, and married. In the year 1797, in company with Dickson, he wintered near Sauk Rapids. When Pike visited the country he was still engaged in trading above the Falls of St. Anthony, and he gave this young officer much information, which he deemed valuable. Returning to Wisconsin he acted as chief justice of Brown county, for a period of sixteen years, and died in 1839, much respected.

While Perlier was wintering on the St. Croix, a broken-down merchant of Montreal, who had married a lady of wealth in that city, a pompous and ignorant man, full of eccentricity, by the name of Charles Reaume, was his companion. To the early settlers of Green Bay he was known as Judge Reaume. While on the St. Croix the following anecdote is related of him :—

" One day he invited Perlier and other traders in the vicinity to dine with him. The guests had arrived, and the venison, cooked in bears' oil and maple sugar was prepared, when Amable Chevalier, a half-breed, told Reaume that there were not plates enough on the table, as there was none for him. 'Yes, there are enough,' said Reaume, sternly; when the half-breed tore from

Reaume's head his red cap, and spreading it upon the table, filled it with the hashed venison. Reaume, in retaliation, seizing a handful of meat, threw it into the half-breed's face. Becoming much excited, it was necessary for the guests to part the belligerents."[1]

In the year 1794, the North-west Company built an establishment at Sandy Lake, with bastions, and apertures in the angles for musketry. It was enclosed with pickets a foot square and thirteen feet in height. There were three gates, which were always closed after the Indians had received liquor. "The stockade enclosed two rows of buildings, containing the provision store, workshop, warehouse, room for clerks, and accommodation for the men. On the west and south-west angles of the fort were four acres of ground, enclosed with pickets, and devoted to the culture of the potato."

The British posts were not immediately surrendered after the treaty of 1783 between Great Britain and America, and led to some ill-feeling upon the part of the United States. When Baron Steuben was sent by Washington, in 1784, to Detroit, to take possession of the fort, the British commandant informed him that he had no authority to deliver up the post, as it was on Indian territory. By the presence of British officials among the Indian tribes, a hostile feeling was maintained towards the citizens of the United States, which led to the wars with the Indians toward the close of the last century.

In the treaty effected by Mr. Jay, Great Britain agreed to withdraw her troops from all posts and places within the boundary lines assigned by the treaty of

---

[1] Wisconsin Historical Society Collections, vol. iii.

peace to the United States, on or before the first day of June, 1796. The treaty also provided that all British settlers and traders might remain for one year, and enjoy all their former privileges without being compelled to be citizens of the United States.

Taking advantage of this clause, the North-west Company, through the Fond du Lac department, dotted every suitable place in Minnesota with trading posts.

They not only encircled the lakes, but did not pay duties nor apply for licenses. At these posts the British flag was hoisted; and they frequently created civil chiefs among the Indians, to whom they presented the colours and medals of his Britannic majesty.

CHAPTER XIII.

On the seventh of May, 1800, the North-west territory, which included all of the western country east of the Mississippi, was divided. The portion not designated as Ohio was organized as the Territory of Indiana.

On the twentieth of December, 1803, the province of Louisiana, of which that portion of Minnesota west of the Mississippi was a part, was officially delivered up by the French, who had just obtained it from the Spaniards, according to treaty stipulations.

To the transfer of Louisiana by France, after twenty days' possession, Spain at first objected; but in 1804 withdrew all opposition.

President Jefferson now deemed it an object of paramount importance for the United States to explore the country so recently acquired, and make the acquaintance of the tribes residing therein; and steps were taken for an expedition to the upper Mississippi.

Early in March, 1804, Captain Stoddard, of the United States army, arrived at St. Louis, the agent of the French Republic, to receive from the Spanish authorities the possession of the country, which he immediately transferred to the United States.

ORGANIZATION OF TERRITORIES.   241

As the old settlers, on the tenth of March, saw the ancient flag of Spain displaced by that of the United States, the tears coursed down their cheeks.

On the twentieth of the same month the territory of upper Louisiana was constituted, comprising the present states of Arkansas, Missouri, Iowa, and a large portion of Minnesota.

On the eleventh of January, 1805, the territory of Michigan was organized.

The first American officer who visited Minnesota, on business of a public nature, was one who was an ornament to his profession, and in energy and endurance a true representative of the citizens of the United States. We refer to the gallant Zebulon Montgomery Pike, who afterwards fell in battle at York, Upper Canada, and whose loss was justly mourned by the whole nation.

When a young lieutenant, he was ordered by General Wilkinson to visit the region now known as Minnesota, and expel the British traders who were found violating the laws of the United States, and form alliances with the Indians. With only a few common soldiers, he was obliged to do the work of several men. At times he would precede his party for miles to reconnoitre, and then he would do the duty of hunter.

During the day he would perform the part of surveyor, geologist, and astronomer, and at night, though hungry and fatigued, his lofty enthusiasm kept him awake until he copied the notes, and plotted the courses of the day.

On the fourth of September, 1805, Pike arrived at Prairie du Chien, from St. Louis, and was politely treated by the traders, Fisher,[1] Frazer,[2] and Woods, who were there at that time.

On the eighth, in two batteaux, with Joseph Renville and Pierre Rosseau as interpreters, he continued his ascent of the river.

On the twelfth he was at the Prairie La Crosse, so called from the Indian game of ball, where he noticed some earth works, and holes that had been dug by the Dahkotahs to screen their wives and children during battle. At this place, Mr. Frazer, of Prairie du Chien, overtook him.

Amid terrific thunder claps, forked lightning, and torrents of rain, he reached, on the seventeenth, Point de Sable, on Lake Pepin, where he took shelter, and remained the rest of the day.

He here found a trader by the name of Cameron, and his son, also a young man, John Rudsdell. The next day he, in company with Cameron, came to Canoe river, where he found a small band under Red Wing, the second war chief of the Dahkotahs.

On the twenty-first he breakfasted at the village of the Kaposia band, which was on the site just below Saint Paul, now known as Pig's Eye. The same day he passed the encampment of a trader, J. B. Faribault,[3]

---

[1] Fisher was a trader at Prarie du Chien until 1815. He then went to the Red River of the North in the service of the Hudson Bay Company. From 1824 to '26, he was at Lake Traverse, the source of the Minnesota. One of his daughters is the mother of Joseph Rolette of Pembina, by a former husband, and she is now married to H. L. Dousman, Esq.

[2] The father of Jack Frazer of Mendota?

[3] "Jean Baptist Faribault is the last survivor of the old traders. He is now more than eighty years of age, and resides at Faribault, in Rice county, with his sons. He is a native of Canada, and removed to this country, in 1798, fifty-seven years ago. He enjoyed considerable advantages of education in early youth. His career in this region has been marked with more of adverse fortune than usually occurs, even in the

which was three miles below Mendota. Arriving at the confluence of the Minnesota and the Mississippi, he pitched his camp on the north-east point of the island. The next day was Sunday, and Little Crow, of the Kaposia village, arrived with one hundred and fifty warriors, ascending the hill which is now covered by Fort Snelling, they saluted him with balls according to their custom. During the day he went up to the Dahkotah village, just above Mendota, to visit Mr. Cameron. On Monday he held a council with the Dahkotahs, and obtained a grant of land for the use of the United States.[1] His speech will always be interesting, as the

perilous life of an Indian trader. Shortly after the close of the war with Great Britain he was robbed by the Winnebagoes at Prarie du Chien, of a large stock of goods, for which he never received any remuneration. Some years subsequently he fixed his residence upon Pike's Island, near Fort St. Anthony (now Snelling), and had barely established himself in his vocation of trader when he was forced by the mandate of the commandant of the fort to abandon his buildings, and to betake himself, with his movable property, to the bottom land on the east side of the Mississippi, where he erected new tenements. The following spring, the water, which was unusually high, carried off his houses and live stock, he and his family escaping in boats, by means of which he was fortunately enabled to save his goods and furs from destruction. Still not discouraged, he built a house at the point now known as Mendota, where he resided many years, except during the winter months, when he assumed charge of his trading post at Little Rapids, on the Minnesota river."—*Sibley's Address.*

[1] Whereas, at a conference held between the United States of America, and the Sioux Nation of Indians, Lieutenant Z. M. Pike, of the army of the United States, and the chiefs and the warriors of said tribe, have agreed to the following articles, which, when ratified and approved of by the proper authority, shall be binding on both parties:

ART. 1. That the Sioux Nation grant unto the United States, for the purpose of establishment of military posts, nine miles square, at the mouth of the St. Croix, also from below the confluence of the Mississippi and St. Peters, up the Mississippi to include the Falls of St. Anthony, extending nine miles on each side of the river, that the Sioux Nation grants to the United States

first expression of the views of the United States to the Dahkotahs:—

"Brothers—I am happy to meet you here at this council fire, which your father has sent me to kindle, and to take you by the hands as our children. We having but lately acquired from the Spanish the extensive territory of Louisiana, our general has thought proper to send out a number of his warriors to visit all his red children; to tell them his will, and to hear what request they may have to make of their father. I am happy the choice has fell on me to come this road, as I find my brothers, the Sioux, ready to listen to my words.

"Brothers—It is the wish of our Government to establish military posts on the Upper Mississippi, at such places as might be thought expedient. I have, therefore, examined the country, and have pitched on the mouth of the river St. Croix, this place, and the Falls of St. Anthony, I therefore wish you to grant to the United States, nine miles square, at St. Croix, and at this place, from a league below the confluence of the St. Peters and Mississippi, to a league above St. Anthony, the full sovereignty and power over said district forever.

ART. 2. That, in consideration of the above grants, the United States shall pay (filled up by the Senate with 2,000 dollars).

ART. 3. The United States promise, on their part, to permit the Sioux to pass and re-pass, hunt, or make other use of the said districts as they have formerly done, without any other exception than those specified in article first.

In testimony whereof, we, the undersigned, have hereunto set our hands and seals, at the mouth of the river St. Peters, on the 23d day of September, 1805.

Z. M. PIKE. [L. S.]
1st Lieut. and agent at the above conference.
                his
LE PETIT CORBEAU. ⋈ [L. S.]
               mark
               his
WAY AGO ENAGEE, ⋈ [L. S.]
               mark

extending three leagues on each side of the river; and as we are a people who are accustomed to have all our acts written down, in order to have them handed to our children, I have drawn up a form of an agreement, which we will both sign in the presence of the traders now present. After we know the terms, we will fill it up, and have it read and interpreted to you.

"Brothers—Those posts are intended as a benefit to you. The old chiefs now present must see that their situation improves by a communication with the whites. It is the intention of the United States to establish at those posts factories, in which the Indians may procure all their things at a cheaper and better rate than they do now, or than your traders can afford to sell them to you, as they are single men, who come far in small boats. But your fathers are many and strong, and will come with a strong arm, in large boats. There will also be chiefs here, who can attend to the wants of their brothers, without their sending or going all the way to St. Louis, and will see the traders that go up your rivers, and know that they are good men.

"Brothers—Another object your father has at heart, is to endeavour to make peace between you and the Chippeways. You have now been a long time at war, and when will you stop? If neither side will lay down the hatchet, your paths will always be red with blood; but if you will consent to make peace, and suffer your father to bury the hatchet between you, I will endeavour to bring down some of the Chippeway chiefs with me to St. Louis, where the good work can be completed, under the auspices of your mutual father. I am much pleased to see that the young warriors have halted here to hear my words this day; and as I know it is hard for a warrior to be struck and not strike again, I will send (by the first Chippeway I meet) word to their chiefs :—That if they have not yet felt your tomahawk, it is not because you have no legs, nor the hearts of men, but because you have listened to the voice of your father.

"Brothers—If the chiefs do not listen to the voice of their father, and continue to commit murders on you and our traders, they will call down the vengeance of the Americans; for they are not like a blind man walking into the fire. They were once at war with us, and joined to all the Northern Indians, were defeated at Roche de Bœuf, and were obliged to sue for peace— that peace we granted them. They know we are not children, but, like all wise people, are slow to shed blood.

"Brothers—Your old men probably know, that about thirty years ago we were subject to, and governed by the king of the English; but he, not treating us like children, we would no longer acknowledge him as father —and after ten years war, in which he lost one hundred thousand men, he acknowledged us a free and independent nation. They know that not many years since, we received Detroit, Michilimackinac, and all the posts on the lakes, from the English, and now but the other day, Louisiana from the Spanish; so that we put one foot on the sea at the east, and the other on the sea at the west; and, if once children, are now men; yet, I think the traders who come from Canada are bad birds amongst the Chippeways, and instigate them to make war on their red brothers, the Sioux, in order to prevent our traders from going high up the Mississippi.

This I shall inquire into, and, if so, warn those persons of their ill conduct.

"Brothers—Mr. Choteau was sent by your father to the Osage Nation, with one of his young chiefs. He sailed some days before me, and had not time to procure the medals which I am *told* he promised to send up, but they will be procured.

"Brothers—I wish you to have some of your head chiefs to be ready to go down with me in the spring. From the head of the St. Pierre, also, such other chiefs as you may think proper, to the number of four or five. When I pass here, on my way, I will send you word at what time you will meet me at the Prairie des Chiens.

"Brothers—I expect that you will give orders to all your young warriors to respect my *flag* and *protection* which I may extend to the Chippeway chiefs who may come down with me in the spring; for was a dog to run to my lodge for safety, his enemy must walk over me to hurt him.

"Brothers—Here is a flag, which I wish to send to Gens de Feuilles, to show them they are not forgotten by their father. I wish the comrade of their chief to take it on himself to deliver it with my words.

"Brothers—I am told that hitherto the traders have made a practice of selling rum to you. All of you, in your right senses, must know that it is injurious; and occasions quarrels and murders amongst yourselves. For this reason, your father has thought proper to prohibit the traders from selling you any rum. Therefore, I hope my *brothers*, the *chiefs*, when they know of a trader to sell an Indian rum, will prevent that Indian from paying his credit. This will break up the pernicious practice, and oblige your father. But I hope you will not encourage your young men to treat our traders ill from this circumstance, or from a hope of the indulgence formerly experienced; but make your complaints to persons in this country, who will be authorized to do you justice.

"Brothers—I now present you with some of your father's tobacco, and some other trifling things, as a memorandum of my good will, and before my departure I will give you some liquor to clear your throats."

On the morning after the council it was discovered that the flag, which had been hoisted from his boat, was gone. Calling the guard he had one whipped for his negligence.

The next day, before he was out of his bed, Little Crow came bustling up from his village, flag in hand, which had been found floating down the river, and he supposed that the whites had all been killed.

On Friday, the twenty-sixth of September, he had transported all of his goods to a post above the Falls of St. Anthony, and then occupied a few leisure hours in writing to his general, and to his wife, who he thought might not see him return from the land of savages.

All the next day and Sunday the soldiers were hard at work dragging the barge over the portage, and when night came they were so fatigued that they could not cook their suppers, and went to sleep. On Monday he encamped on what is now known as Hennepin Island.

Opposite the mouth of Crow river, on the fourth of October, a bark canoe, cut to pieces with tomahawks, and paddles broken, was seen, which appeared as if there had been a fight between Ojibways and Dahkotahs. The next day he passed fortifications, and found five litters in which wounded had been carried, at a place, where five years before there had been fought a severe battle.

On the sixteenth of October, when they awoke in the morning, they were astonished to find that snow had fallen during the night. Pike desired, if possible, to reach Crow Wing, the highest point ever made by traders in their bark canoes, that day, but after the soldiers had worked four hours their limbs were benumbed by the cold.

Going ashore they built a fire, and found the boats were leaking. The sergeant, remarkable for strength, by over exertion burst a blood-vessel, and a corporal also gave evidence of internal injuries.

In view of the unforeseen difficulties, he determined to leave the large boats, and a portion of the men. By the last day of the month a block-house was erected near Swan river, and in his journal[1] he writes:—

"October thirty-first, Thursday.—Enclosed my little work completely with pickets. Hauled up my two boats and turned them over on each side of the gateways; by which means a defence was made to the river, and had it not been for various political reasons, I would have laughed at the attack of eight hundred or a thousand savages, if all my party were within. For, except accidents, it would only have afforded amusement, the Indians having no idea of taking a place by storm. Found myself powerfully attacked with the

[1] The journal and letters of Pike convey so correct an idea of the condition of Minnesota, at the commencement of this century, that we have thought it advisable to give many extracts. Since his day Major Long, Fremont, Allen, Pope, Marcy, Stansbury, and other military officers, by their published journals have made known the region west of the Mississippi.

fantastics of the brain, called ennui, at the mention of which I had hitherto scoffed; but my books being packed up, I was like a person entranced, and could easily conceive why so many persons who have been confined to remote places, acquired the habit of drinking to excess, and many other vicious practices, which have been adopted merely to pass time.

"November twenty-ninth, Friday.—A Sioux (the son of a warrior called the Killeur Rouge, of the *Gens des Feuilles*) and a Fols Avoin came to the post. He said that having struck our trail below, and finding some to be shoe tracks, he conceived it to be the establishment of some traders, took it, and came to the post. He informed me that Mr. Dickson had told the Sioux 'that they might now hunt where they pleased, as I had gone ahead and would cause the Chippeways, wherever I met them, to treat them with friendship; that I had barred up the mouth of the St. Peter's, so that no liquor could ascend that river; but that, if they came on the Mississippi, they should have what liquor they wanted; also, that I was on the river and had a great deal of merchandise to give them in presents.' This information of Mr. Dickson to the Indians, seemed to have self-interest and envy for its motives; for, by the idea of having prevented liquor from going up to St. Peter's, he gave the Indians to understand that it was a regulation of my own, and not a law of the United States; and by assuring them he would sell to them on the Mississippi, he drew all the Indians from the traders on the St. Peter's, who had adhered to the restriction of not selling liquor, and should any of them be killed, the blame would all lie on me, as he had (without authority) assured them they might hunt in security. I took care to give the young chief a full explanation of my ideas on the above. He remained all night. Killed two deer.

"December third, Tuesday.—Mr. Dickson, with one engagee and a young Indian, arrived at the fort. I received him with every politeness in my power, and after a serious conversation with him on the subject of the information given me on the twenty-ninth ultimo, was induced to believe it, in part, incorrect. He assured me that no liquor was sold by him, nor by any houses under his direction. He gave me much useful information relative to my future route, which gave me great encouragement as to the certainty of my accomplishing the object of my voyage, to the fullest extent. He seemed to be a gentleman of general commercial knowledge, and possessing much geographical information of the Western country, of open, frank, manners. He gave me many assurances of his good wishes for the prosperity of my undertaking.

"December sixth, Friday.—I despatched my men down to bring up the other peroque with a strong sled, on which it was intended to put the canoe about one-third, and to let the end drag on the ice. Three families of the Fols Avoins arrived and encamped near the fort: also, one Sioux, who pretended to have been sent to me, from the *Gens des Feuilles*, to inform me that the Yanctongs and Sussitongs (two bands of Sioux from the head of the St. Peter's and the Missouri, and the most savage of them) had commenced the war dance, and would depart in a few days, in which case he conceived it would be advisable for the Fols Avoins to keep close under my protection; that making a stroke on the Chippeways would tend to injure the grand object of my voyage, &c., &c. Some reasons induced me to believe he was a self-created envoy; however, I offered to pay him, or any other young Sioux, who would go to those bands and carry my word. He promised to make known my wishes upon his return. My men returned in the evening without my canoe, having been so unfortunate as to split her in carrying her over the rough hilly ice in the ripples below. So many disappointments almost wearied out my patience; but, notwithstanding, I intend to embark by land and water in a few days.

"December ninth, Monday.—Prepared to embark. Expecting the Sioux, I had two large kettles of soup made for them. Had a shooting-match with four prizes. The Sioux did not arrive, and we eat the soup ourselves. Crossed the river and encamped above the rapids. Wind changed, and it grew cold.

"December tenth, Tuesday.—After arranging our sleds[1] and peroque commenced our march. The sleds on the prairie, and the peroque towed by three men. Found it extremely difficult to get along, the snow being melted off the prairie in spots. The men who had the canoe were obliged to wade and drag her over the rocks in many places. Shot the only deer I saw. It fell three times, and after made its escape. This was a great disappointment, for upon the game we took now we depended for our subsistence. This evening disclosed to my men the real danger they had to encounter. Distance five miles.

"December fourteenth, Saturday.—We departed from

---

[1] Sleds were such as are frequently seen about farmers' yards, calculated to hold two barrels, or four hundred weight, in which two men were geared abreast.

our encampment at the usual hour, but had not advanced one mile when the foremost sled, which happened unfortunately to carry my baggage and ammunition, fell into the river. We were all in the river up to our middles in recovering the things. Halted and made a fire. Came on to where the river was frozen over. Stopped and encamped on the west shore in a pine wood. Upon examining my things, found all my baggage wet, and some of my books materially injured; but a still greater injury was that all of my cartridges, and four pounds of double battle Sussex powder for my own use, was destroyed. Fortunately my kegs of powder were preserved dry, and some bottles of common glazed powder, which were so tightly corked as not to admit water. Had this not been the case, my voyage must necessarily have been terminated, for we could not have subsisted without ammunition. During the time of our misfortune, two Fols Avoin Indians came to us, one of whom was at my stockade, on the twenty-ninth ultimo, in company with the Sioux. I signified to them by signs the place of our intended encampment, and invited them to come and encamp with us. They left me, and both arrived at my camp in the evening, having each a deer which they presented me. I gave them my canoe to keep until spring; and, in the morning, at parting, made them a small present. Sat up until three o'clock, A. M., drying and assorting my ammunition and baggage. Killed two deer. Distance four miles.

"December twenty-first, Saturday.—Bradley and myself went on ahead and overtook my interpreter, who had left camp very early in hopes that he would be able to see the river De Corbeau, where he had twice wintered. He was immediately opposite to a large island, which he supposed to have great resemblance to an island opposite the mouth of the above river; but finally he concluded it was not the island, and returned to camp. But this was actually the river, as we discovered when we got to the head of the island from which we could see the river's entrance. This fact exposes the ignorance and inattention of the French and traders; and, with the exception of a few intelligent men, what little confidence is to be placed on their information. We ascended the Mississippi about five miles above the confluence; found it frozen; but in many places, not more than one hundred yards over; mild and still. Indeed all the appearance of a small river of a low country. Returned and found my party, having broke sleds, had only made good three miles, while I had marched thirty-five.

"December thirty-first, Tuesday.—Passed Pine river about eleven o'clock. At its mouth there was a Chippeway's encampment of fifteen lodges; this had been occupied in the summer, but is now vacant. By the significations of their marks we understood that they had marched a party of fifty warriors against the Sioux; and had killed four men and four women, which were represented by images carved out of pine or cedar. The four men painted and put in the ground to the middle, leaving above ground those parts which are generally concealed; by their sides were four painted poles, sharpened at the end to represent the women. Near this were poles with deer skins, plumes, and silk handkerchiefs. Also a circular hoop of cedar with something attached representing a scalp. Near each lodge they had holes dug in the ground, and boughs ready to cover them, as a retreat for their women and children if attacked by the Sioux.

"January second, 1806, Thursday.—Fine warm day. Discovered fresh sign of Indians. Just as we were encamping at night, my sentinel informed us that some Indians were coming full speed upon our trail or track. I ordered my men to stand by their guns *carefully*. They were immediately at my camp, and saluted the flag by a discharge of three pieces; when four Chippeways, one Englishman and a Frenchman of the North-west Company presented themselves. They informed us that some women having discovered our trail gave the alarm, and not knowing but it was their enemies, they had departed to make a discovery. They had heard of us and revered our flag. Mr. Grant, the Englishman, had only arrived the day before from Lake De Sable; from which he marched in one day and a half. I presented the Indians with half a deer, which they received thankfully, for they had discovered our fires some days ago, and, believing it to be the Sioux, they dared not leave their camp. They returned, but Mr. Grant remained all night.

"January third, Friday.—My party marched early, but I returned with Mr. Grant to his establishment on the Red Cedar Lake, having one corporal with me. When we came in sight of his house, I observed the flag of Great Britain flying. *I felt indignant, and cannot say what my feelings would have excited me to, had he not informed me that it belonged to the Indians.* This was not much more agreeable to me.

"January fourth, Saturday.—We made twenty-eight points in the river; broad, good bottom, and of the usual timber. In the night I was awakened by the cry of the sentinel, calling repeatedly to the men; at length he vociferated, "will you let the lieutenant be burnt to death?" This immediately aroused me; at first I seized my arms, but, looking round, I saw my tents in flames. The men flew to my assistance and we tore them down, but not until they were entirely ruined. This, with the loss of my leggins, moccasins, and socks, which I had hung up to dry, was no trivial misfortune, in such a country, and on such a voyage. But I had reason to thank God that the powder, three small casks of which I had in my tent, did not take fire; if it had, I must certainly have lost all my baggage, if not my life.

January eighth, Wednesday.—Conceiving I was at no great distance from Sandy Lake, I left my sleds, and with Corporal Bradley, took my departure for that place, intending to send him back the same evening. We walked on very briskly until near night, when we met a young Indian, one of those who had visited my camp near Red Cedar Lake. I endeavoured to explain to him, that it was my wish to go to Lake De Sable that evening. He returned with me until we came to a trail that led across the woods; this he signified was a near course. I went this course with him, and shortly after found myself at a Chippeway encampment, to which I believe the friendly savage had enticed me with an expectation that I would tarry all night, knowing that it was too late for us to make the lake in good season. But, upon our refusing to stay, he put us in the right road. We arrived at the place where the track left the Mississippi at dusk, when we traversed about two leagues of a wilderness, without any very great difficulty, and at length struck the shore of Lake De Sable, over a branch of which our course lay. The snow having covered the trail made by the Frenchmen, who had passed before with the rackets, I was fearful of losing ourselves on the lake; the consequence of which can only be conceived by those who have been exposed on a lake or naked plain, a dreary night of January, in latitude 47° and the thermometer below 0. Thinking that we could observe the bank of the other shore, we kept a straight course, and some time after discovered lights, and on our arrival were not a little surprised to find a large stockade. The gate being opened, we entered and proceeded to the quarters of Mr. Grant, where we were treated with the utmost hospitality.

"January ninth, Thursday.—Marched the corporal early, in order that our men should receive assurance of our safety and success. He carried with him a small keg of spirits, a present from Mr. Grant. The establishment of this place was formed twelve years since, by the North-west Company, and was formerly under the charge of a Mr. Charles Brusky. It has attained at present such regularity, as to permit the superintendent to live tolerably comfortable. They have horses they procured from Red River, of the Indians; raise plenty of Irish potatoes, catch pike, suckers, pickerel, and white fish in abundance. They have also beaver, deer, and moose; but the provision they chiefly depend upon is wild oats, of which they purchase great quantities from the savages, giving at the rate of about one dollar and a half per bushel. But flour, pork, and salt, are almost interdicted to persons not principals in the trade. Flour sells at half a dollar; salt a dollar; pork eighty cents; sugar half a dollar; and tea four dollars fifty cents per pound. The sugar is obtained from the Indians, and is made from the maple tree.

"January nineteenth, Sunday.—Two men of the North-west Company arrived from the Fond du Lac Superior with letters; one of which was from their establishment, in Athapuscow, and had been since last May on the route. While at this post I eat roasted beavers, dressed in every respect as a pig is usually dressed with us; it was excellent. I could not discern the least taste of Des Bois. I also eat boiled moose's head, which when well boiled, I consider equal to the tail of the beaver; in taste and substance they are much alike.

"January twentieth, Monday.—The men with the sleds took their departure about two o'clock. Shortly after I followed them. We encamped at the portage between the Mississippi and Leech Lake river. Snow fell in the night.

"January twenty-fifth, Saturday.—Travelled almost all day through the lands, and found them much better than usual. Boley lost the Sioux pipe stem, which I carried along for the purpose of making peace with the Chippeways; I sent him back for it; he did not return until eleven o'clock at night. It was very warm, thawing all day. Distance forty-four points.

"January twenty-sixth, Sunday.—I left my party in order to proceed to a house (or lodge) of Mr. Grant's, on the Mississippi, where he was to tarry until I overtook him. Took with me my Indian, Boley, and some trifling provisions; the Indian and myself marched so fast, that we left Boley on the route, about eight miles from the lodge. Met Mr. Grant's men on their return to Lake De Sable, having evacuated the house this morning, and

Mr. Grant having marched for Leech Lake. The Indian and I arrived before sundown. Passed the night very uncomfortably, having nothing to eat, not much wood, nor any blankets. The Indian slept sound. I cursed his insensibility, being obliged to content myself over a few coals all night. Boley did not arrive. In the night the Indian mentioned something about his son.

"February first, Saturday.—Left our camp pretty early. Passed a continued train of prairie, and arrived at Lake La Sang Sue,[1] at half-past two o'clock. I will not attempt to describe my feelings, on the accomplishment of my voyage, for this is the main source of the Mississippi. The Lake Winipie branch is navigable from thence to Red Cedar Lake, for the distance of five leagues, which is the extremity of the navigation. Crossed the lake twelve miles to the establishment of the North-west Company, where we arrived about three o'clock; found all the gates locked, but upon knocking were admitted, and received with marked attention and hospitality by Mr. Hugh McGillis. Had a good dish of coffee, biscuit, butter, and cheese for supper.

"February second, Sunday.—Remained all day within doors. In the evening sent an invitation to Mr. Anderson, who was an agent of Dickson, and also for some young Indians at his house, to come over and breakfast in the morning.

"February seventh, Friday.—Remained within doors, my limbs being still very much swelled. Addressed a letter to Mr. McGillis on the subject of the North-west Company trade in this quarter.

"February tenth, Monday.—Hoisted the American flag in the fort. The English yacht still flying at the

---

[1] Leech Lake.

top of the flagstaff, I directed the Indians and my riflemen to shoot at it, who soon broke the iron pin to which it was fastened, and brought it to the ground. Reading Shenstone.

"February sixteenth, Sunday.—Held a council with the chiefs and warriors at this place[1] and of Red Lake; but it required much patience, coolness, and management to obtain the objects I desired, viz. That they should make peace with the Sioux; deliver up their medals and flags; and that some of their chiefs should follow me to St. Louis. As a proof of their agreeing to the peace, I directed that they should smoke out of the Wabasha's pipe which lay on the table; they all smoked, from the head chief to the youngest soldier; they generally delivered up their flags with a good grace; except the Flat Mouth, who said he had left both at his camp, three days' march, and promised to deliver them up to Mr. McGillis, to be forwarded. With respect to their returning with me, the old Sweet thought it most proper to return to the Indians of the Red Lake, Red River, and Rainy Lake River. The Flat Mouth said it was necessary for him to restrain his young warriors. The other chiefs did not think themselves of consequence sufficient to offer any reason for not following me to St. Louis, a journey of between two and three thousand miles through hostile tribes of Indians. I then told them, 'that I was sorry to find that the hearts of the Sauteurs of this quarter were so weak, that the other nations would say: what, are there no soldiers at Leech, Red, and Rainy Lakes, who had the hearts to carry the calumet of their chief to their father?' This had the desired effect. The Bucks and

[1] Leech Lake.

Beaux, two of the most celebrated young warriors, rose and offered themselves to me for the embassy; they were accepted, adopted as my children, and I installed their father. Their example animated the others, and it would have been no difficult matter to have taken a company; two, however, were sufficient. I determined that it should be my care, never to make them regret the noble confidence placed in me; for I would have protected their lives with my own. The Beaux is brother to the Flat Mouth. Gave my new soldiers a dance, and a small dram. They attempted to get more liquor, but a firm and peremptory denial convinced them I was not to be trifled with.

"February eighteenth, Tuesday.—We marched for Red Cedar Lake about 11 o'clock, with a guide provided for me by Mr. McGillis; were all provided with snow shoes; marched off amidst the acclamations and shouts of the Indians, who generally had remained to see us take our departure. Mr. Anderson promised to come on with letters; he arrived about twelve o'clock, and remained all night. He concluded to go down with me to see Mr. Dickson.

"February twenty-fifth, Tuesday.—We marched, and arrived at Cedar Lake before noon; found Mr. Grant and De Breche (chief of Sandy Lake) at the house. This gave me much pleasure, for I conceive Mr. Grant to be a gentleman of as much candour as any with whom I had made an acquaintance in this quarter; and the chief (De Breche) is reputed to be a man of better information than any of the Sauteurs.

"March third, Monday.—Marched early; passed our Christmas encampment at sunrise. I was ahead of my party in my cariole. Soon afterwards, I observed smoke on the west shore. I hallooed, and some Indians appeared upon the bank. I waited until my interpreter came up; we then went to the camp. They proved to be a party of Chippeways, who had left the encampment the same day we left it. They presented me with some roast meat, which I gave my sleigh dogs. They then left their camp and accompanied us down the river. We passed our encampment of the twenty-fourth December, at nine o'clock; of the twenty-third, at ten o'clock, and of the twenty-second, at eleven o'clock; here the Indians crossed on to the west shore; arrived at the encampment of the twenty-first December, at twelve o'clock, where we had a barrel of flour. I here found Corporal Meek, and another man from the post, from whom I heard that the men were all well. They confirmed the account of a Sioux having fired on a sentinel, and added, that the sentinel had first made him drunk, and then turned him out of the tent, upon which he fired on the sentinel and ran off, but promised to deliver himself up in the spring. The corporal informed me that the sergeant had used all the elegant hams and saddles of venison which I had preserved to present to the commander-in-chief, and other friends; that he had made away with all the whiskey, including a keg I had for my own use, having publicly sold it to the men, and a barrel of pork; that he had broken open my trunk and sold some things out of it, traded with the Indians, gave them liquor, and this, too, contrary to my most pointed and particular directions. Thus, after I had used, in going up the river with my party, the strictest economy, living upon two pounds of frozen venison a day, in order that we might have provision to carry us down in the spring, this fellow was squandering away the flour, pork, and liquor during the winter, and while we were starving with hunger and cold. I had saved all our corn, bacon, and the meat of six deer, and left it at Sandy Lake with some tents, my mess boxes, salt, and tobacco, all of which we were obliged to sacrifice by not returning the same route we went, and we consoled ourselves at this loss by the flattering idea that we should find at our little post a handsome stock preserved; how mortifying the disappointment! We raised our barrel of flour and came down to the mouth of a little river on the east which we had passed on the twenty-first December. The ice covered with water.

"March fifth, Wednesday.—Passed all the encampments between Pine Creek and the post, at which we arrived about ten o'clock. I sent a man on ahead to prevent the salute I had before ordered by letter; this I did from the idea that the Sioux chiefs would accompany me. Found all well. Confined my sergeant. About one o'clock, Mr. Dickson arrived with the Killeur Rouge, his son, and two other Sioux men, with two women, who had come up to be introduced to the Sauteurs they expected to find with me. Received a letter from Reinville.

"March fifteenth, Saturday.—This was the day fixed upon by Mr. Grant and the Chippeway warriors for their arrival at my fort; and I was all day anxiously expecting them, for I knew that should they not accompany me down, the peace partially effected between them and the Sioux would not be on a permanent footing; and upon this I take them to be neither so brave nor generous as the Sioux, who, in all their transactions, appear to be candid and brave, whereas, the Chippeways are *suspicious*, consequently *treacherous*, and, of course, *cowards*.

"March seventeenth, Monday.—Left the fort with my interpreter and Roy, in order to visit Thomas, the Fols Avoin chief, who was encamped, with six lodges of his nation, about twenty miles below us, on a little river which empties into the Mississippi, on the west side, a little above Clear river. On our way down, killed one goose, wounded another, and a deer that the dogs had driven into an air hole; hung our game on the trees. Arrived at the creek, took out on it; ascended three or four miles on one bank, and descended on the other. Killed another goose. Struck the Mississippi below ———. Encamped at our encampment of the —— of October, when we ascended the river. Ate our goose for supper. It snowed all day, and at night a very severe storm arose. It may be imagined that we spent a very disagreeable night, without shelter, and but one blanket each.

"March eighteenth, Tuesday.—We marched, determined to find the lodges. Met an Indian, whose track we pursued, through almost impenetrable woods, for about two and a half miles, to the camps. Here there was one of the finest sugar camps I almost ever saw, the whole of the timber being sugar tree. We were conducted to the chief's lodge, who received us in the patriarchal style. He pulled off my leggins and moccasins, put me in the best place in his lodge, and offered me dry clothes. He then presented us with syrup of the maple to drink, then asked whether I preferred eating beaver, swan, elk, or deer; upon my giving the preference to the first, a large kettle was filled by his wife, of which soup was made; this being thickened with

NO CHASTITY AMONG SAVAGES. 265

flour, we had what I then thought a delicious repast. After we had refreshed ourselves, he asked whether we would visit his people at the other lodges, which we did; and in each were presented with something to eat; by some with a bowl of sugar, by others, with a beaver's tail. After making this tour, we returned to the chief's lodge, and found a berth provided for each of us, of good soft bear skins, nicely spread, and on mine there was a large feather pillow. I must not here omit to mention an anecdote which serves to characterize more particularly their manners. This, in the eyes of the contracted moralist, would deform my hospitable host into a monster of libertinism; but, by a liberal mind, would be considered as arising from the hearty generosity of the wild savage. In the course of the day, observing a ring on one of my fingers, he inquired if it was gold; he was told it was the gift of one with whom I should be happy to be at that time. He seemed to think seriously, and at night told my interpreter, 'that perhaps his father (as they all called me) felt much grieved for the want of a woman; if so, he could furnish him with one.' He was answered, that with us, each man had but one wife, and that I considered it strictly my duty to remain faithful to her. This he thought strange (he himself having three), and replied that 'he knew some Americans at his nation who had half a dozen wives during the winter.' The interpreter observed that they were men without character, but that all our great men had each but one wife. The chief acquiesced, but said he liked better to have as many as he pleased. This conversation passing without any appeal to me, as the interpreter knew my mind on those occasions, and answered immediately, it did not appear as an immediate refusal of the woman. Continued snowing very hard all day. Slept very warm.

"April eleventh, Friday.—Although it snowed very hard, we brought over both boats, and descended the river to the island at the entrance of the St. Peter's. I sent to the chiefs and informed them I had something to communicate to them. The Fils de Pinchow immediately waited on me, and informed me that he would provide a place for the purpose. About sundown I was sent for and introduced into the council-house, where I found a great many chiefs of the Sussitongs, Gens des Feuilles, and the Gens du Lac. The Yanctongs had not yet come down. They were all waiting for my arrival. There were about one hundred lodges, or six hundred people; we were saluted on our crossing the river with ball as usual. The council-house was two large lodges, capable of containing three hundred men. In the upper were forty chiefs, and as many pipes set against the poles, along side of which I had the Sauteurs' pipes arranged. I then informed them in short detail, of my transactions with the Sauteurs; but my interpreters were not capable of making themselves understood. I was therefore obliged to omit mentioning every particular relative to the rascal who fired on my sentinel, and of the scoundrel who broke the Fols Avoins' canoes, and threatened my life; the interpreters however informed them that I wanted some of their principal chiefs to go to St. Louis; and that those who thought proper might descend to the prairie, where we would give them more explicit information. They all smoked out of the Sauteurs' pipes, excepting three, who were painted black, and were some of those who lost their relations last winter. I invited the Fils de Pinchow,[1] and the son of the Killeur Rouge, to come over and sup with me; when Mr. Dickson and myself endeavoured to explain what I intended to have said to them, could I have made myself understood; that at the prairie we would have all things explained; that I was desirous of making a better report of them than Captain Lewis could do from their treatment of him. The former of those savages was the person who remained around my post all last winter, and treated my men so well; they endeavoured to excuse their people.

"April twelfth, Saturday.—Embarked early. Although my interpreter had been frequently up the river, he could not tell me where the cave (spoken of by Carver) could be found; we carefully sought for it, but in vain. At the Indian village, a few miles below St. Peter's, we were about to pass a few lodges, but on receiving a very particular invitation to come on shore, we landed, and were received in a lodge kindly; they presented us sugar. I gave the proprietor a dram, and was about to depart when he demanded a kettle of liquor; on being refused, and after I had left the shore, he told me, that he did not like the arrangements, and that he would go to war this summer. I directed the interpreter to tell him, that if I returned to the St. Peter's with the troops, I would settle that affair with him. On our arrival at the St. Croix, I found the Petit Corbeau with his people, and Messrs. Frazer and Wood. We had a conference, when the Petit Corbeau made many apologies for the misconduct of his people; he represented to us the different manners in which the young warriors had been inducing him to go to war;

---

[1] Probably the son of the French trader Penneshaw.

that he had been much blamed for dismissing his party last fall; but that he was determined to adhere as far as lay in his power to our instructions; that he thought it most prudent to remain here and restrain the warriors. He then presented me with a beaver robe and pipe, and his message to the general. That he was determined to preserve peace, and make the road clear; also a remembrance of his promised medal. I made a reply, calculated to confirm him in his good intentions, and assured him that he should not be the less remembered by his father, although not present. I was informed that, notwithstanding the instruction of his license, and my particular request, Murdoch Cameron had taken liquor and sold it to the Indians on the river St. Peter's, and that his partner below had been equally imprudent. I pledged myself to prosecute them according to law; for they have been the occasion of great confusion, and of much injury to the other traders. This day met a canoe of Mr. Dickson's loaded with provisions, under the charge of Mr. Anderson, brother of the Mr. Anderson at Leech Lake. He politely offered me any provision he had on board (for which Mr. Dickson had given me an order), but not now being in want, I did not accept of any. This day, for the first time, I observed the trees beginning to bud, and indeed the climate seemed to have changed very materially since we passed the Falls of St. Anthony.

"April thirteenth, Sunday.—We embarked after breakfast. Messrs. Frazer and Wood accompanied me. Wind strong ahead. They out-rowed us; the first boat or canoe we met with on the voyage able to do it, but then they were double manned and light. Arrived at the band of the Aile Rouge at two o'clock, where we were saluted as usual. We had a council, when he spoke with more detestation of the rascals at the mouth of the St. Peter's, than any man I had yet heard. He assured me, speaking of the fellow who had fired on my sentinel and threatened to kill me, that if I thought it requisite, he should be killed; but that, as there were many chiefs above with whom he wished to speak, he hoped I would remain one day, when all the Sioux would be down, and I might have the command of a thousand men of them, that I would probably think it no honour; but that the British used to flatter them they were proud of having them for soldiers. I replied in general terms, and assured him it was not for the conduct of two or three rascals that I meant to pass over all the good treatment I had received from the Sioux nation; but that in general council I would explain myself. That as to the scoundrel who fired at my sentinel, had I been at home the Sioux nation would never have been troubled with him, for I would have killed him on the spot. But that my young men did not do it, apprehensive that I would be displeased. I then gave him the news of the Sauteurs, that as to remaining one day, it would be of no service; that I was much pressed to arrive below; as my general expected me, my duty called me, and that the state of my provision demanded the utmost expedition; that I would be happy to oblige him, but that my men must eat. He replied that Lake Pepin being yet shut with ice, if I went on and encamped on the ice, it would not get me provision. That he would send out all his young men the next day; and that if the other bands did not arrive, he would depart the day after with me. In short, after much talk, I agreed to remain one day, knowing that the lake was closed, and that we could proceed only nine miles if we went; this appeared to give general satisfaction.

"I was invited to different feasts, and entertained at one by a person whose father was enacted a chief by the Spaniards. At this feast I saw a man (called by the French the Roman Nose, and by the Indians the Wind that Walks) who was formerly the second chief of the Sioux, but being the cause of the death of one of the traders, seven years since, he voluntarily relinquished the dignity, and has frequently requested to be given up to the whites. But he was now determined to go to St. Louis and deliver himself up where he said they might put him to death. His long repentance, the great confidence of the nation in him, would perhaps protect him from a punishment which the crime merited. But as the crime was committed long before the United States assumed its authority, and as no law of theirs could affect it, unless it was *ex post facto*, and had a retrospective effect, I conceived it would certainly be dispunishable now. I did not think proper, however, to inform him so. I here received a letter from Mr. Rollet, partner of Mr. Cameron, with a present of some brandy, coffee, and sugar. I hesitated about receiving those articles from the partner of the man I intended to prosecute; their amount being trifling, however, I accepted of them, offering him pay. I assured him that the prosecution arose from a sense of duty, and not from any personal prejudice. My canoe did not come up in consequence of the head wind. Sent out two men in a canoe to set fishing lines; the canoe overset, and had it not been for the timely assistance of the savages, who carried them into their lodges, undressed them, and treated them with the greatest humanity and kindness, they must inevitably have perished. At this place I was informed, that the rascal spoken of as having threatened my life, had actually cocked his gun to shoot me from behind the hills, but was prevented by the others.

"April fourteenth, Monday.—Was invited to a feast by the Roman Nose. His conversation was interesting, and shall be detailed hereafter. The other Indians not yet arrived. Messrs. Wood, Frazer, and myself, ascended a high hill called the Barn, from which we had a view of Lake Pepin; the valley through which the Mississippi by numerous channels wound itself to the St. Croix; the Cannon river, and the lofty hills on each side.

"April fifteenth, Tuesday.—Arose very early and embarked about sunrise, much to the astonishment of the Indians, who were entirely prepared for the council when they heard I had put off; however, after some conversation with Mr. Frazer, they acknowledged that it was agreeably to what I had said, that I would sail early, and that they could not blame me. I was very positive in my word, for I found it by far the best way to treat the Indians. The Aile Rouge had a beaver robe and pipe prepared to present, but was obliged for the present to retain it. Passed through Lake Pepin with my barges; the canoe being obliged to lay by, did not come on. Stopped at a prairie on the right bank descending, about nine miles below Lake Pepin. Went out to view some hills which had the appearance of the old fortifications spoken of; but I will speak more fully of them hereafter. In these hollows I discovered a flock of elk, took out fifteen men, but we were not able to kill any. Mr. Frazer came up and passed on about two miles. We encamped together. Neither Mr. Wood's nor my canoe arrived. Snowed considerably.

"April sixteenth, Wednesday.—Mr. Frazer's canoes and my boats sailed about one hour by sun. We waited some time expecting Mr. Wood's barges and my canoe, but hearing a gun fired first just above our encampment, we were induced to make sail. Passed the Aile Prairie, also La Montagne qui Trompe à L'eau, the prairie De Cross, and encamped on the west shore, a few hundred yards below, where I had encamped on the —— day of September, in ascending. Killed a goose flying. Shot at some pigeons at our camp, and was answered from behind an island with two guns; we returned them, and were replied to by two more. This day the trees appeared in bloom. Snow might still be seen on the sides of the hills. Distance seventy-five miles.

"April seventeenth, Thursday.—Put off pretty early and arrived at Wabasha's band at eleven o'clock, where I detained all day for him; but he alone of all the hunters remained out all night. Left some powder and tobacco for him. The Sioux presented me with a kettle of boiled meat and a deer. I here received information that the Puants had killed some white men below. Mr. Wood's and my canoe arrived.

"April eighteenth, Friday.—Departed from our encampment very early. Stopped to breakfast at the Painted Rock. Arrived at the Prairie Des Chiens at two o'clock; and were received by crowds on the bank. Took up my quarters at Mr. Fisher's. My men received a present of one barrel of pork from Mr. Campbell, a bag of biscuit, twenty loaves of bread, and some meat from Mr. Fisher. A Mr. Jearreau,[1] from Cahokia, is here, who embarks to-morrow for St. Louis. I wrote to General Wilkinson by him. I was called on by a number of chiefs, Reynards, Sioux of the Des Moyan. The Winnebagoes were here intending, as I was informed, to deliver some of the murderers to me. Received a great deal of news from the States and Europe, both civil and military.

"April nineteenth, Saturday.—Dined at Mr. Campbell's in company with Messrs. Wilmot, Blakely, Wood, Rollet, Fisher, Frazer, and Jearreau. Six canoes arrived from the upper part of the St. Peter's with the Yanctong chiefs from the head of that river. Their appearance was indeed savage, much more so than any nation I have yet seen. Prepared my boat for sail. Gave notice to the Puants that I had business to do with them the next day. A band of the Gens du Lac arrived. Took into my pay as interpreter Mr. Y. Reinville.

"April twentieth, Sunday.—Held a council with the Puant chiefs, and demanded of them the murderers of their nation; they required till to-morrow to consider on it; this afternoon they had a great game of the cross on the prairie, between the Sioux on the one side, and the Puants and Reynards on the other. The ball is made of some hard substance and covered with leather, the cross sticks are round and net-work, with handles of three feet long. The parties being ready, and bets agreed upon (sometimes to the amount of some thousand dollars), the goals are set up on the prairie at the distance of half a mile. The ball is thrown up in the middle, and each party strives to drive it to the opposite

[1] Or Jarrot.

goal; and when either party gains the first rubber, which is driving it quick round the post, the ball is again taken to the centre, the ground changed, and the contest renewed; and this is continued until one side gains four times, which decides the bet. It is an interesting sight to see two or three hundred naked savages contending on the plain who shall bear off the palm of victory; he who drives the ball round the goal is much shouted at by his companions. It sometimes happens that one catches the ball in his racket, and depending on his speed endeavours to carry it to the goal, and when he finds himself too closely pursued, he hurls it with great force and dexterity to an amazing distance, where there are always flankers of both parties ready to receive it; it seldom touches the ground, but is sometimes kept in the air for hours before either party can gain the victory. In the game I witnessed, the Sioux were victorious, more I believe from the superiority of their skill in throwing the ball, than by their swiftness, for I thought the Puants and Reynards the swiftest runners. I made a written demand of the magistrates to take deposition concerning the late murders. Had a private conversation with Wabasha.

"April twenty-fifth, Monday.—Was sent for by La Feuille, and had a long and interesting conversation with him, in which he spoke of the general jealousy of his nation towards their chiefs; and that although he knew it might occasion some of the Sioux displeasure, he did not hesitate to declare that he looked on the Nez Corbeau as the man of most sense in their nation; and that he believed it would be generally acceptable if he was reinstated in his rank. Upon my return I was sent for by the *Red Thunder*, chief of the Yanctongs, the most savage band of the Sioux. He was prepared with the most elegant pipes and robes I ever saw; and shortly he declared, that 'That white blood had never been shed in the village of the Yanctongs, even when rum was permitted; that Mr. Murdoch Cameron arrived at his village last autumn; that he invited him to eat, gave him corn as a bird; that he (Cameron) informed him of the prohibition of rum, and was the only person who afterwards sold it in the village.' After this I had a council with the Puants. Spent the evening with Mr. Wilmot, one of the best informed and most gentlemanly men in the place.

"April twenty-second, Tuesday.—Held a council with the Sioux and Puants, the latter of whom delivered up their medals and flags. Prepared to depart to-morrow."

CHAPTER XIV.

The traders of the North-west Company, though they treated Lieutenant Pike with the respect due his commission, and extended to him their hospitality, did not approve of the policy that the United States government were intending to inaugurate.

They were well aware if the system of establishing central depôts of trade, with goods furnished by the government at low rates, was successful, that "their occupation was gone." Influence was consequently employed to prevent the tribes from patronizing the United States factories, and cultivating friendly intercourse with the Americans.

Pike had scarcely disappeared from the waters of the Mississippi, before Dickson, Rolette, and Cameron disregarded the regulations which had been established.

At the commencement of the century Cameron was the principal British trader on the Upper Minnesota, and the spot where he was buried in 1811, is known among voyageurs as "Cameron's Grave." He was a shrewd and daring Scotchman. One of his employees was an old Canadian, familiarly called Milor, who has recently died at Mendota.

He related a circumstance which occurred while in the service of Cameron, which well exhibits the hardships to which the engagées of the fur trade are often exposed.

While at one of the outposts of Cameron, on a tributary of the Minnesota, the winter suddenly set in, and it was impossible to use the canoe. Hoping that there would be a thaw, he and his companions waited from day to day, until their provisions were exhausted. The weather remaining cold, their only alternative was to place their packs of furs beneath the upturned canoe, and seek the shelter of the woods, in the hope that Cameron would send relief.

With their last meal in their pockets, they commenced their journey through the deep snow. Meeting with no game, when they encamped on the evening of the second day, they were compelled by hunger to eat of the bark of a tree.

During the third day two of the party began to fail in strength, and to beg the others to stop and show that they were losing their judgment. Milor gave no heed to their entreaties, but pushing ahead came at dusk to a place sheltered from the piercing wind, and there found an Indian frozen to death beside the remnants of a small fire.

Milor now shouted to his fellow voyageurs, and told them that to stop was to secure a similar fate. Frightened by the scene, they quickened their pace, until late at night. Milor and another succeeded in catching two muskrats, and, building up a good fire, they feasted on one of the rats, and rested till the break of day.

Making a breakfast on the remaining rat, the party resumed their march, Milor encouraging them by saying that they would soon come to a place where there was an abundance of muskrats, and that as soon as they had laid in a supply of them, they would strike for Traverse des Sioux, when they would be sure to hear of Cameron and obtain food.

For several days they found but one muskrat; but on the morning of the eighth day, after they had been marching an hour, Milor, looking attentively in a southeast direction, declared that he saw smoke, and that there must be a fire. This, for a time, had the exhilarating effect of wine; but after two or three hours the sign disappeared, and they began to despond; when the thought came to Milor that if there was a party coming to their relief, they would be on the lookout also. In less than half an hour he had ascended a bluff, and descried a thick column of smoke, about three miles distant. Waving his cap to his companions, and shouting for joy, he hurried in that direction, and found a party who had come to their aid. Two men were there, each with a pack of pork and biscuit, which had been despatched from Traverse des Sioux, while Cameron and three others were expecting to start with an additional supply. When the fatigued party came into camp, they literally danced for joy. Featherstonhaugh, who relates the story, remarks: "This incident is very much to the credit of Cameron, who made so resolute an attempt to relieve his poor engagées, when the chances of success were so few."

As early as the year 1807, it was evident that under some secret influence the Indian tribes of the Northwest were combining with hostile intentions towards the United States. In the year 1809, a trader by the name of Nicholas Jarrot, who frequently visited Prairie du Chien, made an affidavit at Saint Louis, that the British traders at that place were furnishing the Indians with guns for hostile purposes. Messengers from the Prophet, brother of Tecumseh, painted black, were sent among the Ojibways, and in solemn council they told the astonished natives that the Prophet who sent them had been told by one of the great spirits that it was the will of the gods that Indians should live independent of the whites, and return to primitive usages. The flint and steel were to be discarded; and fire obtained as of old, by the friction of two sticks. To those who believed the message, blessings were promised. They also claimed that the Prophet could resuscitate the dead. The late William Warren asserts that a dead child was taken from Lake Ottawa to Keweena, on Lake Superior, for the purpose of having it brought to life by the Prophet; but putrefaction having taken place, the project was abandoned.

At this period, a red-haired Scotchman, of strong intellect, good family, and ardent attachment to the crown of England, was at the head of the Indian trade in Minnesota. Pike, who visited him in 1806, at one of his trading posts near Sauk Rapids, describes him as " a gentleman of general commercial knowledge, and of open, frank manners." Governor Edwards of Illinois, writing to the secretary of war, says: " The opinion of Dickson, the celebrated British trader, is, that, in the event of a war with Great Britain, all the Indians will be opposed to us, and he hopes to engage them in hostility by making peace between the Sioux and Chippeways, and in having them to declare war against us." A source of influence among the Dahkotahs of Minnesota was the fact that he had married a sister of Red Thunder, one of their bravest chiefs, and that the

British government had appointed him agent and superintendent of the western tribes.

On the first of May, 1812, two Indians were apprehended at Chicago, who were on their way to meet Dickson at Green Bay. They had taken the precaution to put their letters in their moccasins, and bury them in the ground, and were allowed to proceed.

A Mr. Frazer, of Prairie du Chien, who was present at the portage of the Wisconsin, when the Indians delivered the letters, stated that Dickson was informed that the British flag would soon be flying on the American garrison at Mackinaw. About this time, Cadotte, Deace, and John Askin were at Fond du Lac, Minnesota, collecting Ojibway warriors. At Green Bay, Black Hawk was formally created commander-in-chief of the Indian forces, by Dickson presenting him with a medal and certificate, a British flag of silk.

The garrison at Mackinaw was composed of fifty-seven soldiers, with a lieutenant in command. Before Lieutenant Hanks was aware that war had been proclaimed by the United States, he was surprised by a force of British soldiers and Indians landing from a ship that belonged to the North-west Company, and numerous batteaux and birch canoes. With the British army were traders who had long been familiar with the tribes of Wisconsin and Minnesota, Askin, Langlade, Michael Cadotte, and Joseph Rolette. The American officer, perceiving the overwhelming force of the enemy, which consisted of forty regulars of the royal veteran battalion, two hundred and sixty Canadians, with their bourgeois or employees, and several hundred Dahkotah, Ojibway, Winnebago, and Menomonee Indians, capitulated without firing a single gun on July the seventeenth, 1812.

An American gentleman, who had been made prisoner, writes from Detroit on August sixth, to the Secretary of War:—

"The persons who commanded the Indians are Robert Dickson, Indian trader, and John Askin, Jr., Indian agent, and son. The latter two were painted and dressed after the manner of the Indians. Those who commanded the Canadians are John Johnson, Crawford, Pothier, Armitinger, La Croix, Rolette, Franks, Livingston and other traders, some of whom were lately concerned in smuggling British goods into the Indian country, and, in conjunction with others, have been using their utmost efforts, several months before the declaration of war, to excite the Indians to take up arms. The least resistance from the fort would have been attended with the destruction of all the persons who fell into the hands of the British, as I have been assured by some of the British traders."

The next year Dickson, Renville, and other Minnesota traders, are present with the Kaposia, Wapashaw, and other bands of Dahkotahs, at the siege of Fort Meigs.

While Renville was seated one afternoon with Wapashaw, and the then chief of the Kaposia band, a deputation came to invite them to meet the other allied Indians, with which the chiefs complied.

Frazer, an old trader in Minnesota, came and told Renville that the Indians were about to eat an American. On repairing to the spot, the flesh was found carved up, and apportioned in dishes, one for each nation present. The bravest man of each tribe was urged to step forward and partake of the heart and head, and only one warrior of a tribe was allowed to partake of these rarities.

Among those assembled there was a nephew of the Kaposia chief, known among the traders as the Grand Chasseur, who was pressed by a Winnebago to partake of the human flesh. In a moment his uncle told him to leave the feast, and, arising, made a speech creditable to his humanity:—

"My friends," said he, "we came here not to eat Americans, but to wage war against them; that will suffice for us; and could we do that if left to our own forces? We are poor and destitute, while they possess the means of supplying themselves with all that they require; we ought not therefore to do such things."

Wapashaw then spoke in these words, "We thought that you, who live near to white men, were wiser and more refined than we are who live at a distance; but it must indeed be otherwise if you do such deeds."

Col. Dickson, sending for the Winnebago, who originated the disgusting feast, asked what impelled him to such a course. To which the savage replied, that it was better for him to kill the American and eat him, than it was for the Americans to burn his house, ravish and murder his wife and daughters.

The citizens of the United States, in the valley of the Mississippi, now began to feel uneasy; and in the Missouri Gazette of July thirty-first, 1813, published at St. Louis, there is a plea by the editor, for the defence of Prairie du Chien:—

"Last winter," he says, "we endeavoured to turn the attention of the government toward Prairie du Chien, a position which we ought to occupy by establishing a military post at the village, or on the Ouisconsin. For several months we have not been able to procure any other than Indian information from the prairie, the enemy having cut off all communication; but we are persuaded that permanent subsistence can be obtained for one thousand regular troops in the upper lake country. At Prairie du Chien there are about fifty families, most of whom are engaged in agriculture. Their common field is four miles long by half a mile in breadth. Besides this field they have three separate farms, and twelve horse-mills to manufacture their produce."

In February, 1814, the Americans captured St. Joseph's, in Lake Huron, not far from Sault St. Marie, and Mr. Bailly and five others connected with the Mackinaw Company were taken prisoners.

On the first of May, 1814, Governor Clark, with two hundred men, left St. Louis, to build a fort at the junction of the Wisconsin and Mississippi. Twenty days before he arrived at Prairie du Chien, Dickson had started for Mackinaw with a band of Dahkotahs and Winnebagoes. The place was left in command of Captain Deace and the Mackinaw Fencibles. The Dahkotahs refusing to co-operate, when the Americans made their appearance they fled. The Americans took possession of the old Mackinaw house, in which they found nine or ten trunks of papers belonging to Dickson. From one they took the following extract:—

"Arrived, from below, a few Winnebagoes with scalps. Gave them tobacco, six pounds powder, and six pounds ball."

A fort was immediately commenced on the site of the residence of H. L. Dousman, which was composed of two block-houses in the angles, and another on the bank of the river, with a subterranean communication. In honour of the governor of Kentucky it was named "Shelby."

The fort was in charge of Lieutenant Perkins, and sixty rank and file, and two gun-boats, each of which carried a six-pounder; and several howitzers were commanded by Captains Yeiser, Sullivan, and Aid-de-camp Kennerly.

The traders at Mackinaw, learning that the Americans had built a fort at the Prairie, and knowing that as long as they held possession they would be cut off from the trade with the Dahkotahs, they immediately raised an expedition to capture the garrison.

The captain was an old trader by the name of McKay, and under him was a sergeant of artillery, with a brass six-pounder, and three or four volunteer companies of Canadian voyageurs, commanded by traders and officered by their clerks, all dressed in red coats, with a number of Indians.

The Americans had scarcely completed their rude fortification, before the British force, guided by Joseph Rolette, Sr., descended in canoes to a point on the Wisconsin, several miles from the Prairie, to which they marched in battle array. McKay sent a flag demanding a surrender; Lieutenant Perkins replied that he would defend it to the last.

At three o'clock, on the afternoon of July seventeenth, the British and Indians attacked the gun-boat of Captain Yeiser; the Indians firing from behind the houses and pickets. The boat moved up toward the head of the village, discharging volleys, which were quickly answered by the British. The enemy now crossed the river, and commenced an attack from the opposite side, which caused Captain Yeiser to run his boat through the enemy's lines to a point a few miles below.

Lieutenant Perkins, in the meantime, fought bravely in the fort for three days and nights. Provisions, ammunition, and water, began to fail, and the enemy were approaching the pickets by mining. He therefore wisely surrendered, capitulating that they were to retain their private property, and not to serve until duly exchanged. After placing them on parol, the British commander escorted them to the gun-boat "Governor Clark," in which they had arrived only a month before, and sent them down the river.

In their descent they were followed by a party of the blood-thirsty savages in canoes, who did not turn back until they reached Rock Island.

About the time of the capture, a detachment of troops were on their way from St. Louis, under the command of a Lieut. Campbell, to strengthen the garrison. Arriving at Rock Island, he held a conference with Black Hawk at his village. A few moments after his departure, runners, by way of Rock River, brought the news to the Sauk village that the Americans had been defeated at Prairie du Chien.

Immediately they started in pursuit of Campbell's party, which they overtook at a small island near the Illinois shore, about three miles above their village. A fierce encounter took place, in which the Americans were worsted. The officer was wounded, several men were killed, and one of their boats captured, so that it became necessary to retreat to St. Louis. Fort Shelby, after the capture, was called Fort McKay. After the attack of Black Hawk on Campbell, the commander of Fort McKay erected a battery, with two twelve-pounders and six painted wooden guns, near Rock Island, on the east side of the river.

Late in August, 1814, Major Zachary Taylor, the late president of the United States, proceeded in some gun-boats to punish the Indians who had attacked Campbell; but on his arrival he was astonished to find the British there with a large force of Indians. It was a bright, beautiful morning in September when the engagement began, and the first cannon ball fired from the British battery passed through one of Taylor's gun-boats, commanded by Captain Hempstead.

Taylor, like Campbell, soon had his boats disabled, and was obliged to drop down the stream about three miles to repair, and attend to the wounded. During the conflict it became necessary for some one to carry a cable from a disabled boat which was drifting towards the Indians to one commanded by Captain Whiteside. A youth of twenty-three, named Paul Harpole, performed the undertaking successfully, but having done this, he lingered and fired fourteen guns which were handed him at the enemy, when he himself was shot. His body, floating down the stream, was seized by yelling savages and cut into many pieces. In the engagement eleven Americans were badly wounded.

Among those who came in Captain Yeiser's gun-boat to St. Louis, after the surrender of Prairie du Chien, was a friendly "one-eyed Sioux," who had behaved gallantly when the boat was attacked by British artillery. In the fall of the same year, this one-eyed Sioux, with another of the same nation, ascended the Missouri under the protection of the distinguished trader, Manual Lisa, as far as the Au Jacques river, and from thence he struck across the country, enlisting the Sioux in favour of the United States, and at length arrived at Prairie du Chien. On his arrival, Dickson accosted him, and inquired from whence he came, and what was his business; at the same time rudely snatching his bundle from his shoulders, and searching for letters. The "one-eyed warrior" told him that he was from St. Louis, and that he had promised the white chiefs there that he would go to Prairie du Chien, and that he had kept his promise.

Dickson then placed him in confinement in Fort McKay, as the garrison was called by the British, and ordered him to divulge what information he possessed, or he would put him to death. But the faithful fellow said he would impart nothing, and that he was ready for death if he wished to kill him. Finding that confinement had no effect, Dickson at last liberated him. He then left, and visited the bands of Sioux on the Upper Mississippi, with which he passed the winter. When he returned in the spring, Dickson had gone to Mackinaw, and Captain Bulger was in command of the fort.

While there, on May twenty-third, 1815, the British evacuated the fort, the news of peace having arrived. As they retired, they fired the fort with the American colours flying; and the brave Sioux, exposing himself to the flames, rushed in and bore off the American flag and an American medal.

This one-eyed Sioux, if Dr. Foster of Hastings is correct, is still living. In an article published in the Minnesota Democrat, May, 1854, he speaks of the signers of the treaty between Pike, on the part of the United States, and the Dahkohtahs, and says:—

"I have omitted till the last, mention of Le Orignal Levé, who, next to Little Crow, appears to have been the most prominent individual present. Pike calls him 'my friend,' and seems to have made him some marked presents—indeed, the Indian relationship and tie of comradeship was probably adopted between them. Pike says he 'was a war chief, and that he gave him my [his] father's tomahawk,' though what he means by that, passes my comprehension. In the table of Indian chiefs, in the appendix to Pike's Journal, he is set down as belonging to the Medaywokant'wans; his Indian name is given as Tahamie, his French as L'Orignal Levé, and his English as the 'Rising Moose,' which is stated to be literally translated.

"I believe this war chief to be identical with the aged Indian, with whom most of the old settlers are familiar by the name of Tah-mah-haw, whose characteristics are one eye, and his always wearing a stove-pipe hat. He is remarkable among the Sioux—and it is his greatest pride and boast, that he is the only American in his tribe. This is explained by the fact, that in the war with Great Britain in 1812, when the rest of the Sioux sided with the British, and when Little Crow, with Joseph Renville, led on a war party to join the British army against us, he refused to participate on that side, and joined the Americans at St. Louis, where he was employed by General Clarke, in the American service.

"He has now in his possession, and carefully keeps a commission from General Clarke, dated in 1814, as a chief of the Sioux; the commission says of the Red Wing band of Indians—which was originally part of Wabashaw's band.

"If he is the same person as L'Orignal Levé, then

Pike and his Indian comrade fought in the same ranks, and the friendship the latter imbibed at Pike's visit for the Americans, stood the test of time and vicissitudes.

"He deserves on this account to receive from the government authorities, special and marked attention.

"Joseph Mojou, an old Canadian of Point Prescott, told me that Tamahaw was called by the voyageurs, the 'Old Priest,' because he was a great talker on all occasions. In Sioux, *tamwamda* means to talk earnestly; to vociferate; and this bears some resemblance to his Indian name as at present pronounced.

"My friend Mr. Hatch informs me, when he traded with the Winnebagoes and with the Sioux of Wabashaw band, he knew him, and has seen his commission from General Clarke. The Winnebagoes, who were acquainted with him, translated his name to mean the *pike* fish, and therefore called him *Nazeekah*—though *tah-mah-hay* and not *tah-mah-haw*, is the word for 'pike' in the Dakotah tongue.

"It may be thought more pains are taken to elucidate this personal history of an old Indian, than the subject warrants. But when we reflect that this old Indian was the contemporary, if not personal friend of Pike; that he and one other Sioux were of all his tribe who sided with the Americans in the war of 1812; there is an interest justly attached to his identity and history, which deserves more than ordinary attention. The other Sioux who, like Tamahaw, joined the Americans in 1812, was Hay-pee-dan, who belonged to Wakootay's band. He is now deceased."

As late as 1817, Colonel Dickson was living in Minnesota, at Lake Traverse, and the Indian agent at Prairie du Chien suspected that he was alienating the

Dahkotahs from the United States, and in company with Lord Selkirk, striving to secure their trade, as the following extract from his letter of February sixteenth, 1818, to the governor of Illinois will show:—

"What do you suppose, sir, has been the result of the passage through my agency of this British nobleman?[1] Two entire bands, and part of a third, all Sioux, have deserted us and joined Dickson, who has distributed to them large quantities of Indian presents, together with flags, medals, etc. Knowing this, what must have been my feelings on hearing that his lordship had met with a favourable reception at St. Louis. The newspapers announcing *his arrival, and general Scottish* appearance, all tend to discompose me; believing as I do, that he is plotting with his friend Dickson our destruction—sharpening the savage scalping knife, and colonizing a tract of country, so remote as that of the Red River, for the purpose, no doubt, of monopolizing the fur and peltry trade of this river, the Missouri and their waters; a trade of the first importance to our Western States and Territories. A courier who had arrived a few days since, confirms the belief that Dickson is endeavouring to undo what I have done, and secure to the British government the affections of the Sioux, and subject the North-west Company to his lordship. * * * * *
Dickson, as I have before observed, is situated near the head of the St. Peter's, to which place he transports his goods from Selkirk's Red River establishment, in carts made for the purpose. The trip is performed in five days, sometimes less. He is directed to build a fort on the highest land between Lac du Traverse and Red

---

[1] Earl of Selkirk. The agent's fears were entirely groundless.

River, which he supposes will be the established line between the two countries. This fort will be defended by twenty men, with two small pieces of artillery."

It is said that after this, Dickson was arrested between the Minnesota and St. Croix, and carried to St. Louis.

Dickson, though an active partisan, is believed to have been a humane man. The American papers were naturally prejudiced against him, and all the cruelties of the savages were charged upon him. Says one editor at that day: "How will the English government, and their agent, Robert Dickson, a native of Scotland, appear when it is announced to the world, that he employed a Sauk warrior to assassinate Governor Clarke at Prairie du Chien? The governor's timely shifting of his sword alarmed and deterred from the commission of the act." There appears to have been no real foundation for any such impression. On the contrary, when Black Hawk expressed a desire to attack the defenceless settlements on the Mississippi, Dickson remonstrated, saying "that he had been a trader on the Mississippi many years; had always been kindly treated; and could not consent to send brave men to murder women and children. That there was no soldiers there to fight, but where he was going to send the Indians there were a number of soldiers, and if they defeated *them*, the Mississippi country should be given up to them."[1]

---

[1] Ramsay Crooks of New York city, in a letter to Hon. H. M. Rice, October 16, 1857, writes.

"I first went to Mackinaw in 1805, as a clerk to Robert Dickson & Co., who were then engaged in the trade with the Indians from the Lakes to the Missouri, and from the Wabash to the boundary between the United States and Great Britain. Dickson's connection as a trader with the Indians was almost entirely with the Sioux, (Dahcotahs) of St. Peters, (Minnesota) * * * *

In 1815, Wapashaw and Little Crow, of the Kaposia band, visited the British post at Drummond's Island in Lake Huron, at the request of the commanding officer, who desired to thank them in the name of his majesty, for the services the Dahkotahs had rendered during the war. After his remark, she pointed to a few presents on the floor, which called forth the following speeches:—

"My Father," said Wapashaw, "what is this I see before me? A few knives and blankets! Is this all you promised at the beginning of the war? Where are those promises you made at Michilimackinac, and sent to our villages on the Mississippi? You told us you would never let fall the hatchet until the Americans were driven beyond the mountains; that our British Father would never make peace without consulting his red children. Has that come to pass? We never knew of this peace. We are told it was made by our Great Father beyond the water, without the knowledge of his war chiefs; that it is your duty to obey his orders. What is this to us? Will these paltry presents pay for the men we have lost both in the battle and in the war? Will they soothe the feelings of our friends? Will they make good your promises to us? For myself I am an old man. I have lived long and always found the means of subsistence, and I can do so still!"

The Little Crow, whose residence at that time was just below St. Paul, on the east side of the river, was more indignant. With vehemence he said, "After we have fought for you, endured many hardships, lost some

I was proud to call Robert Dickson my friend, and I shall ever cherish his memory as a man who exerted himself in restraining the natural ferocity of the Indians on the frontier, in the war of 1812, although he was branded as the worst of savages, at the very time."

of our people, and awakened the vengeance of our powerful neighbours, you make a peace for yourselves, and leave us to obtain such terms as we can! You no longer need our services, and offer these goods as a compensation for having deserted us. But no! we will not take them; we hold them and yourselves in equal contempt!" So saying, he spurned the presents with his foot, and walked away. On the nineteenth of July, at Portage des Sioux, a treaty was concluded between the Dahkotahs of the Mississippi, Minnesota, and the Yankton division, and the United States, in which it was stipulated that there should be perpetual peace between them, and that all previous acts of hostility should be mutually forgiven and forgotten.

After the fame of the North-west Company was established, another association of traders was formed, called the Mackinaw Company. In 1809 Astor organized the American Fur Company, and after two years bought out the Mackinaw Company, and created a new company distinguished as the South-west. During the winter of 1815–16 Congress enacted a law, that no foreigner should engage in the Indian trade who did not become a citizen. Astor, after this, established a company with a former title, the American Fur Company.

The Indian trade of the North-west was so completely in the hands of British subjects, that it was discovered that the trade could not be carried on without their aid, and the Secretary of the Treasury issued a circular, allowing the Indian agents to license interpreters and voyageurs, who might be employed by the American traders.

Under the new arrangements, American citizens began

to identify themselves with the fur trade of Minnesota. As early as 1816 the late Judge Lockwood of Prairie du Chien, in the capacity of clerk, took charge of a trading post, near the sources of the Minnesota. His remarks, in relation to the Indian trade, which are given in his personal reminiscences,[1] show an intimate acquaintance with the trader's life:—

"Tradition says that many years since, when there were many wintering traders in both the Upper and Lower Mississippi, it was the custom of every trader visiting Prairie du Chien, to have in store a keg of eight or nine gallons of good wine for convivial purposes when they should again meet in the spring, on which occasions they would have great dinner parties, and, as is the English custom, drink largely. But, when I came into the country, there were but few of the old traders remaining, and the storing of wine at Prairie du Chien had become almost obsolete, although the traders were then well supplied with wine, and that of the best kind, of which they made very free use. It was then thought that a clerk in charge of an outfit must have his keg of wine; but, after the American Fur Company got fairly initiated into the trade, they abolished the custom of furnishing their clerks with this luxury at the expense of the outfit. As I have already said, the Indian trade of the Mississippi and Missouri and their tributaries was carried on from Mackinaw as the grand depôt of the trade of the North-west.

"The traders and their clerks were then the aristocracy of the country; and, to a Yankee at first sight, presented a singular state of society. To see gentle-

---

[1] Wis. His. Soc. Collections, vol. ii.

men selecting wives of the nut-brown natives, and raising children of mixed blood, the traders and clerks living in as much luxury as the resources of the country would admit, and the engagees or boatmen living upon soup made of hulled corn with barely tallow enough to season it, devoid of salt, unless they purchased it themselves at a high price—all this to an American was a novel mode of living, and appeared to be hard fare; but to a person acquainted with the habits of life of the Canadian peasantry, it would not look so much out of the way, as they live mostly on pea soup, seasoned with a piece of pork boiled down to grease; seldom eating pork except in the form of grease that seasons their soup. With this soup, and a piece of coarse bread, their meals were made; hence the change from pea soup to corn is not so great, or the fare much worse than that which they had been accustomed to, as the corn is more substantial than peas, not being so flatulent. These men engaged in Canada generally for five years for Mackinaw and its dependencies, transferable like cattle to any one who wanted them, at generally about five hundred livres a year, or, in our currency, about eighty-three dollars and thirty-three cents; furnished with a yearly equipment or outfit of two cotton shirts, one three point or triangular blanket, a portage collar, and one pair of beef shoes; being obliged, in the Indian country, to purchase their moccasins, tobacco, pipes, and other necessaries, at the price the trader saw fit to charge for them. Generally, at the end of five years, these poor voyageurs were in debt from fifty to one hundred and fifty dollars, and could not leave the country until they had paid their indebtedness; and the policy of the traders was to keep as many of them in the country as they could; and to this end they allowed and encouraged their engagees to get in debt during the five years, which of necessity required them to remain.

"These new hands were by the old voyageurs called in derision, *mangeurs de lard—pork-eaters*—as on leaving Montreal, and on the route to Mackinaw, they were fed on pork, hard bread, and pea soup, while the old voyageurs in the Indian country ate corn soup, and such other food as could conveniently be procured.[1] These *mangeurs de lard* were brought at considerable expense and trouble from Montreal and other parts of Canada, frequently deserting after they had received some advance in money and their equipment. Hence it was the object of the traders to keep as many of the old voyageurs in the country as they could, and they generally permitted the *mangeurs de lard* to get largely in debt, as they could not leave the country and get back into Canada, except by the return boats or canoes which brought the goods, and they would not take them back if they were in debt anywhere in the country, which could be easily ascertained from the traders at Mackinaw. But if a man was prudent enough to save his wages, he could obtain passage, as he was no longer wanted in the country.

"The engagements of the men at Montreal were made in the strongest language; they bound themselves not to leave the duties assigned them by their employers or assigns either by day or night, under the penalty of forfeiting their wages; to take charge of, and safely keep, the property put into their trust, and to give notice of any portending evil against their employers, or their

---

[1] The experienced *voyageurs* are called *hivernans* or *winterers*, according to Snelling's work on the Northwest.

interests, that should come to their knowledge. It was the practice of the traders, when anything was stolen from the goods during the voyage, whether on the boat or on shore, to charge the boat's crew with a good round price for it; and, if anything not indispensable was accidentally left on shore at the encampment, they did not return for it, but charged it to the crew, as it was understood to be their duty, not the employer's, to see that everything was on board the boat. These people in the Indian country became inured to great hardships and privations, and prided themselves upon the distance they could travel per day, and the small quantity of provisions they could subsist on while travelling, and the number of days they could go without food. They are very easily governed by a person who understands something of their nature and disposition, but their burgeois or employer must be what they consider a gentleman, or superior to themselves, as they never feel much respect for a man who has, from an engagee, risen to the rank of a clerk.

" The traders in this country, at the time I came into it, were a singular compound; they were honest so far as they gave their word of honour to be relied upon; and, in their business transactions between themselves, seldom gave or took notes for balances or assumptions. It rarely happened that one of them was found who did not fulfil his promises; but when trading in the Indian country, any advantage that could be taken of each other in a transaction was not only considered lawful—such as trading each other's credit—but an indication of tact and cleverness in business. Two traders having spent the winter in the same neighbourhood, and thus taken every advantage they could of each other, would meet in the spring at Prairie du Chien, and amicably settle all difficulties over a glass of wine."

After the war with Great Britain, enterprise made a few attempts to develope the resources of the Upper Mississippi. In 1818 the first grist-mill was built at Fisher's Coulée, four miles above Prairie du Chien. The next year the first saw-mill in the country was erected at the Falls of Black river, which was soon burned by the Indians.

While the Ojibways and Dahkotahs now acknowledged the authority of the United States, they still continued their destructive warfare upon each other. Toward the close of the year 1818 one of their terrible conflicts took place, between Lac Traverse and the head waters of the Mississippi. During the summer a Yankton chief, called by the French the Grand, held a council with some Ojibways, and smoked the pipe of peace. When the latter were returning home, some of the Dahkotahs sneaked after them, scalped a few, and took a woman prisoner.

When the receipt of the intelligence reached Leech Lake, thirteen young warriors, whose leader was Black Dog, started for the Dahkotah land, having vowed that they would not return until they had avenged the insult. For four weeks they travelled without meeting any of their foes; but at length, on the Pomme de Terre river, on a very foggy morning, they thought a buffalo herd was in sight, which proved to be a large Dahkotah camp. Some of the latter, who were on horseback, saw them, and gave the alarm. The Ojibways, finding that they were discovered, and that their enemies were numerous, sent one of their number to their homes east of the Mississippi, to announce their probable death. The twelve who remained now began to dig holes in the ground, and prepare for the conflict, from which they could not hope to escape.

Soon they were surrounded by the Dahkotahs; but as they drew nigh many were mortally wounded by the Spartan band. The leader of the Dahkotah party, exasperated by their continual loss, gave orders for a general onset, when the whole Ojibway party were tomahawked in their holes. The thirteenth returned home, and related the circumstances; and though their friends mourned their death, they delighted in their bravery.

CHAPTER XV.

WHILE citizens of the United States and Great Britain, speaking the same language, and having many common associations, were engaged in war near the southern limits of Minnesota, a disgraceful strife was beginning between the employees of the Hudson Bay and North-west Companies, on the northern border.

The channel of trade, west of Lake Superior, followed the line of the Algonquin settlements, and entered the interior chiefly by way of Pigeon river, and the chain of lakes that separates the British possessions from Minnesota.

Veranderie, the French officer, as we have seen in a previous chapter, was the first that pushed his way toward the Rocky Mountains, and is said to have built a fort at the junction of the Assineboine and Red River. As soon as 1762 maps designate Fort la Reine at the confluence, and here at an early period coureurs des bois, from the French establishment at Mackinaw, used to trade with the Omahaws and Assineboines. On the east side of Lake Winnipeg, before the cession of Canada to the English, there was a French post called Maurepas. On the Lake of the Woods there was Fort St. Charles, and in the lake was an island, near the south-eastern extremity, called Massacre Island, from the following circumstance:—

About the year 1750, a birch canoe with eight Frenchmen, left the post on the shores of the Lake of the Woods, and had proceeded to this island, which is not far from the mouth of the river which leads to Rainy Lake. It was quite early when they arrived, and there was not a breeze perceptible. Kindling a fire to cook their repast, the smoke rose like a lofty column, and attracted a war party of the Dahkotahs, who, landing on the opposite side of the isle, surprised the French and massacred them. At the junction of Rainy Lake river with the lake, there was Fort St. Pierre, and at the grand portage of Lake Superior there was the trading establishment of Kamanistigoya. This region of country was claimed by the Hudson Bay Company, under a charter granted to them by Charles II. on May second, 1670; but during the eighteenth century they did not establish posts in the region bordering on Minnesota.

Before the American Revolution, private traders, who obtained their outfits at Mackinaw, gained possession of the trade, and, after the consolidation of several companies with the North-west Company of Montreal in 1783, there was a larger business transacted with the Indians who lived in this region so abundant in furs. At the commencement of the nineteenth century, the Earl of Selkirk, a wealthy, kind-hearted, but visionary nobleman of Scotland, wrote several tracts, urging the importance of colonizing British emigrants in these distant British possessions, and thus check the disposition to settle in the United States. In the year 1811, he obtained a grant of land from the Hudson Bay Company, described as follows:—

"Beginning on the western shore of Lake Winipie, at a point in 52° 30' north latitude, and thence running due west to the Lake Winipigashish, otherwise called Little Winipie, thence in a southerly direction, through the said lake, so as to strike its western shore in latitude 52°, thence due west to the place where the parallel 52° intersects the western branch of Red river, otherwise called Assiniboine river, thence due south from that point of intersection, to the height of land which separates the waters running into Hudson's Bay from those of the Missouri and Missisippi rivers, thence in an easterly direction along the height of land to the source of the river Winipie, meaning by such last-named river the principal branch of the waters which unite in the Lake Saginagas, thence along the main stream of those waters, and the middle of the several lakes through which they pass, to the mouth of the Winipie river, and thence in a northerly direction through the middle of Lake Winipie, to the place of beginning, which territory is called Ossiniboia" or Assiniboia.

Previous to this time the only inhabitants besides the Indians, were Canadians, who, by long intercourse with savages, had learned all their vices, and imitated none of their admirable traits. Unwilling to return to the restraints of well-ordered society, from which they had fled in youth, they were fond of

"Vast
And sudden deeds of violence,
Adventures wild, and wonders of the moment."

They were proud of the title "Gens Libres," the free people.

The offspring of their intercourse with Indian females was numerous. The "bois brulés" were athletic, expert hunters, good boatmen, fine horsemen, and able to speak the native language of both father and mother. Their chief delight and mode of subsistence was in fishing and snaring the buffalo.

In the autumn of 1812, a small advance party of colonists proceeded to a point in latitude 50° north near the confluence of the Assineboine, on the banks of the Red river, whose head waters after heavy rains interlock with those of the Minnesota river, and commenced the erection of houses and preparations for the expected colonists. But their work was soon stopped by a party of men of the North-west Company, attired in Indian costume, ordering them to desist. The affrighted emigrants were persuaded to take refuge at Pembina, Minnesota, by a company of men that they thought were savages. The latter agreed to carry the children, but the men and women were obliged to walk. The exactions of the guides were cruel. One Highlander had to relinquish a gun that had been carried by his father at the battle of Culloden, and which was prized next to the family Bible, and a shrinking woman had to part with the marriage ring which had been placed upon her finger in the bloom of her youth, by a devoted lover in the Highlands. For the sake of creating alarm, the guides would run off with the babes and children, and the distracted mothers refused to be comforted, because their children were not to be seen any more, as they supposed.[1]

[1] "Red River Settlement, by Alexander Ross. London, 1856."

This sport, more worthy of bears than of men, so shocked the nervous system of the more delicate that they never recovered, and found an early and cold grave.

At Pembina the more hardy lived during the winter in tents, and in the spring returned to the colony to resume their labours.

Returning in the spring to the site of the colony, they in the sweat of their brow cultivated the soil, but the fowls of the air anticipated the harvest, and the winter of 1813–14 was again passed at Pembina.[1]

Their success in the chase was however limited, and when they returned to their settlement in the spring they were in appearance half starved, and all tattered and torn.

By the month of September, 1815, the number of settlers was about two hundred, and the colony was called Kildonan, after the old parish in Scotland in which many were born. With increased numbers all things seemed auspicious. Houses were built, a mill was erected, imported cattle and sheep began to graze on the undulating plains. The Highlander was pleased when he discovered that

" Here no stony ground provokes the wrath of the farmer.
  Smoothly the ploughshare runs through the soil, as a keel through the water.
  Here, too, numberless herds run wild, and unclaimed in the prairies;
  Here, too, lands may be had for the asking, and forests of timber
  With a few blows of the axe, are hewn and framed into houses."

[1] This word is pronounced as if written Pembinnaw, and is a contraction of an Ojibway word, the name of a red berry that grows in the vicinity.

The employees of the North-west Company were however exceedingly restive under the march of improvement, and the proprietors of the company suspected that it was a ruse of their powerful rival, the Hudson Bay Company, to oust them from the lucrative posts they were occupying.

As early as 1813 the clerks and engagées of the Montreal traders endeavoured to excite the suspicions of the Indians, but without success.

At a meeting of the partners of the North-west Company, held at Fort William, at the head of Lake Superior, in the summer of 1814, Duncan Cameron and Alexander McDonell were appointed to concert measures to stop the progress of the colony.[1]

About the last of August, they arrived at the North-west Company's post, about a half mile from the Kildonan settlement, at the forks of the Red and Assineboine rivers.

Cameron, during the winter and spring of 1815, with great art obtained the confidence of the Highlanders. He spoke their native Gaelic tongue, extended hospitality to their families, and insinuated rather than evinced direct hostility to the plans of Selkirk. To give the air of authority, he wore a suit of regimentals that belonged to a disbanded corps of voyageurs, and in his communications, subscribed himself "D. Cameron, Captain Voyageur Corps, Commanding Officer, Red

---

[1] Alexander McDonell, in a letter written to a friend at Montreal, from one of the portages west of Lake Superior, says, "You see myself and our mutual friend Mr. Cameron, so far on our way to commence hostilities against the enemy in Red river. * * * * Nothing but the complete downfall of the colony will satisfy some by fair or foul means. So here is at them with all my heart and energy."

River." The fair promises he made unsettled the minds of the colonists, and seduced many to leave the spot. As soon as the free Canadians and half-breeds learned that their employers were not favourable to the colony, they grew insolent. One of the disaffected Selkirkers, by the name of George Campbell, one Sunday, immediately after a sermon had been read in accordance with a venerable Scotch custom[1] to the assembled settlement, rose and read an order issued by Cameron, and directed to the temporary superintendent of the colony, demanding the surrender of their brass field-pieces.

On Monday morning, the governor's house being guarded, the employees of the North-west Company went to the store-house, broke it open, and carried off to their post, field-pieces, swivel, and a small howitzer; in all amounting to nine. This was a signal for the desertion of the disaffected Selkirkers, who repaired to the quarters of the North-west Company.

In the spring of 1815, McKenzie and Morrison, of the North-west Company at Sandy Lake, Minnesota, told the chief Kawtawabetay, that they would give him and his people all the goods or merchandise and rum they

---

[1] The first emigrants were all Presbyterians. Their expected minister having been delayed, a worthy and pious elder, James Sutherland, "was appointed to marry and baptize, from which functions he was never released by the arrival of the ordained minister, in consequence of the difficulties in which the colony was placed. * * * On his arrival at York Factory, the right hand of fellowship was held out to him by the governor-in-chief of the country, as well as by the governor of the colony. These men with their followers gladly heard him expound the Scriptures. * * * * Of all men, clergymen or others, that ever entered this country, none stood higher in the estimation of the settlers, both for sterling piety, and Christian conduct, than Mr. Sutherland."—*Red River Settlement*, p. 31.

had at Leech Lake, Sandy Lake, and Fort William, if they would declare war against the settlers on Red river.[1]

On the morning of Sunday, June the eleventh, a party of North-west employees, armed with loaded muskets, stationed themselves in a grove near the governor's house, and commenced an attack, wounding four inmates, one of whom died. After this unprovoked assault, they demanded Miles McDonell, the governor, who was delivered, and subsequently carried to Montreal. This step did not at all satisfy the traders of the North-west Company, but as soon as the governor was carried off toward Canada by Duncan Cameron, his partner, Alexander McDonell, commenced new aggressions, such as seizing the horses, driving off the cattle, and pillaging the farms of the colonists. Opposite the settlement he erected a battery, upon which he mounted two of the Selkirk field-pieces, and established a camp of about fifty or sixty of the Canadian servants, clerks, and bois brulés.

Dispirited by constant annoyance, the broken-hearted settlers sent word to the head of the North-west Company, that they would leave their farms and homes in a few days. About this time, toward the latter part of the pleasant month of June, two Ojibway chiefs arrived with forty braves, and strange as it may seem, they offered to escort the persecuted colonists with their property to Lake Winnipeg. Guarded by the grim children of the forest from the assault of their foes, they, like the Acadian peasants in Evangeline, were " friendless, hopeless, homeless."

[1] Earl of Selkirk's statement.

"Driving in ponderous wains, their household goods to the sea-shore,
Pausing, and looking back to gaze once more on their dwellings,
Ere they were shut from sight, by the winding road, and the woodland;
Close at their sides, their children ran, and urged on the oxen,
While in their little hands they clasped some fragments of playthings."

After they had embarked in the boats, "sheeted smoke with flashes of flame intermingled," announced that the mill and their houses were fired by the torch of the incendiary.

When the fugitives from persecution had been sometime at the northern extremity of Lake Winnipeg, Colin Robertson, of the Hudson Bay Company, arrived, and offered to lead them back to the settlement from which they had been expelled. Accepting his proposal, they returned, and were soon augmented by a party of emigrants just arrived from the Highlands of Scotland. During the winter of 1810, a majority remained at the mouth of the Pembina river, in Minnesota, for the purpose of hunting the buffalo. But early in the spring they returned to the Kildonan settlement.

In the spring of 1816, Duncan Cameron, who had returned, was arrested by Colin Robertson, and taken towards the coast of Hudson's Bay, for the purpose of being sent to England for trial.

The Earl of Selkirk, hearing of the distressed condition of his colony, sailed for America, and on his arrival at New York, in the fall of 1815, heard that they had been bribed or compelled to leave the settlement.

Proceeding to Montreal, he found some of the settlers who had been under the influence of the North-west Company, in great poverty. While here he gained the information that a remnant of the colony had returned and re-established themselves, and immediately sent an express to announce his arrival and determination to be with them in the spring. These glad tidings were sent by Laguimoniere, who, in the depths of winter, had travelled on foot from the Red River, by way of Red Lake and Fond du Lac, Minnesota, to bring the intelligence to Montreal that the colony had reoccupied their settlement.

The messenger never reached his destination with the kind words of Selkirk. In the night he was way-laid near Fond du Lac, brutally beaten, and robbed of his canoe and despatches. At a council held by the superintendent of Indian affairs, at Drummond's Island, on the twenty-second of July, 1816, an Ojibway chief of Sandy Lake, Minnesota, stated that Grant, one of the North-west Company, offered him two kegs of rum, and two carrots of tobacco, if he would send some of his young men in search of some persons taking despatches to Red River, and pillage the letters and papers. Shortly after this, the chief testified that Laguimoniere was brought in by a negro and a party of Ottawas.

Failing to obtain military aid from the British authorities in Canada, Selkirk made an engagement with four officers and eighty privates, of the discharged Meuron regiment, twenty of the De Watteville, and a few of the Glengary Fencibles, which had served in the late war with the United States, to accompany him to Red River. They were to receive monthly wages for navigating the boats to Red River, to have lands assigned them, and a free passage if they wished to return.

When he reached Sault St. Marie, he received the intelligence that the colony had again been destroyed.

In the spring of 1816, Semple, a mild, amiable, but not altogether judicious man, the chief governor of the factories and territories of the Hudson Bay Company, arrived at Red River. In the month of April he sent a Mr. Pambrun to a trading post on a neighbouring river, and as he was returning with five boats, a quantity of furs, and six hundred bags of pemmican, he was attacked, on the twelfth of May, by an armed party of the adherents of the North-west Company, and captured. This act was in retaliation for the attack made by Robertson on their post, at the junction of the Red and Assineboine rivers, during the previous autumn. On the eighteenth of June a portion of this party left Fort Qui Appele, under the guidance of Cuthbert Grant, Lacerte, Frazer, Hoole, and Thomas McKay, and went toward Red River. Information had been brought by friendly Indians and others, that an attack was intended, and an almost constant watch was kept up night and day, to discover the approach of any of the parties of the enemy. About five o'clock in the afternoon, on the nineteenth of June, a man in the watch-house of the fort of the Selkirkers, called out to Governor Semple that horsemen were approaching. The governor, perceiving with a spy-glass sixty or seventy men, ordered twenty men to accompany him, and meet them. After Semple had proceeded half a mile, some of the settlers were met moving toward the fort, saying that a party was coming with cannon. One of the governor's party was requested to go back and obtain a field-piece from the fort. As the messenger was returning with the cannon, Governor Semple was surrounded. The hostile party first sent forward the reckless son of a Montreal tavern-keeper, to inquire what the governor was about. Semple inquired what his party wanted? Boucher insultingly asked, "Why did you, rascal! destroy our fort?" The governor, laying hold of his horse's bridle, said, "Scoundrel! do you talk thus to me?" Instantly

Boucher sprang from his horse, and the firing commenced. Semple was soon wounded, and called to his men to take care of themselves; but they gathered in a knot around their bleeding leader, and while they collected, the North-west party fired a volley, by which the greater part were instantly killed. The remnant called for mercy, but in vain; all were massacred but four or five. Among those who were spared, was John Pritchard. In his narration he remarks, that " the knife, axe, or ball put an end to the existence of the wounded, and on the bodies of the dead were practised all those horrible barbarities, which characterize the inhuman heart of the savage. The amiable and mild Mr. Semple, with broken thigh, lying on his side, supporting his head upon his hand, said to Grant, the leader of the attacking party, 'I am not mortally wounded, and if you could get me conveyed to the fort, I think I should live.' Grant promised he would do so, and immediately left him in the care of a Canadian, who afterwards told, that an Indian of their party came up and shot Mr. Semple in the breast. I entreated Grant to procure me the watch or even the seals of Mr. Semple, for transmitting them to his friends, but I did not succeed. Our force amounted to twenty-eight persons, of whom twenty-one were killed."

The Indian who killed the kind-hearted Semple was an Ojibway of Minnesota. Schoolcraft, in 1832, says, he saw, at Leech Lake, Majegabowi, the man who had killed Governor Semple, after he fell wounded from his horse.

The morning after the massacre, Grant and Bourassa, with sixteen or seventeen others, insisted upon the abandonment of Fort Douglas, and the settlement.

Two days afterwards the settlers, to the number of two hundred, including women and children, were compelled to embark in boats, to be conveyed to the sea-coast. On the second day's voyage they were met by Norman McLeod, a partner of the North-west Company, with nine or ten canoes, and a batteau with two pieces of artillery, formerly belonging to the Selkirk settlement, and a hundred armed men. As his party perceived the settlers they raised the warwhoop, and McLeod inquired whether Robertson or Semple was in the boats. Informed of the death of the governor, they broke open his trunks, and took his papers.

On his way to Red River, McLeod held a council with the Ojibways at Rainy Lake, and persuaded the Round Lake Chief and some fifteen or twenty others to join his party. Among those who accompanied McLeod in the capacity of clerk was Charles de Reinhard, once a sergeant in the De Meuron regiment. He was sent to a station of the company, at "Bas de la riviere Winipic." In August some deserters from the employ of Owen Keveny, a Hudson Bay trader, arrived there. They told McLeod that they had been badly treated, and he deputed Reinhard to act as constable and seize seize Keveny.

Six bois brulés accompanied him, and he soon returned with the trader, who was then placed in a canoe with three half-breed voyageurs, and consigned to Fort William on Lake Superior. On their way they were met by a partner of the North-west Company, who removed the half-breeds and substituted two Canadians and an Indian, who was to act as guide. The canoe was again met by traders of the company, who ordered them back. The two Canadians, on their return, quar reled with the Indian who left them, and losing their way, they landed Keveny on a small island and deserted him.

Mr. McLellan now started in search of the missing party, and first found the Indian and two Canadians, and at last Keveny, who was with an encampment of Indians. McLellan apprehended him, and purchasing a canoe placed him alone in company with Reinhard, a bois brulé, and an Indian. He then told Reinhard to put Keveny to death at the first favourable spot. A short distance above a deep gorge of granite through which the Winnipeg river rushes, the traveller used to pass a cross, which marked the spot where Keveny's life was taken.

It seems, from the confession of Reinhard, that he had desired to go on shore for a few moments, and when he was returning to the canoe, the half-breed took aim and shot him through the neck. As he fell against the canoe, Reinhard, seeing that he wished to speak, drew his sword, and twice plunging it in his back, soon rendered him speechless.

Joining their employer McLellan, they detailed the circumstances, and a distribution of his bloody clothes and other effects took place. McLellan, opening the writing desk of the murdered man, spent the night in reading and burning his letters and papers. Reinhard, after a protracted trial in Canada, was convicted and executed. During the trial stress was laid upon the question, whether the scene of the murder was in the province of Upper Canada. After much testimony from the best geographers in the country, it was decided that the limits of Canada did not extend to that point.

Previous to the intelligence of the death of Governor

Semple, the Earl of Selkirk had made arrangements to visit his colony by way of Fond du Lac, the St. Louis river, and Red Lake of Minnesota; but he now changed his mind, and proceeded with his force to Fort William, the chief trading post of the North-west Company on Lake Superior; and apprehending the principal partners, warrants of commitment were issued, and they were forwarded to the attorney-general of Upper Canada.

While Selkirk was engaged at Fort William, a party of emigrants in charge of Miles McDonnel, governor, and Captain D'Orsomen, went forward to reinforce the colony. At Rainy Lake they obtained the guidance of a man who had all the characteristics of an Indian, and yet had a bearing which suggested a different origin. By his efficiency and temperate habits, he secured the respect of his employers, and on the Earl of Selkirk's arrival at Red river, his attention was called to him, and in his welfare he became deeply interested. By repeated conversations with him, memories of a different kind of existence were aroused, and the light of other days began to brighten. Though he had forgotten his father's name, he furnished sufficient data for Selkirk to proceed with a search for his relatives. Visiting the United States in 1817, he published a circular in the papers of the Western States, which led to the identification of the man.

It appeared from his own statement, and those of his friends, that his name was John Tanner, the son of a minister of the gospel, who, about the year 1790, lived on the Ohio river, near the Miami. Shortly after his residence there a band of roving Indians passed near the house, and found John Tanner, then a little boy, filling his hat with walnuts which he had picked from a tree. Seizing him, they kept him quiet by threats, and fled. The party was led by an Ottawa Indian, whose wife had lost a son. To compensate for his death, the mother begged her husband to capture one about the same age. To accomplish this was the object of the Indian's visit to the white settlements, and great was the joy of the wife, when he brought her the desired gift. Adopted into the tribe, Tanner grew up as an Indian, and became expert with the gun, and noted for bravery. In time the band with which he was connected wandered into the Red River country. Declining the position of chief which was offered to him, he was esteemed by all of his companions. After Lord Selkirk found his relatives he visited them, but soon returned to the Indian country.

The harvest of 1817 was luxuriant; the seed that had been sown proved good seed, bearing forty and sixty fold, but so little had been sown that it again became necessary for the settlers to pass the winter in hunting.

From Pembina they proceeded into the open prairies of North-western Minnesota, to join a camp of Indian and half-breed hunters. Unprovided with snow shoes, the road was truly a "via dolorosa." Without a particle of food remaining, the half-starved colonists at last reached the long-sought camp.

The night of their arrival was Christmas eve of 1817, and the Indians and mixed bloods were touched by their haggard faces, and shared with them their own scanty fare. The buffalo this winter was very scarce, and the Scotch dragged through it, a set of mere camp slaves.

With the mild rays of the spring of 1818, hope revived, and once more they trudged back to their settlement. They worked with pleasant anticipations as they beheld first the blade, then the ear develope; but, one afternoon, just as the harvest was ripe, and they were about to put in the sickle, "behold, the Lord formed grasshoppers, in the beginning of the shooting up of the latter growth,"[1] and their joy was turned to mourning. The air was filled with these insects; "the earth did quake before them, like the noise of chariots on the tops of the mountains, or like the noise of a flame of fire that devoureth the stubble," was the sound of their movements. When the next morning arose, it was " a day of darkness and of gloominess; a day of clouds and thick darkness," and strong men were bowed down; and, like the Hebrew captives, by the waters of Babylon, they lifted up their voices and wept.

The next year the calamity was worse. "They were produced in masses, two, three, and four inches in depth. The water was infected by them. Along the river they were to be found in heaps like sea-weed, and might be shovelled with a spade. Every vegetable substance was either eaten up, or stripped to the bare stalk; the leaves of the bushes, and the bark of the trees, shared the same fate; and the grain vanished as fast as it appeared above ground. Even fires, if kindled out of doors, were immediately extinguished by them."[2]

The old Highlander understood, as he never had before, the imagery of the prophet, which he had often read in his well-thumbed Bible, for truly "the land was as the garden of Eden before them, and behind them a

---

[1] Amos, chap. vii., verse 2. Joel, chap. ii.   [2] Ross.

desolate wilderness, nothing did escape them." They ran upon the wall; they climbed up on the houses; they entered in at the windows like a thief.

With the whole head sick, and the whole heart faint, the brawny Scotchmen sought once more the plains of Minnesota, and became sons of Nimrod, chasing the deer and the buffalo. But, when they reflected upon the influence of this "vagabond" life upon their children, they were impelled by their consciences to make one more attempt to establish a home for their wives and little ones.

During the winter of 1819-20, a deputation of their number, mounted on snow shoes, passed through the then wilderness of Minnesota, and came to Prairie du Chien, a journey of a thousand miles, to purchase wheat for seed.

In 1820, on the fifteenth day of April, three Mackinaw boats, manned with six hands each, laden with two hundred bushels of wheat, one hundred bushels of oats, and thirty bushels of peas, under the charge of Messrs. Graham and Laidlaw, left Prairie du Chien for Selkirk's colony, on the Red River of the North. Detained by ice at Lake Pepin, they planted the May pole thereon. On the third of May, the boats passed through the lake. The voyage was continued up the Minnesota to Big Stone Lake, from which a portage was made into Lake Traverse, a mile and a half distant, the boats being placed on wooden rollers. Then descending the Sioux Wood river to the Red river, the party arrived at Pembina in safety, with their charge, on the third day of June. Pembina was, at that time, as now, a small hamlet, the rival companies of the North-west and of Hudson's Bay having each a trading post, at the confluence of the stream with the Red river, but on opposite sides. The crop at Selkirk's colony having entirely failed the previous year, the grain was much needed for seed the ensuing season. The trip performed in these boats is worthy of mention, as it is the only instance of heavy articles being transported the entire distance from Prairie du Chien to the Red River settlement, with the exception of the portage between Big Stone and Traverse Lakes by water. Charles St. Antoine, who was one of the crew, is now a citizen of Dahkotah county, and is one of the few survivors of that eventful voyage. The party returned across the plains on foot as far as Big Stone Lake, from which point they descended to Prairie du Chien in canoes.[1]

The cost of this expedition was about six thousand dollars, and was borne by Lord Selkirk.

In 1820, Captain R. May, a citizen of Berne, in the British service, was commissioned by Selkirk to visit Switzerland, and engage persons to repair to his colony.

After years of bloodshed, heart burnings, fruitless litigations, and vast expense, the strife was concluded by compromise. In the year 1821, the two companies, in the language of the articles of settlement, finding " that the competition in the said trade had been found for some years, then past, to be productive of great inconvenience and loss, not only to the said company and association, but to the said trade in general, and also of great injury to the native Indians, and of other persons his Majesty's subjects," they did enter into an agreement for putting an end to competition, and carrying on the trade together.

[1] Sibley's Historical Society Address.

CHAPTER XVI.

THE rumour that Lord Selkirk was founding a colony on the borders of the United States, and that the Hudson Bay Company had posts within the region of country comprised within the boundaries of Minnesota, did not fail to reach the authorities at Washington.

Under the administration of Mr. Monroe, the head of the war department was the intellectual and distinguished John C. Calhoun. At that period he was deeply interested in developing the resources of every section of the Union. During his term of office, the efficiency of the army was increased; the condition of the aborigines noted, and the power of the United States felt in remote regions where it had not been acknowledged.

On the tenth of February, 1819, an order was issued from the war department, concentrating the Fifth Regiment of Infantry at Detroit, with a view to transportation by way of Fox and Wisconsin rivers to Prairie du Chien. After garrisoning that post and Rock Island, the remainder were to proceed to the mouth of the Minnesota, then designated the Saint Peter's, to establish a post at which the head-quarters of the regiment were to be located. About the time of this order, the portion of Illinois territory not included within the state of that name, was attached to Michigan, of which Lewis Cass was governor.

In the spring of 1819, the county of Crawford was organized, which included a large portion of Minnesota. Colonel Leavenworth, with the troops on their way to build the new post at the junction of the Minnesota, brought blank commissions for county officers to be filled up by the inhabitants. With difficulty officers were obtained. Johnson, United States factor, was made Chief Justice of the County Court, and his associates were Michael Brisbois and Francis Bouthillier; Wilfred Owens was appointed Judge of Probate; John S. Findley, Clerk of the Court, and Thomas McNair, Sheriff.

Colonel Leavenworth, having attended to his duties at the Prairie, ascended the Mississippi with his soldiers in keel-boats. The water was so low at that period, that for weeks they "dragged their slow length along," not reaching Mendota until September, the contemplated site for temporary barracks, the remains of which are visible above the present village of Mendota, on the south side of the river. The officers with their wives lived in the boats until rude huts and pickets were erected. Before the quarters were completed, the rigour of winter was felt, and the removal from the open boats to the log cabins, plastered with clay, was considered a privilege. Though the first winter was extremely cold, the garrison remained cheerful, and the officers maintained pleasant social intercourse.[1] During

---

[1] Mrs. Ellet, in a sketch of the wife of the first commissary of this post, says: "Huts had also to be built, though in the rudest manner, to serve as a shelter during the winter, from the

the winter, that dreadful disease, scurvy, appeared among the troops, and raged so extensively, that for a few days military duty was suspended. It is said that "so sudden was the attack, that soldiers apparently in good health when they retired at night, were found dead in the morning. One man who was relieved from his tour of sentinel duty, and stretched himself upon a bench, when he was called four hours after to resume his duties, was found lifeless."[1]

The colonel at this time displayed his humanity, and, with a few friends, spent several days searching the country for antiscorbutics.

In the month of May, 1820, they entered into summer encampment at a spring not far from the old Baker trading house. The camp was named Cold Water. On the tenth of September the corner stone of Fort Snelling was laid. The winter of 1820–21 found them again at the cantonment on the south side of the river; the present fort not being sufficiently advanced for occupation by the troops. The first pine lumber ever

rigours of a severe climate. After living with her family in the boat for a month, it was a highly appreciated luxury for Mrs. Clark to find herself at home in a log hut, plastered with clay, and chinked for her reception. It was December before they got into winter quarters, and the fierce winds of that exposed region, with terrific storms now and then, were enough to make them keep within doors as much as possible. Once in a violent tempest, the roof of their dwelling was raised by the wind, and partially slid off; there was no protection for the inmates, but the baby in the cradle was pushed under the bed for safety. Notwithstanding these discomforts and perils, the inconveniences they had to encounter, and their isolated situation, the little party of emigrants were not without the social enjoyments; they were nearly all young married persons, cheerful, and fond of gayety, and had their dancing assemblages once a fortnight."

[1] Sibley's Address before Minnesota Historical Society.

cut on Rum River was by soldiers for the use of the fortifications.

On the eighteenth of November, 1819, Governor Cass addressed a communication to Mr. Calhoun, secretary of war, proposing an exploration of the territory recently attached to Michigan, for the purpose of becoming better acquainted with the Indian tribes, and its mineral and agricultural resources. The suggestions were approved, and on the morning of July fifth, 1820, the expedition, on the forty-third day of their journey by the lakes from Detroit, entered the St. Louis river of Minnesota. The expedition consisted of Governor Cass, Dr. Wolcott, Indian agent at Chicago and surgeon, Captain Douglass, military engineer, H. R. Schoolcraft, mineralogist, Lieutenant Mackay, James Doty, Esq., secretary, Major Forsyth, private secretary to the governor, C. C. Trowbridge, topographer, besides the voyageurs, soldiers, and Indians, amounting in all to about forty persons.

Three miles above the mouth of the St. Louis they came to an Ojibway village of fourteen lodges. Among the residents were the children of an African, by the name of Bungo, the servant of a British officer who once commanded at Mackinaw. Their hair was curled and skin glossy, and their features altogether African. A short distance above there was the abandoned establishment of the old North-west Company.

On the evening of the first day's ascent of the stream, the expedition lodged at the American Fur Company's houses, twenty-four miles from the lake. The establishment consisted of a range of log buildings, enclosing three sides of a square, open towards the river, and contained the warehouse, canoe and boat yard, and dwelling-house of the resident clerk. The company had also three horses, two oxen, three cows, and four bulls at this post.

On the fifteenth of the month they arrived at Sandy Lake, and were received at the post of the American Company, in the temporary absence of the trader Morrison, by two of his clerks. They occupied the establishment of the old North-west Company, which was built in 1794, and has been described in a previous chapter. On the appearance of the exploring party, in accordance with custom, the Sandy Lake Ojibways saluted them with a discharge of fire-arms loaded with balls.

The population of the Indian village at that time was one hundred and twenty, and their principal men were Broken Arm and De Breche.

On the sixteenth a council was held, and Governor Cass proposed that they should send a deputation of their best men to the mouth of the Minnesota, and conclude a peace with the Dahkotahs, to which they cheerfully consented. The next day the officers of the expedition, with nineteen voyageurs and Indians, and provisions for twelve days, left the post with a view to exploration of the Upper Mississippi. On the nineteenth, the atmosphere in the region of Pokeguma Rapids was so cold that the canoes in the morning were coated with a scale of ice. On the twenty-first of July they reached Upper Red Cedar Lake, which they considered the true source of the Mississippi, and named Cass Lake.

On the north shore of the lake was a village of sixty Ojibways, of whom Wiscoup, or the Sweet, was the chief. Here were found two employees of the Fur

Company, one of whom, during the previous winter, having been caught in a snow storm, had his feet frozen so badly that they had sloughed off. For a time his Indian wife felt an interest in his sad condition, and supported him by catching fish; but at last he became a weariness to her, and she deserted. For months, as he was unable to walk, he had subsisted upon the coarse weeds about his hut.

The expedition discovered him seated on a mat of rushes, in a cabin of bark, with the stumps of his legs wrapped in deer skins. With long beard, sunken eyes, hollow cheeks, and bones ready to protrude through the skin, he was more to be pitied than Job. In the words of the patriarch, his "flesh was clothed with worms and clods of dust; his skin was broken and loathsome; by night he was full of tossings to and fro unto the dawning of the day." The sympathies of the whole party were aroused, and Governor Cass took means to make him comfortable, and have him transported to the Fur Company's post at Sandy Lake.

The next day they commenced the descent of the river, and returned to Sandy Lake on the afternoon of the twenty-fourth. On the twenty-fifth, with a delegation of Ojibways, they entered the canoes once more, and steered towards the fort at the mouth of the Minnesota. The twenty-eighth was passed in hunting buffalo, between Elk river and the Little Falls. Having spent several hours in hunting, they descended the river until three o'clock, when they landed again to hunt at the site of a recent Dahkotah encampment. In the centre of the deserted camp, on a long pole, was a letter of birch bark, addressed to the Ojibways, in which they were informed that a peace party, at the solicitation of the commander of the fort, had proceeded to that spot, but not finding any of their nation, had returned.

On the afternoon of the thirtieth, they reached the garrison at "Camp Cold Water," near the present St. Louis House, near Fort Snelling, and Governor Cass was received with the customary national salute. They found here a busy scene: officers and their men were all occupied. In addition to building the fort, ninety acres of ground were under cultivation, and the soil proved very fertile. Green peas had been ready for the table on the fifteenth of June; the corn was ripe on the fifteenth of July, and the wheat was now ripe for the harvest.

On the first of August, at the winter barracks on the south side of the Minnesota, which were then being occupied by Taliaferro as an Indian agency, a council was held with the Dahkotahs and Ojibways. Governor Cass, Colonel Leavenworth, and other officers represented the United States. Shokpay and other chiefs spoke for the Dahkotahs, and Babasikumsiba for the Ojibways. Though the Dahkotahs agreed to a cessation of hostilities against the Ojibways, they were very indifferent, and some of the chiefs and braves refused to smoke the pipe of peace.

On the second of August, the party continued their descent of the Mississippi, and visited the cave near the upper limits of the city of Saint Paul, which they were erroneously told was "Carver's Cave."[1] Four miles below, at a point now called Pig's Eye, they found the village of Little Crow. "Here," says Schoolcraft, in his narrative of the expedition, is a "Sioux (Dahkotah)

[1] Carver's cave, is in the lower suburb.

band of twelve lodges, and consisting of about two hundred souls, who plant corn on the adjoining plain, and cultivate the cucumber and pumpkin. They sallied from their lodges on seeing us approach, and manifested the utmost satisfaction in our landing. Le Petit Corbeau was among the first to greet us. He is a man below the common size, but brawny and well proportioned; and although rising of fifty years of age, retains the looks and vigour of forty. There is a great deal of fire in his eyes, which are black and piercing. His nose is prominent and has the aquiline curve, his forehead falling a little from the facial angle, and his whole countenance animated, and expressive of a shrewd mind. We were conducted into his cabin, which is spacious, being about sixty feet in length and thirty in width, built in a permanent manner of logs, and covered with bark. Being seated, he addressed Governor Cass in a speech of some length, in which he expressed his satisfaction in seeing him there, and said that in his extensive journey, he must have experienced a good many hardships and difficulties, and seen a great deal of the Indian way of living. He said he was glad that the governor had not, like many other officers and agents of the United States, who had lately visited those regions, passed by without calling. He acquiesced in the treaty which had lately been concluded with the Chippeways, and was happy that a stop had been put to the effusion of human blood. He then adverted to a recent attack of a party of Fox Indians upon some of their people towards the sources of the river Minnesota, in which nine men had been killed. He considered it a dastardly act, and said that if that little tribe should continue to haunt their territories in a hostile manner, they would at length drive him into anger, and compel him to do a thing he did not wish."

The next day they arrived at the village of Remnichah, or Red Wing. Tatankimani, or the Walking Buffalo, one of the signers of the treaty of friendship at Portage des Sioux, in 1815, was the principal man, and about sixty years of age. One of his granddaughters married a Mr. Crawford, who was a prominent British trader during the war of 1812.

On the afternoon of the fourth, they stopped a few minutes at Wapashaw village, the site of the town of Winona; and on the evening of the fifth, their canoes grated on the pebbly banks of the village of Prairie du Chien. At this point Colonel Snelling was met on his way to relieve Lieutenant-Colonel Leavenworth of the command of the troops at Camp Cold Water, opposite Mendota. His wife, a few days after her arrival at the post, gave birth to the first infant of white parents in Minnesota, which, after a brief existence of thirteen months, departed to a better land. The dilapidated monument which marks the remains of the "little one," is still visible in the grave-yard of the fort. Beside Mrs. Snelling, the wife of the Commissary, and of Captain Gooding, were in the garrison, the first American ladies that ever wintered in Minnesota.

Shortly after Colonel Snelling assumed command of the garrison, the Dahkotahs appeared unfriendly. A large body of warriors under the leadership of the celebrated Yankton Wanata, hovered around the barracks for some time, and at last the chief presented himself at the gates, ostensibly desiring to have a friendly talk with the commander. The gates were opened, and sufficient information having been obtained to warrant the suspicion that they meditated an attack, he and his companions were seized, and marched to the council hall under a guard of glittering bayonets. In the council chamber his treachery was fully exposed, and he was deprived of his badges and medals which he had received from the British, and they were destroyed in his presence. In their mortification, the Indians with the chief gashed their flesh with knives. By this decided step, Wanata was impressed with the folly of opposing the United States troops, and from that time showed himself friendly to all American officers with whom he was brought in contact.

Not far from this period two soldiers were shot by a party of Sissetoan Dahkotahs, near Council Bluffs, on the Missouri. The United States authorities, to compel the surrender of the murderers, notified the Sissetoan bands, that no traders should visit them till the guilty ones were delivered.

Deprived of blankets, powder, and tobacco, they held a council, at Big Stone Lake, to determine what should be done, and listened to the arguments of a trader named Colin Campbell. Mahzah Khotah, and another of the band, announced themselves as the guilty ones, and expressed a willingness to deliver themselves to the soldiers, at the mouth of the Minnesota. The aged father of the latter then offered himself as a substitute, which was agreeable to the council. The next day Mahzah Khotah, and the old man, started for the garrison, accompanied by friends and relatives.

On the twelfth of November, 1820, when about a mile distant, the party halted, smoked, and the death dirge was chanted. Blackening their faces, and gashing their arms, as a token of grief, they formed a procession, and marched to the centre of the soldier's parade ground. First came a Sissetoan, bearing a British flag, and then one of the murderers and the aged chief, who had become an atonement for his only son. Their arms were secured by ropes of buffalo hair, and large splinters of oak were thrust through the flesh, above the elbows, to indicate their contempt of death. As they approached, singing death-songs, a company of soldiers was drawn up, and Colonel Snelling came out to meet them. A fire was then kindled, and the British flag burned, after which the medal of the murderer was given up, and then both surrendered themselves. The old chief was detained as a hostage, and the murderer sent to St. Louis, for trial.[1] Placed in a boat, he was rowed by

---

[1] The following letter addressed to the secretary of war, contains most of the facts narrated.

"CANTONMENT ST. PETER'S, November 13, 1820.

"Sir—when I had the honour to address you on the tenth, from the disposition then manifested by the Sussitongs, I had no hope of obtaining the surrender of the murderers of our people on the Missouri, but contrary to my expectation, one of the murderers, and an old chief self-devoted in the place of his son, were voluntarily brought in and delivered up yesterday.

"The ceremony of delivery was conducted with much solemnity. A procession was formed at some distance from the garrison, and marched to the centre of our parade. It was preceded by a Sussitong bearing the British flag; the murderer and devoted chief followed with their arms pinioned, and large splinters of wood thrust through them above the elbows, to indicate as I understood their contempt of pain and death. The relatives and friends followed, and on their way joined them in singing their death-song. When they arrived in front of the guard the British flag was laid on a fire, prepared for the occasion, and consumed; the murderer gave up his medal, and both the prisoners were surrendered. The old chief I have detained as a hostage, the murderer I have sent to St. Lewis, under a proper guard, for trial, presuming it is a course you will approve.

"I am much indebted to Mr. Colin Campbell, the interpreter, for his great exertions in bringing this affair to a speedy issue. The delivery of the murderer is to be solely attributed to his influence over the Sussitongs."

soldiers to the place of destination, but no witness appearing against him, he was discharged, and while returning, is said to have been killed by a frontiersman, in Missouri.

In 1822 a man by the name of Perkins, of Kentucky, obtained permission of Taliaferro, the agent for the Dahkotahs, to build a saw-mill in the Chippeway valley. His partners were Lockwood and Rolette, of Prairie du Chien. For the privilege of cutting timber they agreed to pay Wapashaw's band, who claimed the country, one thousand dollars annually, in goods. The spot selected for the mill, was on a small stream running into the Menomonee, about twenty miles from its mouth.

After the coalition of the two great British Fur Companies, some of those who had been in their service, Renville, Jeffries, McKenzie, and others, in company with a few American traders, formed a new company called the Columbia, whose central establishment was at Lake Traverse. They were licensed by the proper authorities, to trade with the Indians south of the British boundary line. The only rival in the trade, was the American Fur Company.[1] They also had a trading-post on the Minnesota, about a mile above Fort Snelling.

[1] One of their number furnished to the historian of Long's expedition, the following statement of the amount of furs formerly obtained in this region.

Names.	No. of packs.	No. of skins, or wt. of each pack.	Value of pack.	Total.
Beaver	10	100 lbs. weight	$400	$4000
Bear,	20	12 skins	75	1500
Buffalo,	400	10 skins	40	16,000
Martin,	10	100 lbs.	300	3000
Otter	10	100 lbs.	600	6000
Fisher	25		450	11,250
Elk,	40	16 skins	80	3200

FIRST MILL IN MINNESOTA.

It was during this year, the fort being sufficiently completed for occupancy, that the first mill in Minnesota was erected. It was built under the supervision of officers of the fort, on the site of Minneapolis, and was guarded by a sergeant and a few privates.

Joseph R. Brown, now a well known public-spirited citizen, at this time a soldier in the army, in company with a son of Colonel Snelling, and one or two others, explored the rivulet that supplies the cascade of Minne Ha-Ha, as far as Lake Minne Tonka.

The settlers at the Selkirk colony were, as has been seen, reduced to great straits. Owing to their fratricidal strife agriculture had been neglected, and at one time they were forced to live upon salt and lettuce.

Among others at Pembina was a trader by the name of Hess, who, finding provisions scarce, determined to go and join a party who had gone out on a buffalo hunt. He commenced his journey with two daughters and two other settlers. As he had married an Ojibway woman, he travelled through the Dahkotah country with the greatest precaution, knowing the hereditary feud that existed between the nation of his mother's children and

Name.	No. of packs.	No. of skins.	Value of pack.	Total.
Mynx,	10		$200	$2000
Muskrat,	40	500 skins	200	8000
Lynx,	20		280	5600
Swan,	2	60 skins	60	120
Rabbit,	4	400 skins	8	32
Wolverine,	1	400 skins		75
Cowskins,	20	16 skins	80	1600
Wolves,	10		40	400
Moose,	10		80	800
Fox,	5		260	1300
	637			$64,877

the Dahkotahs. On the sixth day of the journey he left his companions to chase some buffaloes that were in sight. He did not return for some time, but after a long ride across the prairie he saw the primitive cart in which his family had travelled, and hoped to find them and recount his success in the hunt. On his approach he found one of his companions scalped, and deprived of both his feet. A few steps beyond, lay one of his beloved daughters with a knife lodged in her heart. He then discovered the lifeless form of his other fellow-traveller, but could not find his second daughter.

Horrified and helpless he returned to Pembina, after travelling three days and three nights on foot, without a morsel of food. Reciting his melancholy story, the settlers were seized with a panic, and not one would accompany him to the scene of slaughter and bury the dead.

Obtaining an intimation that one daughter yet lived, a captive in a Yankton lodge, with the energy of despair he started for the camp, determined to rescue her or to die in the attempt. After a long tramp he descried the cone-shaped teēpeē, and before he reached the spot a Yankton accosted him and asked whether he was a friend or foe. Hess, nerved to the highest physical courage, said, "You know me as your foe; you know me by the name of Standing Bull; you know you have killed one of my daughters and taken the other prisoner." The Dahkotah was impressed by his fearlessness, and extended his hand, and, taking him to the camp, all complimented him. Finding his daughter, he was cheered to learn that she had been treated with kindness. Her owner was at first unwilling to release her, but at last consented for a certain ransom.

Seeking the neighbouring trading posts of the Columbia Fur Company, the traders sympathized with him, and furnished him the necessary amount of goods on a long credit, and bearing the merchandise to the camp, the Dahkotah, true to his word, delivered the daughter; but now the maiden had become attached to those with whom she had been dwelling, and reluctantly left their lodges.

On the appearance of spring in the year 1823, a number of emigrants who had been induced by the prospectus of the Earl of Selkirk's agent to leave their mountain homes in Switzerland, and settle in the valley of the Red river, determined to seek the United States. After a long journey from Pembina, by way of Lake Traverse, they reached what is now Fort Snelling, in a state of great destitution, and were there aided by the officers of the garrison.[1]

---

[1] "In 1823, news was brought by the traders that two white children were with a party of Sioux on the St. Peter's. It appeared from what they could learn, that a family from Red river—Selkirk's settlement—had been on their way to the fort, when a war party of Sioux met them, murdered the parents and an infant, and made the boys prisoners. Col. Snelling sent an officer with a party of soldiers to rescue the children. After some delay in the ransom, they were finally brought. An old squaw, who had the youngest, was very unwilling to give him up, and indeed the child did not wish to leave her. The oldest, about eight years old, said his name was John Tully, and his brother, five years old, Abraham. His mother had an infant, but he saw the Indians dash its brains out against a tree, then killed his father and mother. Because he cried they took him by his hair, and cut a small piece from his head, which was a running sore when he was retaken. Col. Snelling took John into his family, Major Clark the other, but he was afterwards sent to an orphan asylum in New York. The eldest died of lockjaw, occasioned by a cut in the ankle while using an axe. His death-bed conversion was affecting and remarkable. One day, after he had been ill several weeks, he said, 'Mrs. Snelling, I have been a very wicked boy; I once tried to poison my father because he said he would whip me. I

It was during this year that it was demonstrated that it was practicable to navigate the Mississippi from St. Louis to the junction of the Minnesota river. Previously it had been supposed that the rapids at Rock Island would prove an insurmountable barrier. On the second of May, according to a printed announcement, the Virginia, a steamer one hundred and eighteen feet in length and twenty-two in width, drawing six feet of water, left her moorings at the St. Louis levee destined for Fort Snelling.

Among the passengers were Major Taliaferro, the agent of the Dahkotahs; Beltrami, an Italian Count, once a judge of the Royal Court, then a political refugee;[1] Great Eagle, a Sauk chief, returning to his

stole a ring from you which you valued much, and sold it to a soldier, and then I told you a lie about it. I have given you a great deal of trouble. I have been very wicked. I am going to die the day after to-morrow, and don't know where I shall go. Oh, pray for me.'

"His benefactress answered, 'John, God will forgive you, if you repent; but you must pray too, for yourself. God is more willing to hear than we are to pray. Christ died to save just such a sinner as you are, and you must call upon that Saviour to save you.' All his sins appeared to rise before him as he confessed them, and he seemed to feel that he was too great a sinner to hope for pardon. Mrs. Snelling read to him, and instructed him. He never had received any religious instruction, except in the Sunday school taught by Mrs. Clark and herself, and being accustomed to say his prayers with her children, and always be present when she read the church service on Sundays. The next morning after the above conversation, when she asked him how he had rested during the night, he said, 'I prayed very often in the night; I shall die to-morrow, and I know not what shall become of me.' For several hours he remained tranquil, with his eyes closed, but would answer whenever spoken to; then suddenly he exclaimed, 'Glory! glory!' His friend said, 'John, what do you mean by that word?' 'Oh! Mrs. Snelling, I feel so good—I feel so good! Oh! I cannot tell you how good I feel.' "
—Mrs. Snelling's Reminiscences in "*Pioneer Women of the West.*"

[1] "An Italian gentleman came on the boat, who professed to be travelling for the purpose of writing a book, and brought letters of introduction from Mrs. Snelling's friends in St. Louis. The colonel

village from a conference with Governor Clark; and a family from Kentucky, with their children, guns, chests, cats, dogs, and chickens, emigrating to Galena, which was then the extreme frontier. At Dubuque, the Indians held possession of their mines, and watched all who visited them with a jealous eye.

After the steamer had passed the mouth of the Upper Iowa, a grand illumination greeted the appearance of the "great fire canoe," as it glided along the confines of Minnesota. An eye-witness writes: "It was perfectly dark, and we were at the mouth of the river Ioway, when we saw at a great distance all the combined images of the infernal regions in full perfection. I was on the point of exclaiming with Michael Angelo, 'How terrible! but yet how beautiful!'

invited him to his house to remain as long as he pleased, and he was with them several months. He could not speak English, but spoke French fluently, and seemed much pleased when he found his fair hostess could speak the language, she having learned it when a child at St. Louis. A French school was the first she ever attended, and she thus early acquired a perfectly correct pronunciation. She lamented on one occasion to Mr. Beltrami, that her teacher had received his discharge, and was about leaving, and he politely offered his services in that capacity. She was then translating the life of Cæsar in an abridged form, and from the emotion betrayed by the foreigner at a portion of the reading, it was concluded he had been banished from the Pope's dominions at Rome, and that the lesson reminded him of his misfortunes. The passport he showed, gave him the title of 'Le Chevalier Count Beltrami.'

"When at the fort he was busy in collecting Indian curiosities. One day he brought a Sioux chief into Mrs. Snelling's room, who had on his neck a necklace of bears' claws highly polished, saying, 'I cannot tempt this chief to part with his necklace; pray see what you can do with him, he will not refuse you.' 'He wears it,' answered the lady, as a trophy of his prowess, and a badge of honour; however, I will try.' After some time, Wanata said, 'On one condition I will consent: if you will cut off your hair, braid it, and let it take the place of mine, you may have the necklace.' All laughed heartily at the contrivance to get rid of further importunity."—Mrs. Snelling's Reminiscences in *"Pioneer Women of the West."*

"The venerable trees of these eternal forests were on fire, which had communicated to the grass and brushwood, and these had been borne by a violent northwest wind to the adjacent plains and valleys. The flames towering above the tops of the hills where the wind raged with most violence, gave them the appearance of volcanoes at the moment of their most terrific eruptions; and the fire, winding in its descent through places covered with grass, exhibited an exact resemblance to the undulating lava of Etna or Vesuvius. Almost all night we travelled by the light of this superb torch."

The arrival of the Virginia at Mendota, is an era in the history of the Dahkotah nation, and will probably be transmitted to their posterity as long as they exist as a people. They say that some of their sacred men, the night before, dreamed of seeing some monster of the waters, which frightened them very much.

As the boat neared the shore, men, women, and children beheld with silent astonishment, supposing that it was some enormous water spirit coughing, puffing out hot breath, and splashing water in every direction. When it touched the landing their fears prevailed, and they retreated some distance, but when the blowing off of steam commenced they were completely unnerved: mothers forgetting their children, with streaming hair, sought hiding-places; chiefs, renouncing their stoicism, scampered away like affrighted animals.

The peace agreement between the Ojibways and Dahkotahs, made through the influence of Governor Cass, was of brief duration, the latter being the first to violate the provisions.

On the fourth of June, Taliaferro,[1] the Indian agent among the Dahkotahs, took advantage of the presence of a large number of Ojibways to renew the agreement for the cessation of hostilities. The council hall of the agent was a large room of logs, in which waved conspicuously the flag of the United States, surrounded by

[1] Mr. Taliaferro was the first Indian agent in Minnesota, and what is remarkable, he held the office for twenty-one years. Having left the country in 1840, he visited it in 1856, and contributed the annexed reminiscences to the Pioneer and Democrat newspaper, published at St. Paul:—

"It may not be deemed out of place at this period in the rapid and unprecedented growth of cities, towns, hamlets, and population in Minnesota, to refer to, and present date in reference to some of the historical reminiscences of the past.

"There were two expeditions organized—that for the 'Yellow Stone,' in 1818, under Colonel Atkinson, and the second in 1819, under Lieutenant-Colonel Leavenworth, of the Fifth Infantry, to the Falls of St. Anthony, which latter expedition cantoned at the entry of the river St. Peter's, and their first monthly report was dated September thirtieth, 1819. The object of these military movements during the administration of President Monroe, was to open the country to the fur trade, and extend protection to our hitherto defenceless frontiers, north and west. Your humble writer was selected by the president from the army, on the twenty-seventh of March, 1819, and appointed the pioneer Agent for Indian Af-

fairs for the North-west, and established his agency near the Minnesota, and continued his arduous, delicate, and responsible duties under several successive administrations of the General Government, down to the year 1840, when—though appointed for the *sixth term*—he declined longer service, from a rapid decline in health. .

" In the summer of the year 1820, Colonel Snelling relieved Lieutenant-Colonel Leavenworth from the command of what was then called ' Fort St. Anthony,' though not a stone had been set for the permanent work. This was left for the action of the gallant Snelling, who, as acting Assistant Quartermaster, set all hands at work, and laid the corner stone of Fort Snelling on the tenth day of September, 1820, with due ceremonies, in presence of the civil and military officers of the post and several citizens. It is known that in 1805, Pike procured from the Sioux (the chief, 'Little Crow' being present) a cession of nine by eighteen miles, wintered his men below the Sauk Rapids, and returned to St. Louis in the spring of 1806. In excavating the foundation of the circular battery in rear of the commanding officer's quarters, at the foot of a small oak tree, a workman found a black bottle, and upon being

British colours and medals that had been delivered up from time to time by Indian chiefs.

Among the Dahkotah chiefs present were Wapashaw, Little Crow, and Penneshaw; of the Ojibways there were Kendouswa, Moshomene, and Pasheskonoepe. After mutual accusations and excuses concerning the

placed in the hands of Colonel Snelling it was found to contain a synopsis of the grant made to the United States by the Indians.

"To recount all those thrilling incidents, which occurred in the course of the first twenty-one years on this then remote frontier, would fill a volume from our seventeen manuscript journals, in the hands of a ready writer. We would remark upon the ever memorable days the twenty-seventh and twenty-eighth of May, 1827, when the Sioux, shortly after nightfall, fired into the lodges of a party of Chippewas encamped below, and in front of the Agency, killing and wounding some eight or nine—and for this unprovoked attack we caused the offenders to be forthwith given up for this outrage, and insult to our flag and neutrality—and four Sioux were shot, within two hundred paces from the spot on which we now pen this sketch of facts.

"We thought nothing of taking a crew of brave Medawakantons, with Mr. Alexander Farribault as a companion, and passing down to Dubuque, and rescuing a Yankton Sioux prisoner the Sacs and Foxes had captured in 1823,—performing this act of humanity in a few days; evading the vigilance of a party of the Sac braves despatched to intercept and cut us off. It was a dangerous effort, but we determined to risk our lives to save that of a human being, and we landed safely at St. Peter's, and in due season, despatched her off safely to her friends and family on the Des Moines.

"Some are curious to learn how certain locations received designated names. Minnehaha was first indicated as the Little Falls, then as Brown's Falls, in honour of Major General Brown. Lake Calhoun for the distinguished Secretary at the head of the War Department, and other smaller lakes, Harriet, Eliza, Abigail, Lucy, &c., after the ladies of the civil and military officers of the post.

"The first measured distance from Fort Snelling to Fort Crawford (Prairie du Chien), was measured in February, 1822, by Quartermaster Sergeant Heckle, with a perambulator on a wheel, which reported the distance by a sharp crackling every few hundred yards; it was invented by this good old German soldier. The distance was 204 miles.

"Could we write without the use of the personal pronoun, a more connected history of former years might be noted; but in conclusion, it is due the Sioux of your territory to record one fact as to them, and that is, from infraction of the previous treaty, the Dahkotahs lighted the calumet, they having been the first to infringe upon the agreement of 1820. After smoking, and passing the pipe of peace to the Ojibways, who passed through the same formalities, they all shook hands as a pledge of renewed amity.

The morning after the council, Flat Mouth, the distinguished Ojibway chief, arrived, who had left his lodge vowing that he would never be at peace with the Dahkotahs. As he stepped from his canoe, Penneshaw held out his hand, but was repulsed with scorn. The Dahkotah warrior immediately gave the alarm, and in a moment runners were on their way to the neighbouring villages to raise a war party.

On the sixth of June, the Dahkotahs had assembled, stripped for a fight, and surrounded the Ojibways. The latter, expecting the worst, concealed their women and children behind the old barracks which had been used by the troops while the fort was being erected. At the solicitation of the agent and commander of the fort, the Dahkotahs desisted from an attack and retired.

On the seventh, the Ojibways left for their homes; but, in a few hours, while they were making a portage at St. Anthony, they were again approached by the

the commencement of our agency to its close, our frontier pioneers were never even molested in their homes, nor did they shed one drop of American blood; while the Chippewas, Winnebagoes, and Sacs and Foxes, were in the yearly habit of the most revolting and foul murders on all who unfortunately fell in their war path.

"We were in St. Paul on the twenty-fourth of June, the 'widow's son' was Irving's Rip Van Winkle; after a nap of fifteen years, we awoke in the midst of *fast* times. We truly felt bewildered when we found all the haunts and resting-places of the once noble sons of the forest, covered by cities, towns, and hamlets. We asked but few questions, being to our mind received as a strange animal, if nothing worse."

Dahkotahs, who would have attacked them, if a detachment of troops had not arrived from the fort.

A rumour reaching Penneshaw's village that he had been killed at the falls, his mother seized an Ojibway maiden, who had been a captive from infancy, and, with a tomahawk, cut her in two. Upon the return of the son in safety he was much gratified at what he considered the prowess of his parent.

CHAPTER XVII.

THE interesting information procured by the expedition of Lewis and Clarke to the tributaries of the Missouri and Rocky Mountains, and that of Governor Cass through the north-eastern district of Minnesota, induced the United States government to send an expedition to explore the Minnesota river, and the country situated on the northern boundary of the United States between the Red river of Hudson's Bay, and Lake Superior.

The command of the expedition was intrusted to Major Stephen H. Long, and the scientific corps attached were Thomas Say, zoologist and antiquary, William H. Keating, mineralogist and geologist, Samuel Seymour, landscape painter and designer. Late at night, on the second of July, 1823, they arrived at Mendota opposite the fort, and slept in the open air.

On the morning of the third, Colonel Snelling and the five companies of the 5th Infantry, within the fort, were much surprised by the appearance of the exploring party; and, on the afternoon of the ninth of July, they commenced the exploration of the valley of the Minnesota.

Joseph Renville, a bois brulé, after whom one of the counties of the state is named, acted as interpreter and guide; and Joseph, a son of Colonel Snelling, was assistant interpreter, and Beltrami, the Italian refugee, was permitted to accompany the party. To make the examination as accurate as possible, a portion proceeded by land, and a portion in canoes. On the first evening the river detachment encamped near Oanoska, the village known as Black Dog's. The next morning they breakfasted at Penneshaw's. At dinner time they were at Shokpay, called by the French Prairie des Français; this, as well as the other villages, was tenantless, the inhabitants being absent on a hunt.

On the fourteenth, at Traverse des Sioux, the land and river detachments met, and after a reduction of the number of soldiers they united and proceeded by land, having in possession twenty-one horses. They travelled on the south side of the Minnesota, and at the mouth of the Mahkahto passed the residence of the Sissetoan band, one of whose number, in 1820, had been sent to St. Louis to be tried for murdering a white man.

On the twenty-second they arrived at Big Stone Lake, which is considered the source of the Minnesota. Following up the bed of a dried-up stream, they found Lake Traverse, three miles distant. Here they were impressed by beholding within sight the sources of two vast streams, the one discharging its waters in Hudson's Bay, the other in the Gulf of Mexico. At Big Stone Lake, for the first time since leaving the fort, they discovered a large party of Dahkotahs, and, by invitation, the expedition visited their lodges at the lower end of the lake. Upon an island in the lake this band cultivated corn. After being feasted, the party proceeded in the afternoon to a trading post of the American Fur Company, in charge of Mr. Moore, where presents of tobacco were distributed. The traders of the Columbia Fur Company, at Lake Traverse, received the party with a salute, and exhibited the most hospitable disposition. Keating, the historian of the expedition, remarks:—

"The principal interest which we experienced in the neighbourhood of Lake Travers, was from an acquaintance with Wanotan,[1] the most distinguished chief of the Yanktoanan tribe, which, as we were informed, is subdivided into six bands. He is one of the greatest men of the Dahkotah nation, and although but twenty-eight years of age, he has already acquired great renown as a warrior. At the early age of eighteen, he exhibited much valour in the war against the Americans, and was wounded several times. He was then inexperienced and served under his father, who was chief of his tribe, and bore a mortal enmity to the Americans. Wanotan has since learned to form a better estimate of our nation. He is aware that it is the interest of his people to remain at peace with us, and would, probably, in case of another war between the United States and England, take part with the former. Those who know him well, commend his sagacity and judgment, as well as his valour. He is a tall man, being upwards of six feet high; his countenance would be esteemed handsome in any country; his features being regular and well shaped. There is an intelligence that beams through his eye, which is not the usual concomitant of Indian features. His manners are dignified and reserved; his attitudes are graceful and easy, though they appear to be somewhat studied. When speaking of the

[1] This chief's name is spelled Wahnahtah, Wanata, Wanotan.

Dahkotahs, we purposely postponed mentioning the frequent vows which they make, and their strict adherence to them, because, one of the best evidences which we have collected on this point, connects itself with the character of Wanotan, and may give a favourable idea of his extreme fortitude in enduring pain. In the summer of 1822, he undertook a journey, from which, apprehending much danger on the part of the Chippewas, he made a vow to the Sun, that, if he returned safe, he would abstain from all food or drink, for the space of four successive days and nights, and that he would distribute among his people all the property which he possessed, including all his lodges, horses, dogs, etc. On his return, which happened without accident, he celebrated the dance of the Sun; this consisted in making three cuts through his skin, one on his breast, and one on each of his arms. The skin was cut in the manner of a loop, so as to permit a rope to pass under the strip of skin and flesh which was thus divided from the body. The ropes being passed through, their ends were secured to a tall vertical pole, planted at about forty yards from his lodge. He then began to dance round this pole, at the commencement of his fast, frequently swinging himself in the air, so as to be supported merely by the cords which were secured to the strips of skin cut off from his arms and breast. He continued this exercise with few intermissions, during the whole of his fast, until the fourth day about ten o'clock, A. M., when the strip of skin from his breast gave way. Notwithstanding which he interrupted not his dance, although supported merely by his arms. At noon the strip from his left arm snapped off. His uncle then thought that he had suffered enough; he drew his knife and cut off the skin from his right arm, upon which Wanotan fell to the ground and swooned. The heat at the time was extreme. He was left exposed in that state to the sun until night, when his friends brought him some provisions. After the ceremony was over, he distributed to them the whole of his property, among which were five fine horses, and he and his two squaws left his lodge, abandoning every article of their furniture.

"As we appeared upon the brow of the hill which commands the company's fort, a salute was fired from a number of Indian tents which were pitched in the vicinity, from the largest of which the American colours were flying. And as soon as we had dismounted from our horses, we received an invitation to a feast which Wanotan had prepared for us. The gentlemen of the company informed us that as soon as the Indians had heard of our contemplated visit, they had commenced their preparations for a festival, and that they had killed three of their dogs. We repaired to a sort of pavilion which they had erected by the union of several large skin lodges. Fine buffalo robes were spread all around, and the air was perfumed by the odour of sweet scenting grass which had been burned in it. On entering the lodge we saw the chief seated near the further end of it, and one of his principal men pointed out to us the place which was destined for our accommodation: it was at the upper end of the lodge; the Indians who were in it taking no further notice of us. These consisted of the chief, his son, a lad about eight years old, and eight or ten of the principal warriors. The chief's dress presented a mixture of the European and aboriginal costume; he wore moccasins and leggings of splendid scarlet cloth, a blue breech-cloth, a fine shirt of printed muslin, over this a frock coat of fine blue cloth with scarlet facings, somewhat similar to the undress uniform coat of a Prussian officer; this was buttoned and secured round his waist by a belt. Upon his head he wore a blue cloth cap, made like a German fatigue cap. A very handsome Mackinaw blanket, slightly ornamented with paint, was thrown over his person. His son, whose features strongly favoured those of his father, wore a dress somewhat similar, except that his coat was party-coloured, one half being made of blue, and the other half of scarlet cloth. He wore a round hat, with a plated silver band, and a large cockade. From his neck were suspended several silver medals, doubtless presents to his father. This lad appeared to be a great favourite of Wanotan's, who seems to indulge him more than is customary for the Indians to do. As soon as we had taken our seats, the chief passed his pipe round, and while we were engaged in smoking, two of the Indians arose and uncovered the large kettles which were standing over the fire, they emptied their contents into a dozen of wooden dishes which were placed all round the lodge. These consisted of buffalo meat boiled with tepsin, also the same vegetable boiled without the meat, in buffalo grease, and finally, the much esteemed dog meat, all which were dressed without salt. In compliance with the established usage of travellers to taste of everything, we all partook of the latter with a mixed feeling of curiosity and reluctance. Could we have divested ourselves entirely of the prejudices of education, we should doubtless have unhesitatingly acknowledged this to be among the best meat that we had ever eaten. It was remarkably fat, was sweet and palatable. It had none of that dry, stringy character, which we had expected to find in it, and it was entirely destitute of the strong taste which we had apprehended that it possessed. It was not an unusual appetite, or the want of good meat to compare with it, which led us to form this favourable opinion of the dog, for we had, on the same dish, the best meat which our prairies afford; but so strongly rooted are the prejudices of education, that, though we all unaffectedly admitted the excellence of this food, yet few of us could be induced to eat much of it. We were warned by our trading friends that the bones of this animal are treated with great respect by the Dahkotahs; we therefore took great care to replace them in the dishes; and we are informed that, after such a feast is concluded, the bones are carefully collected, the flesh scraped off from them, and that, after being washed, they are buried in the ground, partly, as it is said, to testify to the dog species, that in feasting upon one of their number, no disrespect was meant to the species itself; and partly also from a belief that the bones of the animal will rise and reproduce another one. The meat of this animal, as we saw it, was thought to resemble that of the finest Welsh mutton, except that it was of a much darker colour. Having so far overcome our repugnance as to taste of it, we no longer wonder that the dog should be considered a dainty dish by those in whom education has not created a prejudice against this flesh. In China it is said that fattened pups are frequently sold in the market place; and it appears that the invitation to a feast of dog meat is the greatest distinction that can be offered to a stranger by any of the Indian nations east of the Rocky Mountains."

On the morning of the fifth of August, the expedition arrived at Pembina, a corruption of Anepeminan, an Ojibway word,[1] and were kindly received by Mr. Nolen. This had been the upper settlement of the Selkirk colony, and the Hudson Bay Company had maintained a post here until a few months before the visit of Major Long. Observations made by their own astronomers, led to the supposition that it was within the American boundary line. At the time of the exploration, there were about three hundred and fifty half-breeds residing in fifty or sixty log huts.

The next day after the arrival of the expedition, the buffalo hunters returned from the chase. "The procession consisted of one hundred and fifteen carts, each loaded with about eight hundred pounds of the finest buffalo meat; there were three hundred persons including the women." The number of horses was about two hundred. Twenty hunters mounted on their best steeds rode in abreast, firing a salute as they passed the American camp.

Major Long and his party remained several days, determining the boundary line of the United States. "A flag-staff was planted, which after a series of observations, made during four days, was determined to be in latitude 48° 59' 57½", north. The distance to the boundary line was measured off, and an oak post fixed on it, bearing on the north side the letters G. B., and on the south side those of U. S."

On the eighth of August the United States flag was hoisted on the staff, a national salute fired, and a proclamation made in the presence of all the inhabitants, that all the country on the Red river, above that point,

[1] Pronounced as if written Pembin- naw. Anepeminan, is a red berry, known to botanists as *Viburnim oxycoccos*.

was within the territory of the United States. As far as practicable the expedition commenced their return, along the northern boundary line of what is now Minnesota. At Rainy Lake they found John Tanner, of whom mention has been made in another chapter, and the father of that erratic bois brulé James Tanner, so well known to the older residents of Minnesota, severely wounded, and in a tent attended by two half-breed daughters. An Indian had shot him, and the ball had passed through the right arm and breast. At his request he was transferred to the camp of the expedition. The evening preceding the departure from Rainy Lake, his daughters went over to the Hudson Bay trading-post, to visit an old half-breed woman; but they never returned. All efforts to find them were unavailing, and the father, who was taking them to Mackinaw, to attend a mission school, seemed much distressed. After travelling a few miles with the party, the pain from his wounds was so great, that it was necessary to leave him in the care of one of the employees of the trading-post. It is a little remarkable that Tanner should also have disappeared as mysteriously as his daughters.[1]

At Pembina, Joseph Snelling left the expedition and returned to the fort, his services as interpreter not being needed beyond that point.

Beltrami, the Italian, who had become obnoxious, also detached himself, and conceived the bold project of striking for the most northern point of the Mississippi river. With a "bois brulé," a mule, dog train, and two

[1] It is said that, on the day Mr. Schoolcraft's brother was found killed at Sault St. Marie, the log cabin of Tanner was burned down, and Tanner disappeared. If rightly informed, he had not long before threatened Mr. Schoolcraft.

Ojibways who were going to Red Lake to raise a war party to avenge the death of a companion who had been murdered by the Dahkotahs, he commenced his adventurous journey.

On the fifth day they arrived at Thief river, so called, it is said, from a Dahkotah who for years lurked in the marshes, robbing and scalping his foes as they would pass alone. At this point the half-breed returned with the mule and train to Pembina; and the Italian, finding no trading post here as anticipated, was obliged to proceed with the two Ojibways.

There is much egotism and gasconade in the writings of Beltrami, but it cannot be denied that the Italian was the first to make known to the world the most northern source of the Mississippi, and the region around Red Lake.

As the work written by this foreigner is little known, and not accessible to the general reader, large extracts will be given from his letters to a lady whom he addresses as the Countess:—

"I had been informed at Pembenar that a number of *Bois-bruilés* had proceeded to this confluence in order to erect huts for their winter-hunting establishment, and that some one of them would certainly be able to accompany me, and act as my interpreter, as far as Red Lake; and, if I desired it, still farther; but we found none there. The Cypowais had driven them away, as we were informed by one of the latter, and they were gone to establish themselves about a hundred miles lower down. On the other hand, my interpreter from Pembenar could not possibly continue with me: besides his having to conduct back the mule, other powerful reasons operated to prevent him. I was therefore compelled to decide; and I delivered myself over to the care of my two Indians.

"We had not again proceeded up the river more than two miles before they stopped, and presented an offering of dry provisions and tobacco to *Miciliki*, the Manitou of Waters. This was a stake painted red, and fixed under a kind of *sacellum*, like those of antiquity, and the ceremony is by no means modern. They were, for this once, more generous towards their deities than Indians in such circumstances generally are: the reason is, that their offering was at my expense.

"The frequent rapids which we had met with in the course of five or six miles, and which had compelled us to walk continually in the water, and over pointed and cutting rocks, in order to preserve our canoe from injury, had very much fatigued us, and our appetite also induced us to make a halt: we accordingly did so, and, after eating my repast, I went to sleep beneath a tree, recommending myself to the care of Providence.

"I was awakened by discharges of fire-arms, and, on starting up, perceived five or six Indians on the opposite bank of the river, apparently desirous to cross it. On seeing me they seemed struck with astonishment and terror, and fled with precipitation; one of our Indians was wounded. Those who had fired at them were Sioux. I was already known among the Indians of that nation as the *Tonka-Wasci-cio-honsca*, or *the Great Chief from a far country;* and my tall stature and noble horse had rendered me the more remarked by them, as these are two things of which they are extreme admirers. When they again saw me on this spot, they concluded that the whole expedition was there, and fled with all haste for fear of being recognised. This was the idea that first presented itself to my mind, and I instantly acted upon it. We jumped immediately into our canoe; I performed to the best of my power the labours of the wounded Indian, who had his left arm shot completely through, and his right shoulder grazed. The ball, however, had not touched the bone of the arm, and the wound in the shoulder had injured only the integuments. The juice of some boiled roots was applied as the healing balsam; the down of a swan-skin, which I had purchased at Pembenar, was substituted for lint, my handkerchief served for a bandage, and the bark of a tree called *owigobinigy,* or white wood, answered the purpose of securing the arm in a sling. We kept on our course till evening, and saw nothing more of them.

"My intrepid champions saw nothing but Sioux. The slightest sound from wind or water, the shadow of a tree or of a rock, everything was the Sioux. I discovered that they were plotting against me, for they carefully avoided my looks. I had not the slightest doubt that they meant to leave me on the spot, and determined therefore to make them re-embark, it being more easy to guard them in the canoe. About midnight we stopped. I had but little to fear, being left without my canoe, for I was already well aware that their intention must be to continue their course by land, by a route which would conduct them in two or three days to Red Lake; whereas, were they to proceed by the river they would require more than six. However, I considered that no precaution ought to be neglected by me; I therefore drew the canoe to land, and fastened it to a tree by a cord, one end of which I tied to my leg, and then laid myself down by the side of them in such a manner that they could not rise, even if I should be able to sleep, without waking me. These precautions, and my musket and my sword between my legs, ready for immediate use, kept them quiet the whole night.

"On the following morning they embarked without difficulty. But this was only with a view of reaching a certain point, whence the route by land was shorter. I might have used violence against them if I had chosen, for certainly I had no fear of them; I had even taken the precaution of putting water into their musket barrels: but I should only have exasperated their nation, in a territory where it was now absolute and despotic, and where I could expect no assistance but from my own energies and the care of Providence; I therefore suffered them quietly to go off. They intimated to me, what I was before well aware of, that they were going to leave me. They invited me to follow them, and to leave the canoe, provisions, and baggage, concealed in the brushwood. I deliberated with myself on the subject for a moment: I considered that the river was my best and surest way, that I was in possession of a canoe, provisions, a musket, a sword, and ammunition; whereas, by accepting their invitation, I should be following barbarians who had the cowardice to abandon a stranger, confided to their guardianship at Pembenar by their most intimate friends, one who had treated them as brothers, saved them from the hands of the enemy, healed their wounds, and assisted them kindly with all his means. I should, with wretches of this description, be exposing myself in inextricable forests, in the midst of swamps and lakes, and abandoning to the mercy of a thousand accidents, my baggage, my provisions, and materials for the presents, which are indispensable passports through a savage country. My determination, therefore, was soon fixed: after having vainly endeavoured to make them comprehend that both *Manitous* and men would punish such atrocity, I commanded them by words and signs peremptorily to be gone.

"I imagine, my dear Countess, that you will feel the frightfulness of my situation at this critical moment more strongly than I can express it. I really can scarcely help shuddering, as well as yourself, whenever I think of it. Fortunately, I was not at the time overpowered and confounded. Woe be to us, if in exigencies like this, despair takes possession of our minds. In that case all is completely over with us! * * *

"The solitude I now experienced, which romance-writers would not have found so pleasant and delightful as that which they have been pleased to exhibit in their fictions, impressed me at first with ideas the most dreadful. I must, said I to myself, leave this place some way or other; and I jumped into my canoe and began rowing. But I was totally unacquainted with the almost magical art by which a single person guides a canoe, and particularly a canoe formed of bark, the lightness of which is overpowered by the current, and the conduct of which requires extreme dexterity. Frequently, instead of proceeding up the river, I descended; a circumstance which by no means shortened my voyage. Renewed efforts made me lose my equilibrium, the canoe upset, and admitted a considerable quantity of water. My whole cargo was wetted. I leaped into the water, drew the canoe on land, and laid it to drain with the keel upwards. I then loaded it again, taking care to place the wetted part of my effects uppermost, to be dried by the sun. I then resumed my route.

"You sympathize with the embarrassment in which you conceive I must have been involved, with all my difficulties and want of means for continuing my course. I bore all, however, with great philosophy, and with a resignation which I believe you will readily admit is not very natural to me. I could scarcely help incessantly smiling. I threw myself into the water up to my waist, and commenced a promenade of a rather unusual kind, drawing the canoe after me with a thong from a buffalo's hide, which I had fastened to the prow. The first day of my expedition, the fifteenth of the month, was employed in this manner, and I did not stop till the evening.   *   *   *   *   *   *

"The weather on the second day of my progress was very disagreeable. A storm which commenced before mid-day continued till night. Notwithstanding this, however, I did not relax an instant but to take my food. I saw the hand of providence in the physical and moral vigour which supported me during this dreadful conflict. In the evening I had no access to a more comfortable hearth than on the preceding one. My bear skin and my coverlid, which constituted the whole of my bed, were completely soaked; and, what was worse, the mould began to affect my provisions. I was almost tempted to think that it was all over with my *promenades*, and that I began to *travel*, and that not very *comfortably*.

"On the morning ot the seventeenth of August, the sun's beams gilded the awful solitude by which I was surrounded, and I eagerly availed myself of their influence. I laid out my provisions, baggage, gun, and sword, and stretched myself also at full length under his rays. The powder, which had fortunately been closely confined in tin canisters, was the only thing that escaped the water.

"Necessity makes man industrious, and the necessity I was now under to become so, was great indeed, as otherwise it was impossible for me to continue my progress. The river became narrower and deeper the farther I ascended it, as is the case with all rivers originating in lakes. It was thus absolutely indispensable for me to learn how to guide the canoe with the oar. I set myself, therefore, to study this art in good earnest; and in the afternoon, when I struck my tent, I exerted myself first to pass several deep gulfs, and afterwards to traverse short stages or distances of the river; but the fatigue I endured was extreme, and I preferred returning to my drag-rope whenever the river permitted my walking in it. As appearances seemed to threaten rain, I covered my effects with my umbrella, stuck into the bottom of my canoe. It was singular enough to see them conveyed thus in the stately style and manner of China, while I was myself condemned to travel in that of a galley slave; nor could I help reflecting on those unfortunate victims of despotism which the *restoration* has condemned to drag the vessels on the Danube. As it was of consequence for me to avail myself of everything that could promote cheerfulness and keep up my spirits, I could not help smiling, which I am sure, my dear Countess, you would yourself have done, at the sight of my grotesque convoy. * * *

"The morning of the eighteenth awakened me to my active duties, and I proceeded in my course; and before mid-day fell in with two canoes of Indians. Being alone in a canoe of their nation, with three muskets (for those of my two Indians were in my possession), I might naturally have been apprehensive of exciting their most dangerous suspicions. But, heaven be praised, I entertained no apprehension whatever. I called to them with confidence, while they, struck with wonder at so extraordinary an object, halted on the opposite bank of the river. What astonished them most was my superbly conveyed baggage. They could form no idea of what *that great red skin* (my umbrella) could possibly be, nor of what was placed beneath it; and, observing me walking in the water, they perhaps imagined me to be their *Miciliki*. * * * * *

" I made them comprehend what had occurred to me, and that I wanted one of them to accompany me as far as Red Lake. At first they started immense difficulties; but a woman was captivated by the beauty of my handkerchief, which was hanging from my pocket; a lad was fascinated with the one I had about my neck, and an old man muffled up in a miserable ragged rug, which through its innumerable holes displayed nearly one-half of his person, had already cast his rapacious glance on mine; pretending to search for something in my portmanteau, a bit of calico which casually came to hand excited the full gaze of one of the young girls; and my provisions, which they had already tasted, strongly stimulated their gormandizing appetite: I satisfied the whole of them, and the old man decided to accept my proposal. He took the helm of my vessel, and we set off.

" This assistance extricated me from a situation which certainly was by no means pleasant, and it was so much the more valuable, as it would have been impossible for me to proceed alone, because the river was constantly increasing in depth. Notwithstanding this, however, my mind was in a state of incessant agitation as I proceeded, and I perceived its attention completely occupied about something which it left behind it with regret. It was no difficult matter for me to detect this secret. My mind was, in fact, adverting to the four days of its solitude and independence. I, at that moment, fully comprehended why the Indians consider themselves happier than cultivated nations, and far superior to them.

"It is difficult to meet with a rower as strong as my patriarchal companion, and we advanced at a rapid rate, without stopping, till the evening. Our table was furnished with a couple of ducks: I had fire to make a roast, and I shot them accordingly. Though my bed was without a coverlid (the cunning old fellow having left in his own canoe the one which I had given him), yet wrapping myself, like the Indians, in the skin I wore about me, I lay down to rest very comfortably. In the course of the night I was waked by my cautionary cord; and, at first, I imagined that my pilot was also going to desert me, but it turned out to be occasioned by some large animal who had taken a fancy to my provisions. I gently seized my gun, which I always keep at my side, and in an instant brought him down.

"My Indian, confounded by the report of fire-arms, thought he had been attacked by the Sioux, about whom, not improbably, he had been dreaming, and immediately betook himself to flight. I called out to him, I ran towards him to convince him of his error and restore his confidence, but the forest and darkness concealed him from my view, and thus in a moment my solitude and independence were renewed. However, I could still have smiled at the adventure, if such an expression of feeling had been at all seasonable.

"I waited for him in vain for the remainder of the night. Two discharges of the gun, however, which I fired off immediately, one after the other (considered by them as a signal of friendship), brought him back to his quarters with the dawn of day.

"We searched for the animal I had fired at, which it seems retained strength sufficient to drag itself to a few paces distance among the brushwood, to which traces of blood guided us; it proved to be a wolf. My companion refused to strip the animal of its skin, a superb one, viewing it at the same time with an air of respect, and murmuring within himself some words, the meaning of which will probably surprise you. In fact, the wolf was his *Manitou*. He expressed to it the sincerity of his regret for what had happened, and informed it that he was not the person who had destroyed it.

"On the 19th, my Mentor wanted to play me the trick of handing me over to the charge of another Indian whom he fell in with; but I gave him a frown, and he went on with me. We again made a good day's progress, to which I contributed by rowing to the best of my ability.

"Night arrived without his pausing in his exertions. He gave me to understand that it was indispensable for him to reach the destined place without delay, and appeared excessively eager to rejoin his canoes.

"Much fatigued, and shivering under a cold moist air, with which the night-dews in this country pierce to the very bones, I lay down under my bear skin to sleep. A distant sound awoke me, and I found myself alone in my canoe, in the midst of rushes. On turning my head,

I observed three or four torches approaching me. My imagination had at first transported me to the enchanted land of fairies, and I was in motionless expectation of receiving a visit from their ladyships, or of being addressed, like Telemachus, by the nymphs. They proved, however, to be female Indians, who came to convey my effects, and to guide me to their hut. My Charon, who from purgatory had conducted me to Hell, had applied to them for this purpose, and then hastened his return to his family, who were waiting for him where he first met with me. I was now at Red Lake, at the marshy spot whence the river springs, and about a mile from an Indian encampment.

"I was conducted to a hut covered with the bark of trees, like those which I have already described to you as belonging to the Cypowais, but on a larger scale. I there found fourteen Indians, male and female, nineteen dogs, and a wolf. The latter was the first to do the honours of the house; however, as he was fastened, he could not attack me so effectively as he was evidently desirous of doing, and merely tore my pantaloons, which were, indeed, the only pair I had still serviceable. This wolf was one of their household gods.

"The first two of the Indians that my eyes glanced on were my former treacherous companions: I appeared not to observe them. I desired the women to hang up my provisions to the posts which supported the roof, to preserve them from the voracity of the dogs; and, not having any power to help myself, I lay down in the corner assigned to me in this intolerably filthy stable. When I got up again, you will easily believe that I did not rise alone: thus I incurred an addition of wounds and inflictions on a body which the pointed flints and cutting shells of the river, and the boughs of trees, thorns, brambles, and mosquitoes, had previously converted into a Job.

"On the morning of the twentieth, I desired to be conducted to a bois brulé, for whom I had brought a letter from Pembenar. I was told that he resided at a distance, and that the waters of the lake were in a state of great agitation. I could not even obtain the favour of having him sent for, for this happened to be the day when it was the bounden duty of all the members of the hut to devote themselves to yelling, eating, drinking, and dancing, in commemoration of the Indian killed at the river Cayenne. I quitted the place, and offered the only handkerchief that I had remaining to the first Indian whom I met, and he immediately went off with my letter.

"The funeral ceremony presented nothing more extraordinary than what we have already seen, excepting the pillaging of my provisions in honour of the hero of the fête; and the convulsions of the father and mother composed to quietude by the blowings and exorcisms of the priests, and the wounds inflicted on the arms and legs, the contortions, yellings, and howlings of his relatives. * * * * * * *

"A party of the relatives and friends was gone on an expedition for discovering whether the Sioux had left no remains whatever on the spot where the tragedy had been acted, while my old friend the pilot, as herald-at-arms, had proceeded to rouse the vengeance and implore the succour of some Cypowais Jumpers, who were scattered in various spots about the forests. The doctrine of these Indians is strikingly singular: it is perhaps held by them only, of all mankind. For they seem to recognise rather the immortality of the body than of the soul.

"My bois brulé had now arrived. He was one of the numerous progeny scattered over the country by the vice and immorality of the fur traders. He is the son of a Canadian and a female Indian of the tribe of the Cypowais. * * * * *

"My bois brulé resides about twelve miles distant from this encampment to the south of the lake. The wind was too high for a canoe made of bark, and the lake too violently agitated; we were compelled, therefore, to disembark, and passed the night under an immense plane tree. This plane is, perhaps, the Colossus of the whole vegetable kingdom. The Indians adore it as a Manitou; the ancients would have done the same; and though I am myself a modern, I admire it as one of the most prodigious and most beautiful productions of nature.

"We arrived at his hut on the morning of the twenty-first. Misery might be said to be personified in his family, and in all by which he was surrounded; a wife (the daughter of a father she has never seen) nourishing an infant at her breast, but nearly destitute of nourishment herself, and five naked and famine-struck children, constituted the whole of his property. The uncertain fishery of the lake, and a small quantity of maize, in its green and immature state, furnish the whole means of their subsistence. They are neither civilized nor savage, possessing the resources of neither state, but every inconvenience and defect of both. The worst part of the case is, that this bois brulé has a great deal of natural talent, which serves only to render him more dangerous. He has been taught both to read and write, and has obtained that species of education which just serves to strengthen the innate evil propensities of the man, when unaccompanied by that moral training which is their proper curb and correction: in fact, the obliquity of his character has quite ruined him in the opinion of the traders who have successively employed him; and his crimes obliged him to abscond from Pembenar, where I was informed that I ought to be more on my guard against him than against the Indians themselves. I mention all these circumstances to you, my dear Countess, because, with the truest and noblest friendship, you are desirous of participating, as it were, in every description of danger incurred by me, and in order that those of our mutual friends who may be inclined to engage in the field of adventure like myself, may learn how to meet and overcome the various enemies they may have to encounter. * * *

"But we will now return to the Red river, from which we have somewhat, though not unnaturally, digressed, and which we have surveyed hitherto rather through the imagination than the senses.

"It presents no other extraordinary feature than the very frequent winding of its course, in which perhaps it is scarcely exceeded by the Meander itself. It waters a country uniformly level, and the rapids which we have seen do not lower its level but by the height of its banks. After Robber's river, as you ascend, no other river flows into it. This is more particularly to be noticed, because the English Hudson's Bay Company, according to their theories, have created on their map other Red rivers, with many more tributary streams flowing into it than this has.

"At the distance of about forty miles from the lake,

its banks are lined with impenetrable forests; above, the view is agreeably varied by smiling meadows and handsome shrubbery. On flowing from the lake it passes among rushes and wild rice. It is an error of geographers, founded on the vague information of Indians, that it derives its source from this lake; indeed, a lake which is formed by five or six rivers which flow into it can never be considered as itself the source of any single river. We shall soon have occasion to look farther for this source.

"The lake, by means of a strait, is divided into two ports, one to the north-east and the other to the south-west. Let us proceed to make the circuit of the last, which is certainly the most interesting.

"It receives on the western side the river Broachers (*Kinougeo-sibi*), and that of the Great Rock (*Kisciacinabed-sibi*); to the south, the river *Kahasinilague-sibi*, or Gravel river, near which the hut of my *Bois-brulé* guide is situated; that of *Kiogokague-sibi*, or Gold-fish river; and that of *Madaoanakan-sibi*, or Great Portage river; on the south-east, Cormorant river (*Cacakisciousibi*). A large tongue of land on the E. N. E. forms a peninsula about four miles in length, and of varying breadth, ending in a point towards the west. At a little distance, towards the north, there is another encampment of Indians, consisting of about three hundred persons, the chief of whom is the Grand Carabou (*Kisci-Adike*). The strait is situated to the N. N. E., and there is a small island in the midst of its waters dividing them into two. To the north we find another tongue of land, which serves also to separate the two lakes, and reaches as far as the strait, commencing at the spot whence, as we have seen, Red river, or (more properly speaking) Bloody river, proceeds. The other lake receives, on the east, Sturgeon river (*Amenikanins-sibi*). By the channel of this river, and by means of two portages, there is a communication with Rain river, from whence one can easily communicate with Lake Superior, to the south; and with the waters of Hudson's Bay, by the Lake of Woods, to the north. The waters which flow into Lake Superior on this side, may be considered as the sources of the river St. Lawrence.

"These two lakes are about one hundred and thirty miles in circumference; and Red river traverses about three hundred from the lake to Pembenar; but in a straight line the whole distance scarcely amounts to one hundred and sixty.

"How much has it cost me, my dear Countess, to write you these details! Perhaps as much as it will you to peruse them; for, like all women of spirit, you are fond of the brilliant and romantic. But our geographical friends would accuse me of negligence if I forgot them in a country completely unknown to them, and where no white man had previously travelled. * *

"In the course of an excursion which I made to the south-west, I discovered eight small lakes, undistinguished by names, which all communicate with each other, and of which Gravel river is the outlet. These lakes seem to have been negligently scattered by nature through a territory sometimes gloomy and sometimes gay, varied with hills and dales, and presenting to the eye landscapes the most delightful and enchanting. I resolved to pass a night amidst scenes so uncommonly charming, that I might enjoy as long as possible the exquisite impressions they made upon my mind and senses. I dedicated these lakes to the family to which

I am united by the most cordial friendship; and accordingly gave them the names of Alexander, Lavinius, Everard, Frederica, Adela, Magdalena, Virginia, and Eleonora. The purity of the waters of these lakes I considered a correct image of that of *their* minds; and their union, reminded me of the affection by which the members of this happy family are so tenderly connected.

"I returned to the encampment of Great Hare, to engage an Indian to attend me, together with my bois brulé guide, during the continuance of my excursion, and to purchase the canoe which was the scene of my tragi-comedy on Red river; for I was desirous of having it conveyed, if possible, to my rural cottage, and preserve it with my other Indian curiosities as a memorial and trophy of my labours in these my transatlantic *promenades.* * * * * * * *

"The river of Great Portage is so called by the Indians because a dreadful storm that occurred on it blew down a vast number of forest trees on its banks, which encumber its channel, and so impede its navigation as to make an extensive or great *portage* in order to reach it. The river thus denominated, however, is the true Red, or rather Bloody river. It enters the lake on the south, and goes out, as we have seen, on the northwest. This is the opinion of the Indians themselves, and it is not difficult to find arguments in support of it.

"According to the theory of ancient geographers, *the sources of a river which are most in a right line with its mouth should be considered as its principal sources, and particularly when they issue from a cardinal point and flow to the one directly opposite.* This theory appears conformable to nature and reason; and upon this principle we should proceed in forming the sources of the river of Great Portage. By the name *Portage*, is meant a passage which the Indians make over a tongue of land, from one river or lake to another, carrying with them on their backs their light canoes, their baggage, and cargoes.

"I left Red Lake on the morning of the twenty-sixth. The commencement of *Portage* is between the river so called and Gold-fish river. It is about twelve miles long; and I therefore engaged another Indian, with his horse, to effect it more conveniently. The country is delightful, but at times almost impenetrable. * *

"On the ensuing day, the twenty-seventh, I discharged the supernumerary Indian, with his horse; for, having no provisions but what we could procure by means of our guns, we were already three too many. We crossed the small lake strictly in the direction from north to south; and here we commenced another portage of four miles. * * * * * * *

"At the end of this *corvée* we found the Great Portage river. We embarked and proceeded up its current, crossing two lakes which it forms in its course, each about five or six miles in circumference, and containing patches of wild rice—unfortunately for us not yet ripe. We gave these lakes the name of *Manomeny-Kany-aguen*, or the Lakes of Wild Rice.

"After proceeding upwards of five or six miles, always in a southerly direction, we entered a noble lake, formed like the others by the waters of the river, and which has no other issue than the river's entrance and discharge.

"Its form is that of a half-moon, and it has a beautiful island in the centre of it. Its circumference is about twenty miles. The Indians call it *Puposky-Wiza-*

Kany-aguen, or the *End of the shaking Lands;* an etymology very correct, as nearly all the region we have traversed from the Lake of Pines may be almost considered to float upon the waters. * * * *

"I passed on this spot a part of the day of my arrival and the whole of the succeeding night. On the morning of the twenty-eighth, we resumed our navigation of the river, which enters on the south side of the lake.

"About six miles higher up we discovered its sources, which spring out of the ground in the middle of a small prairie, and the little basin into which they bubble up is surrounded by rushes. We approached the spot within fifty paces in our canoe.

"But now, my dear Countess, let me request you to step on quickly for a moment, pass the short portage which conducts to the top of the small hill, which overhangs these sources on the south, and transport yourself to the place where I am now writing. Here, reposing under the tree, beneath whose shade I am resting at the present moment, you will survey with an eager eye, and with feelings of intense and new delight, the sublime traits of nature; phenomena which fill the soul with astonishment, and inspire it at the same time with almost heavenly ecstasy! This is a work which belongs to the Creator of it alone to explain. We can only adore in silence his omnipotent hand. * *

"We are now on the highest land of North America, if we except the icy and unknown mountains which are lost in the problematical regions of the pole of that part of the world, and in the vague conjectures of visionary mapmakers. Yet all is here plain and level, and the hill is merely an eminence formed, as it were, for an observatory.

"Casting our eye around us, we perceive the flow of waters—to the south towards the Gulf of Mexico, to the north towards the Frozen Sea, on the east to the Atlantic, and on the west towards the Pacific Ocean. * * *

"You have seen the sources of the river which I have ascended to this spot. They are precisely at the foot of the hill, and filtrate in a direct line from the north bank of the lake, on the right of the centre, in descending towards the north. They are the sources of Bloody river. On the other side, towards the south, and equally at the foot of the hill, other sources form a beautiful little basin of about eighty feet in circumference. These waters likewise filtrate from the lake, towards its south-western extremity: and these sources are the actual sources of the Mississippi! This lake, therefore, supplies the most *southern* sources of Red, or, as I shall in future call it (by its truer name), Bloody river; and the most *northern* sources of the Mississippi—sources till now unknown of both.

"This lake is about three miles round. It is formed in the shape of a heart; and it may be truly said to speak to the very soul. Mine was not slightly moved by it. It was but justice to draw it from the silence in which geography, after so many expeditions, still suffered it to remain, and to point it out to the world in all its honourable distinction. I have given it the name of the respectable lady whose life (to use the language of her illustrious friend the Countess of Albany) was one undeviating course of moral rectitude, and whose death was a calamity to all who had the happiness of knowing her; and the recollection of whom is incessantly connected with veneration and grief by all who can properly appreciate beneficence and virtue. I have called the lake, accordingly, Lake Julia; and the sources of the two rivers, the Julian sources of Bloody river, and the Julian sources of the Mississippi, which, in the Algonquin language, means the Father of Rivers. Oh! what were the thoughts which passed through my mind at this most happy and brilliant moment of my life! The shades of Marco Polo, of Columbus, of Americus Vespucius, of the Cabots, of Verazani, of the Zenos, and various others, appeared present, and joyfully assisting at this high and solemn ceremony, and congratulating themselves on one of their countrymen having, by new and successful researches, brought back to the recollection of the world the inestimable services which they had themselves conferred on it by their own peculiar discoveries, by their talents, achievements, and virtues. * * * * * * * * *

"I find it impossible to become weary of examining and admiring the least objects of attention furnished by this scene. The majestic river, which embraces a world in its immense course, and speaks in thunder in its cataracts, is at these its sources nothing but a timid Naiad, stealing cautiously through the rushes and briars which obstruct its progress. The famous Mississippi, whose course is said to be twelve hundred leagues, and which bears navies on its bosom, and steamboats superior in size to frigates, is at its source merely a petty stream of crystalline water, concealing itself among reeds and wild rice, which seem to insult over its humble birth. * * * * * * * * *

"Neither traveller, nor missionary, nor geographer, nor expedition-maker, ever visited this lake. A great many of the stories which find their way into books are invented by the red men, either to deceive the whites,

or to conceal their own belief or their own weaknesses.
* * * The Indians themselves have confessed to me that, when they go down to the traders' settlements, they amuse themselves with gulling their credulity by a number of fables, which afterwards become the oracles of geographers and book-makers. * * * *

"On the fourth of September we struck our tents very early, and arrived in the evening at Red Cedar Lake, so called on account of the number of those beautiful trees, whose dark green foliage overshadows its islands and banks. * * * *

"This lake is the *non plus ultra* of all the discoveries ever made in these regions before my own. No traveller, no expedition, no explorer, whether European or American, has gone beyond this point; and it is at this lake that Mr. Schoolcraft fixed the sources of the Mississippi in 1819. For the more complete celebration of this fortunate discovery, this illustrious epoch, he rebaptized it by the name of Lake Cassina, from the name of Mr. Cass, Governor of Michigan territory, who was at the head of the expedition. Mr. Schoolcraft was the historiographer. * * * *

"At the bottom of this last lake, on the west, is found the entrance of a considerable river, which the Indians call *Demizimaguamaguensibi*, or the river of Lake Traverse. It issues from the lake (the second of that name), twenty miles above its mouth, on the northwest. This lake communicates, in the same direction, by a strait of two or three miles in length, with another lake, which the Indians call *Moscosaguaiguen*, or Bitch[1] Lake, which receives no tributary stream, and seems to draw its waters from the bosom of the earth. It is here,

[1] La Biche Lake, or Elk Lake.

in my opinion, that we shall fix the western sources of the Mississippi.[1] * * * *

"On the night of the seventh I slept at the mouth of Leech river. The lake whence it issues is a new Colchis, where a second Jason found, like the first, a golden fleece; where Mr. Pike fixed the sources of the Mississippi, fourteen years before Mr. Cass fixed them at Red Cedar Lake. This circumstance could not fail of exciting my curiosity, and I determined, in consequence, to go and view the scene which had given birth to the conjectures of the first of my two predecessors. * *

"On the ninth we arrived at Leech Lake (*Kaza-gasguaiguen*), at *Macuwa*, or Bear Island, where we found a considerable band of *Cypowais plunderers*, so denominated from their plundering and murdering the first Canadians who pushed their commerce to such a dangerous distance.

"This band is very numerous and warlike. I found it divided into two factions, one of which is actuated by the spirit of legitimacy, the other by its opposite. The *Pokeskononepe*, or Cloudy Weather, a usurper, contests the crown and empire with the chief *Esquibusicoge*, or Wide Mouth, who possesses them by hereditary right: but as these Indians, beyond all others, require for their head a daring and active man, who can conduct them to victory over the Sioux, by whom they are frequently harassed, instead of an idle and profligate poltroon, always reposing under the shade of his genealogical tree, and destitute of all merit but that allowed him by his flatterers, *Cloudy Weather* has the majority on his side. The government of the United States acknow-

---

[1] Nine years after this suggestion, Allen and Schoolcraft visited the western sources of the Mississippi.

ledges both: *Cloudy Weather*, because he declaims in their favour; and *Wide Mouth*, in order to detach him from the English, to whom he is friendly; but principally, I imagine, from the policy of keeping alive division in a band powerful in force but precarious in attachment. * * * *

"On my arrival among them they were in no little commotion on another subject, involving the two parties in new contention. Cloudy Weather's son-in-law had been killed a few days before by the Sioux, and they had at the same time received intelligence of the affair at Cayenne river, and of what had happened to my two Indians on Bloody river. Wide Mouth demanded an immediate war, and was desirous of forming an army, of which he himself never constituted any part. Cloudy Weather, who is not deficient in sense, suspected that this warlike ardour, this extraordinary eagerness and zeal, were assumed with a view to remove him out of the way, and turn his absence to his injury; and therefore, although the principal person aggrieved, strongly recommended *prudence* and *moderation*. * *

"I was a spectator of the funeral ceremony performed in honour of the manes of Cloudy Weather's son-in-law, whose body had remained with the Sioux, and was suspected to have furnished one of their repasts. What appeared not a little singular, and indeed ludicrous in this funeral comedy, was the contrast exhibited by the terrific lamentations and yells of one part of the company, while the others were singing and dancing with all their might. I was scarcely able several times to refrain from laughing; but the ceremony having some resemblance to the usages of the ancients, who also on such occasions paid and employed together *Tibicenes* and *Præficæ*, my respect for antiquity and antiquaries enabled me to preserve my gravity. At another funeral ceremony for a member of the *Grand Medicine*, and at which, as *a man of another world*, I was permitted to attend, the same practice occurred. But, at the feast which took place on that occasion, an allowance was served up for the deceased out of every article of which it consisted, while others were beating, wounding, and torturing themselves, and letting their blood flow both over the dead man and his provisions, thinking possibly that this was the most palatable seasoning for the latter which they could possibly supply. His wife furnished out an entertainment present for him of all her hair and rags, with which, together with his arms, his provisions, his ornaments, and his mystic medicine bag, he was wrapped up in the skin which had been his last covering when alive. He was then tied round with the bark of some particular trees which they use for making cords, and cords of a very firm texture and hold (the only ones indeed which they have), and instead of being buried in the earth, was hung up to a large oak. The reason of this was, that as his favourite Manitou was the eagle, his spirit would be enabled more easily from such a situation to fly with him to Paradise. Here again we perceive another trait of antiquity, and a rich relish for our antiquarian amateurs, whom, I think, I must at length have completely satisfied. The oak is also among the Indians the tree consecrated to the eagle, that is to say, to Jupiter.

" Mr. Pike, who was at the head of the expedition, despatched by the government of the United States in 1805, to discover the sources of the Mississippi, fixes them at this lake, although the river Leech which flows into it on the N.N.W., ascends more than fifty miles higher up; and although various other rivers, the courses of which are as yet unknown, equally flow into this lake. But it was in winter; the cold was excessively severe, and it is no pleasant or easy matter to discover sources through ice. It is impossible to doubt, that, at a different season of the year, and with a less embarrassing party, Mr. Pike would have pushed his discoveries farther. He was a bold and enterprising man; and his expedition to New Mexico, and his glorious death in the field of honour, merit a place in history. He will always be entitled to the distinction of having been the first who extended his researches so far in regions so wild and repulsive, and that at a time when there existed no fort whatever on the Mississippi."

The following letter, written by William Morrison, an old trader, to his brother, Allan Morrison, published in the Annals of the Minnesota Historical Society for 1856, shows that the lakes of the Upper Mississippi were visited early in the present century by those engaged in Indian commerce:—

"Dear Brother,—In answering your favour of the tenth January, I will pass several incidents that I presume you are well informed of, and give you the time and circumstances that led me to be the first white man that discovered the source of the great Mississippi river. I left Grand Portage, on the north shore of Lake Superior, now the boundary line between the United States and the British Possessions, in the year 1802, and landed at Leech Lake in September or October, the same year. I wintered on one of the streams of the Crow Wing, near its source. Our Indians were Pillagers. In 1803 and 1804, I went and wintered at Rice

Lake. I passed by Red Cedar Lake, now called Cass Lake, followed up the Mississippi to Cross Lake, and then up the Mississippi again to Elk Lake, now called Itasca Lake, the source of the great river Mississippi. A short distance this side, I made a portage, to get to Rice river, which is called the Portage of the Heights of Land, or the dividing ridge that separates the waters of the Mississippi and those that empty into the Red River of the North; thence to Hudson's Bay, the portage is short.

I discovered no traces of any white man before me, when I visited Itasca Lake in 1804. And if the late General Pike did not lay it down as such, when he came to Leech Lake, it is because he did not happen to meet me. I was at an outpost that winter. The late General Pike laid down Cass Lake on his map as the head of the Mississippi river. In 1811-12, I went the same route, to winter on Rice river, near the plains. There I overtook a gentleman with an outfit from Mackinac, by the name of Otesse, with whom I parted only at Fond du Lac, he taking the southern route to Mackinac, and I the northern to head-quarters, which had been changed from Grand Portage to Fort William. This will explain to you that I visited Itasca Lake, then called Elk Lake, in 1803-4, and in 1811-12, and five small streams that empty into the lake, that are short, and soon lose themselves in the swamps.

"By way of explanation, why the late General Pike, then Captain Pike, in 1805, who had orders to stem the Mississippi to its source, and was stopped by the ice a little below Swan river, at the place since called Pike's Rapids, or Pike's Block House, and had to proceed from there to Leech Lake on foot. He had to learn there where the source of the Mississippi was. He went to Cass Lake, and could proceed no further. He had been told that I knew the source, but could not see me, I being out at an outpost. *This want of information made him commit the error; some person, not knowing better, told him there was no river above Cass Lake.* Cass Lake receives the waters of Cross Lake, and Cross Lake those of Itasca Lake, and five small streams that empty into Itasca Lake, then called Elk Lake. Those streams I have noted before, no white man can claim the discovery of the source of the Mississippi before me, for I was the first that saw and examined its shores."

From this digression, let us return to the narrative of Beltrami:—

"On the morning of the fourteenth, I landed at the establishment of the South-west Company, near the exit of the Leech river, in hopes of replacing in some measure my *Bois brulé*. But we found only a single person there, left to take care of the place; and it was quite impossible for him to leave it; I was therefore obliged to go on with *Cloudy Weather* only. However, I obtained all the instructions that were necessary to enable me to proceed with information as far as Sandy Lake; and I found myself gradually more intelligible to my new Indian associate. * * * *

"On the evening of the seventeenth we arrived at Sandy Lake, on the east, which is about one hundred and twenty miles from the last-mentioned place, about three hundred from Red Lake, and about three hundred also from Leech Lake. * * * *

"All the maps, whether of former or recent date, even those constructed conformably to *expeditions*, are exceedingly incorrect with respect to the situation of Sandy

Lake. They place it at the south-east of Lake Leech, though it is nearly at the east; and this error draws after it others respecting its latitude and longitude. I have observed this mistake by the due application of my compass, the result of which corresponds with the opinions of the Indians on the subject, who, indeed, are very seldom deceived in their geographical statements. * *

" After passing the confluence of the Missay-guani-sibi, or River Brandy, on the east, and that of another river, which is unknown, on the west, I approached that grand and interesting spectacle—the Falls of St. Anthony.[1] * * The strength of the current hurried forward our canoe with alarming rapidity; and at length I discerned between the trees, and in a pleasant background, the roof of a house, indicating of course civilized habitation. This was the mill for the garrison at the fort. On reaching this place, my mind, still dwelling on all the grand and terrible scenes which had occurred to me in the course of three months, while traversing eternal deserts, among barbarous tribes and unknown regions, was agitated with emotions which I could scarcely describe or discriminate.

" The sight of this object, which announced my approach to the residence of cultivated man, produced in me a conflict of opposite feelings. I regretted the independence of savage life, while at the same time I experienced a thrill of delight at returning within the sphere of civilized society.

" After having cleared the portage, I completed my Indian toilet for the last time; that is, I shaved myself without either soap or glass, and with razors which were much like saws. I took my bath in the river, and

[1] September thirtieth.

dressed myself as well as I was able, in order to appear at the fort as decently as possible. But I was beset on all sides with dirt and squalidnesss: these perhaps have in fact formed the greatest of my sufferings. My head was covered with the bark of a tree, formed into the shape of a hat and sewed with threads of bark; and shoes, a coat, and pantaloons, such as are used by Canadians in the Indian territories, and formed of *orignal* skins sewed together by thread made of the muscles of that animal, completed the grotesque appearance of my person. I am indebted for my new wardrobe to the fair Woascita, who had compassion on the nakedness to which the thorns and brambles of the forest had reduced me. The Indians attach a high value to the skins of the orignal, which is the most beautiful of quadrupeds, the monarch of reindeer, and only very rarely to be met with. * * * * *

" My Indians announced their approach in the customary manner, that is, by the discharge of guns loaded with ball, and with shouts and chants accompanied by the sound of their harmonious drums.

" Melancholy rumours respecting my safety had been circulated at the fort, and young Snelling, on his return to it, having expressed the apprehensions he felt on my account when we parted at Pembenar, had thus strengthened the belief in them. These gentlemen in fact supposed me to be dead.

" On the arrival of the flotilla all the officers hastened down to inquire about me. They were answered by the supposed dead man himself. While replying to their kind questions I divested myself of the skin covering which I had on, in the disguise of an Indian; a character which my countenance and general appearance greatly contributed to my supporting. I saw in the expression of their physiognomies both a movement of surprise, and sentiments of affection and friendship. The excellent Mr. Tagliawar embraced me in the most cordial manner, and the colonel, his respectable wife, and his children, received me with demonstrations of the most lively joy. I was much moved, and could not help shedding tears of gratitude and attachment. This was the first time since fate began to steep my existence in anguish that I beheld a gleam of those happy moments which, in Italy, friendship always procured for me whenever I returned from my occasional absences. And during the short time that I remained among them I experienced nothing of the constraint, nothing of the cold and formal politeness which Americans in general are accustomed to affect, particularly towards strangers, and which, like a moral rust, tarnishes their natural benevolence and impairs the value of their hospitality."

Dr. Norwood, who was the assistant of Dr. Owens, in the United States' Geological Survey of Minnesota, speaking of his route from Cass Lake, says:—

"Our route from this place led through Turtle river, and the chain of lakes described by Mr. J. C. Beltrami, in 1823, as the 'Julian sources of the Mississippi.' * * * * * The map sketched by him is a tolerably correct one, and appears to have been the source from which Mr. Nicollet derived his information with regard to the route between Cass and Red Lakes."[1]

In the language of Nicollet, the last explorer of the extreme western source of the Mississippi, "I may be mistaken, but it strikes me that American critics have been too disdainful of Mr. Beltrami's book."

---

[1] Owens' Geological Survey of Wisconsin, Iowa, and Minnesota, pp. 322-3.

In the year 1824, a Mr. Findlay left Prairie du Chien in a canoe, and ascended the Mississippi in company with a Canadian named Barrette, and two others. On their arrival at Lake Pepin, they were met by an Ojibway war party from Lac du Flambeau. The Canadian thought he recognised in the party an Indian, who, the the previous winter, had come to the place on Black river where he was cutting lumber, and stole his horse.

Both Findlay and Barrette had partaken freely of whiskey, and, quarrelling with the Indians, they were all killed, and their goods and provisions stolen.

Until the American Fur Company systematized the trade in Minnesota, and Congress took measures to exclude whiskey dealers from the Indians, trade was carried on in a way to make humanity blush. The following letter of Colonel Snelling, addressed to the secretary of war, exhibits the disgraceful condition of affairs at that time:—

"In former letters addressed to the department of war, I have adverted to the mischievous consequences resulting from the introduction of whiskey, and other distilled spirits, into the Indian country. The pretext is, that our traders cannot enter into successful competition with the British traders without it. If the sale of whiskey could be restricted to the vicinity of the British line, the mischief would be comparatively trivial, but, if permitted at all, no limits can be set to it. A series of petty wars and murders, and the introduction of every species of vice and debauchery, by the traders and their engagees, will be the consequence. It becomes, also, a fruitful source of complaint with those engaged in the same trade from the West. The traders who obtain their supplies from St. Louis, pass Fort Snelling, where, in obedience to the orders I have received from the president, their boats are searched, and no spirituous liquors are permitted to be taken further.

"The traders who are licensed for the lakes, spread themselves over the whole country between Lake Superior and the Upper Mississippi; their whiskey attracts a large proportion of the Indians to their trading-houses; and the Western traders not only have to complain of the loss of custom, but, in many instances, the Indians who have obtained their goods of them, are seduced by whiskey to carry their winter's hunt to others. This has long been one of the tricks of the trade. The traders, who are not generally restrained by any moral rules, after they pass the boundary, practise it without scruple, whenever opportunity occurs, and he who has the most whiskey generally carries off the furs. They are so far from being ashamed of the practice, that it affords them subject for conversation by their winter fires. I have myself frequently heard them boast of their exploits in that way. The neighbourhood of the trading-houses where whiskey is sold presents a disgusting scene of drunkenness, debauchery, and misery. In my route I passed Prairie du Chien, Green Bay, and Mackinac; no language can describe the scenes of vice which there present themselves. Herds of Indians are drawn together by the fascinations of whiskey, and they exhibit the most degraded picture of human nature I ever witnessed."[1]

---

[1] Licensed Indian traders among Dahkotahs in 1826:—
P. Prescott, Leaf River.
D. Lamont, Mouth of Minnesota.
J. Renville, Lac qui Parle.
Wm. Dickson, Lac Traverse.
B. F. Baker, Crow Island, Upper Mississippi.
Duncan Campbell, Falls St. Croix.
John Campbell, Mouth of Chippeway.
Francis Grandin, Traverse des Sioux.
Hagan Moores, Lac Traverse.
Louis Provencalle, Traverse des Sioux.

CHAPTER XVIII.

For more than a century there had been a westward tendency in the emigration of the Indian nations, and a frequent source of war among the North-western tribes, was the encroachment upon each other's hunting ground.

In the hope that good might result from well defined boundary lines, on the nineteenth of August, 1825, by order of the authorities at Washington, Governor Clark, of Missouri, and Cass, of Michigan, convened at Prairie du Chien, a grand Congress of Dahkotahs, Ojibways, Sauks, and Foxes, Menomonies, Ioways, Winnebagoes, Pottawottamies, and Ottawas.

After some discussion, it was agreed between the Dahkotahs and Ojibways, that the line dividing their respective countries, should commence at the Chippewa river, half a day's march below the falls, and from thence to Red Cedar river just below the falls, and thence to the Standing Cedar, a day's paddle above the head of Lake St. Croix; thence between two lakes called by the Ojibways, "Green Lakes," and the Dahkotahs, the "Lakes of the Buried Eagles;" and from thence to the Standing Cedar that the Dahkotahs split; thence to Rum river, crossing at Choking Creek, a day's march from its mouth; thence to a point of woods that projects into the prairie a half day's march from the Mississippi; thence in a straight line to the mouth of the first river above the Sauk; thence up that river to a small lake at its source; thence to a lake at the head of Prairie river, a tributary of Crow Wing; thence to the portage of Otter Tail Lake; thence to the outlet of said lake; thence to the Buffalo river, midway between its source and mouth, and down said river to Red river, and down Red river to the mouth of the Outard creek.

The eastern boundary of the Dahkotahs, was to commence opposite the Ioway river, running back to the bluffs, and along the bluffs to Bad Axe river; thence to mouth of Black river; and thence to half a day's march below the falls of the Chippewa.

A few months after the treaty of Prairie du Chien, it was very evident that neither Dahkotah nor Ojibway were willing to be pent up by any boundary lines.

As the Ojibways were dispersed over a great extent of country, it was agreed at Prairie du Chien, that the government of the United States should convene them in 1826, at some point on the shores of Lake Superior. The place selected, was Fond du Lac; and Lewis Cass and T. L. McKenney were the commissioners to assemble the Indians, and conclude the first formal treaty on the soil of Minnesota.

On the twenty-eighth of July, the expedition approached in their barges, with flying colours and martial music, the trading post of Fond du Lac; and for the first time the ears of the Indians of that region were greeted with the tune of "Hail Columbia." On the thirty-first, the commissioner, McKenney, went over to the island opposite the Fur Company's post, to visit an

Ojibway woman who had been scalped when a child, under these circumstances: Having accompanied a band of sixty men, women, and children to the vicinity of the falls of the Chippeway river, they were surprised by a Dahkotah war party which rushed down from the bluffs, and fired into their lodges. The woman, who was then only fourteen years of age, ran towards the woods, and was pursued by a Dahkotah brave, who captured and bound her.

Just then another Dahkotah approached, and struck her with a war club, scalped her, and was about to cut her throat, when he was shot. In the contest for the child, each warrior had taken off a portion of her scalp, and, while they were wrangling, her father had approached and fired his gun, which killed both. When the shades of night came, he went to the spot where he had last seen his daughter, recovered the pieces of her scalp, and, after some search, found her senseless on the snow, about a half mile from the scene of conflict. By proper attention she was restored, and at the time of the treaty of Fond du Lac, she was the mother of ten children, and her skull still bore the marks of violence.

On the second of August the council met, and continued several days. Among those who took a seat was an aged Ojibway woman, from Montreal river. She wore around her neck her husband's medal, and, being very poor, in the place of wampum she laid on the commissioners' table some grass and porcupine quills. In presenting them, she said: " I come in the place of my husband. He is old and blind, but he yet has a mouth and ears. He can speak and hear. He is very poor. He hopes to receive a present from his fathers."

After the usual feastings and speeches, and exhausting of patience, a treaty was concluded on the fifth day of August, which, with some modifications, was ratified by the United States Senate, on the second day of February of the next year.

By an article of the treaty the Ojibways fully disclaimed all connexion with Great Britain, and acknowledged the authority of the United States. At the council there were present deputations from the Minnesota bands at Fond du Lac, river St. Croix, Rainy Lake, Sandy Lake, Leech Lake, Snake River, and Crow Wing.

Supplementary to the treaty was inserted the following clause. "As the Chippeways who committed the murder upon four American citizens, in June, 1824, upon the shores of Lake Pepin, are not present at this council, but are far in the interior of the country, so that they cannot be apprehended and delivered to the proper authority before next summer; and as the commissioners have been specially instructed to demand the surrender of those persons, and to state to the Chippeway tribe the consequence of suffering such a flagitious outrage to go unpunished, it is agreed that the persons guilty of the aforementioned murder shall be brought in, either to the Sault St. Marie, or Green Bay, as early next summer as practicable."

Governor Cass, having determined to return in a bark canoe, contracted with a son of the scalped woman to build one of suitable dimensions, about five feet in width, and thirty-six in length. Immediately a large company of squaws and children commenced the work, for they are the mechanics of every Indian village. Stakes were driven into the ground, the desired length of the canoe, and then rolls of birch bark stripped from the trees unbroken, and stitched together with the roots of the larch, were placed within the enclosure and secured to the stakes. Cross pieces of cedar are now inserted, producing the desired form, and constituting the ribs or framework. The birch bark properly secured to the frame, the stakes are pulled out of the ground, and the seams covered with resin that the water should not enter. After some ornamenting of the sides, it was ready for delivery to Mr. Cass.

> "Thus the birch canoe was builded,
> In the valley, by the river,
> In the bosom of the forest;
> And the forest's life was in it,
> All its mystery, and its magic.
> All the lightness of the birch tree,
> All the toughness of the cedar,
> All the larch's supple sinews;
> And it floated on the river,
> Like a yellow leaf in Autumn,
> Like a yellow water lily."

Not long after the treaty, twenty-nine Ojibways surrendered themselves at Sault St. Marie. After an examination, seven were committed for trial, and confined at Mackinaw. At the next term of court, the judge declined trying the prisoners, in consequence of doubts of jurisdiction; and, during the next winter, they cut their way out of the log jail, and escaped to their distant home.

The year of the treaty of Fond du Lac, was another remarkable year to the Selkirk colony, known to this day as the year of the flood.

In the month of January, it was rumored at the Selkirk settlement, that the hunters who were on the plains of Minnesota in quest of buffalo were starving. The sufferers were from one hundred and fifty to two hundred miles from Pembina, and the only way to carry provisions to them was by dog sleds. The sympathy for their welfare was very great; and even the widow contributed a mite to their relief.

It appears from a statement made by one who was in the colony at the time, that in the month of December, 1825, a snow storm raged with violence for several days, and drove the buffalo out of the hunter's reach. As this was an unexpected contingency, they had no meat as a substitute, and famine stared them in the face.

Says an eye-witness:[1] "Families here, and families there, despairing of life, huddled themselves together for warmth, and in too many cases, their shelter proved their grave. At first the heat of their bodies melted the snow; they became wet, and being without food or fuel, the cold soon penetrated, and in several instances froze the whole body into solid ice. Some again were in a state of actual delirium, while others were picked up frozen to death; one woman was found with an infant on her back within a quarter mile of Pembina. This poor creature must have travelled at the least, one hundred and twenty-five miles in three days and nights. Those that were found alive, had devoured their horses, their dogs, raw-hides, leather, and their very shoes. So great were their sufferings, that some died on the road to the colony after being relieved at Pembina. One man with his wife and three children were dug out of the snow where they had been buried for five days and

[1] Alexander Ross.

nights without food, fire, or light of the sun, and the wife and two of the children recovered."

When the spring came, the melting of the winter's snow produced a still greater calamity. On the second day of May, in twenty-four hours, the Red river rose nine feet; and by the fifth, the plains were submerged. A panic now seized every living thing; dogs howled, cattle lowed, children cried, mothers wept and wrung their hands, and fathers called out to their families to escape to the hills. The water continued to rise until the twenty-first, and houses and barns floated in the rushing waters. On one night a house in flames moved over the waters amid logs and uprooted trees, household furniture, and drowning cattle, reminding one of the day when "the heavens being on fire, shall be dissolved."

The waters began to abate in June; and such is the surprising quickness with which vegetation matures five degrees of latitude north of St. Paul, that barley, potatoes, and wheat sowed on the twenty-second of June, came to maturity.

Misled by the florid representations of one of Lord Selkirk's agents, a number of Swiss arrived in the colony, in 1821. Their occupations had been mechanical, chiefly that of clock making, and they were not adapted for the stern work of founding a colony in the interior of the North American continent.

From year to year their spirits drooped, and, when the Switzers' song of home was sung, they could not keep back their tears.

After the flood, they could no longer remain in the land of their adversity, and they became the pioneers in emigration and agriculture in the state of Minnesota.

At one time a party of two hundred and forty-three departed for the United States, who found homes at different points on the banks of the Mississippi.

Before the eastern wave of emigration had ascended beyond Prairie du Chien, the Swiss had opened farms on and near St. Paul,[1] and should be recognised as the first actual settlers in the country.

The same year of the flood at the Red River settlement, on the twenty-seventh of May, two or three hundred Ojibways had floated down the Mississippi in their canoes, and encamped near a trading-house, on the side of the Mississippi opposite the fort, the ruins of which may be seen east of the ferry-road, on the river bottom.

---

[1] Stevens, in an address on the early history of Hennepin county, says:—

"Strange as it may appear, the immigrants were from the north, all from the Hudson Bay Territory, from which they had been driven by high water. This colony consisted of Louis Massey, Mr. Perry, Pierrie, Garvas, and others. Most of them are now citizens of different parts of the territory and Wisconsin. They settled near where the St. Louis house now stands, and in the vicinity of Kittson's and Baker's landing. Owing to the arbitrary and tyrannical power which then held sway in the territory, they were driven from their homes in 1836 and '37. At that time, and both before and since, the commanding officers at the fort were the lords of the north. They ruled supreme. The citizens in the neighbourhood of the fort were liable at any time to be thrust into the guard-house. While the chief of the fort was the king, the subordinate officers were princes, and persons have been deprived of their liberty and imprisoned by those tyrants for the most trivial wrong or some imaginary offence. Some had their houses torn down; others were more unfortunate, and had their buildings burnt. To the latter class Mr. Garvas belonged. Mr. Perry was the Abraham of Hennepin county. He resided in front of the slaughter-house, near the landing. He pitched his tent after being driven off of his first home on the bank of the brook between the cave and St. Paul. Here he attended to his numerous flocks and cultivated a field, and I think died below St. Paul, near where the large hotel was burnt a year or two since. He was a Swiss by birth. At one time he owned more cattle than all the rest of the inhabitants of what is now Minnesota, if we except Mr. Renville."

They visited the fort for the purpose of smoking the pipe of peace with the Indian agent, and receiving the presents which were annually distributed by the United States government. Their tent-poles were scarcely planted before their arrival was noised among the Dahkotah villages in the vicinity.

In a few hours men in canoes were seen descending the Minnesota, and furious with excitement they entered the slough, on the shores of which the Ojibways were encamped, and commenced an attack upon the unsuspecting Ojibways, scalping their women and children in sight of the windows of the officers' quarters, and the soldiers of the garrison. Their butchery completed, they landed under the walls of the fort, and singing their triumphal songs, proceeded to the undulating prairie just beyond, and danced around the reeking scalps they had taken. As the country was as yet unceded, the United States officers had no proper right of interference.

The following autumn the Ojibway chief Flat Mouth, of Sandy Lake, with seven warriors, and women and children, the whole party amounting to twenty-four, arrived at Fort Snelling one morning at day-break. Walking to the gates of the garrison, they asked the protection of Colonel Snelling and Taliaferro, the Indian agent. They were told, that as long as they remained under the United States flag, they were secure, and were ordered to encamp within musket shot of the high stone walls of the fort.

During the afternoon a Dahkotah, Toopunkah Zeze, from a village near the first rapids of the Minnesota, with eight others, visited the Ojibway camp. They were cordially received, and a feast of meat, and corn, and sugar, was soon made ready. The wooden platters emptied of their contents, they engaged in conversation, and whiffed the peace pipe.

About nine o'clock in the evening they rose and departed; but as soon as they were outside, turned and discharged their guns with deadly aim upon their entertainers, and ran off with a shout of satisfaction. The report was heard by the sentinel of the fort, and he cried, repeatedly, "Corporal of the guard!" and soon at the gates, were the Ojibways, with their women and the wounded, telling their tale of woe in wild and incoherent language. Among others, was a little girl about seven years old, who was pierced through both thighs with a bullet.

Flat Mouth, the chief, reminded Colonel Snelling that he had been attacked while under the protection of the United States flag, and early the next morning, Captain Clark, with one hundred soldiers, proceeded toward Land's End, a trading-post of the Columbia Fur Company, on the Minnesota, a mile above the present residence of Franklin Steele, where the Dahkotahs were supposed to be. The soldiers had just left the large gate of the fort, when a party of Dahkotahs, in battle array, appeared on one of the prairie hills. After some parleying they turned their backs, and being pursued, thirty-two were captured near the trading-post.

Colonel Snelling ordered the prisoners to be brought before the Ojibways, and two being pointed out as participants in the slaughter of the preceding night, they were delivered to the aggrieved party to be dealt with in accordance with their customs. They were led out to the plain in front of the gate of the fort, and when placed nearly without the range of the Ojibway guns, they were told to run for their lives. With the rapidity of deer they bounded away, but the Ojibway bullet flew faster, and after a few steps, they fell gasping on the ground, and were soon lifeless. Then the savage nature displayed itself in all its hideousness. Women and children danced for joy, and placing their fingers in the bullet holes, from which the blood oozed, they licked them with delight. The men tore the scalps from the dead, and seemed to luxuriate in the privilege of plunging their knives through the corpses. After the execution, the Ojibways returned to the fort, and were met by the colonel. He had prevented all over whom his authority extended from witnessing the scene, and had done his best to confine the excitement to the Indians. The same day a deputation of Dahkotah warriors received audience, regretting the violence that had been done by their young men, and agreeing to deliver up the ringleaders.

At the time appointed, a son of Flat Mouth, with those of the Ojibway party that were not wounded, escorted by United States troops, marched forth to meet the Dahkotah deputation, on the prairie just beyond the old residence of the Indian agent. With much solemnity two more of the guilty were handed over to the assaulted. One was fearless, and with firmness stripped himself of his clothing and ornaments, and distributed them. The other could not face death with composure. He was noted for a hideous hare-lip, and had a bad reputation among his fellows. In the spirit of a coward he prayed for life, to the mortification of his tribe. The same opportunity was presented to them as to the first, of running for their lives. At the first fire the coward fell a corpse; but his brave companion, though wounded, ran on, and had nearly reached the goal of safety, when a second bullet killed him. The body of the coward now became a common object of loathing for both Dahkotahs and Ojibways.

Colonel Snelling told the Ojibways that the bodies must be removed, and then they took the scalped Dahkotahs, and dragging them by the heels, threw them off the bluff, into the river a hundred and fifty feet beneath. The dreadful scene was now over; and a detachment of troops was sent with the old chief Flat Mouth, to escort him out of the reach of Dahkotah vengeance.

In the fall of 1826, all the troops at Prairie du Chien had been removed to Fort Snelling, the commander taking with him two Winnebagoes that had been confined in Fort Crawford. After the soldiers left the Prairie, the Indians in the vicinity were quite insolent. About this period a bois brulé from Red river, named Methode, came to the Prairie to reside. In the month of March, 1827, he went to Painted Rock creek, a few miles above on the Iowa side, accompanied by his family, for the purpose of making maple sugar. He not returning as soon as was expected, search was instituted by his friends, when they found him, his children, and his wife with an unborn infant, nearly burned to cinders in their camp—the work of hostile savages.

At the time of the shooting of the Dahkotahs at Fort Snelling, Red Bird, a distinguished Winnebago chief, whose residence was often on Black river, Wisconsin, was on a war party against the Ojibways, in which he was unsuccessful. In some way the Winnebagoes gained the impression that two of their own number who were confined at Fort Snelling, had been delivered to the

Ojibways and scalped; and from that hour they became hostile to the whites.

On the 26th of June, 1827, Red Bird, with two other Indians, entered the dwelling of a trader at Prairie du Chien by the name of Lockwood, who was absent, and loading their guns in the kitchen, proceeded to the bed-room of his wife. On their entrance, she crossed the hall into the store, where she found Duncan Graham, a man of influence with the Indians, who induced them to leave. Thirsting for blood, they proceeded in an easterly direction to a place called McNair's Coulée, where there was an isolated log cabin, in which dwelt a man of mulatto and French extraction, named Gagnier. As Red Bird and his companions entered, Gagnier was sitting on a chest, and near the window; his wife, of French and Dahkotah extraction, was washing; while on the bed lay an infant sleeping. In the cabin there was also a discharged soldier.

Treated with civility, they were asked if they would have something to eat. While the wife was procuring refreshments, she heard the click caused by the cocking of Red Bird's rifle, and in the twinkling of an eye there was a discharge and her husband was dead. One of the other two Indians shot the soldier, and the third, named Wekaw, had his rifle wrested from him by the desperate wife. Unable to cope with three furious savages, she ran to the village and gave the alarm. Returning with a company of armed men, she found her infant with its head scalped, and neck cut, in the bed and still alive. Recovering from these wounds, the daughter still lives, and is now a grandmother.

A little while before this murderous assault two keel-boats had passed Prairie du Chien, on their way to Fort

Snelling with provisions. When they reached Wapashaw village, on the site of the present town of Winona, they were ordered to come ashore by the Dahkotahs. Complying, they found themselves surrounded by Indians, with hostile intentions. The boatmen had no fire-arms, but assuming a bold mien, and a defiant voice, the captain of the keel-boats ordered the savages to leave the decks, which was successful. The boats pushed on, and at Red Wing and Kaposia the Indians showed that they were not friendly, though they did not molest the boats. Before they started on their return from Fort Snelling, the men on board, amounting to thirty-two, were all provided with muskets, and a barrel of ball cartridges.

When the descending keel-boats passed Wapashaw, the Dahkotahs were engaged in the war dance, and menaced them but made no attack. Below this point one of the boats moved in advance of the other, and when near the mouth of the Bad Axe the half-breeds on board descried hostile Indians on the banks. As the channel neared the shore the sixteen men on the first boat were greeted with the war whoop, and a volley of rifle balls from the excited Winnebagoes, killing two of the crew. Rushing into their canoes, the Indians made the attempt to board the boat, and two were successful. One of these stationed himself at the bow of the boat, and fired with killing effect on the men below deck. An old sailor of the last war with Great Britain, called Saucy Jack, at last despatched him, and began to rally the fainting spirits on board. During the fight the boat had stuck on a sand-bar. With four companions, amid a shower of balls from the savages, he plunged into the water and pushed off the boat, and thus moved out of reach of the galling shots of the

Winnebagoes. As they floated down the river during the night, they heard a wail in a canoe behind them, the voice of a father mourning the death of the son, who had scaled the deck, and was now a corpse in possession of the white men. The rear boat passed the Bad Axe river late in the night, and escaped an attack.

It was the day after the murder of Gagnier and Lipcap, the soldier, that the first keel-boat arrived at Prairie du Chien, with two of their crew dead, four wounded, and the Indian that had been killed on the boat. The two dead men had been residents of the Prairie, and now the panic was increased. On the morning of the twenty-eighth of June the second keel-boat appeared, and among her passengers was Joseph Snelling, a talented son of the colonel, who wrote a story of deep interest, based on the facts narrated.

At a meeting of the citizens it was resolved to repair old Fort Crawford, and Thomas McNair was appointed captain. Dirt was thrown around the bottom logs of the fortification to prevent its being fired, and young Snelling was put in command of one of the blockhouses. On the next day a voyageur named Loyer, and the well known trader Duncan Graham, started through the interior, west of the Mississippi, with intelligence of the murders, to Fort Snelling. A company of volunteers soon arrived from Galena, and a few days after four companies of the fifth regiment from Fort Snelling, with Colonel Snelling in command. The citizens had seized De-kau-ray, a Winnebago chief, and retained him as a hostage.

Governor Cass, at the time of these occurrences, was at Butte des Morts, for the purpose of negotiating a treaty, and, proceeding immediately to Jefferson Barracks, a large body of troops, under General Atkinson, were soon on their way to the scene of excitement. A detachment from Green Bay, under Major Whistler, also moved up to the portage of the Fox and Wisconsin rivers. The Winnebagoes were not prepared to engage in war with the United States, and it was decided in council that Red Bird and We-Kaw should surrender themselves to Major Whistler.

Colonel McKinney describes the scene in this language: " On the right was the band of music, a little in advance of the line. In front of the centre, about ten paces distant, were the murderers. * * * * All eyes were fixed on Red Bird, and well they might be, for of all the Indians I ever saw, he is, without exception, the most perfect in form, in face, and gesture. In height he is above six feet; straight, but without restraint. His proportions are of the most exact symmetry; his very fingers are models of beauty. I never beheld a face that was so full of all the ennobling, and, at the same time, the most winning expression.

" During my attempted analysis of his face, I could not but ask myself, Can this man· be a murderer? Is he the same who shot, scalped, and cut the throat of Gagnier? There was no ornamenting of the hair after the Indian fashion, but it was cut after the civilized manner. His face was painted; one side red, the other intermixed with green and white. Around his neck he wore a collar of blue wampum, beautifully mixed with white, which was sewed to a piece of cloth, the width of the wampum being about two inches,—while the claws of the wild-cat, distant from each other about a quarter of an inch, with their points inward, formed the rim of the collar. He was clothed in a Yankton dress, new and beautiful. The material is of dressed elk or deer skin, almost a pure white. * * * * * Across his breast, in a diagonal position, and bound tight to it, was his war pipe, brightly ornamented with dyed horse-hair, the feathers and bills of birds. In one of his hands he held the white flag, in the other the calumet of peace. There he stood. Not a muscle moved, nor was the expression of his face changed a particle. He and We-Kaw were told to sit down. His motions as he seated himself were no less graceful and captivating, than when he stood or walked. At this moment the band struck up Pleyel's Hymn. Everything was still. It was a moment of intense interest to all."

The ceremony of surrender now took place. The Winnebagoes asked kind treatment of the prisoners, and begged that they might not be ironed. Major Whistler said in reply that he would treat them with consideration, and Red Bird standing up said: " I am ready," and was immediately marched off with his accomplice to a tent in the rear and placed under guard.

The prisoners having been handed over to General Atkinson, who had arrived, were conveyed to Prairie du Chien, and delivered to the civil authorities. There they were chained and placed in close confinement, which so chafed the proud spirit of Red Bird, that he soon drooped, and at last died with a broken heart.

CHAPTER XIX.

In the year 1830, steps were taken for another congress of tribes at Prairie du Chien. A few weeks previous to the convocation, a party of Dahkotahs and Menomonees surprised a band of Foxes, who were eating their dinner on an island in the Mississippi, a short distance below the Wisconsin, and killed eight of their chief men. On this account the Fox tribe refused to be present at the council at Prairie du Chien. The M'dewakantonwan Dahkotahs, in a treaty made on this occasion, bestowed on their relatives of mixed blood that tract about Lake Pepin known as the half-breed tract.[1]

During this year another attempt was made to erect a mill on the Chippeway river, Wisconsin. In the month of May, workmen proceeded to the old site on the Menomonee. Three or four Ojibways arrived one night and told them if they did not leave they would kill them. The superintendent (Armstrong) was so much alarmed that he took a canoe and floated down

[1] The tract is described in said treaty as follows: "Beginning at a place called the Barn, below and near the village of the Red Wing Chief, and running back fifteen miles, thence in a parallel line with Lake Pepin and the Mississippi, about thirty-two miles to a point opposite Beef or O'Beuf river, thence fifteen miles, to the Grand Encampment, opposite the river aforesaid."

the river the same evening, and the workmen followed the next day.

In August, one of the proprietors at Prairie du Chien started with other workmen; among others, a discharged soldier by the name of Holmes,[1] under whose supervision the mill was at last constructed; and, by the summer of the next year, had sawed about one hundred thousand feet of lumber.

After the unprovoked attack on the part of the Dahkotahs, which has been related, a continual border warfare prevailed between them and the Ojibways until 1831. War parties of the latter, descending the Chippeway river, constantly lurked around the shores of Lake Pepin, in the hope of obtaining Dahkotah scalps, and endangered the lives of white men ascending or descending the Mississippi.

During the month of April, 1831, the authorities at Washington instructed H. R. Schoolcraft, Indian agent at Sault St. Marie, to proceed to the Upper Mississippi, and use his influence to make peace between the Dahkotahs and Ojibways. The expedition was composed of twenty-seven men, beside a few soldiers under Lieutenant Clary.

Ascending the Mushkeg river, which enters Lake Superior below Bayfield, they passed Lake Kagino, and a chain of small lakes, until they came to the Namekagon, a tributary of the St. Croix. Descending this stream to Lake Pukwaewa, they found a village of fifty-three persons under Odabossa. At this point the expedition divided, a part going to Ottawa Lake by a direct route, and a portion accompanying Mr. School-

This gentleman has since become an active pioneer in Minnesota.

craft down the Namekagon to its junction with the St. Croix, and down that stream to a trading post at Yellow river. On the first of August, Mr. Schoolcraft held a council with the Ojibways at this point.

The Indians, through one of their speakers, referred to an attack that had been made the previous year by the Dahkotahs, on a band of Ojibways and bois brulés, in which four of their friends had been killed, and that the Ojibways had not been in the habit of crossing the boundary line mentioned in the treaty of Prairie du Chien.

At the solicitation of Mr. Schoolcraft, Kabamappa, and Shakoba (the war chief of Snake river), consented to bear wampum and tobacco to the Dahkotah chiefs at Kaposia and Wapashaw village, and invite them to renew the league of friendship.

On the fifth of August, the two detachments of the expedition were re-united at Ottawa Lake, when another council was held at the trading-post with the Indians.

At Lake Chetac, they found the trading-house burned, and village deserted; and while breakfasting on the shores of a little lake below this, eight canoes filled with a returning war party floated into the lake. They were young braves from Ottawa Lake, and had been in pursuit of Dahkotahs near the mill which had recently been erected. On the seventh of August, the expedition arrived at Rice Lake, the residence of a band of warlike Ojibways, much exposed to the Dahkotahs, because they were on the verge of the Dahkotah possessions.

The young chief Neenaba claimed that the saw-mills just erected on the Red Cedar branch of the Chippeway were on their lands, though the Dahkotahs had granted permission, for a certain consideration, to the owners.

At the request to drop his war club, he was confused, and would not receive the proffered presents of a medal and flag until he was pressed by his young warriors. On the next day he came, followed by his braves, with the flag on one arm and the war club in the other hand, and stated that while he accepted the one, he did not drop the other. "He had reflected upon the advice sent by the President, and particularly that part of it which counselled them to sit still upon their lands, but while they sat still, they wished also to be certain that their enemies would sit still."

After this interview, Mr. Schoolcraft visited the mills on the Red Cedar river, which were then in charge of Mr. Wallace.

In 1832, instructions were again issued, ordering Mr. Schoolcraft to visit the tribes toward the sources of the Mississippi. Attached to the expedition, was the late Dr. Douglass Houghton, as botanist, geologist, and surgeon, and the Rev. W. T. Boutwell, now of Washington county, who was appointed by the American Board of Commissioners of Foreign Missions, to explore the field, to observe the condition of the Indians, and the practicability of establishing mission stations. The military escort was in command of Lieutenant James Allen.

On the afternoon of the twenty-third of June, the Fond du Lac trading-house on the St. Louis river, about twenty miles from the mouth, was reached. This was formerly the head-quarters of the fur trade west of Lake Superior; but the American Fur Company removed their depôt to Sandy Lake, because of its more central situation. This department of the Indian trade, included the posts at Fond du Lac, Grand Portage, Rainy Lake, Vermillion Lake, Red Lake, Pembina, Red Cedar, Leech, and Sandy Lakes. The value of furs from all these posts in 1832, was about twenty-five thousand dollars.

On the twenty-first of June, the party were at La Pointe. The chief trader of the place, was the father of the late Mr. Warren, who had thirty or forty acres under cultivation. Among other residents, was the father of his wife, Cadotte, an old French trader, and the Rev. Sherman Hall, now of Sauk Rapids, then a missionary among the Ojibways. His child was said to have been the first child of pure European parents born on the shores of Lake Superior.

On the twenty-fifth of June, the first portage on the St. Louis river was made. The entire length of it is nine miles, and it was necessary to commence carrying the baggage and provisions up a very steep bluff; while the experienced voyageurs ascended with ease, bearing a bag of flour and a keg of pork, the raw recruits of the expedition had stumbling work.

On the twenty-sixth, in the midst of a drenching rain, the men with heavy loads on their backs, waded through mud and water. Some Indian women who were assisting in the portage, carried at once a bag of flour, a trunk, and soldier's knapsack, surmounted by a nursing infant in an Indian cradle.[1] About noon of the next day the end of the difficult portage was reached.

---

[1] "When we stopped at night my men, and even the Canadians, were literally fagged out. Two of the soldiers had snagged their feet, and were disabled, and all of them were galled in the back by the kegs in such a degree as to make their loads very painful. It requires an expe-

Heavy rains fell on the first and second of July, and in reaching the portage of the Savannah, some lost their moccasins, and some a leg of their pantaloons, and all were covered with mud to their waists, so that they were perfect "sans culottes" when they camped at the end of the carrying place.

On the afternoon of July third, reached the trading-post of Mr. Aitkin at Sandy Lake, where they were welcomed by the discharge of muskets, and the hoisting of the American flag. On the ninth, the expedition was at Lake Winnibigoshish, and found a trading-post in the charge of Mr. Belanger, made of logs, with windows of deer skin, surrounded by a little garden, in which were growing tobacco, corn, peas, and potatoes. On the tenth they entered Cass Lake, which Mr. Schoolcraft visited in company with the present secretary of state in 1820. Here were several fine corn fields, which had been cultivated by Indian women. In one of the lodges were three Dahkotah scalps, one of which had been lately taken by the Leech Lake Band. Flat Mouth and one hundred warriors had gone forth to chastise the Dahkotahs for encroaching on his hunting grounds, and meeting a party of the enemy had killed three and wounded others. In the affray a Cass

---

rience of years to habituate men to carrying in this way, and the life and habits of soldiers by no means fit them for such labour. I had four or five Indian women, and as many Indian men carrying for me, and without these I could not have made half the distance. The Indian women carry better than the men, being less indolent and more accustomed to it. I saw a small young Indian woman at the close of the day, carry a keg of one thousand musket ball cartridges, for a distance of one mile without resting, and most of the distance through swamp that was frequently over her knees, and this too, after having carried heavy loads all day."—*Lt. Allen's Journal.*

Lake Ojibway was killed, and when night came there was a grand scalp dance, which an eye-witness has described:—

"Before I had returned to our tent, which is pitched but a few yards from two graves, the greater part of the Indians had here collected, and begun the scalp dance. It was led by three squaws, each bearing in her hand one of the recent scalps. Two or three men sat beating drums and singing, while old and young, male and female, all joined in the song. Occasionally all would become so animated that there would be one general hop, and all at the same time, throwing their heads back, would raise a most horrid yell, clapping the mouth with the hand, to render it, if possible, more terrific. Here were seen little boys and girls, not six years old, all looking on with the most intense interest, imitating their fathers and mothers, and participating in their brutal joy. Thus early do they learn, by precept and example, to imbibe the spirit of revenge and war, which is fostered in their bosoms, and in after life stimulates them to go and perform some deed of daring and blood, which shall gain for themselves the like applause.

"A circumstance which rendered the scene not a little appalling, is, it was performed around the graves of the dead. At the head of those graves hangs an old scalp, some ten feet above the ground, which the winds have almost divested of its ornaments and its hair. The grass and the turf for several yards around, are literally destroyed, and, I presume, by their frequent dancing. One of the scalps I examined. The flesh side had apparently been smoked and rubbed with some material till it was pliant, after which it was painted with vermillion. A piece of wood is turned in the form of a horse-shoe, into which the scalp is sewed, the threads passing round the wood, which keeps it tight. Narrow pieces of cloth and ribands of various colours, attached to the bow, were ornamented with beads and feathers. A small stick, which serves for a handle to shake it in the air when they dance, was attached to the top of the bow by a string. While examining it, a lock of hair fell from it, which the Indian gave me, and which I still preserve."[1]

At two P. M., on July thirteenth, they reached Elk Lake, named Itasca by Mr. Schoolcraft.[2] With the exception of traders, no white men had ever traced the Mississippi so far. The lake is about eight miles in length, and was called Elk by the Ojibways, because of its irregularities, resembling the horns of that animal. Lieutenant Allen, the commander of the military detachment, who made the first map of this lake, thus speaks:—

"From these hills, which were seldom more than two or three hundred feet high, we came suddenly down to the lake, and passed nearly through it to an island near its west end, where we remained one or two hours. We were sure that we had reached the true source of the great river, and a feeling of great satisfaction was manifested by all the party. Mr. Schoolcraft hoisted a flag on a high staff on the island, and left it flying. The lake is about seven miles long, and from one to three broad, but is of an irregular shape, conforming to

[1] Boutwell.
[2] It is asserted that this is a name made up by Mr. Schoolcraft from two Latin words, *veritas caput*. It is true, that by dropping the first syllable of the first and the final syllable of the last word, *Itasca* is obtained; but Mrs. Eastman says, that it is the name of an Indian maiden.

the bases of pine hills which, for a great part of its circumference, rise abruptly from its shore. It is deep, cold, and very clear, and seemed to be well stocked with fish. Its shores show some boulders of primitive rock, but no rock in place. The island, the only one of the lake, and which I have called Schoolcraft Island, is one hundred and fifty yards long, fifty yards broad in the highest part, elevated twenty or thirty feet, overgrown with elm, pine, spruce, and wild cherry. There can be no doubt that this is *the true source and fountain of the longest and largest branch of the Mississippi.*"

Soon after sunrise, on the next day, the expedition turned the bows of their canoes towards the region of civilization. In a little while the canoes were whirling amid splashing rapids, and Allen's capsized. Kegs of pork, loaves of bread, notes of travel, compass, and apparatus, were soon swept out of sight. When the canoe-men are experienced, there is a pleasurable excitement attending the descent of such rapids.

On the afternoon of this day they passed the Dahkotah embankments, which are holes in the earth, where a war party lay in wait for Ojibways descending the rapids, to which allusion has been made in a previous chapter. At ten o'clock at night Leech Lake was reached. In the morning they were welcomed by a salute from the Indians. The chief of the band was Aishkebuggekozh, or Flat Mouth, whose party suffered the dastardly assault at Fort Snelling in 1827. He occupied a log-cabin, twenty by twenty-five feet, which had been presented to him by a trader. He possessed cups, saucers, knives, and forks of European manufacture. At one end of the eating-hall were hung his flags, medals, gun, and scalping knife. Bare-legged and with bare feet, the old chief received his visiters with dignity. He was surrounded by about forty warriors, with standing feathers around their head, and fox tails around their heels. The whole band consisted at that time of over seven hundred men, women and children, and many were vaccinated by Dr. Houghton.

On the twenty-second of July, it being Sunday, the party remained at Baker's trading-post, about fifteen miles below the mouth of the Crow Wing, and here they learned from a small newspaper, which here reached them, concerning the Black Hawk difficulties in Wisconsin. At eight, on Monday morning, they arrived at Little Falls. Says the Rev. Mr. Boutwell, in his journal:—

"At eight we reached the Little Falls. Instead of making a short portage here, as is usual, the water being sufficiently high to clear the canoe from stones, we only put into the current and let her drive. The stream is full of small islands, many of which are covered with a beautiful growth of elm, maple, butternut, and white walnut. The country here is prairie, extending as far as the eye can reach, with here and there a clump of oaks, which at a distance looks like some old New England orchard. *It is the most interesting and inviting tract of country I have ever seen. If there is anything that can meet the wishes, and fill the soul of man with gratitude, it is found here.* What would require the labour of years, in preparing the land for cultivation in many of the old states, is here all prepared to the hand. As far as the eye can reach, is one continued field of grass and flowers, waving in the passing breeze, exhibiting the appearance of a country which has been cultivated for centuries, but now deserted of its inhabitants.

The gentle swells, which are seen here and there, give a pleasing variety. The soil is apparently easy of cultivation,—a black earth and a mixture of black sand. Nothing can be more picturesque or grand, than the high banks at a distance, rising before you as you descend. The islands, in the stream, are most of them alluvial, a soil of the richest quality.

"We have marched thirteen hours and a half to-day, at the rate of ten miles per hour, and are encamped this evening in the dominions of the Sioux, though we have as yet seen none.

"Embarked at five next morning, and marched till twelve, when we reached the Falls of St. Anthony, nine miles above the mouth of the St. Peter's. Our government have here a saw-mill and grist-mill on the west bank of the Mississippi, and also have a large farm. The soldiers are here cutting the hay. For beauty, the country around exceeds all that I can say. These falls are an interesting object to look at, but there is nothing about them that fills one with awe, as do the Falls of Niagara. The stream is divided in about its centre by a bluff of rocks covered with a few trees. The perpendicular fall is perhaps twenty feet on each side of this bluff, at the foot of which there is a shoot of some ten or fifteen feet more in a descent.

"A short portage was made around the falls, when we again embarked in the rapids, and in about an hour reached Fort Snelling. This post is located at the junction of the St. Peter's with the Mississippi. It stands on a high bluff, rising on the north, nearly three hundred feet above the water. The walls of the fort, and of most of the buildings, are of stone. The tower commands an extensive and beautiful view of the adjacent country, and of the Mississippi and St. Peter's rivers. The officers visited us at our tents, invited us to their quarters, and treated us with much kindness and attention.

"After Mr. Schoolcraft had stated to three or four of the principal Sioux chiefs who had been requested to visit him, the object of his tour, and mentioned the complaints which the Ojibwas brought against them for breaking the treaties of Prairie du Chien and Fond du Lac, Little Crow rose and replied, that he recollected those treaties, when they smoked the pipe, and all agreed to eat and drink out of the same dish. He wished the line to be drawn between them and the Ojibwas; the sooner it was fixed the better. He alluded to the late war party from Leech Lake, which had killed two of his nephews, and were now dancing around their scalps; but he did not complain, nor would he go and revenge their death. He denied that the Sioux were in league with the Sacs and Foxes. Black Dog, and the Man-who-floats-on-the-water, also spoke in much the same manner."

After the expedition left Fort Snelling Mr. Schoolcraft pushed ahead, and proceeded without the military escort, by way of the St. Croix to Lake Superior. Near the Falls of St. Croix he met Joseph R. Brown, who had been trading at that point, but was now on his way to establish a new post at the mouth of the river.

Lieutenant Allen was sorely displeased with the summary manner in which Mr. Schoolcraft left him, and in his published report gives full expression to his sentiments.

Early in the spring of 1832, the noted Sauk chief, Black Hawk, raised the British flag, and ascended the

Mississippi with hostile intentions against the frontier settlers. General Atkinson, in the latter part of May, sent an express from Dixon, Illinois, to Prairie du Chien, requesting the Indian agent to procure the services of the Dahkotahs as allies of the United States troops.

On the thirtieth of May, John Marsh, who had accompanied the troops to Fort Snelling in 1819, and Burnett, sub-agent at Prairie du Chien, left that place in a canoe paddled by eight men, to secure the aid of the Dahkotahs. On their way they stopped at the Winnebago village at La Crosse, to inquire if any were willing to join General Atkinson's army on Rock River; Winnieshiek opposed the measure, but the young men agreed to accompany them on their return.

On the first of June, Marsh and Burnett were at Wapashaw Prairie, and found the Dahkotahs fully prepared to go to war against their old enemies. In six days the commissioners returned to the Prairie with eighty Dahkotah and twenty Winnebago warriors.

Marsh, the Dahkotah interpreter, and W. S. Hamilton, marched with the Dahkotahs toward the Pecatonica, and, arriving there the day of the skirmish between General Dodge and the Sauks and Foxes, they gloated over the corpses of their enemies, and, dancing the scalp dance, cut them to pieces.

On the twenty-first of July General Dodge met Black Hawk near an old Sauk village on the Wisconsin and routed him, he retreating north of the Wisconsin, in direction of the Mississippi. As soon as the intelligence of Black Hawk's retreat reached Prairie du Chien, Captain Loomis, now colonel of the 5th regiment United States Infantry, hired the steamboat Enterprise, to proceed to La Crosse, and bring down any Winnebagoes that might be there, lest they should assist Black Hawk in crossing the river. On the thirtieth of July the Winnebagoes and their canoes were at Fort Crawford.

On the first of August, Loomis, one of the officers at Fort Crawford, hired a faster steamboat, called the "Warrior," to ascend the Mississippi. When they came to the mouth of the Bad Axe they discovered Black Hawk's party, who had just arrived with wearied limbs, and diseased and famished bodies. As the steamer approached he told his braves not to shoot, and taking a piece of white cotton placed it on a pole, and signified a desire to come on board; but about this time there was a discharge from the six-pounder on board of the boat, which was returned by Black Hawk's braves.

The steamboat returned that evening to Prairie du Chien, but arrived again the next day, and found that a battle had commenced between the Indians and the regular troops, who had come up to them by land a few hours before. Some of the Indians had fled to the islands of the Mississippi near the Bad Axe, and they were fired at by those on the steamboat.

Batteaux were also sent to the main land to receive and transport the troops of Colonel Z. Taylor and Major Bliss to one of the islands, where a severe fight took place, during which every Indian was killed but one, who made his escape by swimming.[1]

During the fight, General Atkinson came on board of the steamer and remained until the close of the battle. After three hours the battle ended, which was a slaughter rather than a victory.

A writer, in the nearest newspaper,[2] four days after,

[1] Narrative of Captain Este, Black Hawk, and others.
[2] Galena Gazette.

says, "When the Indians were driven to the bank of the Mississippi, some hundreds of men, women, and children, plunged into the river, and hoped by diving to escape the bullets of our guns. Very few, however, escaped our sharp-shooters."

Among those killed on the Wisconsin shore was a mother. Her infant was feeding on her breast, and the bullet had passed through and broken the arm of the child, and penetrated to the heart of the parent. When discovered, the child was alive; it survived the wound, which was attended to by one of the surgeons of the volunteer troops.

Those Indians that escaped the fire from the main shore and steamboat, were met on the west side of the Mississippi by the scalping knife of the Dahkotahs. Wapashaw, with a party of warriors, had arrived during the fight, and they were ordered to pursue those who should escape. Black Hawk, perceiving that all was lost, in forlorn condition fled to the Winnebago village at La Crosse, where the squaws gave him a dress of white deer skin. He was accompanied by the Winnebago chief, One-eyed Dekorrah, to Prairie du Chien, and delivered up to the Americans on the morning of August twenty-seventh.

Black Hawk, on that occasion, is said to have made the following speech :—

"My warriors fell around me; it began to look dismal. I saw my evil day at hand. The sun rose clear on us in the morning, and at night it sunk in a dark cloud, and looked like a ball of fire. This was the last sun that shone on Black Hawk. He is now a prisoner to the white man. But he can stand the torture. He is not afraid of death. He is no coward. Black Hawk is an Indian; he has done nothing of which an Indian need to be ashamed. He has fought the battles of his country against the white men, who came year after year to cheat them and take away their lands. You know the cause of our making war—it is known to all white men—they ought to be ashamed of it. The white men despise the Indians, and drive them from their homes. But the Indians are not deceitful. The white men speak bad of the Indian, and look at him spitefully. But the Indian does not tell lies. Indians do not steal. Black Hawk is satisfied. He will go to the world of spirits contented. He has done his duty—his Father will meet him and reward him. The white men do not scalp the head, but they do worse, they poison the heart—it is not pure with them. Farewell to my nation! Farewell to Black Hawk!"

During the year of the Black Hawk war, the first regular land mail was carried between Fort Crawford and Fort Snelling. The mail carrier was a soldier of the United States' army, and his journeys were on foot. Leaving Prairie du Chien, he crossed to the Iowa side, and then continued on the western side till he came to Fort Snelling. He occupied fourteen days in going and returning, and carried the mail for a period of twelve months.[1] At that time there were no white families in the country. The entire population, beside the soldiers of the fort, were Indian traders.[2]

[1] Smith's History of Wisconsin, vol. i. p. 289.

[2] Licensed Indian Traders in Minnesota, 1833–1834:—

Alexis Bailly, Mendota.
J. R. Brown, Oliver's Grove, Mouth of the St. Croix.
Louis Provençalle, Traverse des Sioux.
J. B. Faribault, Little Rapids of Minnesota.
Hazen Moores, Lac Traverse.
Joseph Renville, Lac qui Parle.
B. F. Baker, Fort Snelling.

In the year 1805, Upper Louisiana was organized as Missouri Territory; and, after the state of that name, was, in 1820, admitted into the Union, the territory beyond its northern boundary, comprising Iowa, and all of Minnesota west of the Mississippi river, was without any organized government. In 1834, the inhabitants petitioned Congress to give them a territorial organization, or attach them to Michigan. For the present it was thought better to pursue the latter course.

In 1836, the territory of Wisconsin was organized, comprising all of Michigan west of the lake of that name; and, in 1838, Iowa was formed, embracing all of the old Missouri Territory beyond the north line of the state of that name.

During the year 1835, an artist of some notoriety, George Catlin, visited Minnesota, and made many sketches which were truthful, and subsequently published many statements which were unreliable.

Featherstonhaugh, in company with Professor Mather, under the direction of the United States government, made a slight geological survey of the valley of the Minnesota.

After Featherstonhaugh returned to England, his native land, he published a work entitled "Canoe voyage up the Minnaysotar," which is only remarkable for its

J. Renville, Jr., Little Rock.
P. Prescott, Traverse des Sioux.
James Welles, Little Rapids.
Joseph R. Brown, Mouth of Chippeway.
W. A. Aitkin, Fond du Lac.
Alfred Aitkin, Sandy Lake.
John Aitkin, Prairie Percée.
Ambrose Devenport, Gull Lake.

Wm. Devenport, Leech Lake.
A. Morrison, Mille Lac.
George Bonga, Lac Platte.
J. H. Fairbanks, Red Cedar Lake.
Louis Dufault, Red Lake.
Wm. Stitt, Lower Red Cedar Lake.
L. M. Warren, La Pointe, Wis.
Chas. Wolfborup, Yellow Lake.

vulgarity, and its attack upon the character of gentlemen who did not show him the attention which he thought he should have received.

The next year, another foreign gentleman visited the country, who was the antipodes to him whom we have just noticed. His name will always be honoured in the university and colleges of the state; and his career will incite others to the culture of those exact sciences, which are so useful in their results to the practical man.

Jean N. Nicollet,[1] with letters of introduction, having arrived in Minnesota, on the twenty-sixth of July, 1836,

[1] Jean N. Nicollet was born in the year 1790, at Cluses, a small town, capital of Fansigny in Savoie. His parents were poor, and he was consequently reduced to the necessity of gaining a subsistence by playing upon the flute and violin, before he had reached the tender age of ten years. He was then apprenticed to a watchmaker, and remained with him until he was eighteen years old, when he removed to Chambry, the capital of Savoie, where he followed his occupation, at the same time prosecuting his studies in mathematics, for his proficiency in which science he received a prize. From Chambry he returned to Cluses, and there gave lessons in mathematics, he himself receiving instruction in Latin and other languages. He continued this course of life for about two years, when he went to Paris and was admitted in the first class of L'Ecole Normale, and soon afterwards he was placed in charge of the mathematical course in the college of "Louis Le Grand."

It was in 1818 that Nicollet published his celebrated letter to M. Outrequin Banquier, "on assurances having for their basis, the probable duration of human life."

From 1819 and 1820, may be dated the commencement of his astronomical labours.

On the twenty-first of January, 1821, between six and seven in the evening, he discovered a comet in the constellation of Pegasus (seen on the same day and at the same hour by Pons at Marseilles), and from his own observations, and those of the astronomers and the observatory, he completed its parabolic elements.

Previous to 1825, M. Nicollet received the decoration of the Legion of Honour, and had also been attached as Professor, to the Royal College of "Louis Le Grand."

Having been unfortunate in speculations which involved others in pecuniary loss, he came to the United States in 1832; poor, but honest.— See sketch in *Annals Minnesota Hist. Soc.*, No. iv. 1853.

left Fort Snelling with a French trader, named Fronchet, to explore the sources of the Mississippi. While at the Falls of St. Anthony, the Dahkotahs pilfered some of his provisions, but writing back to the fort for another supply, he ascended the Mississippi, telescope in hand, and with a trustful, child-like spirit, hoped with Sir Isaac Newton, to gather a few pebbles from the great ocean of truth. After reaching Crow Wing river, he entered its mouth, and by way of Gull river and lake, he reached Leech Lake, the abode of the Pillagers. When the savages found that he was nothing but a poor scholar, with neither medals, nor beef, nor flags to present, and constantly peeping through a tube into the heavens, they became very unruly.

The Rev. Mr. Boutwell, whose mission house was on the opposite side of the lake, hearing the shouts and drumming of the Indians, came over as soon as the wind which had been blowing for several days, would allow the passage of his canoe. His arrival was very grateful to Nicollet, who says: "On the fourth day, however, he arrived, and although totally unknown to each other previously, a sympathy of feeling arose, growing out of the precarious circumstances under which we were both placed, and to which he had been much longer exposed than myself. This feeling, from the kind attentions he paid me, soon ripened into affectionate gratitude."

Leaving Leech Lake with an Indian, Fronchet and Francis Brunet, a Canadian trader of that post, "a man six feet three inches in height, a giant of great strength, and at the same time full of the milk of human kindness," he proceeded toward Itasca Lake. With the sextant on his back, thrown over like a knapsack, a barometer and cloak on his left shoulder, a portfolio under his arm, and a basket in hand holding thermometer, chronometer, and compass, he followed his guides over the necessary portages. After the usual trials of an inexperienced traveller, he pitched his tent on Schoolcraft's Island, in Lake Itasca, and proceeded to use his telescope and instruments.

Continuing his explorations beyond those of Lieut. Allen and Schoolcraft, he entered on the twenty-ninth of August, a tributary of the west bay of the lake, two or three feet in depth, and from fifteen to twenty feet in width. While the previous explorers had passed but *one* or *two* hours at Itasca Lake, he stayed three days with complete scientific apparatus, and sought the sources of the rivulets that feed the lake. With great appropriateness has his claim been recognised by the people of Minnesota, as the individual who completed the exploration of the Mississippi, by giving his name to a county.

Returning to Fort Snelling in the beginning of October, he occupied a room at the stone agency house, a quarter of a mile beyond the gate, where he passed the time in studying the Dahkotah. The latter portion of the winter Nicollet was a guest of Mr. Sibley, at Mendota. That gentleman says:—

"A portion of the winter following was spent by him at my house, and it is hardly necessary to state that I found in him a most instructive companion. His devotion to his studies was intense and unremitting, and I frequently expostulated with him upon his imprudence in thus over-tasking the strength of his delicate frame, but with little effect. When the weather was auspicious, telescope in hand, he would spend hours of the cold winter nights of our high latitude in astral observations. He continued his labours until the opening of spring called him to encounter the privations and sufferings necessarily attendant upon a long sojourn in the wilderness. Such was the enthusiasm of his nature, that he submitted to all physical inconveniences without murmuring, and as of no moment when compared with the magnitude of the enterprise in which he was engaged."

Going to Washington, after his tour of 1836–37, he was honoured with a commission from the United States government, and John C. Fremont was detailed as his assistant. Ascending the Missouri river in a steamboat, to Fort Pierre, he travelled through the interior of Minnesota Territory, visiting the Red Pipe Stone Quarry, which he accurately describes, Minne Wakan, or Devil's Lake, and other important localities.

The map which he constructed, and the astronomical observations which he made, were invaluable to the country.[1]

---

[1] Hon. H. H. Sibley, in his notice of Nicollet, says:—

"His health was so seriously affected after his return to Washington in 1839, that from that time forward he was incapacitated from devoting himself to the accomplishment of his work as exclusively as he had previously done. Still he laboured, but it was with depressed spirits and blighted hopes. He had long aspired to a membership in the Academy of Sciences of Paris. His long continued devotion and valuable contributions to the cause of science, and his correct deportment as a gentleman, alike entitled him to such a distinction. But his enemies were numerous and influential, and when his name was presented in accordance with a previous nomination, to fill a vacancy, he was black-balled and rejected. This last blow was mortal. True, he strove against the incurable melancholy which had fastened itself upon him, but his struggles waxed more and more faint, until death put a period to his sufferings on the eighteenth September, 1844.

"Even when he was aware that his dissolution was near at hand, his

NICOLLET'S DEATH.—AITKIN KILLED.

The Leech Lake Ojibways this year killed the trader[1] in charge of the American Fur Company's post, at that point, and many threatened to drive away the Rev. Mr. Boutwell, and manifested bitter hostility.

thoughts reverted back to the days when he roamed along the valley of the Minnesota river. It was my fortune to meet him for the last time in the year 1842 in Washington City. A short time before his death I received a kind but mournful letter from him, in which he adverted to the fact that his days were numbered, but at the same time he expressed a hope that he would have strength sufficient to enable him to make his way to our country, that he might yield up his breath and be interred on the banks of his beloved stream.

"It would have been gratifying to his friends to know that the soil of the region which had employed so much of his time and scientific research, had received his mortal remains into his bosom, but they were denied this melancholy satisfaction. He sleeps beneath the sod far away, in the vicinity of the capital of the nation, but his name will continue to be cherished in Minnesota as one of its early explorers, and one of its best friends. The astronomer, the geologist, and the christian gentleman, Jean N. Nicollet, will long be remembered in connection with the history of the North-west.

"Time shall quench full many
A people's records, and a hero's acts.
Sweep empire after empire into nothing;
But even then shall spare this deed of thine.
And hold it up, a problem few dare imitate,
And none despise."

[1] Alfred Aitkin.

CHAPTER XX.

THE history of missions among the roving tribes of Minnesota and the regions adjacent, must necessarily be a dark and saddening page. They are all bands without law.

The frontispiece of the first volume of the voyages of Baron La Hontan to the Lakes of the West, published more than one hundred and fifty years ago, is an engraving of an Indian, attired for war, with a bow in one hand and arrow in the other, a statute book under one foot, and a crown and sceptre beneath the other. Over his head is the appropriate motto "Et leges, et sceptra terit:" On laws and sceptres he tramples.

The savages of the north-west, as has been shown, have nothing that corresponds to a civilized government. Their chiefs hold their influence by a trimming and somersaulting which would put the most adroit politician to the blush. Society takes no cognisance of offences, and each man revenges his real or imaginary wrongs. If one is killed, the relative in return goes and kills the person who committed the act. They also hold their property in common. If, on a hunting expedition, a man shoots a deer, he does not claim it as private property, but it is shared with all present. If an industrious person should settle down and cultivate a field of corn and potatoes, custom requires that he should share it with the idler and the passer-by.

The aversion to labour is such that the men ordinarily feel it an insult to be urged to work. Toil is only becoming to women. In addition to these prejudices, when not hunting for wild beasts, they, with the ferocity of wild beasts, hunt for the scalps of their wild neighbours. There is scarcely a large plain in Minnesota that has not been an Aceldama.

The youth from his earliest childhood is trained to delight in war. Bancroft, catching the enthusiasm of the narratives of the early Jesuits, depicts, in language which glows, their missions to the North-west; yet it is erroneous to suppose that they exercised any permanent influence on the Aborigines.

Fond of novelty and attention, the untutored children of the forest for a little while were interested in the pictures and vestments and tales of the "black gown," but they at length grew weary. Marquette, while at La Pointe on Lake Superior, made a fatal mistake as a minister of Christianity. In his narrative he says that he allowed the Ojibways to retain such sacrifices to imaginary spirits as he thought were *harmless*, as if it was possible to serve God and Manitou. After he was driven from the shores of Lake Superior, no further attempt was made to elevate the Aborigines of that region, until the arrival of Protestant missionaries more than a century subsequent.

The devout Romanist, Shea, in his interesting history of Catholic missions, speaking of the Dahkotahs remarks that, " Father Menard had projected a Sioux mission; Marquette, Allouëz, Druilletes, all entertained hopes of realizing it, and had some intercourse with that nation, but none of them ever succeeded in establishing a mission." After the American Fur Company was formed, the island of Mackinaw became the residence of the principal agent for the North-west.

In the month of June of the year 1820, the Rev. Dr. Morse, father of the inventor of the Morseograph,[1] visited the spot, and preached the first Protestant sermon ever delivered in this portion of the North-west. He became quite interested in the condition of traders and natives; and in consequence of his statements, a Presbyterian Missionary Society in the state of New York, sent a graduate of Union College, the Rev. W. M. Ferry, in 1822, to explore the field. In October, 1823, with his wife, he commenced a school, which, before the close of the year, contained twelve Indian children.

Mackinaw being easy of access to the Indians of the Upper Lakes, and the Upper Mississippi, the American Board of Commissioners of Foreign Missions, who had assumed the expense, determined to make it a central station, at which there should be a large boarding-school, composed of children collected from all the North-western tribes, who were expected to remain long enough to acquire a common school education, and a knowledge of manual labour. Mechanics' shops and gardens were provided for the lads, and the girls were trained for household duties. The school, for many years, succeeded admirably; and gained the confidence of traders and chiefs. At times there were nearly two hundred pupils present, representatives of the Ottawas, Ojibways, Dah-

[1] This word is a novelty found at the head of the telegraphic reports of the Philadelphia Public Ledger.

kotahs, Winnebagoes, Pottowattamies, Knistenoes, Sauks, Foxes, and Menomonees. There are those now in Minnesota, surrounded by all the comforts of civilization, who are indebted to this school for their entire education. After a series of years, the plan was modified, the school limited to fifty, and smaller stations commenced in the region between Lake Superior and the Mississippi.

During the summer of 1830, Mr. Warren, the father of the late bois brulé William Warren, came to Mackinaw, with an extra boat, for the purpose of taking a missionary to his post at La Pointe. As there were no ordained ministers that could be spared, the teacher of the boys' school, Mr. Frederic Ayer, now of Belle Prairie, with one of the scholars as an interpreter, returned with the trader to La Pointe, for the purpose of exploring the field.

After surveying the country, Mr. Ayer returned to Mackinaw; but in August of the next year, in company with a graduate of Dartmouth College, the Rev. Sherman Hall and wife, left with the intention of establishing a permanent mission among the Ojibways. The brigade with which they travelled consisted of five boats and about seventy persons. The following extracts from the journal[1] of the first Protestant minister among the Ojibways of the far west, may be perused with interest:—

"August fifth, 1831. The manner of travelling on the upper waters of the great lakes, is with open canoes and batteaux. The former are made in the Indian style, the materials of which are the bark of the white birch, and the wood of the white cedar. The cedar

[1] Rev. Sherman Hall.

forms the ribbing, and the bark the part which comes in contact with the water. These are made of various sizes, from ten to thirty feet in length. The largest are sufficiently strong to carry from two to three tons of lading. They are propelled with the paddle; and when well built and well manned, without lading, will go from eighty to one hundred miles in a day, in calm weather.

"Batteaux are light-made boats, about forty feet in length, and ten or twelve feet wide at the centre, capable of carrying about five tons burden each, and are rowed by six or seven men. They have no deck. Upon articles of lading, with which the boat is filled, is the place for the passengers, who have no other seats than they can form for themselves, out of their travelling trunks, boxes, beds, etc. On these they place themselves in any position which necessity may require, or convenience suggest, with very little regard to gracefulness of position. Such is the vehicle which is to convey us to the place of our destination. In the small compass of this boat we have to find room for eleven persons, including our family and our men, one of whom is an Indian, and four are Frenchmen.

"A person travelling in this region, is obliged to submit to many inconveniences. Here the traveller must take his bed, his house, his provisions, and his utensils to cook them with, along with him, or consent to sleep in the open air on the ground, and to subsist on what the woods and the waters may chance to afford. In short, if he would have anything to make himself comfortable, he must provide himself with it before he leaves home. There are no New England taverns here, at which the traveller can rest when he is weary, and find supplies for all his wants. Journeys are frequent. In this country, people think those near neighbours who live two hundred or three hundred miles distant. A journey of this length, even in the dead of winter, is no more accounted of here, than a ride from one city to another on the sea-coast of the United States, though he who performs it must take his provision and his snow shoes, and march without a track through the unbroken wilderness.

"At night our tent is pitched at some convenient place on the shore. After the tent is raised, a painted cloth is spread within it on the ground. This forms a kind of flooring. On this a carpet of Indian mats, made of a kind of coarse grass or rush, which answers the triple purpose of a carpet, a table, and a bedstead. The bed is composed of several thicknesses of blankets, coverlets, or anything else one may choose to carry for this purpose, with a sufficient quantity of other clothes for covering. Each family of travellers has a willow basket, with a lock and key, sufficiently capacious to hold from one to two bushels, of close texture, which is covered with a swinging lid. This basket answers the purpose of a pantry. This is divided into various departments in the inside, for meat, tea, bread, coffee, and dishes. The cooking is done without, in the open air. With such accommodations a journey of several hundred miles may be performed with tolerable comfort, though at the expense of some inconveniences.

"August thirtieth. After sailing thirty leagues in a day and a half, we arrived at La Pointe, the place of our destination, about noon to-day, all heartily glad to find a resting place, and a shelter from the storm and cold. We were agreeably disappointed on finding the place so much more pleasant than we had anticipated. As we approached it, it appeared like a small village. There are several houses, stores, barns, and out-buildings about the establishment, and forty or fifty acres of land under cultivation.

"September first. This evening we cooked our first meal, and united together around the family altar in our new abode. We returned thanks to God for his goodness in preserving us and bringing us to this place, as we had prayed, and besought his blessing on our future labours."

Mr. Hall immediately established a school for children, and placed it in charge of Mr. Ayer.

The next year, at the urgent solicitation of the trader, Mr. Aitkin, Mr. Ayer went to Sandy Lake and opened a school for the children of voyageurs and Indians.

The Rev. Mr. Boutwell, a graduate of Dartmouth; in the summer of 1832, after his tour with H. R. Schoolcraft, became a colleague of Mr. Hall at La Pointe, and took charge of the school.

In the month of September, 1832, the Rev. Sherman Hall made an exploring tour to Lac du Flambeau, in North-western Wisconsin, and reached the trading-post of Charles H. Oakes, at that place, on the twentieth of the month. His journal is instructive:—

"September eleventh, 1832. I left La Pointe for Lac du Flambeau, accompanied by one man to carry my provisions and baggage. Our journey was partly by water and partly by land, and much of the way through dense forests of tall and heavy timber. Our road was a small foot-path, which has been formed by those who make this wilderness their highway to the interior. The ground in this great forest is not as level as much of the western country. We crossed no high hills, but the surface of the country was continually undulating. The soil appeared to be of excellent quality, and capable of furnishing the means of subsistence for a dense population, if it should be cleared of its present heavy burden of timber, and suitably tilled. It is not stony, though stones are to be found nearly all the way. The country seems to be well watered with clear transparent streams."

Crossing Forty-five Mile Portage, between Montreal river and Portage Lake, at the same time that the gentleman engaged in the fur trade at Lac du Flambeau was conveying his goods to that post, Mr. Hall describes the laborious method of transportation, which is necessarily resorted to in those uncultivated and almost desolate regions.

"All the goods for this department of the Indian trade, together with a considerable quantity of provisions, are carried across this portage on the backs of men. Not a pound of flour, or salt, or butter, or pork, or scarcely any other article of living consumed at the post, except vegetables, a little corn, wild rice, and fish, and a small quantity of wild meat, can be obtained in any other manner. All the tobacco, powder, shot, and balls, used in the trade, and every heavy utensil for household use, and implements for cultivating the ground, which cannot be made by unskilful mechanics on the spot, all the nails and glass for building, and the tools necessary for mechanical purposes, must all find their way through these forests in the same manner. On the other hand, all the furs and peltries collected in the department, many of which are brought some hundreds of miles before they reach Lac du Flambeau, are conveyed to market over the same road, and by the same kind of conveyance.

"The goods are obtained at Mackinaw, and brought through the lake, till they enter the Montreal river, a distance of five or six hundred miles, in boats rowed by men. At the commencement of the portage, they are put up into packs or bales, convenient for carrying, which, in the language of the country, are termed pieces. Each piece is allowed to weigh eighty pounds. A barrel of flour is put into two bags, and each is considered a piece. A keg of pork or a keg of gunpowder is considered also a piece, and a bushel and a half of corn. Two of these pieces constitute each man's load. The carrier uses a collar, which is composed of a strap of leather about three inches wide in the middle, to which smaller straps are attached of a sufficient length to tie round the object to be carried. These straps are tied round each end of the piece, which is then swung upon the back, the lower part resting about on the loins, and the collar is brought over the top of the head. The person, when he takes his load, inclines a little forward, so that it rests considerably on the back, and draws but gently on the collar suspended across the head. After the first piece is thus swung on the back, the second is taken up and laid on the top of it, reaching, if it be large, nearly to the top of the head. I was surprised to see with what ease these men, after they had suspended the first piece, would raise up the second and place it on the top of it. The party consisted of ten men, and each man had ten pieces, or five loads to carry across the portage. They keep the whole of the goods together; that is, each one takes one load and marches with it, the distance of one-half or one-third of a mile, and then returns for a second. This they repeat till all their loads are brought up to this point. Each man's pieces are allotted to him at the commencement of the portage, and he keeps the same through. There are in all one hundred and twenty-two poses, or stopping places, on this portage. The carriers march very rapidly when loaded. About two hundred of these pieces, in goods and provisions, are required for this department annually. When we passed these men, they had been sixteen days on the portage, and had got about two-thirds of the way across it. After they cross this, they have two other portages to make before they reach Lac du Flambeau, one of which is one hundred and fifty or two hundred rods, and the other about three miles in length.

"September twenty-third. I reached the trading-post of Mr. Oakes, by whom I was very kindly received, on the twentieth. The village of the Indians is two or three miles distant from his post. This morning three men, having heard that I had arrived, came, as they said, to see me, and to hear what I had to say to them. Two of them were young men, and the other I should judge to be about fifty, of a straight, well proportioned body and limbs, not very tall, a countenance rather dignified, a keen, arch-looking eye, and a carriage that told him to be a man who claimed some title to chieftainship among his band. I greeted them in a friendly manner, and told them I was glad to see them, and if they would listen, I would tell them something about God and his word."

On the fifteenth of September, 1833, Mr. Ayer arrived at Yellow Lake, also in the extreme north-western portion of Wisconsin, for the purpose of commencing a mission station. In October of the same year the Rev. W. T. Boutwell proceeded to Leech Lake, and established the *first mission in Minnesota west of the Mississippi*. Mr. E. F. Ely[1] became a teacher during this year, at the trading-post of Mr. Aitkin, at Sandy Lake, Minnesota; but the next year opened a school at Fond du Lac, on the St. Louis river.

Calvinism is frequently represented, by those who do not embrace its tenets, as a mere abstract system, only anxious to impress upon the race stern theological formulas; but the journals of its missionaries among the savages are always eminently cheerful, hopeful, and practical. They came to the untutored Indians of Minnesota, not with a long-drawn countenance, and severe exterior, but they came singing songs for the little ones, and teaching the men to plough, and the women to sew and knit.

The following letter, written in 1833, by Rev. Mr. Boutwell, is full of sunshine from one of the dark places of earth, Leech Lake, the abode of the Pillagers, the most savage of all the bands of Minnesota:—

"I arrived at this place October third. Passing for the present in silence the particulars of my voyage, I will proceed directly to give you some account of my reception. When I arrived, the men, with few excep-

---

[1] Letter from Mr. Ely, at Sandy Lake, September twenty-fifth, 1833.

"I arrived at this post September nineteenth, and am happily disappointed in the appearance of the place. I occupy a large chamber in Mr. Aitkin's house, which is both a school-room and lodging-room, commanding an eastern view of Mr. A.'s fields and meadows, and of the lake and hills covered with pines, together with the outlet of the lake running within eighty feet of the house; the Mississippi is about the same distance on the west; and their confluence is about ten rods below. On the twenty-third Mr. Boutwell left us for Leech Lake. My school was commenced on the same day with six or eight scholars. To-day I have had fifteen."

tions, were making their fall hunts, while their families remained at the lake, and in its vicinity, to gather their corn and make rice. A few lodges were encamped quite near. These I began to visit for the purpose of reading, singing, etc., in order to interest the children, and awaken in them a desire for instruction. I told them about the children at Mackinaw, the Sault, and at La Pointe, who could read, write, and sing. To this they would listen attentively, while the mother would often reply, 'My children are poor and ignorant.' To a person unaccustomed to Indian manners and Indian wildness, it would have been amusing to have seen the little ones, as I approached their lodge, running and screaming, more terrified, if possible, than if they had met a bear robbed of her whelps. It was not long, however, before most of them overcame their fears; and in a few days my dwelling (a lodge which I occupied for three or four weeks) was frequented from morning till evening by an interesting group of boys, all desirous to learn to read and sing. To have seen them hanging, some on one knee, others upon my shoulder, reading and singing, while others, whether from shame or fear I know not, who dared not venture within, were peeping in through the sides of the cottage, or lying flat upon the ground and looking under the bottom, might have provoked a smile, especially to have seen them as they caught a glance of my eye, springing upon their feet and running like so many wild asses' colts. The rain, cold, and snow were alike to them, in which they would come day after day, many of them clad merely with a blanket and a narrow strip of cloth about the loins.

"The men at length returned, and an opportunity was presented me for reading to them. The greater part listened attentively. Some would come back and ask me to read more. Others laughed and aimed to make sport, both of me and my book. I heeded as if I understood not. I had been laughed at and called a fool before. Besides, I remembered to have read, 'the servant is not above his master.' The second chief (Riji Osaie), the Elder Brother as he is called, now returned. This chief, though nominally second, is really the first in the affections of the band. He is a man who courts neither the favour, nor fears the frown of his fellow, but speaks independently what he thinks. One morning, after breakfasting with us, I said to him, 'I have come to pass the winter with your trader, and I thought I would teach some of the children to read if their parents were pleased.' 'It is a good thing to instruct the children, and I do not think an Indian in the whole band can be displeased or say a word against it,' replied he. A higher object than this, even this man could not appreciate at present. This was all and even more than I anticipated from him, knowing as I did something of the past history, as well as present disposition of the band. A few days after, as an Indian was leaving with his family for his winter hunt, he came and asked me if I should be pleased to have his little boy, a lad of ten years, remain with me. 'Certainly,' replied I, 'if I had the means of feeding him.' The trader sitting by kindly offered to feed the boy, and the father left him in my care, saying, 'If you will teach him to read as the whites do, I should be so glad I do not know what I could do for you.' He is a lad of much promise, enthusiastically fond of his books, and often expresses a strong desire to learn to read English. It is but about six weeks since he first saw a book in his own language;

yet he now reads and spells in two syllables, counts one hundred in Indian, and forty in English, repeats and sings several hymns in Indian, and is committing the ten commandments. The like request was made by one or two others, but I had no means of my own of either feeding or sheltering them.

"You are now prepared to hear me say from what I have seen, and so far as I am able to judge, the Lord hath opened a door, and apparently preparing the way for you to occupy this field as soon as you can furnish the men and the means. In my opinion the sooner you occupy it the better. The question has often been put to me by the Indians, 'Will you leave in the spring?' 'Will you come back again?' The only reply I could make (but to an Indian of ambiguous interpretation), 'the Lord willing, I will return or send some other person.' That there are individuals who would be unwilling to have their children instructed at present, I have no doubt. I am not without hope, however, that by kindness and a judicious course of conduct, their prejudices would soon give way. I am equally confident also, that there are individuals in the band, and I trust a goodly number, who would be highly pleased to have a kind and judicious missionary located here.

"In relation to their numbers and locality, my journal, now in your possession, may perhaps give you all necessary information. Including the small band on Bear Island, excluded from the estimate, there are at least eight hundred souls belonging to Leech Lake. The Winnipeg and Upper-Red-Cedar Lake bands are distant but a day's march, which in this country and by an Indian is not a matter of reckoning.

"The means of subsistence which the country affords

are not inconsiderable. These are fish, corn, and rice, and they are the almost entire dependence of the traders. Fish is the principal. Not less than thirty thousand were taken this fall for the winter supply of the four houses here. They are called tullibees, the only name save the Indian (Etonibins) that I have ever heard. They will average from one to three pounds as they are taken from the water. The manner of curing them is merely to hang them in the air to freeze—a simple rather than a safe way. The trader with whom I pass the winter has now upon the scaffold about ten thousand. For two weeks past the weather has been quite warm, and he fears, as do his neighbours, that we shall not be able to use them. If fish fail, to say the least, we shall all grow poor, if we do not some of us grow hungry. There was comparatively little corn raised the past season by the Indians, perhaps one hundred and fifty bushels. They are now in the habit of exchanging corn and rice with their traders for strouds and blankets, which, happily for the Indians, have taken the place of liquor, which is now a prohibited article in the trade. I am credibly informed that the exceptions were rare in which an Indian would not give his last sack of provisions for whiskey. Wild rice, an article of much dependence among the Indians, nearly failed the past season on account of high water. Hundreds of bushels of this excellent food are often gathered from the small lakes in the vicinity, and from the deep bays of this lake. Nowhere between Lake Superior and the head waters of the Mississippi has the God of providence so bountifully provided for the subsistence of man as here. In addition to rice and several species of fish which this lake affords, the soil is also of a rich quality and highly

FERTILITY OF SOIL AT LEECH LAKE. 437

susceptible of cultivation. All the English grains, in my opinion, may be cultivated here. At present an Indian's garden consists merely of a few square rods in which he plants a little corn and a few squashes. Very few as yet cultivate the potato, probably for want of seed. Fish, instead of bread, is here the staff of life.

"The traders here have found it impracticable to keep any domestic animal save the dog and cat. For the least offence an Indian here will sooner shoot a horse or cow for revenge than a dog. Still a missionary by the second or third year will be better able to judge than I now can, with how much security he could make the experiment.

"If the Indians can be induced by example and other helps (such as seed and preparing the ground), to cultivate more largely, they would, I have no doubt, furnish provisions for their children in part. If a mission here should furnish the means of feeding, clothing, and instructing the children, as at Mackinaw, I venture to say there would be no lack of children. But such an establishment is not only impracticable here; it is such as would ill meet the exigencies of this people. While a mission proffers them aid, they should be made to feel that they must try at least to help themselves. It should be placed on a footing that will instruct them in the principles of political economy. At present there is among them nothing like personal rights, or individual property, any further than traps, guns, and kettles are concerned. They possess all things in common. If an Indian has anything to eat, his neighbours are all allowed to share it with him. *While, therefore, a mission extends the hand of charity in the means of instruction, and occasionally an article of clothing, and perhaps some aid in procuring the means of subsistence, it should be only to such individuals as will themselves use the means so far as they possess them.* This might operate as a stimulus with them to cultivate and fix a value upon corn, rice, etc., at least with such as care to have their children instructed, rather than squander it in feasts and feeding such as are too indolent to make a garden themselves. It will require much patience, if not a long time, to break up and eradicate habits so inveterate. An Indian cannot eat alone. If he kills a pheasant, his neighbours must come in for a portion, small indeed, but so it is. As it respects furnishing them with seeds and implements of husbandry, this may be done, but only to a certain extent. An Indian would most surely take advantage of your liberality. Every one would come, the last expecting to be served as well, if not better, than the first. The mention of a single fact may throw sufficient light upon this trait in Indian character. While at Sandy Lake, on my way here, I presented a little boy with a shirt. Not half an hour after he had gone out, no less than half a dozen others came for the same favour. But more, I have known boys who had a shirt pull it off and throw it aside, while they would come expecting to get a new one, in case you had made a present to one who had none. They are so jealous, that the utmost precaution must be observed in making a present of the least article to one that you cannot make to another.

"So far as my observation extends, polygamy is more common among this band than any other with which I am acquainted. Not only the chiefs, but all the best hunters who are able to clothe, in their miserable manner, more than one woman, keep from two to five. One individual keeps three who are sisters; and this not being sufficient, has a fourth woman."

In the year 1834, Mr. Boutwell was married at Fond du Lac, to an interesting and educated Anglojibway lady, who died a few years ago. The experiences of married life at Leech Lake, are narrated in his journal published in the Missionary Herald, and are probably the first housekeeping of a couple married according to the rites of Christianity, beyond the walls of Fort Snelling, in Minnesota.

"The clerk very kindly invited me to occupy a part of his quarters, until I could prepare a place to put myself. I thought best to decline his offer; and on the thirteenth instant, removed my effects, and commenced housekeeping in a bark lodge. Then, here I was, without a quart of corn or Indian rice to eat myself, or give my man, as I was too late to purchase any of the mere pittance which was to be bought or sold. My nets, under God, were my sole dependence to feed myself and hired man. I had a barrel and a half of flour, and ninety pounds of pork only before me for the winter. But on the seventeenth of the same month, I sent my fisherman ten miles distant to gather our winter's stock of provisions out of the deep. In the mean time, I must build a house, or winter in an Indian lodge. Rather than do worse, I shouldered my axe and led the way, having procured a man of the trader to help me; and in about ten days had my timbers cut and on the ground ready to put up.

"On the twelfth of November, I recalled my fisherman, and found on our scaffold nearly six thousand tulibees (a kind of fish found in the north-western lakes), for our winter supplies.

"On the second of December, I quit my bark lodge for a mud-walled house; the timbers of which, I not only assisted in cutting, but also carrying on my back, until the rheumatism, to say the least, threatened to double and twist me, and I was obliged to desist. My house, when I began to occupy it, had a door, three windows, and a mud chimney; but neither chair, stool, nor bedstead. A box served for the former, and an Indian mat for the two latter. A rude figure, indeed, my house would make in a New England city, with its deer-skin windows, a floor that had never seen a plane, or a saw, and a mud chimney; but it is, nevertheless, comfortable.

"When I arrived, the Indians, as I expected, were mostly off for their fall hunt. As their gardens were nearly destroyed last summer by the worm, and rice again failed, their families were obliged to go to the deer country, ten days' march from us. This circumstance has tended to remove them, for the time being, from our intercourse and influence. March will bring them back and settle them down around us, at least the major part of them, as they make sugar and cultivate little gardens here and there, where each family chooses.

"Among those whom I have seen, is the Elder Brother, the second chief, who expressed his satisfaction that I had returned, and regretted that he was not present at my arrival, while there remained a few men with whom he would have smoked and spoken on the occasion. The first chief, a few days since, sent me word that he would call his young men together in the spring, when he returns from his hunt. Thus far these two men have taken an honourable and decided course, so far as precept can go, and have given assurance that

FIRST MISSIONS ESTABLISHED AMONG DAHKOTAHS. 441

this should be followed by practice, in case a permanent missionary was located here. What, however, the spring will decide, when the good, bad, and indifferent all meet together, I do not pretend to foretell. The cause is God's, and he will order all things well."

The Jesuits considered the Dahkotahs as the most fierce of all the tribes, and did not venture their lives in their midst, except for a few months by the side of a French officer.

It was not till the year 1834, that any formal attempt was made to instruct them in the arts, letters, or in the morality of the Bible. The Rev. Samuel W. Pond, at that time a layman and school teacher in Galena, Illinois, hearing accounts of the Dahkotahs from Red river emigrants, became interested in their welfare, and wrote to his brother Gideon H. Pond, then a young man in their native place in Connecticut, proposing that they should cast their lot with the Dahkotahs, and try to do them good.

The proposition was accepted, and in the spring of 1834, provided with neither brass, nor scrip, nor purse, he joined his brother at Galena, and embarking on board of a steamer, they arrived at Fort Snelling in May.

They stated their plans to Mr. Taliaferro, the Dahkotah agent, and were treated with kindness by him and Major Bliss, the commander of the fort. Without aid or encouragement from any missionary society, they proceeded to the east shore of Lake Calhoun, on the banks of which and Lake Harriet, dwelt small bands of Dahkotahs, and with their own hands erected a rude cabin on the site of a building in recent times occupied by Charles Musou.

About this period, a native of South Carolina, and

graduate of Jefferson College, Pennsylvania, the Rev. T. S. Williamson, M. D., who, previous to his ordination, had been a respectable physician in Ohio, was appointed by the American Board of Commissioners of Foreign Missions to visit the Dahkotahs, with the view of ascertaining what could be done to introduce Christian instruction. Having made inquiries at Prairie du Chien and Fort Snelling, he reported that the field was favourable. The Presbyterian and Congregational churches, through their joint missionary society, appointed the following persons to labour in Minnesota: Rev. Thomas S. Williamson, M.D., missionary and physician; Rev. J. D. Stevens, missionary; Alexander Huggens, farmer; and their wives; Miss Sarah Poage, and Lucy C. Stevens, teachers; who were prevented during the year 1834, by the state of navigation, from entering upon their work.

During the winter of 1834-35, a pious officer of the army exercised a good influence on his fellow officers, and soldiers under their command. In the absence of a chaplain or ordained minister, he, like General Havelock of the British army in India, was accustomed not only to drill the soldiers, but to meet them in his own quarters, and "reason with them of righteousness, temperance, and judgment to come."[1]

In the month of May, 1835, Dr. Williamson and mission band arrived at Fort Snelling, and were hospitably received by the officers of the garrison, the Indian agent, and Mr. Sibley, then a young man, who had re-

[1] The growling Englishman Featherstonhaugh, whose book has been noticed, became very much offended because this officer did not as he thought sufficiently notice him, and vents his spleen by calling him a long, lean, canting, "psalm-singing major."

cently taken charge of the trading-post at Mendota. On the second Sabbath in June, a Presbyterian church was organized in one of the company rooms of the fort, and the communion was administered for the first time in Minnesota to twenty-two persons of European extraction, composed of officers and soldiers of the army, those engaged in the fur trade, and the mission families. The late Major Ogden, of the army, who died at Fort Riley, here professed his faith in Christianity. Two posts were selected by the missionaries as stations.

The Rev. Mr. Stevens and family proceeded to Lake Harriet, in Hennepin county, and erected a house near the property of Eli Pettijohn; and the Rev. Dr. Williamson and wife, Mr. Huggens, the farmer, and wife, and Miss Poage, proceeded to Lac qui Parle. After a fatiguing journey of seventeen days, without meeting man or beast, they arrived at the lake on the ninth of July, and were warmly welcomed by the well known trader, Renville, whose name is attached to one of the counties of Minnesota.

Immediately after their arrival at the stations, the missionaries began to study the language of the Dahkotahs, and teach the children what they could. In a letter to the Cincinnati Journal, written in November, 1835, Dr. Williamson describes Dahkotah habits as follows:—

"Gathering the corn, as well as whatever else pertains to cultivating the earth, is considered to be the business of the women. They gather it in their blankets, and carry it to the scaffold, on which they stand to drive off the birds. Here it is thrown in a heap exposed to the sun, till the husks begin to wilt. These husks are then stripped from the corn, but most of them still left attached to the cob. The husks of many ears, still fast to the ear, are then platted together into a long string, by which the corn is suspended over a hole to dry. After hanging for several weeks, exposed to the weather till it is entirely freed from moisture, the corn is threshed off the cobs, and put in bags made of skins of small fibres of lynn bark woven together with the fingers.

"The smallest and most unripe ears are prepared in a different way. The husks being entirely torn off, they are boiled. Then the corn is shelled, and dried by being strewed thin where it will be exposed to the direct rays of the sun. When thoroughly dried it is put in bags same as the other. When the corn is sufficiently dried it is put in sacks containing from one to two bushels each, and put away in what are called *caches* by the traders. These are made by digging a circular hole about eighteen inches in diameter, perpendicularly one or two feet deep, and then enlarging it in the form of an earth oven till of sufficient size to contain what they have to put into it. They are usually five or six feet in diameter at the bottom, and as much in depth. The bottom and sides are lined with dry grass, on which the sacks of corn are placed. Dry grass is also put on top of the corn till it is filled, except the perpendicular part. This is filled with earth which is stamped down firmly. Corn thus laid away keeps dry and good from September till April under ground.

"Flesh of every kind is such a rarity with the Dahkotahs of these parts, that they eat every kind of quadrupeds and fowls they can obtain. Not only deer, bear, and squirrels, grouse, ducks, and geese, but muskrats, otters, wolves, foxes and badgers, cranes, hawks, and owls. They eat not only what is properly called the flesh of these animals, but every part which can be supposed to contain nutriment,—the heads, feet, entrails, and the skins, if they be not valuable as an article of traffic. After picking the flesh off the larger bones, they break them and boil them to get any little oil they may contain to mix with their corn. Exclusive of their corn, their food consists in winter chiefly of muskrats, badgers, otters, and raccoons; in the spring, of fish, and roots which the earth produces spontaneously, with some ducks; in the summer, roots, fish, wild pigeons, and cranes; in autumn, wild ducks, geese, and muskrats."

As there had never been a chaplain at Fort Snelling, the Rev. J. D. Stevens, the missionary at Lake Harriet, preached on Sundays to the Presbyterian church, recently organized. Writing on January twenty-seventh, 1836, he says, in relation to his field of labour:—

"Yesterday a portion of this band of Indians, who had been some time absent from this village, returned. One of the number (a woman) was informed that a brother of hers had died during her absence. He was not at this village, but with another band, and the information had just reached here. In the evening they set up a most piteous crying, or rather wailing, which continued, with some little cessations, during the night. The sister of the deceased brother would repeat, times without number, words which may be thus translated into English: 'Come, my brother, I shall see you no more for ever.' The night was extremely cold—the thermometer standing from ten to twenty below zero. About sunrise, next morning, preparation was made for performing the ceremony of cutting their flesh, in order to give relief to their grief of mind. The snow was removed from the frozen ground over about as large a space as would be required to place a small Indian lodge or wigwam. In the centre a very small fire was kindled up, not to give warmth apparently, but to cause a smoke. The sister of the deceased, who was the chief mourner, came out of her lodge followed by three other women, who repaired to the place prepared. They were all barefooted, and nearly naked. Here they set up a most bitter lamentation and crying, mingling their wailings with the words before mentioned. The principal mourner commenced gashing or cutting her ankles and legs up to the knees with a sharp stone, until her legs were covered with gore and flowing blood; then in like manner her arms, shoulders, and breast. The others cut themselves in the same way, but not so severely. On this poor infatuated woman I presume there were more than a hundred long deep gashes in the flesh. I saw the operation, and the blood instantly followed the instrument, and flowed down upon the flesh. She appeared frantic with grief. Through the pain of her wounds, the loss of blood, exhaustion of strength by fasting, loud and long-continued and bitter groans, or the extreme cold upon her almost naked and lacerated body, she soon sunk upon the frozen ground, shaking as with a violent fit of the ague, and writhing in apparent agony. 'Surely,' I exclaimed, as I beheld the bloody scene, 'the tender mercies of the heathen are cruelty!'

"The little church at the fort begins to manifest something of a missionary spirit. Their contributions are considerable for so small a number. I hope they will not only be willing to contribute liberally of their substance, but will give themselves, at least some of them, to the missionary work.

"The surgeon of the military post, Dr. Jarvis, has

been very assiduous in his attentions to us in our sickness, and has very generously made a donation to our board of twenty-five dollars, being the amount of his medical services in our family.

"On the nineteenth instant we commenced a school with six full Indian children, at least so in all their habits, dress, etc.; not one could speak a word of any language but Sioux. The school has since increased to the number of twenty-five. I am now collecting and arranging words for a dictionary. Mr. Pond is assiduously employed in preparing a small spelling-book, which we may forward next mail for printing.

"Since the Indians have returned to their village, I have felt it important to spend the Sabbath at the station generally. I have determined on going to the fort only on one Sabbath in each month. We have not yet been able to collect the Indians together, to give them religious instructions on the Sabbath, for want of an interpreter."

During the year 1836 a Presbyterian church was organized at Lac qui Parle, and the bois brulé trader, Renville, became a member, and subsequently his wife, the first pure Dahkotah that ever professed, and the first that ever died in the Christian faith.

During the year 1837 Mr. G. H. Pond offered his services as farmer and teacher at Lac qui Parle, and Mr. S. W. Pond became a teacher in the mission at Lake Harriet. The mission was also strengthened by the arrival of Rev. Stephen R. Riggs, a graduate of Jefferson College, Pennsylvania, and his wife. After remaining some time at Lake Harriet, Mr. and Mrs. Riggs went to Lac qui Parle.

CHAPTER XXI.

MINNESOTA has ever been a favourite ranging-ground of the buffalo. This animal does not appear to have roamed in what is now called Canada, and, previous to the visit of Perrot to the region of Lake Michigan, but little was known concerning its habits. Two centuries ago, in a description of New York, it is said "traders who come from a great distance make mention of *lions*' skins, which will not be bartered because they are used for clothing, being much warmer than others." These supposed lions' skins were evidently buffalo robes. Joliet and Marquette, descending the Mississippi, in 1673, saw these animals; and the latter, in his journal, says:—

"We call them wild cattle because they are like our domestic cattle; they are not longer, but almost as big again, and more corpulent; our men having killed one, three of us had considerable trouble in moving it. The head is very large, the forehead flat, and a foot and a half broad between the horns, which are exactly like our cattle, except that they are black and much larger. Under the neck there is a kind of large crop hanging down, and on the back a pretty high hump. The whole head, the neck, and part of the shoulders are covered with a great mane like a horse's; it is at least a foot long, which renders them hideous, and, falling over their eyes, prevents their seeing before them. The rest of the body is covered with a coarse, curly hair like the wool of our sheep, but much stronger and thicker. It falls in summer, and the skin is then as soft as velvet. At this time the Indians employ the skins to make beautiful robes, which they paint with various colours."

The first engraving of the buffalo is found in the book of travels of Hennepin. In 1677 La Salle was in France, and represented to Colbert, the minister, that he wished to continue discoveries where commerce in the skins and wool of the buffalo might establish a great trade and support powerful colonies.

For many years the half-breeds of the Hudson Bay Company have subsisted by hunting the buffalo on the plains of Minnesota, and their encroachments on the territory of the United States have been a just ground of complaint.[1] With the commencement of each spring these hunters commence preparations for their campaign, and about the month of June they march forth to the plains. Their carts are truly primitive, having the appearance of being made before the days of Tubal Cain. Not a particle of iron fastens them together. The wheels are without tires, and wooden pegs take the place of iron spikes. Into the shafts an ox is harnessed with gearing made of raw hide, and with this vehicle they travel hundreds of miles. Women and children

---

[1] The following list gives an idea of the extent of the hunting by British half-breeds in Minnesota. The number of carts for the first trip of each year is given:—

In 1825, there were 680 carts.
" 1830, "   "   820 "
" 1835, "   "   970 "
" 1840, "   " 1210 "

accompany the hunters, and, as they wind over the prairies in their gay hunting attire, they appear like bold crusaders on a pilgrimage. When they halt for the night, the carts are arranged in the form of a circle, with the shafts projecting outward, and within this wooden cordon the tents are pitched at one end, and the animals tethered at the other extremity—when danger is anticipated. The camp is under complete organization. At a meeting of the hunters, chiefs are nominated, one of whom acts as chief captain. The rules formed by the council of captains are implicitly obeyed.[1] At the hoisting of the flag in the morning all hands are "up and doing," and at the lowering of the flag all halt for the night and pitch their tents. The flag, to these modern sons of Ishmael, is what the pillar of cloud was to the camp of the children of Israel.

On the fourth of July, 1840, there was a grand buffalo chase near the Cheyenne river in Minnesota. An eye-witness[2] describes the scene:—

"At eight o'clock, the whole cavalcade made for the buffalo; first at a slow trot, then at a gallop, and lastly at full speed. Their advance was on a dead level; the

---

[1] In 1840, the following were some of the rules of the camp, as determined at Pembina:—

1. No buffalo to be run on the Sabbath day.
2. No party to fork off, lag behind, or go before, without permission.
3. No person to run buffalo before the general order.
4. Every captain with his men, in turn to patrol the camp and keep guard.
5. For the first trespass against these laws, the offender to have his saddle and bridle cut up.
6. For the second offence, the coat to be taken off the offender's back, and cut up.
7. For the third offence, offender to be flogged.
8. Any person convicted of theft, even to the value of a sinew, to be brought to the middle of the camp, and the crier to call out his or her name three times, adding the word "Thief," at each time.

[2] Alexander Ross.

plain having no hollow or shelter of any kind to conceal their approach. When within four or five hundred yards, the bulls began to curve their tails and paw the ground, and in a moment more the herd take flight, and the hunters burst in among them and fire. Those who have seen a squadron of horse dash into battle may imagine the scene. The earth seemed to tremble when the horses started; but when the animals fled, it was like the shock of an earthquake. The air was darkened, and rapid firing at last became more faint, as the hunters became more distant."

During the day, at least two thousand buffaloes must have been killed, for there were brought in to the camp that evening 1375 tongues. The hunters are exceedingly expert; with their mouth full of balls, they load and fire on the gallop. The carts follow out after the hunters and bring in the carcasses, and for several days there is a busy scene in camp. Much of the meat is useless in consequence of the heat of the season; but the skins are dressed, the tongues cured, and pemmican prepared.[1]

The last buffalo seen below St. Paul east of the Mississippi, was in 1832, in the neighbourhood of Trempe à l'Eau.

The history of Minnesota is now beginning to be identified with those who are its citizens, and still in the vigour of life.

The duty of the historian is simply to narrate facts;

---

[1] Pemmican is a staple to the hunter and voyageur. It is made by boiling the tallow of the buffalo, and mixing with it shreds of meat. Sacks of raw hide are then made, into which the preparation is poured in a fluid state.

and his views concerning living men, and their public acts, are not to be expected.

During the year 1836, a Mr. Dickson, styling himself General of the Indian Liberating Army, with several others, appeared in the Red River settlement, and endeavoured to enlist the settlers in a project to unite all the Indian nations under a common government, of which he was to be the head, with the title of Montezuma the Second. His officers were dressed in showy uniforms and glittering epaulettes.[1] Before they arrived at Red river, the cold weather came, and the leader had his toes frozen off, which crippled him as well as the whole enterprise.

The latter part of the following winter, one of the expedition, Martin McLeod, who has since become one of our most active citizens, and whose name is attached to a county, left Red river for the United States, on snow shoes. His two companions, a Polander and an Irishman, both perished in a snow storm near Cheyenne river. He and his guide, Pierre Bottineau,[2] were twenty-six days without seeing a living soul; and after being five days without food, ate one of their dogs, and at last reached the trading-post of the Hon. Joseph R. Brown, at Lake Traverse.

In the month of February, 1837, missionaries sent out by the Evangelical Society at Lausanne, Switzerland, arrived and located at Red Wing and Wapashaw villages; but after a few years of toil, they abandoned the attempt to ameliorate the condition of the Dahkotah. About the same time a Methodist mission was

---

[1] *Martin's Hudson's Bay*, London.
[2] Now a resident of St. Anthony.

commenced at Kaposia, afterwards moved to Red Rock, after a large expenditure, was finally abandoned.

The year 1837, forms an era in the history of Minnesota, as the first steps were then taken for the introduction of the woodman's axe, and the splash of the mill-wheel.

Governor Dodge, of Wisconsin Territory, convened the Ojibways at Fort Snelling, and made a treaty by which the pine forests of the valley of the St. Croix and its tributaries were ceded to the United States.

A deputation of Dahkotahs the same year proceeded to Washington, and in the month of September, concluded a treaty by which they ceded all their lands east of the Mississippi, including all of Washington and Ramsey counties, to the United States.

J. B. Faribault and Pelagie, his wife, presented a claim to the United States government for the island in front of Fort Snelling, which Pike had purchased. The claim was based upon a grant made by the Dahkotahs in 1820.[1]

After the treaties with the Indians were concluded, Messrs. Baker, Taylor, and Franklin Steele made a claim, and commenced the improvement of the valuable water-power at the Falls of St. Croix.

Among visiters of note this year was the distinguished novelist, Maryatt. Like all mere tourists, he has been

---

[1] Extract from papers presented to the secretary of war by Alexis Bailly, and S. C. Stambaugh, prosecutors of the claim. Grant confirmed by Indians August ninth, 1820:—

"Also we do hereby reserve, give, grant and convey, to Pelagi Faribault, wife of John Baptist Faribault, and to her heirs for ever, the island at the mouth of the river St. Pierre, being the large island, containing by estimation, three hundred and twenty acres. * * * * * * The said Pelagi Farribault being the daughter of François Kinie, by a woman of our nation."

betrayed into inaccuracies; and yet it is interesting to note the impression produced by an intelligent mind at that period—when the country was still in possession of savages.

The winter of 1837-38 was one of suffering among the Dahkotahs of the Upper Minnesota. Famine, and the loathsome disease small-pox, made its appearance at Lake Traverse, and produced wailing, weeping, and gnashing of teeth. The disease was communicated by some who had been on a steamboat on the Missouri, and they were swept off by scores. In addition to famine and pestilence, the war whoop was again raised.

On the first of August, 1838, a small hunting party left Lac qui Parle, accompanied by Mr. Gideon H. Pond, who was desirous of becoming more thoroughly acquainted with Dahkotah modes of life. In the fall of 1837, Hole-in-the-day, a distinguished Ojibway chief, father of the young man who now bears that name, had smoked the calumet with the Dahkotahs, and promised to meet them the next spring, and make them presents for the privilege of hunting on their lands.

After travelling for a few days, the hunting party separated, and a portion proceeded in advance. Three lodges of men, women, and children remained. The afternoon of the day of the division of the party, eleven Ojibways came to the advance lodges. They were received as friends : two dogs were killed, and they feasted. Hilarity ended, the Dahkotahs lay down to sleep. When all was silent, the guests arose and scalped men, women, children, and infants, nearly the whole camp. Among those who escaped, was a mother. While fleeing, her babe was shot in her arms, and she was wounded.

Hastening behind a tree, she eluded the enemy, and watched them in their fiendish work.

After they left the scene, she returned to the lodges, and remained till the dawn of day. Fastening two poles, after the manner of Indians, to a horse, she placed on them a wounded boy, and her scalped little ones, and proceeded in search of the party that had gone ahead. At length finding them, she told her tale of woe. Mr. Pond, in company with an Indian, immediately repaired to the scene of carnage, and found several bodies who had passed from the sleep of life to the sleep of death, without opening their eyelids. Hastily digging a grave, the severed limbs, heads, and mangled bodies of eleven Dahkotahs were interred, and covered with a buffalo skin tēēpēē. On the fourteenth of April the survivors returned to Lac qui Parle, and the intelligence caused "wailing and weeping."

In the month of August, a war party left Lac qui Parle to retaliate for the April slaughter. Discovering five or six Ojibways, they attempted to scalp them, but all escaped their hands but a woman. About to become a mother, she swam a stream with difficulty, and sank down on the opposite bank exhausted. Her pursuers soon tore her scalp from her head, and then, ripping open her body, dashed the unborn babe to pieces.

The Ojibways, at Pokeguma, became very much afraid that the Dahkotahs of the Mississippi would now attack them. Dancing the war dance, they were unfriendly to the mission at their lake; shooting cattle, and dashing a canoe to pieces. They also threatened to drive the missionaries and all others from the country.

Finding some lumbermen, in anticipation of the ratification of the treaty of 1837, cutting trees at the mouth of Snake river, they pursued them. The men fled down the St. Croix in their canoes, and, at the imminent risk of their lives, floated over the falls, where their canoe sunk, but they were unhurt.

A few miles below the falls they were met by the first steamboat that had ever ascended the St. Croix, bringing the welcome news of the ratification of the treaty, which had been made at Fort Snelling the year before, and ratified by the Senate on the fifteenth of June, 1838. This boat brought to the country Orange Walker, Samuel Burkleo, and others who were interested in the Marine Mills in Washington county.

After the unprovoked attack of Hole-in-the-Day, beyond Lac qui Parle, some Dahkotahs met an Ojibway, near the grave-yard, at Fort Snelling, and killed him. The murderers were for a time confined in the guard-house of the fort, but at last set at liberty. During the month of June, 1839, hundreds of Ojibways arrived at Fort Snelling, under the erroneous impression that they were to receive their annuities there. While there, the neighbouring Dahkotahs visited them. They drank, they feasted, they danced together. Two sons of the Ojibway, murdered near the grave-yard the year before, took the occasion to go and weep over the burial-place of their father. The thought of their murdered parent excited a desire for revenge; and, that night secreting themselves near a frequented trail at Lake Harriet, at the next day's dawn they shot and scalped one of that band named "Badger," who was starting to hunt. The friends of the murdered one soon brought him home, wrapped in his blanket.

Yeetkadootah, or Red Bird, a near relative, approaching, removing the ornaments from the corpse, kissed it, and said he would die for it.

His voice was now lifted up for war. Raising a party, he crossed the Mississippi at Fort Snelling, in pursuit of the Ojibways, who had departed for their country the day before. While assembled on the east bank of the Mississippi they bound themselves to kill all. The Ojibways had gone partly by the St. Croix, and partly by the Mississippi, to their villages. Red Bird determined to follow the party that had ascended the Mississippi.

The same day warriors from Kaposia, and the other villages in the vicinity of the fort, followed the trail leading through St. Paul, in search of the Ojibways that had gone in that direction. Travelling until night, they found the Ojibways sleeping in the ravine near the penitentiary at Stillwater. Perceiving that there was a white man, an old trader (Mr. Aitkin), in the enemy's camp, they postponed their attack until dawn of the next day, as they did not wish to injure him.

At daybreak, the first intelligence of the presence of the Dahkotahs was a volley of musket balls poured from the bluffs into the midst of the Ojibway camp.

The Ojibways, fighting bravely, retreated to the shore of the lake, and endeavoured to escape in their canoes; but, before the conflict was over, forty or fifty of their number were slain. Ten or fifteen Dahkotahs were killed and wounded.[1]

About the time that the battle of Stillwater ended, Yeetkadootah's party came up to the women and child-

---

[1] The one-legged Indian, known to the citizens of St. Paul as Lame Jim, lost his leg by a wound in this battle.

ren of the Ojibways, who were making a portage on Rum river, while the men were absent hunting deer. With lance, scalping knife, and tomahawk, in a brief period they made bloody work. In their haste to take scalps, it is said they scalped one of their own number.

Yeetkadootah, on horseback, approaching a wounded Ojibway, who still held his gun in his hand, was shot through the neck, just as he was alighting to scalp him.

It is said that while the Ojibways were at Fort Snelling, a young Dahkotah brave had wooed an Ojibway maiden, and was loved in return. In the heat of the battle he found his tomahawk raised to strike a woman, and behold, it proved to be her whom he had loved. She begged to be his captive, but it had been agreed that there should be no quarter. As he could not save her he passed on, and in an instant, one in the rear cleft her skull with the sharp tomahawk. From these two engagements the Dahkotahs brought back ninety-one scalps, and were frantic with glory.

In 1836, before the Indian title was extinguished, settlers located on the tract of land on the east side of the Mississippi, between St. Paul and Fort Snelling. By the treaty of September, 1837, made by the Dahkotahs with the United States, which was ratified by the Senate on the fifteenth of June, 1838, the Indian title to the tract in question ceased.

In March, 1838, the commander at Fort Snelling selected this land as a part of a military reservation. Consequently, it was withheld from sale. Those who had made claims upon it, were much dissatisfied, and evinced a disposition to resist. Orders were issued from the war department, to the United States Marshal of

Wisconsin, to remove the intruders.[1] The greater portion of the settlers were Swiss, and after all of their migrations from Switzerland, via Hudson Bay Company's possessions, to the present desirable location, they were loath to depart. The troops were summarily called out from the fort on the sixth of May, 1840, and the settlers with undue haste removed, and on the next day the troops destroyed their cabins, to prevent re-occupation.

[1] Order for removal of squatters on Military Reserve, Fort Snelling:—

"WAR DEPARTMENT,
Oct. 21, 1839.

"Sir—The interests of the service, and the proper and effective maintenance of the military post at Fort Snelling, requiring that the intruders on the land recently reserved for military purposes, opposite to that post east of the Mississippi river be removed therefrom, the President of the United States directs that when required by the commanding officer of the post you proceed there, and remove them under the provisions of the act of March third, 1807, entitled 'An act to prevent settlements being made on lands ceded to the United States, until authorized by law.'

"You will satisfy yourself of the shortest period within which the intruders can make their arrangements for removal, and depart from the reservation without serious loss or sacrifice of the property which they may have to take with them, and you will promptly make known to them that it is expected they will not delay beyond that period; as should they do so, it will become your duty to remove them by military force. It is hoped, however, that a resort to such force for this purpose which by the Act above-mentioned the President is authorized to employ, will not be necessary; but that they will promptly depart, on being informed of the determination of the executive, not to permit them to remain. Should you however be unfortunately obliged to use force in order to accomplish the object, you are authorized to call for such as you may deem necessary on the commanding officer at Fort Snelling. In this event you will act with as much forbearance, consideration, and delicacy as may be consistent with the prompt and faithful performance of the duties hereby assigned to you, first fully and mildly explaining the folly of resistance on their part, and your own want of discretion in the matter. Very respectfully, your obedient servant,

J. R. POINSETT.

Edward James, Esq.,
United States Marshal for the Territory of Wiskonsan, Peru."

During the summer of 1840, a tragic and melancholy occurrence took place on the plains of Minnesota. On the sixth of June, Thomas Simpson, the youthful, educated, and adventurous explorer, who had discovered and named Victoria Land, in the Arctic Regions, left Fort Garry, in the Red River settlement, to visit England, by way of the traders' route through Minnesota. He left the settlement with quite a number, but anxious to behold Great Britain, from which he had been absent for years, they travelled too slow, and he moved on in advance with a Canadian, two half-breeds, and a lad, the son of one of the latter.

His movements were those of one whose mind was excited, and in two days he had advanced one hundred miles. He then complained of sickness, and said he would never recover; and when told that there was a physician at the mission-house of Lac qui Parle, he replied "that he did not wish a doctor." At his urgent solicitation, his guides turned back on the fourteenth of June, and an hour and a half after the setting of the sun, they encamped near Turtle river. While two of the men and the lad were busy in raising the tent, one of them, named Bird, was shot, and instantly died, and on turning around, the others saw Simpson fire at a half-breed, named Legros, father of the boy, and in a few minutes he expired. The boy and surviving guide ran off, when Simpson called out that their lives were safe, and that he had shot the others because they intended to murder him on that night, and take the papers on his recent Arctic explorations.

Before Legros died, he called his son and kissed him. Bruce, the remaining guide, and lad, that night mounted their horses, and proceeded toward the main camp that they had left a few days before. Relating their strange story, five accompanied them to the scene of the disaster. As they approached the cart the next day, on their return, a shot was fired, as they at first supposed at their party. Drawing nigh with great caution, crawling through the grass on their stomachs, they discovered Mr. Simpson stretched out, with one leg across the other, the butt end of his gun between his legs, the right hand with the glove off directed to the trigger, all the head above the nose blown off, and his nightcap some yards distant with a bullet hole in it, and some of his hair attached. Since Bruce and the son of Legros left the night before, the body of one of the guides had been covered with the tent, and the poles laid on the top, and the body of the other had been covered with a blanket, and a pillow placed beneath the head. From the beaten path it was supposed that he had passed the whole night in walking between these two dead bodies. It was a tragic scene. The moon that night shone brightly. The faithful dog of one of the party remained watching, and Simpson, with his over-tasked mind, gibbered over the corpses, and wrapped them up, filled with some strange fancy.

On the fifteenth of June, Simpson, only thirty-two years of age, and his two guides, were wrapped up in the same winding-sheet, the cover of the tent, and deposited in the same grave. The news of this tragedy did not reach Red river until the party returned from Fort Snelling, in the month of October. A medical gentleman with some men then proceeded to the grave, and disinterring the bodies, made a post mortem examination, which corresponded with the deposition of

Bruce, as given before Mr. Sibley at Mendota in July. His body was conveyed to Red river, and there re-interred.[1]

The Dahkotahs in the neighbourhood of Lakes Harriet and Calhoun, through fear of their enemies, after the troubles of 1839, began to reside on the banks of the Minnesota, near Oak Grove.

On the seventeenth of June, 1840, four Ojibways who had secreted themselves about two miles below Mendota, on the Mississippi, killed and scalped a Dahkotah man and woman.

Joseph R. Brown, who since 1838 had lived at Chan Wakan, on the west side of Grey Cloud Island, this year made a claim near the upper end of the city of Stillwater, which he called Dahkotah, and was the first to raft lumber down the St. Croix, as well as the first to represent the citizens of the valley in the legislature of Wisconsin.

On the second of September, of this year, the Rev. Mr. Riggs, of the Lac qui Parle mission, accompanied by the mission farmer, Mr. Huggens, made a tour to the Missouri, in company with a party of Indians on a buffalo hunt.[2]

Until the year 1841, the jurisdiction of Crawford county, Wisconsin, extended over the delta of country between the St. Croix and Mississippi. Joseph R. Brown, having been elected as representative of the

---

[1] Alexander Simpson, in "*Life and Travels of T. Simpson*," Bentley, London, 1845, conveys the impression that he was murdered by the half-breeds. Ballantyne, in "*Hudson's Bay*," has the same opinion, but Ross, in "*Red River Settlement*," who was a justice of the peace, and examined the eye-witnesses, thinks he became deranged, and shot his guides and himself.

[2] An interesting account of this journey is published in the *Missionary Herald*, Boston, 1841.

county, in the territorial legislature of Wisconsin, succeeded in obtaining the passage of an act on November twentieth, 1841, organizing the county of St. Croix, with Dahkotah designated as the county seat.

At the time prescribed for holding a court in the new county, it is said that the judge of the district arrived, and to his surprise, found a claim cabin occupied by a Frenchman. Speedily retreating, he never came again, and judicial proceedings for St. Croix county ended for several years.

After the Ojibway slaughter of 1839, the missionaries removed from Lake Harriet to the stone building above Fort Snelling, now known as the St. Louis House. Early in the spring of 1841, in a thicket in the vicinity, three Ojibway warriors lay watching for scalps. At length Kaibokah, a Dahkotah chief, with his son, and another man, passed. The chief and his son were both shot, and their foe escaped in a canoe to the east bank of the Mississippi. For this act retaliation soon took place.

Pokeguma is one of the "Mille Lacs," or thousand beautiful lakes for which Minnesota is remarkable. It is about four or five miles in extent, and a mile or more in width. Its shores are strewn with boulders that in a past geologic age have been brought by some mighty impetus from the icy north. Down to the water's edge grow the tall pines, through which, for many years, the deer have bounded, and the winds sighed mournfully, as they wafted away to distant lands the shriek of many Dahkotah or Ojibway mothers, caused by the slaughter of their children.

This lake is situated on Snake river, about twenty miles above the junction of that stream with the St. Croix. Though as late as the year 1700, the Dahkotahs resided in this vicinity, for a long period it has been the abode of their enemies, the Ojibways.

In the year 1836, missionaries of the American Board of Foreign Missions connected with the Congregational and Presbyterian denominations, came to reside among the Ojibways of Pokeguma, to promote their temporal and spiritual welfare. Their mission-house was built on the east side of the lake; but the Indian village was on an island not far from the shore. In a few years, several Indian families, among others that of the chief, were induced to build log houses around the mission. The missionaries felt, to use the language of one of them, that "the motives of the gospel had no more influence over the Indian, in themselves considered, than over the deer that he follows in the chase." They therefore first encouraged the Indian to work, and always purchased of him his spare provisions.

By aiding them in this way, many had become quite industrious. In a letter written in 1837, we find the following : "The young women and girls now make, mend, wash, and iron after our manner. The men have learned to build log houses, drive team, plough, hoe, and handle an American axe with some skill in cutting large trees, the size of which, two years ago, would have afforded them a sufficient reason why they should not meddle with them."

On May fifteenth, 1841, two young men had gone, by order of Mr. Russell, now of Sauk Rapids, then Indian farmer at Pokeguma, to the Falls of St. Croix, after a load of provisions. On the next day, which was Sunday, the news arrived there, that a Dahkotah war party, headed by Little Crow, of the Kaposia band, whose face is so familiar to the older citizens of St.

Paul, was on the way to their village. Immediately they started back on foot to give the alarm to their relatives and friends.

They had hardly left the Falls, on their return, before they saw a party of Dahkotahs, stripped and bedaubed with vermillion, and preparing themselves for war. The sentinel of the enemy had not noticed the approach of the young men. A few yards in front of the Ojibway youth sat two of the sons of Little Crow, behind a log, exulting, no doubt, in anticipation of the scalps in reserve for them at the lake. In the twinkling of an eye, these two young Ojibways raised their guns, fired, and killed both of the chief's sons. The sentinel, who had by his carelessness allowed them to pass, was a third son. The discharge of the guns revealed to him that an enemy was near, and as the Ojibways were retreating, he fired, and mortally wounded one of the two.

Fiendish was the rage of the Dahkotahs at this disastrous surprise. According to custom, the corpses of the chief's sons were dressed, and then set up with their faces towards the country of their ancient enemies. The wounded Ojibway was horribly mangled by the infuriated party, and his limbs strewn about in every direction. His scalped head was placed in a kettle, and suspended in front of the two Dahkotah corpses, in the belief that it would be gratifying to the spirits of the deceased, to see before them the bloody and scalpless head of one of their enemies.

Little Crow, disheartened by the loss of his two boys, returned with his party to Kaposia. But other parties were in the field. The Dahkotahs had divided themselves into three bands; and it was the understanding that one party was first to attack Pokeguma, and then retire. After the Ojibways supposed that the attack was over, the second party was to commence their fire, and after they had ceased to fight, the third party was to begin to slaughter.

The second party proceeded as far as the mouth of Snake river, but, supposing that the Ojibways had discovered them, they turned back, and upon their arrival at the Falls of St. Croix, they were still more chagrined, by hearing of the death of the sons of the Kaposia chief.

It was not till Friday, the twenty-first of May, that the death of one of the young Ojibways sent by Mr. Russell, to the Falls of St. Croix, was known at Pokeguma. The murdered youth was a son of one of those families who had renounced heathenism, and whose parents lived on the lake shore, in one of the log buildings, by the mission-house. The intelligence alarmed the Ojibways on the island opposite the mission, and on Monday, the twenty-fourth, three young men left in a canoe to go to the west shore of the lake, and from thence to Mille Lac, to give intelligence to the Ojibways there, of the skirmish that had already occurred. They took with them two Indian girls, about twelve years of age, who were pupils of the mission school, for the purpose of bringing the canoe back to the island. Just as the three were landing, twenty or thirty Dahkotah warriors, with a war whoop emerged from their concealment behind the trees, and fired into the canoe. The young men instantly sprang into the water, which was shallow, returned the fire, and ran into the woods, escaping without material injury.

The little girls, in their fright, waded into the lake;

and as in Indian warfare it is as noble to kill an infant as an adult, a delicate woman as a strong man, the Dahkotah braves, with their spears and war clubs, rushed into the water after the children and killed them. Their parents upon the island, heard the death cries of their children; and for a time the scene was one of the wildest confusion. Some of the Indians around the mission-house jumped into their canoes and gained the island. Others went into some fortified log huts. The attack upon the canoe, it was afterwards learned, was premature. The party upon that side of the lake were ordered not to fire, until the party stationed in the woods near the mission commenced.

There were in all one hundred and eleven Dahkotah warriors, and the fight was in the vicinity of the mission-house, and the Ojibways mostly engaged in it were those who had been under religious instruction. The rest were upon the island. During the engagement, an incident occurred, as worthy of note as some of those in Grecian history.

The fathers of the murdered girls, burning for revenge, left the island in a canoe, and drawing it up on the shore, hid behind it, and fired upon the Dahkotahs and killed one. The Dahkotahs advancing upon them, they were obliged to escape. The canoe was now launched. One lay on his back in the bottom; the other plunged into the water, and, holding the canoe with one hand, and swimming with the other, he towed his friend out of danger. The Dahkotahs, infuriated at their escape, fired volley after volley at the swimmer, but he escaped the balls by putting his head under water whenever he saw them take aim, and waiting till he heard the discharge, when he would look up and breathe.

After a fight of two hours, the Dahkotahs retreated with a loss of two men. At the request of the parents, Mr. E. F. Ely, now of Oneota, from whose notes the writer has obtained these facts, being at that time a teacher at the mission, went across the lake, with two of his friends, to gather the remains of his murdered pupils. He found the corpses on the shore. The heads cut off and scalped, with a tomahawk buried in the brains of each, were set up in the sand near the bodies. The bodies were pierced in the breast, and the right arm of one was taken away. Removing the tomahawks, the bodies were brought back to the island, and in the afternoon were buried in accordance with the simple but solemn rites of the Church of Christ, by members of the mission.

It is usual for Indians to leave their murdered on or near the battle-field, with their faces looking towards the enemy's country; and on Wednesday the Ojibways started out in search of the Dahkotahs that had been killed. By following the trail, they soon found the two bodies, and scalped them. One of the heads was also cut off, and brought to the island, to adorn the graves of the little girls. To a North-western savage, such a head-stone at a daughter's grave is more gratifying than one of sculptured Italian marble. Strips of flesh were fastened to the trees. A breast was also taken, and cooked and eaten by the braves to express their hatred to the Dahkotahs.

The mother and wife of the young man who had been killed by Little Crow's third son, were each presented with a hand. These women had been accustomed to attend preaching at the mission-house, and knew the principles of the Prince of Peace. Though they had, in 1839, lost many relatives by an attack from the Dahkotahs, on Rum river, they engaged in no savage orgies, but, withdrawing to their wigwam, they placed the hands of their foes upon their knees, gazed in silence, then wrapped them in white muslin and interred them. Such is one of the many similar scenes that have occurred in our own territory within ten years. Governor Ramsey, the president of the Historical Society, in his address of 1851, well remarked that the region between the Falls of St. Croix and Mille Lac, was a "Golgotha"—a place of skulls.

The sequel to this story is soon told. The Indians of Pokeguma, after the fight, deserted their village, and went to reside with their countrymen near Lake Superior.

In July of the following year, 1842, a war party was formed at Fond du Lac, about forty in number, and proceeded towards the Dahkotah country. When they reached Kettle river they were joined by the Ojibways of St. Croix and Mille Lac, and thus numbered about one hundred warriors. Sneaking, as none but Indians can, they arrived unnoticed at the little settlement below St. Paul, commonly called "Pig's Eye," which is opposite Kaposia, or Little Crow's village. Finding an Indian woman at work in the garden of her husband, a Canadian, by the name of Gamelle, they killed her; also another woman, with her infant, whose head was cut off. The Dahkotahs, on the opposite side, were mostly intoxicated; and, flying across in their canoes but half prepared, they were worsted in the encounter. They lost thirteen warriors, and one of their number, known as the Dancer, the Ojibways are said to have skinned.

The year of the Pokeguma battle, Governor Doty visited the Dahkotahs, and negotiated a treaty with the several bands at Wapashaw, Mendota, and Traverse des Sioux, by which the country west of the Mississippi would have been ceded, but the United States Senate did not ratify it.

During the winter of 1842-3, Mr. Ayer visited Red Lake, whose waters flow into the Red River of the North, with the view of ascertaining the practicability of missionary operations there. The chief received the proposition with favour, and thus addressed his warriors :—

" My braves! I should be ashamed to suffer one who has come so far to visit us to turn back again. We should not turn him away. We would not treat our trader in this way; we should run to meet him. My braves! you have listened to what he said. I believe what he says. Let us try him four years, and if we do not find him true, then we will send him away."

On the 17th of April he made a second visit, accompanied by Mr. Spencer, and Mr. E. F. Ely. The latter two immediately commenced assisting the Indians in their ploughing and in preparations for putting in a crop. The months of February and March, 1843, were exceedingly severe, the thermometer ranging lower than ever before recorded. The snow had fallen to such depths that the snow shoe was not very serviceable, and the waters were so troubled by high winds that it was difficult for the Indians to spear the fish through the holes cut in the ice. The Dahkotahs were brought to the verge of starvation, some bands being reduced to the necessity of subsisting on a syrup made of hickory chips, or boiled bitter sweet. The United States government, in view of their peculiar necessities, granted them twenty-five hundred dollars worth of provisions, powder, and clothing.

During the summer the Rev. Mr. Riggs, on his return from a visit to Ohio, commenced a mission station at Traverse des Sioux. His family and the Rev. Mr. Hopkins and wife proceeded to Lac qui Parle. While drawing to the close of their last day's journey, three young Dahkotahs, who had been on a visit to Ohio, hurried on in advance. Shortly two Indian lads said that, while drinking at a little stream, they had heard the report of fire-arms, and had seen Ojibways. The intelligence was confirmed by the return of one of the three who had gone ahead, who said that he had conversed with the Ojibways, and had been saved by his white man's dress. In a little while the travellers beheld on an eminence fifteen or twenty Ojibway warriors, who retreated as they approached. Crossing the Maya-wakan, they found the two corpses of the young Dahkotahs. Taking the wagon cover for a winding-sheet, the missionaries wrapped one of the bodies and proceeded toward Lac qui Parle. The Indians there having gained intelligence of the attack, rushed forth to meet them, and were enraged because the whites had not pursued the Ojibways.

On the tenth of October, 1843, was commenced a settlement which has become the town of Stillwater. The names of the proprietors were John McKusick from Maine, Calvin Leach from Vermont, Elam Greeley from Maine, and Elias McKean from Pennsylvania. They immediately commenced the erection of a saw-mill, and made improvements which fixed the point as the centre of the lumbering interests of the valley of the St. Croix.

On the eleventh of August, 1844, Captain Allen, with fifty United States dragoons, left Fort Des Moines, Iowa, and passed through the south-western portion of Minnesota; but, the guide having left them soon after they commenced their march, they wandered through the country in great uncertainty. After floundering through marshes, they came, as they supposed, to a tributary of the Minnesota; and, on the tenth of September, about latitude 45°, they found the Big Sioux, and there, for the first time since they started, met a party of Dahkotahs.

B. Gervais, during this year, moved to a point five miles north-east of St. Paul, known as Little Canada, and erected the first mill in Minnesota beyond the military reservation of Fort Snelling.

In the summer of this year, a party of drovers, on their way from the South to Fort Snelling with cattle, lost their way, and were captured and maltreated by the Sissetoan Dahkotahs. As soon as the intelligence reached the fort, troops were despatched in pursuit of the offenders, who were captured, but subsequently escaped.

The United States, having learned that the half-breed hunters of Red River settlement were killing thousands of buffalo annually in Minnesota, sent a military expedition to the valley of the Red river, under the charge of Captain Sumner of the dragoons. They left Fort Atkinson, Iowa, on the third of June, 1845, and, marching through the interior, reached Traverse des Sioux on the twenty-fifth. Proceeding to Lac qui Parle, a council was held with the Dahkotahs of that vicinity. Although they had difficulty with the half-breeds of the North, in consequence of hunting buffalo in their country, they did not wish the United States to interfere. On the fifth of July, another council was held at Big Stone Lake, but it was unsatisfactory.

The next day they marched northward, and, on the eighth, while Captain Sumner was holding an informal council in the saddle, three of the murderers of the drover (Watson) and party, who had escaped the previous autumn from Colonel Wilson's detachment of the First Infantry, boldly walked into council. Immediately they were recognised and arrested. The excitement for a few moments was intense, but Sumner told them that it was useless to talk at that time, as he would be there again in about a month. The prisoners then accompanied the troops to Minne Wakan[1] Lake, about the 48th degree of latitude, which was reached on the eighteenth. In this vicinity they struck the trail of the hunters, and soon met a deputation of them with an interpreter. The next morning Captain Sumner proceeded to their camp, which was composed of one hundred and eighty men. In his interview with them he found them frank and sensible. They told him that they had been trained to the hunter's life from childhood, and knew no other occupation, and that the buffalo was their only subsistence, and they desired to know whether they would be received as citizens, if they moved within the American lines. The officer told them that he was not authorized to express any opinion on such points, but advised them to write a letter to Washington.

[1] Devil's Lake.

The expedition returned to Traverse des Sioux on the seventh of August, and was surprised at seeing two fine horses, that belonged to the officers of Captain Allen's company, and some mules, among the Indians. The thieves were arrested and sent down to Fort Snelling.

In the spring of 1845, one of Good Road's band of Dahkotahs was killed by Pillagers at Otter Tail Lake. Not long after, a party of Ojibways came to Fort Snelling, and to protect them from the exasperated Dahkotahs, Captain Backus quartered them within the walls.

In the month of March, 1846, Joseph Renville, of Lac qui Parle, whose name one of the counties of the State bears, died. Previous to the ratification of the treaty of 1837, he was, perhaps, the most prominent citizen in Minnesota.[1]

---

[1] Joseph Renville was of mixed descent, and his history forms a link between the past and the present history of Minnesota. His father was a French trader of much reputation. His mother was a Dahkotah, connected with some of the principal men of the Kaposia band. He was born just below the town of St. Paul, about the year 1779, during the war of the American Revolution. At that time, there was probably not a white family residing in the whole of that vast territory that now comprises Northern Illinois, Wisconsin, Iowa, and Minnesota, excepting officers of the British army.

Accustomed to see few European countenances, in sports, habits, and feelings he was a full Dahkotah youth. As often happens, his mother deserted her husband, and went to live with one of her own blood. The father, noticing the activity of his son's mind, took him to Canada before he was ten years of age, and placed him under the tuition of a priest of Rome. His instructor appears to have been both a kind and good man, and from him he received a slight knowledge of the French language, and the elements of the Christian religion. Before he attained to manhood, he was brought back to the Dahkotah land, and was called to mourn the death of his father.

At that time, there was a British officer by the name of Dickson, who lived in what is now Minnesota, and the head of an English Fur Company. Knowing that young Renville was energetic, he employed him as a "coureur des bois." While

The year that the Dahkotahs ceded the land east of the Mississippi, a Canadian Frenchman, by the name of Parant, the ideal of an Indian whiskey-seller, erected

a mere stripling, he had guided his canoe from the Falls of Pokeguma to the Falls of St. Anthony, and followed the trails from Mendota to the Missouri. He knew by heart the legends of Winona, and Ampato Sapawin, and Hogan-wanke-kin. He had distinguished himself as a brave, and also became identified with the Dahkotahs more fully by following in the footsteps of his father and purchasing a wife of that nation.

In 1797, he wintered, in company with a Mr. Perlier, near Sauk Rapids. The late General Pike was introduced to him at Prairie du Chien, and was conducted by him to the Falls of St. Anthony. This officer was pleased with him, and recommended him for the post of United States Interpreter. In a letter to General Wilkinson, written at Mendota, September ninth, 1805, he says: "I beg leave to recommend for that appointment, a Mr. Joseph Renville, who has served as interpreter for the Sioux last spring at the Illinois, and who has gratuitously and willingly served as my interpreter in all my conferences with the Sioux. He is a man respected by the Indians, and I believe an honest one."

At the breaking out of the last war with Great Britain, Col. Dickson was employed by that government, to hire the warlike tribes of the North-west to fight against the United States. Renville received from him, the appointment and rank of captain in the British army, and with warriors from the Wapashaw, Kaposia, and other bands of Dahkotahs, marched to the American frontier.

In 1822 he became a member of the Columbia Fur Company. Shortly after, the American Fur Company of New York, of which John Jacob Astor was one of the directors, not wishing any rivals in the trade, purchased their posts, and good-will, and retained the "coureurs des bois." Under this new arrangement, Renville removed to Lac qui Parle, and erected a trading-house, and here he resided until the end of his days.

Living as he had done, for more than a half century among the Dahkotahs, over whom he exercised the most unbounded control, it is not surprising that in his advanced age he sometimes exhibited a domineering disposition. As long as Minnesota exists, he should be known as one given to hospitality. He invariably showed himself to be a friend to the Indian, the traveller, and the missionary. Aware of the improvidence of his mother's race, he used his influence towards the raising of grain. He was instrumental in having the first seed corn planted on the Upper Minnesota. An Indian never left his house hungry, and they delighted to do him honour. He was a friend to the traveller. His conversation was intelligent, and he constantly commua shanty at what is now the principal steamboat landing in St. Paul. Ignorant and overbearing, he loved money more than his soul. Destitute of one eye, and

nicated facts that were worthy of record. His post obtained a reputation among explorers, and their last day's journey to it was generally a quick march, for they felt sure of a warm welcome. His son was the interpreter of Nicollet, that worthy man of science who explored this country in connection with Fremont. This gentlemen, in his report to Congress, pays the following tribute to the father and son:—

"I may stop a while to say, that the residence of the Renville family, for a number of years back, has afforded the only retreat to travellers to be found between St. Peter's and the British posts, a distance of seven hundred miles. The liberal and untiring hospitality dispensed by this respectable family, the great influence exercised by it over the Indians of this country in the maintenance of peace and the protection of travellers, would demand, besides our gratitude, some especial acknowledgment of the United States, and also from the Hudson's Bay Company."

The only traveller that has ever given any testimony opposed to this is Featherstonhaugh, a dyspeptic and growling Englishman, whose book, published in London in 1847, and styled a 'Canoe Voyage up the Minnay Sotor,' betrays a filthy imagination. He remarks:—

"On reaching the fort, Renville advanced and saluted me, but not cordially. He was a dark, Indian-looking person, showing no white blood, short in his stature, with strong features and coarse black hair. * * * * * I learnt that Renville entertained a company of stout Indians to the number of fifty, in a skin lodge behind his house, of extraordinary dimensions, whom he calls his braves, or soldiers. To these men he confided various trusts, and occasionally sent them to distant points to transact his business. No doubt he was a very intriguing person, and uncertain in his attachments. Those who knew him intimately, supposed him inclined to the British allegiance although he professes great attachment to the American government, a circumstance, however, which did not prevent him from being under the surveillance of the garrison at Fort Snelling."

He was also a friend to the Missionary of the Cross. Until the year 1834, no minister of the church, made arrangements to devote his life to the spiritual and temporal welfare of the Dahkotahs.

The Rev. T. S. Williamson, M.D., of the Presbytery of Chilicothe, arrived at Fort Snelling in 1834; then returned to the East, and in 1835 came back with assistant missionaries. Renville warmly welcomed him, and rendered him invaluable assistance in the establishment of the missions. Upon the arrival of the missionaries at Lac qui Parle, he provided them with a temporary home. He acted as interpreter, he

the other resembling that of a pig, he was a good representative of Caliban.

In the year 1842, some one writing a letter in his assisted in translating the Scriptures, and removed many of the prejudices of the Indians against the teachers of the white man's religion. His name appears in connection with several Dahkotah books. Dr. Watts' second Catechism for children, published in Boston, in 1837, by Crocker & Brewster, was partly translated by him.

In 1839, a volume of extracts from the Old Testament, and a volume containing the Gospel of Mark, was published by Kendell & Henry, Cincinnati, the translation of which was given orally by Mr. Renville, and penned by Dr. Williamson. Crocker & Brewster, in 1842, published Dahkotah Dowanpi Kin, or Dahkotah Hymns, many of which were composed by the subject of this sketch. The following tribute to his ability as a translator, appeared in the Missionary Herald of 1846, published at Boston:—

"Mr. Renville was a remarkable man, and he was remarkable for the energy with which he pursued such objects as he deemed of primary importance. His power of observing and remembering facts, and also words expressive of simple ideas, was extraordinary. Though in his latter years he could read a little, yet in translating he seldom took a book in his hand, choosing to depend on hearing rather than sight, and I have often had occasion to observe, that after hearing a long and unfamiliar verse read from the Scriptures, he would immediately render it from the French into Dahkotah, two languages extremely unlike in their idioms and ideas of the words, and repeat it over two or three words at a time, so as to give full opportunity to write it down. He also had a remarkable tact in discovering the aim of a speaker, and conveying the intended impression, when many of the ideas and words were such as had nothing corresponding to them in the minds and language of the addressed. These qualities fitted him for an interpreter, and it was generally admitted he had no equal."

It would be improper to conclude this article without some remarks upon the religious character of Renville. Years before there was a clergyman in Minnesota, he took his Indian wife to Prairie du Chien, and was married in accordance with Christian rites by a minister of the Roman Church. Before he became acquainted with missionaries, he sent for a large folio Bible in the French language, and requested those connected with him in the fur trade to procure for him a clerk who could read it. This Bible was probably the first Bible in Minnesota, and in itself valuable for its antiquity. It was printed at Geneva, in 1588, and had a Latin preface by John Calvin, the great Reformer.

The writer, in 1853, requested Dr. Williamson, of the Dahkotah Mission, to procure this same copy for the Historical Society. At his soli-

groggery, for the want of a more euphonious name, designated the place as "Pig's Eye," referring to the peculiar appearance of the whiskey-seller. The reply

citation, one of the sons of the late Mr. Renville, brought it to the Mission House at Lac qui Parle, to be forwarded to St. Paul. Before an opportunity occurred, the Mission House, with all of its contents, was consumed by fire.

After the commencement of the mission at Lac qui Parle, his wife was the first full Dahkotah that joined the Church of Christ, of whom we have any record. She was also the first Dahkotah that died in the Christian faith. Before she had ever seen a teacher of the religion of Christ, through the instruction of her husband she had renounced the gods of the Dahkotahs. The following is an extract from a translation of Mr. Renville's account of his wife's death:—" Now, to-day, you seem very much exhausted, and she said 'yes; this day, now God invites me. I am remembering Jesus Christ who suffered for me, and depending on him alone. To-day I shall stand before God, and will ask him for mercy for you, and for all my children, and all my kinsfolk."

Afterwards, when all her children and relatives sat round her weeping, she said, "it is holy day, sing and pray." From very early in the morning, she was speaking of God, and telling her husband what to do. Thus she died "when the clock struck two."

Like Nicodemus, one of the rulers of Israel, he loved to inquire in relation to spiritual things. Of independent mind, he claimed and exercised the right of private judgment in matters of faith.

In 1841, he was chosen and ordained a ruling elder, and from that time, till his death, discharged the duties of his office in a manner acceptable and profitable both to the native members of the church and the mission.

After a sickness of some days, in March, 1846, his strong frame began to give evidence of speedy decay. He was aware he was soon to take "his chamber in the silent halls of death," but he knew "in whom he had believed," and went,

"Not like the quarry slave, at night
Scourged to his dungeon; but sustained and soothed,
Like one who wraps the drapery of his couch
About him, and lies down to pleasant dreams!"

Dr. Williamson thus narrates the death-scene: "The evening before his decease, he asked me what became of the soul immediately after death? I reminded him of our Saviour's words to the thief on the cross, and Paul's desire to depart and be with Christ. He said, 'That is sufficient,' and presently added, 'I have great hope I shall be saved through grace.' Next morning (Sunday) about eight o'clock, I was called to see him. He was so evidently in the agonies of death, I did not think of attempting to do anything for him. After some time, his breathing becoming easier, he was asked if he

to the letter was directed in good faith to " Pig's Eye," and was received in due time.

In 1842, the late Henry Jackson, of Mahkahto, settled at the same spot, and erected the first store on the height just above the lower landing; and shortly

wished to hear a hymn. He replied, 'Yes.' After it was sung he said, 'It is very good.' As he reclined on the bed, I saw a sweet serenity settling on his countenance, and I thought that his severest struggle was probably past, and so it proved. The clock striking ten, he looked at it and intimated that it was time for us to go to church. As we were about to leave, he extended his withered hand. After we left, he spoke some words of exhortation to his family, then prayed, and before noon calmly and quietly yielded up his spirit."

Sixty-seven years passed by, before he closed his eyes upon the world. The citizens of Kentucky delight in the memory of Daniel Boone; let the citizens of Minnesota not forget Joseph Renville, though he was a " bois brulé."

His descendants are still living among the Dahkotahs. The son who bore his name, died on February eighth, 1856, in the neighbourhood of the mission at Payutazee. The Rev. S. R. Riggs, in a communication to the St. Paul Daily Times, remarks:—

" The deceased was about forty-seven years of age, a son of Joseph Renville, who died at Lac qui Parle some years since, and whose memory is identified with the past history of Minnesota. Inheriting from his father many noble and generous qualities, unfortunately for himself and family, the habits of the Indian trade in which the deceased was educated, were not such as enabled him to gain a comfortable livelihood by labour. After the death of his father, he removed with his family to the Mississippi, and resided for some time at Kaposia, with Little Crow's band, many of whom were his mother's relatives. Soon after the cession of this Minnesota country to the United States, he with a younger brother, and cousin of the same family name, removed up to the neighbourhood of Fort Ridgley. When they attended the payment at Yellow Medicine, he was already far gone in the disease which has just terminated his earthly career. Here, in the house of a younger brother, and with other relations, he with his family found a temporary home, and a place to die. Through the kindness of friends and neighbours, they have not wanted. It has been pleasant to see that former kindnesses received from the family when his father was a prince in wealth among them, have not been entirely forgotten by the Dahkotahs, but have been returned now to the son in his sickness."

after, Roberts and Simpson followed, and opened small Indian trading shops. In the year 1846, the site of St. Paul was chiefly occupied by a few shanties, owned by "certain lewd fellows of the baser sort," who sold rum to the soldier and Indian. It was despised by all decent white men, and known to the Dahkotahs by an expression in their tongue, which means, the place where they sell minne-wakan.[1]

The chief of the Kaposia band in 1846, was shot by his own brother in a drunken revel, but surviving the wound, and apparently alarmed at the deterioration under the influence of the modern harpies at St. Paul, went to Mr. Bruce, Indian agent, at Fort Snelling, and requested a missionary. The Indian agent in his report to government, says:—

"The chief of the Little Crow's band, who reside below this place (Fort Snelling) about nine miles, in the immediate neighbourhood of the whiskey dealers, has requested to have a school established at his village. He says they are determined to reform, and for the future, will try to do better. I wrote to Doctor Williamson soon after the request was made, desiring him to take charge of the school. He has had charge of the mission school at Lac qui Parle for some years; is well qualified, and is an excellent physician."

In November, 1846, Dr. Williamson came from Lac qui Parle as requested, and became a resident of Kaposia. While disapproving of their practices, he felt a kindly interest in the whites of Pig's Eye, which place was now beginning to be called, after a little log chapel

---

[1] Supernatural water.

which had been erected by the voyageurs, St. Paul's.[1] Though a missionary among the Dahkotahs, he was the first to take steps to promote the education of the whites and half-breeds of Minnesota. In the year 1847, he wrote to Ex-Governor Slade, President of the National Popular Education Society, in relation to the condition of what has subsequently become the capital of the state.[2]

---

[1] St. Paul was then called St. Paul's, because at that time reference was had to the chapel of St. Paul, the designation of the log church.

[2] The letter of Dr. Williamson gives, probably, the first description of the hamlet of St. Paul as it was in 1847:—

"My present residence is on the utmost verge of civilization, in the north-western part of the United States, within a few miles of the principal village of white men in the territory that we suppose will bear the name of Minnesota, which some would render 'clear water,' though strictly it signifies slightly turbid or whitish water.

"The village referred to has grown up within a few years in a romantic situation on a high bluff of the Mississippi, and has been baptized by the Roman Catholics, by the name of St. Paul. They have erected in it a small chapel, and constitute much the larger portion of the inhabitants. The Dahkotahs call it Im-ni-ja-ska (white rock), from the colour of the sandstone which forms the bluff on which the village stands. This village has five stores, as they call them, at all of which intoxicating drinks constitute a part, and I suppose the principal part, of what they sell. I would suppose the village contains a dozen or twenty families living near enough to send to school. Since I came to this neighbourhood I have had frequent occasion to visit the village, and have been grieved to see so many children growing up entirely ignorant of God, and unable to read his Word, with no one to teach them. Unless your Society can send them a teacher, there seems to be little prospect of their having one for several years. A few days since, I went to the place for the purpose of making inquiries in reference to the prospect of a school. I visited seven families, in which there were twenty-three children of proper age to attend school, and was told of five more in which were thirteen more that it is supposed might attend, making thirty-six in twelve families. I suppose more than half of the parents of these children are unable to read themselves, and care but little about having their children taught. Possibly

In accordance with his request, Miss H. E. Bishop came to his mission-house at Kaposia, and, after a short time, was introduced by him to the citizens of St. Paul. The first school-house in Minnesota besides those connected with the Indian missions, stood on the site of the First Presbyterian Church, and is thus described by the teacher:—

"The school was commenced in a little log hovel, covered with bark, and chinked with mud, previously used as a blacksmith shop. It was a room about ten by twelve feet. On three sides of the interior of this humble log cabin, pegs were driven into the logs, upon which boards were laid for seats. Another seat was made by placing one end of a plank between the cracks of the logs, and the other upon a chair. This was for the priest might deter some from attending, who might otherwise be able and willing.

"I suppose a good female teacher can do more to promote the cause of education and true religion than a man. The natural politeness of the French (who constitute more than half the population) would cause them to be kind and courteous to a female, even though the priest should seek to cause opposition. I suppose she might have twelve or fifteen scholars to begin with, and if she should have a good talent of winning the affections of children (and one who has not should not come), after a few months she would have as many as she could attend to.

"One woman told me she had four children she wished to send to school, and that she would give boarding and a room in her house to a good female teacher, for the tuition of her children.

"A teacher for this place should love the Saviour, and for his sake should be willing to forego, not only many of the religious privileges and elegances of New England towns, but some of the neatness also. She should be entirely free from prejudice on account of colour, for among her scholars she might find not only English, French, and Swiss, but Sioux and Chippewas, with some claiming kindred with the African stock.

"A teacher coming should bring books with her sufficient to begin a school, as there is no book-store within three hundred miles."

visiters. A rickety cross-legged table in the centre, and a hen's nest in one corner, completed the furniture."[1]

St. Croix county, in the year 1847, was detached from Crawford county, Wisconsin, and reorganized for judicial purposes, and Stillwater made the county seat. In the month of June the United States District Court held its session in the store-room of Mr. John McKusick; Judge Charles Dunn presiding. A large number of lumbermen had been attracted by the pineries in the upper portion of the valley of St. Croix, and Stillwater was looked upon as the centre of the lumbering interest.

The Rev. Mr. Boutwell, feeling that he could be more useful, left the Ojibways, and took up his residence near Stillwater, preaching to the lumbermen at the Falls of St. Croix, Marine Mills, Stillwater, and Cottage Grove. In a letter, speaking of Stillwater, he says, " Here is a little village sprung up like a gourd, but whether it is to perish as soon, God only knows."

For a long time it had been thought expedient to change the location of the Winnebago Indians, from the neutral ground of Iowa, to a point more remote from white men. By the terms of a treaty, made at Washington in October, 1846, they agreed to recede from their possessions, in Iowa, in the year 1848. Hon. Henry M. Rice had selected for them a new home, and with difficulty obtained it from the Ojibways, between the Sauk and Long Prairie, and Crow Wing rivers.

In the spring of 1848 their agent, Mr. J. E. Fletcher, discovered that a large portion of the tribe were desirous of emigrating to the Missouri, and grumbled at the preparations to remove northward. The treaty granted

---

[1] "*Floral Sketches*," by Miss H. E. Bishop, p. 87.

twenty thousand dollars to the Indians, to pay the expenses of their removal to their new location, to be paid after they arrived there. As no one was willing to trust Indians, for large amounts, Mr. Rice, and a few others, were obliged to advance the supplies necessary for the support of the tribe.

The difficulty in relation to subsistence being overcome, it was agreed that the tribe should move in two parties, one in canoes and boats up the Mississippi, in charge of Mr. Rice, the other by land, under the direction of Agent Fletcher. When the appointed time came to start, June the sixth, 1848, the Indians dallied, and the agent grew impatient, and, in the hope of hurrying them, had their baggage placed in the wagons, which was as quickly thrown out again by the savages. The agent sent for the troops at Fort Atkinson, and the Indians made ready for battle. The troops remained drawn up in hostile array until dark; the next day an appeal was made to the stomach of the Winnebagoes, always potent: beef was plentifully distributed, and a calm ensued.

The land party now agreed to move, provided they could join the river detachment at Wapashaw Prairie. At Wapashaw they arrived without any trouble, and found Mr. Rice, with his division of the tribe, and the company of volunteers that had accompanied him, waiting for their appearance. Almost the entire nation, with the exception of Little Hill, instead of encamping on the river bank, near the whites, sought the land beneath the bluffs, thus causing a creek and slough to intervene.

Pleased with the appearance of the prairie, where the town of Winona now stands, they purchased it of Wapashaw, the Dahkotah chief, and expressed their determination not to move a step further. Wapashaw and his band uniting with them, they made war speeches, prepared for battle, and worked themselves into frenzy. Mr. Rice, perceiving that this was a critical juncture, chartered a steamboat that happened to be there, and it was hurried to Fort Snelling.

By request, Captain S. H. Eastman came down with a company of infantry, and a party of Dahkotahs from the Minnesota river, who came to welcome the Winnebagoes, and say that they would be pleased to have them, in the place of the Ojibways, for their neighbours on the north. The company of volunteers from Crawford county, the United States dragoons from Fort Atkinson, and the infantry from Fort Snelling, and sixty armed teamsters, were now placed under the command of Eastman. The Indians, arrayed on the other side of the slough, numbered about twelve hundred. The next day was appointed for a council, between the Winnebagoes and the Dahkotahs of the Minnesota river.

The day was one of those beautiful days in June which so charm the resident of Minnesota, and the troops were all drawn out ready for service at a moment's warning; the teamsters, near the wagons, under Mr. Culver, now of St. Paul, on the right, the infantry in the centre, with two six-pounders charged with grape; the dragoons on the left. About ten o'clock in the morning, the Indians, chiefly on horseback, painted and decked with all their war ornaments, marched around the head of the slough toward the camp.

A mile from the council ground they halted, and sent forward a deputation to ask "Why the array of glittering muskets, as they supposed they were coming to council, and not to fight?" Captain Eastman replied, "that he was prepared for either: if they wished to hold a council, they would not be molested." Permission being granted, they rode around the arranged council ground and returned. In a moment the whole cavalcade, twelve abreast, were in motion toward the United States troops; and as the terrific war whoop was sounded, the Americans began to think that they might feel the scalping knife. Everything was made ready for the worst: the cannon were loaded, and soldiers stood by with the lighted matches, waiting for the voice of command.

While the council was proceeding between the Dahkotahs and Winnebagoes, an Indian and a soldier met, and were about to fight. Should either party fire, the slaughter would be instantaneous, as both sides knew; and the excitement for a moment was intense. By the timely interposition of Mr. Rice and others, the Indian and soldier were led away, and the danger passed.

During the rest of the day the Indians were in council, but, sustained by Wapashaw, they still remained firm in their determination not to leave *that* prairie. Little Hill, and a small band of Winnebagoes, had never sympathized in the revolt; and at last, Agent Fletcher, taking them on board of a steamboat, carried them up to Fort Snelling, leaving matters at Wapashaw in charge of Mr. Rice.

This sudden movement was a great surprise to the disaffected, and by the efforts of Mr. E. A. Hatch, S. B. Lowry, George Culver and others, they began to waver, and by the time the boat came back seventeen hundred were ready to embark; the remainder retreating towards the Missouri river or into Wisconsin. Mr. Rice, with a lieutenant and two soldiers, now proceeded to the lodge of Wapashaw, and arresting him, he was sent a prisoner to Fort Snelling.

About the first of July, the Winnebagoes began to move again; but on their route, those who had charge of the Indians were much annoyed by creatures that were destitute of the instincts of manhood, selling liquor to them. As a precaution against further difficulty, orders were given to destroy all the whiskey that was discovered on the line of march. About the first of August they arrived at Watab in their new country, on the west side of the Mississippi, above St. Cloud.[1]

[1] For the facts concerning the removal, I am indebted to a manuscript kindly furnished me by Mr. Rice. George Culver, of St. Paul, and to conversations with Hon. Henry M. Rice.

CHAPTER XXII.

THREE years elapsed from the time that the Territory of Minnesota was proposed in Congress to the final passage of the organic act. On the sixth of August, 1846, an act was passed by Congress authorizing the citizens of Wisconsin Territory to frame a constitution, and form a state government. The act fixed the St. Louis river to the rapids, from thence south to the St. Croix, and thence down that river to its junction with the Mississippi, as the western boundary.

On the twenty-third of December, 1846, the delegate from Wisconsin, Morgan L. Martin, introduced a bill in Congress for the organization of a territory of Minnesota. This bill made its western boundary the Sioux and Red River of the North. On the third of March, 1857, permission was granted to Wisconsin to change her boundary, so that the western limit would proceed due south from the first rapids of the St. Louis river, and fifteen miles east of the most easterly point of Lake St. Croix, thence to the Mississippi.

A number in the constitutional convention of Wisconsin were anxious that Rum river should be a part of her western boundary, while citizens of the valley of St. Croix were desirous that the Chippeway river should be the limit of Wisconsin. The citizens of Wisconsin Territory, in the valley of the St. Croix, and about Fort Snelling, wished to be included in the projected new territory, and on the twenty-eighth of March, 1848, a memorial signed by H. H. Sibley, Henry M. Rice, Franklin Steele, William R. Marshall and others, was presented to Congress, remonstrating against the proposition before the convention to make Rum river a portion of the boundary line of the contemplated state of Wisconsin. The petitioners remark:—

"Your memorialists conceive it to be the intention of your honourable bodies so to divide the present territory of Wisconsin as to form two states nearly equal in size as well as other respects. A line drawn due south from Shagwamigan Bay, on Lake Superior, to the intersection of the main Chippeway river, and from thence down the middle of said stream to its debouchure into the Mississippi, would seem to your memorialists a very proper and equitable division, which, while it would secure to Wisconsin a portion of the Lake Superior shore, would also afford to Minnesota some countervailing advantages. But if the northern line should be changed, as suggested by the convention, Minnesota would not have a single point on the Mississippi below the Falls of St. Anthony, which is the limit of steamboat navigation. This alone, to the apprehension of your memorialists, would be a good and sufficient reason why the mouth of Rum river should not be the boundary, as that stream pours its waters into the Mississippi nearly twenty miles above the Falls. Besides this, the Chippeway and St. Croix valleys are closely connected in geographical position with the Upper Mississippi, while they are widely separated from the settled parts of Wisconsin, not only by hundreds of miles of mostly waste and barren lands, which must remain uncultivated for ages, but equally so by a diversity of interests and character in the population."

On the twenty-ninth of May, 1848, the act to admit Wisconsin changed their boundary line to the present, and as first defined in the enabling act of 1846. After the bill of Mr. Martin was introduced into the House of Representatives in 1846 it was referred to the Committee on Territories, of which Mr. Douglas was chairman. On the twentieth of January, 1847, he reported in favour of the proposed territory with the name of Itasca. On the seventeenth of February, before the bill passed the House, a discussion arose in relation to the proposed names. Mr. Winthrop of Massachusetts proposed Chippeway as a substitute, alleging that this tribe was the principal in the proposed territory, which was not correct. Mr. J. Thomson of Mississippi disliked all Indian names, and hoped that the territory would be called Jackson. Mr. Houston of Delaware thought that there ought to be one territory named after the "Father of his country," and proposed Washington. All of the names proposed were rejected, and the name in the original bill inserted. On the last day of the session, March third, the bill was called up in the Senate and laid on the table.

When Wisconsin became a state the query arose whether the old territorial government did not continue in force west of the St. Croix river. The first meeting on the subject of claiming territorial privileges was held in the building at St. Paul, known as Jackson's store, near the corner of Bench and Jackson streets, on the bluff. This meeting was held in July, and a convention was proposed to consider their position. The first public meeting[1] was held at Stillwater on August fourth, and Messrs. Steele and Sibley were the only persons present from the west side of the Mississippi. This meeting issued a call for a general convention to take steps to secure an early territorial organization, to assemble on the twenty-sixth of the month at the same place. Sixty-two delegates answered the call, and to the convention a letter[2] was presented from Mr. Catlin, who

---

[1] Among those present, were W. D. Phillips, J. W. Bass, A. Larpenteur, J. McBoal, and others from St. Paul.

[2] "MADISON, August 22, 1848.
Hon. Wm. Holcombe:

"Dear Sir: I take the liberty to write you briefly for the purpose of ascertaining what the citizens of the present Territory of Wisconsin desire in relation to the organization of a territorial government. Congress adjourned on the fourteenth instant, without taking any steps to organize the Territory of Minnesota, or of amending the act of 1836, organizing Wisconsin, so that the present government could be successfully continued.

"I have given Mr. Bowron, by whom I send this, a copy of Mr. Buchanan's opinion, by which he gives it as his opinion that the laws of Wisconsin are in force in your territory; and if the laws are in force, I think it is equally clear that the officers necessary to carry out those laws are still in office. After the organization of the State of Michigan, but before her admission, Gen. G. W. Jones was elected by the Territory of Michigan (now State of Wisconsin), and was allowed to take his seat.

"It is my opinion that if your people were to elect a delegate this fall, he would be allowed to take his seat in December, and then a government might be fully organized: and unless a delegate is elected and sent on, I do not believe a government will be organized for several years. You are aware of the difficulty which has prevented the organization of Oregon for two years past; and the same difficulty will prevent the organization of Minnesota. If Mr. Tweedy were to resign, (and he would if requested), I do not see anything to prevent my issuing a proclamation for an election to fill the vacancy, as the acting governor; but I should not like to do so unless the people would act under it, and hold the election.

"If a delegate was elected by colour of law, Congress never would inquire into the legality of the election.

"It is the opinion of almost all this way that the government of the Territory of Wisconsin still continues, although it is nearly inopera-

claimed to be acting governor, giving his opinion that the Wisconsin territorial organization was still in force. The meeting also appointed Mr. Sibley to visit Washington and represent their views; but the Hon. John H. Tweedy having resigned his office of delegate to Congress on September eighteenth, 1848, Mr. Catlin, who had made Stillwater a temporary residence, on the ninth of October issued a proclamation ordering a special election at Stillwater on the thirtieth, to fill the vacancy occasioned by the resignation. At this election Henry H. Sibley was elected as delegate of the citizens of the remaining portion of Wisconsin Territory. His credentials were presented to the House of Representatives, and the committee to whom the matter was referred presented a majority and minority report; but the resolution introduced by the majority passed, and Mr. Sibley took his seat as a delegate from Wisconsin Territory on the fifteenth of January, 1849.

Mr. H. M. Rice, and other gentlemen, visited Washington during the winter, and, uniting with Mr. Sibley, used all their energies to obtain the organization of a new territory.

On the third of March, 1849, a bill was passed organizing the Territory of Minnesota,[1] whose boundary

tive, for want of a court and legislature.

"I write in haste, and have not time to state further the reasons which lead me to the conclusion that the territorial government is still in being; but you can confer with Mr. Bowron, who, I believe, is in possession of the views and opinions entertained here on the subject.

"I shall be pleased to hear from you at your earliest convenience.

"Yours very respectfully,
"JOHN CATLIN."

[1] Boundaries of the Territory of Minnesota:—

"Beginning in the Mississippi river, at the point where the line of forty-three degrees and thirty minutes of north latitude crosses the

on the west extended to the Missouri river. At the time of the passage of the bill, organizing the Territory of Minnesota, the region was little more than a wilderness. The west bank of the Mississippi, from the Iowa line to Lake Itasca, was unceded by the Indians.

At Wapashaw was a trading-post in charge of Alexis Bailly, of whom mention has been made, and here also resided the ancient voyageur, of fourscore years, A. Rocque. At the foot of Lake Pepin was a store-house kept by Mr. F. S. Richards. On the west shore of the lake lived the eccentric Wells, whose wife was a bois brulé—a daughter of the deceased trader, Duncan Graham. The two unfinished buildings of stone, on the beautiful bank opposite the renowned Maiden's Rock, and the surrounding skin lodges of his wife's relatives and friends, presented a rude but picturesque scene. Above the lake was a cluster of bark wigwams, the Dahkotah village of Raymneecha, now Red Wing, at which was a Presbyterian mission-house. The next settlement was Kaposia, also an Indian village, and the residence of a Presbyterian missionary, the Rev. T. S. Williamson, M. D.

same, thence running due west on said line, which is the northern boundary of the State of Iowa, to the north-west corner of the said State of Iowa, thence southerly along the western boundary of said State to the point where said boundary strikes the Missouri river, thence up the middle of the main channel of the Missouri river, to the mouth of White Earth river, thence up the middle of the main channel of the White Earth river to the boundary line between the possessions of the United States and Great Britain; thence east and south of east along the boundary line between the possessions of the United States and Great Britain, to Lake Superior; thence in a straight line to the northernmost point of the State of Wisconsin in Lake Superior; thence along the western boundary line of said State of Wisconsin, to the Mississippi river; thence down the main channel of said river to the place of beginning."

On the east side of the Mississippi, the first settlement, at the mouth of the St. Croix, was Point Douglas, then, as now, a small hamlet. At Red Rock, the site of a former Methodist mission station, there were a few farmers. St. Paul was just emerging from a collection of Indian whiskey shops, and birch-roofed cabins of half-breed voyageurs. Here and there a frame tenement was erected; and, under the auspices of the Hon. H. M. Rice, who had obtained an interest in the town, some warehouses were being constructed, and the foundations of the American House were laid. In 1849, the population had increased to two hundred and fifty or three hundred inhabitants, for rumours had gone abroad that it might be mentioned in the act, creating the territory, as the capital.

More than a month after the adjournment of Congress, just at eve, on the ninth of April, amid terrific peals of thunder and torrents of rain, the weekly steam-packet, the first to force its way through the icy barrier of Lake Pepin, rounded the rocky point, whistling loud and long, as if the bearer of glad tidings. Before she was safely moored to the landing, the shouts of the excited villagers announced that there was a Territory of Minnesota, and that St. Paul was the seat of government. Every successive steamboat arrival poured out on the landing men big with hope, and anxious to do something to mould the future of the new state.

Nine days after the news of the existence of the Territory of Minnesota was received, there arrived James M. Goodhue with press, types, and printing apparatus. A graduate of Amherst College, and a lawyer by profession, he wielded a sharp pen, and wrote editorials, which, more than anything else, perhaps, induced emigration. Though a man of some glaring faults, one of the counties properly bears his name. On the twenty-eighth of April, he issued the first number of the " Pioneer."[1]

On the twenty-seventh of May, Alexander Ramsey, the governor, and family arrived at St. Paul, but, owing to the crowded state of the public-houses, immediately proceeded in the steamer to the establishment of the fur company known as Mendota, at the junction of the Minnesota and Mississippi, and became the guest of the Hon. H. H. Sibley.

For several weeks there resided, at the confluence of these rivers, four individuals who, more than any other men, have been identified with the public interests of Minnesota, and given the state its present character. Their names are attached to the thriving counties of Ramsey, Rice, Sibley, and Steele.

> " As unto the bow, the cord is,
> So unto the man is the woman,
> Though she bends him, she obeys him,
> Though she draws him, yet she follows,
> Useless each without the other ;"

Therefore we venture, fully aware of the extreme delicacy of the undertaking, to attempt a portrait, not only of these citizens, but of those who are their wives,

---

[1] By advertisements in its columns, David Lambert, deceased, and William D. Phillips, of Washington City, appear as the only lawyers; J. W. Bass and Lott Moffett, keepers of houses of entertainment ; Forbes, Myrick, Simpson, Fuller & Brother, and David Olmsted, as traders; John J. Dewey, as doctor ; Miss Bishop as school teacher; and Rev. E. D. Neill, as a resident clergyman ; W. H. Nobles, and D. C. Taylor, as blacksmiths; John R. Irvine, as plasterer ; C. P. Lull, as house builder ; B. W. Brunson, surveyor.

and who must always be considered as among the prominent early settlers.

Alexander Ramsey is still in the prime of life, and was born near the city of Harrisburg, Pennsylvania. Blessed with worthy and industrious parents, he was not trained to habits of idleness. From an early period, he betrayed a fondness for reading, and amid difficulties which would have deterred many, he persevered until he succeeded in entering Lafayette College, at Easton, Pennsylvania. Circumstances were such that he remained but a brief period. A correspondent of the Public Ledger, of Philadelphia, under date of April fourth, 1849, thus writes:—

"By untiring industry and perseverance, he struggled through the study of law, and was admitted to the bar of Dauphin county. The first public office ever held by him, was that of Secretary of the Harrison Electoral College of 1840. A month afterward, in January, 1841, he was elected Clerk of the House of Representatives of Pennsylvania. In 1843, he was nominated by the Whig Conference as a candidate for Congress, to represent the district, embracing the counties of Dauphin, Lebanon, and Schuylkill. He was elected by a decisive majority; and in Harrisburg, his place of residence, which before had given a Democratic majority, there was a large vote in his favour. His course in Congress was marked rather by a practical business devotion to his duties, than by any effort at oratorical display. He was nominated and re-elected for a second term; and in 1846, declined in favour of another. He is social and good-humoured, but cool, cautious, shrewd, and persevering. He is a man of very large perceptive powers, and of much grasp of intellect; altogether what might be termed a man of a good deal of force of character. He speaks well, not eloquently; but to the point, quite as fluently in German as in English." No longer

> "In the land of the Dahkotahs,
> Lives the arrowmaker's daughter,
> Minnehaha, Laughing Water,
> Handsomest of all the women;"

Yet the first governor of the territory appears to have received from some one, as good advice as Old Nokomis gave to Hiawatha:—

> "Bring not here an idle maiden,
> Bring not here a useless woman,
> Hands unskilful, feet unwilling.
> Bring a wife with nimble fingers,
> Heart and hand that move together,
> Feet that run on willing errands."

His wife is Anna E., the daughter of Hon. Mr. Jenks, of Newtown, a former member of Congress from Bucks county, Pennsylvania. At the time of his marriage in 1845, she was eighteen years of age. Accompanying her husband to Minnesota, when it was chiefly occupied by savages, removed from the associations of her childhood, she with great cheerfulness adapted herself to her new position. Queenly and attractive in appearance, she well fulfilled the duties of a governor's wife. Affable, open-hearted, and well informed, she immediately became a favourite, not only with "those in authority," but also with the plain frontiersman. Domestic in her tastes, she is best appreciated by those who know her most intimately.

Henry Hastings Sibley was born in Detroit, in 1812. His father was a native of Massachusetts, and one of the early settlers of Michigan, having been a member of the first Legislative Assembly of the North-west Territory, which met at Cincinnati. Subsequently he was delegate to Congress, and Judge of the Supreme Court of Michigan. His mother was a native of Rhode Island, who removed with her parents at an early age to Ohio. Educated at the celebrated Moravian School at Bethlehem, and in the city of Philadelphia, she was refined and accomplished, and trained her children well.

When the subject of this sketch was eighteen years of age, he became a clerk of Mr. Stewart, a gentleman of probity and intelligence, who had charge of the depôt of the American Fur Company at Mackinaw. In the year 1834, when but twenty-two years of age, Mr. Sibley commenced his residence at Mendota, as clerk of the American Fur Company's establishment. After this company failed in 1842, the inventory was purchased by P. Chouteau, Jr., and Co., of St. Louis, and Mr. Sibley continued the business until he became a delegate to Congress in 1848–49, which post he held for several years, and faithfully discharged its duties. After a long delay, he has been declared by the board of canvassers the governor of the state.

Mr. Sibley's wife is a native of Pennsylvania, and the sister of Mr. Franklin Steele. Married at an early age, she also gracefully accommodated herself to the novelty of frontier life, although, living immediately opposite to Fort Snelling, she found some congenial society among the families of the officers. Sprightly in disposition, and devoted to her children, her venerable mother and her husband, her house is a happy home.

Henry M. Rice, one of the representatives of the state in the Senate of the United States, is a native of

SKETCH OF HENRY M. RICE.   499

Vermont, although his life, from youth, has been passed in the far West. With much foresight, and quick in execution, he has always been prominent in developing the resources of the state he represents. The following sketch, published a few years ago, gives the views of one of Mr. Rice's friends:—

" He settled here when there were no white men in the territory, except Indian traders, missionaries, and soldiers; and during his long residence, has been noted as the promoter of every enterprise tending to develop the hidden wealth of Minnesota, and attract hither immigration from other portions of the country. Two years ago, he was elected to Congress by an overwhelming vote; and then commenced a series of labours on his part which will make him long remembered in the territory as the most efficient of representatives. The pre-emption system he caused to be extended to unsurveyed lands; the military reserves opened to actual settlers; land offices to be established; post routes opened out and offices established; millions of acres of lands to be purchased from Indians, and thrown open to settlers; and thousands of dollars to be appropriated to the construction of government roads. Nor was this all: legislation for the benefit of individuals entitled to it, was secured, and no exertion ever spared, in Congress and out of it, at the executive departments or elsewhere, that would benefit the territory. The heavy immigration of the past two years is as strong proof as could be desired that Minnesota is regarded as the chosen spot of the West, either for immigrants seeking to establish themselves, or capitalists desiring investments; and for much of this heavy immigration, we cannot help thinking our territory is indebted to the late delegate;

the beneficial legislation he procured for us, rendered Minnesota indeed a land of promise.

"Mr. Rice possesses in a great degree the qualities necessary to make a good delegate. His winning manners secure him hosts of friends, and enable him to acquire great influence; his business habits, industry, and perseverance, insure the accomplishment of whatever he undertakes, while his perfect knowledge of the wants of the territory, prevents his efforts from being misdirected. His political opinions are those of a National Democrat—coinciding with those of the president and heads of departments, a majority of the Senate, and a respectable and united minority in the House—which will successfully combat a divided majority."

In the year 1849 Mr. Rice was married to Miss Matilda Whitall, whose family reside in the vicinity of Richmond, Virginia. Youthful, graceful in bearing, and with warm impulses, her houses in Washington and St. Paul have always been an agreeable resort to her husband's friends. With a disposition to be identified with whatever will promote the interests of her husband, she proves a valuable wife as well as attentive mother.

Franklin Steele is a native of Lancaster county, Pennsylvania, and, when a youth, was advised by Andrew Jackson, late President of the United States, to identify himself with the West. John H. Stevens, Esq., of Glencoe, formerly a clerk of Mr. Steele's, in a lecture before Hennepin County Lyceum, says:—"The day he landed at Fort Snelling, the Indians had concluded a treaty with the whites, by which the St. Croix Falls were ceded to the latter. Mr. Steele went over; liked the place much, made a claim, hired a large crew of men, put Calvin A. Tuttle, Esq., now of St. Anthony, at their head, and commenced in earnest to build mills. Upon being appointed sutler to the army at Fort Snelling, he disposed of the St. Croix property, and became interested on the east side of St. Anthony Falls. He has continued to make this county his home ever since his first arrival in the territory. Mr. Steele has been a good friend to Hennepin, and as most of the citizens came here poor, they never had to ask Mr. Steele a second time for a favour. Fortune has favoured him, and while many a family has reason to be thankful for his generosity and kindness, he has constantly made money."

Mrs. Franklin Steele is a native of Maryland, and was a Miss Barney, a relative of the naval officer whose name is associated with the glory of our marine. Commanding in person, and well educated, she has been much admired in society.

About the last of May, 1849, the Dahkotahs of the Kaposia band, just below St. Paul, performed one of their peculiar ceremonies. A short distance from their lodges they formed an elliptical enclosure with willow bushes stuck in the ground. In the centre was placed a large buffalo fish on some green fern, and a cat-fish on a bunch of dry grass. A small arbour was placed over the fish. At one end of the enclosure was a tēēpēē, in which were men singing Hah-yay, Hah-yay, Hoh, Hoh, Hoh, Hoh-ah. Soon six men and three boys issued with bent bodies and long, dishevelled hair, who moved around the enclosure, keeping their faces as much as possible in the direction of the fishes. Then a tall man, of threescore years, painted entirely black, appeared with a small hoop in each hand, walking " on all fours," and howling like a bear. Entering within the enclosure of willow branches, he moved around as if scenting something. While thus occupied, two more made their appearance smeared all over with white clay, one representing a grizzly bear, the other, with a tail suspended from his breech cloth, and body bent, represented a wolf. The other Indians danced and sang for two or three hours, while these men as beasts prowled around the fishes, pawing, snuffing at them, and then retreating. At last one of the bears crept up to one of the fish, and, after much growling, bit off a piece, and went round the ellipse chewing. The other bear then bit the remaining fish. These signals caused all the dancers to follow, and flesh, fins, bones, and entrails were all devoured without being touched by the hands. The sacred men also prayed to the spirits of the fish, and the object of the feast, was supposed to be, to induce a change of weather.

On the first of June, Governor Ramsey, by proclamation, declared the territory duly organized, with the following officers: Alexander Ramsey, of Pennsylvania, Governor; C. K. Smith, of Ohio, Secretary; A. Goodrich, of Tennessee, Chief Justice; D. Cooper, of Pennsylvania, and B. B. Meeker, of Kentucky, Associate Judges; Joshua L. Taylor, Marshal; H. L. Moss, Attorney of the United States.[1]

---

[1] *A Proclamation, by Alexander Ramsey, Governor of the Territory of Minnesota.*

TO ALL WHOM IT MAY CONCERN.

Whereas by an act of the Congress of the United States of America, entitled "*An act to establish the Territorial Government of Minnesota,*" approved March third, 1849, a true copy whereof is hereto annexed, a government was erected over all the country described in said act to be called "The Territory of Minnesota;" and whereas the following named officers have been duly appointed and commisssioned under the said act as officers of said government, viz:

Alexander Ramsey, Governor of said Territory, and Commander-in

On the eleventh of June, a second proclamation was issued, dividing the territory into three temporary judicial districts. The first comprised the county of St. Croix; the county of La Pointe, and the region north and west of the Mississippi, and north of the Minnesota, and of a line running due west from the headwaters of the Minnesota to the Missouri river, constituted the second; and the country west of the Mississippi, and south of the Minnesota, formed the third district. Judge Goodrich was assigned to the first, Meeker to the second, and Cooper to the third. A court was ordered to be held at Stillwater on the second Monday, at the Falls of St. Anthony on the third, and at Mendota on the fourth Monday of August.

On the sixth of June, Major Wood left Fort Snelling, charged with the duty of making a military examination of the country in the vicinity of Pembina, in view of establishing a military post there. Captain Pope, of the topographical engineers, accompanied the expedition, and his report, published by Congress, is valuable

Chief of the Militia thereof, and Superintendent of Indian affairs therein,

Charles K. Smith, Secretary of said territory,

Aaron Goodrich, Chief Justice, and David Cooper and Bradley B. Meeker, Associate Justices of the Supreme Court of said territory, and to act as Judges of the District Court of said territory,

Joshua L. Taylor, Marshal of the United States for said territory,

Henry L. Moss, Attorney of the United States for said territory,

And said officers having respectively assumed the duties of their said offices according to law, said territorial government is declared to be organized and established, and all persons are enjoined to obey, conform to, and respect the laws thereof accordingly.

Given under my hand, and the [SEAL.] seal of said Territory, this first day of June, A. D. 1849, and of the Independence of the United States of America the seventy-third.

By the Governor,   ALEX. RAMSEY.
    CHAS. K. SMITH, *Secretary.*

in information, concerning the adaptation of the Red River valley for agricultural purposes.

Until the twenty-sixth of June, Governor Ramsey and family had been guests of Hon. H. H. Sibley, at Mendota. On the afternoon of that day they arrived at St. Paul, in a birch-bark canoe, and became permanent residents at the capital. The mansion first occupied as a gubernatorial mansion, is the small frame building, on Third, between Robert and Jackson streets, subsequently known as the New England House.

A few days after, the Hon. H. M. Rice and family moved from Mendota to St. Paul, and occupied the house he had erected on St. Anthony street, near the corner of Market.

On the first of July, a land office was established at Stillwater, and A. Van Vorhees, after a few weeks, became the register.

The anniversary of our National Independence, was celebrated in a becoming manner at the capital. The place selected for the address, was a grove that stood on the sites of the City Hall and the Baldwin School Building.

In pursuance of a requirement in the organic act, the sheriff of St. Croix was ordered to take a census of all inhabitants.[1]

[1] The result was as follows:—

Names of Places.	Males.	Females.	Total.
Stillwater,	455	154	609
Lake St. Croix,	129	82	211
Marine Mills,	142	31	173
St. Paul,	540	300	840
Little Canada and St. Anthony,	352	219	571
Crow Wing and Long Prairie,	235	115	350
Osakis Rapids,	92	41	133
Falls of St. Croix,	15	1	16

On the seventh of July, a proclamation was issued, dividing the territory into seven council districts, and ordering an election to be held on the first day of August, for one delegate to represent the people in the House of Representatives of the United States, for nine councillors, and eighteen representatives to constitute the Legislative Assembly of Minnesota.

Shortly after his arrival, Governor Ramsey recognised a new hereditary chief of the Wahk-pay-koo-tay band of Dahkotahs, named Wa-min-di-yu-ka-pi, by investing him with a sword and a soldier's medal. He was a fine looking youth, and a few weeks after this honour he and seventeen others were slaughtered in broad daylight, by a party of Indians they met near the headwaters of the Des Moines river. The Dahkotahs took four scalps, and the citizens of St. Paul, during the quiet nights of that summer, could hear the noise of the scalp dance at Kaposia.

Names of Places.	Males.	Females.	Total.
Snake River,	58	24	82
La Pointe County,	12	10	22
Crow Wing,	103	71	174
Big Stone Lake and Lac qui Parle,	33	35	68
Little Rock,	20	15	35
Prairieville,	9	13	22
Oak Grove,	14	9	23
Black Dog Village,	7	11	18
Crow Wing, east side,	35	35	70
Mendota,	72	50	122
Red Wing Village,	20	13	33
Wabeshaw and Root River,	78	36	114
Fort Snelling,	26	12	38
Soldiers and women and children in forts,	267	50	317
Pembina,	295	342	637
Missouri River,	49	37	86
	3067	1713	4680

During the latter part of July, a band of Sissetoan Dahkotahs, near Big Stone Lake, proceeded to a buffalo hunt. Unsuccessful, they were obliged to eat their dogs and tipsinna.[1] One day they were startled by a horseman galloping across the plain in the direction of their camp. On his approach, they saw he was a Red River half-breed, who had formerly lived in their country. He had come to tell them that the Ojibways were in the neighbourhood, and contemplated an attack. The Dahkotahs had just hid their women and children in holes, and covered them with brush-wood, when the enemy came in sight. A few of the bravest Dahkotahs went out to meet the foe, and the fight commenced near a rivulet, in the valley of the Cheyenne. The leader, after fighting bravely, found himself surrounded by the Ojibways, who had concealed themselves in the grass. While in the act of raising his head to draw the stopper from his powder-horn, he was shot through the brain. His little son, not ten years of age, seeing his father fall, rushed to the corpse, and after clasping it, he lay by its side, and fired at the enemy until aid came from

---

[1] The Tipsinna, or Dahkotah turnip, grows only in the high and dry prairie. It seeks the high points and gravelly hills, where it continues to grow in size from year to year, increasing with every summer that passes over it. The root is roundish or oval, and of various sizes, according to its age. It has a thick, hard rind, which the Dahkotah usually remove with their teeth. During the months of June and July, when the top can be easily discovered in the grass, the Indians of the Upper Minnesota depend, very much, for their subsistence on the tipsinna. They eat it both raw and cooked. This root has lately acquired a European reputation. Mr. Lamare Picot, of France has, within a few years past, introduced it into his native country, and the Savans of Paris, it is said, have given it the name of "Picotianna." It has been supposed that this dry prairie root might yet take an important place among the vegetables which are cultivated for the support of human life; but this expectation will probably end in disappointment.

the Dahkotah camp, and his corpse was cared for by friends. After skirmishing till dusk, the Ojibways retreated with three killed. The Dahkotahs lost the same number.[1]

In this month the Hon. H. M. Rice despatched a boat laden with Indian goods from the Falls of St. Anthony to Crow Wing, which was towed by horses after the manner of a canal boat.

The election on the first of August, passed off with little excitement, Hon. H. H. Sibley being elected delegate to Congress without opposition.[2] David Lambert, on what might, perhaps, be termed the old settlers' ticket, was defeated in St. Paul, by James McBoal. The latter, on the night of the election, was honoured with a ride through town on the axle and fore-wheels of an old wagon, which was drawn by his admiring, but somewhat undisciplined friends.

J. L. Taylor having declined the office of United States Marshal;[3] A. M. Mitchell, of Ohio, a graduate of

---

[1] Communication in Minnesota Pioneer, September 19, 1849.

[2] The vote in St. Paul was:—

Delegate to Congress,	H. H. Sibley,	188
Councillors,	W. H. Forbes,	187
"	J. McBoal,	98
"	D. Lambert,	91
House of Representatives,	B. Brunson,	168
" "	P. K. Johnson,	104
" "	H. Jackson,	165
" "	J. J. Dewey,	171
" "	J. R. Brown,	84
" "	A. G. Fuller,	24

Unsuccessful in *Italics*.

[3] The following exhibits the result of the first census, along with the vote cast for the Delegate to Congress on the first August, 1849, arranged under the counties into which the territory was subsequently divided by the first Legislature:—

West Point, and colonel of a regiment of Ohio volunteers in Mexico, was appointed, and arrived at the capital early in August.

There were three papers published in the territory soon after its organization. The first was the Pioneer,[1] issued on April twenty-eighth, 1849, under most discouraging circumstances. It was at first the intention of the witty and reckless editor to have called his paper "The Epistle of St. Paul." About the same time there was issued, in Cincinnati, under the auspices of the late Dr. A. Randall, of California, the first number of the Register. The second number of the paper was printed at St. Paul, in July, and the office was on St. Anthony, between Washington and Market Streets. About the first of June, James Hughes, now of Hudson, Wisconsin, arrived with a press and materials, and established the Minnesota Chronicle. After an existence of a few weeks these papers were discontinued; and, in their place, was

Co. Seats.	Counties.	Males.	Females.	Vote for Del.
St. Paul,	Ramsey,	976	564	273
Stillwater,	Washington,	821	291	213
Sauk Rapids,	Benton,	249	108	18
Mendota,	Dahkotah,	301	167	75
	Wahnatah,	344	182	70
Wabashaw,	Wabashaw,	246	84	33
Pembina,	Pembina,	295	342	—
	Itasca,	21	9	—
	Mankato,	—	—	—
		3253	1687	682
		1687		

Total population, June 30, 1849, . . . 4940

[1] The press used in printing the "Pioneer" is said to have been the first ever used north of Missouri, and west of the Mississippi. It was purchased in Cincinnati in 1836, and first used in printing the Dubuque Visitor, published by John King.

SESSIONS OF THE FIRST COURTS.

issued the "Chronicle and Register," edited by Nathaniel McLean and John P. Owens.

The first courts, pursuant to proclamation of the governor, were held in the month of August. At Stillwater, the court was organized on the thirteenth of the month, Judge Goodrich presiding, and Judge Cooper, by courtesy, sitting on the bench. On the twentieth, the second judicial district held a court. The room used was the old government mill at Minneapolis. The presiding judge was B. B. Meeker; the foreman of the grand jury, Franklin Steele. On the last Monday of the month, the court for the third judicial district was organized in the large stone warehouse of the fur company at Mendota. The presiding judge was David Cooper. Governor Ramsey sat on the right, and Judge Goodrich on the left. Hon. H. H. Sibley was the foreman of the grand jury. As some of the jurors could not speak the English language, W. H. Forbes acted as interpreter. The charge of Judge Cooper was lucid, scholarly, and dignified. At the request of the grand jury it was afterwards published.

R. G. Murphey, the United States' agent for the Dahkotahs, used commendable diligence during this year in checking the whiskey traffic, and in inducing the Indians to renew their temperance pledges. Under the influence of a vile class of whiskey sellers that infested the neighbourhood of what is now the capital of Minnesota, the Dahkotahs, a few years before this, were a nation of drunkards. Men would travel hundreds of miles to the "place where they sell Minne-wakan," as they designated St. Paul, to traffic for a keg of whiskey. The editor of the Dahkotah Friend says:—

"Twelve years ago they bade fair soon to die, all together, in one drunken jumble. They must be drunk—they could hardly live if they were not drunk. Many of them seemed as uneasy when sober as a fish does when on land. At some of the villages they were drunk months together. There was no end to it. They would have whiskey. They would give guns, blankets, pork, lard, flour, corn, coffee, sugar, horses, furs, traps, anything for whiskey. It was made to drink—it was good —it was wakan. They drank it—they bit off each other's noses—broke each other's ribs and heads—they knifed each other. They killed one another with guns, knives, hatchets, clubs, fire-brands—they fell into the fire and water, and were burned to death and drowned —they froze to death, and committed suicide so frequently that, for a time, the death of an Indian, in some of the ways mentioned, was but little thought of by themselves or others. Some of the earlier settlers of St. Paul and Pig's Eye remember something about these matters. Their eyes saw sights which are not exhibited now-a-days."

The reform was commenced through the influence of the missionaries, Mr. Sibley, and Mr. Murphey's predecessor.

On one occasion Agent Murphey met a Sissetoan Dahkotah, a few miles above Mendota, returning home with a supply of "fire water." A wagon happening to pass at the time, he secured the fellow, and returned with him in the vehicle toward Fort Snelling; but, in passing a wooded ravine, the Indian, a most active and athletic man, succeeded, by a desperate exertion, in leaping from the wagon, and, dashing into the woods, made his escape. During the summer a steamboat landed in the night at Raymneecha (Red Wing), and a

MEETING OF FIRST LEGISLATURE. 511

son of one of the chiefs, told his father that the band were obtaining whiskey at the boat. The chief was indignant, and, awaking the Indian farmer, he went to the landing, and told the crew that he would cut the boat loose unless they immediately removed.

On Monday, the third of September, the first Legislative Assembly convened in the "Central House," a building which answered the double purpose, of capitol and hotel. On the first floor of the main building was the secretary's office and Representative chamber, and in the second story was the library and Council chamber. As the flag was run up the staff in front of the house, a number of Indians sat on a rocky bluff in the vicinity, and gazed at what to them was a novel, and perhaps saddening scene; for if the tide of emigration sweeps in from the Pacific as it has from the Atlantic coast, they must diminish.

The legislature having organized, elected the following permanent officers: David Olmsted, President of Council;[1] Joseph R. Brown, Secretary; H. A. Lambert, Assistant. In the House of Representatives, Joseph W. Furber was elected Speaker; W. D. Phillips, Clerk; L. B. Wait, Assistant.

On Tuesday afternoon, both houses assembled in the

[1] Councillors.	No. of District.	Residence.	Age.	Place of Nativity.
James S. Norris,	1	Cottage Grove,	38	Maine.
Samuel Burkleo,	2	Stillwater,	45	Delaware.
William H. Forbes,	3	St. Paul,	38	Montreal, C.
James McC. Boal,	3	"	38	Pennsylvania.
David B. Loomis,	4	Marine Mills,	32	Connecticut.
John Rollins,	5	Falls of St. Anthony,	41	Maine.
David Olmsted,	6	Long Prairie,	27	Vermont.
William Sturges,	6	Elk River,	28	Up. Canada.
Martin McLeod,	7	Lac qui Parle,	36	Montreal, C.

dining hall of the hotel, and after prayer was offered by Rev. E. D. Neill, Governor Ramsey delivered his message. The message was ably written, and its perusal afforded satisfaction at home and abroad.

The members of the first legislature were generally acquainted with each other previous to their election, and there was but little formality manifested in their proceedings. A child of one of the members having died, the House of Representatives[1] adjourned to attend the little one's funeral.[2]

[1] Representatives.	No. of District.	Residence.	Age.	Place of Nativity.
Joseph W. Furber,	1	Cottage Grove,	36	N. H.
James Wells,	1	Lake Pepin,	46	N. Jersey.
M. S. Wilkinson,	2	Stillwater,	30	New York.
Sylvanus Trask,	2	"	—	"
Mahlon Black,	2	"	—	Ohio.
Benjamin W. Brunson,	3	St. Paul,	25	Michigan.
Henry Jackson,	3	"	42	Virginia.
John J. Dewey,	3	"	—	New York.
Parsons K. Johnson,	3	"	—	Vermont.
Henry F. Setzer,	4	Snake River,	—	Missouri.
William R. Marshall,	5	Falls of St. Anthony,	25	
William Dugas,	5	Little Canada,	37	L. Canada.
Jeremiah Russell,	6	Crow Wing,	—	
L. A. Babcock,	6	Sauk Rapids,	29	Vermont.
Thomas A. Holmes,	6	"	44	Pennsylvania.
Allen Morrison,	6			
Alexis Bailly,	7	Mendota,	50	Michigan.
Gideon H. Pond,	7	Oak Grove,	39	Connecticut.

[2] Extract from the Journal of the House, October fourth, 1849:—

Mr. Wilkinson offered the following:—

"Whereas, by the sudden and mysterious dispensation of Providence, one of our brother members of this house, has been *painfully*(?) bereaved by the death of a beloved member of his family, and feeling a deep sympathy for our worthy brother in his bereavment, therefore

Resolved, That when this house adjourn, that it adjourn until tomorrow morning at ten o'clock, and that the members be requested by the speaker to attend the funeral of the daughter of the Hon. B. W. Brunson, at one o'clock."

FIRST COUNTIES.—RED PIPE STONE.

The first session of the legislature adjourned on the first of November. Among other proceedings of interest, was the creation of the following counties: Itasca, Waubashaw, Dahkotah, Wahnahtah, Mahkahto, Pembina, Washington, Ramsey, and Benton. The three latter counties comprised the country that up to that time had been ceded by the Indians on the east side of the Mississippi. Stillwater was declared the county seat of Washington; St. Paul, of Ramsey; "and the seat of justice of the county of Benton, was to be within one-quarter of a mile of a point on the east side of the Mississippi, directly opposite the mouth of Sauk river."

The day of elections after the year 1849, was appointed to be on the first of September.

A warm interest was manifested in the common school system, and an able report on the subject was made to the Council by the Hon. M. McLeod, chairman of the committee.

A joint resolution was passed, ordering a slab of the red pipe stone to be forwarded to the Washington Monument Association.[1]

---

[1] Mr. McLeod submitted the following communication from the Hon. Henry H. Sibley, which
On motion of Mr. McLeod, was ordered to be read and entered on the minutes of the council:—

MENDOTA, Sept. 11, 1849.
To the Honourable, the Legislative Council of Minnesota Territory:
The undersigned having seen a notice in the public journals some time since, signed by the general agent of the Washington Monument Association, to the effect that a portion of rock from each state, would be received to be used in the construction of the monument, has caused to be procured from the quarry, about two hundred miles distant, a specimen of the Red or Pipe stone, which is peculiar to our territory, to be proffered for that purpose. Believing it to be meet and proper that Minnesota should not be backward in her contribution to a work which is intended to perpetuate the memory of the "Father

The stone for ages has been used by the Dahkotahs and other tribes for the manufacture of pipes, and is esteemed "wakan." In the State Cabinet of Albany there is a very ancient pipe of this material, which was obtained in the Seneca country, and the tradition is that it was taken from the Dahkotahs.

Charlevoix, in his History of New France, speaking of the pipe of peace, says: "It is ordinarily made of a species of red marble, very easily worked, and found beyond the Mississippi among the Aaiouez (Ioways)." Le Sueur speaks of the Yanktons, as the village of the Dahkotahs at the Red Stone-quarry. It is asserted that in days gone by hostile nations used to assemble at this quarry, and obtain the material for pipes without mo-

of his Country," and that the offering should be that of the constituted authorities of the territory, rather than the act of a private individual, I have hereby the honour to present the specimen of rock to your honourable body, for your acceptance, to be disposed of in such manner as your wisdom may suggest.

The slab is about two and a half feet in length, and a little over one and a half in breadth, and two inches in thickness. In the last particular it does not meet the requirements of the Association; but, apart from the impracticability of transporting a huge mass of stone, weighing nearly, if not quite, half a ton, if of the dimensions stated, to so remote a point as Washington City, it is known that the strata of pipe stone rarely, if ever, exceed three inches in thickness. In length and breadth, it is believed, the specimen will come up to the standard, and can be so used as to face a solid block of granite or other material, and thus answer the proposed end.

In conclusion, I would beg leave to state, that a late geological work of high authority, by Dr. Jackson, designates this formation as *Catlinite*, upon the erroneous supposition that Mr. George Catlin was the first white man who had ever visited that region; whereas, it is notorious that many whites had been there and examined the quarry long before he came to the country. This designation is therefore clearly improper and unjust. The Sioux term for the stone is Eyanskah, by which, I conceive, it should be known and classified.

I have the honour to be,
Very respectfully,
Your obedient servant,
H. H. SIBLEY.

lestation. Whether facts will sustain the tradition may be doubtful.

The first canto of the "Song of Hiawatha" gives an impressive picture of the conclave of natives at "the great Red Pipe Stone Quarry."[1]

Nicollet, in his admirable report, remarks: "This red pipe stone, not more interesting to the Indian than it is to the man of science, by its unique character, deserves a particular description. In the quarry of it which I had opened, the thickness of the bed is one foot and a half, the upper portion of which separates in thin slabs, whilst the lower ones are more compact. As a mineralogical species it may be described as follows: compact; structure, slaty; receiving a dull polish; having a red streak; colour, blood red, with dots of a fainter shade of the same colour; fracture, rough; sextile, fat, somewhat greasy; hardness, not yielding to the nail;

---

[1] "Down the rivers, o'er the prairies,
Came the warriors of the nations,
Came the Delawares and Mohawks,
Came the Choctaws and Camanches,
Came the Shoshonies and Blackfeet,
Came the Pawnees and Omahaws,
Came the Mandans and Dacotahs,
Came the Huron and Ojibways,
All the warriors drawn together,
By the signal of the Peace-Pipe,
To the mountains of the prairie,
To the great Red Pipe Stone Quarry.
* * * * *
Gitche Manito, the mighty,
The creator of the nations,
Looked upon them with compassion,
With paternal love and pity;
* * * * *
Spake to them with voice majestic
As the sound of far off waters,
* * * * *
O my children! my poor children!
Listen to the words of wisdom,
Listen to the words of warning,
From the lips of the Great Spirit,
From the Master of Life, who made you;
I have given you lands to hunt in,
I have given you streams to fish in,
I have given you bear and bison.
I have given you roe and reindeer,
I have given you brant and beaver,
Filling the marshes full of wild fowl,
Filled the rivers full of fishes;
Why then are you not contented?
Why then will you hunt each other?
I am weary of your quarrels,
Weary of your wars and bloodshed,
Weary of your prayers for vengeance,
Of your wranglings and dissensions;
All your strength is in your union,
All your danger is in discord;
Therefore be at peace henceforward,
And as brothers live together,
Bathe now in the stream before you,
Wash the war paint from your faces,
Wash the blood stains from your fingers,
Bury your war clubs and your weapons,
Break the red stone from this quarry,
Mould and make it into peace-pipes,
Take the reeds that grow beside you,
Deck them with your brightest feathers,
Smoke the calumet together,
And as brothers live henceforward!"

not scratched by selenite, but easily by calcareous spar; specific gravity, 2.90. The acids have no action upon it; before the blow-pipe it is infusible, *per se;* but with borax gives a green glass."

The committee on seal recommended as a device an Indian family, with lodge and canoe, encamped, a single white man visiting them, and receiving from them the calumet of peace. The report was accepted, and the committee discharged. During the following winter, Governor Ramsey and the delegate to Congress devised at Washington the territorial seal. The design was: Falls of St. Anthony in the distance; an emigrant ploughing the land on the borders of the Indian country, full of hope, and looking forward to the possession of the hunting-grounds beyond. An Indian, amazed at the sight of the plough, and fleeing on horseback towards the setting sun.

The motto is, "Quo sursum volo videre," I wish to look beyond; indicative of the disposition of the pioneer to be constantly pushing into an unsettled country. By mistake of the engraver, the original seal of state reads Quo sursum *velo* videre; and for two or three years it puzzled all Latin scholars to translate it for their own comprehension, or that of the "vulgum pecus."

The Historical Society, in their publication for the year 1856, had an engraving of the seal with the motto correctly spelled; and since then the difficulty has been rectified to some extent.

The wife of Captain S. Eastman, who was formerly in command of Fort Snelling, a lady of fine literary qualifications, who, with her husband, has done more than any one to illustrate Dahkotah-land and Dahkotah-life, prepared a poem on the "Seal of Minnesota," about the time it was designed.[1]

When the Territory of Minnesota was organized, the Indian title had been extinguished to but a small portion of the country. The ceded region was chiefly east of the Mississippi, being bounded on the north by a line extending east from the mouth of the Crow Wing river to the western boundary line of Wisconsin. The lands above were occupied by the Ojibways.

It therefore seemed very desirable to make room for the rushing emigration to procure the right of occupancy to the lands in possession of the Dahkotahs west

---

[1] Give way, give way, young warrior,
    Thou and thy steed give way—
Rest not, though lingers on the hills
    The red sun's parting ray.
The rocky bluff and prairie land
    The white man claims them now,
The symbols of his course are here,
    The rifle, axe, and plough.

Not thine, the waters bright whose laugh
    Is ringing in thy ear;
Not thine the otter and the lynx,
    The wolf and timid deer.
The forest tree, the fairy ring,
    The sacred isle and mound
Have passed into another's hands—
    Another claimant found.

Give way, give way, young warrior—
    Our title would you seek?
'Tis " the rich against the poor,
    And the strong against the weak."
We need thy noble rivers,
    Thy prairies green and wide,
And thy dark and frowning forests
    That skirt the valley's side.

The red man's course is onward—
    Nor stayed his footsteps be,
Till by his rugged hunting ground
    Beats the relentless sea!
We claim his noble heritage,
    And Minnesota's land
Must pass with all its untold wealth
    To the white man's grasping hand.

Give way, give way, young warrior,
    Thy father's bones may rest
No longer here, where earth has clasped
    Them, closely to her breast—
Here, were thy fiercest battles fought—
    Here, through the valleys rung
The voices of the victors brave,
    As they their triumph sung.

Here, too, with long and braided hair,
    Thy maidens in the dance
Rivalled the wild deer's fleetest step,
    The wild deer's brightest glance.
And here they gathered oft at eve
    From aged lips to hear
How flowed the warrior's heart's best blood,
    How fell the maiden's tear.

Give way—I know a thousand ties
    Most lovingly must cling,
I know a gush of sorrow deep
    Such memories must bring.
Thou and thy noble race from earth
    Must soon be passed away,
As echoes die upon the hills,
    Or darkness follows day.

Yet hear me still, young warrior,
    Thou and thy steed give way—
Rest not, though lingers on the hills
    The red sun's parting ray.
The rocky bluff and prairie land
    The white man claims them now,
The symbols of his course are here—
    The rifle, axe, and plough.

of the Mississippi, and in the valley of the Minnesota. Governor Ramsey and Ex-Governor Chambers of Iowa were appointed Commissioners to treat with the Dahkotahs. They repaired to Mendota during the session of the legislature; but in consequence of the absence of many Indians on their fall hunt, and other circumstances, they did not wholly comply with their instructions. They however made a treaty for the purchase of what is known as the half-breed tract of Lake Pepin.

Previous to the session of the legislature, there had been no organization of any political party in the territory. On the evening of September twenty-fourth, a Democratic caucus was held at the house of H. M. Rice, at St. Paul, on St. Anthony near Market street, and it was determined to call a mass meeting of Democrats. On October twentieth,[1] the first party convention assembled in the ball-room of the American House. Henry Jackson was Chairman, pro tem., and as permanent officers were chosen James S. Norris, President; John A. Ford, S. Trask, W. Dugas, H. N. Setzer, James Wells, John Rollins, and A. Morrison, Vice-Presidents; B. W. Lott, A. Larpenteur, H. A. Lambert, and John Morgan, Secretaries. The Minnesota Pioneer was de-

[1] "At a Democratic caucus held at the house of Henry M. Rice, on Monday evening, September twenty-fourth, 1849, the undersigned were appointed a committee to call a Mass Meeting of the Democracy of the Territory of Minnesota.

"Believing that the safety and integrity of our party, and the permanent interests of our infant territory, demand that the party lines be henceforth drawn, we extend a cordial invitation to our Democratic brethren in all parts of the territory, to assemble in mass meeting at St. Paul, on Saturday, the twentieth day of October, to take measures to secure a permanent and thorough organization.

W. D. PHILLIPS, 3d Dist.
JOHN ROLLINS, 5th "
J. S. NORRIS, 1st "
S. TRASK, 2d "
H. N. SETZER, 4th "
T. A. HOLMES, 6th " "

clared to be the organ of the party, and from that period there was manifest a different spirit in the conduct of public affairs.

On Friday evening, David Lambert, Esq., who had been prominent in the meetings that led to the organization of the territory, under the influence of that mania, which hurries so many of our public men to the grave, jumped from a steamer, on which he was returning from Galena, and was drowned.[1]

During the session of the legislature, considerable discussion arose in relation to the right of the territory, to expend the twenty thousand dollars appropriated in the organic act for a capitol, at the temporary seat of government. Joseph R. Brown, desiring information, wrote to the secretary of the treasury, who decided that the money could only be appropriated at the permanent seat of government.[2]

---

[1] His friend, the editor of the Pioneer, in his paper of November eighth says:

"Mr. Lambert was about thirty years of age, was prosperous in business, and acknowledged to be a man of superior abilities. He had suffered some wounds in his domestic relations, which made him misanthropic, reckless, and miserable. We should characterize him as a man of very remarkable conversational talent, and when he devoted himself to literary pursuits he was considered a very promising writer. Mr. L. graduated at Washington (Trinity) College, Hartford, Ct. He published a newspaper at Little Rock, Ark., and, afterwards published the Wisconsin Inquirer at Madison."

[2] TREASURY DEPARTMENT,
Oct. 30, 1849.

Sir:—Your letter of the eleventh inst., is received, inquiring whether "the twenty thousand dollars appropriated for the erection of public buildings in Minnesota can be expended previous to the location of the permanent seat of government by a vote of the people?"

It is provided by the thirteenth section of the act to establish the territorial government of Minnesota, approved third of March, 1849, that the Governor and Legislative Assembly shall, at such time as they shall see proper, prescribe by law, the manner of locating the permanent seat of government of said territory by a vote of the people. "And the

On the fourth Monday of November, the elections for the officers of the new counties took place.[1]

In the month of November, the first meeting in relation to the establishment of public schools, was held in the small school-house that stood on St. Anthony street, near the First Presbyterian Church. Previous to this, the English schools, in the white settlements, had chiefly been taught by teachers who had been sent out by the National Society of Popular Education: Misses Bishop and Scofield having taught at St. Paul, Miss A. Hosford[2] at Stillwater, and Miss Backus at St. Anthony.

sum of twenty thousand dollars out of any money in the treasury not otherwise appropriated, is hereby appropriated and granted to said Territory of Minnesota, to be applied by the Governor and Legislative Assembly to the erection of suitable public buildings at the seat of government."

In view of the antecedent, and the object of this appropriation, the Department cannot doubt that the public buildings in question, can only be erected at the permanent seat of government, located as prescribed. Of course the reply to your inquiry must be, that nothing can be expended from this appropriation until after the location shall be duly made.

Very respectfully,

Your obedient servant,

W. M. MEREDITH,

Secretary of the Treasury.

JOSEPH R. BROWN,

St. Paul, M. T.

[1] The vote in Ramsey county was as follows:—

		St. Anthony.	St. Paul.	Total.
Register,	Day,	39	172	211
"	Phillips,	30	69	99
Sheriff,	Lull,	17	172	189
"	Irvine,	33	60	93
"	Brisette,	19	2	21
Treasurer,	Simpson,	69	240	309
Commissioners,	Roberts,	57	202	259
"	Godfrey,	19	123	142
"	Gervais,	31	167	198
"	Banfill,	37	70	107
"	Russell,	54	108	162
Judge of Probate,	Lambert,	34	149	183
"	Lott,	33	93	126

[2] Mrs. H. L. Moss.

ST. ANTHONY LIBRARY ASSOCIATION.

In the month of December, the St. Anthony Library Association, which had been incorporated by the legislature, commenced a series of lectures. The introductory was delivered by the Rev. Mr. Neill, and part of it was published, as a supplement, in the annals of the Historical Society for 1850. Among other lecturers, were the Rev. Mr. Gear, Chaplain of Fort Snelling, and Wm. R. Marshall, Esq. The association was the first institution of the kind, excepting the Historical Society, in Minnesota; and had a small library of valuable standard works.

CHAPTER XXIII.

By the active exertions of the secretary of the territory, C. K. Smith, Esq., the Historical Society of Minnesota[1] was incorporated at the first session of the legis-

---

[1] The Chronicle and Register of January fifth, 1850, has the following editorial:—

"The first public exercises of the Minnesota Historical Society, took place at the Methodist Church, St. Paul, on the first inst., and passed off highly creditably to all concerned. The day was pleasant, and the attendance large. At the appointed hour,—the President and both Vice-Presidents of the society being absent; on motion of Hon. C. K. Smith, Hon. Chief Justice Goodrich was called to the chair. The same gentleman then moved that a committee, consisting of Messrs. Parsons K. Johnson, John A. Wakefield, and B. W. Brunson, be appointed to wait upon the Orator of the day, Rev. Mr. Neill, and inform him that the audience was in waiting to hear his address.

"Mr. Neill was shortly conducted to the pulpit; and after an eloquent and appropriate prayer by the Rev. Mr. Parsons, and music by the band, he proceeded to deliver his discourse upon the early French Missionaries and voyageurs into Minnesota. It was a highly creditable production; and we hope the society will provide for its publication at an early day. In truthfulness to history—candour and liberality of sentiment—and strength, and beauty of composition, it commended itself to all present.

"After some brief remarks by Rev. Mr. Hobart, upon the objects and ends of history, the ceremonies were concluded with a prayer by that gentleman. The audience dispersed highly delighted with all that occurred.

"The occasion owed much of its interest to the presence of the far-famed 'Sixth Infantry Band,' now stationed at Fort Snelling. They 'discoursed most eloquent music' at appropriate intervals throughout the exercises. We have never heard a band anywhere that appeared more

lature. The opening annual address was delivered in the Methodist church at St. Paul, on the first of January, 1850.

At this early period the Minnesota Pioneer issued a Carrier's New Year's Address, which was amusing doggerel. The reference to the future greatness and ignoble origin of the capital of Minnesota is as follows:—

The cities on this river must be three,
Two that *are* built and one that is to be.
One, is the mart of all the tropics yield;
The cane, the orange, and the cotton-field;
And sends her ships abroad and boasts
Her trade extended to a thousand coasts;
The *other*, central for the temperate zone,
Garners the stores that on the plains are grown;
A place where steamboats from all quarters, range,
To meet and speculate, as 'twere on 'change.
The *third will be*, where rivers confluent flow
From the wide spreading north through plains of snow;
The mart of all that boundless forests give
To make mankind more comfortably live,
The land of manufacturing industry,
The workshop of the nation it shall be.
Propelled by this wide stream, you'll see
A thousand factories at St. Anthony:
And the St. Croix a hundred mills shall drive,
And all its smiling villages shall thrive;
But then *my* town—remember that high bench
With cabins scattered over it, of French?
A man named Henry Jackson's living there,
Also a man—why every one knows L. Robair;
Below Fort Snelling, seven miles or so,
And three above the village of Old Crow?
Pig's Eye? Yes; Pig's Eye! That's the spot!
A very funny name; is't not?
Pig's Eye's the spot, to plant my city on,
To be remembered by, when I am gone.
Pig's Eye, converted thou shalt be, like Saul:
Thy name henceforth shall be St. Paul.

On the evening of New Year's day, at Fort Snelling, there was an assemblage which is only seen on the outposts of civilization. In one of the stone edifices belonging to the United States there resided an unassuming gentleman of integrity who had dwelt in Minnesota since the year 1819, and for many years had been in the employ of the government. In youth he had been a member of the Columbia Fur Company, and conforming to the habits of traders, had purchased a Dahkotah wife who was wholly ignorant of the English complete masters of their profession, the celebrated Styermarkich not excepted.

"The Society has made a most auspicious commencement. Let it be carried forward energetically, and its good results will be felt and appreciated by generations that will occupy our place centuries to come."

language. As a family of children gathered around him he recognised the relation of husband and father, and conscientiously discharged his duties as a parent. His daughter at a proper age was sent to a boarding-school of some celebrity, and on the night referred to was married to an intelligent young American farmer. Among the guests present were the officers of the garrison in full uniform, with their wives, the United States Agent for the Dahkotahs, and family, the bois brulés of the neighbourhood, and the Indian relatives of the mother. The mother did not make her appearance, but, as the minister proceeded with the ceremony, the Dahkotah relatives, wrapped in their blankets, gathered in the hall and looked in through the door.

The marriage feast was worthy of the occasion. In consequence of the numbers, the officers and those of European extraction partook first; then the bois brulés of Ojibway and Dahkotah descent; and, finally, the native Americans, who did ample justice to the plentiful supply spread before them.

The union has been blessed, and the bride, now a mother, in the fear of God, is training up her little ones, who bid fair to be useful and industrious citizens.

Until the close of the year 1849 the only roadway in winter to the settlements of Wisconsin and Iowa was the ice of the Mississippi. Late in December, after five weeks' work, a road was marked out from Prairie du Chien to Hudson, Wisconsin, and the hauling of supplies by land was commenced. The mail service[1] during the

---

[1] Proposals for carrying mail in Minnesota, 1850:—
From St. Paul at 6 A. M., once a week, Monday:
By Lake St. Croix, Nelson's Landing, La Cross, Wis., and Lansing;
To Prairie du Chien by 6 P. M. next Sunday, 270 miles;

year 1850 was very meagre. The first murder case was brought before Judge Cooper, at the February term of the court, at Stillwater.

On the afternoon of the twelfth of September, a number of boys were playing on the bluff in St. Paul, near the corner of St. Anthony and Franklin streets, opposite the stone block, now occupied by the carpet rooms of O. King. One of the number, Isaiah McMillan, seeing another, by the name of Heman Snow, approaching with a press-board before his face, said he would shoot him, and taking aim with a gun, he had in his hands, fired. The shot entered the right eye and left cheek of Snow, who was a lad about twelve years of age, and after a few hours he expired. The counsel for the prosecution were Messrs. Bishop and Wilkinson, and for the defendent Messrs. Ames and Moss. From the testimony adduced, it was not clear that there was malice prepense, and the jury brought in a verdict of manslaughter, with a recommendation that the court would inflict the least possible penalty under the law. The boy was sentenced to one year's imprisonment. As there was no prison in which to confine him, he was sent up to Fort Snelling, and subsisted at the expense of the soldiers, and by permission of the colonel, was

And back between 6 A. M. Monday and 6 P. M. next Sunday.
Proposals for more frequent supply will be considered.
From St. Paul at 6 A. M., once a week, Monday;
To Fort Snelling by 8 A. M., 6 miles;
And back between 10 A. M. and 12 M.
Proposals for more frequent supply, stating the number of trips, times of departure and arrival, will be considered.
From St. Paul at 6 A. M., once a week, Monday;
By Stillwater and Marine Mills;
To Falls of St. Croix by 12 M. next day, 49 miles;
And back between 2 P. M. Tuesday and 6 P. M. next day;
With one additional weekly trip from St. Paul to Stillwater.

occasionally allowed to make himself useful by sawing wood.

In the month of April, there was a renewal of hostilities between the Dahkotahs and Ojibways, on lands that had been ceded to the United States. A war prophet at Red Wing, dreamed that he ought to raise a war party. Announcing the fact, a number expressed their willingness to go on such an expedition. Several from the Kaposia village also joined the party, under the leadership of a worthless Indian, who had been confined in the guard-house at Fort Snelling, the year previous, for scalping his wife.

Passing up the valley of the St. Croix, a few miles above Stillwater, the party discovered on the snow the marks of a keg and foot-prints. These told them that a man and woman of the Ojibways had been to some whiskey dealer's, and were returning. Following their trail, they found on Apple river, about twenty miles from Stillwater, a band of Ojibways encamped in one lodge. Waiting till daybreak of Wednesday, April second, the Dahkotahs commenced firing on the unsuspecting inmates, some of whom were drinking from the contents of the whiskey keg. The camp was composed of fifteen, and all were murdered and scalped, with the exception of a lad, who was made a captive.

On Thursday, the victors came to Stillwater, and danced the scalp dance around the captive boy, in the heat of excitement, striking him in the face with the scarcely cold and reeking scalps of his relatives. The child was then taken to Kaposia, and adopted by the chief. Governor Ramsey immediately took measures to send the boy to his friends. At a conference held at the governor's mansion, the boy was delivered up, and on being led out to the kitchen, by a little son of the governor, since deceased, to receive refreshments, he cried bitterly, seemingly more alarmed at being left with the whites than he had been while a captive at Kaposia.

From the first of April the waters of the Mississippi began to rise, and on the thirteenth, the lower floor of the warehouse, now occupied by William Constans, at the foot of Jackson street, St. Paul, was submerged. Taking advantage of the freshet, the steamboat Anthony Wayne, for a purse of two hundred dollars, ventured through the swift current above Fort Snelling, and reached the Falls of St. Anthony. The boat left the fort after dinner, with Governor Ramsey and other guests, also the band of the sixth regiment on board, and reached the falls between three and four o'clock in the afternoon. The whole town, men, women, and children, lined the shore as the boat approached, and welcomed this first arrival, with shouts and waving handkerchiefs.

On the afternoon of May fifteenth, there might have been seen, hurrying through the streets of St. Paul, a number of naked and painted braves of the Kaposia band of Dahkotahs, ornamented with all the attire of war, and panting for the scalp of their enemies. A few hours before, the youthful and warlike head chief of the Ojibways, "Hole in the Day," having secreted his canoe in the retired gorge which leads to the cave in the upper suburbs, with two or three associates had crossed the river, and, almost in sight of the citizens of the town, had attacked a small party of Dahkotahs, and murdered and scalped one man. On the receipt of the news, Governor Ramsey granted a parole to the thirteen Dahkotahs confined in Fort Snelling, for participating in the Apple river massacre. On the morning of the sixteenth of May, the first Protestant church edifice completed in the white settlements, a small frame building, built for the Presbyterian Church, at St. Paul, was destroyed by fire, it being the first conflagration that had occurred since the organization of the territory.

One of the most interesting events of the year 1850, was the Indian council, at Fort Snelling. Governor Ramsey had sent runners to the different bands of the Ojibways and Dahkotahs, to meet him at the fort, for the purpose of endeavouring to adjust their difficulties. We give the account of the proceedings, as reported in the Minnesota Pioneer:—

"Tuesday morning, June eleventh, was one of the sweetest days of the month. By nine o'clock in the morning, a large concourse of persons had assembled at Fort Snelling, from various quarters, and especially from St. Paul, to witness the council. Fort Snelling is at the extreme angle of a high table land, between the Mississippi and the St. Peter's—a beautiful elevated plain, covered with grass as far as the eye can extend. Near the bank of the Mississippi, and distant from the fort a few hundred yards, are the stables of the garrison, and on the open space between the garrison and the stables were the encampments of the Chippewas, and there was the council ground. Captain Monroe was present with a small detachment of infantry, and a few troops were ready for service in the fort, as well as artillery. The Chippewas were lying about their tents, seeming quite contented, laughing, talking, playing together, and some gambling in various ways. There seemed nothing surly or stoical in their countenances. A message was at length sent by the governor to notify the Sioux that they would be expected in half an hour, if at all.

"At length they made their appearance a mile distant, upon a brow of the hill across the St. Peter's. The few infantry present, on the approach of the Sioux, were extended in an open line, nearly from the Fort to the stables, so as to form a separation between the Chippewas in their rear and the advancing band of the Sioux, numbering perhaps three hundred, a large portion on horseback, armed and painted, who by this time were rushing up on the plateau, screaming and whooping horribly, themselves loaded with jingling arms and ornaments, and their horses with bells on, the whole of them rushing on at full speed and making a feint as if they would pass around the stable, turn the right flank of the infantry, and attack the Chippewas; but they were only showing off; having, in fact, all due respect for those ugly cast iron orators of Uncle Sam's. The line of Chippewas remained where it was at the time of the grand entree (for we can compare it to nothing it so much resembled as a grand entree into a stupendous circus), they continuing to dance and shout, and brandish their weapons as if aching for an onslaught. Among them, conspicuous as Achilles in the battle of Troy, stood the young Pillager chief, Sitting-in-a-row, standing six and a half feet in his moccasins, well proportioned, and weighing two hundred and twenty pounds, who takes his name, perhaps, from the fact that he is equal to a man or two beside himself. The Sioux soon fell back and formed a line; they discharged their pieces in a scattering fire along the line. The Chippewa line returned their salute; after which Uncle Sam replied by the mouth of one of his cast iron orators, who were so persuasive in Mexico. The representation of a white flag then appearing between the two opposing lines, the Chippewas first and next the Sioux, marched away and stacked their arms. Then returning, the two lines advanced until they reached the file of infantry which separated them, when the chiefs and braves met at the centre between the lines, and, advancing, went through the ceremony of shaking hands. The governor then took his seat in a marquee, with Captain Todd, Captain Monroe, Mr. McLean, Mr. Prescott, Sioux Interpreter, Mr. Warren, Chippewa Interpreter, W. B. White, Esq., Secretary of the Council, and the Sioux chiefs occupying one side, while the Chippewas occupied the other side of the marquee; besides which some small space was occupied by several ladies who were present, just in front of the Sioux.

"His excellency, the governor, having given notice that the council was now open, then made substantially the following speech, through the interpreters, who both seemed very prompt and accurate in translating. Mr. Prescott speaking the harsh, guttural, clucking language of the Sioux, and Mr. Warren, an educated half-breed Chippewa, rolling off the euphonious sentences in the Chippewa tongue, with the utmost fluency:—

"Chiefs, braves, and head men of the Chippewa nation, and chiefs, braves, and head men of the Sioux nation: You are here, under the flag of our Great Father, the president, to see if you can settle your difficulties and bury the hatchet. I hope this will be done, and that peace will be made, for the sake of your poor bleeding wives and children. Long ago, the white children of your Great Father, lived far off and only heard of the outrages you committed upon each other;

but now they live amongst you, and all around you. They see the reeking scalps of your victims. Things are now changed. The whites are upon the Mississippi, the Missouri, the St. Peter's, every where. They witness what you do. They will not suffer these atrocities; if they did, the Great Spirit would not smile upon them. To many of you, this may seem harsh. If we only wanted your lands, we would give you firearms and let you kill each other. You know at what trouble and expense your Great Father has been to keep ardent spirits away from you, which would, if not thus prevented, soon destroy you, if we wanted only your lands. You well know the power of your Great Father; that he has ten thousand villages, each larger than all the villages together of either of your tribes; and that his people not only live upon the land, but upon the ocean, sailing upon long voyages; that all you see here of the Great Father's villages, are few and small, but that it is not so elsewhere. Your white brethren are proud to be the children of so great a Father, and no doubt, you, his red children, are proud of it. Your Father is not only great, but good. He loves his red children as well as his white, or he would let them go to war. He regards both of your tribes with equal favour. Under his flag he has red, white, and black children, all whose different interests he protects. Numerous as you are, yet when compared to all the tribes under his protection, you are but as a single blade of grass to a whole prairie. [Here some interruption occurred by the Sioux outside, riding about on horseback. They were required to dismount.] I do not say these things by way of boast, but to let you know that your Great Father is able to enforce any treaty you may make. I am aware that complaints are made on both sides, that the treaty has not been enforced; but as I told you, his business extends so far that he has to do it by agents and officers, who sometimes neglect to do their duty; that the Great Father has now sent an agent, who thinks as I do, that it is right that your old troubles should be buried. A treaty between you, made in 1843, is now in full force, but it has been so long neglected, that we do not like to make it a rule of redress. Your Great Father prefers that you settle these troubles yourselves. If you say you are hereditary foes and cannot make a permanent peace, it is not true. The two nations next in power to this, France and Great Britain, were foes for many hundreds of years, but are now friends, peaceful and happy, without wars. You should leave off wars and learn that a bushel of potatoes is worth more to one who is hungry than a pile of eagle plumes. Long ago the white race had your notions about labour, but now they are changed. Your Great Father knows that when you strike, you often kill those who have treated you as friends; that three-fourths of the scalps you take are those of women and children, who could not and would not hurt you. Amongst the whites, he who should kill a woman or a child would be considered less than a dog. Your Great Father is determined that you shall not scalp women and children. You have a treaty in force, but your Great Father prefers that you settle matters and make a new treaty. I should be glad to send him word that you had buried the hatchet. There are many bleeding hearts here, but you must forgive and forget. To assist in shaping a treaty, I recommend that each nation appoint a committee of three or five men to assist—submitting it afterwards to yourselves to decide upon.

"*Hole-in-the-day.*—All men that live have minds of their own, and had better settle their own affairs.

"After some explanation, the committee was agreed to. The following gentlemen were appointed: On the part of the Sioux, W. H. Forbes, O. Faribault, and Captain Monroe, United States Army; on the part of the Chippewas, Mr. Warren, Mr. Beaulieu, and Captain Todd. Bad-Hail, a saucy-looking Sioux orator, then stepped up and asked that another commissioner, Mr. Alexander Faribault, might be appointed on their part. The governor replied, that he would submit their proposition to the magnanimity of the Chippewas. At this time the Sioux arose, with a great deal of talk, and left the council *en masse.* Upon inquiry, it seems that their highnesses had taken offence at the presence of the ladies in council; and word came in that 'they thought they were to meet Chippewas in council, not women.' Hole-in-the-day adroitly turned the matter to his own advantage, saying very politely, *that he was happy to see so many sweet women there, and that they were all welcome with their angelic smiles, to a seat on his side of the council.* The ladies, however, chose to withdraw, the young Chippewa chief shaking each one cordially by the hand. The Sioux having returned, the governor rebuked them sharply for their act of disrespect to the council, saying, that if they withdrew again in that manner, he would enforce the treaty of 1843. Bad-Hail said they wanted time to consider, and that a treaty could not be made in a day. After this little interlude, the council proceeded, the Chippewas consenting to the appointment of the fourth commissioner on each side. Rev. Mr. Gear was appointed on the part of the Chippewas; for the Sioux, A. Faribault. The council then adjourned to meet at ten o'clock on Wednesday morning."

On Wednesday, after much talking, as is customary at Indian councils, the two tribes agreed as they had frequently done before, to be friendly, and Governor Ramsey presenting to each party an ox, the council was dissolved.

On Thursday, the Ojibways visited St. Paul for the first time, Hole-in-the-Day being dressed in a coat of a captain of United States infantry, which had been presented to him at the fort. On Friday, they left in the steamer Governor Ramsey, which had been built at St. Anthony, and just commenced running between that point and Sauk Rapids, for their homes in the wilderness of the Upper Mississippi.

The summer of 1850 was the commencement of the navigation of the Minnesota river by steamboats. With the exception of a steamer that made a pleasure excursion as far as Shokpay, in 1842, no large vessels had ever disturbed the waters of this stream. In June, the "Anthony Wayne," which a month previous had ascended to the Falls of St. Anthony, made a trip. On the eighteenth of July she made a second trip, going almost to Mahkahto. The "Nominee" also navigated the stream for some distance.

On the twenty-second of July the officers of the "Yankee," taking advantage of the high water, determined to navigate the stream as far as the size of the boat would allow. The author was one of the numerous party of exploration, and he here inserts impressions in the form they were written at that time, when the whole country west of the Mississippi was in possession of the barbarians.

As there was some danger in navigating a stream, whose waters had never been disturbed for any distance by the paddles of the "fire canoe," we did not ascend on the first evening more than twenty-five miles above the fort. At early dawn on Tuesday, the steamer was again in motion, and curved around the numerous short bends of this zig-zag stream, with wonderful ease. The scenery, the farther we advanced, became more varied and beautiful. Here there was an extensive prairie, "stretching in graceful undulations far away;" there a wide amphitheatre encircled by cone-shaped hills, and inviting the agriculturist to seek shelter for himself and his cattle; owing to the high tide of water, we passed quite early in the morning some rapids without any difficulty. During the day we met with little to excite us. Now and then, we would pass an Indian in his canoe, who, frightened by the puffing and novel appearance of the boat, had crouched behind the overhanging boughs of the weeping willow. Upon the south bank of the river, eighty-five miles from Fort Snelling, within a few yards of some ledges of fawn-coloured limestone, there enters a little stream of clear and pure water, which Featherstonhaugh, who explored the country some years ago, named "Abert's Run." In the afternoon, we passed a bluff of sand and limestone, similar to those so frequent on the Upper Mississippi, which is called White Rock. About twelve miles beyond this, we came to Traverse des Sioux, where we did not stop, as we were anxious to ascend as far as possible by sunset. The wood we had taken with us began to grow scarce, and a little distance above this point the boat stopped, and the crew and many of the passengers began to chop wood.

While engaged in this occupation, some two or three Dahkotah Indians, painted and plumed, and covered with perspiration, galloped up on their Indian ponies. To pacify them, and pay for the wood which it was necessary to take from their lands, the party presented them with some sacks of corn, and treated them to a glass of fire water, which was entirely unnecessary. At dusk the boat tied up, in front of a beautiful prairie, elevated some seventy feet above the river; and there those whose tastes and principles permitted, danced until the heat and the mosquitoes forced them back to the boat. The view from this prairie was exceedingly interesting. It was bounded by a belt of woodland, and upon the opposite side, were slopes most beautifully rounded. Upon its surface, jutting from the green sward, were boulders of every size and shape, looking in the dark as if the cattle had come down from a thousand hills, and were in repose.

As the writer sat upon the deck, he could but be interested in looking over the party and seeing how well they harmonized, born, as they had been, in various parts of the continent, and educated under diverse influences. Among the party was one who had been an aid of General Harrison, and at a later day our ambassador at the court of Russia; another who had graduated at West Point and the Yale Law School, and who had been wounded while in command of a regiment at Monterey.

Among the half-breeds was one who had been the guide and interpreter of Nicollet, while engaged in scientific explorations in the valley of the Minnesota;

also one by the name of Renville, the son of one of the most intelligent and benevolent half-natives who ever dwelt in the Dahkotah country.

Before sunrise on Wednesday morning, the boat had left her moorings, and was proceeding onward. At breakfast time we had reached the highest point to which a steamboat had ever ascended, a feat that was accomplished the week previous by the "Anthony Wayne."

About nine and-a-half, A. M., we passed the Blue Earth river. The latitude of this point is about forty-four degrees, being nearly one degree lower than the mouth of the Minnesota. Our course until now was south-westerly, but henceforward it is north-westerly. After passing the Blue Earth, the Minnesota is much narrower, and the bends so numerous that the boat did not go in one direction at any one time for more than five minutes. During the morning, the report was raised that some buffaloes were grazing in the distance, and, for a time, there was quite an excitement; but the nearing of the boat, and the use of the spy-glass, dispelled our hopes, and exhibited in their stead huge boulders scattered among the prairie grass. At night, we arrived near the mouth of the Cotton Wood river, about two hundred miles from Fort Snelling. The day had been intensely hot, the thermometer having been at one hundred and four degrees in the shade; and as soon as the sun had set a cloud of mosquitoes enveloped us. The cabins were smoked, and the mosquitoes beat with green boughs, but they could not be forced to retreat. They looked upon us as intruders, and seemed determined to make us smart, and leave their impression.

The ice, too, had failed, and the ladies of the party began to feel that there was more reality than poetry in an exploring expedition into an uncivilized country. A meeting was called to see if the captain should turn back, but the majority decided to go on. That night few of the male members of the party entered their state-rooms, but nearly all wrapped in mosquito-bar were stretched upon the hurricane deck, vainly endeavouring to sleep. When Thursday's sun arose, the boat was not in motion. The crew were worn out by their extra labours, and even those of the passengers who had been anxious to navigate farther, had been brought to terms by the severe wounds that had been inflicted upon them by the mosquito.

It is quite a coincidence that Major Long and his party, twenty-seven years before, suffered the same inconvenience, near the same place, by the same insect. Says his narrative: "We never were tormented at any period of our journey, more than when travelling in the vicinity of the St. Peter's. The mosquitoes rose all of a sudden. We have been frequently so much annoyed by these insects, as to be obliged to relinquish an unfinished supper, or to throw away a cup of tea which we could not enjoy. To protect our feet and legs we were obliged to lie with our boots on."

While at breakfast, to the satisfaction of all parties concerned, the prow of the boat turned once more towards the land of civilization and comfort. At dinner time we turned into the Blue Earth river. This is a rapid stream, with pebbly banks, and the principal tributary of the Minnesota. The scenery around it is picturesque, and it will always be viewed with interest because of a French fort or trading-post having been built here one hundred and fifty years ago. Upon the banks of the Blue Earth, the party gathered some tolerable specimens of agate and carnelian, and a dark substance resembling cannel coal, but probably lignite. It was the discovery of this mineral, no doubt, that led some of the old travellers to mark on their maps a coal mine on the Minnesota, a few miles above Fort Snelling.

Just at dark, the boat reached Traverse des Sioux. This is one of those spots which nature has marked out for a town of some importance. It derives its name from the fact, that for a long period it has been a crossing-place of the Sioux or Dahkotahs. The landing here is easy, the soil is fertile, woodland is convenient, and from a ridge of two hundred feet in elevation, there is a creek affording a great amount of water power, and easily accessible from the river. The spot is now occupied by an Indian village of a portion of the Dahkotahs, a trading-house, and three neat and plain white buildings occupied for mission purposes by the missionaries. There are many acres of land in cultivation, presenting quite an air of comfort and of civilization. As it had been some time since we had any ice, most of the passengers left the boat, and walked to the mission premises, where they found a well of clear and cool water, and to which they did ample justice.

Instead of returning to the boat, the writer passed the evening with the Rev. Mr. Hopkins, the missionary of the American Board in charge of this station. His wife, in the course of conversation, mentioned that the Indians could not conceive of the object that led the white men to navigate a stream which was not theirs; and that the children had been in through the day, to tell her how terribly frightened they had been by the steam-whistle; and to inquire whether it was a human being or the boat that made such an unearthly noise.

Leaving Traverse des Sioux early on Friday morning, we passed during the day some ancient mounds of the same kind as those scattered through Wisconsin and Illinois. Inasmuch as the Smithsonian Institution has volunteered to publish a description of the earth-works near Lake Pepin, and mounds in other parts of Minnesota, it is to be hoped that some gentleman of leisure will sketch and prepare descriptions of them.

In the middle of the afternoon, we stopped at Six Village, the largest village of the Dahkotahs. About three hundred warriors, squaws, and children were on the bank, eager to see the wonder. As the steam-whistle screeched it was amusing to see the boys and girls tumbling over each other in their haste to escape. The chief soon stepped on board and demanded a present, for the privilege of navigating the river. He also contended that a canoe had been broken; but as he did not give the company ocular evidence of the fact, they did not pay him; but presented him with some pieces of calico, provisions, and a box of Spanish green. Since 1847, the American Board has had a missionary residing here, the Rev. S. W. Pond. The population around him, within four or five miles, is about six hundred; and at a little distance is another band of two hundred and fifty. Sixteen miles below this is a fourth mission station. The missionary in charge is the Rev. G. Pond. He has resided with the Indians for many years, and is one of the best speakers of their language.

Though there are four stations on the Minnesota river, and two on the Mississippi below St. Paul, the prospects of the Dahkotah mission are not bright. The male portion of the nation, with but few exceptions, have an inveterate hatred of the Christian religion, and look upon the missionaries as intruders who drink their water and plough their soil, but give nothing in return. The few that would gladly listen to instruction are deterred from the fear of ridicule and persecution.

After a rapid run of nine miles from the village at which the Rev. Gideon Pond resides, we came once more in sight of the stars and stripes floating from the walls of Fort Snelling.

At an early bed hour, on Friday night, the steamboat was moored at the landing of St. Paul.

It had been demonstrated that steamboats of light draught could navigate the Minnesota, by the removal of a few obstructions, at all stages of water, to Traverse des Sioux, and even to the Blue Earth river. In a year or more the Dahkotahs will make a treaty and leave the land of their ancestors, and then, in an incredibly short period, the war whoop, the scalp dance, the skin lodge, and the canoe, of the red man, will give place to the lowing of cattle, the hum of children conning their lessons in the school-house, the neat village church, with its spire pointing heavenward, and a frugal and industrious American husbandry. The foreign missionary will soon give way to the home missionary, and what a field is the Territory of Minnesota for the latter to work in! Like the people of the northern latitudes of Europe, the future population of Minnesota will be hardy and intelligent. They will crave a learned and zealous ministry. The towns now settled are like what Stockbridge, Massachusetts, was a century ago, filled with Indians and white land speculators, and a few church members. We would have labour here in the home field, just such missionaries as Jonathan Edwards and his wife, the beautiful and holy Sarah Pierpont, who was such a valuable helpmeet in spiritual as well as temporal things, Whitfield is said to have offered up a prayer that God would send him just such a daughter of Abraham to be his wife. Minnesota does not desire ministers that will leave the East, because they possess narcotic properties; she does not want men who will love New England or any other section so as to be unfitted to construct society out of the "rude and jostling materials" which will here abound; she does not want heralds of salvation to come here and sow wheat upon a quarter-section, but to sow the seed of God beside all waters; she does not want firm partisans of any school or ism, but men who will advocate a broad and comprehensive Christianity; she does not want young men to come within her borders, because they think that to their friends they will appear more comely and brilliant, upon the principle that "distance lends enchantment to the view;" but she desires, in view of the fact that Indian claims will be soon extinguished, scholars who have bathed themselves in the learning of the inspired writings; gentlemen like Paul who will be highminded, willing to work with their own hands rather than cringe, glorying in being able to visit some rude cabin, to whisper consolation, and thinking themselves happy when they can gain the ear of an Agrippa, Felix, Drusilla, or Bernice. In fine, Minnesota desires for her future population a ministry who, in the true sense, can be "all things to all men."

As the time for the general election in September approached, considerable excitement was manifested. As there were no political issues before the people, parties were formed based on personal preferences. Among those nominated for delegate to Congress, by various meetings, were H. H. Sibley, the former delegate to Congress, David Olmsted, at that time engaged in the Indian trade, and A. M. Mitchell, the United States' marshal. Mr. Olmsted withdrew his name before election day, and the contest was between those interested in Sibley and Mitchell. The friends of each betrayed the greatest zeal, and neither pains nor money were spared to insure success. Mr. Sibley was elected by a small majority.[1] For the first time in the territory, soldiers at the garrisons voted at this election, and there was considerable discussion as to the propriety of such a course.

Miss Fredrika Bremer, the well known Swedish novelist, visited Minnesota in the month of October, and was the guest of Governor Ramsey.[2]

---

[1] The following are the returns of the late election for Delegate, as filed in the office of the Secretary:—

Precincts.	Sibley.	Mitchell.
St. Paul, . . .	151	153
St. Anthony, . .	64	110
Little Canada, .	44	8
Stillwater, . . .	117	59
Marine, . . .	17	4
Falls St. Croix, .	17	0
Snake River, . .	10	0
Prairie, ...	54	24
Sauk Rapids, . .	3	60
Swan River, . .	22	56
Crow Wing, . .	8	48
Elk River, . . .	16	8
Nokaseppi, . .	36	26
Lac qui Parle, .	12	0
Mendota, . . .	78	3
	649	559

[2] St. Paul, as described by the novelist of Sweden, in 1850, and St. Paul in 1858, with its gas lamps and public edifices, are very different places:—

"Scarcely had we touched the shore, when the governor of Minnesota, and his pretty young wife, came on board and invited me to take up my quarters at their house. And there I am now; happy with these kind people, and with them I make excursions into the neighbourhood. The town is one of the youngest infants of the Great West, scarcely eighteen months old; and yet it has in a short time increased to a population of two thousand persons, and in a very few years it will certainly be possessed of twenty-two thousand; for its situation is

During November, the Dahkotah Tawaxitku Kin, or the Dahkotah Friend, a monthly paper, was commenced, one-half in the Dahkotah and one-half in the English language. Its editor was the Rev. Gideon H. Pond, and its place of publication at St. Paul. It was published for nearly two years, and, though it failed to attract the attention of the Indian mind, it conveyed to the English reader much correct information in relation to the habits, the belief, and superstitions, of the Dahkotahs.

On the tenth of December, a new paper, owned and edited by Daniel A. Robertson, late United States' marshal, of Ohio, and called the Minnesota Democrat, made its appearance.

as remarkable for its beauty and healthiness, as it is advantageous for trade.

"As yet, however, the town is but in its infancy, and people manage with such dwellings as they can get. The drawing-room at Governor Ramsey's house is also his office, and Indians and workpeople, and ladies and gentlemen, are all alike admitted. In the mean time, Mr. Ramsey is building a handsome, spacious house upon a hill, *a little out of the city* [now in the middle of the west end of the city], with beautiful trees around it, and commanding a grand view of the river. If I were to live on the Mississippi, I would live here. It is a hilly region, and on all sides extend beautiful and varying landscapes.

"The city is thronged with Indians. The men, for the most part, go about grandly ornamented, with naked hatchets, the shafts of which serve them as pipes. They paint themselves so utterly without any taste, that it is incredible. Here comes an Indian who has painted a great red spot in the middle of his nose; here another who has painted the whole of his forehead in lines of black and yellow; there a third with coal black rings round his eyes. * * * * The women are less painted, with better taste than the men, generally with merely one deep red little spot in the middle of the cheeks; and the parting of the hair on the forehead is dyed purple. There goes an Indian with his proud step, bearing aloft his plumed head. He carries only his pipe, and when he is on a journey, perhaps a long staff in his hand. After him, with bowed head and stooping shoulders, follows his wife, bending under the burden which she bears. Above the burden peeps forth a little round-faced child, with beautiful dark eyes."

During the summer there had been changes in the editorial supervision of the "Chronicle and Register." For a brief period it was edited by L. A. Babcock, Esq., who was succeeded by W. G. Le Duc.

About the time of the issuing of the Democrat, C. J. Henniss, formerly reporter for the United States Gazette, Philadelphia, became the editor.

The first proclamation for a thanksgiving day was issued in 1850 by the governor, and the twenty-sixth of December was the time appointed, and it was generally observed.

CHAPTER XXIV.

On Wednesday, January first, 1851, the second Legislative Assembly[1] assembled in a three-story brick build-

---

[1] The following persons composed the second Legislative Assembly:—

Councillors.	No. of District.	Residence.	Age.	Place of Nativity.
James S. Norris,	1	Cottage Grove,	39	Maine.
Samuel Burkleo,	2	Stillwater,	46	Delaware.
William H. Forbes,	3	St. Paul,	35	Montreal, C.
James McC. Boal,	3	"	39	Pennsylvania.
David B. Loomis,	4	Marine Mills,	33	Connecticut.
John Rollins,	5	Falls of St. Anthony,	42	Maine.
David Olmsted,	6	Long Prairie,	28	Vermont.
William Sturges,	6	Elk River,	32	Up. Canada.
Martin McLeod,	7	Lac qui Parle,	36	Montreal, C.

Representatives.				
James Wells,	1	Lake Pepin,	47	N. Jersey.
John A. Ford,	1	Red Rock,	38	New York.
M. E. Ames,	2	Stillwater,	30	Vermont.
Sylvanus Trask,	2	"	30	New York.
Jesse Taylor,	2	"	45	Kentucky.
Benjamin W. Brunson,	3	St. Paul,	26	Michigan.
J. C. Ramsey,	3	"	29	Pennsylvania.
Edmund Rice,	3	"	30	Vermont.
H. L. Tilden,	3	"	32	Connecticut.
John D. Ludden,	4	Marine Mills,	32	Massachusetts.
John W. North,	5	Falls of St. Anthony,	35	New York.
Edward Patch,	5	"	27	"
S. B. Olmstead,	6	Belle Prairie,	36	"
W. W. Warren,	6	Gull Lake,	26	L. Superior.

ing, since destroyed by fire, that stood on St. Anthony street, between Washington and Franklin. D. B. Loomis was chosen speaker of the Council, and M. E. Ames speaker of the House.[1] This assembly was characterized by more bitterness of feeling than any that has since convened. The previous delegate election had been based on personal preferences, and cliques and factions manifested themselves at an early period of the session.

On the morning of January sixteenth, an editorial appeared in the Pioneer grossly attacking the character of one of the judges of the territory. Every word was barbed, and naturally irritated the brother of the judge, who was then absent at Washington. Meeting the editor near the building used as the capitol, a rencontre took place in which Mr. Goodhue was severely stabbed in the abdomen, and the other party was shot. Among other exciting topics was the election of public printer. The candidates were the editors of the Pioneer, Democrat, and the Chronicle and Register; the Whig members coalescing with the friends of Mr. Sibley, the editor of the Pioneer was elected.

The locating of the penitentiary at Stillwater, and the capitol building at St. Paul gave some dissatisfaction. By the efforts of J. W. North, Esq., a bill creating the University of Minnesota at or near the Falls of St. Anthony was passed and signed by the governor. This institution, by the constitution recently adopted

Representatives.	No. of District.	Residence.	Age.	Place of Nativity.
D. T. Sloan,	6	Little Rock,	36	New York.
David Gilman,	6	Watab	39	"
Alex. Faribault,	7	Mendota,	46	Minnesota.
B. H. Randall,	7	Fort Snelling,	27	Vermont.

by the vote of the people, is now the state university, and is entitled to the two townships of land granted for that purpose.

The apportionment bill, based on the census of 1850, led to a bitter personal discussion, but was passed on Saturday, March twenty-ninth. The opponents of the bill in the House of Representatives, seven in number, on the same day resigned their seats. They contended that the census was incorrect; that Benton county, with four thousand acres under cultivation, by the bill had but one half the representation that Pembina county had, where there were but seventy acres under cultivation, and more than one-half of that belonging to one individual. They also urged the fact that, excepting soldiers, at least seven-eighths of the population were Indians, and that the legislature had no authority over the unceded lands.[1]

---

[1] Correspondence in relation to points in dispute:—

"HOUSE OF REPRESENTATIVES,
"WASHINGTON, Feb. 27, 1851.
"Hon. James Thompson, Chairman of the Judiciary Committee:

"DEAR SIR:—There are questions mooted among the people of Minnesota, as to the extent of the authority conferred by the Organic Act, upon the Legislative Assembly of the territory, and other matters connected with the exercise of that jurisdiction on the Indian country, which comprises all the region west of the Mississippi. The distinguished position you occupy as the head of the Judiciary Committee, and your acknowledged eminence as a lawyer, will invest your opinion with great weight in the settlement of the points referred to. I have the honour, therefore, to request that you will reply to the following queries, to wit:—

"First: Does, or does not the organic act of Minnesota, grant to the Legislative Assembly full jurisdiction over all the country embraced within the limits of the territory, restricted solely by provisions of Indian treaties conflicting with it, should such exist?

"Second: Does, or does not the organic act secure to all the people, living as well on the unceded as the ceded lands, the right of representation in the Assembly, and of voting at all elections, subject only to the restrictions of the laws to

SUFFERING AND SICKNESS OF OJIBWAYS.

The Ojibways of Red, Cass, Leech, and Sandy Lakes suffered much during the winter of 1850–51. About the first of October, 1850, the Indians collected at the new agency at Sandy Lake, to receive their annuities,

regulate the qualifications of voters, and are not elections held on the unceded lands made equally valid and legal by the provisions of the organic law, with those held on the ceded country?

"An early reply to the questions will be gratefully acknowledged by,

"Yours, very respectfully,
"H. H. SIBLEY."

—

"WASHINGTON, Feb. 28, 1851.
"Hon. H. H. Sibley, Delegate from the Territory of Minnesota:

"DEAR SIR:—I have examined, though briefly, the law organizing the Territory of Minnesota, in relation to the questions you propound in your note of yesterday. I was surprised that any question of the kind could arise in the mind of any one. I had been one of the committee that framed the law in question, and I presume that no one of that committee ever doubted that the legislative power of the territory extended to the entire limits of the territory, restricted only to 'rightful subjects of legislation, consistent with the Constitution of the United States, and the provisions of this act,' and subject to the approval of Congress. Nothing of course could be done by the legislature of the territory in regard to the Indian tribes, as this subject belongs exclusively to Congress, but that the territory, in all its parts, was devoted to the same legislative control, is proved by the provision that every free white citizen of the age of twenty-one years, who shall have been a resident of the territory at the time of the passage of the act, shall be entitled to vote at the first election. All could vote; the consequence of which is apparent—that all, in contemplation of law, were to be represented. Subsequent legislatures could regulate the qualifications of voters, but in the territory, and in any part of it, the right of voting would remain, and of course the right of representation.

"This short view of the subject answers the points made in your note. The organic law of the territory regarded the entire territory in precisely the same light—all parts of it entitled to representation—all male citizens of twenty-one years of age, being free, no matter where situated or living, being entitled to vote. The legislation over the whole territory is a complete right in the territorial legislature, subject only to the restrictions implied in the exclusive right of Congress to regulate the intercourse between the Indian tribes. Excuse the imperfections of this note, written in the midst of a boisterous debate.

"With great respect,
"I am truly yours,
"JAMES THOMPSON."

supposing that they would be immediately paid. To their disappointment they were kept waiting for seven or eight weeks, and while there measles and dysentery carried off hundreds. Some of the provisions received at the payment appear in some way to have been damaged, and this increased the mortality. The wife of a missionary, writing from Red Lake, on the first of February, says:—

"Many of the Indians who attended the payment last fall at Sandy Lake, will remember the place for a long time as the burying-place of their friends. The Indians gathered there to receive their annuities about the first of October, expecting payment to take place in a few days; but they were put off from time to time for two long months, and then were obliged to leave, having received but a part of their dues. During their stay there, the dysentery and measles prevailed, and carried off great numbers of them; many others were attacked, and in this state were obliged to start for their respective homes. Provisions were so scarce that they could not procure food for their journey home, and many of them died on the way. It is reported that more than five hundred have died since the sickness commenced.

"To give you an idea of their suffering, I will furnish you with an account of one family, near neighbours of ours.

"This family consisting of a man and his wife, two children, and his wife's brother, started from Sandy Lake in health, with food enough for their journey, if they had not been detained on their way. About half-way from Sandy Lake to Leech Lake, the wife's brother was taken sick, and detained them several days, when he died; they buried him and came on. Three days' march from Leech Lake, the two children were taken sick, the oldest a boy of twelve years old (who, by the way, was the best boy we have known in the country, a member of our school, one we had hoped to educate), the other a girl two years old. At this time their food was all gone. The father was obliged to carry his sick son, and the mother the daughter, until the last night before they reached Leech Lake, when the boy died. The next morning they set off again, the father carrying the corpse of his son, and the mother a sick child. About noon the girl died, but they came on until they reached Leech Lake, bringing the dead bodies of their children on their backs.

"Another man started from Sandy Lake for Cass Lake with his sister, in company with another family. He was taken sick soon after he left Sandy Lake, but travelled on until about half-way to Leech Lake, and died. The next morning the family went on. The sister remained by the body alone, one night and two days, when some Indians came along and buried it.

"There are more Indians about us this winter than there have been any winter before, since I have been in the country. Many have come here from Leech Lake, Cass Lake, and Lake Winnepec, to live by begging, having nothing to eat at home. Probably not less than forty families are wintering here from other bands. Many of them were intending to go to the plains, but so many are sick, and the snow so deep, that they dare not start out. This band last fall, had provision enough to make them comfortable for the year, but having so many beggars to live upon them, they will all be out by sugar-making."

Hole-in-the-day, the Ojibway chief, addressed the

legislature in relation to the wants of his people. The speech at the First Presbyterian Church, attracted a great crowd. He in true Indian style narrated the suffering of his people, and begged in the inimitable manner of his race; and a committee was appointed to solicit subscriptions for their relief. During the winter, hunger is said to have driven some to cannibalism.[1]

---

[1] Extract from Minnesota Democrat, July 29, 1851:—

"Last winter an old man and woman of the Pillager Band of Chippewa Indians, with two married daughters, went from Leech Lake to Lake Itasca, to spend the winter. The husbands of the daughters were not with them—one had four and the other five children, varying in age from one to eighteen years.

"They were reduced to a starving condition, and the mothers commenced killing and eating their children! They fed voraciously upon the flesh of their children, and became passionately fond of it. All of the children were despatched and eaten, but one, a boy about eighteen years of age.

"In the latter part of winter his mother called him to her, and requested him to put his head in her lap, under pretence of desiring to look for vermin, as is the custom among the Indians. The boy complied. The mother had some molten lead at hand, which she poured into his ear, and killed him. His cries of agony alarmed the old people. The old man told his wife to go and see what was the matter. She went and looked into the door of the lodge, and there saw the woman with the body of the boy on the fire, singeing his hair off. She said to her, 'Come in, and get some—it is good;' and narrated to her mother how she had killed the boy.

"The old woman returned, and informed the old man what had taken place. He went to the lodge with his gun, and shot her. He did not kill her immediately, but despatched her with an axe. Before this happened, there were two men with their wives encamped in the same vicinity. One of the men was led to mistrust that they were eating the children, from the fact of their being missed, and also from the signs of plenty indicated by the personal appearance of the women. He told the other what he suspected, and expressed a desire to go to some other place, and asked him to raise camp, and leave with him.

"He agreed to leave, and requested the other to go and encamp at a spot named, saying that he would join him next day. He waited at the place appointed several days, and ultimately moved on without him. The man and wife, who remained, have never been heard from.

"A blanket, recognised as belong-

A spirited debate occurred on February sixth, 1851, in the House of Representatives of the United States, previous to the passage of the bill granting two townships of land for the use and support of a University in Oregon and Minnesota, and authorizing the legislatures of those territories to make necessary laws to protect the school sections.

The bill before the House also granted to Oregon and Minnesota the privilege of leasing their school lands for four years before they were sold.

Mr. Bowlin, of Missouri, chairman of the committee on public lands, moved that all relating to the leasing of the lands should be stricken out. Mr. Sibley, in reply, contended that the provision in the bill was almost an exact transcript of acts that had been passed in relation to Michigan and Wisconsin.

The second section of the bill provided, that when a *bonâ fide* settlement was made on any school sections previous to survey, that the settler should have the right to enter the land.

Mr. Wentworth, of Illinois, was opposed to touching the school lands. He remarked:—

"When a man squats upon the school lands, there is a higher law that takes him off. So far as I am concerned, whenever a territorial bill comes up here containing a provision in relation to school lands similar to that contained in this, I shall feel compelled to oppose it. I would leave the matter to the townships. If

ing to them, was found near the place. It is supposed that they met the same fate as the children.

"The husband of the surviving woman returned to his lodge, at Itasca Lake, in the latter part of winter, and finding out what had been done with his children, killed his wife with his knife and tomahawk. The old people, and the man who killed his wife, returned to Leech Lake, where they now are."

when the townships are organized they choose to let men squat on their school lands, it is their business, not the business of Congress. I remember well, that in order to encourage education in the Territory of Minnesota, we gave them another section, twice as much as other states have received; and now they come here and ask us to give settlers the privilege of squatting on those lands. I should have been willing to have given them twice as much land as they have received for school purposes; but I would not have voted to give them any, if I had thought squatters should settle on the lands before they were surveyed."

Mr. Stevens, of Pennsylvania, moved to strike out the word "Minnesota" from the section. He said:—

"I make this motion, for the purpose of destroying the section. I understand the law to be, that any man who squats upon the public land, in any of the new states or territories, before it is surveyed, is entitled to no pre-emption right. He is a wrongdoer, a trespasser. But if he settles down after the land is surveyed, he gets his pre-emption right. This section proposes to give to this wrongdoer a right to take possession of the lands devoted to sacred charity, if I may call it charity, for school purposes. * * * * I believe there is no law which gives a right of pre-emption to settlers upon unsurveyed lands. I may be wrong in this."

Mr. Fitch—"You are decidedly wrong."

Mr. Stevens—"I am informed by a gentleman behind me, who, I believe, is right, that there is no law which gives a right to unsurveyed land but the 'higher law,' which the gentleman from Minnesota speaks of, the law of the bowie-knife. Now, I think that we ought not to recognise *that* kind of higher law at any rate. If we are to recognise a higher law above, we are not at any rate to recognise a higher law below. I cannot go for that. I hope the whole bill will be killed."

Mr. Sibley, in reply, said:—

"That the 'higher law' to which he had referred was not any law of violence, nor that of the bowie knife, as stated by the gentleman from Pennsylvania, nor a law from below, but the law of public opinion, of public sentiment; a higher law which he believed existed elsewhere in this country as well as in Minnesota."

Mr. Stevens's motion prevailed. Mr. Bowlin of Missouri moved to strike out all in the bill relative to the leasing of the lands, which was agreed to, and the bill passed in a modified form.

During the Legislature the publication of the "Chronicle and Register" ceased.

About the middle of May a war party of Dahkotahs discovered near Swan river an Ojibway with a keg of whiskey. The latter escaped with the loss of his keg. The war party, drinking the contents, became intoxicated, and, firing upon some teamsters they met driving their wagons with goods to the Indian Agency, killed one of them, Andrew Swartz, a resident of St. Paul. The news was conveyed to Fort Ripley, and a party of soldiers, with Hole-in-the-Day as a guide, started in pursuit of the murderers, but did not succeed in capturing them. Through the influence of Little Six, the Dahkotah chief, whose village was at, and named after him, Shokpay, five of the offenders were arrested and placed in the guard-house at Fort Snelling. On Monday, June ninth, they left the fort in a wagon guarded by twenty-five dragoons, destined for Sauk Rapids for trial. As they departed they all sung their death song, and the coarse soldiers amused themselves by making signs that they were going to be hung. On the first evening of the journey the five culprits encamped with the twenty-five dragoons. Handcuffed, they were placed in the tent, and yet at midnight they all escaped, only one being wounded by the guard. What was more remarkable, the wounded man was the first to bring the news to St. Paul. Proceeding to Kaposia, his wound was examined by Dr. Williamson, and then fearing an arrest, he took a canoe and paddled up the Minnesota. The excuse offered by the dragoons was, that all the guard but one fell asleep. Had they lived in ancient Rome they would all have slept the sleep of death for their negligence.

The first paper published in Minnesota, beyond the capital, was the St. Anthony Express, which made its appearance during the last week of May.

The most important event of the year 1851 was the treaty with the Dahkotahs, by which the west side of the Mississippi and the valley of the Minnesota river were opened to the enterprise of the hardy emigrant. The commissioners on the part of the United States were Luke Lea, Commissioner of Indian Affairs, and Governor Ramsey. The place of meeting for the upper bands was Traverse des Sioux. The commission arrived there on the last of June, but were obliged to wait many days for the assembling of the various bands of Dahkotahs.

Steps had been taken for the observance of the fourth of July, by those associated with the commissioners, but that day proved to be one of sadness. Mr. Goodhue, who was on the spot, writes to the "Pioneer," of which he was the editor:—

"Instead of the joyous festivities we had this day anticipated, the sudden death, by drowning, this morning, before breakfast, of the Rev. Mr. Hopkins, resident missionary here, has thrown over our whole encampment a shadow of gloom. A multitude of men and women of both races ran to the spot to search the water for his body. His clothes were found upon the bank of the river, or, rather, the bank of a slough, near the bed of a pretty strong current of water. A little Indian girl says she saw him wading breast deep toward shore, and that looking again, after filling her pail with water, she saw only his hands above water. As he could not swim, he was, doubtless, drowned by wading into a deep hole. Search has been made all day with nets and hooks, and by Indians diving, but, as yet, in vain. Mr. Hopkins was a good man, and left a most amiable wife, and four children." Under date of July seventh, he writes:—
"Suddenly, news arrives in camp that the body of the lamented Mr. Hopkins is caught in a drag-net; and, instantly, the most of our company, and hundreds of Indians, are running from all directions to the spot. The body being washed was removed to the mission-house, amid much silent grief, while a very aged squaw indulged in piteous lamentations, which affected every listener, saying, 'He was my son; he was very kind to me; he provided for me when I was hungry and needy.' This afternoon we are engaged in the mournful duty of burying this good man, who, buried in the seclusion of savage life, spent the flower of his days in a work as disinterested as that which made Howard immortal."

For several days there had been violent rains and thunderstorms, and the Dahkotahs supposed that the Great Thunder Bird had dashed his wing upon the head of the Blue Earth river, and broken up fountains which had caused the rise in the waters. One day there was a propitiatory dance to Wahkeenyan, the God of Thunder.

On the afternoon of July twelfth the dance was commenced. The spot selected was nearly a half mile from the river bank. The commissioners and their party, and perhaps one thousand Dahkotahs, were present. The dance was performed within a circular enclosure made of the limbs of the aspen stuck in the ground, interwoven with four arched gateways, forming an area like a large circus. A pole was planted in the middle of the area, with an image cut out of bark, designed to represent the Thunder Bird, suspended by a string at the top. At each of the arched gateways stood another pole and image of the same description, but smaller than the one in the centre. Near the foot of the central pole was a little arbour of aspen bushes, in which sat an ugly-looking Indian with his face blackened, and a wig of green grass over his head, who acted as sorcerer, and uttered incantations with fervent unction, and beat the drum, and played on the Indian flute, and sung by turns, to regulate the various evolutions of the dance. Before this arbour, at the foot of the central pole, were various mystical emblems; the image of a running buffalo cut out of bark, with his legs stuck in the ground, also a pipe and a red stone shaped something like a head, with some coloured down. At a given signal by the conjurer, the young men sprang in through the gateways, and commenced a circular dance in procession around the conjurer, who continued to sing and beat his drum. After fifteen or twenty minutes, the dancers ran out of the ring, returning after a short respite. The third time a few horsemen, in very gay fantastic costume, accompanied the procession of dancers who were within, by riding outside of the enclosure. The last time a multitude of boys and girls joined the band of dancers in the area, and many more horsemen joined the cavalcade that rode around the area, some dressed in blue embroidered blankets, others in white. Suddenly several rifles were discharged at the poles upon which the Thunder Birds were suspended, knocking them down, and the sacred dance ended.

On the eighteenth of July, all those expected having arrived, the Sissetoans and Wahpaytoan Dahkotahs assembled in grand council with the United States commissioners. After the usual feastings and speeches, a treaty was concluded on Wednesday, July twenty-third. The pipe having been smoked by the commissioners, Lea and Ramsey, it was passed to the chiefs. The

---

[1] The treaty is in substance as follows:—

Perpetual peace.

The cession of all the Sioux lands east of Sioux river and Lac Traverse. The line then runs up the head waters of Otter Tail Lake, thence down from the head of Watab river to the Mississippi.

The cession embraces the entire valley of the Minnesota, and the eastern tributaries of the Sioux river, and is estimated to contain 21,000,000 acres.

The Indians reserve a tract on the Minnesota, about one hundred miles in length, and twenty in breadth. This reserve commences at the mouth of Yellow Medicine river, and extends up the Minnesota ten miles on each side to Lac Traverse.

The Indians are to receive $1,665,000, as follows:

To be paid after their removal to the reservation, $275,000, and

To be expended in breaking land, erecting mills, and establishing manual labour schools, $30,000, amounting to $305,000.

The balance of $1,360,000 to be invested at five per cent. for fifty years, which will give an annual income of $68,000, to be paid as follows:

In cash, annually	$40,000
Goods and provisions,	10,000
Civilization fund,	12,000
Education,	6,000
	68,000

paper containing the treaty[1] was then read in English, and translated into the Dahkotah by the Rev. S. R. Riggs. This finished, the chiefs came up to the secretary's table and touched the pen; the white men present then witnessed the document, and nothing remained but the ratification of the United States Senate to open that vast country for the residence of the hardy emigrant.

During the first week in August, a treaty was also concluded beneath an oak bower, on Pilot Knob, Mendota, with the M'dewakantonwan and Wahpaykootay bands of Dahkotahs. About sixty of the chiefs and principal men touched the pen, and Little Crow, who had been in the mission-school at Lac qui Parle, signed his own name. Before they separated, Colonel Lea and Governor Ramsey gave them a few words of advice on various subjects connected with their future well-being, but particularly on the subject of education and temperance. The treaty was interpreted to them by the Rev. G. H. Pond, a gentleman universally conceded to be the most correct speaker of the Dahkotah tongue of any who are not natives.

The day after the treaty these lower bands received thirty thousand dollars, which, by the treaty of 1837, was set apart for education; but, by the misrepresentations of interested half-breeds, the Indians were made to believe that it ought to be given to them to be employed as they pleased.

The next week, with their sacks filled with money,

After fifty years all payments to cease, and the principal of $1,360,000 to revert to the government.

The intercourse laws, so far as relates to the introduction and sale of ardent spirits, shall be continued in full force, until changed by legal authority.

they thronged the streets of St. Paul, purchasing whatever pleased their fancy. Many desired horses. Now an Indian always purchases a horse on a different principle from a white man. If he desires a white horse, all other considerations are secondary. He may be awkward in gait, or slow in motion; these are all outweighed by the colour that he desires. Another one will want a long-tailed horse, and, if such an animal can be found, but few questions are asked in relation to his age or freedom from trick. The week subsequent to the treaty there was a general clearing out of worn-out nags from the livery stables of the capital; and, when the cavalcade started for the Indian country, in John Gilpin style, it was a scene to excite the laughter of a stoic. Many departed empty-handed, and, if they had not given a kingdom, had given their all for a horse that would die, under Indian treatment and grooming, in a few months.[1]

[1] By the treaty signed at Mendota, August fifth, the above-named bands ceded to the United States all their lands in Minnesota and Iowa.

A reserve is granted them on the Minnesota river, commencing at Little Rock, which is about fifty miles by land from Traverse des Sioux, and extending up the river ten miles wide on each side to Yellow Medicine and Chatanba rivers, to which they are to remove within one year after the ratification of the treaty.

On the ratification of the treaty, the chiefs were paid the sum of two hundred and twenty thousand dollars, to be used by them in the purchase of provisions, to defray the expenses of their removal, and settle their affairs generally.

In opening farms, erecting mills, smith-shops, and school-houses, is to be expended thirty thousand dollars.

In annuities to be continued fifty years:

In agricultural fund . $12,000
In goods and provisions 10,000
In education 6,000
In cash 30,000

By the two treaties concluded between the United States and four divisions of the Dahkotah tribe, about thirty millions of acres of land have been added to the possessions of the United States, and most of it is in Minnesota. Much of it is of an excellent quality, well tim-

A few days before the treaties, one of the Dahkotah missionaries at Shokpay's village, now a flourishing town, the county seat of Scott county, writes:—

"Our situation is in many respects unpleasant. We have no persons residing with us, and no white neighbours within sixteen miles. This is much the largest band of the Dahkotahs, on the Minnesota or Mississippi, and they all dwell within a hundred rods of our door, some of them much nearer. We have great reason to be thankful for the degree of peace and security we enjoy whilst living in the midst of so many savages; but we are continually annoyed in a thousand ways. They are almost universally thieves and beggars; and, though we endeavour to have as little property exposed as possible, we are obliged to be continually on the watch. My wife has been only a mile from home in three years, and, when the Indians are here, I seldom go out of sight of the house, unless I am obliged to do so. Few days pass in which they do not commit some depredation. I do not mention these things by way of complaint. We are annoyed much less than we might reasonably expect in such circumstances; and we should feel contented and cheerful in our situation, if the Indians would only listen to the gospel of our Lord and Saviour Jesus Christ."

On the seventeenth of September, a new paper was commenced in St. Paul, under the auspices of the "Whigs," and John P. Owens became editor, which relation he sustained until the fall of 1857.

The election for members of the legislature and bered and well watered. It is an inviting country to cramped-up New England farmers, who dig among the rocks and hills. Here is room enough, a rich soil, and healthy climate.

county officers occurred on the fourteenth of October; and, for the first time, a regular Democratic ticket was placed before the people. The parties called themselves Democratic and Anti-organization, or Coalition.

In the month of November Jerome Fuller arrived, and took the place of Judge Goodrich as Chief Justice of Minnesota; and, about the same time, Alexander Wilkin was appointed secretary of the territory in place of C. K. Smith.

The eighteenth of December, pursuant to proclamation, was observed as a day of thanksgiving.[1]

---

[1] *A Proclamation, by Alexander Ramsey, Governor of the Territory of Minnesota.*

"The Harvest is past, the Summer is ended;" the corn and the wheat that stood thick upon our fruitful soil, have been "gathered into the garner." Once more, "cold out of the North" has come; "frost is given, and the breadth of the waters is straitened." Before the year closes, it seems a becoming act for the people of Minnesota, by public assembly and solemn observance, to unite in giving thanks to Him "who crowneth the year with goodness," and whose blessings "are more in number than the sand."

In accordance, therefore, with a time-honoured, and now general custom of the states of the Republic, I respectfully recommend to the people of this territory the observance, in the way that to them is most appropriate, of Thursday, the eighteenth day of December, as a day of Praise and Thanksgiving.

Given under my hand, and the great seal of the Territory, [SEAL.] at St. Paul, this third day of December, in the year of our Lord one thousand eight hundred and fifty-one.

ALEX. RAMSEY.

By the Governor:
ALEXANDER WILKIN, *Secretary.*

564   HISTORY OF MINNESOTA.

CHAPTER XXV.

THE third Legislative Assembly commenced its sessions in one of the edifices on Third below Jackson street, which now forms a portion of the Merchants' Hotel, on the seventh of January, 1852.[1]

[1] Councillors.

Name	No. of District.	Residence.	Occupation.
Elam Greeley,	1	Near Stillwater.	
D. B. Loomis,	1	Marine,	Lumber Merchant.
G. W. Farrington,	2	St. Paul,	Merchant.
William H. Forbes,	2	"	Indian Trader.
W. L. Larned,	3	St. Anthony.	
L. A. Babcock,	4	St. Paul,	Lawyer.
S. B. Lowry,	5	Watab,	Indian Trader.
Martin McLeod,	6	Oak Grove,	Indian Trader.
N. W. Kittson,	7	Pembina,	Indian Trader.

Representatives.

Name	No. of District.	Residence.	Occupation.
Mahlon Leavitt,	1	Stillwater,	Lumber Dealer.
Mahlon Black,	1	"	Lumber Dealer.
Jesse Taylor,	1	"	
John D. Ludden,	1	Marine,	Lumber Dealer.
Charles S. Cave,	2	St. Paul,	Saloon Keeper.
W. P. Murray,	2	"	Lawyer.
S. D. Findlay,	2	Near Fort Snelling,	Indian Trader.
J. W. Selby,	2	St. Paul,	Farmer.
J. E. Fullerton,	2	"	Merchant.
S. W. Farnham,	3	St. Anthony,	Lumberman.
J. H. Murphy,	3	"	Physician.
F. S. Richards,	4	Lake Pepin,	Trader.

ST. PETER'S DISCONTINUED IN PUBLIC DOCUMENTS. 565

This session, compared with the previous, formed a contrast as great as that between a boisterous day in March and a calm June morning. The minds of the population were more deeply interested in the ratification of the treaties made with the Dahkotahs, than in political discussions. Among other legislation of interest was the creation of Hennepin county, the passage of an act punishing trespassers on school lands, and the postponement of the election of delegate to Congress until October, 1853. An important liquor law was also passed, subject to a vote of the people, similar in its provisions to what is known as the Maine Liquor Law. The election was ordered to be held on the first Monday of April, and if the majority of citizens were in favour, it was to be in force after the first of May.

Among the memorials to the Congress of the United States, was one relative to the name of the Minnesota river. Ever since the acquisition of this country by the United States, it had been called the St. Pierre by the French voyageurs, and Anglicized by the Americans into St. Peter's. The memorial states that the stream was named after Mons. St. Pierre, who was *never* in this country, which is incorrect. It then asserts " that Minnesota is the true name of this stream, as given to it in ages past, by the strong and powerful tribes of

Representatives.	No. of District.	Residence.	Occupation.
James Beatty,	5	Itasca,	Farmer.
David Day,	5	Long Prairie,	Physician.
James McBoal,	6	Mendota,	Painter.
B. H. Randall,	6	Fort Snelling,	Clerk.
Joseph Rolette,	7	Pembina,	Clerk.
Antoine Gingras,	7	"	Hunter.

aborigines, the Dahkotahs, who dwelt upon its banks, and, that not only to assimilate the name of the river with that of the territory and future state of Minnesota, but to follow what we conceive to be the dictates of a correct taste, and to show a proper regard for the memory of the great nation whose homes and country our people are soon to possess, we desire that it should be so designated." The memorial was considered by the Senate, and a law passed ordering the word St. Peter's to be discontinued in public documents, and Minnesota employed in its place.

The first report of the Superintendent of Public Instruction was presented at this session. As a portion of it may be interesting to the future educators of the state, we insert extracts.

"Owing to the rapid increase of population in districts Nos. 2 and 3, in the county of Ramsey, the present school accommodations have proved wholly inadequate. About the close of the past year, it became necessary for the trustees of each district to rent a room and employ a female assistant teacher to instruct the less advanced pupils.

"Before another year elapses, it may be found that the present school-houses in Stillwater, St. Anthony, and St. Paul, are too contracted; but it is hoped that there will be no unnecessary multiplication of school districts in these towns. The money necessary to build two small school-houses in different parts of a town, can be much more advantageously employed in erecting a single edifice upon some central and commanding site, containing several rooms.

"In this way, a town not only secures a building

that is attractive to the sight, but, by employing a male principal, with a female assistant or assistants, considerably reduces the expenses of education.

"As there are already towns that have more than one district, your attention is called to the propriety of introducing a section in the school law, allowing primary school districts in the same town, the privilege of establishing a grammar school for the older and more advanced children of their several districts.

"And in this connexion it may be well to suggest the repeal of all laws granting to school districts the power of conferring degrees or granting diplomas. To grant such high powers to the trustees of a common school district, who are elected annually, not by those who feel a lively interest in education, but ' by every inhabitant over the age of twenty-one years, who shall have resided in any school district for three months immediately preceding any district meeting, and who shall have paid, or shall be liable to pay, any taxes, except road taxes,' is to degrade education, and burlesque the University of Minnesota, to whose regents such powers more properly belong.

"The buildings that have been erected for school purposes are far in advance of the log huts that were formerly erected by pioneer settlers, as school-rooms for their 'little ones,' and which even the cows of the farmer might blush to own as their resting place.

"In saying this, however, it is not to be understood that they can receive no improvement. Nearly all, like the barns, remain unpainted, and are destitute of all those surrounding conveniences which are so necessary to cultivate neat and modest habits in youth. The trustees have, in almost every instance, neglected to plant shade and ornamental trees, and, unless some care is shown, it will not be long before the school-houses will look as dilapidated as the drunkard's dwelling.

"It is strange that 'fathers who know how to give good gifts to their children,' almost invariably neglect to furnish their offspring with a school-house that is calculated to make the associations with their studies pleasant, or to teach them the principles of correct architecture, or give them a single idea of beauty.

"'Barnard's School Architecture' is a book that a trifling sum will purchase, and, in the erection of school-houses in our new settlements and villages, it is desirable that the trustees should follow some of the plans there detailed. It is, therefore, suggested that the trustees of each school district purchase a copy for the school library. Before we pass from the subject of school architecture, it is proper to call your attention to the importance of trustees securing larger lots for school buildings.

"One of the largest school lots in the territory is that of district No. 5, in Ramsey county, and yet the building appears to be squeezed into the back ground by the pressure of a building on each side.

"To make a full man, the boy must be developed physically as well as intellectually; and the village which would have its youth prosper most in school hours, should take care in this new country, where land is not held at an exorbitant price, that the school-house be situated in the centre of at least an acre lot. Nothing raises a population so much in the estimation of a traveller or emigrant, as to see a crowd of boys issuing from a pleasant school-house, to play during the recess upon a capacious lawn.[1]

"The vocation of teacher is a noble one. He is far from being a drone in society, but is eminently one of the class of producers. His duties are such as often to require 'an angel's wisdom;'

> "For he does the work
> Deputed by the parent, still uncheered
> By that rich filial love, whose magic makes
> All burdens light."

"In many states he is forbidden the social position to which, if competent, he is entitled, and looked upon as a servant, rather than an equal, and therefore receives but a servant's wages.

---

[1] *Table representing the condition of School Districts in the Territory of Minnesota, January, 1852.*

	School-House—by whom owned.	When built.	Cost.	Dimensions.	Size of Lot.
WASHINGTON CO.					
Point Douglas, Cottage Grove,	Priv. property			16 by 18 ft.	
[No school building erected, or school kept.]					
Stillwater,	District	1848		20 by 30 ft.	50 by 150 ft.
Marine Mills,	do.	now building		20 by 30 ft.	75 by 150 ft.
BENTON COUNTY.					
[No returns received.]					
RAMSEY COUNTY.					
District, No. 1.					
St. Paul, " 2.	District	1850	$600	18 by 36 ft.	50 by 150 ft.
do. " 3.	Priv. individual	1848	$400	20 by 24 ft.	
do. " 4.	[No returns.]				
St. Anthony, " 5.	District	1849	$600	24 by 34 ft.	1-4th acre.
do. " 6.	None				
District " 7.					
do. " 8.	[No returns.]				

"Immediately after the organization of our school districts, the ground was taken by the friends of education, that so valuable a member of society as the faithful teacher should receive at least the wages of an ordinary day labourer."

On Saturday, the fourteenth of February, a dog-train arrived at St. Paul from the north, with the distinguished Arctic explorer, Dr. Ray. He had been in search of the long-missing Sir John Franklin, by way of the Mackenzie river, and was now on his way to England.

During the same month, Captain Simpson, of the Corps of Topographical Engineers, United States Army, made the first reconnoissance of the country between Watab and the Winnebago Agency at Long Prairie. One of the party gives a sketch of the exploration in the Minnesota Pioneer:—

"Securing for guides the noted old Ojibway, of Crow Wing, White Fisher, and a half-breed, Johnson, the party and guides started from Sauk Rapids, on Monday, February second. On the next Thursday evening they camped on a little branch of Two Rivers. The next Friday, the fifth day out, came into a high maple region, and one large marsh, which they crossed on the ice; but on examination, discovered where two points of high timber ground approximated each other; and here one hundred and fifty feet of log-way might be necessary. After this, it was all maple high land until they camped.

"The next day, Saturday, they only proceeded three miles, crossing one little stream, and encamped at the Birch Bark Fort Lake, on a singular neck of land between the lake and a succession of marshes extending far to the northward. Here they remained until Tuesday, one of the number returning to Sauk Rapids with the team for further supplies. They found here a camp of ten lodges of Chippewas, who were living fat on plenty of white fish, and a bear they had just killed. The country on this part of the route seemed alive with game—deer tracks and other tracks in every direction. So far from the Winnebago country being destitute of game, it is full of it; but the tribe are too indolent to hunt it. Birch Bark Fort they calculated was from twenty to twenty-four miles from the Rapids; while it was about fifteen miles further to the Agency. It is a noted Indian pass—the remains of two war forts constructed of birch trees being seen in the vicinity. One was erected a great many years ago by the Sioux; and the other more recently by Strong Ground, the brother of old Hole-in-the-Day.

"Starting again on Tuesday, their route that day was over high rolling dry land, all the way, with occasionally a little run to cross; they made but six miles and camped. The next day, Wednesday, the route continued good—only meeting one place, where log-waying, about one hundred feet, will be required. They now came to a magnificent and beautiful sheet of water, some fifteen miles in length, and five or six wide, the northern shore rising almost into mountainous height; the water clear and transparent, and abounding in luscious white-fish; and beautified by several islands with bluff shores, one of them booming mountain-like out of the water more than one hundred feet; and all wooded to the tops with red cedar. The only name the Chippewas have for this fine lake, is 'The Lake where there is Red Cedar;' but there being a dozen lakes of this name, besides the great Red Cedar Lake up the Mississippi, this amounts to no distinctive name at all; and we have, therefore, called it Neill's Lake, in honour of the Rev. Edward D. Neill, of St. Paul, Territorial Superintendent of Common Schools. A large unnamed lake, with islands in it, which is, perhaps, intended to represent Neill's Lake, is set down in Nicollet's map (from reports of Indians merely—he never was there), as discharging its water into the Watab river. This is discovered to be an error. It really empties into Sauk river.

"The party passed to the northward of Neill's Lake. The next day, Thursday, they found small, open, dry prairies, for four miles before reaching the south-east corner of Round Prairie, and thence continuing northward, they arrived without further difficulty at the Agency."

The election on the first Monday in April for the approval or rejection of the Liquor Law interested all classes of citizens. It was a theme of conversation with mothers and daughters, and the subject of discourses in the pulpits of both the Protestant and Roman Catholic clergy, all heartily co-operating. When it was discovered that Ramsey county had voted in favour of the law, all the church bells at the capital about nine o'clock at night, rang a simultaneous peal of joy.[1]

Before the ratification of the treaties with the Dahkotahs, impatient pioneers had gone in and possessed the land. Among the earlier settlements commenced

[1] The Vote on the Liquor Law :—

Counties.	For.	Against.	Counties.	For.	Against.
Ramsey,	528	496	Chisago,	13	3
Washington,	218	68	Benton and Cass,	62	91
Dahkotah,	32	4		853	662

on the Minnesota, were those of Mahkahto, Traverse des Sioux, Kasota, Louisville, and Shokpay. A pioneer, by the name of Mackenzie, had a claim on Eden Prairie, and near by, on a lake in the woods, were other claimants. The first settlement of any magnitude, on the west bank of the Mississippi, was made on Rolling Stone Creek, just above Winona. The colony was from New York city and vicinity. Inexperienced in frontier life, with theoretical rather than practical views, many of them shrunk from the hardships which every pioneer must endure, others sickened and died, and what was begun in so much hope soon dwindled away. The place for the town was not judiciously selected, though the name, "Rolling Stone," in view of the results, was not wholly insignificant.

On the fourteenth of May, an interesting lusus naturæ occurred at Stillwater. On the prairies, beyond the elevated bluffs which encircle the business portion of the town, there is a lake which discharges its waters through a ravine, and supplies McKusick's Mill. Owing to heavy rains the hills became saturated with water, and the lake very full. Before daylight the citizens heard the "voice of many waters," and looking out, saw rushing down through the ravine, trees, gravel, and diluvium. Nothing impeded its course, and as it issued from the ravine it spread over the town site, covering up barns and small tenements, and continuing to the lake shore, it materially improved the landing, by a deposit of many tons of earth. One of the editors of the day, alluding to the fact, quaintly remarked, that "it was a very extraordinary movement of real estate."

During the summer, Elijah Terry, a young man who had left St. Paul the previous March, and gone to

Pembina, to act as teacher to the mixed bloods in that vicinity, was murdered under distressing circumstances. With a bois brulé he had started to the woods on the morning of his death, to hew timber. While there he was fired upon by a small party of Dahkotahs; a ball broke his arm, and he was pierced with arrows. His scalp was wrenched from his head, and was afterwards seen among Sissetoan Dahkotahs, near Big Stone Lake.

About the last of August, the pioneer editor of Minnesota, James M. Goodhue, died. The deceased was born in Hebron, N. H., March thirty-first, 1810. His parents possessed the strong faith and stern virtue of the Puritans, and felt that an education was the greatest treasure they could give their children. After passing through preparatory studies, he entered Amherst College, where he listened to the lectures of the distinguished geologist, Hitchcock, and other devout men of science. In the year 1832, he received a diploma from that institution. It was his desire to have attended a meeting of his surviving classmates in the halls of his "Alma Mater;" but another summons came to take "his chamber in the silent halls of death."

Having studied law, he entered upon the practice of the profession. He became an editor unexpectedly to himself. Having been invited to take the oversight of a press, in the lead region of Wisconsin, during the temporary absence of its conductor, he discovered that he increased the interest of the readers in the paper. From that time he began to pay less attention to the legal profession, and was soon known among the citizens of the mines as the editor of the Grant County Herald, published at Lancaster, Wisconsin. While residing at this place, he became interested in the territory "of sky-tinted waters" (Minnesota). With the independence and temerity of one Benjamin Franklin, he left Lancaster as suddenly as the ostensible editor of the New England Courant left Boston, and he arrived at the landing of what is now the capital of Minnesota, with little more money and few more friends than the young printer who landed at Market street wharf, in the capital of the then youthful territory of Pennsylvania.

In April, 1849, he found St. Paul nothing more than a frontier Indian trading settlement, known by the savages as the place where they could obtain Minne Wakan, or whiskey, and wholly unknown to the civilized world. When he died, with the sword of his pen he had carved a name and reputation for St. Paul, and he lived long enough to hear men think aloud and say, that the day was coming when school-boys would learn from their geography that the third city in commercial importance, on the banks of the mighty Mississippi, was St. Paul. His most bitter opponents were convinced, whatever might be his course towards them, that he loved Minnesota with all his heart, all his mind, and all his might.

When, in the heat of partisan warfare, all the qualities of his mind were combined to defeat certain measures, the columns of his paper were like a terrific storm in midsummer amid the Alps. One sentence would be like the dazzling arrowy lightning, peeling in a moment the mountain oak, and riving from the topmost branch to the deepest root; the next like a crash of awful thunder; and the next like the stunning roar of a torrent of many waters.

The contrarieties of his character often increased his

force. Imagining his foes to be Cossacks, he often dashed among them with all the recklessness of Murat. The fantastic magnificence of his pen, when in those moods, was as appalling in its temerity as the white ostrich feather and glittering gold band of Napoleon's famed marshal.

His prejudice was inveterate against sham and claptrap. He refused to publish many of the miserable advertisements of those quacks, who seek to palm off their nostrums upon young men, diseased through their own vices. When a "stroller" for a living, or a self-dubbed professor, came to town, he sported with him as the Philistines with blind Samson. By sarcasm and ridicule, "Jarley, with his wax works," was made to decamp.[1]

[1] His love for a joke frequently led him to sacrifice truth. In his paper of February twentieth, 1850, with all gravity he has a paragraph, headed Singular Petrifaction, and adds, that "at the mouth of Crow River there are several petrifactions in the shape of men and horses." A man in St. Louis about establishing a museum, saw the paragraph, and wrote a letter to the editor. The letter appeared in the paper of May 16th, with an editorial, entitled "Stone Cavalry Wanted."

"We have received the following letter from a gentleman in St. Louis. In answer to it, we can only say, that it is generally understood here in St. Paul, that the secretary of the territory had all the petrifactions in question (four horses and riders, beside a few fragments), raised at the expense of the treasury, and put in a small new stable, erected for the purpose, in the rear of the Central House, St. Paul, at an expense of four hundred and thirty-one dollars to the government, which has been duly audited and allowed in his accounts. Secretary C. K. Smith, who is also secretary of the Minnesota Historical Society, is now absent. On his return, a few weeks hence, a letter addressed to him on the subject, will no doubt receive prompt attention. Crow Wing river is one hundred and twenty-eight miles above Saint Paul. To prompt further search for similar petrifactions at the mouth of the Crow Wing, we will now make an offer of fifty dollars for each sound petrified horse, mare, or gelding, the same for each perfect petrified man or woman, and half that price for ponies and children, delivered in

When untrammelled by self-interest or party ties, his sentiments proved that he was a man that was often ready to exclaim:—

"Video meliora proboque;
Deteriora sequor."

At the November Term of the United States District Court, for Ramsey county, a Dahkotah, named Yu-ha-

boxes on the bank of the river, ready to be shipped down to St. Anthony, on the steamboat Governor Ramsey, in good condition.

"ST. LOUIS, April 27, 1850.
"Sir:—You will, I hope, excuse the liberty I take of addressing this letter to you, being an entire stranger to you. My object in writing it is to inquire of you some particulars with respect to a notice I observed in the St. Louis *Union* of the twenty-ninth inst., copied from your paper, of a number of petrifactions, in the shape of men and horses, which are said to be at the bottom of Crow river, near its mouth. If not too much trouble, will you be good enough to let me know, at your earliest convenience, more about the matter, and if there is any possibility of getting at them?

"I am about establishing a museum in this city, and am desirous of collecting all the natural curiosities I can get for the same. If there are any specimens of fossils, minerals, or in fact anything in the way of curiosities in your neighbourhood, that could be sent to this city, I would pay liberally for them.

"Trusting that I may, at some future time, have it in my power to reciprocate the favour,
I remain, dear sir,
Yours most respectfully."

The Philadelphia North American, receiving the hoax, writes:—

"*The Crow River Petrifactions.*—The petrified men and horses, recently discovered at the bottom of Crow river, Minnesota, near its mouth, have been housed in a building near St. Paul, erected for the purpose, and are under the care of the territorial officers. There are four horses with their riders."

Goodhue, feeling that he had carried his joke far enough, publishes the above paragraph in his paper of June twentieth, and adds:—

"Yes; but as oats in St. Paul are scarce at one dollar per bushel, the secretary enlisted them in the new company of dragoons, and they were shipped down on the Dr. Franklin, No. 2, last week, under command of Captain Garland, U. S. A., to hunt the Sacs and Foxes out of Iowa."

And thus ended the Horse Marine Story.

zèe, was tried for the murder of a German woman. With others she was travelling above Shokpay, when a party of Indians, of which the prisoner was one, met them; and, gathering about the wagon, were much excited. The prisoner punched the woman first with his gun, and, being threatened by one of the party, loaded and fired, killing the woman and wounding one of the men.

On the day of his trial he was escorted from Fort Snelling by a company of mounted dragoons in full dress. It was an impressive scene to witness the poor Indian half hid in his blanket, in a buggy with the civil officer, surrounded with all the pomp and circumstance of war. The jury found him guilty. On being asked if he had anything to say why sentence of death should not be passed, he replied, through the interpreter, that the band to which he belonged would remit their annuities if he could be released. To this Judge Hayner replied, that he had no authority to release him; and, ordering him to rise, after some appropriate and impressive remarks, he pronounced the only sentence of death ever pronounced by a judicial officer in Minnesota. The prisoner trembled while the judge spoke, and was a piteous spectacle. By the statute of Minnesota, one convicted of murder cannot be executed until twelve months have elapsed, and he was confined until the governor of the territory should by warrant order his execution.

Judge Hayner, having been appointed chief justice in the place of Fuller, whose nomination was not confirmed by the United States Senate, on an appeal of Alexis Cloutier, who had been fined twenty-five dollars for violating the liquor law, decided that the legislative power was vested by the organic act, in the Governor and Legislative Assembly alone, and that they had no power to delegate their authority to the people; that the act in question was an attempt at such transfer of power, and was consequently null and void.

CHAPTER XXVI.

THE fourth Legislative Assembly convened on the fifth of January, 1853, in the two story brick edifice at the corner of Third and Minnesota streets. The Council chose Martin McLeod as presiding officer, and the House Dr. David Day, Speaker. Governor Ramsey's message was an interesting document, and thus eloquently concluded:—

"In concluding this my last annual message, permit me to observe that it is now a little over three years and six months since it was my happiness to first land upon the soil of Minnesota. Not far from where we now are a dozen framed houses, not all completed, and some eight or ten small log buildings, with bark roofs, constituted the capital of the new territory, over whose destiny I had been commissioned to preside. One county, a remnant from Wisconsin territorial organization, alone afforded the ordinary facilities for the execution of the laws; and in and around its seat of justice resided the bulk of our scattered population. Within this single county were embraced all the lands white men were privileged to till; while between them and the broad rich hunting grounds of untutored savages, rolled the River of Rivers, here as majestic in its northern youth, as in its more southern maturity. Emphatically new and wild appeared everything to the incomers from older communities; and a not least novel feature of the scene was the motley humanity partially filling these streets—the blankets and painted faces of Indians, and the red sashes and moccasins of French *voyageurs* and half-breeds, greatly predominating over the less picturesque costume of the Anglo-American race. But even while strangers yet looked, the elements of a mighty change were working, and civilization with its hundred arms was commencing its resistless and beneficent empire. To my lot fell the honourable duty of taking the initial step in this work by proclaiming, on the first of June, 1849, the organization of the territorial government and consequent extension of the protecting arm of law over these distant regions. Since that day, how impetuously have events crowded time! The fabled magic of the eastern tale that renewed a palace in a single night, only can parallel the reality of growth and progress.

"In forty-one months the few bark-roofed huts have been transformed into a city of thousands, in which commerce rears its spacious warehouses, religion its spired temples, a broad capitol its swelling dome, and luxury and comfort, numerous ornamented and substantial abodes: and where nearly every avocation of life presents its appropriate follower and representative. In forty-one months have condensed a whole century of achievements, calculated by the old world's calendar of progress—a government proclaimed in the wilderness, a judiciary organized, a legislature constituted, a comprehensive code of laws digested and adopted, our population quintupled, cities and towns springing up on every hand, and steam with its revolving wings, in its season, daily fretting the bosom of the Mississippi, in bearing fresh crowds of men and merchandise within our borders.

"Nor is that the least among the important achievements of this brief period, which has enabled us, by extinguishing the Indian title to forty million acres of land, to overleap the Father of Waters, and plant civilization on his western shore. Broad and beautiful, by universal concession, are these newly acquired lands— the very garden spot of the north-west, as explorers have pronounced them—and it is scarcely surprising, though less than six months have elapsed since the ratification of the treaties by the Senate, that the keen-eyed enterprise of our race has within them already planned towns, built mills, opened roads, commenced farms, the nucleus of many a happy home.

"But it is, however, in their initiatory stages only, we can consider the present growth and advancement of our territory in all the constituents of national and individual prosperity. Our brief, though energetic past, foreshadows but faintly the more glorious and brilliant destiny in store for us in the future; nor is prophetic inspiration necessary to foretell it. It is written so plainly that he who runs may read it. It is written in the advantages nature has so liberally bestowed upon us; by a beautiful country, unqualified by the drawback of much waste land, with an universally fertile soil, where prairies, 'that blossom as the rose,' with groves and woods are proportionately intermingled; while dotting it over, in refreshing profusion, are gem-like lakes, and intersecting its map, at convenient distances, are crystal streams whose precipitous waters afford elements out of which to create future Lowells and Manchesters.

"It is written in our geographical position, in the centre of our continent, at the head of the Mississippi valley, and enfolding either bank of the great river with its very head springs, even as its delta is embraced on both sides by our sister Louisiana. It is written in our proximity to Superior's inland sea, and the abundant mines of rich ores possessed alike by its northern, as by its southern shores—mines, whose workmen it will be our inevitable lot to feed and clothe.

"And it is written likewise, on a thousand features of interest and advantage incident to our territory; in our extensive pineries, the livelihood of hardy lumbermen, and a future chief resource for building purposes of the people of the great valley below us; in the many opportunities for manufacturing establishments offered by our magnificent water powers, and the ease with which the Mississippi enables us to procure the material, and export the products of factory labour; in our salubrious climate, insuring a healthy, hardy, and numerous population, and in the immediate advantage to our early growth and prosperity, which follows the expenditure of a quarter of a million of dollars annually by the national government, for the benefit of the Indian tribes in our midst.

"That which is written is written—the life of a short generation will realize it. In ten years a state—in ten years more half a million of people, are not extravagant predictions. In our visions of that coming time, rise up in magnificent proportions, one or more capitals of the North, Stockholms, and St. Petersburgs, with many a town besides, only secondary to these in their trade, wealth, and enterprise. Steam on the water and steam on the land, everywhere, fills the ear and the sight. Steamboats crowd our waters, and railroads intersecting in every direction, interlink remotest points within and without our territory. The blue waters of Lake Superior and the red-tinged floods of the Mississippi are united by iron bands, and a south-eastern line connects St. Paul direct with Lake Michigan.

"The great New Orleans and Minnesota Railroad pours into its depôt, somewhere on the Upper Minnesota river, passengers and products from the far sunny South, to receive in return, for ultimate ocean transit perhaps, furs and merchandise from the polar circle, which steamboats on the Red River of the North, or a railroad on its banks, have just brought from Selkirk, or the plains of distant Athabasca. Let none deem these visions improbable, or their foreshadowing impracticable. Man, in the present age, disdains the ancient limits to his career; and in this country, especially, all precedents of human progress, growth of states, and march of empires, are set aside by an impetuous originality of action, which is at once both fact and precedent. Doubtless an overruling Providence, for inscrutable purposes, has decreed to the American nation this quicker transition from the wilderness of nature to the maturity of social enjoyments—this shorter probation between the bud and green tree of empire; and it well becomes us therefore, in our gratulations upon present prosperity, and in our speculations upon greater power and happiness in the early future, to render humble, yet fervent thanks 'unto Him who holdeth nations in the hollow of his hand,' and shapes out the destinies of every people."

Two subjects came before the legislature affecting

domestic happiness. The large majority of citizens petition that a liquor law might be enacted that would be free from the objections existing against the law of the previous session. A bill was proposed by the friends of temperance, but it failed to pass.

During this session, an estimable citizen, the late Bishop Cretin, in accordance with an understanding with the other bishops of the Roman Catholic branch of the Church in this country, caused petitions to be presented, asking a division of the common school fund.

Mr. Murray, from the select committee to which was referred sundry petitions for a change in the school law, made the following report:—

"A majority of the committee to whom was referred sundry petitions from the citizens of St. Anthony, St. Paul, and Little Canada, praying a modification of the present school law, beg leave to report:

"That while they have been unable to give the matters set forth in the petitions, that attention and investigation which their importance as affecting the rights and interests of so large and respectable a number of the citizens of this territory, would demand, it is evident to them that the petitioners have just grounds of complaint, and that the present school law is defective in this: that while a revenue is derived from every taxpayer of this territory, to support and maintain common schools, more than one-third of the entire population of this territory have never derived any benefit from the large amounts paid for that purpose.

"Your committee believing that duty demands a conciliation of law with individual liberty and freedom of conscience; and where any law does not, by reason of its imperfections, meet the wants and situation, and the thousand circumstances which diversify human character and pursuits, or where it fails to benefit communities or denominations, by reason of a conscientious belief in opposition thereto, in common with their fellow-citizens, their case, of right, ought to be provided for by such legislation as is consistent with the welfare of every other citizen, and of the whole.

"Your committee, therefore, ask leave to introduce the accompanying bill, and recommend its passage."[1]

The moderate of all denominations, and the friends of the American system of public instruction, were surprised at the introduction of a bill with such features as

---

[1] The following is the bill as originally introduced by the Committee:—

"*No.* 18, (*H. of R.*)—*Introduced by Mr. Murray, from Select Committee to which was referred sundry petitions on the subject, February sixteenth,* 1853. *Read first and second times, and laid on the table to be printed, February sixteenth,* 1853: —A BILL AMENDATORY OF THE SCHOOL LAW:

"*Be it enacted by the Legislative Assembly of the Territory of Minnesota:*—Sec. 1. That all communities of any denomination, willing to have a school of their own, in which religious instruction will be taught as well as other branches of education, be authorized to do so, and their schools shall be entitled to all the benefits accruing to district schools.

"Sec. 2. All schools well organized, and composed of at least twenty-five children, shall receive a part of the school money, according to the number of children regularly attending the said school.

"Sec. 3. It shall be the duty of the trustees of any school district to issue warrants upon the treasurer for the proportionate share of money coming to any school as aforesaid, on application of the teacher or trustees of said school. Provided, that said teacher or trustees shall prove by the affidavit of at least one person, the number of scholars in regular attendance, which number shall be at least twenty-five.

"Sec. 4. Such schools as only are composed of at least twenty-five children, and are kept in operation at least four hours every day, during five days of every week, shall be considered well organized schools, and entitled to a share of the school fund.

"Sec. 5. All acts and parts of acts, contravening the provisions of this act, are hereby repealed.

"Sec. 6. This act to be in force from and after its passage."

that introduced by Mr. Murray, and it led to considerable discussion.[1]

The region west of the Mississippi was divided, by the legislature, into the following counties: Dahkotah, Goodhue, Waupashaw, Fillmore, Scott, Le Sueur, Rice, Blue Earth, Sibley, Nicollet, and Pierce.

The Baldwin School, the male department of which is now under a separate charter, and known as "The College of St. Paul," was also incorporated at this session of the legislature, and was opened the following June.

On the ninth of April, a party of Ojibways killed a Dahkotah, at the village of Shokpay. A war party, from Kaposia, then proceeded up the valley of the St. Croix, and killed an Ojibway. On the morning of the twenty-seventh, a band of Ojibway warriors, naked, decked, and fiercely gesticulating, might have been seen in the busiest street of the capital, in search of their enemies. Just at that time a small party of women, and one man, who had lost a leg in the battle of Stillwater, arrived in a canoe from Kaposia, at the Jackson street landing. Perceiving the Ojibways, they retreated to the building now known as the "Pioneer" office, and the Ojibways discharging a volley

---

[1] "No. 18, (H. of R.) 'A bill amendatory of the School Law,'

"Was taken up.

"The question then recurring on ordering the bill to a third reading,

"And the ayes and noes being called for and ordered, there were ayes 5, noes 12.

"Those who voted in the affirmative were,

"Messrs. Lott, Murray, Noot, Oliver, and Rolette—5.

"Those who voted in the negative were,

"Messrs. Ames, Dutton, Ludden, McKee, Randall, Russell, Ramsey, Stimson, Truax, Wells, Wilcox and Speaker—12.

"So the House refused to order the bill to be read a third time."

through the windows, wounded a Dahkotah woman who soon died. For a short time, the infant capital presented a sight similar to that witnessed in ancient days in Hadley and Deerfield, the then frontier towns of Massachusetts. Messengers were despatched to Fort Snelling for the dragoons, and a party of citizens mounted on horseback, were quickly in pursuit of those who with so much boldness had sought the streets of St. Paul, as a place to avenge their wrongs. The dragoons soon followed, with Indian guides scenting the track of the Ojibways, like bloodhounds. The next day they discovered the transgressors, near the Falls of St. Croix. The Ojibways manifesting what was supposed to be an insolent spirit, the order was given by the lieutenant in command, to fire, and he whose scalp was afterwards daguerreotyped, and appeared in Graham's Magazine, wallowed in gore.

During the summer the passenger, as he stood on the hurricane deck of any of the steamboats, might have seen, on a scaffold on the bluffs, in the rear of Kaposia, a square box covered with a coarsely fringed red cloth. Above it was suspended a piece of the Ojibway's scalp, whose death had caused the affray in the streets of St. Paul. Within was the body of the woman who had been shot in the "Pioneer" building while seeking refuge. A scalp suspended over the corpse is supposed to be a consolation to the soul, and a great protection in the journey to the spirit land.

On the accession of Pierce to the Presidency of the United States, the officers appointed under the Taylor and Fillmore administrations were removed, and the following gentlemen substituted: Governor, W. A.

Gorman, of Indiana;[1] Secretary, J. T. Rosser, of Virginia; Chief Justice, W. H. Welch, of Minnesota; Associates, Moses Sherburne, of Maine, and A. G. Chatfield, of Wisconsin. One of the first official acts of the second governor, was the making of a treaty with the Winnebago Indians at Watab, Benton county, for an exchange of country.

At the close of the summer the Dahkotahs began to leave their ancient villages, and move to the reserve on the Upper Minnesota. Their locations on the Mississippi and Minnesota, previous to this period, was as follows:—

The Kiyuksah band, called by that name, signifying "relationship overlooked," because they disregard the Dahkotah custom, and marry their relatives, lived below Lake Pepin. Their chief Wapashaw lived in the vicinity of Winona, and they hunted on the Chippeway river and branches.

At the head of Lake Pepin, where the town of Red Wing now stands, was the Raymneecha band. They were so designated because their village was near a hill (Ha), water (min), and wood (chan). The chief was Wah-koo-tay, the uncle of the celebrated half-breed Jack Frazer.

Four miles below St. Paul dwelt the Kaposia band. The signification of Kaposia is "light," and applied because of the agility with which they travelled. Their chief was called by the whites Little Crow, after his ancestor. His real name is Tahohyahtaydootah, "His

---

[1] Governor Gorman was born in Fleming Co., Ky., but for many years was a resident of Indiana. During the Mexican war, at the battle of Buena Vista, he commanded the Rifle Battalion, and in 1849 he was elected as a member of Congress from the sixth Indiana district.

Scarlet People." The first village on the Minnesota was on the south side, and known as Black Dog's, about four miles above Mendota.

At Oak Grove and vicinity lived Good Road's band, and the band driven by the Ojibways from Lake Calhoun.

The Tintatonwan band occupied the site of Shokpay, and their principal chief was Shokpaydan, or Little Six.[1]

During the year 1853 an exciting topic of conversation was an alleged fraud, said to have been perpetrated by Governor Ramsey, H. H. Sibley, H. L. Dousman, Franklin Steele, and others, in the payment of the Dahkotahs at Traverse des Sioux, in the autumn of 1852. Charges were made against Governor Ramsey by an Indian trader named Madison Sweetser, who had come into the country after the treaty, and was not satisfied with the mode of payment. At the request of Mr. Sibley, then a delegate to Congress, Senator Gwin moved that the Senate of the United States investigate the alleged fraud. Commissioners were appointed to proceed to Minnesota, and examine all the facts in the case. A large number of witnesses testified, and on the twenty-fourth of February, 1854, the Committee of

---

[1] Presbyterian missionaries and assistants among the Dahkotahs, in 1850-53 :—

LAC QUI PARLE.—Stephen R. Riggs, Moses N. Adams, *Missionaries;* Jonas Pettijohn, *Assistant;* Mrs. Mary Ann C. Riggs, Mrs. Mary A. M. Adams, Mrs. Fanny H. Pettijohn, Miss Sarah Rankin.

TRAVERSE DES SIOUX.—Rev. Robert Hopkins and Mrs. Agnes Hopkins, Alexander G. Huggins, *Assistant;* Mrs. Lydia P. Huggins.

SHOKPAY.—Samuel W. Pond, *Missionary;* Mrs. Cordelia F. Pond.

OAK GROVE.—Gideon H. Pond, *Missionary;* Mrs. Sarah P. Pond.

KAPOSIA.—Thomas S. Williamson, M. D., *Missionary and Physician;* Mrs. Margaret P. Williamson, Miss Jane S. Williamson.

RED WING.—John F. Aiton, *Missionary;* Joseph W. Hancock, *Licentiate;* Mrs. Nancy H. Aiton, Mrs Hancock.

Indian Affairs of the Senate, to whom the testimony taken by the commissioners appointed by the President of the United States was referred, reported "that they have carefully examined all the testimony taken by the commissioners during nearly three months in session at St. Paul, and have arrived at the conclusion that the conduct of Governor Ramsey was not only free from blame but highly commendable and meritorious. Not one of the charges preferred against him has been sustained by the testimony. On the contrary, the witnesses of the complainants themselves, in almost every instance, have negatived them, proving conclusively that he neither violated the stipulations of the treaties as understood by the parties to them, nor was governed in his conduct by motives other than such as entitle him to commendation, both as a man and an officer."

On the twenty-ninth of June, D. A. Robertson, who by his enthusiasm and earnest advocacy of its principles had done much to organize the Democratic party of Minnesota, retired from the editorial chair and was succeeded by David Olmsted.

At the election held in October, Henry M. Rice and Alexander Wilkin were candidates for delegate to Congress. The former was elected by a decisive majority.[1]

[1] The official vote was:—

	Rice.	Wilkin.		Rice.	Wilkin.
Ramsey,	880	292	Fillmore,	161	12
Benton and Cass,	233	38	Nicollet,	81	00
Hennepin,	160	30	Chisago,	41	8
Sibley,	13	2	Washington,	288	147
Wabasha,	10	24	Itasca,	18	00
Dahkotah,	114	46	Pembina,	60	68
Scott,	51	9			
Blue Earth,	16	12	Total,	2149	696
Le Sueur,	23	8			

CHAPTER XXVII.

WITH the advent of a new governor, a different arrangement of parties in a territory naturally follows.

During the early periods of a territorial government, citizens are so much occupied with local and personal interest, as not to feel the interest in national politics which is witnessed in the Atlantic States.

From the previous chapters it appears that the exciting question of the year 1851 was the apportionment bill of the legislature of that year, allowing citizens on the unceded lands a representation.

The year 1852 was characterized by the discussion on the liquor question, and the passage of a law prohibiting the sale of intoxicating beverages, except for medicinal, mechanical, and sacramental purposes. The year 1853 was one of bitter personal controversy, and parties were known as Fur Company and Anti-Fur Company.

The year 1854 witnessed entirely new coalitions. Those who had previously stood shoulder to shoulder were found withstanding each other to the face. On the one side are ranged Ramsey, Rice, and Robertson; on the other side, Sibley and Gorman.

The fifth session of the legislature was commenced in

the building just completed as the Capitol, on January fourth, 1854. The President of the Council was S. B. Olmstead.[1]

Governor Gorman delivered his first annual message on the tenth, and with his predecessor urged the importance of railway communications, and dwelt upon the necessity of fostering the interests of education, and of the lumbermen.

The exciting bill of the session was the act incorpo-

---

[1] COUNCIL.

	Age.	Birth-place.
S. B. Olmstead,	41	Otsego Co., N. Y.
J. R. Brown,	48	York Co., Penn.
I. Van Etten,	27	Orange Co., N. Y.
N. W. Kittson,	40	Sorel, Canada.
A. Stimson,	37	York Co., Me.
W. P. Murray,	28	Butler Co., Ohio.
W. Freeborn,	37	Richland Co., Ohio.
J. E. Mower,	36	Somerset Co., Me.

HOUSE.

	Age.	Birth-place.
R. Watson,	28	Scotland.
Cephas Gardner,	53	N. H.
W. A. Davis,	31	St. Louis, Mo.
Levi Sloan,	31	Schoharie Co., N. Y.
W. H. Nobles,	36	Genesee Co., N. Y.
Wm. McKusick,	28	Maine.
D. G. Morrison,	27	Fond du Lac, M. T.
C. P. Stearnes,	46	Berkshire Co., Mass.
N. C. D. Taylor,	42	Belknap Co., N. H.
Peter Roy,	26	Rainy Lake, M. T.
John Fisher,	29	Canada West.
H. Fletcher,	35	Maine.
R. M. Richardson,	36	Pickaway Co., Ohio.
J. H. Day,	33	Virginia.
O. M. Lord,	27	Wyoming Co., N. Y.
Louis Bartlette,	33	Montreal, C. E.
H. S. Plumer,	25	Sheffield Co., N. H.
Wm. Noot,	43	Prussia.
Joseph Rolette,	32	Prairie du Chien.

rating the Minnesota and North-western Railroad Company, introduced by Joseph R. Brown. It was passed after the hour of midnight on the last day of the session. Contrary to the expectation of his friends, the governor signed the bill.

On Friday, the third of March, the Presbyterian mission-house at Lac qui Parle was burned. Two of the children of the Rev. Mr. Riggs went into the cellar to procure some vegetables for their mother; bearing a lighted candle, they unintentionally communicated fire to the hay, and soon the house was in flames. Nearly everything was destroyed. The missionary, in a letter, says: " A few books were thrown out of the window, Gesenius' Hebrew Lexicon and a few others, but neither my Hebrew Bible, Septuagint, Vulgate, French Bible, nor Greek Testament, nor a single copy of the English Scriptures, were saved. A short time since I had, at the request of Dr. Williamson, obtained of Mr. M. Renville his father's large French Bible, for the library of the Minnesota Historical Society. It was printed at Geneva, Switzerland, in 1588, if I remember correctly, and was not only the oldest, *but probably the first Bible in Minnesota*. For its historical value we all very much regret its loss. * * * * * When Paul and those who sailed with him were shipwrecked on the island of Melita, he says, 'The barbarous people showed us no little kindness.' How often have I thought of this within a few days! While some of the Dahkotahs came, both during and after the fire, to steal, the majority exerted themselves to save for us what could be saved."

During the same month Joseph R. Brown, who had been editor of the Pioneer, was succeeded by Earle S. Goodrich, the present conductor of the paper.

Tuesday, the eighth of June, is a day that will long be remembered by the early settlers of Minnesota. Mr. Farnham, the builder of the Rock Island Railroad, to mark the era of its completion, with princely liberality, extended an invitation to hundreds of "the wise men of the East," to accompany him, via the Chicago and Rock Island Road, on a pleasure excursion to the Upper Mississippi. At the wharf at Rock Island, the company found five large steamers ready to receive them. Among the guests were some of the prominent statesmen, divines, scholars, editors, and merchants of the land.[1] Passing through Lake Pepin, on a beautiful night, the steamers quietly approached each other, and being fastened together, the signal was given for a general exchange of visits from boat to boat. The scene of grandeur and excitement, as these boats moved through the lake, side by side, with their precious freight, will probably never be repeated. Arriving near St. Paul a day sooner than was anticipated, the firing of a cannon on board of the steamer in advance, created considerable surprise and confusion, as the preparations for the proper reception of one thousand guests were not completed. All felt that they could not return without beholding the Falls of St. Anthony, and yet appropriate vehicles were very scarce. Though a man could have given a kingdom, he could not have obtained a horse for himself. The ride to St. Anthony was however accomplished,

---

[1] Ex-President Fillmore.
George Bancroft.
Professor Silliman.
Edward Robinson, LL. D.
Professor Gibbs, Yale College.
Professor Larned, Yale College.
Professor Parker, Harvard.

Professor H. B. Smith, New York.
Rev. Dr. Vermilye.
Rev. Dr. Spring.
Rev. Dr. Bacon.
Charles Sedgwick.
Miss Catharine Sedgwick, and many others.

after a fashion. A Galena editor thus described the scene:—

"The 'March to Finchley' was nothing compared to our motley cavalcade. Here was a governor astride a sorry Rozinante of which even the great Don would have been ashamed; here an United States Senator, acting the part of footman, stood bold upright in the baggage boot of a coach, holding on by the iron rail surrounding the top; here the historian of whom the country is justly proud, squatted on the top of a crazy van, unmindful of everything but himself, his book, hat, and spectacles; there a hot-house flower, nursed in some eastern conservatory, so delicate and fragile that a falling leaf might crush it, but a beautiful specimen of the feminine gender withal, would be seated over the hind axle of a lumber wagon, supported on each side by opera glass exquisites, who only wondered 'why the devil the people in this country didn't send to New York for better carriages?' and whose groans between every jolt, furnished amusement for the more hardy of the party; here some corpulent madame, whose idea of a ride is bounded by luxuriant cushions, shining hammer cloths, spirited horses, and obsequious flunkies, was seated in a hard bottom chair, in an open one-horse wagon, first cousin to her husband's vegetable drag, or perhaps his pedlar's cart, before riches came to bless them (about which she has forgotten of course), here she was, surrounded perhaps by the *canaille* whom she has learned in latter days to despise, dragged along at a snail's pace by one old mare, with a crazy, foolish, wickering colt alongside, to torment her and to make the driver curse; there a politician who has ridden successfully more than one easy hobby, would have been glad to ride a rail. The scene was animated and amusing!"

In the afternoon the steamers proceeded to Fort Snelling, and the gates being thrown open, the fort was completely stormed. As the fair company retired from the green sward, within the walls, the fort never seemed so lonely to the young lieutenants, and that night memory brought the light of other days around them. Returning to St. Paul before dark, the citizens and the guests repaired to the Capitol. The more grave listened to speeches in the Senate Chamber, from Ex-President Fillmore, and Bancroft the historian, while the more gay tripped it, in the Supreme Court Room. At midnight the guests embarked on their respective steamers, whose bows were soon turned towards the homes of the visiters.

On the following Sunday, a clergyman, who had not been able to give his usual attention to study, preached a discourse suggested by the occasion, which was published in one of the St. Paul papers, and was severely criticised by the Daily Times of New York city, as inappropriate to the pulpit. From the fact, that it led to some profitable discussion on what a sermon should be, we give an abstract. The texts were:—

"Isaiah xl. 3. The voice of him that crieth in the wilderness, Prepare ye the way of the Lord, make straight in the desert a highway for our God. Every valley shall be exalted, and every mountain and hill shall be made low; and the crooked shall be made straight, and the rough places plain.

"Judges v. 6. In the days of Shamgar the son of Anath, in the days of Jael, the highways were unoccupied and the travellers walked through byways."

The introduction was in these words:—

"The Prophet Isaiah, in uttering this language, foretold in figurative expressions, the pioneer work of John the Baptist, yet it primarily was applied to the return of the Hebrews from their captivity in Babylon.

"Not only in the days of Shamgar, but during all of the earlier periods of the history of the world, there was but little international intercourse. The means of transportation were exceedingly limited, and there were few roads that were common thoroughfares for nations.

"Here and there, over the mountains and through the valleys, there were the trails of the hunter and restless adventurer, and pathways of sheep and their shepherds, but seldom was there a highway of any costliness extending beyond the national boundaries. It was the policy of the day to intrench or wall themselves around, and cut off the intercommunication of the people. When, therefore, great bodies of men were necessitated to move toward some distant land, a preparatory work was needed. Pioneers preceding the army or caravan, made highways for their passage, smoothing down the rough hills and filling up the marshy valleys.

"Diodorus, an ancient historian, in giving an account of Semiramis, Queen of Babylon, says: 'In her march to Ecbatane, she came to the Zarcean mountain, which, extending many furlongs, and being full of craggy precipices and deep hollows, could not be passed without taking a great compass. Being therefore desirous of leaving an everlasting memorial of herself, as well as shortening the way, she ordered the precipices to be digged down and the hollows to be filled up, and at a great expense she made a shorter and more expeditious road, which to this day is called from her the road of Semiramis.'

"Babylon was separated from Judea by a wide and dreary country, and no doubt pioneers were literally sent on before to 'make straight in the desert a highway.'

"Since the advent of the year eighteen hundred and fifty-four, the community in which we dwell have been greatly interested in the propositions for making a straight iron highway from the head of Lake Superior to this point on the Mississippi, and from hence to the waters of the Pacific, connecting with bracelets of iron the Naiads of the St. Lawrence, Mississippi, and Columbia.

"Every mail is watched with eagerness, in the hope that it may bring the intelligence that the National Congress has taken measures for exalting the valleys and lowering the hills and mountains that lie between our Mediterranean and Pacific.

"The week that has passed has been signalized by the arrival of hundreds of our fellow-countrymen on an excursion in boats as far excelling in splendour the renowned barges of the luxurious Cleopatra, as those surpassed the osier vessels of the Briton, or the birchen canoe of the Ojibway,—who have been gratified and astonished by a continuous journey in a steam vehicle from the shores of the Atlantic to the head of navigation of the mighty Mississippi, in the brief space of a few days.

"'To every thing there is a season, and a time to every purpose under heaven,' saith Ecclesiastes.

"Fatigued with the multiplied duties of last week, unfitted for severe thought, and believing that the theme can be appropriately discussed, without infringing upon the sacredness of the day, or deviating from the dignity of the pulpit, we enter upon the consideration of railways and other modes of international communication, in the higher and religious aspects."

The preacher proceeded to show that they decrease idleness; expand the mind of the nation; were aids to contentment; rode over sectional prejudices; promoted a common healthful public sentiment; and lastly, were agencies in the promotion of pure and undefiled religion. Under this head the clergyman remarked:—

"First: They draw the emigrant population to certain localities. Before the mountains were depressed, and the valleys exalted, and the rough places made plain, the roads were so unbroken that the farmer moving into a new land, was not attracted by the beaten path, but he branched off in the direction inclination prompted. Settlements consequently were much scattered, and it was difficult for him who longed to proclaim the unsearchable riches of Jesus Christ to discover the abiding places of the lost sheep of Israel. It was almost impossible in the first period of the settlement of a new country to pass from house to house, on account of the impassable state of the road. But the condition of affairs has changed.

"The emigrant population of the Atlantic and European states are drawn as if by magnetic influence along the great iron railway leading from the eastern cities of commerce to the remotest west. In this way, made acquainted with the sections of land in the vicinity, and knowing the advantages of a railway in finding a market for produce, they settle along the line of the great inland road, and the labourer in Christ's cause, finds the fields white for the harvest, and numbers in the same neighbourhood to whom the gospel should be preached. By these highways he is enabled to advance along with, or before the wave of emigration, and commence turning the wilderness into the garden of the Lord, before the rank weeds of error have taken deep root.

"Had the means of conveyance to this town not been expeditious, the ministers of Jesus Christ, would not have been here at the laying of the foundation stones of our territorial existence, and years would have probably elapsed before so many temples erected to the worship of the true and living God would have been visible, or the community reached its present position in the scale of civilization.

"Secondly: They aid religion by proving *antidotes to bigotry*. When the wagon drawn by oxen was the mode of conveyance to a new country, but few penetrated the wilds of the west, except those who had been driven away from the homestead of their fathers by poverty or other misfortune.

"Far away from all refining influences, they rapidly degenerated; their children, debarred the knowledge of the common school, grew up without education, and were semi-barbarous. The only religious teachers they possessed were those who came to them because they knew they were ignorant and ripe for error, or because their own ignorance had rendered them unfit for the exercise of the ministry where there was intelligence. Under the guidance of these, they grew up with strong prejudices towards those who attempted to present the truth in a different light, or a more polished dress, or wore a blacker coat. The religion they possessed was tinctured with the quintessence of bigotry.

"Through the influence of railways and steam carriages, this state of things has been almost dissipated.

"The very year a town starts into existence, the inhabitants are visited by religious teachers of various schools of belief. The student who has been disciplined in the college, and who has studied the Bible systematically, as well as he who has hurried from the work-bench into the pulpit, stand side by side.

"He who defends the general teachings of Calvin, and he who eulogizes Wesley, appear before the same audience, perhaps upon the same Sabbath. It will not do for either to show an improper spirit, or an unwise sectarian zeal. Men who listen to the herald of salvation in such circumstances are not won to Christ by a minister of the gospel depreciating his fellow-ministers. They are impenitent under discourses in which there is an attempt to prove that none are safe out of the line of a certain succession, or off of certain platforms of faith. They demand that those truths shall be preached which will convince them that religion is adapted to expand the mind, and promote man's highest well-being. They become acquainted with the writings of Fenelon and Pascal, Leighton and Taylor, Edwards and Chalmers, Wesley and Fletcher, and love them not because of denominational peculiarities, but because of their likeness to Jesus. The contractedness that in days gone by was manifested in places that were settled almost exclusively by Scotch Presbyterians, English Puritans, and Wesleyan Methodists, in this progressive age will now disappear, and religion will assume a higher and more effective, because a more scriptural type.

"Thirdly: Religion is promoted by the construction of expeditious routes of travel, because there is a great saving of time. The days that were once lost by a minister in passing from preaching station to preaching station, are saved upon a line of railway, or a river navigated by regular steamers. He can accomplish in a few hours what once occupied as many days, and thus he has more time for study, prayer, and meditation.

"Under the improved system of travelling, a man like the eloquent Dr. Duff, can cross the ocean, and one Sunday hold the attention of thousands on the Atlantic coast, and on the next be discoursing to an audience equally interested far away in the valley of the Mississippi, and ere long a divine can pass his third Sabbath with the future dwellers on the mountain tops of Oregon, and the fourth Sabbath, address a congregation on the Pacific coast.

"Finally, our great thoroughfares are destined to facilitate intercourse with the Pagan world of Asia, and hasten the approach of Millennial glory.

'Coming events cast their shadows before.'

"For more than two centuries an impression has prevailed that the welfare of the whole globe would be promoted by a channel of travel through North America, connecting the western settlements of Europe with the eastern nations of Asia. The island of Montreal was named by Robert de La Salle, 'China,' to commemorate his cherished plan of civilizing and evangelizing the great empire of that name, by establishing a channel of communication through this continent. Hennepin, the first European that ever ascended the Mississippi, and the discoverer of the Falls of St. Anthony, was a Franciscan priest, despatched by the adventurous La Salle to explore a route to Japan, which he thought could be found in this direction.

"The first British subject that entered Minnesota, about a century ago, predicted that there would be 'a short cut made from New York to Green Bay,' and had no doubt, to use his own words, 'that mighty kingdoms would emerge from these wildernesses, and stately palaces and solemn temples with gilded spires rending the skies, supplant the Indian huts, whose only decorations are the barbarous trophies of their vanquished enemies.' Returning to London, he formed a plan, with the aid of a member of Parliament, 'that would disclose new sources of trade, promote many useful discoveries, and open a passage for conveying intelligence to China and the English settlements in the East Indies, with greater expedition than a tedious voyage by the Cape of Good Hope or the Straits of Magellan.'

"Had not the American Revolution taken place, it was designed to have built a fort at Lake Pepin, to have proceeded up the river St. Pierre (now known by its original name, Minnesota), then up a branch of the Missouri, till they discovered, as they supposed they could, the river Oregon, down which they expected to sail into the Pacific.

"One year ago, we witnessed a civil and military expedition start forth from our vicinity, by order of the United States, in search of the long-desired thoroughfare to the Pacific. The commander of that expedition[1] has returned to Washington, by the way of San Francisco, and reports that such a route is entirely practicable.

"On Thursday of the last week, men distinguished in the professional, scientific, and commercial circles of the country, visited us, and felt that the day was not

[1] Governor Stevens.

far distant when the waters of Superior and Pacific would be bound together. Let this only occur, and who can doubt that the Redeemer's kingdom will be extended, that—

> "From Java to the furthest West
> The heavenly light shall reach,
> And truth divine its power attest
> In every clime and speech."

"A Pacific Railroad would be a voice in the wilderness, saying, 'Prepare ye the way of the Lord, make his paths straight. Every valley shall be filled, and every mountain and hill shall be brought low; and the crooked shall be made straight, and the rough ways shall be made smooth; and all flesh shall see the salvation of God.'

"In view of the good results, it becomes Christians to watch with interest the enterprises of the day. Every great invention is an aid to the cause of religion. The telescope, the printing press, the telegraph, the ocean steamers, a Pacific Railway, are ordained by God, not for the pulling down but the upbuilding of religion—they are all working together to produce the grand consummation of giving the kingdoms of this world to Christ—of bringing about the day when all will cry:—

> "Worthy the Lamb, for he was slain for us;
> The dwellers in the vales and on the rocks
> Shout to each other, and the mountain tops
> From distant mountains catch the flying joy;
> Till, nation after nation taught the strain,
> Earth rolls the rapturous hosanna round."

"With a few remarks we close the discourse.

"In such a fast age every Christian must be up and

doing. It is high time to awake out of sleep. We must gird ourselves up for the race, and pray earnestly that we may not as a Church of Christ be found lagging when all things else are advancing with accelerated speed. This one thing we ought to do—'Forgetting those things which are behind, and reaching forth unto those things that are before, we should press toward the mark for the prize of the high calling of God in Christ Jesus.'

"It would be doing violence to my own feelings, and a neglect of ministerial duty, if I should conclude this discourse without reminding this audience that this world is a great station-house, in which we are awaiting the approach of the cars that lead to 'that bourne from whence no traveller returns,' but through which every traveller passes to regions of bliss or despair.

"My hearers! some of you have tickets that will lead you to hell. The car of death is hastening on, swifter than an eagle hasteneth to its prey, or any 'lightning train.' Before it arrives we urge you to change that ticket. Christ is always in his office. He says, 'If any man knocketh, the door shall be opened.' If any man asketh, he will change his ticket, and that 'without money and without price.'

"Hasten before it is too late. Now! now! now! 'is the accepted time, and now is the day of salvation.'"

On the twenty-ninth of the month of this excursion, Congress passed an act to aid the Territory of Minnesota in the construction of a railroad therein, which was approved by the President, and directions were issued from the General Land Office to the offices in Minnesota, withdrawing from sale a city, certain townships on the line of the proposed road. The citizens of Minnesota received the intelligence with joyful enthusiasm, but the Greek proverb,

Πολλα μεταξυ, πελει κυλικος και χειλεος αχδου,

there's many a slip between the cup and the lip, was soon fulfilled.

On the twenty-fourth of July, in the House of Representatives of the United States, Mr. Washburne, of Illinois, rose to a question of privilege. He said the House, on the twenty-ninth of June, passed the bill granting lands to Minnesota, to aid in the construction of railroads, and a material alteration had been made since its engrossment. The bill was introduced here by the Committee on Public Lands. It was drawn up by a gentleman from Minnesota, who was well acquainted with the subject, and who had frequent consultations with him (Mr. Washburne) concerning its provisions. Minnesota had chartered a company with most extraordinary powers, granting to it all the lands which have been or may hereafter be donated to that territory for the construction of railroads. The House, to avoid this, added a proviso that said lands shall be subject to the disposition of any future legislature for the purpose aforesaid. Nor shall they inure to the benefit of any company hereafter to be constituted or organized. This was the way the bill was originally framed, to prevent the company from receiving the benefit of the grant. The first alteration he noticed was the striking out of the word "future," but this he believed was made by the committee. The second alteration, which he charged with being made after the bill was engrossed, was the changing of the word "or" to the word "and," so as to read "constituted and organized company." This company, not being constituted and organized, expects to hold these lands under the bill, and hence he charged this object in the alteration. The word was in a hand different from that of the engrossment. This was a matter affecting deeply the proceedings of the House, and it was due that an examination should be made, as the records of this House have been mutilated.

Mr. Washburne said he understood the bill was altered after it was sent from the House to the Senate. He offered a resolution for the appointment of a select committee to inquire into the fact which he brought before the House, with power to send for persons and papers, and to examine witnesses under oath.

Mr. Stevens, of Michigan, rose to make a personal explanation with reference to the subject on which the special committee had a short time since been ordered to be appointed. He intended to make his statement on honour. After the Minnesota Land Bill had been sent to the Committee on Public Lands, of which he is a member, it was referred to him for his individual action on it. Gentlemen who were connected with the bill called on him, and requested that certain alterations should be made in the third section before he returned the bill to the committee. The alterations desired were explained. One of them was to affect the subject of legislation in Minnesota in relation to lands granted by Congress, and he, with his own hands, struck from the original bill the word "future." The other was the alteration of the word "or" to "and," and he thought proper it should be made, and he supposed he had made it. He presented the bill with some explanation to the Committee on Public Lands, which approved of it. He then reported it to the House. It passed, and was sent to the Senate. After getting there, his attention was called to the bill. It was remarked that the alteration which he said he had made, he did not make, or that the bill did not contain the alteration. He conferred with one or two gentlemen of the Senate, and told them frankly that when he reported the bill to the Committee on Public Lands, he made the alterations, or intended to do so. Subsequently one of the Senate clerks came to him in the lobby fronting the centre door. He met General Patton, who held out the bill, and pointing out the third section, asked him whether it was right. To which he (Mr. Stevens) replied it was not right as it passed from the Committee on Public Lands, and according to his recollection, he further said, "You will find, if you look at the original draft, the word 'and' instead of 'or' is there." He went to the desk of the House engrossing clerk (Mr. Sperle), where the matter was talked over. He there stated he had supposed he had made the alteration in the original draft, and thought he voted for the bill thus amended. The question came up as to whether the alteration could be made, and several Senators said it was a mere verbal alteration, and they had frequently made such.

Mr. Forney said he did not know whether the bill could be altered. But Mr. Patton said, "We frequently make such alterations." Whereupon Colonel Forney remarked, "Then perhaps it would be better the alteration should be made." He (Mr. Stevens) left, and he supposed the alteration was made in consequence of what had taken place. He wished to withhold nothing, but to state the facts. However much he may have erred, he wished to state them frankly. If he had sinned, it was an error of judgment, nothing more. He was perfectly certain that Colonel Forney, in giving his sanction to the alteration, supposed he was right and justified in so doing. He wished here to say, this was the first and last interview he had with Colonel Forney on the subject. So help him God, he did not then know of any design in having the bill changed from its original form; he said the only interest he had in the bill was to connect the waters of the Mississippi with the lake and steamboat navigation, and thereby benefit other states, and the substitution of the word "and" for "or" could not affect the original purpose.

On the morning of August the third the bill was repealed, and the news was quickly transmitted by the energetic delegate of Minnesota, Hon. H. M. Rice.[1]

The Minnesota and North-western Railroad Company contended that they had complied with the provisions of the act of Congress, and that that body had no right to repeal. A complaint was brought before

---

[1] WASHINGTON, Aug. 3, 1854, 1 o'clock, P. M.

Dear Sir:—This morning the select committee reported that the word "and" between the words "constituted" and "organized" had been substituted for the word "or," but exonerated Gen. Stevens and the clerk of the House—and recommended that the word "or" be reinstated. Mr. Letcher's (of Virginia) repeal bill was introduced and carried by a large majority—so the House has repealed the Minnesota land grant. The testimony taken by the committee will be printed—a copy of which I will send you as soon as possible—then the people of Minnesota can judge for themselves. A motion is now before the House to discharge the clerk of the House, Col. Forney.

The vote to repeal was 109 to 56.

The vote for expelling Col. Forney was ayes 18, nays 154.

The Senate must now act in regard to the repeal of the grant—its non-concurrence will save the grant—but it is impossible for me to now give a conjecture of its probable action. To-morrow will tell the tale: the result will be forwarded by telegraph. Many able lawyers are of the opinion that Congress has not the power to repeal the act. That, however, is a question to be settled hereafter.

In haste, respectfully yours,
H. M. RICE.
D. Olmsted, Esq.

Judge Welch, at a session of the United States District Court, in Goodhue county, against the company. The complaint alleged that the company had cut and carried off five hundred trees, the property of the United States, in Goodhue county. On the fourth of November, Chief Justice Welch gave judgment in favour of the railroad company. The case was carried up to the Supreme Court of Minnesota, on December sixth, which confirmed the decision of Chief Justice Welch. Chancellor Walworth, and other jurists of New York, furnished written opinions that Congress had no right to repeal the act. The case was then taken to the Supreme Court of the United States.[1]

On the afternoon of December twenty-seventh, the first public execution in Minnesota, in accordance with the forms of law, took place. Yuhazee, the Dahkotah who had been convicted in November, 1852, for the murder of a German woman, above Shokpay, was the individual. The scaffold was erected on the open space, between the Franklin House and the rear of Mr. J. W. Selby's enclosure. About two o'clock, the prisoner, dressed in a white shroud, left the old log prison, near the court house, and entered a carriage with the officers of the law. Being assisted up the steps that led to the scaffold, he made a few remarks in his own language, and was then executed. A disgraceful rabble surrounded the scaffold, and none of the decencies of law were manifested on the occasion. Says an editor, "liquor was openly passed through the crowd, and the last moments of the poor Indian were disturbed by baccha-

---

[1] At the December Term, 1855, Supreme Court of the United States, the attorney-general moved to dis- continue the case, which motion was granted.

nalian yells and cries. Remarks too heartless and depraved, in regard to the deceased, to come from men, were freely bandied. A half-drunken father could be seen holding in his arms a child eager to see well; giddy and senseless girls chatted with their attendants, and old women were seen vying with drunken ruffians for a place near the gallows." Numerous ladies sent in a petition to the governor, asking the pardon of the Indian, to which that officer made an appropriate reply.[1]

---

[1] EXECUTIVE DEPARTMENT, M. T.,
ST. PAUL, Dec. 28, 1854.

Ladies:—I have the honour to acknowledge the receipt of your petition, asking me, as the executive of the territory, to pardon the Indian now under sentence of death, or to commute his punishment to imprisonment for life in the penitentiary.

I cannot conceal the sympathy I feel, in common with each of you, on this melancholy subject; and I find it even more difficult to reject the prayer of those whose hearts are always first in missions of mercy; those who are always first to imitate the divine character and forgive. Those whose gentle hands smooth the brow of the sick and afflicted. Those who are first to console even in the last hours of trial. And this petition is a high compliment to these many virtues, and even a still higher one to the benevolence of your hearts. "To forget is a virtue; but to forgive is divine." But, ladies, I deeply regret, that, in accordance with what I deem to be my duty to the country, and the general peace of society, I cannot consistently grant the prayer of your petition.

The murder for which this unfortunate child of nature is condemned, was without a shadow of excuse. It was seemingly deliberate, and his victim was of your sex, innocent and defenceless. She was murdered by the side of a poor, but no doubt fond and devoted husband, while in the public highway, wending their course to a new home.

If such criminals should be allowed to escape the stern demands of the law, others of his savage tribe might be tempted to hope for a like release, and commit a like offence; and the danger of such results would be far greater from Indians than from civilized man.

Every effort that can be has been made to save him by the law. An impartial jury of the country gave him a fair trial, and found him guilty. And there is no just reason known to stay the execution of the penalty of the law.

With sentiments of the highest personal regard,

I am, most respectfully,
Your ob't serv't,
W. A. GORMAN.

To Mrs. Julia E. Fillmore, Mrs. Anna E. Ramsey, Mrs. E. R. Holliushead, and others.

CHAPTER XXVIII.

THE discussion concerning the charter of the Minnesota and North-western Railroad Company did not terminate with the year 1854.

The sixth session of the legislature convened on the third of January, 1855. S. B. Olmstead was elected President of the Council, and C. Gardner Speaker of the House.

About the last of January, the two houses adjourned one day to attend the exercises occasioned by the opening of the first bridge of any kind over the mighty Mississippi ever completed, from Lake Itasca to the Gulf of Mexico. It is made of wire, and at the time of its opening, the patent for the land on which the west piers were built had not been issued from the Land Office, a striking evidence of the rapidity with which Minnesota is being developed.

The governor, in his message to the legislature, took strong ground against the railroad charter, and in the United States House of Representatives a resolution was passed declaring the charter of the Minnesota and North-western Company null. On the twenty-seventh of February, the United States Senate refused to approve of the resolution that had passed the House, annulling the charter of the company. The news that the charter was not annulled caused great rejoicing among the friends of the railroad, and on Saturday night, March twenty-fourth, there was a general illumination of the principal stores and residences of the capital.

Governor Gorman having vetoed a bill passed by the Minnesota legislature, amending the act incorporating the Minnesota and North-western Railroad Company, it was again passed in the legislature on February twenty-first, by a two-thirds vote, and became a law.

On the twenty-ninth of March, a convention was held at St. Anthony, which led to the formation of the Republican party of Minnesota. This body took measures for the holding of a territorial convention at St. Paul, which convened on the twenty-fifth of July, and William R. Marshall was nominated as delegate to Congress. Shortly after the friends of Mr. Sibley nominated David Olmsted and Henry M. Rice, the former delegate was also a candidate. The contest was animated, and resulted in the election of Mr. Rice.[1]

[1] Vote for Delegate:—

Counties.	Rice.	Marshall.	Olmsted.	Counties.	Rice.	Marshall.	Olmsted.
Blue Earth,	54	52	12	Nicollet,	85	34	39
Brown,*	30			Olmsted,*			100
Benton,	195	52	121	Pierce,			
Carver,	37	28	33	Pembina,	46		
Cass,	57			Rice,	50	226	48
Chisago,	104	61	11	Renville,			
Dahkotah,	153	161	331	Ramsey,	735	510	529
Dodge,	48	49	1	Scott,	190	125	127
Doty,*	100			Stearns,	125	7	42
Davis,				Sibley,	96	4	1
Fillmore,	185	151	9	Superior,*	200		
Freeborn,				Steele,			
Faribault,				Todd,	9		
Goodhue,	184	126	1	Wabashaw,	18	103	30
Hennepin,	358	415	80	Winona,	132	134	57
Houston,*	115	16		Washington,	292	121	37
Itasca,				Wright,	11	63	18
Le Sueur,*	56	55	19				
Mower,*	40				3705	2493	1746

* Incomplete.

About noon of December twelfth, 1855, a four horse vehicle was seen driving rapidly through St. Paul; and deep was the interest when it was announced that one of the Arctic exploring party, Mr. James Stewart, was on his way to Canada with relics of the world-renowned and world-mourned Sir John Franklin. Gathering together the precious fragments found on Montreal island and vicinity, the party had left the region of icebergs on the ninth of August, and after a continued land journey from that time had reached St. Paul on that day *en route* to the Hudson Bay Company's quarters in Canada.

The seventh session of the Legislative Assembly was begun on the second of January, 1856, and again the exciting question was the Minnesota and North-western Railroad Company.

John B. Brisbin was elected President of the Council, and Charles Gardiner, Speaker of the House.

Governor Gorman, in his annual message, devoted much space to railroad projects, and expressed his opposition to the Minnesota and North-western Railroad. Contrary to what the community had anticipated, on the last night of the session, the governor signed a bill giving an extension of time to the company. With the announcement of the approval, he submitted the following message:—

"I have this day approved and signed an act, entitled 'An act granting an extension of time to the Minnesota and North-western Railroad Company, and for other purposes.'

"This bill is satisfactory so far as the resulting interest is concerned, yet there are not such guards as in my judgment should be thrown around so important an interest as is involved in this company's charter.

"I have, from the beginning of this railroad question, earnestly sought the permanent welfare of Minnesota, and in conjunction with many faithful and upright men in public and private life, finally succeeded in procuring two per cent. upon the gross proceeds, receipts, and income of said road.

"This percentage, if the road is ever built, is to be applied to the governmental expenses of our future state, and must yield ample means in a few years to relieve our fellow-citizens from all state taxes for state purposes, and must be admitted by all as an important event to the tax-payers of our country.

"If, on the other hand, said company shall not construct the road nor get the land, nothing can be lost to the people. I have yielded other objections, because three several legislatures have passed favourably upon this company's charter and amendments, and I feel that each favourable amendment should not be lost, because others are desirable. Strong professions of ample capacity to build this road have been made; we shall now see how far they are to be realized; I confess that my confidence in these professions is still feeble.

"The means used to accomplish ends by this company have never met my approval, and I trust never will; but if they shall fairly and legally get possession of the lands granted by Congress to aid in constructing said road, I trust we shall have no cause to regret having urged the demands of the people for the interest and guards we have succeeded in throwing around their corporate powers. Trusting to the calm and considerate judgment of my fellow-citizens, and especially to

LIST OF LEGISLATORS OF 1856.   617

the members of the legislature, I leave the future to develop its results."[1]

[1] *List of Members of the Seventh Session of the Legislative Assembly of Minnesota.*

COUNCIL.

NAMES.	COUNTY.	POST-OFFICE.	AGE	CONDI'N.	NATIVITY.	OCCUPATION.
Balcomb, Saint A. D.	Winona	Winona	26	married	New York	Farmer
Bailley, Henry G.	Dahkotah	Hastings	27	married	Minnesota	Merchant
Dooley, Samuel	Scott	Louisville	57	married	Kentucky	Farmer
Flandrau, Charles E.	Nicollet	Traverse d'Sioux	26	single	New York	Lawyer
Freeborn, William	Goodhue	Red Wing	30	married	Ohio	Farmer
Hanson, D. M.	Hennepin	Minneapolis	28	married	Maine	Lawyer
Ludden, John D.	Chisago	Taylor's Falls	35	single	Massachusetts	Lumberman
Lowry, William D.	Olmsted	Rochester	34	married	Pennsylvania	Farmer
Rollins, John	Ramsey	St. Anthony	48	married	Maine	Farmer
Rolette, Joseph	Pembina	Pembina	35	married	Wisconsin	Indian trader
Setzer, Henry N.	Washington	Stillwater	31	married	Missouri	Lumberman
Stone, Lewis	Benton	Royalton	60	widow'r	New York	Farmer
Tillotson, Benj. F.	Fillmore	Richland	35	married	Ohio	Farmer
Thompson, C. W.	Houston	Hokah	30	single	Canada	Miller
Brisbin, John B., President.	Ramsey	St. Paul	29	married	New York	Lawyer

HOUSE OF REPRESENTATIVES.

NAMES.	COUNTY.	POST-OFFICE.	AGE	CONDI'N.	NATIVITY.	OCCUPATION.
Boutillier, C. W. Le	Ramsey	St. Anthony	27	married	Isl'd of Jersey	Physician
Bradley, James T.	Hennepin	Minneapolis	36	married	Connecticut	Carriage m'kr
Buck, C. F.	Winona	Winona	28	married	New York	Lawyer
Burdick, R. C.	Pembina	Pembina	21	single	Michigan	Indian trader
Cleaveland, Arba	Carver	Chanhassen	36	married	Massachusetts	Farmer
Covel, Wm. B.	Mower	Frankfort	25	single	New York	Surveyor
De La Vergne, A. F.	Le Sueur	Le Sueur	40	married	New York	Shoemaker
Dunbar, Wm. F.	Houston	Caledonia	31	married	Rhode Island	Farmer
Farnham, Sumner F.	Ramsey	St. Anthony	35	married	Maine	Lumberman
Galbraith, Thos. J.	Scott	Shakopee	29	married	Pennsylvania	Lawyer
Gere, William B.	Fillmore	Chatfield	26	single	Pennsylvania	Farmer
Gibbs, O. C.	Dahkotah	St. Paul	28	married	Vermont	Farmer
Grant, Charles	Pembina	St. Joseph	30	married	Red River, B.P.	Indian trader
Hartenbower, J. H.	Olmsted	Pleasant Grove	27	married	Kentucky	Farmer
Haus, Reuben	Ramsey	St. Paul	37	married	Pennsylvania	Carpenter
Holland, J. M.	Scott	Shakopee	24	single	Maryland	Lawyer
Hubbell, J. B.	Dodge	Mantorville	36	married	New York	Farmer
Hull, Samuel,	Fillmore	Carimona	47	married	Pennsylvania	Farmer
Hunt, Thomas B.	Carver	Chaska	24	married	Canada	Lawyer
Ide. J. C.	Rice	Farribault	45	married	Vermont	Mechanic
Jackman, H. A.	Washington	Stillwater	36	married	Maine	Lumberman
Johnson, Parsons K.	Blue Earth	Mankato	39	married	Vermont	Tailor
Kirkman, James	Wabashaw	Wabashaw	31	married	Canada	Blacksmith
Knauft, Ferdinand	Ramsey	St. Paul	31	married	Prussia	Carpenter
Lott, B. W.	Ramsey	St. Paul	25	single	New Jersey	Lawyer
McLeod, George A.	Nicollet	Traverse d'Sioux	35	married	Canada	Merchant
Murphy, M. T.	Dahkotah	Mendota	24	single	Ireland	Farmer
Nobles, Wm. H.	Ramsey	St. Paul	37	married	New York	Miller
Norris, James S.	Washington	Cottage Grove	40	married	Maine	Farmer
Pierce, T. W.	Hennepin	Minneapolis	30	married	Pennsylvania	Carpenter
Sturgis, William	Benton	Little Falls	38	married	Canada	Farmer
Taylor, Nathan C. D.	Chisago	Taylor's Falls	45	single	N. Hampshire	Lumberman
Thompson, M. G.	Houston	Brownsville	26	married	New York	Lawyer
Thorndike, F.	Hennepin	Elm Creek	29	married	Maine	Farmer
Van Vorhes, A.	Washington	Stillwater	60	married	Pennsylvania	Gunsmith
Wilkinson, Ross	Ramsey	St. Paul	35	married	Pennsylvania	Farmer
Wilson, John L.	Stearns	St. Cloud	35	married	Maine	Architect
Gardiner, Charles, Speaker.	Goodhue	Westervelt	40	married	New York	Lawyer

During the session of 1856, there was some conversation about the division of the territory by an east and west line, and forming a new territory north of the forty-sixth degree of latitude, but no definite action was taken. But in the summer the question of a state organization was for the first time formally agitated in a series of earnest articles in the newspaper, from the pen of John E. Warren.

This year was comparatively devoid of interest. The citizens of the territory were busily engaged in making claims in newly organized counties, and in enlarging the area of civilization.

On the twelfth of June, several Ojibways entered the farm house of Mr. Whallon, who resided in Hennepin county, on the banks of the Minnesota, a mile below the Bloomington ferry. The wife of the farmer, a friend, and three children, besides a little Dahkotah girl, who had been brought up in the mission-house at Kaposia, and was so changed in manners that her origin was scarcely perceptible, were sitting in the room when the Indians came in. Instantly seizing the little Indian maiden, they threw her out of the door, killed and scalped her, and fled before the men who were near by in the field could reach the house.

The procurement of a state organization, and a grant of lands for railroad purposes, were the topics of political interest during the year 1857.

The eighth Legislative Assembly convened at the capitol on the seventh of January, and J. B. Brisbin was elected President of the Council, and J. W. Furber, Speaker of the House.

A bill changing the seat of government to St. Peter, on the Minnesota river, passed the House.

On Saturday, February twenty-eighth, Mr. Balcombe offered the following resolutions :—

"*Resolved*, That the Hon. Joseph Rolette be very respectfully requested to report to the Council, Bill No. sixty-two Council File, entitled 'A Bill for the removal of the Seat of Government for the Territory of Minnesota,' this day; and that should said Rolette fail so to do before the adjournment of the Council this day, that the Hon. Mr. Wales, who stands next in the list of said Committee on Enrolled Bills, be respectfully requested to procure another truly enrolled copy of the said bill, and report the same to the Council on Monday next.

"*And be it further Resolved*, That the secretary of the Council is very respectfully requested to give said bill, after it has been signed by the Speaker of the House, and President of the Council, to the Hon. Mr. Wales, to deliver to the Governor for his approval."

Mr. Setzer, after the reading of the resolutions, moved a call of the Council, and Mr. Rolette was found to be absent. The chair ordered the sergeant-at-arms to report Mr. Rolette in his seat. Mr. Balcombe moved that further proceedings under the call be dispensed with, which did not prevail. From that time until the next Thursday afternoon, March the fifth, a period of one hundred and twenty-three hours, the Council remained in their chamber without recess. At that time a motion to adjourn prevailed. On Friday, another motion was made to dispense with the call of the Council, which did not prevail. On Saturday, the Council met, the president declared the call still pending. At seven and a half P. M., a committee of the House was announced. The chair ruled, that no communication from the House could be received while a call of the

Council was pending, and the committee withdrew. A motion was again made during the last night of the session, to dispense with all further proceedings under the call, which prevailed, with one vote only in the negative.

Mr. Freeborn, from the committee on enrolled bills, made the following report:—

" The Committee on Enrolled Bills would respectfully report, that owing to the absence of the chairman of this committee, Bill No. (62) sixty-two, Council File, being a bill for the removal of the seat of government of the Territory of Minnesota, introduced by Mr. Lowry on the sixth of February, 1857, has not been reported by this committee back to the Council. Your committee would further state that the above-named bill might have been reported back to the Council at this time, but that after examining the enrolled copy of said bill, which was delivered to this committee with the engrossed bill, by the secretary of the Council, in presence of the enrolling clerk of the Council, and carefully comparing the same, we find numerous errors in the enrolled copy—some portions of the engrossed bill being left out of the enrolled copy, and matter being inserted in the enrolled copy which is not in the engrossed bill. Your committee cannot, therefore, report the said Bill No. 62, C. F., as correctly enrolled, but retain the same in our possession, subject to the order of the Council.

" All which is respectfully submitted."

Mr. Ludden moved that a committee be appointed to wait on the governor, and inquire if he had any further communication to make to the Council.

Mr. Lowry moved a call of the Council, which was

ordered, and the roll being called, Messrs. Rolette, Thompson, and Tillotson were absent.

At twelve o'clock at night the president resumed the chair, and announced that the time limited by law for the continuation of the session of the territorial legislature had expired, and he therefore declared the Council adjourned without day.

The excitement on the capital question was intense, and it was a strange scene to see members of the Council, eating and sleeping in the hall of legislation for days, waiting for the sergeant-at-arms to report an absent member in his seat.

During the spring and early summer, the public mind was indignant at an atrocity perpetrated in the extreme south-western frontier of Minnesota, the recital of which causes the blood to curdle, and the mind to revert to the border scenes of the past century, which occurred in the valley of Wyoming. In the north-western corner of Iowa, a few miles from the Minnesota boundary, there is a lake known as Spirit Lake. In the spring of 1856, persons from Red Wing had visited this place, and determined to lay off a town. In the winter of 1857, there were six or seven log cabins on the borders of the lake. About fifteen or twenty miles north, in Minnesota, there was also a small place called Springfield.

For several years, Inkpadootah, a Wahpaykootay Dahkotah, had been roving with a few outlaws, being driven away from their own people by internal difficulties. These Indians were hunting in north-western Iowa, when one was bitten by a white man's dog, which he killed. The whites then proceeded to the Indian camp, and disarmed them, but they soon supplied themselves again. After this, they arrived on Sunday, the eighth of March, at Spirit Lake. They proceeded to a cabin, where only men dwelt, and asked for beef. Understanding, as they assert, that they had permission to kill one of the cattle, they did so, and commenced cutting it up, when one of the white men came out and knocked down the Dahkotah. For this act the settler was shot, and another one coming out of the cabin, he was also killed. Surrounding the house, the Indians now fired the thatched roof, and as the men ran out all were killed, making the whole number eleven.

About the same time, the Indians went to the house of a frontiersman, by the name of Gardner, and demanded food, and all the food in the house was given to them. The son-in-law, and another man, left to go and see if all was right at the neighbouring cabin, but they never came back. Toward night, excited by the blood they had been spilling through the day, they came back again to Mr. Gardner's house, and soon killed him, and despatching his wife, and two daughters, and grandchildren, carried off Abby, the surviving daughter. The next day, they continued their fiendish work, and brought into camp Mrs. Thatcher and Mrs. Noble. That day a man by the name of Markham visited the house of Gardner, and saw the dead bodies. Secreting himself till night, he came to the Springfield settlement in Minnesota, and reported what he had seen. Three miles above the Thatcher family on the lake, there lived a Mr. Marble.

On Thursday, the twelfth of March, an Indian, who had been on friendly terms with Marble's family, called at his house, and (as near as Mrs. Marble, with her imperfect knowledge of the language, could make out) told them that the white people below them on the Lake had been *nippoed* (killed) a day or two previously. This aroused the suspicion of the Marbles, and none the less that the great depth of the snow made it almost impossible to get out and ascertain the truth of the story. The next day (the thirteenth), quite early in the forenoon, four Indians came to Marble's house and were admitted. Their demeanour was so friendly as to disarm all suspicion. They proposed to swap rifles with Marble, and the terms were soon agreed upon.

After the swap, the chief suggested that they should go out on the lake and shoot at a mark. Marble assented. After a few discharges they turned to come in the direction of the house, when the savages allowed Marble to go a few paces ahead, and immediately shot him down. Mrs. Marble, who was looking out of the cabin, saw her husband fall, and immediately ran to him. The Indians seized her and told her that they would not kill her, but would take her with them.

They carried her in triumph to the camp, whither they had previously taken three other white women, Mrs. Noble, Mrs. Thatcher, and Miss Gardner.

Inkpadootah and party now proceeded to Springfield, where they slaughtered the whole settlement, about the twenty-seventh of March. When the United States troops arrived from Fort Ridgely, they buried two bodies, and the volunteers from Iowa buried twenty-nine others. Besides these, others were missing. The outlaws, perceiving that the soldiers were in pursuit, made their escape. The four captive women were forced by day to carry heavy burdens through deep snow, and at night-fall they were made to cut wood and set up the tent, and, after dark, to be subject to the indignities that suggested themselves to savages. When food began to fail, the white women subsisted on bones and feathers.

Mrs. Thatcher was in poor health in consequence of the recent birth of a child, and she became burdensome. Arriving at the Big Sioux river, the Indians made a bridge by felling a tree on each side of the river bank. Mrs. Thatcher attempted to cross, but failed, and, in despair, refused to try again. One of the men took her by the hand, as if to help her, and, when about midway, pushed her into the stream. She swam to the shore, and they pushed her off, and then fired at her as if she was a target, until life was extinct.

"In the early spring it was next to impossible to make any considerable efforts for their rescue; and it was not known what direction the captors had taken. Time passed on. Two military expeditions reached the place where the massacre took place, but did nothing, except to bury the slain. Early in the month of May, two young men from Lac qui Parle, who had been taught by the mission to read and write, and whose mother is a member of our church,[1] while on their spring hunt, found themselves in the neighbourhood of Inkpadoota and his party. Having heard that they held some American women in captivity, the two brothers visited the camp,—though this was at some risk of their lives, since Inkpadootah's hand was now against every man,—and found the outlaws, and succeeded in bargaining for Mrs. Marble, whom they first took to their mother's tent," and then brought her to a trading-house at Lac qui Parle, when she was visited by those connected with the mission at Hazelwood, and clothed once more in civilized costume. On her arrival at the hotel at St. Paul, the citizens welcomed her, and presented

[1] Letter of Dr. Williamson.

RESCUE OF WHITE WOMEN FROM CAPTIVITY.

her with a thousand dollars. The desire to rescue the two surviving white women now became intense.

One night a good Indian, named Paul by the whites, an elder of the mission church, came into the mission-house and said:—

"If the white chief tells me to go, I will go." "I tell you to go," replied Mr. Flandrau, then Dahkotah Agent. With two companies he started next day, with a wagon and two horses, and valuable presents. After a diligent search the outlaws were found on the James river with a band of Yanktons.

A few days before Mrs. Noble had been murdered, a Yankton, who had lost his legs by disease, had purchased the two women. One night Mrs. Noble was ordered to go out, and be subject to the wishes of the party. She refusing to go, a son of Inkpadootah dragged her out by the hair and killed her. The next morning a Dahkotah woman took Miss Gardner, the sole surviving captive, to see the corpse, which had been horribly treated after death.

Paul, by his perseverance and large presents, at length redeemed the captive, and she was brought to the mission-house, and from thence she visited St. Paul, and was restored to her sister in Iowa.

For some days previous to the first of July it had been reported that one of Inkpadootah's sons was in a camp on the Yellow Medicine river. A message was sent to the agent, Flandrau, who, with a detachment of soldiers from Fort Ridgely, and some Indian guides, soon arrived and surrounded the lodges. The alarm being given, Inkpadootah's son, said to have been the murderer of Mrs. Noble, ran from his lodge followed by his wife. He concealed himself for a short period in the brush by the water, but was soon ferreted out and shot by United States soldiers.

The rest of the outlaws are said to be west of the Missouri, and that they may yet meet the punishment which they so richly deserve for their horrible barbarity, is the wish of every righteous man.

On the twenty-third of February, 1857, an act passed the United States Senate, to authorize the people of Minnesota to form a constitution, preparatory to their admission into the Union on an equal footing with the original states. And at the close of the session another act passed, making a grant of land in alternate sections, to aid in the construction of certain railroads in the territory.

Governor Gorman called a special session of the legislature, to take into consideration measures that would give efficiency to these acts. The extra session convened on April twenty-seventh, and a message was transmitted by Samuel Medary,[1] who had been appointed governor in the place of W. A. Gorman, whose term of office had expired. An act was passed to execute the trust created by Congress; and the lands, under certain conditions, were given to certain chartered railroad companies. The extra session adjourned on the twenty-third of May; and in accordance with the provisions of the enabling act of Congress, an election was held on the first Monday in June, for delegates to a convention which was to assemble at the capital on the second Monday in July. The election resulted, as was thought, giving a majority of delegates to the Republican party.

At midnight previous to the day fixed for the meet-

[1] He acted as governor for a few months only.

ing of the convention, the Republicans proceeded to the capitol, because the enabling act had not fixed at what hour on the second Monday the convention should assemble, and fearing that the Democratic delegates might anticipate them, and elect the officers of the body. A little before twelve, A. M., on Monday, the secretary of the territory entered the speaker's rostrum, and began to call the body to order; and at the same time a delegate, J. W. North, who had in his possession a written request from the majority of the delegates present, proceeded to do the same thing. The secretary of the territory put a motion to adjourn, and the Democratic members present voting in the affirmative, they left the hall. The Republicans, feeling that they were in the majority, remained, and in due time organized, and proceeded with the business specified in the enabling act, to form a constitution, and take all necessary steps for the establishment of a state government, in conformity with the Federal Constitution, subject to the approval and ratification of the people of the proposed state.

After several days the Democratic wing also organized in the Senate chamber at the capitol, and, claiming to be the true body, also proceeded to form a constitution. Both parties were remarkably orderly and intelligent, and everything was marked by perfect decorum. After they had been in session some weeks, moderate counsels prevailed, and a committee of conference was appointed from each body, which resulted in both adopting the same constitution, on the twenty-ninth of August. According to the provision of the constitution, an election was held for state officers and the adoption of the constitution, on the second Tuesday, the thirteenth of October. The constitution was adopted by almost a unanimous vote. It provided that the territorial officers should retain their offices until the state was admitted into the Union, not anticipating the long delay which has been experienced.

The first session of the state legislature commenced on the first Wednesday of December, at the capitol, in the city of St. Paul; and during the month elected Henry M. Rice and James Shields as their Representatives in the United States Senate.

On the twenty-ninth of January, 1858, Mr. Douglas submitted a bill to the United States Senate, for the admission of Minnesota into the Union. On the first of February, a discussion arose on the bill, in which Senators Douglas, Wilson, Gwin, Hale, Mason, Green, Brown, and Crittenden participated. Brown, of Mississippi, was opposed to the admission of Minnesota, until the Kansas question was settled. Mr. Crittenden, as a Southern man, could not endorse all that was said by the Senator from Mississippi; and his words of wisdom and moderation during this day's discussion, are worthy of remembrance. On April the seventh, the bill passed the Senate with only three dissenting votes; and by the time that this history is published, Minnesota will be recognised as one of the United States.

THE END.

MID-AMERICAN FRONTIER

An Arno Press Collection

Andreas, A[lfred] T[heodore]. **History of Chicago.** 3 volumes. 1884-1886

Andrews, C[hristopher] C[olumbus]. **Minnesota and Dacotah.** 1857

Atwater, Caleb. **Remarks Made on a Tour to Prairie du Chien:** Thence to Washington City, in 1829. 1831

Beck, Lewis C[aleb]. **A Gazetteer of the States of Illinois and Missouri.** 1823

Beckwith, Hiram W[illiams]. **The Illinois and Indiana Indians.** 1884

Blois, John T. **Gazetteer of the State of Michigan,** in Three Parts. 1838

Brown, Jesse and A. M. Willard. **The Black Hills Trails.** 1924

Brunson, Alfred. **A Western Pioneer: Or, Incidents of the Life and Times of Rev. Alfred Brunson.** 2 volumes in one. 1872

Burnet, Jacob. **Notes on the Early Settlement of the North-Western Territory.** 1847

Cass, Lewis. **Considerations on the Present State of the Indians,** and their Removal to the West of the Mississippi. 1828

Coggeshall, William T[urner]. **The Poets and Poetry of the West.** 1860

Darby, John F[letcher]. **Personal Recollections of Many Prominent People Whom I Have Known.** 1880

Eastman, Mary. **Dahcotah:** Or, Life and Legends of the Sioux Around Fort Snelling. 1849

Ebbutt, Percy G. **Emigrant Life in Kansas.** 1886

Edwards, Ninian W[irt]. **History of Illinois, From 1778 to 1833:** And Life and Times of Ninian Edwards. 1870

Ellsworth, Henry William. **Valley of the Upper Wabash, Indiana.** 1838

Esarey, Logan, ed. **Messages and Letters of William Henry Harrison.** 2 volumes. 1922

Flower, George. **The Errors of Emigrants.** [1841]

Hall, Baynard Rush (Robert Carlton, pseud.). **The New Purchase:** Or Seven and a Half Years in the Far West. 2 volumes in one. 1843

Haynes, Fred[erick] Emory. **James Baird Weaver.** 1919

Heilbron, Bertha L., ed. **With Pen and Pencil on the Frontier in 1851:** The Diary and Sketches of Frank Blackwell Mayer. 1932

Hinsdale, B[urke] A[aron]. **The Old Northwest:** The Beginnings of Our Colonial System. [1899]

Johnson, Harrison. **Johnson's History of Nebraska.** 1880

Lapham, I[ncrease] A[llen]. **Wisconsin:** Its Geography and Topography, History, Geology, and Mineralogy. 1846

Mansfield, Edward D. **Memoirs of the Life and Services of Daniel Drake.** 1855

Marshall, Thomas Maitland, ed. **The Life and Papers of Frederick Bates.** 2 volumes in one. 1926

McConnel, J[ohn] L[udlum.] **Western Characters:** Or, Types of Border Life in the Western States. 1853

Miller, Benjamin S. **Ranch Life in Southern Kansas and the Indian Territory.** 1896

Neill, Edward Duffield. **The History of Minnesota.** 1858

Parker, Nathan H[owe]. **The Minnesota Handbook, For 1856-7.** 1857

Peck, J[ohn] M[ason]. **A Guide for Emigrants.** 1831

Pelzer, Louis. **Marches of the Dragoons in the Mississippi Valley.** 1917

Perkins, William Rufus and Barthinius L. Wick. **History of the Amana Society.** 1891

Rister, Carl Coke. **Land Hunger:** David L. Payne and the Oklahoma Boomers. 1942

Schoolcraft, Henry R[owe]. **Personal Memoirs of a Residence of Thirty Years With the Indian Tribes on the American Frontiers.** 1851

Smalley, Eugene V. **History of the Northern Pacific Railroad.** 1883

[Smith, William Rudolph]. **Observations on the Wisconsin Territory.** 1838

Steele, [Eliza R.] **A Summer Journey in the West.** 1841

Streeter, Floyd Benjamin. **The Kaw:** The Heart of a Nation. 1941

[Switzler, William F.] **Switzler's Illustrated History of Missouri, From 1541 to 1877.** 1879

Tallent, Annie D. **The Black Hills.** 1899

Thwaites, Reuben Gold. **On the Storied Ohio.** 1903

Todd, Charles S[tewart] and Benjamin Drake. **Sketches of the Civil and Military Services of William Henry Harrison.** 1840

Wetmore, Alphonso, compiler. **Gazetteer of the State of Missouri.** 1837

Wilder, D[aniel] W[ebster]. **The Annals of Kansas.** 1886

Woollen, William Wesley. **Biographical and Historical Sketches of Early Indiana.** 1883

Wright, Robert M[arr]. **Dodge City.** 1913